America's
Deceit

JOHN A. GAETANO

"Your story is our priority"

LitPrime Solutions
485c US Highway 1 South
Suite 100
Iselin, NJ 08830
www.litprime.com
Phone: 1-800-981-9893

Published by LitPrime Solutions: 09/20/2024

ISBN: 979-8-88703-378-5(sc)
ISBN: 979-8-88703-379-2(e)

Library of Congress Control Number: 2024913584

Table of Contents

"Of the more than 450 books written on the Kennedy Assassination, *America's Deceit* is the only one to explore the full truth regarding the death of our thirty-fifth president. Backed by thirty years of careful research, John Gaetano brilliantly dismantles the 'lone gunman' theory. To this day, Gaetano is convinced that Lee Harvey Oswald did *not* kill JFK, and he presents a huge mass of evidence to support his conviction. For any concerned citizen who seeks the detailed truth behind the tragic event of November 1963, *America's Deceit* is a treasure—a truly stunning work of in-depth research. Here is the gloves-off book that conspiracy buffs have been waiting for. It's a mind-blower!"

William F. Nolan, Author of_Logan's Run

This book is dedicated to the Children:

To John F Kennedy, Jr.

May God bless him and may he rest in peace.

To Caroline Kennedy Schlossberg

and her dear mother, Jackie.

To June and Rachel Oswald

and their mother, Marina Oswald Porter

Acknowledgments

A special thanks to Miles Liptak, in Los Angeles, California, for whose help in editing I express an immense gratitude. May God bless him.

I also want to thank Terray Kashuba very much for all of his help.

Thank you Marlene Thomas, in Spokane, Washington, for helping me in the beginning stages.

I send my love to those I miss: Deanna Jurgens, Robert and Martha Sterling, Dr. Thelbert and Doreen Roberts, my friend Curt Donner in Spokane, and also from Spokane, Will Murray, and to my brother, James Gaetano in Tampa Bay, and in Los Angeles, Steve Maggio and family, Kari Morsell, Arne Manson, Gideon and Penny Karpovsky, Mark Stein (Where are you?), the Scott family, especially the girls, Natassia and Sheena who will always remain special in my life. A nod to my friend, John Mitry and to a special girl, Stephanie Zimbalist.

An abundance of thanks to the late Marty Feldman and Hal Ashby for being my mentors and inspiring me to put my ideas down on paper. May God bless Jimmy and Gloria Stewart for my introduction to Hollywood. In remembrance Dean, Paul Martin Jr. who's friendship came too late and to his father. My appreciation to the Frank Capra family, especially to Lucille, and to Sir Alfred, and Alma Hitchcock. And finally, my thanks to Mr. Cary Grant for just being my friend.

"Let us have faith
that right makes might
and in that faith
let us to the end
dare to do our duty
as we understand it!"

-- Abraham Lincoln

Forward

On an early evening in June of 1992 in Little Rock, Arkansas, a man who served as Governor for the last twelve years, the youngest ever to be elected to that office in the nation's history, was being prepped for the presidency of the United States. If he were to win, he would become the second youngest elected President, breaking the current record held by Theodore Roosevelt. John F. Kennedy was the youngest President ever elected, and still stands today. Bill Clinton was no Kennedy, but that did not stop the media from having a field day trying to evoke the possibilities.

Simultaneously, another event was developing-- one that had indirectly disturbed this country for over twenty-nine years. It concerned a motion picture about the murder of John F. Kennedy, our Thirty-fifth President of the United States, titled simply *JFK*. It caused quite a stir and controversy throughout the world, more so with our government, although many people did rally around and support its writer and director, Oliver Stone.

The movie, *JFK*, created enough controversy in the film industry to rival Orson Welles' release of his masterpiece *Citizen Kane*, fifty years earlier in 1941, or the release of Frank Capra's masterpiece, *Mr. Smith Goes To Washington* in 1939. The United

States Senate tried to ban the 1939 film before its release. It was the people themselves in this country that made *Mr. Smith* the second most applauded and respected film of that year. The other film that caused a stir in 1939 and rose to become the number one film of all time was, *Gone With the Wind*. Today, in this country, *Citizen Kane*, considered the second greatest film of all time, is to many worldwide, number one.

Like *Mr. Smith,* when *JFK* was released in 1991, it drew tremendous contempt from every corner of the government. But, the people who saw the movie and discovered all the unanswered questions it posed complained loudly enough to demand answers. Changes occurred, and the government files ordered sealed until the year 2039 were opened. The files were from agencies that included the CIA, the FBI, and the Warren Commission. This seven member panel, with the conclusion of their report, said a lone gunman had assassinated the thirty-fifth President. The Warren Commission then ordered certain records sealed within all capacities of the government. Those who would not have access to the records would include future committees such as the Rockefeller Commission, the Church Hearing and the Senate and House Select Committee on the Assassinations of John Kennedy, Martin Luther King Jr. and Robert Kennedy. Even the Dallas police records from 1963 were closed.

To get the government to open these files, Oliver Stone and we the people had to go before Congress and the Senate subcommittees to meet them with our request for the truth. It was an interruption that disturbed the present Commander In Chief then, President George Bush. He wanted those files to remain suppressed.

President Bush, a former CIA director himself, in the end would lose this battle and with it his second term as president, but he would not lose the war. Before he left office, he appointed five colleagues to supervise and decide what files could be released and what files to be withheld for National Security reasons. You will run into the term "National Security" often throughout this story. These words are repeatedly used within our government to hide something that we the people pay so much for. Funny, isn't it-- we pay our government to spy, deceive, steal, and even set the wages people get and yet we're the ones who continue to go along with it. But I'm not laughing, and I'm sure you're not, either.

By October 21, 1992, the man who caused this storm over twenty-five years earlier and who was the focus of the film, *JFK,* would die. He would write a book about his trial and tribulations called *On the Trail of Assassins*, a story occurring between 1963 and 1970. His name was James Garrison, a former World War II hero, an FBI agent, the District Attorney for New Orleans, and, at the time of his death, a Federal Judge.

Though this story you will read has little to do with Oliver Stone's stand for justice or his film, it does have something to do with the subject matter. Long before we even thought of the words, "assassin" or "Vietnam," JFK's death marked an end to our belief in for a bright future and our innocence.

This is a story about people who, like the Garrisons of the world, risk their lives for honor and truth-- for which this country represents, but is no longer required today for some to abide by. What you will read is fiction mixed with fact. The scary part is sorting out which is which. Those who know the truth will have no problem.

I will not blame the reader if he or she does not like what they will read. But, I believe everyone is entitled to their opinion. Much of what you will read has been bottled up within me for over thirty years of my life. It started as a screenplay in 1983, and for over ten years I've had encouragement by those who know my feelings to put this all down on paper. My friends know I have a lot to say because of my own research and background and relationships in the film industry, from all the people I've crossed paths with from Honolulu to Washington, D. C., from Texas to Arkansas. In the film industry, you meet all kinds of people including outsiders who want to finance your work. Some of these people have worked or were working for our government in high places. How they found me is another story in itself, but was actually simple. The motion picture industry is really a small community, especially if one has been involved in it as long as I have. These contacts may also be very close to personalities such as Marilyn Monroe, Sinatra or even Peter Lawford who was doing commercials prior to his death. In my early years in the film industry, I had to supplement my income by doing bit parts in movies, television, and-- yes-- even commercials.

When any of my contacts found out I was a writer, they would seek me out, usually out of necessity, and approach me discreetly to reveal stories and information they found difficult to keep to themselves. When the opportunity arose and these people found someone who really cared about what they had to say; they confided in me. If they hadn't, they would have taken their secrets to their graves. They expressed the concern that someday I might bring out the truth if I wrote a novel or movie script. I had every intention to, but I had my own personal demons to fight. All I did was continue to bottle it up. One reason for this was to protect my sources until I gathered enough pieces of the puzzle, a puzzle I continued to put together for over thirty years.

This is the second time I wrote the foreword to this novel. I originally wrote the first after finishing chapter seven, not knowing whether I was actually going to complete my story. When I did, I expanded it.

Although this is a book of fiction, my friends have told me to stick to non fiction. I know there was no way I could do that, but after the book *The Dark Side of Camelot*, written by Pulitzer-prize winning author Seymour Hersh, came out, I had to ask whether this book really belonged in the nonfiction category. Then weeks later, I was amazed to find out that not only Hersh, but Peter Jennings came out with another destructive piece on the myth of John F. Kennedy's legacy. I could not believe a top anchor man from ABC News would stoop so low to destroy a man who brought honor to the Presidency of the United States and died a martyr by an assassin's bullet. I'm not saying Kennedy was perfect, he was not, but he was one president who provided strength and union to the young people of our country during the twentieth century. The polls put him on top.

Seymour Hersh says he spent five years researching the dark side of our thirty-fifth president. For what? To prove he was someone who actually deserved to be assassinated? This is how Hersh and Jennings came off with their investigations. But look whom their sources are: the CIA, the secret service, Mayor Daley's people in Chicago, of which Daley happened to have ties to Sam Giancana and to the mob, and a woman called Judith Campbell Exner who recently died as I wrote this novel's foreword.

Judith Campbell Exner seems to be the only woman to come forward publicly to talk about her relationships to both the President of the United States and the number one mob boss in the country since Al Capone, Sam Giancana. Both Kennedy and Giancana had been introduced to Mrs. Campbell, separately by their mutual friend Frank Sinatra, the chairman of the board, the man who sat and sang with presidents, popes, and the mob, as well as the pimps and paupers of "that's life!" The trouble with Judith Campbell Exner was that as she told her story again and again, she told it each time differently. First, it was how the mob was in bed with the CIA, then after the Church and Senate hearings it was the Mafia in bed with JFK. Her stories grew tremendously from a mole hill to a very large mountain one couldn't climb.

Today, her story is she didn't sleep with Sam, but it was Sam, and her who slept with John Kennedy. I'm being facetious, of course. It is this lady, or broad, as Sinatra used to say, a Beverly Hills debutante, a wife to a small time actor, William Campbell, who gave herself to the big boys of Vegas who is not only the instigator, but the focal point that ties Kennedy to the actual reason Hersh said JFK became President of the United States.

Throughout the years, the more attention Judith Campbell Exner demanded, the bigger her stories became. And they changed on a whim, to the point if she could not get attention, she would even come out to say, I'm doing this or I'm saying this, because I am dying of cancer and I want the truth to come out before I die. It's been over ten years now and Exner finally succumbed to cancer in September, 1999. What Mrs. Exner is saying is "I am somebody too, and I was an instrument that helped change history. I should be appreciated and never forgotten." Some of her stories may have some credence and truth to it, I dedicated no more than a page or two to Mrs. Exner in my novel because she was a tool used by others and not mentioned here for what she thought or said. If she really knew the truth, she may have misgivings in what she had said to a Kitty Kelly or a Seymour Hersh or even to *20/20*.

Ironically, as you read my novel, remember this is a book of fiction, though Hersh's book is not! I did not change a word of my story since new information has emerged in the last eighteen months, including new evidence showing Gerald Ford, a Warren Commissioner, and the future Vice-President and President of the United States, was the instigator behind developing Spector's magic bullet theory.

From papers of the late Lee Rankin, head counsel for the Commission, he stated Gerald Ford had changed the bullet location originally in Kennedy's autopsy report on the back spine to the neck of the spine to fit counsel member Arlen Spector's location to support what we now know as the "Magic Bullet theory." Arlen Spector is now the Senator of Pennsylvania.

A lot happened since I completed what would be my first book of fiction. I started writing *America's Deceit* out of anger and frustration offended by the book, *Case Closed*, by Gerald Posner, and the fact our former President, Bill Clinton stated publicly, he believed Lee Harvey Oswald was Kennedy's assassin-- something I privately feel that he doesn't believe. The other reason is that of a short, but tough as nails Texan by the name of Ross Perot.

New facts continue to surface, showing Kennedy would not embark on a War in Vietnam and that all American soldiers and advisors were returning to the United States by the end of 1965. Jackie Onassis is gone. Recent Kennedy family members have also died including John Kennedy Jr., and one of Kennedy's closest friend and aid, David Powers.

I'll always remember back to 1974 when I was in Honolulu, Hawaii before Nixon's resignation. I had dinner with a retired British Secret Service agent, and we discussed the Kennedy assassination and Kennedy's legacy: will Kennedy be remembered for the Bay of Pigs, or for his Assassination? This gentleman explained it this way: Kennedy, no matter what type of human being he was, will always be remembered in history through the eyes of the most distinguished dignitaries of the world-- through Churchill, Charles DeGaulle, Douglas MacArthur, Harry Truman, and Eisenhower. All these great men left an indelible stamp of approval of John Kennedy, even Nixon himself who, following the Watergate years, changed his opinions of the man.

Nixon's attitude of his rival, in the 1990's before his death had only kudos to say about Kennedy the man and his Presidency. Why? Because Nixon, after traveling throughout the world in his final years as a spokesman, would hear often from world leaders how truly loved and respected Kennedy was-- a man Nixon was jealous of all his political life. It was scary. Nixon sometimes seemed proud to have known the man. Nixon again received attention by those who wanted to know the Kennedy mystique through his own eyes.

Even to his death Nixon would not speak ill of his rival. So, why do people speak ill of Kennedy today by those who really didn't know him? Those who might have met him or worked with him surely might have had these negative feelings, but these are not the close individuals like the MacNamara's, the Schlisinger's, Sorenson's, nor even his widow, the late Jackie Kennedy Onassis who knew him best, nor even the many women he was purported to sleep with. I think James Garner's character in the movie, *My Fellow Americans*, comically showed it best *á la* Clinton.

There was a time when the American people looked up to the Presidency. We, as a nation, respected the President. We saluted him, we praised what the red, white, and blue colors on our flag symbolized and how it represented this beautiful country of ours. But following the Kennedy assassination, Johnson and Nixon changed all that.

Kennedy might have been the womanizer they say he was, but apparently those women who didn't have an affair with him wish they had! No one accused him of sexual harassment, no one accused him of indecent exposure; no one called him anything. As a kid, I remembered how women wanted him and wanted to love him. I heard the same remarks years later when I worked in the film industry. His rivals always knew this, his opposition knew this, the media as well, but no one said or would do anything about it. They all had respect for the man.

This was a man who was loved worldwide more than any President in history. John Kennedy adored the American People so much so, he went out of his way not to disappoint them. Sadly, it would be too late when he finally discovered the true meaning of his Presidency.

The Press of yesteryear loved the man and their President and could have exploited the situation if they wanted to, if there were really anything to exploit. Today's anchors and news reporters do not know him and use an innuendo to top their ratings, or they continue to lead us by offering only the government's point of view of who did or did not murder our thirty-fifth President of the United States. This is what Seymour Hersh's job finished doing and he got paid millions of dollars up front to fulfill his contract. Again, how ironic.

This novel is about a Pulitzer Prize winning photo journalist who had written the government's point of view for twenty-five years concerning Oswald's lone gunman stance. It is about what happens to him that forever changes his opinion, his life, and those who meet him. It is about our country and the facade we all lived behind those years following Kennedy's assassination. I feel sorry for those people who know the truth and continue to hide behind it. I commend those people who dedicated their lives these last thirty-five years by continuing to smash that facade into a thousand pieces, because of what John Kennedy said just weeks prior to Dallas. He prepared to expose the CIA for what the agency had really become and the lies and corruption that both Kennedy brothers found themselves facing. John F. Kennedy's words: "*I will splinter the CIA into a thousand pieces and blow them into the winds.*" He would be dead within three weeks after he uttered them. Who is fooling who? All you people need to do is read the historical transcripts and listen to the tape recordings to know Johnson, to know Nixon, to know John Kennedy. Only then you will know the truth and what might have been the deepest darkest secret that haunted Nixon to the end of his life and that he took with him to his grave.

John A. Gaetano

2000

No matter whether you believe John Kennedy was one of the greatest Presidents in the history of this country; I want the people who read this book to come away satisfied with the fact that they will now know who killed him. There will be those who will read this book who will probably hate this author. To those people, know this: I finished writing the last chapter while in Orlando, Florida sometime late in October, 1996, two weeks away from former President Clinton's reelection for his second term. Unless you read each chapter, you will not understand the final chapter or how I knew the outcome.

It may come as a surprise or a shock, but at least 90% of the forty-one chapters have a clue to the piece of the puzzle which you will be able to determine and understand the ending. I want to thank the Mark Lanes, the David Liftons, and Robert Grodens for supplying pieces of the puzzle over the years. But, what you didn't know were pieces supplied by what was taken for granted by those who were assassinated. I'm referring to Kennedy and Oswald and even Jack Ruby himself who predicted his own death before he could get a second trial.

Piece by piece, dot to dot, the reader has a chance to finally expose the many people who were involved in this conspiracy. Then one can understand why those Presidents who followed Kennedy were capable of easily covering up one of the greatest of all unsolved political murders.

In playing the game of six degrees of separation, we can review the last forty years in the history of the United States and see how everything, form Watergate to Iran-Contra and even up to 9/11 and Bush's war on Iraq ties to the John F. Kennedy assassination. May God Bless those who will try to stop what is about to happen next.

John A. Gaetano
2003

Final Author's Note

From ancient times, man has tried to control the destiny of other human beings by depriving them of liberty and compelling them to obedience. Slaves have been forced to work and to serve to the utmost of their masters; prisoners have been chained to row in the galleys; even Jesus was forced to carry the cross at his own execution. Today, men as well as women are still inducted into the armed forces and sent thousands of miles away from their homeland to create chaos, take lives, and lose their own.

In 1975 during the Rockefeller Commission, it was the first time that the committee heard that the CIA was involved in mind control. Many people believed after the CIA had openly confessed to its conspiracy of mind control and publicly disclosed its interest in it, that it had ceased its activities. The earlier CIA records, however, contain many termination dates for aspects of secrecy termed 'Operation Mind Control,' yet evidence clearly to the contrary suggests that it continued far past the thirty years when they said it began. The reason we now know this and it has come to the surface is that in 1964 J. Lee Rankin, the Head Counsel for the Warren Commission, was told, based on President Lyndon Johnson's public declaration, that the commies sent Lee Harvey Oswald back to the United States as a brainwashed 'Manchurian Candidate' to assassinate President Kennedy. On that theory, Rankin asks the now new CIA Director; Richard Helms for all information they had on the KGB program on mind control. Now what Helms would never admit at the time is that the CIA was far ahead of the U.S.S.R. when it came to mind control. Not until twelve years later when they investigated JFK's assassination, following the release of the Rockefeller Commission Report and the subsequent investigations by Senator Church's and

Congressman Pike's committees. A public accounting was made and apologies given, and the intelligence was reprimanded, but do you think they stopped after this—not by a long shot.

In July, 1977, following a wave of resignations in the Carter administration and in the CIA's clandestine services, CIA Director Adm. Stansfield Turner informed the Senate Intelligence Committee that the whole story had not been told, although the case has been put to rest. Turner informed both the committee and the White House that additional information had been brought to his attention that proved that the CIA had given many mind-controlling drugs to research scientists throughout the nation, to untold number of Americans, be it drug addicts, prison systems, terminal cancer patients as well as college students in high profile Universities and in soldier experimentations on military bases.

The result was headlines in the press about the CIA and drugs, including the LSD incident in an experiment that took place back in the early 50's that killed a man who the CIA had under their mind control experimentation and had lied about his death as a suicide. The Family of the man could sue after almost 20 years of secrecy. The senate passed the bill for compensation in a wrongful death in the amount that reached into the seven figure range that was cut in half by Congress. Another suit followed in another undisclosed case, but somehow the CIA has never been accountable for anyone's demise since. In my book, you will see what they are truly getting away with. The two words were commonly linked: drugs and the CIA, but few newsmen made the connection between drug tests and behavior control or mind control. Drugs would be prominently linked to them in the mid-late 1980's that made up the Iran-contra scandal.

If a prospective agent cannot be recruited by an appeal of patriotism, he is bribed. If he refuses to be bribed, he is blackmailed. If he cannot be blackmailed, he is 'programmed.' This is where our mind and our souls are taken away from us, we the people, by our own government. It is not brainwashing, it is much worse. It is like transplanting our brain, like setting it in a mason jar, letting them use and abuse it for their own benefit. Without drugs or hypnosis, your mind is already being controlled when you watch television. It is in the ads you watch, the sit-coms, and even some of the movies you watch. Your mind is always being controlled one way or another by the images on the screen. It is known as total 'mind control' and it has been going on since World War II ended, used specifically by our government agencies. During World War II it was called propaganda—both sides of the war used it, ours being Navel Intelligence and the OSS—Office of Strategic Services, what is now the CIA. For that prospective agent I mentioned above, if all fails for him, if he cannot be programmed then he is simply killed, for it must not be known that he had ever been approached. So important is 'National Security.'

The secret government within these agencies often has worked against our own President. It has, we know with the many crimes they have committed on record, worked against the U.S. constitution and the American people. It began in this country fifty years ago and on November 22, 1963, when those human scum in control took out our 35th President of the United States and splattered him in the front pages not only here in this country but also in the front pages of all over the world.

Since then this secret government from within has needlessly caused the death of innocent citizens and people who were working as patriots, just as it has tortured and murdered those who stood in the way or got in their way. Documented atrocities and criminal blunders have been constantly revealed by Congressional investigations. Like them, we the people turn a blind eye—no one in the last 50 years has been brought to trial for John F. Kennedy's murder, though James Garrison surely tried. The Warren Commission was not a court of law, and no trial has ever taken place and there is no statute of limitations when it comes to murder. I would think that those born in the last three generations who didn't experience that time would be certainly very confused if anything. The 'National Security Act' has contributed to the cancer of these intelligence agencies – and they have only thrived more each decade.

I've kept a secret for many years of my life. Based on the above I can now tell you that not only Shirhan Shirhan was mind controlled to shoot at Robert F. Kennedy but in March of 1981, like Shirhan who didn't kill Bobby Kennedy, John Hinckley fired a pistol and shot every bullet hitting Press secretary James Brady and a Secret Service agent. Ronald Reagan however was shot by a different bullet and a different gun. Hinckley to this day has never gone to trial and is not in prison. He, in thirty-one years, has never been interviewed. He spends holidays with his family.

Reading my book and based upon what you just read you will figure out the *why*, the *how*, and maybe if you are smart enough the *who*. In the end, history will be set straight and the truth will win out. Nobody leaves this world alive. Before I finish with my final word, you will finally get to read my book and will be able to tie together dot by dot the story how those in our own government did ambush and kill President John F. Kennedy.

Since my last book that was to be released back in 2007, but never was, there are those who did come out with their books that continue to lie to you, including Gerald Posner who actually changed history for the moment writing his fantasy books. I'll let you compare my novel with his nonfiction. Robert Blakely of the House Select Committee recently came out and said that CIA had lied to him. Duh! A startling revelation isn't it! Then there is Vincent Bugliosi and Mark Fuhrman both claiming in their books that Oswald acted alone and the Warren Commission is correct, Bugliosi gave it to you in 1652 pages while Fuhrman in just over 200. You will read about my take on Fuhrman in the aftermath at the end of this book. Now there is Bill O'Rielly, coming off a best selling book called "The Assassination of Lincoln." He is coming out with his take on Kennedy as I write this. I used to watch Mr. O'Rielly when I was in the film industry when he was far left on the tv show *Hard Copy*. He did a pretty good job of reporting and I witnessed his investigation on Kennedy with subtlety. When H. W. Bush became President in 1988, I noticed O'Rielly heading for the middle between the far right and the far left. When W. Bush became President in 2000, O'Rielly went to the far right for the next eight years. Today, he has moved to the middle. We will see whether his far right comes out again or if he will play it safe where he is now, near the middle.

I would like to make my last acknowledgments and thanks to William F. Nolan whose generous input, inspiration and friendship gave me that extra boost of life that I didn't know I had left in me. Once again, to Miles Liptak for his bad taste in people; namely me, for the help he constantly gives me through the years, his editing and screening of my work. To John Thamm who introduced me to the work of his friend, Walter Bowart that inspired me to write this foreword you have now read. Thamm was a friend to Norman Mailer who proclaimed to the world since the '70's--and even to the end at his death in 2008--that Lee Harvey Oswald shot Kennedy and that the Warren Commission is correct, Thamm knows different, and now I know too!

Ted Kennedy, when he died, left a last will and testament stating (now see whether you can guess. I'm going to control your mind right now--his statement was, repeat after me...) Lee Harvey Oswald killed his brother from that sixth floor book depository building in Dealey Plaza and that the Warren Commission was correct. Where did I hear that before, or am I being programmed to control you the reader as you now decipher my story. But, you will have to enter these pages with caution. Another important thing--after JFK was shot, the news media reported on national television that three shots rang out in Dallas that day. How did they know that and who told them to report this? Witnesses present reported more shots and even thought firecrackers were being set off. Just maybe we were all under mind control that day. When Dan Rather lied to us about the Zapruder film for the next 12 years then who knows what else was a lie.

My thanks to Stanley Kubrick for our evening together in March of 1976 who provided me with information he had not realized, nor did I, until two years later in 1978. I believe God brought us together that evening because two of the many subjects we discussed I was told all my life never existed. This conversation changed the direction I took in my search for the truth and finished with the story you will read. I believe that the information Stanley wanted to be brought out in his work may have lead to his untimely death, since he has been wanting to make a film about this subject matter since his beginning as a filmmaker as far back as 1952. And only those very close to him would know what I am talking about. You will find out about one of these subjects we discussed in my book, and that subject is the Tri-lateral Commission. The other subject, which now I believe goes hand in hand with the first, I would finally see twenty-three years later, ending up in his film *"Eyes Wide Shut"* in 1999. The reason I say this concerning his untimely death is that Stanley was a stickler about editing his own films and never got to edit this particular film. You will read about my evening and conversation with Stanley Kubrick, in an upcoming autobiography which I will soon be writing about my life in the film industry,

John A. Gaetano
September 2012

At the time of this book's latest publishing we have passed the 60th anniversary of John F. Kennedy's death. Who knows how long it will be before the real truth comes out.

"So that thou incline thine ear unto wisdom and
apply thine heart to understanding."

--Proverbs

"Ye shall know the truth....
and the truth shall make you free...."

The above words, spoken by Our Lord, Jesus Christ, from the book of St. John 8:32, represent the motto of the CIA, considered one of the safeguards of our United States Government. At the main entrance of the building in Langley, Virginia, the words are engraved and set in the cornerstone. If we had the privilege to enter this American Institution, you and I as American citizens would have the opportunity to reflect on these words in stone and see the large engraved emblem set in the floor and encircled with inscription: "The Central Intelligence Agency of the United States of America."

PROLOGUE

It was a late spring evening in June 1992, when an American Airliner touched down at the airport in Little Rock, Arkansas. Michael Bradley emerged from the terminal with a single overnight bag in his hand. He had been a handsome man in his youth, but now, at forty-two, his features had matured to a more rugged, weary look. He whistled for a yellow cab and climbed in.

"Where to, sir?" the cabby asked.

"Tenth and Parkson," he said wearily, leaning back in his seat. He had an appointment with the Powell, Leland, Vincent and Eisenbaum Law Firm in downtown Little Rock. The cab driver intuitively knew his customer wasn't in the mood for talking and drove in silence to their destination.

It was dark when Bradley arrived and paid the cab driver off. A light still glowed within the building, still open for business. With his luggage in hand, he entered.

The first thing that caught Michael Bradley's attention was that the inside of the building didn't resemble a law firm. It looked like one of the campaign headquarters for the Democratic candidate for President. Posters of William Jefferson Clinton were tacked on the walls and campaign literature were stacked in boxes on the desk. Several people, stuck behind desks, working the late shift were making calls on the phone. He paused at a desk, behind which a large poster announced "Clinton for President."

The receptionist smiled at him. "Welcome Mr. Bradley, nice to see you again!" she said cheerfully. She picked up her phone. "Mr. Vincent? Michael Bradley has arrived. Sure, fine..." The receptionist gave Bradley a surprised look. "Wow, that's a first! You can go right in without waiting..." As Bradley reached for the doorknob, the receptionist spoke up again. "Would you care for some coffee?"

Bradley grinned in response, "Boy, I think the Airline did me in with their coffee. Maybe you can get me a Seven Up to settle my stomach." He opened the door and walked into the office.

Frank Vincent stood from behind his desk, beaming as he greeted him, "Good to see you again, Michael!" Vincent was a few years older than Bradley and a senior member of this established law firm.

"Me too, Frank." The two shook hands and Vincent led Bradley to a chair.

"Well, how do you like our campaign headquarters?"

"So I've noticed," Bradley told him, chuckling. "You caught me by surprise on that one."

The receptionist knocked on the door and entered with a can of Seven up and a glass on a tray. She brought it over to Bradley. "Here you go, Mr. Bradley." She smiled at him and departed the room.

"Want a Bourbon to go with that Seven Up, my boy?" Vincent asked as he picked up his own drink from his desk. Bradley knew now why his friend was a little happier than usual to see him.

"Well, my boy," Vincent continued, "What brings a fine Indiana lawyer like you to Little Rock, Arkansas. I thought there were plenty of ambulances to chase in your own home state."

"You're right on that account, Frank, but this isn't a social call."

"Hmmm... You did say on the phone it was news that couldn't wait."

"Yes, I did," Bradley replied. He glanced over to see whether the door was closed. "What I have to tell you concerns matters of significant importance-- issues which have affected the national security of this country... And it also involves your friend...the one whose face is on all those campaign posters you have out there..."

Frank Vincent's smile faded to a thin, hard line. He put his drink back down on his desk. "Why don't you tell me all about it," he said, suddenly sober.

* * *

Two months later in the small town of Madison, Indiana, the hometown of Michael Bradley, certain events were set in motion to irrevocably change his life and the lives of others.

It was the month of August, and the local news reported the President of the United States, George Bush, was heading for the biggest challenge of his career. He had stiff competition with a man named Bill Clinton who became the 1992 Democratic candidate for President, whose popularity threatened to steamroll over Bush's campaign strategy.

But on this hot August night in the city center of Madison, the thoughts of the people were not on the presidential candidates. The fuse had been lit back in 1988 and Michael Bradley prepared for its explosive result. All hell would break loose in this quiet town.

Michael Bradley drove his '88 Bentley down the street and parked two blocks from the Greyhound Bus terminal. He turned the ignition off and stared ahead at the beige brick building a few streets away. A bus pulled into the entrance way and moved around to the back debarkation area.

Bradley sat in the driver's seat, breathing hard. He was scared, and there was an edge of desperation about him. He took a moment and forced himself to think seriously of what he would do. He faced a decision that could finally end his career. *It's not only my life, but the lives of others,* he thought to himself. He had reviewed his plan of action over and over in his mind, but there was always that little bit of doubt that pestered him, like a puppy nipping at his heels. He knew what he was doing was important. *This is the beginning of a wake-up call for the country. Will it come to its senses, or would it be suppressed in the name of National Security?* He grimaced to himself, the thoughts spinning around and around in his brain. *Only a new President would be able to make that decision now.*

He picked up his cellular phone and dialed. Anyone walking by on the sidewalk would think he was praying the way he held it close to him.

"I'm ready," was all he said into the receiver. He hung up the phone and placed it in his jacket pocket. He reached for a can of Classic Coke in his cup holder and took a last swig from it.

He got out of his car, crossed the dimly lit street and entered a phone booth near the corner. As he fed the change into the phone and dialed, he glanced back at the bus terminal. A woman's voice came on the line.

"Michael?" the voice answered promptly as if expecting his call.

"Catherine, it's set. It looks like the coast is clear," he said nervously. "Are you okay?"

From the tone of her voice, Michael understood she was upset. "Michael, I can't go through with this! I'm worried! It's dad...he's been missing five days now, what if they have him?"

Michael impatiently interrupted, "Forget about your father!" Immediately, he knew he shouldn't have used that tone of voice. He chose his next words carefully so he wouldn't upset her further. "Listen to me, Catherine. The old goat can take care of himself!"

Catherine disagreed, "No! Michael...you don't understand! Senator Fuller is dead. They found his body today, and Dad's voice was on Fuller's office recorder as the last person he met with. Now, my father has disappeared!"

The news caught Michael totally off guard. "The Senator is dead? God damn!" He felt that things were really getting out of control now. "Catie, you've got to listen to me. If your father has disappeared, it might be his doing. That's one thing I know about him. And...realistically, Catie, if he is dead...well, I think you better start thinking about all of us who are still alive. You know it won't stop here. It's not like...okay, we better stop now, and hope it will all go away. They've been getting away with this type of thing for over thirty years now! You've got to go through with this! Please, Catherine! We can stop them, at least we can try! Your father didn't tell us he would back out, did he? We've started the ball rolling and if he's still with us, he'll do his part. He wouldn't want you to quit now! We're here to make a difference. We're here to prove all those people who have died over the years did not die in vain... Some of them believed, like us, Catie!"

Michael could hear Catherine's sobs over the phone. "I'm scared, Michael!"

"And you're saying I'm not, Catie?" Michael's eye caught a movement in the street. A tan Dodge Dart slowly drove by and turned a corner. "We all are! Now you know what Karl went through. Right now, John Modini is risking his life-- again-- and for what? He's proven we were right about Karl, and now he wants to sacrifice his life to not only to save our lives, but the future of this country... So a lot is at stake. Trust me, I know you, Catie," he assured her, "You'll be fine!"

Catherine remained silent on the other end of the line, letting his words sink in. Michael heard her take a deep breath. Michael spoke again, this time with emotion in his voice, "I love you; Catherine!"

Her voice finally responded. She had finally made her decision. "How much time before I enter the terminal?"

Michael smiled, grateful of her decision. "That's my girl! Give me ten minutes and you're on your own." Michael listened for her response, but she didn't answer. "Catherine...are you still there?"

"Yes, I'm just wiping my tears... I love you, too, Michael! God bless!" She hung up on her end.

Bradley stared at the receiver, knowing full well the pressure she was under. For a few moments, he felt the twinge of guilt and regretted what he was putting her through. She was actually putting her life on the line for him. But there was no other way to end this situation. They had to go through with their plan no matter what happened.

He dialed 911, and checked his watch. It read 8:50 p.m. When the Madison Police Department answered, Michael spoke in a quick and intense tone, "Listen carefully. There is a bomb in the Greyhound bus terminal. It is scheduled to go off in fifteen minutes at exactly 9:05 p.m. It will kill everyone inside the building if it isn't evacuated immediately."

Michael hung up the phone, feeling his heart pounding in his chest. Then he switched to his cellular phone and dialed again. "Fifteen minutes, go!" Sliding his cellular back into his coat pocket, he hurried from the booth and into the street.

Then suddenly, from out of the darkness, two men approached him dressed in business suits. Michael was nervous, but tried not to look suspicious. He was confident these men didn't know what he was involved in.

One of them removed an identification card and a badge from his suit pocket and identified himself and his partner. "We're Federal Agents... Are you Michael Bradley?"

Michael raised an eyebrow coolly and smiled, "Wow! You guys startled me! Ah...no, no...I'm sorry. You must have mistaken me for someone else... My name is Doug Stanton... Sorry, excuse me!" Michael walked past the two men and headed down the street to the bus terminal without looking back. He thought he was having an anxiety attack and tried to control his breathing.

The two men started following him. He heard his name shouted, but ignored it. He hurried along the sidewalk to the corner, hoping to put some distance between him and the men.

As he stepped into the crosswalk, one of the men yelled out, "Don't take another step, Mr. Bradley!"

Michael halted in mid stride and stopped. Then a strange feeling came over him as though some sixth sense warned him of danger. Had it been the authoritative note in the man's voice?

His eyes misted over as he whispered to himself, "Please God, let me get through this!" Michael squeezed his eyes tightly, hoping the men would just disappear. The street became silent as the two men approached him from behind.

Michael opened his eyes and decided to face them. He faced them, but the agents continued to stare him down, to intimidate him. "I have an appointment," he told them.

The second Federal Agent reached into his unbuttoned coat and pulled out a gun, "I think not...Mr. Bradley!"

"Look," Michael began, "I already told you, I am not--"

The agent fired his gun once, but Michael didn't even see the flash from the muzzle. The bullet struck Michael between the eyes, killing him instantly. The noise of the gunshot echoed in the dark empty streets and faded before his lifeless body hit the ground.

* * *

Eight months later in Washington D.C. on a sunny April day in 1993, a dark gray government car pulled up to the White House gate. It received permission to pass on through and drove up the path to the historic structure. Two agents from the Federal Bureau of Investigation inside the car gawked at the scenery outside. They felt that it was a rare privilege to be driven on the grounds of this historic structure. Of course, they told themselves; it was all within the guidelines of doing their duty. It was their first time here and prepared themselves to conduct a proper interview with one of the men closest to the President.

Once they entered the White House, the agents were escorted through the corridors, now presided over by a newly elected President, Bill Clinton. The FBI agents exchanged glances as they stopped before a stenciled door reading, 'Frank Vincent - Special Counsel to the President.'

A black Marine nodded, bid the two men adieu and departed.

Frank Vincent was sitting behind his desk and writing a memo when Schneider, his assistant knocked and entered

"You told me to let you know when the two FBI men arrived..." Schneider ventured, hoping he didn't disturb his boss.

Vincent sighed, "Please send them in." He got up from his desk as Schneider led the two FBI agents into the room.

This is agent William Rutland, and this is agent Phyllip Shayne. Schneider introduced them to Frank Vincent.

Vincent greeted them with a handshake and a smile, "What brings you gentlemen here today? Please, sit down..." he gestured to a couch against the wall.

Schneider moved to the door. "If you need anything," he said to Vincent, "I'll be right outside." He closed the door behind him.

The two men seated themselves on a couch near a window with a picturesque view of Pennsylvania Avenue. Agent Rutland was very impressed with the surroundings, and he expresses it, "I have to say that this is my first time."

Vincent gave him a puzzled look.

The agent explained, "I mean here...in the White House... It's really a thrill!" Even his partner nodded.

Vincent smiled, "Yes, for me, too. I have to agree with you." He understood what Rutland meant. He felt the same way when he first moved into his White House office. He leaned back against the front of his desk in a casual pose. "What can I do for you, gentlemen?"

The second agent, Shayne spoke up, "We don't want to take up too much of your time, Mr. Vincent, but we've been asked to reopen the Michael Bradley case. Ever since his homicide last year, there have been more questions about his death than answers. Surprisingly, many people across the nation, including the Miami Police Department, are very disturbed by his death. We're wondering why? Apparently, Michael Bradley was a friend of yours, sir. While going through his calendar notes for last June, we discovered he paid a visit to you in Little Rock."

Vincent pursed his lips and turned from the men. "I see," was all he said.

Agent Shayne continued, "We're trying to follow up on all the leads we can. So if you can give any information on his visit..."

Vincent responded suddenly, avoiding the question, "Yes, yes, he was a friend of mine. I was in total shock when I first heard of the circumstances of his death."

The first agent interrupted him, "Excuse me, was he such a good friend, sir, enough to give you information to keep in his trust?"

Vincent didn't realize the Federal Agents would be so direct, so soon. He answered as best he could, "Yes, in a manner of speaking. At the time, I did not take everything he said seriously, but now I have come to believe it is something to be considered. I'm afraid his death has haunted me ever since I heard of it."

The second agent became curious. "Can you discuss any of what Bradley said in this conversation to you? Did he happen to mention something about a certain letter?" Shayne left the sentence unfinished.

Vincent crossed to the window and looked out beyond the White House fence to the streets and buildings in the distance. He seemed lost in thought, as though he didn't hear the question, staring straight ahead.

Agent Shayne exchanged glances with his partner. "Sir, has this information you carry have anything to do with the President or his knowledge of--"

"I'm sorry gentlemen," Vincent came out of his comatose-like stare and flashed one of his gracious smiles, "Any of the conversations between Mr. Bradley and myself are confidential. It's something that I must work out for myself. Maybe in due time I might be able to answer you. Now do you gentlemen have anything else to ask?"

The smiles left the agents lips. The men were visibly bothered because they couldn't get the information they wanted. They rose from the couch to leave. "We feel, sir, whatever information he has given you, might have gotten him killed," Rutland said handing Vincent his card. "If you change your mind, please contact us at this number." The two agents shook his hand and thanked him.

"One more question; sir..." Shayne said before opening the door. "Before Bradley died, were you aware of any connection between Bradley and Oliver Stone, the film director who went to the Congress and the Senate to open the Kennedy files?"

Vincent gave them a quick smile and shook his head, "No, gentlemen, I assure you. Mr. Bradley and I have never met or spoken with Mr. Stone!"

The agent continued to press, "Do you know anything about Stone or his film?"

Vincent shook his head, "No, only a little. In '91, the government secretly tried to suppress the film, *JFK*. They had a spy at the studio that kept an eye on Stone while he was making the movie. They had no plans to release it, but it got out of hand, partly because Stone and the producers planned to sue the studio. Now this is only rumor, mind you, but someone in the government gave the word to release the film! Did they get cold feet? Did they want to confuse the public? Who knows? Maybe the plan then was to do what they did to Mr. Garrison in 1969, to campaign to destroy Mr. Stone and his movie."

Vincent visibly showed his impatience to the two agents. "That is all I have heard, gentlemen. Some of it may be true and some of it not. Coincidentally, while Stone was up on the hill, Mr. Bradley was killed, but believe me, no paths have ever crossed between myself, Mr. Bradley or Mr. Stone."

Agent Rutland remarked, "This entire investigation seems to be built on rumor. We're only seeking to find the truth here." He thanked Mr. Vincent again for his time and departed, still in awe of his surroundings.

Vincent closed the door behind them and frowned. Was this just a routine inquiry, or was something sinister in the works? Frank Vincent didn't have long to wait before his suspicion was confirmed.

The summer of '93 wound to an end in Washington D.C., and a few months later, the headlines of The Washington Post flashed the daily headline: *Frank Vincent, Special Counsel to the President, found dead in park outside Washington, D.C.*, while another copy read: *Bullet hole in head of Special Counsel to the President, apparent suicide, gun found beside body.* Other national headlines read: *Suicide note found in pieces twenty-four hours later. Office files missing. President in flux over Special Counsel's suicide and present investigation!*

Then on November 21, 1993, the newspaper reported an unrelated, yet important story: *President agrees with Warren Commission findings on eve of the thirtieth anniversary of JFK Assassination,* while other headlines read: *Arlen Spector's magic bullet rides again, his theory is alive and well as a book: 'Case Closed' points to Oswald as lone assassin, proves there was no conspiracy! Computer analyses now proves again, without a shadow of a doubt, Lee Harvey Oswald alone assassinated President Kennedy. KGB defector tells all to the author of book, Gerald Posner who confirms, OSWALD CAPABLE GUNMAN.*

Dan Rather televising CBS news gave Gerald Posner recognition in discrediting all conspiracies, including Oliver Stone's fantasy movie, *JFK*, and the humiliation of three witnesses, including a deaf mute who like the others, gave testimony concerning the assassination before millions of television viewers.

A commentator from a local news station reported this story on the air. "Dan Rather seemed overjoyed as if Posner was his Messiah, and his book was the Bible, by actually discrediting a deaf mute on television that had been consistent in his testimony about eye-witnessing a man with a rifle behind the grassy knoll."

The reporter continued, "As an American citizen I ask how does this Harvard graduate get to interview a Russian defector who had been under surveillance, incarcerated, and on the payroll to the CIA since his defection in the mid 1960's? Was Posner on that sixth floor with Oswald? How ironic that the District Attorney and future Federal Judge, Jim Garrison, had no such cooperation from the Government he was working for! So I ask the question now who is Posner working for? Certainly not for himself!"

Chapter One

"Disclosure"

It was in early Fall of 1981 that Private First Class Daniel Conrad of the United States Marine Corps walked into the Congress of the United States of America to present his case before the House Subcommittee on East Asian and Pacific affairs. Father Conrad in full uniform nervously sat down next to his attorney. The lawyer whispered into his ear, explaining the formalities to come.

Congressman Roy Hitchcock, the Chairman of the House Subcommittee banged his mallet and asked for the House to come to order.

"Now that we have Father Daniel Conrad present we may begin...if that is all right with you, sir. We have a full day, Father, and allocated enough time for you as our first priority of the day. I hope you respect our position, sir, though you wear a uniform of the Marine Corps that we address you as Father, for we are well aware of your position with the Roman Catholic Diocese."

Father Conrad slowly rose before the members of the Subcommittee. He looked around the room, glancing at the few people in the galleries and was surprised to recognize a familiar face. Senator Gerald Fuller, a distinguished looking gentleman, was present as a spectator at the proceedings.

Father Conrad turned his attention to the Congressmen before him. "Gentlemen, far as I'm concerned you have called me everything in the book these past few weeks. I am not here to be defined as anything, but to preserve the lives and rights of those soldiers eagerly awaiting your help and response. I am here for them as a soldier, but you may address me by any title, formal or informal, before this House as long as I can speak here today with respect and without rude interruptions or outbursts, as the people I represent have outlined for me."

The chairman nodded to the other members of Congress present on the Subcommittee, and they returned the gesture. Then he acknowledged Father Conrad. "Father, we are in agreement you shall have the respect of the Committee and the privilege to speak your mind without interruption as long as you keep your presentation time to the allotted fifteen minutes. If you agree with this stipulation, then you may proceed. You have the floor, sir"

"This arrangement is fair. I'll say everything I have to in this appropriate time period." Father Conrad took out his notes and glanced over them. He really didn't need them. He knew what he wanted to say. Everyone was quiet as he began his statement: "I want to outline what I know about American prisoners who are alive and being held against their will in Vietnam. Allow me to call to your attention the attached *Washington Times* article dated May 21, 1981, as an accurate summary of what I saw and heard of other American prisoners of war while I was in Vietnam. I am concerned you as Congressmen have not taken steps to bring my brothers, our fellow American prisoners, home. It's time for you to outline what act ions you had taken, besides holding hearings and writing letters, to rescue these live POW's! I fought Communists in a war, gentlemen, in Southeast Asia in which you, those of you in Congress, had started and then walked away from in 1973. To make things worse, you left me, as well as many other Americans, behind!"

In a few brief sentences, Father Conrad had their attention. "I have been told repeatedly by officials of the U.S. Government to remain silent and only privately discuss my knowledge of Americans who were held back as prisoners by the Vietnamese. Since both Presidents Nixon and Ford have...been less than truthful about presenting this issue to the American people, and after waiting through a half decade of silence, I decided to disclose to the public my firsthand knowledge of other Americans still in prison camps in Vietnam! An article was written in the *Wall Street Journal*, based on my evidence. Much to my surprise, I received little attention from Congress despite this alarming disclosure. Between 1973 and 1978, I alone had witnessed sixty to seventy American prisoners in captivity.

"Earlier this spring I held a news conference in Washington, D.C. and gave names, dates and locations of the Americans whom I knew were still in Vietnam to Congressman William Henley for transmittal to President Reagan, who I respected very much, our concern. To date, I am

2

given to understand that the advisors to the President have refused to permit a meeting between the President and Congressman Henley to discuss the issue of any live POW's I saw! I cannot understand why a President who declared the POW/MIA problem to be this nation's highest national priority, would allow his advisors to stop this important information from reaching him! Is this fair, gentlemen, for those of us who voted for the President to be treated in this manner as though we didn't exist?

"Prior to today's testimony, I met in a closed session with members of the Senate and the House Subcommittee. After what I understood as an intense lobbying effort by some of my friends to set up this meeting, I, for the life of me and the life of our lord, Jesus Christ, do not and cannot understand what you are hiding! I was interrupted and instructed by both Congressmen Thomas and Senator Gerald Fuller, not to pursue this matter."

Father Conrad felt the Senator's presence in the gallery. Fuller just glared at him silently as he continued his speech. "In an elevator with both branches of government present, they asked me *not*-- I'm appalled to say-- to discuss openly my sightings of live American prisoners of war held in Vietnam. I cannot understand why our government wants to keep it quiet."

He gestured angrily to the members of House Subcommittee, "*You* have left live American POW's in Vietnam and have not taken steps to rescue them!"

A senior congressman from the panel joltingly spoke out at Conrad, interrupting him, "I believe you've made your point more than once here, Father Conrad!"

Father Conrad stared for the moment at the Congressman who broke his train of thought. Chairman Hitchcock quickly raised his voice, "I wish to apologize to P.F.C. Conrad on behalf of my colleagues' sudden outburst." He nodded to Conrad. "Would you please proceed with your statement?"

Father Conrad clenched his teeth, hiding his frustration. He took a moment to compose his thoughts, shuffling his notes. He asserted a change of demeanor and composure and then continued, "I freely volunteered to come forward in open session and swear under oath these American POW's I spoke with and saw with my own eyes want to come home to America! They *want* to be rescued! You simply cannot write these live Americans off as war casualties! I understand it was you, Congressman Hitchcock and Congressman Simmons who wanted to see me only in a closed executive session-- and it took an arm and a leg to get me here before all of you today. I believe no American should have to go through what I did to get the attention of the United

States Congress, so listen closely gentlemen! The only reason I came forward six months ago, with a public disclosure of my eyewitness accounts of United States POW's, was to help in bringing these Americans home. I should not be ignored or hidden away in a back room, and told by Congressmen and Senators to be quiet! It's my understanding, from other POW's as well, we received better treatment when it was widely known we were important to the American Public-- it would be a betrayal of American values and the Constitution of the United States if you as Congressmen were not doing everything you could in your power to bring these Americans home to their families.

"It has been six long months now since I came forward. As I pray to God, I wish to be told three things: What have you done to bring these Americans home? Why did you walk away and leave us there? And why do you want to hide from the American public the proof the government left live American prisoners of war still in Vietnam? Please, in the name of our Lord, Jesus Christ, tell me!"

The Congressmen stirred uneasily in their seats, murmuring among themselves. Father Conrad had made his point.

"This plea concludes my speech here today. I am prepared to testify in open session before the American people so they can judge the truthfulness of my information. I am unable, nor will I state my case with you, or anyone from now on, behind closed doors. I would like you to write or respond publicly to the three questions I have asked of this Subcommittee today. Thank you for allowing me to be here today, to acknowledge my concerns. Please, gentlemen, I pray...bring home the live prisoners of war! I ask you in God's name, Amen!"

* * *

On Sunday afternoons in Salem, Oregon, in the fall 1963, it was customary for teenagers to go to the local downtown theater, the Bijou, for an afternoon of entertainment. This was especially true for a young man of thirteen who had no other pressing desires or girlfriends to contend with, and plenty of time to consume. In this chilly month of October, he took an advantage of the opportunity to enjoy viewing the weekend films. He knew the days were numbered before the heavy snowfall of winter came, and his trips to the theater would dwindle to zero.

The weekend matinee at the theater offered plenty of entertainment. It featured a cartoon, a newsreel and a World War II film called *The Great Escape*. Last summer's hit, *McLintock,*

4

featuring John Wayne, was the second feature. This thirteen-year old boy had already watched it three times and been back now for his forth. He couldn't pass up a John Wayne western like that on a double feature bill for only thirty-five cents, could he?

But as the young man settled back in the theater seat, waiting for Steve McQueen and John Wayne to appear, it was the *March of Time* type newsreel that sparked his interest. He had always shown a curiosity in history, so he watched, engrossed with the subject matter. The screen gave a presentation of John F. Kennedy's first 1,000 days in office. Kennedy, from 1961 to the present. Not only that, he watched a familiar hero of his, J. Edgar Hoover, the head of the FBI, in conference with the President and his brother Attorney General, Robert F. Kennedy. A year earlier this thirteen-year old had seen the Warner Brothers classic, *The FBI Story,* which motivated him to want to be an FBI agent for the government of the United States.

The screen introduced General Douglas MacArthur emerging from the Oval Office of the White House and into the garden followed by President Kennedy. The announcer from the soundtrack reported the events,

"After concluding over a three-hour talk, General Douglas MacArthur, invited today for a luncheon with the President, was apparently impressed with the youngest elected President of the United States. President Kennedy later expressed a warm admiration for this reactionary old soldier. This was the President's second meeting with General MacArthur. The first time was in New York City after the Bay of Pig's disaster."

The young man in the theater seat hung on every word. The announcer continued, "Today MacArthur told Kennedy he was extremely critical of the military advice the President had been getting from the Pentagon, blaming the military leaders of the previous ten years, who he said had advanced the wrong younger officers. 'You were lucky,' MacArthur commented, 'to have this mistake happen in Cuba, where the strategic cost was not too great.' MacArthur implored the President to avoid a U.S. buildup in Vietnam, or any other part of the Asian mainland, because he felt the domino theory was ridiculous, especially in a nuclear age. MacArthur continued to point out there were too many domestic problems in this country-- the urban crisis, the ghettos, and the economy which should have far more priority than Vietnam. Kennedy came out of the meeting stunned from the General's remarks that a man such as MacArthur should give him such unmilitary advice. It impressed the President enormously.

"In 1962, Kennedy inspected his newly-developed soldiers, the Green Berets, as the State

5

Department announced an increase in its American military advisors in South Vietnam to bolster the Vietnamese government of Diem against Ho Chi Minh's Communist North. But this was also the year of October 1962, and the Cuban Missile Crisis became the biggest challenge for the President."

Photos flashed across the screen of missile silos in Cuba. The Pictures were taken from the U-2 Reconnaissance spy plane. "As Kennedy confronted the Russian Premiere Nikita Khrushchev in the showdown of a lifetime, this became the greatest threat in history of the cold war since World War II! Dr. Martin Luther King, Jr. visited the White House as J.F.K. received the leader of *The March on Washington* on August 28, 1963. Just a month earlier the President had signed the instruments of ratification for the Nuclear Test Ban Treaty and announced this was the happiest day of his life. As this fall lead to the conclusion of the President's 1000 days in office, the Kennedy brothers attended a Washington charity benefit for Universal's Stanley Donen film: *Charade* to be released at Christmas time starring Cary Grant and Audrey Hepburn. The Attorney General and the President commented about its star and their favorite actor, Cary Grant. Bobby laughed while he explained, 'At least once a month the President and I call Cary at his home on the coast just to listen to his voice.'"

The young man left the double feature late that afternoon, not realizing what the coming weeks would develop. His thoughts were not on the two movies, but the newsreel and the news concerning his President. It was a turning point and put a lasting mark on him for the rest of his life. John Modini would have no idea why God picked him to become involved in what would become the greatest mystery and puzzle of the Twentieth Century.

* * *

Something awful had been brewing in the South, something that could have been prevented, something of a wake-up call for both the Treasury Department and the Justice Department to be well aware of. Something that would be a warning for us all that the mood of this country was heading towards a change-- a frightening course no one could imagine except for those who were involved. Just thirty years earlier in 1932, the Lindbergh kidnapping case took center stage. It became a national mystery which still, to this day, remains to many as unsolved.

Now a new mystery was developing and threatened to become one of the most controversial unsolved cases in history. It was the one mystery in which the government had no interest in solving, and would do everything in its power to hide from the American people. My name is Raymond Corrigan. I work with the Miami Police Department. I'm sure there are many people out there still walking around with a story to tell about what happened that day, but for me it started on my first night's assignment with the MPD narcotics squad. It was a late, sultry fall evening in downtown Miami Beach, Florida on November ninth, 1963.

Roy Orbison singing *Running Scared* was playing loudly from an RCA pocket radio. A man walked alone, the music echoed, coming from his windbreaker, as he trudged down the street. He carried two sacks full of burgers from an all night diner. The man approached a car parked on the street facing the beach. The man reached the curbside window of two men sitting in a metallic blue Dodge Dart. These men were narcotics officers on a stakeout. The burger man, also on stakeout, handed one of the two bags to the officer sitting on the passenger side, wearing an earphone.

The man behind the wheel spoke out, "Do you mind?" The burger man didn't connect. The officer behind the wheel continued, "Could you turn off the 'Big O'? It might look a little suspicious!"

"Oh, you mean Roy Orbison? Sure! Sorry!" He turned off the radio.

The narcotics officer behind the wheel smiled, "So you're the new man assigned to the shittiest job on the Miami P.D. payroll-- next to a desk job that is. What's your name, kid?"

The burger man leaned into the window on the passenger side of the car. "The name is Corrigan."

The officer took off his earphones. "Well, welcome aboard the night shift, Corrigan. I'm Ramrod, and this is Wishbone."

Corrigan shook Ramrod's hand and nodded to Wishbone. "I get it-- 'Rawhide,' right? I was just transferred to your unit. I heard that you guys are the best!"

Ramrod laughed, "Hey, Wishbone, did you hear that, we're famous!"

Wishbone half smiled, "Don't get too excited kid, tonight is just another boring night. Don't mind it though, you'll get used to it. It gets worse as it rolls on!"

Corrigan's enthusiasm almost faltered, "Well, I better get back. My partner must be starving. Catch you guys, later!"

"Yeah, sure kid," Wishbone responded, "maybe we can go in style tomorrow night. Prime rib...sounds pretty good! Think about it kid!" He laughed as Corrigan headed out across the street.

Corrigan's partner, Gary, sat in a basement apartment of a Miami hotel called "*The*

7

Sunflower." Gary had a tape recording device set up, listening in on one of their informants talking to an unidentified man. Instead of writing down any information of importance, Gary worked on the day's crossword puzzle. A tape recording machine was running, getting the conversation on tape.

Corrigan entered the room with their sack of burgers. "I just met the rest of the team. Nice guys... Anything yet?" Corrigan was excited to be part of this sting operation.

Gary put his crossword puzzle down, anxious for dinner. "Nothing yet, boring...just some political organizer. I think it's for some Segregationist Party." Gary unwrapped his burger, losing his enthusiasm. "Great! Burgers again! It's either burgers or pizza! When do you think the department will break down and let us have steak and lobster?"

Corrigan answered curtly, "Maybe when you make Captain, sir. Then you can change the rules and be responsible for raising everybody's taxes. It's the taxpayers who furnish these elaborate burgers."

Gary scoffed. "Yes, me raising taxes? That'll be the day!" He bit into his burger, then suddenly just as fast, spit it back out.

"What is it?"

Gary adjusted his headphones, listening intently.

"Are you all right, sir?" Corrigan remarked, concerned.

Gary halted Corrigan with his upraised hand, "Shut the fuck up and listen to this!" He switched the sound to a small speaker box so Corrigan could hear and turned up the volume.

He heard an unidentified man speaking, "...A plan to kill the President is in the works... Kennedy will be shot with a high powered rifle from an office building. The gun that is to be used will be disassembled, taken into the building, and then reassembled and used for the murder! They will pick up somebody within hours...just to throw the public off!"

Gary was stunned by what he heard. "My God! Is this some sort of joke?" He quickly picked up the day's newspaper, and searched through it. He stopped at the headline: *President to arrive in Miami on the eighteenth.*

Corrigan read the caption and looked at Gary turning pale, "Shit! What's the procedure for something like this?"

Gary quickly reacted, "We'd better bring in the Secret Service on this--!" He nervously contemplated his next move, not believing what he just heard. "Son of a bitch!" he said to himself.

Corrigan could only wonder what was to happen next.

Chapter Two

"Garrison"

Three years later during the late afternoon of October 29th, 1966, gunshots sounded from the studio office of Lieutenant Commander William B. Pitzer, within the National Navel Medical Center in Bethesda, Maryland. But no one apparently heard them. Pitzer was found dead. Three government institutions investigated the incident. First was Navel Intelligence, followed by The Navel Investigative Service, an informal Board of the NNMC, and finally the Federal Bureau of Investigation. Whether these institutions realized it or not, all three investigations ominously came to the same conclusion. The final report stated the wound to Lieutenant Pitzer's head was self inflicted. Suicide. The Military had handled the autopsy. Navel intelligence would not release Pitzer's body or allow Mrs. Pitzer or their children to see or receive his body for the funeral arrangements. When Mrs. Pitzer asked for her husband's wedding band, her request was denied. The incident was hushed up to avoid public attention. The government, by their decisions and their actions, considered this case closed.

* * *

A few months later in Miami, during a warm January winter in 1967, a new plain clothed Corrigan entered the Miami Police Department with the day's newspaper in hand and on his mind. He nodded to his fellow officers who watched him moving at a fast pace toward their superior's office.

Corrigan entered and sat down, tossing the newspaper on his superior's desk. A photo of Jim Garrison, District Attorney of New Orleans, was the focus of the article on the front page. Behind Corrigan, outside the office, Gary and other members of the department crowded around to watch.

Captain Cummings looked down at the paper and sipped his hot coffee. "So?" was his only response.

Corrigan became a little upset, "Well, what are you going to do about it?"

Captain Cummings pushed the paper away. "Is there anything in this story concerning the Miami P.D.?"

Corrigan maintained his cool, "No, but if they shut this Garrison up and make trouble for him like they did to us, they could do it to anyone!"

"What the hell do you want me to do?" Captain Cummings yelled, "Those people in Washington can do anything they want! As long as I don't have to deal with them, I mind my own business!"

Corrigan noticed he had gathered an audience behind him. Although the door was closed, he couldn't help feel the tension developing in the room. He tried to be diplomatic about it. "Look, sir, we handed over a tape to the FBI four years ago and for some reason it never reached the hands of the Warren Commission. Why? It comes to light there are people connected to Kennedy's death who are suddenly dying. Why? Now, Jack Ruby keels over with cancer! This is our President we are talking about sir! I want to know why the government is trying to discredit and destroy a district attorney who works for them?"

The Captain spoke sharply, "Oh, maybe the fool wants to become Governor or some high powered Senator."

Corrigan shook his head, "Where does it say Garrison announces his candidacy for anything? All I'm saying, Captain, is that we think the people have a right to know." He turned to the others and acknowledged them, "They're backing me on this sir-- the others in this department. And we'd like an answer."

The Captain gazed at the front page of the newspaper in contemplation. His eyes finally connected with Corrigan. "What do you want from me?"

Corrigan straightened up and demanded, "To go public with the tape and permission to release a proclamation. All that I am asking for is just a statement sir, we handed the tape over to the

FBI and it exists. Let the media handle it from there!"

His superior scrutinized Corrigan again. Corrigan pressed on to make his point, "I don't like what they're doing to Garrison. And if it were you, or one of us, I'd hope to see the department backing us."

"Even if it meant going home one day to find your family totally dismembered?" The Captain asked cautiously,

Corrigan raised his eyebrow, then bluffed his way through. "They can't kill us all, sir!"

"Don't be surprised!" his Superior snapped back. Tense seconds passed as Captain Cummings thought it over. "Okay, Corrigan, it's your head in a sling. You have my blessings. Go ahead and jerk off with this, but just check to be sure the M.P.D. handed the tape over to the FBI, per regulations-- no speculations or conclusions!"

Corrigan felt overwhelmed at his victory, "No sir, none. The tape says what it says. The public and the media will do that for us, easily!"

"Wait," The Captain stopped Corrigan as he was ready to leave. "You go ahead, but remember, I don't want any part of it!"

Corrigan grinned and nodded his head in thanks. He left the room with a satisfied confidence, and was pleased to receive handshakes and pats on the back from his friends and coworkers for a job well done.

* * *

1967 was the year of upheaval, the flower child, Vietnam escalation, The Beatles and The Doors. It seemed everyone sang of San Francisco and peace and love on the Pacific West Coast, while on the East Coast the politicians and generals concerned themselves with an overseas war.

The news of the Vietnam war was diverted into the background as the sunny afternoons brought out the best during spring break, including songs about a white rabbit, about beach boys, surfers, and sun worshipers living on love in Southern California.

One particularly beautiful landmark between San Francisco and Los Angeles was Santa Barbara. Unlike the humidity of Miami, Santa Barbara was the Mecca of the coastline resorts. It had all the warmth, comfort, and fresh air where, like in Miami, the rich and famous lived and vacationed all year around. The old Summer Spanish Fiestas were as famous here down on State Street as Mardi Gras was down in New Orleans-- and just as proud.

Northeast, above Santa Barbara, lay San Simeon, the famous William Randolph Hearst Castle, used as a metaphor for Orson Welles' motion picture masterpiece, *Citizen Kane*. Ironically, Hearst destroyed people's lives for years in his newspapers and hoped to do the same to Welles, and RKO Radio Pictures, the studio that produced *Kane*. But in the end, the film would become what critics now proclaim the greatest American film. Hearst eventually destroyed himself in the process. His castle stood erected as a monument to Hollywood's scandalized past where the Hollywood elite once partied.

On April seventh, between San Simeon and off the coast of Santa Barbara, an afternoon dinner party was held at a beautiful large and luxurious house with a view of the beach. Cars were parked by a valet. Guests were greeted as they arrived at the entrance.

A young man of seventeen attended this plush party and attempted to remain inconspicuous, trying to avoid any encounters with anyone who caught sight of him. His luck ran out when the hostess, a beautifully sun-tanned fiftyish year-old woman named Julia spotted him.

"John... John! Over here, darling... I want you to meet some very special people who have just arrived."

John Modini half smiled and dropped his head, "Yes, Aunt Julia."

Aunt Julia put her arm around him and whispered to him, "John, you've got to be a little more peppy than this. This isn't a funeral party. These people are influential. They could help you up the road of life!" She perked up as she turned to her guests and smiled at two she recognized. "Congressman Fuller! I want you to meet my youngest sister's child, my nephew, John Modini. John is down visiting us from Oregon on his spring break. He's a big senior this year! John, this is Gerald Fuller and his wife, Caroline. They presently reside in Washington D.C. Now, Gerald, John is President of his school, isn't that right, John?"

"Well..." John Modini started, but couldn't get a word in edgewise.

Julia continued, "So politics is something you two have in common. Meanwhile, I'll busy myself in the kitchen. We've got to get more steaks on the barbecue. Caroline, would you mind helping me with the hors d'oeuvres? Thank you, you're a dear!"

As the two women departed, Modini politely smiled. Congressman Fuller tried to fill the void, "So...you're the school president, that's quite an honor at your age. You--"

Modini cut in, "Actually, sir, I'm only the class president."

Fuller smiled, "And I am only a congressman," he laughed. "Still, just the same, very impressive. It shows you have ambition, character, spunk. So you're planning on going into politics, are you?"

John Modini's eye caught a movement at the doorway entrance. He noticed a very pretty girl, young, blonde, and about thirteen years old, enter with her father. He was immediately attracted to her lovely figure, but his concentration remained on Fuller's question, "Not exactly, sir. I don't really know what I want to do. I like photography. I'm not really interested in politics, sir. I just like to help people and maybe change things for the better."

Fuller was impressed by the young man's candor, "Well, that's definitely what I try to do. It's all part of politics, son..."

Modini looked at Fuller, "No offense, sir, but politics to me is about taking and not giving."

John's Uncle George interrupted the conversation, arriving with two more guests. "Well, well... How are you two getting along? You've met my nephew?"

Fuller responded to George's question, "Yes, yes, John is a fine boy!"

Uncle George winked at Modini while presenting his new guests. "Gerry, I believe you know Judge Kencade and his beautiful daughter, Catherine? They've come all the way from Madison, Indiana."

It was the same girl who had arrived only moments before with her father. *So Catherine Kencade is her name*, John Modini thought. *I won't forget that.* The girl looked even prettier up close.

John Modini glanced away before she realized he was staring at her. This was the type of girl he would like to spend with. Someone he wouldn't mind getting to know better. But he remembered his manners. He focused his attention on the girl's father, the judge, tall and lanky and in his mid-fifties.

Gerald Fuller shook Judge Kencade's hand with enthusiasm. "Hank! You old goat, how in the heck are you?"

Judge Henry Kencade smiled. "Fine, just fine, Gerry...and you?" Kencade said, a bit red faced.

"Never felt better, especially after this last election," said Fuller. "It was nip and tuck there for a while but it's fine now, just fine. Caroline is around here somewhere."

Modini gave a cordial smile to Catherine who reluctantly returned it. She looked as though she weren't pleased to be here.

"Judge," George said, putting a hand on Modini's shoulder, "I want you to meet my nephew. He's visiting us for a few days from Oregon. John, this is Judge Henry Kencade, who's taking a small vacation from his state of Indiana with his daughter Catherine."

Modini shook hands with the judge, "How do you do, sir?"

Kencade reciprocated and introduced his daughter, "A pleasure. My daughter, Catie..."

"I'm pleased to meet you, Catherine," he said, extending his hand. He took the opportunity to look without embarrassment into her eyes.

"Catie," she said bluntly, hardly making eye contact. "I like to be called Catie." She reluctantly shook his hand, nodded and looked away, like one who was snobbish and spoiled.

"Kencade, you're doing well these days," Fuller said politely. Then he smiled at the young girl. "Well... Catherine-- Catie-- You've grown into a beautiful young woman since the last time I saw you."

Catherine brightened up at Fuller's cordial remark. "Thank you, Congressman," she responded with a smile. "I believe I'm surviving."

John Modini stared at Catherine with confusion. He felt a pang of jealousy because Congressman Fuller seemed to captivate her attention. He almost wondered what he was doing wrong to make a good impression.

Fuller saw his wife in the crowd and gestured to her. "Caroline, look who's here. Good old Hank. And would you take a good look at Catherine, his daughter!"

Caroline looked Catherine up and down, "I see... Nice to see you again, Catie."

"Nice to see you, too. Excuse me everyone. I'm going to mingle with the crowd." She moved to a table serving punch.

Caroline resumed her conversation. "Hello, Hank. I'm sorry about Martha. She was a good friend to me."

Kencade nodded, "Thank you, Caroline, she still is."

Caroline excused herself and joined the other guests.

"I'm sorry Hank, about Martha's health, I hear she's in a convalescent home."

Kencade nodded, "It's pretty bad... That's why I brought Catie out here. She didn't know that her mother tried to commit suicide."

John Modini felt awkward listening in on a personal conversation that had little to do with him. As he excused himself, he heard Fuller say to Kencade, "Come on, Hank, let's get ourselves a dry martini and let the young be young." Modini headed off in Catherine's direction.

Catherine held a plastic cup with punch and was conversing with two other guests. Modini helped himself to some punch then waited near by. When the two guests finally left, Modini finally summoned up the courage to move over to her. He was sure she was aware of his presence, but chose to ignore him.

Modini nervously made the first move to open a conversation. "So, you're from Indiana, huh? I've seen *The Music Man*...and heard the song, *Gary, Indiana*. What year are you in at school?"

Catherine hardly glanced at him. She was busy looking at two young male college students in the crowd. "I'm thirteen if that's what you want to know."

John Modini smiled, "I'm here from Oregon, visiting my Aunt and Uncle on spring break. I can show you around the place, if you'd like..." he offered.

Catherine put her plastic cup down on the table. "Excuse me, it's really boring hanging out here, so if you don't mind..." Without waiting for a reply from Modini, she walked away from him as he looked on in bewilderment.

"Sure..." John Modini watched her cross the room and smile at the two college students. The two men responded by looking at each other, wondering who this gorgeous creature was. After a few words, the three went out the back door, heading for the beach.

Two hours later, near sunset, most of the guests were outside, partying on the beach, or barbecuing, swimming, or playing a volleyball game. A football sailed overhead as Modini walked past the two college students chasing Catherine into the surf. One of them picked her up and tossed her into a wave.

Aunt Julia was concerned with John's moodiness. She approached her nephew, passing two guests reading and discussing the front page headlines of that day's newspaper. "John, why aren't you out swimming or playing football with the other young folks? You're supposed to be enjoying yourself."

John Modini tried to be diplomatic about the situation. "Oh, I'm just doing some thinking right now, Auntie. I might join in later."

"You seem to be thinking all day! You're not ill are you, dear?"

"No, Aunt Julia. I'm fine."

Julia gave him a concerned look. "Now, John--" she began. She was planning to say something when she saw Congressman Fuller, Caroline, and Judge Kencade approaching.

Fuller had one too many drinks, and he interrupted Julia in passing, "Now here, for example, is a handsome young man who knows what he wants out of life, don't you, son?" He spoke up to his wife and Judge Kencade, indicating John Modini. "Tell me, John, what do you think you'll be doing a year from now in 1968?"

Modini found the question tantalizing as he looked at Julia for his answer. "That's the 64,000 dollar question, sir. I really don't know. I'll probably get drafted!"

Fuller's eyes opened in surprise, "Well, I hope you're not one of those who are thinking of skipping out of town if duty calls-- scrambling for the Canadian border, are you, son?"

Modini laughed. "I've never thought of that, sir," he replied, "I always thought that it was my duty to serve my country if I were called."

Fuller straightened up and smiled, "That's the spirit, son!" He put his arm around him, "Now this is the kind of American allegiance that should be in all our young kids throughout this nation. Some of the students are totally out of control, too spoiled! Free love my ass! They seem to forget about our flag and what it stands for, about Ma and her apple pie!"

The two men with the newspaper joined the group after overhearing Fuller giving his little speech. Fuller continued, speaking to this impromptu crowd. "Those kids need their butts kicked occasionally. If they only could have witnessed what we went through during World War II. Isn't that right, Hank?"

Judge Kencade nodded, but didn't say anything.

"Maybe it's because of headlines like this, Congressman!" One of the guests with the newspaper handed it to Fuller, showing him the day's front page. "What about this, Congressman? Is there any truth in what this man Garrison says? Is the government hiding something from us? Is there such a conspiracy?"

Fuller read the headlines: "New Orleans District Attorney, Jim Garrison and his office announce they have solved the case of Kennedy's assassination and charging Clay Shaw with conspiracy in the murder of John F. Kennedy!"

Fuller blinked and responded angrily, "Garrison's a total crackpot! Don't believe any of this crap you read from this, folks!" He slapped the newspaper. "Believe me...this character will be driven out of office and put away into a booby-trap where he belongs. I guarantee you!" He saw

17

Henry Kencade looking at him and lowered his voice. "Sorry, Hank," he said apologetically, "I hope you don't take offense concerning the Mrs...!"

"Don't worry about it, Gerry"

Again, Fuller turned to the others, "But I don't take very lightly to the word 'conspiracy,' and people like this Garrison fellow-- scum like him only crave publicity for their own benefit!"

The second man stopped him, "But sir, he's a District Attorney, a man who works for our government!"

Fuller spit on the ground, "Not *my* government! Believe you me, when this is over and done with, he'll forever regret the black spot he put on this country!"

John Modini became very ill at ease listening to Fuller's ranting. He decided to move off, to disappear down to the beach, distancing himself from the party, and people in general. It was arguments like this that really upset him.

The sun set on the ocean and the darkness came within the hour. The night air brought with it the smell of a bonfire. A large one took center stage on the quiet beach, smoking and crackling with dry driftwood. It became a gathering place for the guests seeking warmth and the company of other people.

John Modini reappeared from his solitary stroll, still keeping his distance from the others as he walked around the fire. He saw the two young college students who earlier had been with Catherine had now paired up with two other young ladies from the party. Uncle George and Aunt Julia were roaming around, chatting with their guests, including Caroline Fuller who was drinking a bit more than she could handle.

George, who sipped a bottle of Coors, spotted Modini, heading for the house. He called out to him, "John...! Where are you going? Come and join us!"

Modini waved at him, "I'll be back, Uncle George, I need to hit the head." George responded by saluting him with his bottle of Coors.

Modini walked up to the house. He heard music coming from the inside. Someone had turned on the stereo, and a Dean Martin song was playing. In another room, he heard Jim Morrison and The Doors blasting from a portable radio. A strange mix, he thought as he paused on the enclosed patio, and looked down at the sparking bonfire on the beach below.

Modini turned and stumbled over a cushion someone had carelessly thrown on the floor. He caught himself in time, almost awakening Judge Kencade who was lying on a sofa in a deep sleep.

Modini quietly passed by him and entered the house through the patio's sliding glass doors. Nobody seemed to be around, so Modini walked in the direction of The Doors music which he found, surprisingly, coming from his bedroom. There, he found two young couples sitting huddled together snorting coke and smoking marijuana. One of the girls smiled while offering him a toke.

"No thanks..." Modini told her. He excused himself and departed, heading to the master bedroom, where the Dean Martin music was originating. He noticed the bathroom was unoccupied and entered. He turned on the light, closed the door and relieved himself. After washing his hands he discovered there were no towels and searched for one in the cupboard. Then, unexpectedly, he heard giggling coming up through an air vent in the floor. Modini listened for a moment. The noises were low, but Modini could tell it was a female's voice.

Before Modini could close the cupboard door he clearly heard a man's voice say the words, "I won't tell anyone if you don't...it will just be our little secret!"

A female's voice replied, "Will it hurt?"

The man's voice responded, "Only the first time, baby!"

Modini closed the cupboard and opened the bathroom door. He looked into the master bedroom and saw the television set was turned off. He shook his head and continued through the house.

He listened carefully, but couldn't hear anything now. Just the music. Still, he was determined to find the source of those voices.

Modini walked out the front door hearing Dean singing, "You're nobody until somebody loves you," with the added background sound of crickets accompanying the music. It was dark now, and nobody was around.

He walked around the side of the house and passed a lit basement window covered by curtains. Then he heard the voices again. They were muffled, coming from inside. Modini got down on his hands and knees and attempted to peer in through the curtains of the window, sure the voices came from down there.

The voices spoke again, but Modini couldn't understand what they were saying. Curiosity got the best of him, and he tried the window. It wasn't latched. Very carefully, he pulled the glass open a crack.

He heard a girl's laughter, then silence.

Carefully he leaned away from the window and broke a twig from a bush growing along the side of the house. He took the twig and poked it under the open window and brushed the curtain to one side, just enough to see two bodies. It was a man on top of a woman. They were in the act of having sex.

Modini was riveted to the spot, feeling both excitement and embarrassment along with a pang of guilt, so much so, he suddenly blushed. Hardly breathing now, he looked closer to see whether he could tell the identity of the lovers.

And when he discovered whom they were, he received the shock of his life. He immediately recognized Congressman Gerald Fuller as the man, but what was more incredible was the sight of the woman who was enjoying the pleasure of this clandestine rendezvous.

When Fuller drew back to kiss his partner, John Modini was shocked to see the other body was not of an older woman, but none other than thirteen-year-old Catherine Kencade.

Chapter Three

"The Serial Killer"

The wooden gavel hammered down on the judge's desk, almost cracking the wooden block. The uproar of the disgruntled spectators in a midwestern courtroom refused to subside. Judge Henry Kencade repeatedly called for order, but the noise continued. A courtroom drama was unfolding here, twenty-one years later in a Madison, Indiana courtroom in the early spring of 1988.

Michael Bradley, the Defense Attorney, stood at his table trying to regain the attention of the court. As the noise quieted down, Bradley addressed the court. "Your Honor--"

But the Judge would not hear him. The Honorable Henry Kencade, a man now more cantankerous and outspoken than he was two decades ago, interrupted Bradley and reprimanded the spectators for their noisy disturbance. "I will not have another word said in this courtroom or I will throw every one of you out."

The Judge turned and fixed his eyes on the woman who caused the disruption, standing beside Bradley. "Mrs. Rogers. I will not tolerate this conduct in my courtroom-- ever!" Judge Kencade was extremely agitated.

Mrs. Catherine Rogers had become the focal point of the Judge's wrath. She was in her mid-thirties, and dressed smartly for the courtroom: navy blue suit and jacket and neatly arranged blonde hair. She stood at the defense table, her eyes glittering with anger. There was a challenge, and something bordering on hostility, in the tightness of her lips.

Michael Bradley couldn't help notice the defiant look in Catherine's face. He was relieved she was on his side. Only a few minutes earlier he had completed his closing argument to the jury. He was defending a serial killer, a man by the name of Karl Hunter.

The defendant, the accused killer, Karl Hunter sat at the defense table, stiff, emotionless, staring at his folded hands on the table top. The man was deliberately ignoring all the commotion. It had been an uphill battle for Bradley to defend the man. Hunter did nothing, said nothing, and offered nothing for his defense. He let Bradley do it all.

Bradley had to argue the point that circumstantial evidence was all that pointed to the guilt of his client. He was being tried for the murders of two separate women. Bradley knew if Hunter were convicted, the press would have a field day. And it was almost certain the authorities would blame Hunter for the twenty-three other unsolved murders that fit the same *modus operandi.*

Michael Bradley had spoken over two hours, alone, giving his closing argument. Occasionally he would steal a glance at the courtroom door behind him, as if expecting someone. It was only after he completed his closing argument and rested when Catherine Rogers entered the courtroom. It was late afternoon, and tension was heavy in the air as the trial neared its end.

"Would you excuse me a moment, your Honor," Bradley asked. The Judge nodded his head.

Catherine hurried to Bradley's side and sat at the table. She opened her briefcase, showed him some papers, and exchanged intense whispers.

"I'm sorry, but I was delayed at the lab," Catherine explained. "They took forever..."

"But I just finished my closing argument," Bradley said, incredulously. "I never expected–" he swallowed hard. "It might be too late!"

"Well, you've got to do something-- right now!" Catherine told him, desperately.

Bradley faced Judge Kencade. "Your Honor... This may seem a bit unusual, but I beg the court's indulgence. My assistant, Mrs. Catherine Rogers, has some information, which I believe is relevant to the court."

"And what information is that," Judge Kencade asked.

"I'll...I'll have Mrs. Rogers explain it to you."

Catherine Rogers addressed the Judge, holding the papers in her hand. "Your Honor. I have just received the results from the new tests taken of the blood evidence at the scene of Mary Cardwell's murder, one of the women our client is accused of killing. And I'm here this afternoon to introduce it as evidence. The preliminary results show what may be a third type of blood present

22

at the scene of the crime."

Judge Kencade held up his hand. "Stop right there, Mrs. Rogers!"

Catherine ignored him. "The prosecution has established that Mary Cardwell's blood and my client's blood are the same, type 'O'--"

"Did you hear what I said?" The Judge's temper was rising by the second.

"Judge Kencade!" she said impulsively, "My client was accused of acting alone. If there's evidence of a third person's blood, then it's plain to see more than one person was involved--"

"That is enough, Mrs. Rogers!" The Judge's face was livid. "Mr. Bradley, Mrs. Rogers... Meet me at the side bar."

Bradley and Catherine exchanged uneasy glances and crossed to the side of the Judge's bench.

Kencade was outraged. "What kind of a stunt are you pulling, Bradley?"

"This is no stunt, sir. I'm sorry you perceive it as one," Bradley looked anxiously at Catherine.

Catherine understood his discomfort and took over. "Your Honor, I apologize for my untimely interruption, but I believe this evidence is critical to our client's case."

"If this evidence was so critical, why wasn't it introduced months ago, when this trial started."

"Michael Bradley hired me to review all the evidence that the authorities gathered, not only what the prosecution introduced. I had been studying the case independently, and it was only last night I discovered certain blood tests were both misfiled and mislabeled. I took them to a lab to rerun the tests."

Bradley spoke up, "Your Honor, she tried to get this evidence here in time. It was a long shot to see whether anything new turned up. Had I known something would be discovered, I wouldn't have rested my case. I think we--"

"It's too late!" the Judge glared at him. "You've had -- what -- seven months to present your case and challenge the prosecution. Now, in the closing phase of the trial you wish to delay it further?"

Bradley shook his head, "Not at all, Your Honor. Mrs. Rogers and I are doing everything we can in the best interests of our client. We've already discussed this before, in your private chambers. My client refuses to cooperate with his defense--"

"Just because your client is reluctant to assist you in his own defense doesn't matter! You work around it! Now it's over, Mr. Bradley. You have already rested your case."

"Then I'll make a motion to reopen it," Catherine spoke up. "Karl Hunter is being denied a fair trial." She could not understand why Kencade was dismissing such critical legal proof.

A long moment passed as the Judge stared at her. Then he made up his mind. "Your request to admit new evidence is denied! This conference has ended."

Kencade moved back to his chair while Bradley and Catherine resumed their positions at the defense table. The Judge addressed the court stenographer. "Let the record show the request by the defense to admit new evidence has been denied." He had to wait a moment as a murmur went through the courtroom. "Is there anything else you want to say, Mr. Bradley?"

Bradley shook his head. He looked at Catherine.

"Based upon new evidence, I wish to reopen this trial," Catherine said loudly, suddenly defying the Judge's wishes.

Judge Kencade banged his gavel. "Your motion to reopen this trial is denied, Mrs. Rogers," he said, infuriated. Another buzz went up from the spectators in the back of the courtroom. They were puzzled and confused.

"But, Your Honor--"

Then Judge Kencade lost it. "Do you understand me, Mrs. Rogers? If you think you can come here on your high horse from the state of Washington at this late date to disrupt this trial--"

Bradley again raised his voice, interrupting, "Your Honor, please!"

Kencade trembled with rage. "Another word from you Mr. Bradley, I'll lock you up myself!" The Judge jerked his head around and glared down at Catherine. "Now, Mrs. Rogers, is that all you wish to say?"

Catherine drew herself up to her full height. "With all due respect, your Honor, you don't seem to understand what I'm trying to do here today-- and now your reactions have become obvious to us as to the rest of the people in this room. This court is trying a man with extreme prejudice. This man, the defendant, is not receiving a fair trial in this courtroom! I'm filing for a mistrial and ordering you to step down immediately. This entire proceeding appalls me!"

The people in the courtroom spoke out loudly, interrupting the proceedings. Again the gavel pounded.

One man particularly, wearing sunglasses and sporting a very scruffy beard, sat in the

24

reporter's seats. He had the credentials but looked out of place, watching and listening to what was happening, instead of taking notes. He seemed to be viewing the events in the courtroom as if were a stage play performed before him-- a play where the ending was already known.

Judge Kencade rose from his seat. "Mrs. Rogers you are in contempt of this court!" he yelled through the uproar. "I fine you five-hundred dollars and a night in jail! The court is adjourned until nine a.m. tomorrow morning!"

Catherine reeled in shock. She had expected some type of overbearing response from the judge, but nothing severe as this.

Judge Kencade threw his gavel down furiously and departed to his chambers.

As the jury filed out in one direction, The reporters in attendance hurried from the courtroom with their scoops.

The prosecution lawyers just stared, nonplused, amazed at what had just taken place in the courtroom. As Bradley whispered something in Hunter's ear, one eye was still on the prosecution. "I think...we just spooked them," he told Hunter. "And don't worry about the theatrics you just saw. We still have a few options left."

Hunter remained silent. He didn't even nod his head. Two police guards appeared and escorted the accused serial killer from the room.

Another police officer put handcuffs on Catherine Rogers and led her away. Bradley found it difficult to watch her go. She forced a smile and gave him a thumbs-up gesture as she disappeared out the door.

* * *

Later that evening Karl Hunter lay on his prison cell cot in the county jail smoking a cigarette, oblivious to the numerous articles headlining the evening newspapers: *Serial Killer Trial Nears End,* and *Courtroom Erupts As Defense Asks To Admit New Evidence,* and *Protest By War Vets Across The Country.*

At the same time in the city hall jail cell, Catherine Rogers was busy writing detailed notes on small scraps of paper, ignoring her recently arrived dinner meal. Finishing a cigarette, she promptly put it out in her mashed potatoes.

"Since when do you smoke?" Michael Bradley saw her give a start. He had surprised her by his visit.

Catherine turned and smiled at him through the bars. "I don't," she answered. "I stopped ten years ago, but it was either this or the blue plate special they distribute to their guests here." She started gathering her bits of paper together. "Michael, I've been writing these notes for you. I think we can get that mistrial. I want you to take them back to your office and prepare the papers to remove Judge Kencade from the bench. You don't have much time, so--"

Bradley cut in quickly, "No matter what I say or do-- what *we* say or do-- Kencade will allow the jurors to start their deliberations tomorrow. But I'll prepare your argument anyway. I just wanted to say thank you for coming, and I'm sorry for what's happened!"

Catherine crossed over to Bradley. Leaning through the bars, she kissed him on the cheek, then handed him her notes, "Mr. Bradley, it was worth it just to see the Judge's face when I entered the courtroom and sat down at your defense table!"

Bradley smiled, "*Our* defense table!"

Catherine shook her head in disagreement, "No, Michael, it's all yours, I'm just here to assist you. Now you better get going...and take this pen. I had to bribe a guard to get it. I had to promise him I wouldn't try to commit suicide with it."

"Then I guess I'll be off. I'll see you tomorrow," Bradley turned to go.

"Michael," Catherine made him pause. "There's something I have to ask you. What *you* think? Do you think Hunter is guilty?"

Bradley stopped short of his exit. He thought a moment before answering. "I don't know. He's a strange one. He's highly intelligent, a very smart man-- a hero in the Vietnam war-- yet there's something mysterious about him as well. He's accused of being a serial killer and blamed for over two-dozen deaths, but he won't talk or say anything to help his case. He won't even tell me *why* he won't talk."

"That is strange..."

"And to top it all off, he refused to take the stand, although it meant saving his life. There's no doubt he's hiding something...or maybe protecting someone. I don't know..."

"I haven't been working for you long, but the more I dig into this case, the less I like it." Catherine shook her head.

Bradley smiled. "You were the one who insisted I hire you. What you've done so far for this case has been a great help."

"I wish I could do more," Catherine said.

"Maybe...maybe you can," Bradley said, getting a sudden idea. "What if you try a last minute plea to get something out of him? I could probably arrange for you to talk to him in person."

"Me?" Catherine became apprehensive. "I don't know-- I mean, do you think it would be a good idea?"

"Why not? It's worth a try-- that is, if you don't mind speaking face to face with a man accused of murdering twenty-five women?"

Catherine winced at his failed attempt at humor. "After facing Judge Kencade, I don't think that would be a problem at all," she shot back.

Bradley smiled. "Good night, Catherine. See you at nine a.m. sharp. Don't be late!"

Catherine shivered and looked reluctantly around her cell, "I'm not going anywhere. I'll see you tomorrow!" She watched Bradley walk away from her cell, then worried about what would happen in the morning.

* * *

At nine a.m. the courtroom was crowded again. Everyone talked among themselves as they waited for Judge Kencade to enter from his chambers.

The cameras flashed outside the courtroom as Catherine Rogers hurried down the corridor, and entered the courtroom. She barely had time to seat herself next to Michael Bradley. As he handed Catherine her briefcase, the court clerk stepped into the room.

"Will everyone present please rise," the clerk said. As everyone stood, Judge Henry Kencade entered, and a hush fell on the courtroom.

Kencade took his seat behind the bench, banged his gavel, and announced, "Court is now in session." Everyone sat down, but Michael Bradley remained standing. His thirty-eight-year old client, Karl Hunter, sat poised next to him. Bradley awaited recognition from the judge but was ignored. "May I speak, sir, your Honor?" Bradley finally ventured.

Kencade's disdain was still visible on his face, "No you may not! Now sit down Mr. Bradley!" Bradley did what he was told. Kencade went on. "The next time there are any sudden outbursts like yesterday from any of the spectators, I will have this courtroom cleared. And if any of the attorneys, *including Mr. Bradley and Mrs. Rogers*, should speak out of turn, contrary to my wishes, I will not only remove them from my court but suspend them for a time of my choosing.

27

Now is that understood, Mr. Bradley, Mrs. Rogers?"

They both answered contritely. "Yes, your Honor."

The man with the scruffy beard and sunglasses entered the courtroom and discreetly showed his press identification card to a police officer. The officer let him through, and the bearded man took his seat.

Judge Kencade continued. "Now we'll get on with the proceedings!" He turned to the twelve jurors as they finished seating themselves, "I'm sorry ladies and gentlemen of the jury, I shall ask you to disregard all statements you heard yesterday and everything you witnessed in this courtroom, including yesterday's requests to introduce new evidence *both* by the defense and prosecution."

A gasp came from the gallery, and a protest was voiced from the lead prosecutor. "Your Honor, I realize closing arguments have been made but perhaps on this occasion we could--"

Again the Judge's gavel banged down, "Sit down, Lloyd! This is my last warning before expelling those who protest from this courtroom!"

Everyone settled down and the court resumed its session. Kencade proceeded, "Again, disregard yesterday's remarks and only consider the evidence presented to you these last few weeks. Thank you. Ladies and gentlemen!" The Judge looked at the notes in front of him.

Bradley exchanged an anxious glance with Catherine as Kencade proceeded. "The court now considers a date for deliberation to form your verdict following the prosecution and the defense's final arguments. The date is set for Monday at 8:00 a.m."

Kencade struck the gavel. "Court is dismissed until Monday morning!" He looked straight at Catherine Rogers. "Oh, by the way, Mrs. Rogers, I know why you were brought here...but it's not going to work!" He struck the gavel one last time then exited to his chambers.

Everyone in the courtroom was shocked at the abruptness of the Judge's decision, including the jury who stared back in confusion as they exited to leave.

"Why did he postpone the jury deliberation?" Catherine asked Bradley.

"I don't know," he replied. Bradley was just as stunned as she was. As Catherine watched, Kencade entered his chambers. Before he shut the door, their eyes locked. Kencade hesitated for the space of a heartbeat. There appeared a momentary twinge of guilt visible on his features. Then he nodded to Catherine and closed the door.

As the last of the jury members filed through the door, their eyes focused on the defense table and Kencade's closed chamber door. The reporters scattered like rats, eager to get to their telephones, the news crews rushed to get their story on the afternoon television.

The courtroom galleries of spectators were baffled by the sudden conclusion of the proceedings and talked among themselves. They exited the courtroom, one by one, until all except one individual remained seated. It was the man with the sunglasses and beard. He stared at the accused, the defendant, Karl Hunter.

Two officers stood by, ready to take Hunter to his cell, waiting for Bradley to finish talking to him.

Catherine waited with Bradley, while the two officers took Hunter into custody. All this was visible to the man sitting in the gallery in the back of the room.

Hunter was prepared to walk through his door with his guards, but stopped short, glancing back to notice Catherine sorting through some papers in her briefcase. He turned a little more and saw the last person left in the spectator's gallery. A smile came over Karl's face for the first time in months, and he lifted his head in a quick nod. Then he proceeded through the door and to his cell. Neither Catherine nor Bradley noticed this.

Catherine picked up her briefcase and kissed Bradley on the cheek. "I'll see you back at the office." She headed down the aisle, passing the bearded gentleman with the sunglasses. Sensing his eyes focused on her, she kept them straight ahead as she went through the courtroom doors to avoid his gaze.

Outside, Catherine was bombarded by the sudden assault of the TV news media, rushing to her and shouting questions. The Vietnam veteran protesters were there, too, and they joined in, denouncing the kind of trial taking place, concerning one of their own being railroaded to death row on trumped-up charges.

A Women's protest group held their signs protesting the proceedings, blaming attorney Catherine Rogers for sidetracking a sure fire conviction of a mass murderer. One sign significantly stated: MRS. ROGERS SHOULD BECOME VICTIM #26 FOR DEFENDING SERIAL KILLER!

Inside the courtroom, the bearded man took off his sunglasses and wiped the tears from his eyes. Then he buried his head in his hands. Twenty years had been good to this man. Even with an unkempt beard on his face, the man's handsome features stood out in fresh contrast.

Bradley noticed the man's behavior in the back of the room and became concerned. He

29

approached him slowly. "Can I be of any assistance?"

The man stiffened at the sudden sound of Bradley's voice, and refused the courtesy. He looked up at Bradley with his tearstained eyes and asked one question, "Who was that woman?"

Bradley was intrigued by his query. "Do you mean Catherine Rogers?" He looked down at the man's press pass. "You're a reporter. There was a statement released by my office--"

"No, I mean why is she here?" the stranger asked.

Bradley became a little suspicious of this gentleman's curiosity. "Mrs. Rogers was a prosecuting attorney in Seattle, Washington," he cautiously responded. "She's now a defense attorney. Her field of expertise is...well, serial killers. She is a personal friend of mine. We went through law school together at Gonzaga University in Spokane, and she's here to assist me in this case."

Bradley felt a little uncomfortable with this conversation, yet he couldn't help bragging about Catherine. "That's about all I can tell you. You're not one of those investigative journalists, are you?" It was more of a statement than a question.

The stranger looked up at Bradley. "One time I was, but not now..."

There was something about the man who caught Bradley's interest. He didn't fit the mold of other reporters. "Then what brings you here?" Bradley asked.

The man gave a weary gesture with his hand. "I guess you can say that I'm just drifting right now. I'm a bum!" He gave a forced laugh at his own assessment of himself, and even Bradley had to laugh with him.

"A bum, huh? Well, I must say, your clothes certainly don't flatter you." Then Bradley asked, "Are you a Vet?"

The man lifted an eyebrow. "You can tell? I've seen some action in my time. How about you?"

Bradley laughed. "No, I just made it after they stopped the lottery."

The man sighed, then got up to leave. "Good for you!" He reached out to shake Bradley's hand.

They both clasped each other's hands and Bradley asked, "Do you mind if I ask your name? I'm Michael Bradley."

The man's voice got serious. "Yes, I know. I hope...well, never mind. Pleased to meet you. My name is Modini...John Modini. I better not keep you from your work. Thanks for your concern." He headed for the doors.

Bradley was a little disheartened by Modini's mood. "By the way, Mr. Modini," he called after him, "If you're not covering this story, why are you here?"

Modini paused with his hand on the door. "If I told you, Mr. Bradley, you would know all my secrets." He disappeared through the doors.

Bradley watched him leave and muttered to himself, "Interesting, these vets, but weird!"

Chapter Four

"The Phone Number"

John Modini proceeded to a small restaurant bar not far from the courthouse. He asked for change to use the phone and entered the phone booth in the back of the room. He dialed long distance to Salem, Oregon, where he spoke with his secretary.

He spilled the circumstances of the day's events in the courtroom, giving a brief summary of how a simple serial murder case could elicit such legal complications. His so-called "secretary"-- a word he used only as a code-- also happened to be his mother.

"I want you to come home now, Jack." She always called him Jack-- his nickname-- when she worried. "You have to take your mind off all this! You've been through so much already. Staying there will only cause you more pain and conflict!"

Modini disagreed, "No, mother...I can't! I have to see this through... You have to understand that! Please, don't worry about me!"

"Well, I can't help worry just the same, son!" his mother was silent a moment, "All right, but please do me this one favor... Do you have something to write with?"

"Yes, what is it?" Modini asked. He took out a pen and tore a piece of paper from the phone book.

The operator broke in, "Please deposit another two dollars and twenty-five cents for the next three minutes."

"Please reverse the charges," Modini's mother promptly told the operator. "Are you

32

ready, Jack?"

"Yes mother, give it to me..." Modini scribbled on the page to make sure he had ink in his pen.

"You know Martha Phillips?" his mother continued.

"Barely, it's been years, but what about her?" Modini looked back at the bar, impatient for a drink. He fished in his back pocket for his wallet.

His mother resumed, "I want you to call her. Martha told her sister in Fort Worth you were a free-lance journalist and could be trusted. She doesn't want to go to the authorities or the newspapers on this. She feels you'll do the right thing if you believe her. It could be something big, from what Martha says, Jack!"

Modini, waited for the punch line, but there was only silence. He watched the bartender pouring a drink for a customer. "Well, what is it? I don't have time to go calling anyone in Fort Worth... I--"

His mother stopped him. "Jack, I don't know what it's about. She wouldn't even tell her own sister over the phone. At least give Martha Phillips a call. Do that much!"

Modini sighed. He felt that he was being sidetracked again. His mother's voice cut through his thoughts. "Jack, if it's money, I can send some money to you!"

Modini thumbed through his wallet, spotting two five-dollar bills. "No, Ma, I'm fine, Ma... I'll be all right. Yes, tell me the number. Yeah...yeah I've got it." He shoved the piece of paper next to the bills in his wallet. "I'll try to call her... Good-bye, Ma!" Modini hung up and dropped his head in defeat. He needed money desperately, but his pride prevented him from taking money from his mother. She always had a sixth sense to know when he needed it. But he had asked for it too often in the past. He would not give in this time.

Modini exited the phone booth and headed for a bar stool. He ordered a gin and tonic and handed the bartender one of the fives. "Make it a double...with four olives!" he told the bartender.

The bartender gave a double take.

"Dinner!" Modini explained.

* * *

A Honda Prelude drove through an upper middle-class residential section of Madison and pulled into the driveway of a white-columned house. Parking next to the garage, A woman emerged from the car and locked it. As she headed for the front door, the porch light sensor clicked on revealing her features. It was Catherine Rogers, the attorney from Washington State.

As Catherine pulled out a set of keys and entered the front door, she set her briefcase down on a table stand near a coat tree hanger in the inside foyer. She made herself at home, and headed straight into the kitchen where she made herself a Tom Collins.

After taking a strong gulp of her drink and swishing the ice cubes with her pinkie finger, she climbed the staircase in the front of the house to the second floor.

As she reached the top of the staircase, she called out, "Dad! Dad, are you home?" A faint voice came from one of the rooms down the hallway, "In your mother's bedroom, dear..."

Catherine paused at the top of the hallway and looked around, staring at how much the house had changed over the years. She noticed her father had hung new pictures in the upstairs hallway. She moved down the hallway to her mother's bedroom.

The bedside light was on, and a man's oversized shadow was thrown on the wall. The man took a shirt from a dresser drawer and placed it neatly into a large hard-side suitcase.

Catherine hesitated, more annoyed than surprised. "Dad... What are you doing?

The man took a tie from the closet to match the shirt he just packed and put it in with the rest of his wardrobe. His suitcase was almost full. He stopped a moment and responded to Catherine's question, "I'm packing dear! I have an urgent appointment."

And Judge Henry Kencade finally summoned the courage to turn and face his daughter, Catherine.

"But you promised we--" Catherine stopped. "Where are you going now?" she asked, with restraint in her voice.

Kencade closed and locked his suitcase, "I have a nine o'clock meeting tonight with Senator Fuller. I'm taking a seven-thirty flight to Washington!"

"But why, dad?" Catherine said exasperated. "Why tonight-- for God's sake-- of all nights? We need to talk! We were supposed to have dinner together this evening?"

Kencade answered with a calm but insistent tone, "I'm disappointed too, Catie. I know we had plans, but what I have to do is urgent. I'll have a late dinner with Gerry, stay at The Garden overnight, and you..." he kissed her on the forehead. "You and I will dine tomorrow night. And then we will talk."

A taxi horn honked outside. "My taxi... Good night dear, the house is yours!" Kencade took the suitcase and left, leaving his daughter standing there alone in the room.

* * *

At the downtown Madison YMCA Hotel for men, John Modini paced back and forth outside on the sidewalk, contemplating his current situation. Putting it off no longer, Modini climbed the stairs of the hotel and entered through one of the heavy double doors. He headed to the front desk where, almost hidden from sight, a desk clerk sat in a low chair, staring at the antics of The Three Stooges on a portable tv. Only the top of his head was visible.

Modini was annoyed, waiting for the desk clerk to acknowledge his presence. All he wanted to do was pick up his mail and phone messages and go to his room. "Any messages for me?" he asked, raising his voice.

The desk clerk barely looked up. "Could ya' hold it a minute, Mac, dis is a great pitcher."

Modini, hiding his impatience, shifted around to see some of the clientele hanging out, A few were sitting and watching a basketball playoff on the big tv set in the lounge. Some of the renters had their separate radios and music blasting in different corners of the room. Several of the basketball crowd weren't putting up with it and argued with the music crowd. There was a noisy paddle tennis game going on in an adjacent room.

A resident with a thick beard came downstairs from the hotel section and approached Modini for a cigarette: "Sorry, don't smoke..." Modini said, backing away from his pungent odor.

The desk clerk interrupted, "Mr. Houdini...!"

"The name's Modini!" he corrected

The desk clerk smirked. "Sorry about that, but you've already been locked out of your room. It says here on the register you owe thirty-five for this week's rent..."

Modini was afraid of this. "I know. I'll have it for you tomorrow...cut me some slack."

The desk clerk wasn't sympathetic. "I'm sorry, but them's the rules! I was told by my boss that come Friday-- that's today-- you pay up or they lock you out of your room!"

Modini took a contrite attitude, "Isn't there a way you can unlock my room, just for tonight?"

The desk clerk got edgy. He wanted to get back to his program. "If you got the bread, I can make a call, 'cause everyone's gone home for the weekend. They told me you had to pay by five o'clock, today or they're locking you out. It's now a quarter to eight. So what do you want me to

35

do?"

The bearded resident interrupted. "Hey! Man! Do you have an entire cigarette?" he asked the desk clerk.

The clerk was agitated now. "Scram, Sam! You know I don't smoke, and I'm tired of telling you that!" Sam moved away, grumbling. The desk clerk continued with Modini. "Now, Modini...sorry 'bout that but, what can I do? Dem's the rules!"

Modini turned and walked away humiliated. He had no money and nowhere to stay. He felt that he was being watched by every bum, derelict and common resident as he walked to the entrance. He imagined they must be thinking, "You're going to end up just like us, sucker!"

He stopped at a pay phone. He wanted to leave the place, but there was one last obligation he had to fulfill. He searched in his pocket for the piece of paper with his mother's message. He began dialing Martha Phillips in Salem, Oregon, but got cold feet and hung up. He reconsidered, then dialed again, feeding most of his loose change into the phone.

"Hello," a woman's voice answered.

Modini cleared his throat, "Yes, is this Martha Phillips?"

Again, the timid voice responded, "Yes, this is she..."

"This is John Modini, Mrs. Phillips. May I call you Martha? My mother asked me to give you a call. She said you needed to speak with me about an important matter... Yes... Well, I believe I just have enough for a minute or so... Oh, yes, in Indiana... Madison, okay... Fine, the number here is area code 317-555-4130..." Modini hung up the phone and waited for her to call back. Seconds later the phone rang.

Modini picked up the phone. "Hello?"

It was Martha Phillips calling back. "I'm sorry for all the precautions, but I believe my sister's life could be in danger. I'm afraid she might be killed if what she knows should ever get out..." Mrs. Phillips told him in an excited voice.

Modini's face became tense, pressing the phone tightly to his ear. He thought this might be some kind of joke, but he remained courteous and played to her conversation.

"But...Martha... I don't know what I can do... I don't know what this is all about! Why the big secret?"

"I told her you know what she should do, and that she could trust you-- and not to break this information until she spoke with you first!"

36

"Thank you for your confidence," Modini said, trying to calm her down, "but, just tell me what your sister has done? What kind of trouble is she in?"

Mrs. Phillips snapped at him. "I'd rather not say over the phone because I think it might be tapped!"

Modini stared at the receiver a second, thinking this little old lady was over reacting. "Tapped?" he said in disbelief. "What are you talking about? This isn't 'Kojak,' Mrs. Phillips. Why would anyone want to tap your phone?"

"Please! Believe me, John. You must call on her...fly down there to Fort Worth and see her...help her!" This time he could hear the fear in her voice. It didn't sound as if she were joking. He felt she really believed what she was saying. He wanted to help, but could only think of his own present predicament.

"Mrs. Phillips, ma'am... I don't know if I can do anything right now. I'm kind of busy and I'm a little tight with money--"

"If it's money you need," Mrs. Phillips interrupted, "there's no problem... But please call her. It will help her, and I know it may help you. I'm sorry, but I shouldn't say any more. I have to go. Please, think about what I said. Let your curiosity make the decision. Good-bye, Mr. Modini!" Mrs. Phillips hung up.

Modini shook his head feeling both surprised and confused. He didn't need any more complications in his life right now. He had enough troubles going for him. He hung up the phone and left the YMCA.

Later that evening, at 8:55 p.m., John Modini waited in line in the front of an art theater. The marquee read: The Japanese masterpiece, Akira Kurosawa's *Seven Samurai*.

A gruff, dirty, bearded man in his forties, wearing a small poncho over his torso as if he were in a to a spaghetti western, cut ahead of Modini and made his way to the box office. Modini was too tired to make a scene, so he let the man have his way.

The man presented himself by spitting out his words to the box office lady, "One, please!"

The lady took in his bad breath as well. "That'll be four dollars and fifty cents..."

The bearded man smiled, "God is paying for it!"

Modini looked up in disbelief as did a couple standing behind him.

The box office lady humored him, "Right? That'll be four...fifty!"

The bearded man's eyes grew large as he explained, "You don't understand, I'm here because God sent me... He came to me and said, I must see this movie and I was to be given a ticket and entrance to this grandiose film-- and he would take care of the cost!"

The box office lady was actually being patient and gave a wink to Modini and the couple behind him. "Yes, well..." she said to the man in the poncho, "You see, sir, we have to pay for all the lights on our Marquee and the electricity inside at the concession stand. "Yes, well..." she said to the man in the poncho, "You see, sir, we have to pay for all the lights on our Marquee and the electricity inside at the concession stand. And then there's the movie print, the use of the theater and the wages of the projectionist, the manager, the assistant manager, and finally the person who makes your life easy to walk into this theater-- me!" The lady leaned forward and lowered her voice, speaking in a confidential tone. "Sir, if you get God to do all that then I'll let you and anyone else in. You go now and get God to do that, okay?"

The bearded wonder listened intently and after taking it all in, responded, "Right!...Okay!" He hurried off down the street. Modini and the rest of the line watched him and shook their heads as he went.

* * *

It was in an upper middle-class neighborhood, where the white-columned house of Judge Kencade sat dark in the quiet night air with one light shining from the front porch. In the kitchen, Catherine poured a cup of coffee for herself lit only by the stove light, then leaned against the sink counter. She took a sip, her mind in deep thought. The kitchen phone rang, almost making her spill her coffee.

She grabbed it on the second ring. "Yes, I mean hello, I'm sorry... Oh, hi, Frank...not good, and you? No, please Frank, not tonight... It just wouldn't be good, that's why! I'm going to stay this weekend. I'm worried about Dad. Not only that, they changed the venue on us. The jury starts deliberation next week. I have to go see our client tomorrow upstate. Yes. I've decided to remain here with Michael. He needs me..."

There was a long pause as she listened to Frank's reply. She interrupted sharply. "Well, maybe we should call it quits then!" Catherine choked on her next words, "I don't know... Just what is our relationship, Frank?" She became angrier and more intense as she spoke. "All right! Fly back to Seattle! If ever I'm in need of a good fuck, I'll call you!"

She slammed the phone down, "Bastard!" Her hands were trembling as she let go of the phone.

Three breaths later the phone rang again. She jumped, hesitated, then angrily answered it. "Now I told you no! Go find someone else to fuck tonight! What? Oh! Dad...? Hi...I'm sorry... Ah no, no, it's just--" Catherine took a deep breath, trying to recover. "I just broke up with my boyfriend. No... No... It wasn't going well with us anyway..."

Judge Kencade was on a private phone in the VIP section of the plush Carlisle hotel restaurant where he was staying. "I'm sorry to hear that things aren't going well. Catie, I just called to see how you are. I-- I wanted to apologize about tonight, and about yesterday in court! No, I'm fine. I'm having dinner with Gerry Fuller now. Yes, we're about to wrap it up soon. Then I'll have some time to relax. I'm planning to take my evening walk, maybe over to the Lincoln Memorial. Yeah, yeah, I'll be careful. I'll get to bed early. I have a breakfast meeting tomorrow at eight fifteen. Then I'll see you tomorrow night. Right... Eight o'clock for dinner!"

There was an awkward pause. Kencade tried to rid himself of the guilt feeling. "Catie! I know I don't need to say this, but I'm truly sorry this case has...well, I guess what I want to say is, you do what's best. You always were a fighter. I... Catie... Never stop, no matter what happens. I know you're helping those who desperately need it."

Catherine held the phone, listening to her father express his buried feelings. It became quiet on the other end. "Daddy, are you still there?" Tears ran down her cheeks. Finally, Catherine heard her father's voice again,

"Yes dear, I just want to...welcome you home, it's been a long time... I'll see you tomorrow night!"

Catherine called out before her father hung up, "Dad! I love you...!" But there was no reply, only silence. The other end had disconnected. Catherine hung up the receiver and stared into the darkness outside the kitchen window. She picked up her coffee and slowly sipped it.

* * *

Judge Henry Kencade walked through the hotel restaurant and joined Senator Fuller who was ten years his junior, and sat with another gentleman of Italian descent in his mid-sixties. Fuller smiled, winking at the gentleman, standing for Kencade as he arrived at their table. The Italian gentleman remained seated.

Fuller seated himself, closely watching Kencade. "So...how's Catherine? It must be at least ten years since I last saw her..."

Kencade straightened up, "Yes, that's about right, that's when her mother died... in '78..."

Fuller looked away, trying to be sensitive and cordial. "Your daughter has become quite famous in the Northwest. I've heard and read several articles about her in the last few years." His tone became more serious, "How is she taking this-- the Hunter case? She can't harm the progress of it, could she?"

Kencade shot a serious glance at Fuller and the other gentleman. "She's not taking it well at all...no. She thinks this fellow sittin' back in our famous Indiana prison, the one you and your people want on the hot seat, is innocent, Senator...and she feels a bit discouraged. Not by this twisted legal system of ours, no-- but by me! She thinks, I'm the one who's defeating her when it's this damn system that is tearing us apart!"

Fuller shifted his eyes to the other gentleman who remained silent then flicked them back to Kencade, "Yeah, well...it'll work itself out. It'll be over soon. Like you said yourself, by the end of the week! Then we'll finally rid ourselves of this dark cloud hanging over us once and for all!" Fuller waved his fist at the Italian gentleman, emphasizing they would beat this.

Kencade wasn't so sure, and the Italian gentleman sensed this. He asked, "What's the matter Judge?"

Kencade squinted his eyes, knowing he had to level with the men in front of him. "No, Gerry, we're not quite rid of this problem, yet... Catherine's a tough lady-- maybe too tough! You just said she's been getting recognition lately. Well, to tell you the truth, she can still legally maneuver to get that mistrial!"

Fuller straightened up in his seat and appeared very uncomfortable. "What do you mean? What could she do? Hank, this case has been cut and dry all the way! This is your baby!"

Kencade lifted his head in recognition, nodding, "I'm her father. She's for the defense... As judge on this case, I may have to step down from the bench. There's a conflict of interest!"

The Italian gentleman now interrupted, "Mr. Kencade, let's cut to the chase. Are you in with us or not? There is a lot riding on this conviction as you well know. You are in charge of this case. We expect Hunter to be found guilty and given the proper sentence." The Italian gentleman exchanged a knowing glance with Fuller, then again addressed Kencade. "There's enough for all of us...and then some. There's so much to gain that you won't have to bother with another case or courtroom trial for the rest of your lifetime-- or for that matter, your daughter's, or your

40

grandchildren's lifetime!

Kencade raised his eyebrows, "That's quite a proposition you have, sir. And I was prepared to go along with it, but you see, my daughter has a mind of her own. As for myself," Kencade's irritation showed, "If you're talking bribery--"

Fuller interrupted nervously, "Hey! Nobody is talking about bribery here!"

The Italian gentleman smiled and leaned forward. "Rumor has it you want to become a Supreme Court judge, a representative of this wonderful country of ours. I know many influential people. I can make that happen for you. But then I can make your worst nightmare happen too! It's your choice!"

Kencade got to his feet in protest. "I don't like being threatened, Mr...! Understand this, when I say I like my work, that means I like being a judge and no one will change that but me! I'll make the decisions in the Hunter case-- not you, nor anyone else!"

Fuller grabbed Kencade's arm. "Please, Hank! We've talked about this! Now, think about how much you are in this already! It's important we get this trial over with! Do me a favor and sleep on it tonight. Let me know what you decided in the morning..."

Kencade looked down at Fuller and gestured to the Italian gentleman. "Who is this man? What is his position here?"

The Italian gentleman reclined in his seat, as if making himself more comfortable. "Let's leave it at that, shall we, your Honor? It's unnecessary to know my position. Just be aware lot of important people are counting on you. You would be amazed to find out whom! For your own protection, I suggest you take the easy path. Lets close the Karl Hunter case once and for all! Otherwise...let's say...you might encounter some people who think it's time for you to retire!"

Kencade pulled his arm free from Fuller's grasp. His eyes blazed in a manner as if he were going to condemn them. "I know a threat when I hear one." He turned to Fuller. "I'm just surprised I had to hear it come from you, too, Gerry! Shame on you!" Kencade walked away from them and out of the restaurant.

The two men just looked at each other. Fuller, a bit nervous, spoke first, "I-- I thought I had him on our side. Maybe he'll change his mind by tomorrow."

The Italian gentleman took out a cigar from a silver cigar case. "I don't think Kencade will want to change his mind-- especially after your less than subtle approach. No...I'm afraid we lost him... It's too bad, really..."

Fuller reached over with a lighter and lighted the man's cigar. "What now?"

The Italian Gentleman took a few puffs and smiled at Fuller. "Not to worry. He'll be back...and then he'll play ball for us!"

* * *

It was close to midnight and Judge Henry Kencade felt the need to walk the anger off. The Judge was striding in the cool night air, taking in deep breaths. His eyes were set in one direction as he approached the goal he had set for himself earlier, the Lincoln Memorial.

Kencade stood before it, facing Lincoln himself, in his bigger than life pose. Kencade's face still held an almost awed expression as if he were remembering how it used to be when he first came to Washington D.C., standing here in his younger years, gazing upon the likes of Lincoln's face. Abraham Lincoln was one of the most important figures of this country, and Kencade felt proud and patriotic just for the privilege of standing in front of the statue.

"Well, Mr. Lincoln, nothing changes much, does it?" he said to himself. He glanced around and continued his stroll, watching the other people, mostly young lovers, using the area as a rendezvous for love-making. He checked his watch and decided it was time to turn in for the night.

It took only a few minutes for Kencade to cross the bridge over Lake Potomac. He thought out loud, "A year from now, Ronald Reagan will be out as President and a new administration will be in session. Should I take my leave as well?" This was one of the things Henry Kencade mulled over in his mind as he headed back to his hotel.

A quick movement up ahead caught his eye. On one side of the bridge he spotted two people, one was a woman who seemed to be fighting off another person. Kencade tried to comprehend what was happening as he got closer to them. His fears became a reality as he saw the man with a knife threatening the young woman. That's why he didn't hear her cry out or make any sound to draw attention.

The attacker suddenly pulled the woman closer, and she screamed. Kencade raced across the street, yelling to the assailant to stop. He had no intention of putting himself in danger. All he wanted to do was chase the woman's assailant away.

As he paused in the middle of the road, there came the sound of a racing motor. Kencade turned to the roaring sound. The bright lights of a car switched on and flashed across his face, blinding him. Kencade angled away, but the speeding car anticipated his move and aimed at him.

Kencade's adrenaline already was making his blood race. He reacted swiftly, leaping out of the way. But the car hit him a glancing blow on the side of his hip, twirling him around, knocking him to the pavement. He hit his head hard on the concrete road.

Kencade raised his head and struggled to get to his feet when the pain hit him. With blurred vision, he saw the girl rushing to him. She was a brunette with long hair that swung out behind her as she ran. Her attacker was nowhere in sight, and Kencade was momentarily relieved. The girl reached down to help him. And then the pain in his head stuck him again, and everything became fuzzier. His eyes wouldn't focus. Everything swirled before his eyes.

Before darkness overtook him, the last words he heard from the girl were, "Sir! Are you all right? Sir...can you hear me?" The girl yelled for help and assisted him to his feet. She brought his arm around her, and he leaned on her for support. They headed off the street, and walked toward the spiraling decay of darkness.

* * *

At 2:45 a.m. in the Art Theater in Madison, Indiana, John Modini fell asleep during the end of the second run of the three hour showing of *Seven Samurai*. As the movie ended and the credits concluded, the auditorium lights came on overhead. A police officer on his nightly beat pounded the theater seats with his nightstick. Modini, totally out of it, didn't hear the noise. The officer strolled down the aisle and struck his nightstick against Modini's seat, jolting him out of his sleep. Modini awakened with a start, his muscles tense and his heart pounding. Then he realized where he was and yawned. He watched the officer continue to bang his stick, kicking people out of the theater. After he had calmed down, Modini left the theater.

A short time later, Modini found himself again pacing in front of the Madison YMCA, trying to decide whether he should enter or not. The cold night air was slowly making up his mind for him. It was after 3:00 a.m. and he tried to get his second wind.

Modini entered the YMCA entrance and saw the new desk clerk who took over the graveyard shift. The clerk's name was Miles and Modini knew he was more lenient than other clerks who followed the rules and regulations to the letter.

Modini strolled up to the desk and acted as a regular resident if it were normal for him to come in so late. There was no curfew, and the desk was opened twenty-four hours. He moved slowly and casually, so not to give the impression he was locked out of his room.

Miles recognized Modini as he passed the desk. "Mr. Modini, how do you do?" he said flippantly, almost pleased to see him. "I see we have a letter here in your box," he took it out and held it up. "Western Union! Someone must like you...and, unfortunately, there's also a notice reminding you that you owe this last week's rent!"

Modini felt his world caving in. He thought he might have a chance to sleep on the sofa in the lobby, but that wasn't allowed by nonresidents. Feeling weary and tired, he replied, "Yes, I'm aware..." He took the printed notice, then paused to look at the Western Union envelope. "When did this arrive?"

Miles shrugged. "I presume this afternoon. It was here when I stared my shift."

Curious now, Modini opened the envelope, and found two hundred dollar bills in cash and a letter, addressed from his mother.

"There should be a time on there...stamped somewhere." The desk clerk remarked.

Modini looked at the envelope. "Yeah, it says two p.m.!" Modini was really irritated. "That figures! Just great...!" He shoved one of the bills towards Miles. "This should take care of my bill. Now is there any way I can get some sleep around here?"

Miles gave Modini his receipt and change. He opened a drawer and took out a ring of room keys. "Sure, I'll let you in your room." Modini gave him a double take, "But I thought--"

Miles walked with Modini up the stairs to his room. "Did the clerk on the evening shift tell you he couldn't open up your room?" Miles asked. Modini nodded. "Well, just chalk him up as a jerk! They call this the Young Men's Christian Ass... Remember what the YMCA used to represent!"

Modini snorted. "Greed. The old YMCA went out with prohibition. They decided if the churches could make money without government interference, why couldn't they?"

Miles unlocked Modini's door and left. A few minutes later, Modini walked into the community shower room. He took off his robe, hung it up, removing a half pint of bourbon from the pocket. With a cautious look around, he downed half of it. Modini knew any kind of liquor or booze wasn't allowed in the YMCA, so he had to be very discrete when he disposed of it. He placed the bottle back in his robe and proceeded into the shower stall. He turned on the water and adjusted the shower head, allowing the hot water flow over his head. He closed his bloodshot eyes in half ecstasy, half sadness, letting the water run down his body. He leaned his back against the wall, then slowly slid down to the floor, staring outward at nothing, thinking. The past few days have finally taken their toll. Soon he began to cry, oblivious to the world around him, depressed about his dismal situation.

Thirty minutes later, Modini entered his room, a towel wrapped around him. He checked on his bedside table for the Western Union letter and read it again: "Please call Mary Ann Sweeney in Fort Worth, Texas. This is her number 817-555-4207. I tried to call you, but you weren't in. This is my friend Martha's sister. She tells me she'll only talk to you. Hoping you're fine, son. Your mother, with love. P.S. I know you have no more money, call me if you need more."

Modini put the letter down. Like it or not he knew what he had to do next. He switched off the night light and slipped into his bed and fell into a soundless sleep.

Chapter Five

"Karl Hunter"

It was 8:00 a.m. when Catherine Rogers left her father's house, briefcase in hand, and got into her rented Honda. She turned on the car radio and pulled out of the driveway. The past day's events of the trial were broadcast on the news. They covered her appearance in court, her history as a prosecutor and defense attorney in the state of Washington, as well as the fact she was Judge Henry Kencade's daughter. And the question asked was should Judge Kencade step down from the bench now that Catherine Rogers was working for the defense. The news broadcast concluded with a psychological profile and condition of the defendant, her client, Karl Hunter.

The psychological profile was broadcast in the Madison YMCA an hour later, as Modini descended the stairs from his room to the main floor. He walked through the lobby, not paying any attention to the broadcast.

A ringing pay phone contributed to the general noisy atmosphere of the lobby. The morning desk clerk yelled out for someone-- anyone-- to answer it.

Modini crossed over to the coffee machine and put some change into it. He felt as though he woke up with his head in a vice. He took a slow sip from his coffee and grimaced at the bad taste, practically knowing what to expect, hoping this time for a miracle.

The bearded resident from the night before appeared and decided to answer the ringing phone. "Huh? What? Who?" The resident yelled out, "Hey... Anyone by the name of Modini here?"

Modini reluctantly took it. "Who is it?"

"Hey, I don't know!" the resident shrugged. "How am I supposed to know? Some broad says it's important!"

"Thanks." Modini smiled at the man.

The resident didn't leave. "Can I borrow a smoke?"

Modini gave him a dirty look. "Sorry. Like I told you last night, I don't smoke." He turned his attention to the phone. "Hello, yes... This is he... Oh, Mrs. Sweeney... Yes, I talked to your sister, right!" He listened patiently for a moment, then interrupted abruptly. "Now come on, Mrs. Sweeney, not you too! What's with you ladies and this phone-tapping paranoia?"

Mrs. Sweeney's voice replied, "Please, just listen!"

Modini, still annoyed at this game she was playing, listened courteously.

"There's an airline ticket waiting for you at the airport in your name. Fly here, when you reach Fort Worth. Call the service desk and give your name only to a woman named Joyce. There will be a message for you where to find me!"

Modini was upset. "What's with the cat and mouse mystery, Ma'am? What's going on? I just can't fly to Fort Worth, Texas and--"

Sweeney stopped him. "It concerns something you are very much interested in, something you have written about that happened over twenty-five years ago down here on 'one-one, two-two!'"

Modini thought for a moment, "One-one... Two-two... One-one, two-two? You mean eleven...twenty two? You mean, John F. Kennedy... The date of his assassin--"

A click, was heard at the other end of the line. Mrs. Sweeney had hung up. Modini looked at his phone receiver in bewilderment.

* * *

At 10:40 a.m. the same morning at the Watergate Hotel in Washington D.C., a murder was discovered. During the decade of the seventies, the circular and curved building was once known as the most controversial hotel in the world. It became famous as the headquarters for the Democratic Convention in 1972. An office utilized by its chairman, Lawrence O'Brien, was broken into. O'Brien was a one-time chairman for the Presidential election committees for both John and Robert Kennedy. He kept, under lock and key, private information about the current President of the United States, Richard Nixon. The President was a man who wanted these secrets very badly, so badly, he would take actions which would cause him to be the first President in history to resign from office. Now, a second scandal would take place at the Watergate hotel, one that involved a bizarre murder.

A pigeon flew to a window of the Watergate Hotel and fed off the birdseed put there each morning by the owner of that apartment. But it was the adjacent apartment next door that would become of the main center of interest.

Inside, clothes were strewn on the floor, both male and female. They were scattered over the room leading to the bed. And upon the bed it had a large nine-inch switchblade knife stuck upward through the covers. A bloody hand reached out to the handle of the knife, touched it, then pulled away quickly, realizing what it was. The knife was a vertical blur to Judge Kencade who had just awakened from a deep sleep. His head pounded and as his vision came into focus. The judge stared at the knife with a mixture of fear and incredulity. He had only seen large and deadly weapons like that when admitted for evidence in his courtroom trials.

His hands and body were bloodied from the knife sticking into the nude body of a woman, lying spread-eagle next to him on the bed.

Kencade sat up in the bed, the terror of the situation bringing him to the verge of panic. He recognized the woman on the bed as the brunette girl who helped him to his feet after he was struck by the car the night before. He tried to sort out the events of the previous evening, but his thoughts were in disorder.

"Oh, God..." Kencade said to himself. It was as if he were trapped in a nightmare happening to somebody else. Before he could get out of bed, he was startled by pounding on the door.

Muffled voices yelled from outside the corridor. "Open up! Police!"

Kencade, now overwhelmed with fear and panic, swung his bloodstained body out of bed. And then came the loud crash-- the sound of the door breaking and the police entering the room.

* * *

It was earlier that morning when Catherine Rogers drove her Honda through the maximum security entrance of the State Penitentiary near Fort Wayne, Indiana. As a precaution she had to go through the usual security procedures allowing her access inside this institution.

Catherine sat in a glass-cased cubicle and waited to meet her client. There were phones on each side of the thick glass for her and the prisoner to converse on. She was very nervous, though she did everything she could to keep those around her from noticing. She took her pencil out and started to scribble her thoughts on her yellow note pad.

A guard brought her client to his side of the cubicle window. She picked up her phone and waited.

Karl Hunter sat in the cubical seat but did not reach for his phone.

"Pick up your phone," Catherine demanded.

Hunter just stared, ignoring her.

"Please pick up your phone," Catherine insisted, without raising her voice. She wasn't there to argue with him. "I didn't come all this way for nothing!"

For a moment Hunter didn't respond, looking away. Then he sighed and reluctantly put the receiver to his ear.

"Thank you, Mr. Hunter" Catherine said. "I want you to know that I am filing an appeal for you. Meanwhile, I'm calling for a mistrial. Did Michael tell you I'm taking over your case? He'll still be your attorney, but if we get our mistrial, I'll be representing you."

Hunter calmly listened to Catherine's nervous introduction, paying most of his attention to her features-- her face, her eyes, her skin, her hair-- almost as if he were admiring her beauty and dismissing what she had to say.

But Catherine had more on her mind than to let his roving eye distract her. She had a lot to say and was determined to get through to him. "Karl!" she addressed him by his first name, hoping it would make a difference, "Karl, I need your help! There's something happening...something I don't understand... Maybe you can help me.'"

Karl Hunter's eyes came back to hers. He was listening.

"During the last week of the trial, enough circumstantial evidence was introduced by the prosecution, to throw a cloud over your defense. Michael said it was like trying to stop an avalanche. Part of that evidence included the mislabeled blood type that put you solely at the scene of one of the murders. Most of it is circumstantial, but it was enough to overwhelm Michael's defense strategy. Do you know anything about this? Do you have any idea where it's coming from or where the prosecution is getting this information? Please, Karl, you've got to talk to me. You've done nothing to defend yourself of all the charges they've brought against you! I need your testimony *now* before a grand jury. Why won't you talk to anyone?"

Hunter tilted his head calmly, and spoke for the first time. "It doesn't matter! I'm a *dead* man already! If you want to help me, you've got to get me out of here now. They're going to kill me!"

Catherine was totally confused by his unexpected request. "What are you talking about? Who's going to kill you? If it's the other prisoners you're concerned about, I can have you moved to another section of the prison."

"No!" Hunter responded angrily. He banged his fist on the counter, making Catherine jump. "I can handle myself here with the prisoners! I'm not concerned with them!"

Catherine appealed to his desperation. "Then who's trying to kill you?"

Hunter stopped and looked at her, almost becoming very concerned and protective toward her. "I can't tell you that. You'd be in danger-- and I still don't even know whether I can trust you... You understand? It could be anybody...anytime... My killer can even be you!"

Catherine spoke carefully, convinced his paranoia had gotten out of control. "Mr. Hunter, believe me, I'm not here to kill you, I'm here to help you. You're well protected in here. You're in a tight security cell that no one can get to! Michael made sure of that!"

"Ma'am, don't you get it? From what you are telling me--" Hunter paused a moment, searching for words. "Can't you see? You say you're my attorney-- you say you want to help me..." he turned away controlling his emotions with difficulty. "I didn't kill any of those girls! You have to believe that first..."

"I want to, Mr. Hunter, I do!" Catherine said frankly.

"Then you'll have to believe me that I'm being set up...framed! If you want to help me as you say you do, then start by getting me outta here and fast! I'm a dead man! They'll get me no matter how protected I am. Just get me out! At least I'll have half a chance if no one knows where I am. Right now you're making things worse for me!"

Catherine listened to his raving, trying to understand his point of view. "I'll try Karl, that's all I can tell you for now. I'm sorry, but I'll do what I can to get you transferred somewhere. But you must tell me...who is 'they'? Who are these...people who want to kill you?"

Karl looked her straight in the eye. "Ask your father, he's working for them!"

Catherine was startled. "What? I don't understand! Just what do you mean by that?" She had the distinct feeling he was playing mind games with her.

Karl raised an eyebrow and grinned. "Got you stirred didn't I? Well...it doesn't matter if you're my counselor or not! I'm dead meat anyway. Listen to me, Rogers. Your father and those who put me in this position have a stake in my conviction and death sentence! So for your own sake, if the time comes-- and it may come soon-- and you hear that I'm dead...I want you to play along with what they say. It will probably be reported as a suicide...but know in your heart that it *wasn't* suicide and remember what I have said. Someday maybe you and everyone else will know the truth!"

"What's that supposed to mean?" Catherine had made an honest effort to help him, but instead he repaid her by ranting like someone who was mentally unstable.

"How good is your memory?" Hunter asked.

"Pretty good. What do you want to know?"

"I mean are you good at memorizing things?"

Catherine frowned. She didn't know what he was getting at. "Yes, I'm pretty good at memorizing," she told him.

Hunter took out a piece of paper from his shirt pocket. He unfolded it and pressed it flat against the window for her to read. It was written in neat block letters: "An envelope, addressed to H. Kencade at Madison Post Office Number 8."

Hunter concluded. "Go there only if I die, otherwise, forget I ever existed... Please, for your own sake!" He took the piece of paper, folded it, then put it into his mouth and swallowed it. "Good-bye C.R.!" Hunter said, then hung up his phone and got up from his chair.

"Wait...! Wait!" Catherine shouted, but Hunter couldn't hear her. She pounded on the glass window. He gave her one brief glance as he was escorted out of the room by the guard. Catherine watched in frustrated silence as the door closed behind them.

In the Warden's office, his secretary, Miss Trenton, was buzzed by her boss. The nervous voice of warden Henry Pierce came over the desk intercom. "Miss Trenton, would you please inform Catherine Rogers, I'd like to see her immediately in my office, once she finishes interviewing her client, thank you!"

Miss Trenton looked up at Catherine Rogers standing in front of her. Miss Trenton smiled at Catherine, winking at her as she spoke into the intercom, "Sir, she's here now, waiting to see you."

Mr. Pierce met Catherine at the door inside his office, his face heavy with concern.

"Catherine...won't you please come in. I was just trying to get in touch with you... I hope everything went well for you."

Catherine followed the warden into his office. "Mr. Pierce... I need to ask you for a favor. It's very important."

"What is it," Pierce was preoccupied, distracted.

"I want you to transfer Karl Hunter from his cell as soon as—" But Catherine never finished her sentence.

"Excuse me, Mrs. Rogers..." the Warden said as he moved around his desk, interrupting her. "I just got a phone call from Michael Bradley's Law Firm. I'm afraid it's bad news... It's about your father...he's been arrested in D.C."

"What?" Catherine said, momentarily stunned. "What were the charges?" she asked quickly.

"They say he was booked for murder!"

Catherine couldn't believe what she just heard, "I don't understand. Why-- What happened?"

It was hard for Pierce to say the words. "They said he killed a prostitute!"

Chapter Six

"The Phone Operator's Secret"

The tires of the Delta Airliner screeched as they touched the ground at the Fort Worth Airfield in Texas. It was a warm and bright early Sunday afternoon, and there were no crowds at the airport this time of day. Not many passengers on this flight Modini thought as he came through the terminal, carrying a small carry-on bag over his shoulder. The flight made him weary, and he just wanted to get this day over with. He searched for the nearest information desk and got the information Mrs. Sweeney had provided for him to rendezvous with her. Modini hailed a taxi to take him to his destination.

The taxi drove up to a small modest home in a low to middle-class residential neighborhood, and Modini exited, paying the driver. As the cab departed he looked apprehensively at Mrs. Sweeney's two story house and felt he would regret coming here.

It was Modini's nature to have a kind heart for the elderly, but he almost felt as though he was taking advantage of the old woman. Everything was paid for on this trip, and he had nothing to lose. This is why his guilty conscience bothered him.

Before Modini reached the top of the stairs, a woman, about fifty-nine years of age, opened the door to him. "You must be John Modini? The gentleman from Oregon?"

Modini extended his hand to her, "Yes, and you must be Miss Sweeney?"

The woman gave him a look as if he should know he made a mistake. "No, I'm her cousin June. I'll take you to her. She's waiting for you in my guest house in back."

Modini followed her through the house, out the back door and through a garden with a white painted gazebo at the far end. He came to feel less tense because of the serene surroundings. He actually had a smile on his face as he approached the guest house. A sixty-seven-year old woman greeted him at the door. "Miss Mary Ann Sweeney?" Modini asked.

Sweeney nodded in recognition, "Mr. Modini!"

Modini extended a friendly hand. "A pleasure..." Modini greeted her, not really knowing what to say or expect. Miss Sweeney had aged into a cute elderly lady, not the hard-as-a-rock woman he expected to see. He could picture her immediately as being a beauty when she was in her youth.

Miss Sweeney nodded thanks to her cousin.

Modini saw June disappear quickly back into the house. "I hope I wasn't rude to your cousin," he said.

"Oh, no, she's fixing us a lunch. I would ask you inside--" here she gestured to her little guest house, "--but since it's such a pleasant afternoon I was wondering if you would walk with me through the garden?"

"Sure, I'd be happy to." As Modini took Miss Sweeney's arm to escort her into the garden, he felt composed enough to ask her a personal question, "Am I correct in saying you've never been married?"

Miss Sweeney smiled, "Yes, I've never married, not that I couldn't or wouldn't, mind you. I had beaus in my time who've asked me, but I could never make up my mind when the opportunity arose."

Modini felt a little embarrassed. "I hope I didn't offend you, it's just that I was wondering why such an attractive lady as yourself never married. You must have been a very independent woman." She smiled and Modini smiled back. "Hey, what am I saying-- I'm not married either! I guess there's still a chance for me," he joked.

Miss Sweeney laughed. "Oh, you men, you can marry at any age. It's the women who, if they waste their time, will miss out. Women have only a certain time to make their mark in life. Once it's gone...well, we learn to cope by ourselves. Some of us regret it because there are no children we wish who can take care of us in our old age. Those are the consequences, Mr. Modini, of making those weighty decisions in life. I'm not saying I haven't made as many wrong or right decisions, it just so happens to be what it is. If I had a family, I can honestly say you and I would probably never have the opportunity to meet like this. It's because I have no family I can say certain things to you. I can explain why I've asked you down here. I imagine you have better things to do with your life than coming down here to Texas to talk to an old woman."

Modini laughed, "Well, Miss Sweeney, I did have my doubts at first, but I go on gut feelings." He glanced around, noticing they were alone. "And my gut feeling is, you do what your mother tells you to do. And if anyone wants me bad enough to fly me to them, it must be important. Now my instincts might not be right all the time, but it doesn't matter because it's times like this I'm brought back down to earth. I can honestly say, I'm glad I came to visit you."

As the two of them strolled down the garden path, a peacefulness came over Modini. This afternoon's meeting meant a lot to Modini as it did her. As the two of them reached the end of the garden, they entered the gazebo. It was freshly painted and had a table with two folding chairs set up in the center of it. As they sat down, Modini saw Miss Sweeney's cousin emerge from the house carrying a tea tray. June set the refreshments down on a small table and headed back to the house.

Modini sipped his iced tea as Miss Sweeney spoke in a candid tone. "My cousin, June, doesn't know why I asked you here. She had never known-- like anyone else-- what I know and will tell you. I've asked her to stay in the house while you and I are in conference, so don't think she's being strange or anything like that. Now, what I'm about to say is still unexplained. I hope after all these years you'll know why I've kept quiet about it, and then you'll understand!"

Modini politely interrupted. "Miss Sweeney, before you continue-- and don't misunderstand me, I do want to hear what you have to say-- but, why tell *me*? Why not tell the police or some other newspaper writer your secret? Why choose me?"

Mary Ann Sweeney responded genially to a perfectly understandable question. "Because, dear, I know I can trust you-- and It's not just because you're Marion Modini's son, my sister's best friend...but you're a journalist yourself. I've read some of your work, and I know you can be and will be objective to what I have to say. You need not believe me, but I know in the end you'll do the right thing." She put down her iced tea glass and took a deep breath. "Right now, you probably believe the opposite of what I'll tell you, mainly because in the last twenty-five years a lot had been said about the Kennedy thing I feel is untrue. And I want to set the record straight!"

"You, of course, mean the Kennedy Assassination."

"Yes. I'm one who had been trying to avoid the issue and continue to do so. But what I don't understand is the misinformation spread on and on about Mr. Oswald by our own government. I feel that no one will really know the truth about him. Even the Warren Commission never wanted to take my testimony when they came down to interview Jack Ruby." She placed a friendly hand on his arm. "If you want me to stop, Mr. Modini, I will and you can go on your way!"

"No, no!" Modini quickly replied, "I want to hear what you have to say. Please, Miss Sweeney...go on!"

Mary Ann Sweeney paused a moment to collect her thoughts. "On November 22, 1963," she began slowly, "that night after the Kennedy assassination, Lee Harvey Oswald had been arrested and incarcerated in a cell on the fifth floor of the Dallas City Hall. Police Chief Curry gave instructions that the prisoner was allowed all the rights and privileges entitled to him. And exercising those rights, Lee Oswald asked to use the telephone. It was on Saturday, November 23, the day after the assassination of President Kennedy, he made two phone calls, one at four p.m. and the other at 8 p.m.-- both to Ruth Paine...the woman who owned the house where Oswald's wife, Marina, was living. He talked to her about his search for legal assistance. During one of those calls he did get to talk to Marina and told her not to worry, that everything will be taken care of. He said he couldn't believe what was happening, and that this was a mistake, which he was telling everyone here at City Hall all along--"

Modini broke in, "Excuse me, Miss Sweeney. How do you know all this? You speak as though you were right there!"

Mary Ann Sweeney smiled and nodded in agreement. "I was..." She saw Modini's surprised reaction. "I'm sorry, let me explain. I was one of the switchboard operators on duty both nights at City Hall. I was waiting for you to ask that question."

Modini was very impressed and listened intently as she continued her story. "Now, the Dallas Police records show the calls he made, but...what they don't show is a...third call he tried to make later that Saturday night-- maybe between ten and eleven p.m. He failed to complete it and that's probably why there's no record of it, but that's where the mystery really begins. Until now, supposedly everything you can find on Oswald is in the records. Except for his interrogation Which was never recorded-- at least not that we know of..." She paused, her forehead wrinkling with concern.

"Don't you think someone would have recorded something, especially since the President of the United States was just killed? I've often wondered if there were some recording of Oswald somewhere hidden away we weren't allowed to hear. I raise this point because-- for one, it is not like the Dallas Police Department to interrogate someone, even the smallest criminal, without proof to protect themselves. To tell you the truth, I don't think any police department in this country would have let an opportunity like this go. In the forty-eight hours Mr. Oswald was incarcerated, the police say only a few handwritten notes were made! The reason I am saying this Mr. Modini, is that it was just taken for granted any prisoner's voice would be recorded. There's no way the Dallas Police Department would not have a record of it, and the answer for this inconsistency, Mr. Modini, may be in that third call Mr. Oswald made that night..."

She was quiet for the moment. Modini took the opportunity to satisfy his concern. "This is the first time I've ever heard of a 'third' call by Oswald. What happened that night, Miss Sweeney?"

The elderly woman looked straight into Modini's eyes. "There was another operator on duty with me that night, Mrs. Trudy, who has passed on, bless her soul... She died a few years back in her sleep...and with her, our secret. Mrs. Trudy had been told beforehand that law enforcement officers-- to tell you the truth I think they were really Secret Service men-- would be coming to listen in on Oswald's phone calls. And *they did* come. Two men arrived, showed their credentials to Mrs. Trudy, and were placed into a room next to the switchboard. I felt that they had to be Secret Service because, while waiting, I heard them talking about all the security lacking with so many important people in town. J. Edgar Hoover had been in town having dinner with the oil man Clint Murchinson, and they mentioned Nixon had been there with the mayor's brother."

"Who was the mayor then?" Modini asked.

"I believe, Mayor Cabell. Yes...apparently his brother and Mr. Nixon had once worked together."

Modini's eyes lighted up. "The man in the Eisenhower administration! Yes that would be General Cabell, Deputy Director of the CIA. He was fired by Kennedy after the Bay of Pigs, or I should say resigned along with the director of the CIA, Allan Dulles and Richard Bissell."

She stopped him here, "Dulles? That's one of the three men who refused to take my statement! The others were Gerald Ford and Mr. Warren. They had just turned down Jack Ruby's request to take him to Washington D.C. for protective custody. Ruby told them he wouldn't talk unless they brought him to Washington. He told them he would be killed if they left him here in

Dallas."

Modini thought this was more than enough for him to take in all at once, but Mary Ann Sweeney wasn't through. She still had not told him why he was here.

"You met with these three from the Warren Commission?"

Miss Sweeney admitted it willingly, "Yes, they took my statement but didn't bother to pursue it further, not with any of us, so I didn't show them what I had. By this time they were convinced of only one thing, that Lee Harvey Oswald was the lone assassin. It mattered only to them how they could tie up any loose ends. It seemed that the questioning was only one sided. I wanted to ask who was defending Mr. Oswald, or who was speaking for him?"

Modini asked curiously, "Please continue. What happened next?"

Her voice became serious. "Okay. I think it was between 10:45 p.m. and 11:00 p.m. Saturday night. A red light began blinking on the panel of our switchboard, showing that someone was placing a call from the jail telephone."

Her eyes focused in the distance as she described the events in the switchboard room at the Dallas City Hall on Saturday evening, November 23, 1963. Twenty-five years younger and, at the age of forty-two, she was fortunate to have her looks from her youth. Both Mrs. Trudy and she were handling the outgoing calls from the switchboard. It was Mrs. Trudy who took charge as she opened her key. Mary Ann Sweeney, meanwhile, listened in with curiosity.

"A strange thing then occurred," she explained. "Mrs. Trudy spoke with the two officers eavesdropping in the next room and told them Oswald had asked her to place the expected call. I was dumbfounded at what happened next. Mrs. Trudy opened the key to Oswald and told him, 'I'm sorry, the number doesn't answer!' She hadn't even put the call through, she then unplugged and disconnected Oswald! A few minutes later, Mrs. Trudy tore the page out and off her notation pad and threw it in the wastepaper basket. Later that evening, I remembered to retrieve the note as Mrs. Trudy took her break. It was the phone number Oswald had called. I kept it all these years, I guess, as a souvenir of the time..."

She reached into her garden apron and showed a small envelope. She took out the same note, unfolded it and handed it to him. "This shows that Lee Oswald booked a call that nobody wanted anyone to know about. The area code is 919 as you can see, and it was a person to person to somebody called either Herty or Hertig. Apparently, Mrs. Trudy was unclear on the exact name."

Modini asked, "And the area code? Where's the location?"

"Raleigh, North Carolina! That's as far as I got. I was scared..." Miss Sweeney took a deep breath to help calm her nerves. Modini could see she was visibly upset. He took her hand and comforted her as she finished. "I left it alone all these years. In fact, Mrs. Trudy never knew I'd taken the note from the wastebasket. I still believe to this day those two men, those secret service agents, or whoever they were, told Mrs. Trudy to scuttle that call. And I don't know why. I never asked her and never wanted to, but I can say this, if there were ever a possible answer to whom Oswald was-- the answer I feel could be in that number..."

Chapter Seven

"The Killing Zones"

The wheels of the 747 came down, locked in position and hit the landing strip at Washington D.C.'s National Airport. A short time later, Catherine Rogers disembarked from the plane and hailed a yellow cab to the Justice Department.

The Justice Department Jail door opened and Catherine entered carrying her briefcase. She introduced herself to a group of officers on duty. They took her briefcase and slid it on through x-ray machine.

"Did he have any visitors," Catherine asked the Officer-in-charge.

"No," came the reply. "He's not allowed to have any visitors or see any family members until he speaks with council."

"But I *am* counsel!" Catherine gave the officer a stern look.

The Officer-in-charge regarded her skeptically. "You're his daughter *and* his attorney?"

Catherine answered sarcastically. "Yes I am. Do I have to show you my credentials?"

"Yes...you do, lady!" the officer demanded.

She took a card from her briefcase and showed him her identification from her purse.

The officer grimaced, then nodded his approval. "Just doing my job, Mrs. Rogers. You know the rules."

Catherine was a bit upset at the delay. "Just show me to my client, please!"

Another officer accompanied Catherine to a jail cell where she saw her father, Judge Henry Kencade sitting on a cot, facing the wall, his head in his hands. The officer banged his keys on the cell door to get his attention. "Sir! Your counsel has arrived..."

Kencade turned around in his cell, pulling his hands from his face, and saw his daughter. He recognized her and attempted to wipe the tears from his eyes, but could not hide his embarrassment in seeing her.

Catherine bit her lip, trying to calm herself. She addressed the attending officer, almost whispering under her breath. "God damn it! Does he have to be in there?"

The officer, felt a bit of sympathy for her. "You know the rules, ma'am...as an attorney." He opened the cell door. "Hell...! I can take you both to a more private room if you like?"

Catherine nodded as if to say please, and wiped away her own tears welling up in her eyes.

In a more private area, in a small conference room, Catherine and her father sat down at a large table with six chairs.

"Thank you," Catherine said to the officer. He left them alone, locking the door. Catherine watched her father's eyes following the officer's exit then suddenly return to hers.

"I didn't want you to be here or see me like this," Kencade said.

"Then why did you insist on staying here, dad?" Catherine snapped back. Her voice was taut with emotion. "Why aren't you taking the bail offered you? Don't you want to get out of here, for God's sake?"

Kencade studied his daughter's face for a moment, then spread his hand in a gesture of futility. "God forgive me, Catie... I-- I believe I'm guilty!"

* * *

On Monday morning John Modini went out for a stroll and finished his walk in the center of Dealey Plaza. The Dallas, Texas sun provided only a little of the warmth from the chilliness Modini felt on his first walk through-- what he considered-- this historical site where John F. Kennedy was assassinated.

An elderly gentleman kept pace beside him, a witness to the crime of twenty-five years ago.

As they reached a certain point in an area across the street from the grassy knoll, Modini stopped and remarked to his companion, "George, I appreciate the time you're taking to talk to me." He looked around at the park-like setting. "I can't get over it. Dealey Plaza is so small!"

George smiled. "Yes, it is, everyone gets fooled once they see it. It's bigger than life when you see it on the TV set..." He raised his hand and pointed across the street to the grassy knoll. "I was standing over there... I heard four distinct shots and saw smoke come from up there on the hill, from behind that fence..."

Modini stared across the street. His face paled as he heard this description. Then bits and pieces-- sharp cuts and flashes of unwanted memory-- intruded into his consciousness. They were his memories and recollections from a horrible episode in his youth, stretching back to 1969 in a country on the other side of the world-- Vietnam.

Private First-class John Modini and the rest of his platoon had been on patrol when they traveled through what they suspected was a Viet Cong village. Platoon Sergeant Contos had warned Modini and the men to stay alert for any signs of trouble, but the men took the advice with a grain of salt. Their platoon had been on missions for three solid months and the only time they fired their weapons was for idle target practice.

"Hey, Sergeant..." Modini sprinted up the worn village path until he reached his platoon leader. "What's the big idea? We patrolled this village last week. I thought we were all finished with this area..."

The Sergeant halted at the edge of the village-- a small collection of weary huts. "Look around, Modini, and tell me what you see?" Sergeant Contos said. "Never mind-- I'll tell you. Women and children-- that's all. The men are all gone. Their husbands and brothers are probably Viet Cong. Yeah, that's right. That's why we're here again...and maybe we'll be here

next week as well. Now shut up and--"

Those were the last words Contos ever said. As Modini watched in disbelief, the

Sergeant's face exploded with blood as his head snapped back. Modini watched the horror

unfolding before his eyes as the soldier's lifeless body crumpled slowly to the ground.

Modini screamed out in terror, backing away quickly from him, trying to tell someone

what had happened. But everyone around him was running for cover to hide from the sniper fire.

Modini moved to his buddy's body, now knowing there was nothing he could do. He looked down.

There was blood and brain debris splattered all over himself

Then he heard the sound of gunfire in the distance. He swung his head around,

incredulously searching for the source of the sound. He saw a low wood-slatted fence stretching

across the top of a low hill nearly fifty yards away.

When Modini saw the thin haze of smoke floating above the worn picket tops, he realized

where the enemy was hiding. He dived for cover only moments before the sniper fire resumed,

spraying bullets through the air where he had just stood.

When John Modini opened his eyes, he found himself back in Dealey Plaza. Only a few seconds had passed since he had squeezed his eyes shut, trying to blot out the memories. He stared fearfully at the grassy knoll and at the fence as if he were ready to be ordered to take it on command.

George, the man beside him, wasn't aware of Modini's recall and continued. "Something very peculiar happened just as the smoke cleared from the grassy knoll. I followed a police officer up to the top of the hill and entered the parking area behind the stockade fence. The officer pulled his pistol from his holster. Just then a man appeared and showed his credentials. He said he was Secret Service Agent, and proceeded to point to the fifth floor window of the book depository. The officer took the hint and rushed inside, but as I turned from the officer to look for the Secret Service man, I realized he had disappeared. I mean, he was *no where* in sight! Later we were told that *no* Secret Service Agents were on the premises! They were all either with the President on their way to Parkland Hospital or with Vice-President Johnson. The authorities and the Warren Commission all said I was mistaken, but I tell you and anyone else that wants to know, I was here, Mr. Modini, they were not! They say everyone witnessed the shots from the depository, then why did everyone I witnessed run up there to the grassy knoll? Why did that policeman run up here? Why did I? Then they find a rifle on the sixth floor, not the fifth floor. First, it was a German Mauser then it was the Italian Mannlicher. I tell you, Mr. Modini, there was never a better shell game going on here that day! I saw what I saw, I heard what I heard...and it was *not* echoes!"

That evening John Modini sat in the center of a small screening room and viewed a never-before-seen film print for the first time. A darkened screen showed a pristine, unedited, uncut, computer-enhanced blowup print of the Zapruder Film, the actual footage of the Kennedy Assassination. It was never as riveting as it was until now.

Modini's face projected pain and anguish as he watched the motorcade drive past the front of the school book depository with Kennedy disappearing behind the Stemmons Freeway sign.

When he stood in Dealey Plaza, Modini remembered the Stemmons sign was no longer there.

"Can you hold it there a second?" Modini said. The film continued to run several seconds. He felt shock as he watched Kennedy grabbing for his throat as if he had caught something sharp in it, and moves forward. Here, the film froze in mid-motion, Kennedy's arms were spread like an eagle, his hands on his throat.

Another man near back of this screening room came forward, "What is it, Mr. Modini?"

Modini turned to the gentleman. I was in Dealey Plaza earlier today, and I noticed there was no Stemmons sign... Why?"

The gentleman came down to Modini's seat. He was holding a remote control in his hand. "Not many people notice or realize this, Mr. Modini. That's a good question. The sign was taken down and destroyed soon after the assassination, just like the President's car. That too, was taken away, sent to Denver, broken down and reconstructed. Why, too? The only explanation, Mr. Modini, is if both the sign and the car were left intact and used as exhibits for examination, Arlen Spector would have a hard time explaining his magic bullet theory."

Modini studied the freeze frame of Kennedy. "You're saying there might have been traces of a bullet fragment on that sign?"

The man also looked at the screen. "Yes, Mr. Modini, and in the car as well. Only John Connally can protest this magic bullet theory since he has claimed from the beginning, he was shot by a separate bullet."

The man continued, "It's not John Connally's testimony that the Government believes, but an attorney for the Warren Commission who was never inside that car, never experienced in being shot first hand. Yes, that's the man history will claim who solved the Oswald problem, a man who today is a United States Senator. You'll see! Look at Kennedy here, what is he doing?"

Modini turned his attention back to the frozen screen.

The man continued. "If I had just come in this room, I would say President Kennedy looked as though he just got a chicken bone stuck in his throat. That's what I see. You notice he leaned back and then forward just before the film stopped. To me, that means Mr. Kennedy was shot first from the front! Notice here... he first stiffens up with his throat, as a bullet enters through it, then there's a motion forward and toward the front seat. Another bullet from behind caused that to happen, a bullet probably in his upper back but not in his neck, since you never ever see the President reach behind himself. And remember the Parkland doctors always said from the beginning a bullet had entered his throat from the front, and they had to open that wound wider to give him a tracheotomy. Our own police department first announced the shots came from the front. Bethesda Hospital in D.C., where they gave Kennedy's autopsy, thought the front hole was a wound blasted outward from a bullet from behind. The Doctors didn't know it had been a tracheotomy until the next morning when Dr. James Humes called Parkland and was told about it. The next thing we heard years later was that the original autopsy report was burnt, and never shown to anyone. They then reconstructed a new one to satisfy those concerned with our doctor's tracheotomy. But they still can't explain it today. Instead of finding answers to Kennedy's death, those doctors at Bethesda who did the autopsy, actually sealed Kennedy's fate of how, why, and when. We will never know the truth of what happened over twenty-five years ago." The man raised his remote control and pushed a button. "Now watch this..."

The freeze frame started and Kennedy continued with his movement. The motorcade was suddenly interrupted. Even Modini, who was concentrating on the screen, knew what to expect, was startled. Kennedy's head took up much of the screen. In never-before-seen footage, in extreme close-up, the President's head jerked back and the right side exploded with a red smear.

Modini reacted, jerking back in his own seat, as his mind again flashed back to images of Vietnam in 1969. He saw Sergeant Contos standing next to him near the Viet Cong village. The sniper fire from the Cong struck the Sergeant's face, ripping apart his head.

Modini's face turned white. He could only say, "Oh, My God!" Kennedy's head was almost blown off the same way. Modini saw the reaction of the people around the motorcade, hitting the ground for cover.

Mrs. Kennedy crawled onto the back trunk of the limousine to retrieve her husband's skull fragment and brain tissue, grabbing for it as Secret Service Agent Hill ran, and leaped aboard the back of the moving vehicle and pushed her back into her seat. Hill sprawled over the couple, and the limousine sped through the freeway underpass with only the shoe of the President visible sticking up.

"Oh, my God!" was all that Modini could say in a shaken voice.

* * *

A pair of legs dangled in the air in a prison cell. One end of a bed spring was wrapped around the window bars and the other around the neck of a dead man. As the cell door was opened, a slash of light from the corridor fell across the man's face, revealing it to all those present. The dead man was Catherine Rogers' client, Karl Hunter.

* * *

A 747 airliner headed westward into the night. Inside the American aircraft, a stewardess moved down the aisle to the first-class section. She puffed up two pillows for her special passengers who were asleep, Catherine and Judge Kencade, whose head was resting upon his daughter's shoulder. Catherine was taking him home...

Chapter Eight

"The Priest And The MIA's"

John Modini sat and stared out the window of an eastward bound train. He appeared to be in an almost trance like state. In the distance he heard the thin, shrill sound of the train's whistle as the cars entered a tunnel. The darkness took Modini by surprise, and his thoughts suddenly went back seven years to a letter he had received from Father Conrad. What the letter had said and what occurred during that winter evening in March in 1982 had a profound effect on him.

In a Catholic cathedral in the New England state of Vermont, the congregation had settled in their pews for an evening of worship. The sermon went well, and as the church music concluded, the priest, Father Conrad, appeared before them at the pulpit. He began his sermon by speaking out about the controversial POW/MIA matter as pertained to his participation as a soldier in Vietnam.

Father Conrad was in his early thirties and spoke with authority and experience. "Let us pray, people, that we American citizens do not turn our backs on those who were left behind in that war in Vietnam. And let us support our present veterans who have suffered since returning to our own country these last few years.

"Let us pray that Jesus Christ will guide and protect those that were left behind after the fall of Saigon, that Jesus Christ will guide those in our government to seek the truth and not hide behind a shield that reads National Security..."

A gentleman in the congregation suddenly rose from his pew, waiting to be noticed by Father Conrad. When a break in the prayer came, Father Conrad looked over his congregation briefly, and noticed the one man who stood out. He watched the man as he moved into the center aisle and disappeared to the back of the Cathedral. Father Conrad finished his prayers. "Help those, Lord who served and sacrificed their lives for you and our children. Seek and ye shall find truth and the truth will set you free!"

Later in the evening as the congregation departed from the cathedral, many parishioners greeted and thanked and shook the hand of Father Conrad. As Father Conrad waved to the last of them, he closed the doors of the cathedral with a warm smile on his lips. He started his rounds, checking to see whether everyone had gone or if anyone strayed behind.

Everything seemed quiet, but he thought he noticed a blinking light in the confessional box. Father prepared himself and approached the confessional. He entered and gave the Holy Mary's and proceeded with his unexpected parishioner. "May you confess your sins in the name of the Father, of the Son, and of the Holy Ghost. May they be forgiven!"

The man on the other side in the confessional box remained silent. Father again asked, "May I hear your confession?"

Again, silence.

Father Conrad pressed on. "Have you come to confess your sins, sir?"

The man finally spoke, "My confession, Father, is...that you have given your last sermon. You've been warned, and I don't have to tell you we mean business!"

Father Conrad reacted calmly to the man's threat. "Who are you to come here and behave like this? You can't threaten me or the Church, sir! God in the end has full power of what is the truth...and believe me, it will be told!"

The man laughed. "Not from you, Father. In twenty-four hours your life will never be the same. They will put you in the seat where I'm sitting this moment and ask you to confess! In your last hours as a priest, you will be degraded and humiliated by a series of revealing articles appearing in newspapers all over the country. And they will continue to appear until you're stripped of your collar and congregation!"

As the man laughed again, Father Conrad remained in his box and prayed for his indiscretions.

The man continued to laugh as he exited. He yelled, "YOU'RE GOING TO FIND YOURSELF IN HELL, FATHER! IN HELL!" Father Conrad listened to the man repeat his ravings until he exited the building.

That evening Father Conrad told Modini about the strange occurrence in the confessional. Modini found it hard to believe-- until the man's predictions began coming true...

John Modini's face reflected on the glass of the train window. The countryside appeared in a sudden rush as the train exited the tunnel, whistle blasting. The motion of the train relaxed Modini, and his mind started to wander again.

This time he was thinking of his boss, a well-known publisher who had his office on the top floor of a high-rise building in New York City. Inside the office, Michael Huxley, Modini's boss, a middle aged, craggy faced man, was clearly upset. He paced in front of his desk and yelled at Modini, pausing between breaths to glance out at the view from his office window. It was midday and cloudy outside, Modini recalled. He sat uncomfortable and remained quiet in a chair, listening to the man bellow.

Modini tuned him out and studied the walls of the office. On display were a variety of photos, awards, plaques, and framed magazine covers. These exhibits were evidence enough that this office housed a highly respected magazine publisher in the tradition of *Time*, *Life*, and *Look*.

Mr. Huxley stopped pacing for a moment and confronted Modini. "I am your editor and I am your friend, but this has gone too far, John! I've given you everything you asked for. But no, you had to ruin all that! You don't deliver a God-damn story for three months now. First, it was this priest in New England who you claimed was in trouble. I bent over backward for you so you could pursue the story. Why? Because you told me he was your friend!"

As the publisher continued to rant, Modini thought about the very subject. He was very familiar with the Father Conrad story. Father Conrad had sat at his desk and written a letter to John Modini and addressed it to his magazine publisher. Then he sealed the envelope and stamped it with the Church's signature. With the letter in hand he took a walking tour of his church, taking his time and admiring it as if it were the last time he would see it. He kneeled down at the statue of the Virgin Mary holding the baby Jesus and spent a few minutes in prayer. Taking his coat, he then exited the Church into the cold winter night. Father Conrad finally dropped the letter in a corner post office box and continued his walk in the beautiful New England night air.

Snow flakes fell out of the cold night sky as Father Conrad came to a bridge in the city overlooking a river. He looked up into the sky and smiled and let the snow fall down upon his face. A tower clock broke the silence, ringing the hour of three a.m.

Father Conrad continued on his journey until he reached the center of the bridge, then paused. There was no one in sight. He took a hold of the metal balustrade and climbed onto a tier.

The wind was blowing colder now. Father Conrad peered downward to the rushing river below. He took his cloth and kissed it and did the same with his cross. Tears welled from within his tired eyes. He looked to God and the heavens above him. "Please, forgive me, Father...for the sin I'm about to commit." He closed his eyes and pushed himself away from the tier of the bridge and fell downward to his death into the rushing water.

Modini's eyes became moist as he recalled the fate of Father Conrad. His publisher, Mr. Huxley, continued with his pacing and yelling. "You're one of my best people here! I gave you four weeks off to get this other problem off your chest...this obsession you have, John, on this mass murder thing in some small fucking town in Indiana! Well, It's getting out of hand! I say, right now, close the door on it! Just forget it and go back to work! You hear me?" Mr. Huxley stared at him, but he wasn't getting any response. "Well, speak to me, John...Damn it!"

Modini avoided eye contact, not responding. His fingers twiddled. He fought to keep his eyes from breaking into tears. The publisher sat down in his seat behind his desk. He saw this meeting was going nowhere. "Okay, John... Get the fuck outta my office...you're fired!"

Total darkness again and the shrill sound of the train's whistle blasted again as the train exited another tunnel. Modini continued to stare out of his window as a voice continued within his mind, the same words over and over, "You're fired! You're fired!"

But it was another voice above him who interrupted his reflection. This second voice repeated, "Sir, are you all right? Can I get you something, sir? Sir...!"

Modini jumped up, awakening from his daze. The purser of the train stood over him, "Can I help you, Sir?"

Modini forced a smile and shook his head, "Thanks... No, I'll be all right..."

The purser nodded. "Your ticket, Sir? How far will you be traveling?"

Modini handed the purser his ticket. "Raleigh... Raleigh, North Carolina!" When the purser left, Modini continued to stare out the window. The train moved steadily through the darkness and across the countryside.

* * *

The same evening, Catherine drove her bright red Honda Prelude to her father's house in Madison. It was close to midnight as her car pulled into the driveway. Both Catherine and Judge Kencade exited the car and walked silently to the house. As they reached the front door, they heard the phone ringing inside.

"Who is phoning at this time of night?" Catherine was perturbed.

"Just let it ring, it'll stop soon enough," her father sounded a bit tired. The key turned in the lock and the two entered the house. The phone stopped ringing. Catherine picked up the daily newspaper from off the doorstep and closed the door behind them.

What neither Catherine nor Kencade saw was a car parked across the street from the Kencade house, watching them. A man lighted up a cigarette, and settled back, observing the house.

72

Catherine set the paper down on the side-table and hung up both her and her father's coats. The Judge wearily began to ascend the staircase to the second floor. She called up after him. "Dad...! Will you be all right?"

The Judge turned around to snap at her. "Yes, I still have my faculties... They haven't put me away in a mental institution yet, for not knowing how to climb a set of stairs on my way to my own toilet!"

Catherine corrected her father, "'Bathroom,' Dad."

The Judge reached the top of the stairs. "You call it what you want and I'll call it what I like... It's a God-damned toilet!"

The phone started ringing again. Catherine picked up the receiver. "Yes, Michael? She answered, recognizing Bradley's voice. "Why are you...what is it?"

"I just wanted you to know I'm still at the office and if you need anything, I'm here for you. You know that. I checked your flight, and I knew you'd be getting in late. I'm sorry, Catherine, that this had to happen-- especially now of all times. It's sick!"

Catherine agreed, "You didn't need to stay at the office, Michael. You should be at home in bed. Why are you still there?"

Michael Bradley dismissed her question. "Well, I just want to close it out so you wouldn't need to do any of the paper work. I've got to say we did have them there for a moment. I don't know, maybe it's a blessing for all of us. Who knows?"

Something wasn't right with the conversation. Catherine was confused. "Michael, either I'm just too tired or I don't know what you're talking about. Are you talking about father or what?"

"Catherine, no... Oh, my God!" Bradley replied, his voice startled, "I thought you heard... It's all over the newspapers--"

Catherine reached over to the table where she placed that day's newspaper and opened it up. The front page read: SUICIDE: On eve of conviction, serial killer found dead, hanging from cell!"

She dropped the phone and read on. "Karl Hunter, accused serial killer, veteran of Vietnam conflicts and awarded the Congressional Medal of Honor for his distinguished bravery in combat, died today in his cell, a suicide by strangulation."

Chapter Nine

"Oswald vs. Gerald Ford"

Michael Bradley's Michael Bradley's office was on the top floor of a high-rise building in the city center of Madison, Indiana. His office space took up the entire floor, providing six attorneys each with their own office, a screening room, and two conference rooms. Almost every major area was prominent with colors of burgundy, with shades of gray and olive green to break up the monotony.

Catherine sat at the head of a conference table with all six attorneys in attendance, two of which were women, and one counsel was black. Bradley was at the other end, acting the role of spokesperson. All were aware of what had transpired in the last two days.

One attorney, Mr. Hyduk, announced, "Today could well be considered our 'Black Monday!'" He compared the news to the Wall Street disaster. He turned to his black colleague and nodded, "No offense to our esteemed colleague here, Mr. Booker."

Mr. Booker laughed at the comment with snickers coming slowly from the others.

"The police report says Karl Hunter strangled himself with the bedsprings from the mattress they provided for him because of his bad back." Michael Bradley said. He kept the rhythm moving as he spoke, setting down some material, passing it on around. "Apparently he had an old war wound and it says here <u>you</u> requested it!" Bradley looked at Catherine as she gave a startled look.

"I think I would remember something like that," Catherine replied. "I do know I requested his transfer so no one would know his whereabouts, and I was told by the Warden he would process it. But there was nothing about a mattress, unless he requested it.

Catherine stopped, remembering the words of Karl Hunter: "If you find I'm dead, believe it not to be suicide...but play along as if it is!" Catherine closed her eyes, trying to arrange her thoughts in order.

Bradley crossed over to her. "Catherine, are you all right?"

She opened her eyes and saw Bradley standing next to her. She forced a smile. "Yes, Michael, I think so... For now, anyway!"

* * *

Meanwhile, at ten a.m. in Raleigh, North Carolina, John Modini dialed a phone number in an outdoor phone booth. The sky outside looked as though it wanted to pour rain, but something was holding it back. Mary Ann Sweeney's piece of paper was in Modini's hand. He heard a young child's voice answer the phone. "Hello," the tiny voice said.

"Hello... Can I speak with your mother or father, please?" He heard the child yell to his mommy to come to the phone.

"Yes, Hello? A woman's voice answered. "Who is this please?"

Modini responded, "Ma'am, I'm not sure if I dialed right. Is your number...843-1964? Oh, it is... So this is a family residence? For how long has that been? In the last two or three years? No, Ma'am, I'm calling because a family member had once lived here in Raleigh at this number... Yes, I'm passing through... Oh, really... This number was not originally at this address. Would you know maybe where it originated from? No? Well, thank you. I really appreciate this very much... Sorry for the bother."

76

Modini took the piece of paper with Miss Sweeney's strange number and stared at it, trying to figure out what to do next. He leafed through the phone book until he found the address of Raleigh's Public State Library.

A half hour later Modini entered the State Library and headed straight for the information desk.

"Excuse me, Ma'am," he asked the lady sitting behind the counter. "But do you have a telephone directory going back to 1963?"

The lady behind the desk replied, "I'm sure we do, but why not first try the phone company itself. It may save you some time if they have a record of what you're looking for."

Modini thought her suggestion made sense. "Thank you, I think I'll just do that." Then he remembered to ask another question, one just as important. "Oh... Ma'am, do you...have all the twenty-six volumes of the Warren Commission Report?"

The lady escorted Modini to the back of the library and pointed down an aisle of books to where he might find them. He thanked her and examined the bookshelves until he found on the bottom of one of the shelves what he was searching for-- all twenty-six volumes, side-by-side. He took one volume out and opened it. He leafed through the chapters, then scanned the other books, checking each index, searching for a particular one. His finger stopped at one heading. He opened the book to the chapter headed: "Lee Harvey Oswald, His Life History"

Modini looked at Oswald's chronology from the day he defected October 1959 to his return in the Spring of 1962. He noticed the year describing his movements in 1960 was totally missing. "So much for the chronology," he said to himself. "Right here, something is not right! What is the basis for this chronology?"

His finger moved down the page: "...that Oswald's transfer to Minsk in the USSR in January of 1960 on, until his return to Moscow in 1961 is not included in his 'historic diary.'" Modini's eyes widened with surprise. "A diary? The Warren Commission had based its judgment on this historic diary? A diary automatically *assumed* to be the assassin's?"

77

Modini voiced his thoughts aloud until someone near him asked him politely to be quiet. *If this is really Oswald's diary, why would 1960 be omitted? Modini thought to himself. Oswald would not omit a whole year, even parts of it, unless he was a prisoner bound with shackles all that time. More likely, someone had deliberately taken that year out! But why? For what reason-- National Security? If there weren't something to hide, it meant there would be more reason for the Commission to want us to believe Oswald did it. Or what if the Commission just took the word of whoever provided this diary that there was no information pertaining to 1960? But what about Marina Oswald? Surely, she could provide information on the missing year-- especially if she were threatened with deportation. She would say and do almost anything to protect herself and her children, her two girls. Yes... why wasn't there a statement provided by Marina? Why didn't she just leave and return to her country, knowing she must be the most hated woman in the United States at that time? Why?*

Modini leafed through a few more pages. *I see,* he continued to think to himself. *It says here they didn't meet until spring of 1961... Oh, of course not, she wouldn't be able to know what he did in 1960. Her word wouldn't mean anything since she didn't come into the picture until afterward. Is that what the Warren Commission would like us to do-- only believe this diary and forget 1960 as though it didn't exist? It doesn't matter if Oswald is the assassin. It doesn't matter as long as the Commission tells you it is! But the diary must continue when he returns to Moscow and meets Marina and everything seems again hunky-dory for Oswald as he writes...*

Modini came across a page reproducing Oswald's defection letter. He read through it slowly. *Funny, but this doesn't make sense. Oswald's defection letter was written by an intellectual who could have come out of Harvard... But Oswald's diary seemed to be written with a sixth grade mentality. The words in the diary were misspelt, and it was very inarticulate, whereas the defection letter is very articulate! Is this diary written by the same man? He was nineteen when he defected and twenty-two when he returned to the United States. You don't become dumber when you age, unless Communism turns you into a blubbering idiot! Who wrote this chronology for the Commission?*

Modini leafed through the credentials of the members of the Commission and found Commission member Gerald Ford's name attached to the chronology. *Gerald Ford? The man who would be the future President of the United States?*

Modini's eyes kindled as he noticed the name of Attorney Arlen Spector as one who assisted Ford with the chronology. *Hmmm...our magic bullet expert! I can't believe this! I'm such an idiot!*

Modini turned to another page and found an interesting excerpt. "The following was a description by Warren Commission member, Representative Gerald R. Ford, Republican Congressman from Michigan. He wrote an article published in *Life Magazine* one month after Chief Justice Earl Warren handed over to President Johnson the final report on the 26 volumes of the Warren Commission. The date of the published article, October 2, 1964 (later to be noted in his book *Portrait of an Assassin* read: 'There was the mother, Mrs. Marguerite Oswald, a singularly angry woman whose strange attitudes and actions provided an appropriate background for the strange son she had shaped. Mrs. Oswald's irrational allegations caused one of the most persistent and dangerous and completely untrue rumors, that Lee Harvey Oswald was, or had been an agent of the U.S. Government!'"

Modini continued reading. "Ford wrote further: 'Oswald's mother appeared in a black dress and at the time I noted on a pad that she was aggressive, dogmatic, difficult! She told wild stories, frequently forgot her point, meandered through blind and unproductive asides. When we tried to get her back on the track, she denounced us for interrupting.'"

It seems Mr. Ford was none too sympathetic to this woman's feelings or the ordeal she was going through. After all, he must think she wasn't a human being any more! And Mr. Ford would be our future President!

Modini continued with Ford's essay: 'Ford described Marina Oswald, the wife at the hearings, thus: Then there was also Oswald's handsome Russian wife, a quiet young woman

79

whom, first, seemed simple and direct and eager to cooperate, but who, as time went on and conflicts began to develop in her testimony, emerged as a complex and even mysterious person.'

Modini stopped here and commented sarcastically, "Where's his description of her small little mustache and the knife that appears, from just a click of her heel, at the toe of her high-top laced Russian boots whenever a Commissioner stepped out of line!" Modini frowned and shook his head. "Mr. Ford, were you an example of what to expect from the other six commissioners?"

Modini continued to flip pages, stopping at: "Marguerite Oswald talking to Chief Justice Warren and J. Lee Rankin, General Counsel of Commission at the Warren Commission Hearings starting Monday, February 10, 1964: ...kept insisting that her son had been a Secret Service agent for this country, and that at age sixteen, Lee Harvey was influenced to read communist literature, part of the procedure for becoming an agent. He began reading his brother's Marine manual, and one year later entered the Marine Service at age seventeen."

Modini flipped to the chronology and read. "After training in this country, Oswald was sent to Atsugi, Japan, a Navy base used also by Marine squadrons. He was a member of Marine Air Control Squadron No. 1, which directed aircraft by radar communicating with the pilots by radio. This was also a major top secret program and base for U-2 flights. The U-2 aircraft at this time in history, was a top priority target of the KGB..."

How convenient for someone! Modini thought, his fingers taking a walk to another page. *Oswald, on January 30, 1962 sent an angry letter from Russia, concerning his 'undesirable' discharge from the Marine Corps Reserve because of his defection, to John B. Connally who at the time had resigned his post as Secretary of the Navy to run for Governor of Texas.*

Modini halted and became agitated by the last part of Oswald's chronology and took out a note pad and started writing. 'Call mother.' Then he read on. "Meanwhile, this same month, after not hearing from her son in over a year after his defection, Mrs. Oswald went to Washington to contact President Kennedy, knowing in her heart her son to be an agent." Modini again halted and flipped back pages of the chronology until he found: "October 1960, Marguerite Oswald wrote to her son telling him of his dishonorable discharge from the Marine Corps and the newspapers here labeling him a traitor..."

Modini went back to the section on John Connally's letter from Oswald-- though not the actual letter itself-- and checked the chronology date: January 30, 1962. *Either this date had been a misprint, or the people reading this were taking the word of Ford and the attorney, Spector, as well as the Commissioners. Was this a contradiction, or did Oswald take almost a year and a half to write Connally about his discharge? Or is there something wrong with that missing year in this 'historic diary' the Commissioners claim is their Bible?* Modini noticed that letters written by Oswald were not consistent with this one. *Why,* he asked himself.

Modini took a couple of the reports with him to a copy machine and copied specific pages. One of them he marked at the bottom 'Look at interrogation of Oswald, P. 268 WCR (Warren Commission Report). This page was the Oswald letter to Connally interpreted by Ford with an added note: "...that this letter Oswald sent to Connally stating his dishonorable discharge from the Marines was a mistake written by Oswald, when in actuality the discharge was 'undesirable,' a less derogatory characterization." Another mistake by Oswald within this letter was that Oswald thought the then Governor of Texas, John Connally, was still the Secretary of the Navy!

"Wait a minute!" Modini remembered. "Connally didn't become Governor of Texas until January 1963! This whole matter doesn't make sense!"

Modini took out the note pad he wrote 'Call mother' on and added 'Connally letter.' This was something he planned to look into.

Chapter Ten

"Nixon's Little Secret"

The clock tower on top of the United States Post Office in Madison, Indiana, read 4:45 p.m. The late afternoon clouds were darkening, giving a hint they could burst at anytime.

Catherine sat stuck within the five o'clock rush hour traffic and contemplated what she would do next. She stared at that clock tower through her windshield and continued to ponder until a car eased out of a parking place in front of the post office. The words of Karl Hunter came back to her: *"Go there only if I die, otherwise, forget I ever existed! Good-bye, C.R.!*

Suddenly, in a burst of determination, Catherine swerved out of traffic and squeezed into the vacant parking spot in front of the post office. As she exited her Honda, a clap of thunder roared overhead. She looked above her as the skies opened up. She ran up the stairs and entered the United States Post Office before she got wet.

She waited in line until the postmaster called her up to the window marked Registered Mail and Packages. "Yes, ma'am...may I help you?" the postmaster said smiling.

Catherine started to perspire, although it was not warm inside the building. She felt a little uncertain if what she was doing was right.

"Are you okay, ma'am?" The postmaster asked.

"Yes!" Catherine said, almost forcing the words out. "I'm here to pick up a registered envelope!" She calmed down and smiled at the postmaster as she noticed his reaction.

The postmaster became somewhat relaxed after seeing her smile and asked, "And your name, please?"

Catherine laughed, "Excuse me... I'm sorry, my mind's elsewhere. I mean it's under the name H. Kencade..."

The postmaster excused himself and disappeared in the back room. Catherine glanced around to look at everyone standing in line. She felt a little anxious as she waited. The postmaster brought back a large 8 x 10 manila envelope to the window, "Yes, this is it, it's been here quite a long time. You just need to sign here." He gave her a pen to use. Catherine signed the receipt and thanked him, taking the thick envelope.

Catherine ran to her car through the pouring rain as she tried to protect herself as well as the packaged envelope in her hand. Once inside her car, Catherine stared at the envelope. It was addressed to H. Kencade, written in neat strokes with a marking pen. Her fingers tested the envelope. It was closed by the two folded metal tabs and not sealed shut. She pulled open the top and looked inside. There were two envelopes inside. She took them out. The first one was brown and bulky, and had the name *H. Kencade* on it. The second was a regular letter and was addressed to an unfamiliar attorney and his law firm in New York City. This letter was postmarked over some twenty years ago but never opened. She stared closely, trying to discern the date. "Either 1965 or '66..." Then she saw a note attached to the bottom of the first letter. It reads: "Open first!"

Catherine tore open the first envelope and removed an audio cassette, the only thing inside. She looked it over. It had no label or markings. She inserted it into the car tape deck. For a few seconds there was silence, then she was startled to hear Karl Hunter's voice coming from the car speakers.

"Important!" Karl's voice began with a warning. "Do not read the second letter in your possession! I know its contents, and it is for your protection you do not know what it contains!

This information can cause you great harm if anyone should find out you have it."

Catherine reached out to adjust the volume of Karl's recorded voice.

"You, Judge Henry Kencade, will have to decide whether you're going to read the second letter at the conclusion of this tape. If you do, you will have to live with the consequences of your actions. I would recommend against it, because what you don't know can't hurt you."

Catherine listened intently, concentrating on the words of her deceased client to her father.

"By now, it is obvious I'm dead, otherwise, you wouldn't be listening to this tape. This is just a warning to you-- from beyond the grave, so to speak-- that your life could be in danger if you do not take my words seriously."

Catherine, disturbed and upset by Karl Hunter's remarks, punched the tape button and stopped the tape. Only the sound of the rain splattering on her windshield broke the silence. She looked around at the people and cars on the rain-drenched street. An illogical fear grew within her, as if she expected someone to be watching her as she sat in her car.

She closed her eyes for a few seconds and the continuous pounding of the rain seemed to calm her, instead of increase her anxiety. Finally, she took a deep breath and pressed the play button.

Karl Hunter's voice came from the speaker again: "...The letter addressed to the attorney in New York is of no significance anymore. The letter has not been delivered for over two decades, and the attorney is dead. Only the contents are of any value, and if revealed to anyone, that person would be as good as dead!"

Catherine's brow furrowed with concern. *What did Karl mean by that*, she wondered.

"The man who wrote the letter is...well, for now, I'll just call him Mister X. He is a man well known within the American Intelligence circles. At the time of the Kennedy Assassination, he was in North Africa and was held in jail in Tangier by Moroccan Security Police in connection with the President's murder. And because of the information in this letter, now in your custody, Mister X was released from the Moroccan prison with the assistance of the CIA by an operative using the code name: QJ/WIN. For your own protection, I will not identify him, since at the time I'm recording this, I believe he is still alive..."

Catherine was totally in absorbed as if she were listening to 'Mystery Theater' or some Orson Welles thriller on radio. She was hypnotized by Karl Hunter's voice, even as she tried to determine the thrust of his message. The soul of Karl Hunter had somehow come alive and totally captured her attention.

"This operative was a narcotic smuggler for the CIA, and OAS activist, and has also used an alias, the name of Michael Roux," Hunter continued. "QJ/WIN was a key agent in the CIA's 'Executive Action' program, formed to plan and execute assassinations of foreign leaders. Roux was in Dallas on the day of the Kennedy assassination! Coincidence?

"Roux or QJ/WIN, his boss in the CIA's Assassination Department was William Harvey. I say 'Assassination Department' not in jest because most people think that's what the CIA does. The Central Intelligence Agency is not and cannot be used for assassination purposes-- the CIA's purpose is for spying and intelligence only, outside the U.S.A. on foreign ground. But in the mid-50's a secret assassination department was formed under then Vice-President Richard Milhous Nixon, with Allen Dulles then the CIA director, and Deputy Director Cabell, all in attendance. Its purpose was the elimination of leaders from small foreign countries with the intention of the CIA putting in their own elected puppet presidents or dictators!

If one would take the time and research our government policy between 1954 and the election of Kennedy in 1960, one would be amazed the sudden influx of foreign countries new leadership and the fact the association of our government contributed in helping the progress of those countries. Just go back to the Shah of Iran and Guatemala, even Vietnam!"

Outside the car, a flash of lightening startled Catherine. Thunder cracked and the skies got darker. It was still pouring rain. Catherine decided to leave the post office before the weather became any worse. She started the car and pulled into traffic. A second car parked across the street spotted Catherine taking off and quickly did a U-turn and trailed her.

Inside Catherine's car, Karl Hunter's voice continued: "As I said, Roux's boss in this department of the CIA was William Harvey. His specialty was the agency's Cuban operations and the plots to assassinate Fidel Castro, whose okay came straight from the White House. It was of special interest to Nixon who was angry with Castro's betrayal, since it was Nixon who helped Castro take over Cuba from its former Dictator, Batista.

"Castro betrayed Nixon and angered the Mafia who smuggled, along with the CIA, guns and money, acting as bagmen to Castro to gain his control of power and without the world's knowledge. It would have been another coup for the CIA. The Mafia's would have gained control of Havana's gambling, prostitution and drug trades, but Castro reversed all this, when he threw out all mob figures or locked them up and turned to Russia for help and Communism.

"Since it was the United States that put Castro into position and power, our government now wanted to reverse it. Ironically, this situation placed Nixon in a very high level position. He had a good chance to be the next president of the United States, since he was the number one crime fighter against communism, which was now potential threat located just ninety miles off Miami Beach, Florida. If the fight against communism in the motion picture industry and our own military became fruitless and an embarrassment to our country during the past decade, our government decided this would not. Then Cuba became the real thing...and Nixon now had an excuse to bend the rules. Those rules would develop into the international incident known today as the Bay of Pigs! And those who were in charge of putting Castro into his leadership position, were now going to take him out. These men included names familiar to all of us like E. Howard Hunt and Frank Sturgis, two men supposedly linked to Dallas and the date of November 22, whose names will always be linked as two of the plumbers arrested at Watergate in 1972. They'll always be known as Nixon's men and their affiliations go back to 1955 when the CIA created the code name 'Executive Action' for assassination."

Catherine continued to drive down the street, listening to the taped message. Although the traffic was a little slower and heavier, the same car at the post office still followed her.

"It was William Harvey who was in personal touch with John Rawalson, an alias for Johnny Roselli," Karl Hunter clarified. "Rawalson, or I should say Roselli, was the gangster used as liaison man between the CIA and the Mafia in the murder plot against Castro, assisted by mobster Santos Trafficante out of Florida. Robert Blakley and the House Select Committee on John Kennedy's assassination in '78 used their conclusions to involve the Mafia. Since there was proof a fourth shot was fired upon the motorcade that fateful day in Dallas, a conspiracy existed-- not within the government, but within this country's Mafia, a group, in the eyes of J. Edgar Hoover and the FBI that supposedly didn't exist until Fall of 1963.

"The CIA, the FBI, and Deputy Director Richard Helms, to name a few. Helms who later became Nixon's man following in the steps of the Johnson administration-- and it's former director Allen Dulles who was fired by Kennedy following the Bay of Pigs fiasco, also became a member of the Warren Commission. How convenient, right? All the agencies and people I mentioned were involved in the cover up. They all kept secrets and hid reports from the Warren Commission! They did not do anything to help resolve the conspiracy. Among the things they concealed was the fact that Jack Ruby who assassinated Lee Harvey Oswald worked for Sam Giancana, the number one Mafia boss out of Chicago. And the fact that Ruby visited the Mafia boss, Santos Trafficante, while in a Havana prison, and who, with the liaison, Roselli, was involved with the CIA in its Castro murder plots.

"Roselli, the key contact man who was killed before testifying in 1976 for the House Select Committee, stated, 'Ruby was ordered to eliminate Oswald.' Remember, Judge Kencade, Mister X, is someone whose real identity will never be exposed except through this second letter you now have in your possession. I know him personally, and that's why, if you are listening to me now, I am probably dead.

If you think this is a fantasy, think back... Hasn't our government been brainwashing the country with countless lies over the past twenty-five years? Oh, yes, you're probably thinking, I wrote the letter, but once you read it, you and every forensic scientist and writing analyst in the nation will conclude that a 13 or 14 year old child could not have written such a letter or had the information it holds...no, not even the CIA. They can deny it all they want, but by this exposure, like Kennedy himself said just prior to his assassination, 'the CIA will be splintered into a thousand pieces.' And believe me, it would be best for the country if it were, so as to weed out those corrupt elements within our own government.

"If you want to know the truth about the identity of Mister X, keep in mind the fact he holds the keys to the deaths of Sam Giancana the night before his testimony before the Senate Select Committee on Kennedy's assassination in June 1975. He knows information about Johnny Roselli's death the following year prior to his testimony in '76, and the death of officer J.D. Tippit in 1963 following Kennedy's assassination. He knows the details about Jack Ruby's death in prison in 1967, and the mysterious death of Naval Commander William B. Pitzer who was found in his own office at the Bethesda Naval Hospital in Maryland. The government said he killed himself with a gunshot wound to the head, by a gun fired by a right hand, though the commander was left handed. His body was never returned to his family and has since disappeared.

"The body of Clay Shaw also vanished after his mysterious death in 1974. It was during the Rockefeller Commission and Church Hearings, former CIA Director Richard Helms confessed that Clay Shaw was in truth a CIA operative who denied for years, he ever worked for or was connected to the Intelligence Agency. Clay Shaw had lied at the Garrison trial in '69.

"Do you see how it works, Judge? If you want to cover up something in the government all you do is to form a committee. First, the Warren commission was created to cover up Kennedy's death for 'national security' reasons. They expelled the Senate, the Congress, and even the Dallas Police Department, which had the most to gain, in investigating the murder of the President Kennedy right in their own back yard. Then in 1974 and '75 the Rockefeller Commission was formed because of the Pentagon Papers leak concerning the CIA's 'Executive Action' program, of which CIA Director Bill Colby confirmed at the hearings. This was followed by his removal by President Ford and peaked the interest of the theorists, commenting that if the CIA were secretly out there in the world assassinating world leaders, why couldn't this same program turn on our own President. If you read between the lines, what they were saying all along was the CIA committed the act of eliminating JFK!

"Again, the Church Hearings were held in 1976 to squelch any rumors that 'Executive Action' had turned on our President, and a newly appointed CIA Director was to confirm this was not possible. This former Texas oil man, George Bush, came before the hearings to state that although the CIA did have a program that did exist, known as 'Executive Action,' and had since been shut down, the CIA, known as 'The Company,' was thoroughly cleaned up. He, himself, George Bush, had searched and found *no* link to the 'Executive Action' program or any CIA involvement with the assassination of JFK!"

There was a momentary pause on the tape. "Tell me, Judge, how does a Texas oil man become a CIA Director, the head of the most secret organization in our government? An organization that had secretly fraternized with a few wealthy Texas oil men. Here's a man whose only link to becoming a government official was through Richard Milhous Nixon...and would eventually become the President of the United States. Ask Bush whom George DeMohrenschildt is. You'll be surprised at his connection. DeMohrenschildt's death was caused by a gunshot wound to the head, like most of the others ruled a suicide prior to an appearance he was to have made before the House Select Committee in 1977. How convenient for those who still control this country and continue the cover up!

"...Again, if you dare to know the truth and are willing to suffer the consequences, you can open the letter. Otherwise, this so-called 'land of the free and home of the brave' is really masking a sick country! Shit...and we call it 'America, the Beautiful!' Be careful, Judge! This is just one victim you didn't or could not save! Now try, if you have a heart at all, to save this country by doing so, you may have to sacrifice yourself...like me!"

It was evening now, and Catherine parked her car in the pouring rain in the Greyhound Bus terminal parking lot. The other car following her pulled into the same parking lot but kept a safe distance, far enough away not to be noticed. The headlights, shined at her car. Only a dark silhouette of a man was discernible behind the wheel.

Inside the bus station, Catherine deposited change into a key deposit box and opened it up. She took the sealed second letter from her purse, placed it into a plastic bag and closed it. Catherine hesitated, staring at it with curiosity, then decided to do what she came there to do. She placed the letter into the deposit box, locked it and dropped the key into her purse.

Catherine left the terminal and drove off. The second car continued to follow her. Catherine pulled up to her father's house and parked in the driveway. The man inside the second car watched as she entered the house, then drove on and disappeared down the street.

Catherine slipped off her coat and put her purse on the side table. Her eye caught the newspaper, and she opened it to the front page story describing how Karl Hunter committed suicide in his cell. She could feel her temper rising the more she thought about it. She headed upstairs to the second floor, newspaper and envelope in hand.

She entered her father's bedroom through the opened door and found him in bed with his glasses on, reading a book. Catherine threw the newspaper on his lap so he could see the headlines. "Dad, what do you know about this? And don't give me any of your bullshit, either!"

Judge Kencade was stunned for a moment as he looked up at her, "Don't use that tone of voice to me again!" He said, his voice hardening. He slowly set his book down and picked up the newspaper, adjusting his glasses. His brow furrowed as he read. "I have no idea what you mean, Catie! What's this got to do with me?"

Catherine let her anger get the best of her. "Oh, come off it, your Honor! Do you mean to tell me you don't know why my client-- the man you were ready to convict-- was murdered in a top security cell?"

Her father calmly responded, "I know you're upset dear...but it says here, right here in the newspaper, death by suicide, not murder. Now, unless you have other information to the contrary," Kencade said in a much stronger tone, "Where do you come off at me with this murder crap?"

Catherine stood her ground. "Bullshit!"

Kencade ignored her outburst. "Suicide happens all the time in prisons, you know that!"

"Bullshit!" Catherine shot back. "Not to my clients, it doesn't! Now, I want the truth, dad! My client told me this weekend he was being set up to be killed and asked me to get him out. Now he's dead. On top of this, some girl picks you up after an accident and you get charged with her murder! Too many things are happening to make me believe they're just coincidences!"

The Judge resented his daughter's questioning. "Catie, I told you what happened. What are you suggesting? That I was set up or framed by that girl?"

Catherine suddenly looked at her father strangely. "It's funny you should say that. Karl Hunter used almost those exact words. Dad, tell me...what are you trying to hide? Are you saying you still believe your story-- that you didn't know what you were doing and somehow you grabbed a knife and accidentally stabbed this girl in...a blackout? Twenty-seven times? Where did the knife come from, dad?"

Kencade, went on the offensive, "I don't know...I don't know! That girl...she helped me... She picked me up off the street when I was injured. That's all I can remember. Why would I kill her?" Kencade's voice dropped. He stared straight ahead. "But I must have... I must have..."

Catherine sat down on the bed beside her father and put her hand on his shoulder and looked into his eyes, "What else, father? Think! What else do you remember?"

Kencade just shook his head, "He had a knife..."

"He?" Catherine responded. "You mean the man attacking the girl?"

"Yes!" Kencade concurred.

Catherine tried to calm her voice, "Dad, listen carefully... The last thing Karl Hunter said before I left him, when I asked him why he thought someone would kill him...he said for me to-- to *ask* you!"

Kencade gave his daughter an astonished look. Catherine continued, "He also said if he should die, I was to go to the Post Office where I'd find an envelope addressed to you, under H.

Kencade. There were two letters in the manila envelope. In one of them was a tape recording. She took the tape from her purse. "This is the tape from the letter with your name on it."

Kencade stared at the strange tape his daughter held. His curiosity got the best of him. He took the tape from her and slipped it into the stereo cassette player on his bedside table. He gazed at his daughter as Karl Hunter spoke to him.

* * *

At ten p.m. in a small downtown diner in Raleigh, North Carolina, John Modini sat down for a late dinner. He stretched out his tired body in one of the booths and stared at his note pad, trying to organize the information he had been collecting. A television set was on at the other end of the diner. The news was on the air, but the sound was so low Modini couldn't hear it.

A customer sitting across from him slid out of his booth and threw down his newspaper. Modini's eye caught a partial headline: "DIANA'S MASS MURDERER FOUND."

As the waitress served him a cheeseburger and coke, Modini slipped his note pad into his pocket. He took a bite from the burger and tilted his head to stare at an article on the front page of the discarded paper.

He got out of his booth, burger still in hand, and picked up a tabloid newspaper. It read: "Indiana's mass murderer found dead in cell only hours prior to verdict." The article continued, "Apparent suicide by strangulation." Below this another story in bold letters: "TRIAL JUDGE HENRY KENCADE FREED ON HIS OWN RECOGNIZANCE. Judge goes on rampage and kills prostitute as trial of serial killer nears end."

Modini heard the name "Kencade" and glanced up to notice a news anchor on the television set was reporting the same story. A picture of Judge Kencade was superimposed over the anchor's shoulder.

"Would you turn up the volume, please," he asked the waitress.

The waitress complied, and the newscaster repeated what Modini had just read, adding,

"Judge Kencade, accused in the stabbing death of a known prostitute, Rita Stebbings, has been released on his own recognizance. Henry J. Kencade is now in the custody of his daughter, Catherine Rogers, one of the attorneys for Karl Hunter. Kencade who had been on the 'A List' to become the next Supreme Court Justice will be arraigned in the next two days. Mrs. Rogers had no comment at this time."

"In other news out of the state of Indiana, Vice-President Bush who is the Republican front runner for President, is considering an Indiana hometown boy, Dan Quayle, as his candidate for Vice-President."

All Modini could say, staring up at the set was, "His daughter?" Then he murmured to himself, "Catherine Rogers is Catie Kencade?" Modini recalled the thirteen-year-old girl at the beach front party over twenty-one years ago. He paused a moment in thought, then turned his mind to more important matters.

He headed straight to the phone booth, cheeseburger in hand, and dialed. "Yes, Directory Assistance, please..." He pulled out his note pad again and searched for a pencil.

"Thank you...yes, I was asked to call this number for-- Well, the kind of information I need is probably a strange request to you. How do you go about finding a number that existed around twenty-five years ago, one that might have changed a couple times since then?" Modini looked on one of the pages of his note pad and noticed his reminder to 'call mother' "...Call the directory library between the hours of 8:30 a.m. and 4:45 p.m. The address? Okay...shoot... Fine, and I thank you very much. What? Well, sort of, you could say it is for some kind of reunion..."

Modini hung up and dialed again. "Yes, person to person to Marian Modini... John Modini! Mother! You're up? Oh, I guess you would be. I'm three hours ahead of you! Yes! I just heard. I know, I know, but I'm going to look into it. There's no way Karl took his own life! Mom, I was sidetracked because of you, coming down here to see Miss Sweeney. No, I'm in Raleigh, North Carolina. It's a long story. I saw her a couple of days ago! Yes, she's very nice." He patiently waited to speak again.

"Mom, I need you to do something for me. You remember dad's things you put away in the basement or garage. I don't know. Remember, just before he passed away he had a box he wanted me to have and I always refused to look at it? He kept it a big secret all these years. Yes, the Kennedy box with Martin Luther King and Bobby Kennedy's assassination articles! Yes, you're right, I always disagreed with him. Yes, I ridiculed him, too. Don't rub it in. I write what I believe, mother, and I still believe I'm right, but...he's finally going to have his due...at least for the next few days anyway. No writer wants to be challenged, especially when he thinks he's right. I'm only doing this for Miss Sweeney.

"Now, the box, mother...inside it there's a pamphlet. Dad showed it to me years ago. It has Kennedy's picture on the front-- pictures of the assassination and some of Oswald. I want you to fax me the letters inside the pamphlet, the ones Oswald wrote. I believe there are two of them, but the one I'm interested in is the one he wrote John Connally from Minsk, Russia. Yes, the Texas Governor. I want you to fax it to...now write this down...to Max Slaton in D.C. at the U.S. Bureau of Records. Yes, in Washington D.C.! I don't have the number, but you can call and get it. I'll be there tomorrow afternoon.

"Mom, it's a pamphlet. Dad got it the year after he deserted us. He said he bought it two weeks after the assassination. Someone was peddling them to make a quick buck, I imagine. It has always puzzled me these last few years that someone could release so much information on Oswald and had capabilities and the resources to almost...campaign to destroy and convict Oswald before the Government could legally try him. Come to think of it, the Warren Commission wasn't even formed when this pamphlet was being sold on the street. Only that Congress and the Senate were planning to form committees to investigate!"

He listened to his mother's question. "Yes, I'll call you when I find out more about Karl. Even if I have to go to the Pentagon and make a scene, Karl will have his due process! Thanks, mother, I'll call you in a few days."

Modini hung up and took a bite of his now cold cheeseburger. "Ah, about as cold as my life," he said, shaking his head. He continued to munch on it in the privacy of his phone booth as he contemplated the death of Hunter.

* * *

In the late evening at the Kencade house in Madison, Indiana, Catherine sat in her father's bedroom sipping a cup of coffee. Karl Hunter's recording had just ended. Judge Kencade took out the cassette tape and handed it back to Catherine. "You don't really believe this...do you, Catie?" He commented.

Catherine, weary from all the events of the day, stood up to face her father again. "I don't know what to believe anymore... Hunter might have just said those things in anger, probably because the way life was treating him, for all I know. But why on tape? How could he possibly exploit this after his death? It doesn't make sense! One thing I know for sure-- my client is dead...and he certainly predicted it to me, didn't he?"

Judge Kencade responded, but not in the way Catherine expected. "What about this other letter you mentioned? What does it say?"

Catherine paced nervously. "I don't know, I didn't want to read it!"

Kencade watched her pace, "So, you're afraid? Although Hunter's dead, he's still got you spooked..."

Catherine, turned on him, "You're damn right I'm spooked, but not because of what you think!"

Kencade raised his eyebrows. "Then what, for instance, Catie...that you just might find me involved-- that I'm part of this scam of his! If that's it, you're totally wrong, Catherine — all wrong! I have nothing to do with what this crackpot has said or written! This is something someone insane would do! I've had cases like this up to my wing-wang, for God's sake! Who do you take me for?"

Catherine stopped pacing. "Would you have given Karl Hunter that chance, or even half a

95

chance? Would you have allowed us, <u>him</u>, to plead insane?"

The Judge would not and did not answer her question.

Catherine continued. "You think you're so smart, don't you?"

This time in trepidation, Kencade answered her, "No, Catherine, I don't...I don't feel so smart at all..."

Chapter Eleven

"The Colonel's Agenda"

On Tuesday On Tuesday morning at ten a.m. in Raleigh, North Carolina, John Modini stared at the gray stone building across the street. He tightened his jaws as he realized he was at an impasse, and he didn't know what to do. Modini checked his watch for the time. He had a flight to catch before the noon hour. He studied the building again before heading off. The building was the headquarters of U.S. Navel Intelligence.

The airplane Carrying John Modini flew northbound, its destination was Washington D.C. Modini found the opportunity to sleep in the coach section of the TransWorld Airliner.

In the front of the plane in the first-class section, A man the same age as Modini, dressed in a Marine uniform, signaled one of the beautiful brunette flight attendants. As she approached him, Colonel Roger Tracy stood, taking his hat off.

"Excuse me, Miss," Tracy said in a flirtatious manner, "but would you direct me to the rest rooms?"

"Why certainly, sir," the flight attendant replied and escorted him to the rest rooms in the rear of the airliner.

As the Marine headed down the aisle, his eyes checked out the people in their seats. Then he spotted a familiar face: John Modini.

"Thank you," Tracy said to the attendant, politely excusing himself. He stopped to gaze down at Modini who was dead asleep.

Tracy hadn't seen him in two decades and was amazed how unchanged the man looked. Modini apparently had dozed off earlier during the flight. As Tracy stared at the man, his recollection took him back to the year 1969 and Vietnam,

Roger Tracy remembered the year 1969 and Vietnam. He recalled the very moment Private First-class Modini had screamed for someone to help his dead comrade whose head had just been blown off by a sniper fire. It was an incident indelibly etched into his memory.

* * *

Lance Corporal E 3 soldier Roger Tracy saw Modini's face become a mask of horror. Modini fell backward and saw the other soldiers in his platoon running from the enemy fire. A thin haze of smoke drifted above the fence on the hill. Modini, covered with blood, dived for cover, and was ready to scramble away, when Tracy stopped him.

"Move forward," Corporal Tracy, yelled. He was the Platoon Front-man. "Move forward and head for cover!" he ordered Modini. "We're sitting ducks out here!" At that very second sniper fire missing the both of them by inches, hitting the ground next to them.

Modini, still in shock, did what he was told and the two men scattered behind a dirt pile for cover, joining two more soldiers. Tracy recognized the both of them from the back, although he saw only the helmets covering their heads.

The first soldier, a Lance Corporal, motioned to the fence on the hill. "There, up behind the fence, I see smoke from his gun. He's there all right!"

Modini couldn't tear his eyes off the fence. He looked like a young kid, more terrified than ever. It was as if death himself waited behind that fence, ready to strike him down.

Lance Corporal Karl Hunter turned around. He also saw the fear on Modini's face. It was the fear that more often than not sent men to their deaths. "My God, Jack...are you all right?" Hunter asked Modini. "You're white as a ghost!"

Modini moved his mouth. His words were forced. "Karl! Platoon Sergeant Contos-- his, his head...isn't on his body anymore!"

Hunter grabbed him by the shirt and shook him. "Jack! Snap out of it! Forget it! There's nothing we can do about it! Understand? We've got to save our own skins now!"

Hunter glanced up at the fence. As far as the men could determine, the attack was coming from that specific location.

"You hear me, Jack?" Hunter shouted to John Modini. "Soldier, I need your help! You've got to cover me!"

Hunter gave a nod to the other soldier with him, Private First-class Daniel Conrad. "Conny, I want you to stick like glue to Jack. Now, Jack, you and Conrad have to cover me! Are you with me, Jack?" Modini managed to nod his head. Hunter smiled, "Great, now you and Conrad are taking the right flank!" He yelled over to Tracy, "Tracy, I'm playing Frontman, take left!"

Hunter gripped his rifle and readied himself to make the run up the hill. He glanced to both Conrad and Modini. "I'm going 'round back to flush out that Mother-Fucker! I'll see you guys in hell!"

Bullets started splattering around him as Hunter made his move to the right flank. All the men could hear as Hunter sprinted off was his voice calling to him, "Cover me, Jack!"

Hunter dodged the bullets and ran for cover as Modini aimed his rifle along with Conrad, spraying bullets at the fence in a short burst of firepower. Hunter, taking the long way around, headed covertly to his destination, just behind and above the fence. He inched his way forward until he had a full view from the opposite side where a sniper might hide. There was no one in sight. The sniper was not where Hunter thought he would be.

Confused, but cautious, Hunter continued his search by angling around, keeping himself down and inconspicuous. He tried to figure where this ghost-out-of-the-blue could be.

Meanwhile, Modini and Conrad had stopped firing. Modini called out over the silence." Hunter! Are you all right?" But there wasn't any answer.

Tracy was becoming impatient. A few moments later he spoke up. "We can't just stay here forever," he announced, preparing a plan in mind. "I think we should make ourselves visible for our friend and draw their fire, what'd 'ya think?"

Conrad responded, "What about Karl?"

Tracy spat, "Fuck 'em! Like Hunter said, I'm not spending the rest of my life here! I'll take the left flank. You guys take the right! See 'ya!"

Tracy dashed to the left as Modini cried out, "Roger, wait a minute!" But it was too late. Tracy was off and running. He kept low, advancing through the tall grass around the foot of the hill. He hoped Modini and Conrad would work up their courage to make their move to the right flank.

They did. Modini and Conrad became visible from Karl's point of view, from above the fence as he watched the two ascend the hill in his direction. Seconds later, a machine gun fired, raking the dirt in front of the soldiers. They fell on their bellies for cover, effectively pinned down.

Hunter frantically searched for the point where the gunfire came from. He heard the weapon clearly but couldn't get a fix on its location.

From his position, Tracy could see both Modini and Conrad. Then he realized something had happened. Modini was staring at his leg where blood stained his clothing. Then he heard Modini yell. "Conny, I've been hit! Tracy! Hunter! I've been hit! I'm hit... God help me!" Modini screamed, panicking.

Hunter scanned the area around the fence below him, but still couldn't see anyone shooting from it. He was confounded by this and heard Modini screaming out, but didn't know what he was saying. Hunter had to do something...and fast. Reluctantly, he came to the only decision he could. He stood up to face his deadly ghost and became an open target.

Roger Tracy crawled forward up the hillside from the left. Hunter noticed the movement from his standing position, and Tracy became visible to him. Suddenly, directly below him, Hunter saw the ground and foliage rising from a small section near the back side of the fence. The small bushes and brush in front of the fence camouflaged the enemy. Automatic weapons, barely visible, poked out of a three-inch trapdoor space from underneath the ground. Hunter smiled at this extraordinary sight and quietly descended a narrow path toward the enemy.

The weapons from the trap door took aim at Corporal Tracy and opened fire, pinning him down. Tracy refused to be a sitting duck and rolled to his left, dodging the deadly bullets, then dived for cover.

Hunter's boots stopped behind the trap door and kicked off the brush, and dirt covered bamboo platform above the enemies' underground bunker. Then blasted away with his machine gun at two armed snipers and a half dozen other Vietnamese soldiers inside the pit, killing all of them in one long bloody sweep of his weapon. He paused only for a few moments as he slammed new clips into his rifle and continuing firing down into the hidden bunker. When Hunter exhausted all his ammo, he raised his rifle and waved it in the air, giving out a yell as if he were the king of the mountain.

Tracy slowly picked himself off the ground and watched in amazement as Hunter demonstrated his victory by yelling and jumping up and down like a Banshee. John Modini wasn't even paying attention. He was too busy gripping his bloody leg in agony as Conrad helped him to his feet.

Modini managed a painful grin, and managed to yell out, "Hunter! You son of a bitch!"

Tracy hollered up, "You got 'em all, Hunter?"

Hunter, dancing away in celebration, responded, "You damn right! The mother-fuckers! They were a piece of cake!"

Conrad didn't make any comment. "Let's get out of here..." he said to Modini.

* * *

Modini suddenly woke up as the airliner was still in motion flying northbound to D.C. His eyes focused on a Marine in uniform, a familiar face, now aged twenty years, staring down at him.

Colonel Roger Tracy smiled, "Hello, Corporal Modini. Or, I should say, civilian Modini?"

Modini was genuinely surprised to see him. "My God, Roger... Roger Tracy?"

Tracy corrected him, "Colonel Roger Tracy. So...you haven't forgotten me all these years?"

Modini sat up amazed. "Wow, no...as a matter of fact, I was just thinking about you, recently...this is amazing!"

Tracy just continued to smile, noting the empty seat next to Modini. "Oh, really? Mind if I...sit down?"

Modini almost in awe, nodded. "Sure, let's have a drink. So, you're still with the Marines and you're a Colonel now, too! In the Pentagon?"

Tracy twirled his cap, "No, Naval Intelligence! I'm on my way to Andrews Air Force Base."

"Impressive," Modini said, a bit surprised, "Congratulations."

Tracy just broke into a smile, "I deserve it, thank you! So, how the hell are you?"

Modini shrugged. "How do I look?"

Tracy studied him seriously. "Like Hell! Like one too many martinis," Tracy laughed.

Modini motioned a stewardess over. "That reminds me..."

The brunette stewardess who had helped Tracy earlier, returned. "Playing musical chairs, Colonel?" she winked at Tracy.

"No, just catching up with an old war buddy," Tracy answered.

"Is there anything I can get you two gentlemen?" she asked.

"Scotch and soda for me, and your undivided attention, if it's anyway possible?" Tracy returned her wink.

The stewardess blushed at this. "Well, you definitely have it now, Colonel...and you, sir?"

Modini smiled at her. "Ah, just plain scotch for me, please!" As the two men watched her depart, Modini added, "I see you're still the ladies' man!"

"Have you ever known me to waste time on a great piece of ass like this before?" Tracy was very smug and sure of himself. "No, and you never will!"

Modini became curious now, "So, you've never been married, huh?"

Tracy slapped his leg with assurance, "Sure I have. I have a boy and a girl to boot!"

The stewardess returned with their drinks. Tracy slipped her a twenty and told her to keep the change. She thanked him for his generosity and departed. Tracy changed the subject as he watched her walk back down the aisle, "You treat 'em like queens at first, then when you have them in your grasp, you shit on their face!"

John Modini raised his eyebrows. "Is this your expert analysis on the subject, Doctor Tracy?"

Tracy replied very confidently. "Believe me, she wants me to shit on her face."

"Really? How interesting." Modini thought Tracy might be putting him on, but realized he probably wasn't. He had positively possessed the same crude personality as Modini remembered. "I'll have to remember that one."

Tracy nodded. "You must get them all the time in your business. I've heard you're a big shot writer for some big time magazine."

Modini stared at the drink in hand. "In the past tense," he raised his glass, "...was! I got fired! Cheers!" And he gulped down his drink. "I think I'll have another."

Tracy watched Modini in a concerned way. He came down off his high horse for an instant. "Is that why you're on the bottle? Don't you think you've had enough?"

Modini leaned over to him. "Colonel, tell me..." he said glancing at the brunette stewardess for Tracy to get the point, "..has your wife ever asked you whether you've had enough?"

And on Roger Tracy's expression, John Modini smiled.

* * *

An hour later the aircraft came down for a rough but safe landing, bouncing its passengers in their seats as it landed at the Washington D.C. Airport. Tracy and Modini departed separately from the plane, but not before the stewardess could slip the Colonel a note with a returned smile.

The passengers entered the arrival area and some exited to claim their baggage. Modini connected with Colonel Tracy again with a group heading for baggage claim, though Modini had no baggage except for the tote bag he was carrying.

Tracy took the opportunity to open the conversation again. "On the plane, you mentioned you recently thought of me..."

John Modini wouldn't make this easy for him. "Yeah, so?"

Tracy took it another step, "I'd like to know what my old war buddy had on his mind."

Modini just cut to the chase. "Quit playing games with me, Tracy-- Colonel! I think you know! You damn well know, as a matter of fact!" There was a hidden tension in his voice.

Tracy remained silent upon Modini's sharp reply. They continued walking to their destination. The good old boy charm left Tracy as it became very apparent the two men did not like one another.

Tracy finally responded, "Oh! You mean about our pal, our good buddy-- the big hero that won the Medal of Honor, the Audie Murphy and Sergeant York of Vietnam. The same man who also supplied every Tom, Dick and Mary in our platoon with every drug from hashish to heroin and cocaine!" Tracy spat out the words. "The prick deserved what he got!"

Modini stopped and grabbed Tracy's arm. "But he saved my life! He saved Conny's life and saved your life, Tracy! He fuckin' saved your life!"

Tracy pulled his arm out of Modini's grasp and moved on, "Fuck Him! Karl Hunter was a Goddamn pimp and drug dealer. He probably killed over a hundred girls and women out there because he couldn't get his prick up!" People were starting to stare the two men as they reached the baggage claim area.

As they waited for their luggage next to the baggage turnstile, two men entered from the taxi and limo service area and approached them.

"Colonel Tracy?" one of the men asked, showing his FBI credentials.

"Yes," Tracy answered. He turned to Modini. "Excuse me..." Tracy proceeded to converse with the agents as they escorted him to a third man. The Colonel shook hands with this man, and Modini recognized him although he hadn't seen him in person since 1967. It was Senator Gerald Fuller. Tracy and Fuller shook hands again and departed as Tracy returned to retrieve his bags at the turnstile.

Modini's curiosity was more than peaked by this incident. "Why are you here, Tracy? Why are you in Washington?"

Tracy's reply wasn't as abrupt as Modini expected, but was surprisingly cordial. "Business, you know. Military matters."

John Modini's persistence didn't change. He was still as curious as ever. "Since when do you take a commercial airliner instead of a military plane to Andrews Air Force Base?"

Tracy didn't want to pursue the matter. They went out though the doors to the curbside where cars and taxis were picking up the arrivals.

"Why the concern? There could be a dozen reasons, and some of them might be top secret! We don't always do things by the book. Maybe I don't like the food on those transport planes."

Modini glared at him and shook his head. "Okay, forget it," he said sarcastically. "It was nice seeing you again and congratulations for making Colonel. I'll be seeing 'ya!"

Modini departed and Tracy hesitated for a moment before moving after him. "Now wait, Modini. We both started on a good foot and then got off on the wrong one. I don't want you to go away mad. You and I might have had our differences in the past, but we're what's left of the old platoon-- so you're all that I got left. This may sound silly to you coming from me, but you know it's true. So, I'm asking you nicely, as a friend. How about having dinner with me tonight. What'll you say? I'll get a couple of girls for us, and we'll talk, get drunk-- whatever you want-- talk about old times...all right?"

Modini felt apprehensive about Tracy's sudden change of heart. He shook his hand. "I'll think about it," was all Modini said.

Tracy became more persistent. "I'm staying at the Sheraton," he told Modini. "Where are you staying? What hotel?"

Modini just looked at his watch for time. "I don't know. I'll keep in touch."

Tracy wouldn't give up. "I'll tell you what, I'm making reservations for eight o'clock at The Velvet Fountain. Try to be there. Okay, Modini?"

Modini sighed and stared after him.

Tracy assumed he had gotten through to him and nodded. He hurried to the curb as a black limo arrived.

John Modini saw the limo driver hurry around to open the car door for Tracy. A hand from inside the car reached out and greeted Tracy as he got in. Before the door closed, Modini saw the two FBI agents seated inside as well. As the Limo speeded off, Modini removed a small notebook and pen and jotted down the limousine's license plate number.

At the nearest pay phone Modini dialed a number from the small black address book he carried. "The United States Bureau of Records, may I help you?"

Modini settled himself and smiled. "Yes, I'd like to speak with Max Slaton, please!"

"Please wait a moment," The voice said, and soon Max Slaton came on the line.

"Max Slaton here, can I help you?"

"Max! It's me...John Modini!" he was pleased to hear Slaton's voice.

Max went ape on the other end of the line. "Wop! Is it really you? Where are you?"

"I'm here, Max, in D.C., at the airport. Modini was happy to hear an encouraging voice. "I need your help."

"Just name it," Max said eagerly, "I owe you, old boy! Where in the hell have you been, it's been ages! I heard rumors that you were canned, or maybe downsized is the word from your magazine, or am I mistaken?"

Modini didn't want to get into it. "Yeah, yeah, I'll tell you later over a beer. Listen, Max, I need you to get me access to the National Archives Building."

Max, amused answered, "Fine, no problem. What's the topic?" Modini is quiet for a moment then answered, "Kennedy. I'd like to look at some of the Warren Commission materials. And I need to find some information through the Freedom of Information Act. This can't wait"

Max responded, "All right, I'll do what I can. With your credentials, it should be okay. Is this for the twenty-fifth anniversary coming up?" Modini had forgotten about the fact. "Well, yes and no, I'm just doing a favor for someone."

Max was excited to help out and added, "John, I could do you one better. Is today a good day for you?"

"This afternoon, if I could," Modini hoped.

"Like I say, no problem, but do you mind having company? I know a guy who may be a lot of help to you. What he has to say could put a good slant on your story. His name is Richard Franklin. He's an attorney who worked for Ted Kennedy's Presidential Campaign. He also has read your articles and always said he wanted to meet you to discuss your point of view. John, listen to this, he was one of the attorneys for the House Select Committee on Kennedy and Martin Luther King-- and does he have a story to tell you!"

Modini made up his mind. "Yes, if he wants to meet me fine, I have no difficulty with that. I'll probably be around a couple of days-- which reminds me-- my mother! You should be expecting a fax from her today. It concerns Lee Harvey Oswald. Please hold onto it for me and I'll get it when I meet you later...for beer."

Max laughed, "No problem, I'll watch for her fax. Meanwhile, expect Franklin to get hold of you! I'll tell him to call you at the Archive Building."

"Thanks Max. I'll see you soon," Modini said and hung up the phone.

* * *

It was a bright and sunny day in Madison, Indiana when a gentle looking man about thirty-years old entered Michael Bradley's office high-rise building to check the directory. After finding the floor number of Bradley's office, the man entered an elevator and pressed the appropriate button. Entering the office lobby, he approached a young female secretary at her desk.

She looked up and smiled, "Yes, may I help you, sir?"

The gentleman casually looked around the lobby at the impressive and expensive interior design, then answered the woman. "I want only to speak with the woman attorney who is representing that rapist murderer!"

Chapter Twelve

"Mothers Know Best"

It was after two in the afternoon when John Modini reached the National Archives Building in Washington, D.C. Modini went through all the usual security procedures, culminating the process by getting clearance to a top floor section of the building.

After exiting an elevator, Modini headed down a long corridor until he reached a man sitting all alone at the end of it.

The curator watched Modini approach and centered his attention on the welcomed visitor. It was as if his boring existence and quiet surroundings had been awarded with a ray of sunshine. He rose as Modini stopped before him.

"I take it you are Mr. MacIntosh?" Modini asked.

The man agreed pleasantly, beaming with delight. "Correct! What can I do for you, sir?"

Modini explained, "I was told you were the curator who could help me view the State Department files on Lee Harvey Oswald. I'm interested in any film or tapes you may have on the Warren Commission hearings."

MacIntosh was silent for a moment. "Well, I'll do my best to help you. Keep in mind there's some material not available for another fifty years or so you'd be out of luck there."

MacIntosh opened a door into a huge room exhibiting more than Modini can handle. "This is the main research room."

Modini, after looking the room over in awe, turned to MacIntosh. "All this...huh? This must be the place where 'Citizen Kane' got the idea to store the treasures of his private world."

MacIntosh gave him a puzzled look, "Excuse me, sir?"

"Never mind," Modini remarked, "it's only a joke. Just point me in the right direction and I'll see what I can accomplish."

MacIntosh led the way. "I'll help you find all the materials you need," he assured Modini, chuckling. "After all, I know where all the bodies are buried."

MacIntosh and Modini went into a boardroom set with a screening facility, and television monitors for video and audio playbacks. Modini began by showing MacIntosh a list of written material and tapes he wanted to review.

Next, Modini was offered a compilation within a montage of clips on the Warren Commission hearings and started with their second, but actually first full month of hearings marked as the three-day interview with Marguerite Oswald, dated February 10, 1964. The Commission members present were headed by Chief Justice Earl Warren and J. Lee Rankin, General Counsel of the hearings.

Modini was provided the actual transcripts, but more important he watched the tape of Marguerite Oswald, mother of Lee Harvey Oswald, on a large monitor screen. At one point she turned the table on the commissioners and questioned them.

Modini saw and heard for the first time, Chief Justice Warren say to her in mid-conversation: "Please don't turn this into examining the Commission. You may go ahead and tell what you want, but don't question the Commission, Mrs. Oswald!"

Marguerite Oswald gave Chief Justice Earl Warren a look of disdain because she was prevented from saying what she truly felt. After all, it wasn't her idea to be here to satisfy the Commissioner's whim or his ego, to attest the fact her son was an assassin. To her, it was a mother's duty to suspect her son was being used as a scapegoat. She continued her questioning.

"I ask your Committee members to recall my daughter-in-law...after what would be contrary testimony to my testimony."

Chief Justice Warren responded. "I could give you no assurance of this."

Marguerite Oswald stuck to her guns. "I see no reason then for my testimony!"

Chief Justice Warren tried to be diplomatic about this predicament. "Certainly you should have some confidence in a Commission that is appointed by the President (Johnson) and not try to tie our hands in a way that would be contrary to the manner in which commissions normally proceed?"

Marguerite was angry. "Marina is changing her testimony! Why? Everything was Mama, and we were going to live together and I told you they took her from me and I didn't see her-- then Marina's testimony was not this testimony the first three days. I have testified, and she has testified differently than me. I don't know of all of her testimony but the first three days, this was not her husband's rifle at the police station, and she admitted, but it wasn't her husband's rifle. She was going to live with her Mama, and everything was fine, and then when I told you the way they did, then Marina turned against me. You no have work, and from that time Marina has been changed to a different personality."

J. Lee Rankin stepped in. "What are you saying, Mrs. Oswald?"

Marguerite quickly responded, "Let's admit, sir, Marina has been changing to a different personality! Sir, my son is a Secret Service Agent for this country, I believe...I am going to say it as strongly as I can that I-- and I have stated this from the beginning-- that I think our trouble in this is in our own government, and I suspect the two Secret Service agents assigned to myself and Marina and the children after the assassination of conspiracy with my daughter-in-law in this plot."

She continued, "Lee was set up and it is quite possible these two Secret Service men are involved. I have reason to think so. I am not a detective, and I don't say it is the answer to it, but I must tell you what I think because I am the only one that has this information. I cannot prove these things, and he is not perfect, but if my son was involved, he could not have killed the President alone-- if he did it! Because it is utterly impossible! And I do not believe that my son did it! Gentlemen of the Commission, if that were his rifle, would his rifle be in the sixth floor window of the depository unless you want to say my son was completely out of his mind-- and yet there has been no statement to that effect. I am convinced my son was framed and that Marina Oswald, my daughter-in-law, along with Ruth Paine, the woman she was staying with, was brainwashed by the Secret Service to believe whatever they were told!"

Modini, focused on this conversation, was amazed at what he heard and could only say, "Remarkable!"

* * *

Catherine Rogers put some files into her briefcase. She was ready to deposit Karl Hunter's audio tape into it, but stopped. She decided to visit her father in his bedroom.

The Judge was watching a basketball game on his TV set when Catherine interrupted with tape in hand, "Dad, will you be all right while I'm gone? I'm just going to the office for a couple of hours."

Judge Kencade felt as though he was being treated as a child and became irritated. "Yes, Catherine...I'll be all right. I'm not going to cut my throat while you're gone."

Catherine gave him a stern look. "Seriously, dad, I never gave it a thought, but if you want to be nasty about it, go right ahead! I just want to remind you to be packed when I return. We have to be in Washington tomorrow at the Justice Department for the Grand Jury, remember?"

The judge nodded, "Yes, yes...now go, leave me alone.!"

Catherine thought about the tape in her hand. "Another thing I need to know, dad. It's about the tape. Remember when Karl Hunter mentioned a Naval Commander named William Pitzer?"

The judge appeased his daughter. "Yes, what about him?"

"Well, we know he worked out of Bethesda Naval Hospital. Was he a doctor? I'm confused to why Karl mentions him. What is this man's connection?"

The judge answered his daughter as if she were crazy. "Are you kidding? This Hunter character has you fooled! This is crap! For one, I have no idea why he gave me this tape, and I don't know how it would have helped his case or stopped him from getting the electric chair. I don't know of any William Pitzer, and I don't care! It's simple enough, dear, if you want to continue with this charade all you do is to call Bethesda or go to the library and find out if he ever existed! Now, have I answered your questions?"

Catherine was frustrated, yet saddened by her father's answer and turned to go. But before she left the room, she paused.

"Just to set the record straight, it's because of Karl's death we have this tape and the letter, not the other way around. He was warning you of something! I guess until we read that letter we'll never know what it was, will we?"

The judge was silent, but turned his head half a degree toward her, acknowledging she made her point. Catherine reluctantly left the room.

* * *

Max Slaton watched the fax machine at the U.S. Bureau of Records in Washington, D.C. as three copies came out of the machine. Two were written by Oswald from Minsk, Russia. The other was a cover letter from Marian Modini to Max.

Max handed the letters to Richard Franklin, an African-American attorney who put them in his briefcase. "Perfect, I'll stop by the National Archives and see Mr. Modini. I'm going to have a dialogue with him and before I get done with him he'll be converted."

"Well, I wish you luck," Max smiled.

Franklin mock-saluted him and exited out of his office. Max yelled out, "Remind him he can't get away from me without having that beer!"

In the Archive Screening Room, Modini scratched his head as he watched the screen. J. Lee

Rankin continued to speak with Marguerite Oswald in the interview: "Mrs. Oswald, after the defection, it was January, 1961. You hadn't heard from your son for over a year. You traveled to Washington to contact President Kennedy. Could you elaborate on that?"

Marguerite Oswald was pleased to answer this question. "Yes, I went to ask for my son's return since I didn't know if he were alive or dead and I was ill at the time. Not able to speak with the President, I wanted the Secretary of State, Rusk-- but he was in a conference and so Mr. Boster talked to me. I explained to him everything and within the hour I was meeting three gentlemen in the White House. I remember Mr. Boster telling me when I arrived, 'Mrs. Oswald, I'm awfully glad you came early because we are going to have a terrible snowstorm and we have orders to leave early in order to get home.' So he called Mr. Stanfield. The arrangements have been made. Now, the other man...I don't have that name here for you, Mr. Rankin.

Rankin answered her. "Is it Mr. Hickey?"

Marguerite Oswald agreed, "Yes, Mr. Hickey! You are correct. So, then we were in conference. So, I showed the papers, like I am showing here, and I said, 'Now I know you are not going to answer me, Gentlemen, but I am under the impression that my son is an agent.' They said, 'Do you mean a Russian Agent?' I said, 'No, working for our government, a U.S. Agent!' And I want to say this: that if he is, I don't appreciate it too much because I am destitute and just getting over a sickness, on that order. I had the audacity to say that. I had gone through all of this without medical, without money, without compensation. I am a desperate woman, so I said that."

Rankin interrupted here. "What did they say to you?"

Marguerite Oswald tried to make herself more comfortable in her seat and continued, "They did not answer that. I even said to them, 'No, you won't tell me.' So, I didn't expect them to answer that."

"Do you mean you were seeking money from them?" Rankin suggested.

Marguerite became perturbed by this remark. "No, sir! I didn't think that my son should have gone to a foreign country and me being alone. What I was saying was that I think my son should be home with me, is really what I implied."

Justice Warren now comes into this line of questioning, "Did you tell them that?" he asked.

Marguerite Oswald turned to Warren, but explained to all of them as they stared at her, "In the words I said before, I didn't come out and say, 'I want my son home.' But I implied that if he was an agent, that I thought that he needed to be home."

Rankin changed his course of questioning. "Mrs. Oswald, this report says here, you were suspicious at the way you had been treated when you arrived in Washington, calling it 'the red carpet treatment.'"

Marguerite handled this question as if with great authority and confidence. "Let's say, Gentlemen, if a woman gets on the phone at nine o'clock and has an appointment at 11 o'clock with three big men from the government. That is wonderful treatment. Now, would they probably do that to anybody? I don't know..." Marguerite Oswald eyed him with very serious consternation. "I haven't been that fortunate before!"

Rankin smiled and eased into his reply, "Well, that shouldn't be held against them that they treated you nicely."

"No, I have told you Mr. Rankin, they were most gracious to me." Marguerite Oswald explained herself carefully as if Rankin weren't listening to what she was saying. "The Administration was most gracious to me."

Rankin continued to interpret, "I don't see why you should think that because they treated you nicely that was any sign your son was an agent."

Marguerite again tried to explain herself, feeling contempt toward Rankin. "Well, maybe you don't see why, but this is my son... And this is the way I think, because I happen to know of the other things that you don't know-- the life and everything. I happen to think this, and this is my privilege, sir, to think this way... And I can almost back it up with these things. This is a stranger to you folks, but this is a boy I have known from a child!"

John Modini pushed a button to stop the projection for the moment to stand and stretch. He paced back and forth thinking, then turned on the projector again as Mrs. Oswald spoke. "Now you want to know why I think my son is an agent, and I have been telling you all along. Here is a very important thing why my son was an agent. On March 22, I received a letter of his address and stating that my son wishes to return back to the United States. You have that, sir?"

Rankin answered her, "Yes!"

She proceeded. "On April 30, he marries a Russian girl, approximately five weeks later. Now why does a man want to come to the United States five weeks later. Here is proof: April 30, 1961, is the wedding date! Marry a Russian girl? Because I say — and I may be wrong-- the U.S. Embassy has ordered him to marry this Russian girl... And a few weeks later, May 16, 1961, he is coming home with the Russian girl. And, as we know, he does get out of the Soviet Union with the Russian girl with money loaned to him by the U.S. Embassy. I may be wrong, gentlemen, but two and two in my books make four!" She stopped, and the members of the Commission just stared at her, stunned by this. She then continued, "Now you have a five-week period in here where he suddenly met Marina and married her before coming back to the United States."

Warren interjected here, "Mrs. Oswald, I think it is a very serious thing to say about your son that he would do a thing like that to a girl!"

Modini reacted to Warren's comment. He couldn't believe the statement he just heard and spoke aloud, "Are you kidding me?"

Marguerite Oswald responded to Warren on the screen, "No, sir, it is not a serious thing! I know a little about the CIA, the U-2, Gary Powers and things that have been made public. They go through any extreme for their country."

Modini his hand on his chin, reacted to this, sitting forward. "I can't believe this!"

Marguerite Oswald doesn't stop. "I do not think that would be serious for him to marry a Russian girl and bring her here, so he would have contact. I think that is all part of an agent's duty."

Warren responded, "You think that your son is capable of that?"

Marguerite had never been so sure of herself as she stood her ground with the Chief Justice, "Yes, sir, I believe to this day my son was an agent!"

* * *

The clock read three-thirty p.m. in the lobby of Michael Bradley's top floor law office. Sherry Keller, the secretary fiddled with her pencil nervously. As the head receptionist, she turned her attention to the gentleman who arrived two hours earlier, sitting and waiting patiently for Catherine to arrive, and addressed him again, "I'm sorry you're waiting so long. Would you like to come back another time? I can make an appointment for you."

"No, no... That's quite all right. What I have to say to Mrs. Rogers is important, so I'd rather wait." The neatly dressed gentleman put on a pair of eyeglasses and stood up to view the photographs on the lobby wall.

"Then would you like a cup of coffee or a beverage?" Sherry asked.

The gentlemen smiled. "Would a glass of water be of any trouble?" he inquired. Across the room, the elevator bell sounded. They heard Catherine chatting with someone in the hallway.

The gentleman went back to retrieve his briefcase at the couch and stood at attention for her entrance.

The lobby door, stenciled with 'Bradley/Lobe and Assoc., Attorneys at Law' opened and Catherine entered, heading straight for the secretary's desk and asked, "Any messages, Sherry?" She didn't notice the gentleman present.

Sherry handed Catherine her messages. "Yes, lots, about a dozen, Mr. Newmyer called three times from Washington about you and Judge Kencade's appearance before the grand jury tomorrow. If you can't reach him, it's scheduled for ten a.m. tomorrow and he wants you and Judge Kencade to meet tonight for dinner and strategy. The time should be in one of those notes. Your father wants you to call him as soon as you can! Her eyes stared past Catherine's shoulder,

117

"This gentleman has been waiting for over two hours to see you.",

Catherine turned around and was startled to find the gentleman standing right behind her. "Oh, I'm sorry, I didn't see you. Yes, can I be of help to you?"

The gentleman, polite, yet cautious, glanced suspiciously at her secretary then to Catherine. "I need to talk to you in private...please!" The tone of his voice was serious.

Catherine answered, cautious herself. "Well, sir, I do have a deadline to make. I really don't have any time today. Late Thursday afternoon is the best I can do--"

The man stopped her short and demanded, "No, it's got to be now! I have some very important information for you!"

Sherry spoke up, "Do you want me to phone--"

Catherine intervened discretely, "That's quite all right, Sherry." Catherine was still wary, but decided to play it cool. "Sir, what is this regarding?"

The gentleman got to the point. "It's my daughter. I believe she might have been a victim of your client!"

"My client?" Catherine asked, puzzled.

"Karl Hunter!" The man said bluntly.

Catherine raised an eyebrow. "Sir, I'm sorry..." she responded, a little unsettled at his revelation. "You need to see the District Attorney's office. You see, I'm for the defense-- or I should say was, that is. Perhaps you want to go there?"

The gentleman still persisted. "No, no, I'll only talk to you, I need you to see her, to talk to her! She won't talk to me!"

Catherine, a little bewildered, replied. "Sir, let me understand this right. You're saying your daughter is alive?"

The gentleman nodded. "Yes, she's alive! Now, may I speak to you in private, please?"

"Yes...sure," Catherine exchanged a glance with her secretary. "Ahh...Sherry? We'll be in Michael's office. Please sign him in. By the way, sir...what is your name?"

He held out his hand. "My name is Ziegler...Joseph Ziegler." Catherine shook his hand.

"Catherine Rogers..." she introduced herself. "Mr. Ziegler, you sign in with Sherry and she'll escort you to our office...all right?" She crossed the main lobby and went down the corridor to Michael Bradley's office.

She took off her coat and gloves, then proceeded to his desk where she prepared herself for Mr. Ziegler. Sherry guided Mr. Ziegler into the office moments later.

"Thank you Sherry," she said to her secretary. Sherry left, leaving the door ajar.

Catherine motioned to a chair. "You may sit here if you like." Mr. Ziegler looked back to confirm Sherry was gone before he decided to sit in response to Catherine.

As he did, Catherine felt comfortable to speak. "Mr. Ziegler, I'm curious about you. The reason-- and you may know this already-- is that none of my client's suspected victims were found alive! So you can see how astonishing this news is to me. You say your daughter might have been a victim of my client? Well, Mr. Ziegler, I have to ask you, are you aware that my client is dead?"

Mr. Ziegler nodded. Catherine closed her eyes a moment feeling a mixture of grief and anger, but calmed herself to be as diplomatic about this situation as she could. "Did you know if you had come to this office earlier, or the District Attorney's office, you could have saved an innocent man from being sentenced to death?"

Mr. Ziegler answered her calmly. "Why? So my testimony should set him free? I doubt that! He's guilty! He deserves to die for what he has done to my daughter! How dare you! Don't preach to me about innocence! My daughter was only twelve years old. How more or less innocent could that be, tell me!"

Catherine's reply showed her concern and sympathy. "She's alive, Mr. Ziegler. She's alive... Doesn't that mean something?"

Mr. Ziegler opened his briefcase and took out an unmarked half inch video cassette and handed it to Catherine. "You tell me?" he said coldly.

Catherine examined the video cassette, then took him into the boardroom and slipped the

119

cassette into a VCR. Picking up the remote control, she pressed play.

Catherine moved to the opposite side of the table from Ziegler and waited for the image to brighten on the monitor screen. When the picture came on she was stunned by what she saw. The images on the monitor showed young girls, ages from eleven to fourteen, in sexual acts with older men. Catherine turned away, nauseated by the sight.

The images triggered Catherine's thoughts back twenty-one years to that traumatic day when she lost her virginity in the basement bedroom of that beach house in Santa Barbara. She remembered asking Congressman Fuller, *"Will it hurt?"* And she remembered his reply, *"Only the first time, baby. This will be our little secret..."*

Catherine faced the pictures on the monitor again. She saw Ziegler watching her. "Why are you showing me this perverted--"

Ziegler interrupted. "Look... Look there on the screen! That's why!"

Catherine's eyes widened in disgust as she recognized Karl Hunter enter the room with a twelve-year old girl, a small half-Caucasian and Asian child. He began taking her clothes off,

"That girl...that's my daughter, Carrie," Ziegler said tearfully. He removed his handkerchief and dabbed his eyes.

When the girl was stripped, Hunter forced her stomach-down onto the bed and strapped her hands to the bedpost. Catherine watched in horror as Hunter slid his belt out of his pants and started whipping her. After finishing with his torture, he held her down and forced himself upon her.

Catherine couldn't take it any more. She pressed the button on the remote control and turned the tape off. She was shaken, not only for the memories they kindled, but also for realizing the pornography she had viewed was an illegal piece of evidence.

Mr. Ziegler was openly crying. All the man's emotions were open and exposed. Catherine's rage turned to sympathy for him, knowing how much pain he must have endured watching his daughter suffer so. "My God, Mr. Ziegler, where did you get this tape?"

Through his tears he told her, "It was delivered in the mail to me one day."

"Could you positively identify the girl on that tape as your daughter?" Catherine asked.

"Yes!" was all Ziegler could say.

Catherine took the cassette out of the VCR and handed it back to Ziegler. She continued to probe. "When was this tape made-- how long ago?"

"This happened over seven months ago, and since then she won't see me or talk to me anymore!" Ziegler pleaded to Catherine, "You've got to help me and my daughter."

Catherine moved to Ziegler and put her arm around him for comfort. "Where is she now? Who's taking care of her?" Catherine asked.

Ziegler wiped the tears from his face. "She's thirteen years old now and...and I can't be her daddy anymore... I-- She's in a mental institution!"

Catherine patted him on the back. "And her mother, your wife, is she Asian? Where is she?"

"Her mother died in Vietnam. I brought her home at the time President Reagan got into office. My-- My daughter was a good girl and in the American schools, she had the highest point average in her class."

"What can I do to help," Catherine asked.

Ziegler suddenly brightened up. "Would you please...just come to see her? Just talk to her? She needs a woman who can understand what she has gone through! I need you to tell her she can trust her own father...that I love her so much and need her!"

Catherine smiled. "Don't worry, Mr. Ziegler, I think I can do that. I'll tell you what...I have to be in Washington tonight and tomorrow. I'll be back Thursday morning. Why don't you give me the address of the hospital where she is staying and I'll meet you there. Let's say, this time, three o'clock Thursday afternoon. Will that be okay?"

Ziegler stood up. He was a very happy man. "You'll really be there... Promise?"

Catherine shook his hand and repeated his last word, "Promise! Write down all the information I need to know, I'll be there!"

Ziegler took her hand and kissed it in an old-fashioned way and thanked her again before he departed, leaving the video cassette on the conference table.

Catherine, with all the problems she faced, still felt good about what she had done. A smile brightened on her face as she picked up the phone to call Sherry to ask her to finish up with Mr. Ziegler and get her father on the phone. Catherine opened her briefcase and put Ziegler's cassette inside.

The phone in the office rang. She picked it up. "Hello...Father? Yes, I did. I believe I owe you an apology." Tears came into Catherine's eyes. "Don't ask me why. It's just that I understand now about you and Mother. I know Mother loved me, and she did what she did, like you, to protect me. And you did what you had to do to protect me. I wanted to say Mother was right. I do love her and...I love you, dad...forever."

Catherine stopped her chin from trembling and wiped the tears from her eyes. "I'm sorry I took so long to realize it. but...you were right about everything! Yes, I'll pick you up soon. Just be ready. We'll lick this together, won't we?"

Chapter Thirteen

"The House Select Committee"

Jack Ruby's face filled the screen in the screening room at the National Archives Building in Washington, D.C. In a rare 1965 interview in Texas, Ruby spoke with reporters following a hearing for a new trial for the murder of Lee Harvey Oswald: "The only thing I can say is everything pertaining to what's happened has never come to surface... The world will never know the true facts of what occurred-- my motive. In other words, I am the only person in the background to know the truth pertaining to everything relating to my circumstances..."

A reporter asked a question, "Do you feel the truth will ever come out?"

Ruby answered fastidiously and to the point. "No! Because unfortunately, these people who have so much to gain and have such an ulterior motive to put me in the position I'm in, will never let the true facts come aboveboard to the world..."

A second reporter asked, "How high up are these people?"

Ruby's response was, "As high as you can go!"

"Are you saying this is a complete conspiracy, Mr. Ruby?" asked a third reporter.

Ruby, cool, calm, and collected, answered as if waving it off. "I have been used for a purpose! I was framed into killing Oswald! If you knew the truth, you would be amazed!"

A voice-over narrator, took over and disclosed Ruby's background following the interview.

John Modini was so riveted by this presentation he didn't notice or hear someone enter the room. The man slipped to the back of the room, as if not to disturb anyone. The narrator was saying: "Jack Ruby succumbed to cancer in January, 1967, just as New Orleans District Attorney James Garrison was about to reopen the Kennedy case..."

Modini turned off the monitor and switched on the lights. He stretched, knowing he had enough for the day. An African-American gentleman standing near the back of the room, watching and studying him suddenly spoke up, "Quite a show, wasn't it?"

He Startled Modini. "I didn't know anyone else was watching," Modini said, staring at the African-American gentleman behind him.

"I'm sorry," the man said, coming forward. Modini saw he was thin and tall and carrying a briefcase. "I didn't want to disturb you while you were watching. You seemed to be very focused on this last piece on Ruby. I've seen it a dozen times and I still can't ever get over the fact Warren and Ford never took the advantage of bringing this man to Washington for questioning. He warned them he would die if they didn't, and would not answer them if they didn't. They told him they did not have the authority to take him to Washington, and it was impossible. They said he was crazy!

The mystery man gestured toward the screen. "Can you believe, Mr. Modini, that Earl Warren gave Ruby a clean bill of health in his twenty-six volume report? The head of the Commission and our future President, Gerald Ford, had *carte blanche* with a Commission controlling the final outcome of the murder of our thirty-fifth President. They made the world to accept it. They actually got away with a line like that...that they *did not have the authority* to bring Jack Ruby, the man you just saw on this monitor screen, to Washington D.C. for questioning.

"Ruby provided us with the biggest sneak preview if ever there was one; a conspiracy to kill...to murder the President of the United States! One thing's for sure, he was right about his own death! He did die, didn't he?"

The man forward now, to Modini, his hand out, "Excuse me, Mr. Modini, the name is Richard Franklin..." He saw Modini recognize the name. "I believe, Max Slaton told you about

124

me."

Modini smiled and shook Franklin's hand. "Oh, yes... You're the one from the House Select Committee."

"Right, he told you then. Does that mean you have an open mind to talk to me?"

Modini laughed. "If you took the time to read my articles, I can bear your rhetorical comments."

Franklin took some papers out of his briefcase. "Great! In that case Max asked me to give you this..." he said, handing Modini the fax letters from his mother. "I was curious what you were going to do with these?"

Modini looked at the copies and noticed Connally's letter. It was the one thing he needed to see right away but didn't expect the other letter, written by Oswald from Minsk, Russia to Senator John Tower in Washington, D.C. He was astonished.

"I thought you would be surprised as I was," Franklin commented. "Was it just a coincidence that Oswald wrote to Tower, who today just happens to be the Chairman of the Senate Committee on Iran Contra and the Senate Liaison to the CIA? This is the man who took George Bush out of the loop and guaranteed him as this nation's next president. The same Vice-President, the people of this country labeled for the past eight years as a wimp that couldn't get elected dog catcher if he tried. But don't be surprised if Tower will be right there next to him, that I guarantee you!"

Modini, wide-eyed, said, "What, as CIA Director?"

Franklin stared at Modini, shaking his head. He lifted his hands and smiled.

Modini waited Franklin's next move, but Franklin seemed to be waiting for him. Modini offered his hand and Franklin slapped it. "You're catching on, Mr. Modini. You must be psychic! So, tell me, why the big urgency on the letters?"

John Modini turned the question back to Franklin, "You tell me. What did the House Committee think?"

"Why does it matter? What is it going to prove," Franklin started in. "You're not going to agree with that *Time Magazine* article written two years ago stating John Connally was Oswald's real target, not Kennedy? That guy was a nut case!"

Modini disagreed. "No, no, nothing like that. It was about Oswald asking for help to get out, telling them he was falsely accused as a defector. But there's a letter written prior, asking to defect. Why? Was the defection letter written by someone else?"

Richard Franklin almost freaked out. "Wait, wait a minute! Aren't you the one who wrote the Bible on the subject stating Oswald was the lone gunman?"

Modini gave Franklin an awkward look, then grinned, "Yes. I wrote many articles over many years stating that belief. And I thought so too, until I found out that title really belongs to Gerald Ford."

Both men laughed, and Franklin added, "I think you might be okay after all. I thought you might be a bit difficult. Do proceed..."

Modini tried another scenario. "If Oswald wrote these letters-- which I believe he did-- it's hard to believe this is the same man who wrote the quote 'historic diary' and the previous defection letter. One was written by an illiterate and the other by a Harvard graduate, which neither fits Oswald's profile-- especially based on these letters," he said waving the two letters from Connally and Tower.

Franklin seemed to be impressed so far. He asked him to elaborate more. Modini complied, "Well, the 'historic diary' would explain why Ford chose that direction because he thought the whole Oswald family was total nut cases and repeated it constantly, but he never explained the defection letter. He just accepts it. And it's funny! You don't see much of the actual writings of Oswald displayed in the Warren report, but you do see the defection letter associated with Oswald along with bits and pieces of the diary, but only when depicted as being stupid or a nut!"

"And what about these two letters?" Franklin asked.

"That's just it. These letters say a lot-- it's not what Oswald writes about, but what Gerald

Ford and Arlen Spector did with the letters in the report."

Franklin frowned. "You're saying, the Commission-- wanting to play God-- changed the letter's interpretation in the report so to suit their profile of Oswald?"

Modini smiled. "No... They changed the *chronology* of the report, to fit Oswald's profile as a nut in Russia that defected."

Franklin became confused. "I think you lost me!"

"Okay...here," Modini explained, "In the report, I've read Oswald's chronology, from the day he defected in October '59, to his return from Russia in May '62. Missing from the chronology was the entire year 1960! Why? Well, let's say Ford and Spector who wrote Oswald's chronology, based their whole report on Oswald's 'historic diary' and Marina Oswald's recollections and testimony. The Commission stated Marina did not meet Lee Harvey Oswald until March of 1961 and married him one month later in April. The couple was supposed to return to the United States soon after, but couldn't because Marina was suddenly with child.

"So My question is what happened to Oswald between the time he arrived in Russia in '59 and the time he met Marina in 1961?

"In 1960, Oswald was sent to Minsk from Moscow instead. Why? And why is 1960 not a part of this 'historic diary'? If you were writing a diary you might forget or skip a day or two, or maybe even a week, but not a month, and certainly not a year, unless you're hanging in irons on some prison wall or being interrogated to death in some tiny room.

"Oswald lived in Minsk with a good job and a nice apartment flat, better than the people he worked side by side with. Oswald should have included this in his diary! But that's why I believe there was no 'historic diary' at all. Maybe we should call it a 'prehistoric diary,' since it appears it was made up. Let's say Oswald was writing his memoirs as he said in Connally's letter. He didn't say a diary, but he, thinking more as a novelist, like Hemingway, wrote everything on a piece of paper-- his thoughts-- his life in exile. When it's all on paper, like these letters, then its possible someone took these memoirs and decided to forge his writings to make what?"

Franklin nodded and finished his sentence, "This 'historic diary' would be easy to make him illiterate, although it contradicts his defection letter."

"Yes!" Modini moved on. "Exactly, but you have these attorneys working on the legal aspect of the report like Spector and Ford. How many people will read this report, though it was condensed by the *New York Times* and was an immediate best seller? Today 90% of the people have never read it. It may be in law schools and law firms across the nation, but no one, especially an attorney in 1963, would dispute something that couldn't be proven because the government told him what the truth was. So you, as an American, believe whatever the government tells you, period! And that was what Rankin, David Belin, Arlen Spector, and the rest did. They had the people's respect for the United States government as their ally."

Then Modini concluded, "When I researched my report on Oswald as the lone gunman, even I hadn't read the complete report and the people believed me!"

Franklin laughed. "Yes, but you always agreed with the government's report. As long as you printed their side, your views and opinions were accepted everywhere in the newspapers and magazines. You were their public relations!"

Modini had to agree. "Yes, but it took only one man to come out and challenge the report, and he started the controversy. Before Jim Garrison, there was Mark Lane!"

"An attorney!" Franklin added.

"Yes, I believed in this country, Mr. Franklin, When I served in Vietnam, I believed I had to defend every inch of it." Modini said emphatically. "I believed our government and policies were one, that our country was the figurehead for truth around the world. I never wanted our leaders or politicians who represented my country to be destroyed.

"I admired John F. Kennedy. He brought faith to me and represented what our country stood for, but Vietnam and Watergate and now, Iran Contra, changed all that! The word 'truth' doesn't seem to belong in this country's vocabulary anymore," Modini admitted.

Franklin gave Modini an admirable look. "Congratulations, Mr. Modini. You've now come down to the level of us little folk. I praise you for being so honest and sincere. I can't wait to see what you'll write in your next article. To me, you were always the devil's advocate to us conspiracy theorists. But before I show you something that may be of interest to you, especially since you served in Vietnam, I have to ask you something about these letters. Do they contain any information that might be of any value?"

Modini reminded him of the chronology. "You remember, the year 1960 was missing from his diary, and Oswald's writings were only based on letters he wrote to his mother or brother or the consulate. None of those letters were recorded in the chronology. They were only hearsay through Ford and Spector's own words throughout their report. These men showed us only what they <u>wanted</u> us to see! They didn't want you to see any more letters than what was actually used in the report to accuse Oswald as the lone gunman. This lone gunman scenario was based on one thing and one thing only-- Arlen Spector's 'magic bullet theory!' If you can believe this theory, then you can make believe Oswald was on that sixth floor with a rifle with no fingerprints! Meanwhile, it's enough to wonder who supplied Oswald's 'historic diary' in the first place!

"In the report it states police officials and Chief Curry approached Oswald with that infamous picture, the one showing Oswald holding the rifle in the backyard. That photo gained nationwide attention on the front cover of *Life Magazine* and would convict Oswald in the eyes of the public before the Warren Report ever got released. By the way, it was only six months following the assassination of these two men, Kennedy and Oswald that the public was forced to be satisfied with President Johnson's findings and made him a sure sweep over Senator Goldwater in the election of 1964. Oswald told the police officials if they gave him some time he would prove to them that it was a faked picture. His head was superimposed on someone else's body. I was shocked because I didn't know this was ever in the report, and this was the only piece of evidence I ever was skeptical about.

"I was first interested in photography as a kid and that *Life Magazine* cover has bothered me to this day. And to hear Oswald deny it was a revelation. So I thought to myself, why not the diary? They had this photo first, and soon after they had Marina Oswald's possible confession that she took the picture. And then later another picture shows up, and Marina didn't remember taking more than one picture! But the Commission brought her in just the same to authenticate that she did. Then somewhere in 1970-71, *another* picture appears out of nowhere. It seems that Marina Oswald had become quite the photographer, but by this time we were led to believe she was mistaken, and she didn't realize how many pictures she took.

"I wouldn't be surprised if there are more undiscovered pictures, but only time will tell. Now, I don't know what to believe. I mean, all they had to do was threaten Marina with deportation and she'd say something like, 'If you say my husband killed the President and all this so-called evidence you provided, then I love America, I do what you say.' In the beginning, she spoke very little English, so why not provide the diary like the photo? If these investigators found a photo, why not the diary? The only answer is there was no diary because it became an invention only after the Warren Commission was formed, like these letters, except these letters were authentic, and I believe the diary wasn't."

"So who provided the diary," Franklin asked.

Modini shrugged. "Who really knows? Someone from Commissioner Allen Dulles' group? The CIA? Hey, we all know from the Pentagon Papers that the CIA forged letters and documents to beef up the Vietnam War. Why not this 'historic diary'? They could get away with this diary, but they could never get away with using these letters-- and I mean these actual letters-- not the written statements typed up. You see, if the actual letters were used with Oswald's own handwriting in the Warren Report, the whole chronology would have fallen apart based on three major reasons: first, the skeptics would have found it phony immediately, second..." Modini reached into his tote bag and took out some pages he had photocopied from the Warren Commission. He leafed through the chronology section, found the year 1962, January, and asked Franklin "Read the page that concentrates on Connally's letter."

Franklin took the pages and read what the Commission wrote:

"Late in January, Oswald received a letter from his mother telling him he had been given a dishonorable discharge from the Marines (the discharge had actually been 'undesirable,' a less derogatory characterization). This apparently revived his fear of prosecution, and on January 30, he wrote to his brother for more information. On the same day he wrote also to John B. Connally, Jr., then Governor of Texas whom Oswald believed was still Secretary of Navy. The letter read: 'I wish to call your attention to a case about which you may have personal knowledge since you are a resident of Ft. Worth as I am.'"

Franklin stopped here, stunned, "Hold on a minute! Let me see the copy of the original letter." Franklin's eyes read it quickly, stopping where Oswald addressed Mr. Connally as Secretary of Navy. This is where the Commission said Oswald was mistaken since Connally was the Governor of Texas and not the Secretary of the Navy. Then Franklin's eyes shifted back to the letter where Oswald recorded his Marine Number, his address in Minsk, Russia, and dated the letter, January 30, 1961. And Franklin nodded, noticing an error.

Modini knew they were both in agreement after seeing the error in the chronology. Modini waited for Richard Franklin to verify it. "Someone wants you to think that Oswald wrote this a year ahead of its time. Why?" Franklin asked. "Whose truth are we to believe? Did they make a mistake or did Oswald?"

Modini answered him disconcertingly. "Does it matter what Oswald says or does? The Commission was in control of Oswald's destiny from the beginning! Read the rest, you'll find more."

Franklin continued reading Oswald's letter:

"In November 1959 an event well publicated (sic) in the Ft. Worth newspapers concerning a person who had gone to the Soviet Union to reside for a short time (much in the same way E. Hemingway resided in Paris).

"This person in answers to questions put to him by reporters (sic) in Moscow criticized certain facets of American life. The story was blown up into another 'turncoat' sensation, so the

Navy department gave this person a belated dishonorable discharge?"

Franklin stopped again and added, "The Commission says he was wrong, it was an 'Undesirable' discharge?"

Modini again nodded. "Yes, but does it matter what Oswald says? The Commission wants the reader to think Oswald constantly contradicted himself, although Oswald responded to a letter his mother sent him in October, 1960, concerning the newspaper article from September, 1960. You see Oswald's letters dated. The Commission doesn't tell you it is dated-- only that it is January, and in *their* chronology it is 1962. Now I can believe Marguerite Oswald's letter might have taken a couple months to reach Oswald, but a year and two months? No! I can't believe that scenario, but go on, read!"

Franklin picked up where he left off. "...Although he had received an honorable discharge after three years service on September 11, 1959 at El Toro, Marine Corps base in California. These are the basic facts of my case. I have always had the full sanction of the U.S. Embassy, Moscow USSR and hence, the U.S. Government. Inasmuch as I am returning to the U.S.A. in this year with the aid of the U.S. Embassy, bring with me my family (since I married in the U.S.S.R.) I shall employ all means to right this gross mistake or injustice to a *bona fide* U.S. Citizen and ex-serviceman. The U.S. government has no charges or complaints against me. I ask you to look into this case and take the necessary steps to repair the damage done to me and my family. For information I would direct you to consult the American Embassy, Chikovski St. 19/21, Moscow, USSR."

Then the Warren Report reads: "Connally referred the letter to the Department of the Navy, which sent Oswald a letter stating that the Department contemplated no change in the undesirable discharge. On March 22, Oswald wrote to the Department insisting his discharge be given a further full review. The Department promptly replied it had no authority to hear and review petitions of this sort and referred Oswald to the Navy Discharge Review Board. Oswald filled out the enclosed application for review in Minsk but did not mail it until he returned to the United States."

Richard Franklin gave the copy of the report back to Modini and continued his thought. "Well, from Oswald's point of view, he's saying he wasn't a defector though it lets Connally know this through some code in a third person, inferring, of course, himself."

Modini jumped in. "Remember, I suspected he did...that he was writing his memoirs-- and those pages turned into this 'historic diary' for the Warren Commission."

Franklin asked to see the page in the report that actually showed the real defection letter written by Oswald and read: 'November 3, 1959'.

"*I, Lee Harvey Oswald, do hereby request that my present United States citizenship be revoked. I appeared in person, at the Consulate Office of the United States Embassy, Moscow, on Oct. 31st, for the purpose of signing the formal papers to this effect. This legal right I was refused at that time.*

I wish to protest against this action, and against the conduct of the official of the United States Consular service who acted on behalf of the United States Government.

My application, requesting that I be considered for citizenship in the Soviet Union is now pending before the Supreme (sic) Soviet of the...U.S.S.R. In the event of acceptance, I will request my government to lodge a formal protest regarding this incident."

Lee Harvey Oswald

Franklin squinted his eyes in confusion. "Here you have someone very intelligent, like yourself, speaking on behalf of himself to give up his American citizenship-- though the terminology he uses here was too pat for a person who just arrived in the Soviet Union for the first time. Gerald Ford, in the chronology, was feeding us a split personality, a 'Dr. Jekyll and Mr. Hyde'. One minute he's intelligent in the way he speaks, then, as in the 'historic diary,' he's an idiot with misspelled words in every sentence. But this letter had one misspelled word where Connally's had two maybe three, and that defection letter was worded longer. If he were illiterate, he had to be programmed or rehearsed. Oswald, either way, had some help in writing this letter! What else was wrong with the Connally letter?"

Modini showed Franklin the last paragraph where it talked about Oswald returning to the United States with his family (since he married in the U.S.S.R.) to repair the damage done to him and 'my family'. "The question arises <u>when</u> was Oswald married?"

Franklin tried for the answer, but it didn't come to his mind quickly. He gave it a shot. "It was common knowledge in all the books written about Oswald that-- and even Oswald's mother said it-- It was just a month of courtship and bamm-- they were married!"

"Yes, it was 1961 in the month of March," Modini explained. "Today, all the historical records say-- including the Warren Report, and the words of Marina Oswald, 'it was March they met.' In April '61, and Oswald said here he was already married."

Richard Franklin agreed, "That's right, so he must have been married in 1960 sometime..."

Modini jumped back in, "Well, there's part of your missing year 1960 from the chronology. It wasn't even mentioned by the Commission, but read what Oswald says here and look at Senator Tower's letter." Franklin took the Tower letter and read:

"Address to:
Senator John Tower
Washington D.C.
Lee H. Oswald
St. Kalinina 4-24
Minsk, USSR

Dear Senator Tower,

My name is Lee Harvey Oswald 22, of Fort Worth up till October 1959, when I came to the Soviet Union for a residenual (sic) stay. I took a residenual (sic) document for a non-Soviet person...Living for a time in the U.S.S.R. The American Embassy in Moscow is familiar with my case.

Since July 20th 1960, I have unsuccessfully applied for a Soviet Exit Visa to leave this country, the Soviets refuse to permit me and my Soviet wife, (who applied at the U.S. Embassy Moscow, July 8, 1960 for immigration status to the U.S.A.) to leave the Soviet Union..."

Modini stopped Franklin from reading further and pointed out, "There, right there... See 'my Soviet wife, July 8, 1960 applied for status'. One, they were married in 1960, so the Commission was trying to hide something. Either the letters are phony, which I can't see why, or the Commission was lying here. Again why? And two, here Oswald showed us what he was doing in 1960-- but 1960 was not included in the chronology, why? Hey! Wait a minute, Mr. Franklin. Here is the section I found in my photocopies, the section where Tower's letter was mentioned on page 308, and Connally's letter was on Page 309."

Franklin continued to read. "According to the Warren Commission, Tower's letter was written first and received near the end of January 1962, which would be the exact same time as Connally's letter. In fact, where's the letter? They mention it but, it's not even printed here. Look, it just reads: *Late in December, Oswald wrote a letter to Senator John G. Tower of Texas, which was received in Washington near the end of January. He stated he was an American Citizen, and the Soviet Government refused to permit him and his wife to leave the Soviet Union. He asked Senator Tower to raise 'the question of holding by the Soviet Union of a citizen of the U.S. against his will and expressed desires'. The letter was referred to the State Department and no further action concerning it was taken."*

Modini interjected, "Why not?"

Franklin read on. "On December 25, Marina was summoned to the Soviet Passport Office and told the exit visas would be granted to her and her husband. She was surprised, having doubted she would ever be permitted to leave."

Again Modini added, "I'm sure she was, and so am I!"

Richard Franklin continued, "Oswald wrote to the Embassy on December 27, asking for Visas and his passport be extended without another trip to Moscow. He added, however, he would come to Moscow if this would expedite the processing of his application."

"In his diary," Franklin stopped and repeated, "...in his diary he wrote, 'It's great (I think?).'" Franklin turned to Modini and said, "I don't get it. Where's mention of the rest of the letter? This is only half of it. And there are no dates!"

Modini concurred, "Notice again it's 1962. Even at the mention of the letter someone wants to deceive us, this time on purpose, by not allowing the full letter to be known. They don't want us to know it's a year earlier, stating he married in 1960. The letter was conveniently lost in the Commission report. It's in here and we need to find it, but at least now we can see they didn't follow through by printing the complete letter, because someone would spot what we just did!

"Without Oswald's actual letter, we can't fit Oswald's true actions into the Commission's chronology. We may find the full letter later, but as long as Tower's letter follows their chronology we won't notice the errors!

"These letters were brought forth to the attention of the Commissioners after their interview, or I should say the 'reprogramming' of Marina! They always had a set path for Oswald which meant they had to screw the chronology and botch the theories. This became a mistake for them. Certain members of the Commission never knew of the mistake because they were never told of it. I'm giving them the benefit of the doubt. Or, perhaps, Ford and Spector and maybe others knew what they were doing since the actual letters aren't here to prove one way or the other-- which

136

meant some members of the Commission <u>did</u> deceive and cover up a major point concerning their remarkable assassin! Now, go ahead, read the rest of Tower's actual letter where you left off at Marina's applying for her immigration status to the U.S.A."

Franklin found the paragraph where he left off and read:

> *"I am a citizen of the United States of America (Passport No.*
> *1733242, 1959) and I bessech (sic) you, Senator Tower, to rise (sic) the*
> *question of holding by the Soviet Union of a citizen of the U.S., against his*
> *will and expressed desires.*
>
> > *Yours Very Truly, Lee Harvey Oswald"*

Franklin shook his head, "Mr. Modini, this part was all they mention in the chronology, and you're right, someone was deliberately hiding something! Why let us see Connally's full letter and not Tower's?"

"Look, Connally's letter never mentions the date 1960, Tower's does," Modini pointed out. "Plus both have to look as though it were 1962 to fit *their* chronology of Oswald, not Oswald's! You have to remember, the whole report is based on only one theory, Arlen Spector's 'magic bullet theory.' If you believe that, then you have to believe the government's investigation of Oswald is true. As you now can see, these two letters alone could tear apart the whole twenty-six volumes of this report and you have your conspiracy without hidden gunman behind grassy knolls, or faked documents, and autopsy reports, 'magic bullet theories,' or Connally's bullet on the stretcher at Parkland Hospital."

Franklin added, "For which evidence has surfaced to prove it wasn't even Connally's stretcher where this mystery bullet was supposedly found!" Franklin took some papers out of his briefcase and gave them to Modini. "I guess I won't need to debate you on this." Franklin handed the papers to Modini.

Modini gave it a quick glance. It was a Top Secret document that had been unsealed and declassified for The House Select Committee in the year 1976. Before Modini could see what was in it, MacIntosh entered the room.

"Excuse me, gentlemen, the National Archives Building is now closing."

John Modini and Richard Franklin exchanged glances. They made plans to continue their conversation elsewhere.

* * *

It was a starry evening as the two men stood outside the National Archives Building. Modini read the top secret document Franklin had given him. It was drawn up by Secretary of State, McGeorge Bundy, and had President Lyndon Johnson's signature attached, dated November 26, 1963. It reminded Modini of the fact, the night of the assassination on November twenty second, Johnson sent a group of Cabinet members to Honolulu, Hawaii to stay the weekend and on through Kennedy's funeral, to set the stage for the basis of what would be the beginning of the Vietnam War.

Modini was shaken by what he had in his hand and asked the question, "Why? Why, if you had this information during the House Select Committee, didn't the Committee bring this out in the open? The public has the right to know, our Veterans have the right to know why we were fighting over there! My God, this document could have saved many veteran's anguish, those from mental disorders and breakdowns and even those who were driven to suicide. It took years to discover those with post traumatic syndrome."

Richard Franklin agreed. "Tell me about it! Do you know how often I wanted to bring this and other information out into the open from behind the closed doors of the House Select Committee? Senators, Congressmen and attorneys, law officers, and anyone who had a position on that Committee or worked for a Committee member had to be sworn to secrecy, before they could ever be a part of this Committee, for national security reasons."

"I thought this was an open Committee for the public to witness how this investigation worked?"

"Yes, that was the basis of the Committee when Congressman Henry Gonzalez of San Antone, Texas was to head it," Franklin said. "We had Robert Groden and Jim Garrison to participate, then when the government brought in Richard Sprague from Philadelphia as head counsel, all hell broke loose. First, a disagreement ensued-- a battle concerning the appropriation of monies, who was to spend it, and what direction the Committee's would go. This included not only the investigation on the murder of John F. Kennedy, but of Reverend Martin Luther King, Jr. and Bobby Kennedy. But someone behind the scenes upset the barrel of apples. Garrison was gone and so were many conspiracy theorists, whom this Committee was supposed to be for. Sprague's boss, we find out, was Arlen Spector. The congressman Henry Gonzalez of from San Antone was no longer in charge. Louis Stokes, from Ohio who was handling Martin Luther King's case, took over. Then Robert Blakley appeared, whom we thought was the Messiah because he once worked for Bobby Kennedy during his brother's administration. So who comes along with Blakley? None other than our old buddy, ...yes, the man who would direct the Committee to its wrong conclusion-- yours truly, Arlen Spector!"

Modini's head shook, realizing the full potential of a coverup. "If the shoe fits, why change it? Spector was the string here, appointed by David Belin, Richard Nixon's lawyer, on the Warren Commission who followed up on both the Rockefeller Commission and the Church hearings during the Ford administration and now was on the House Select Committee on Assassinations. Follow that up with Senator of Pennsylvania, and what next, President?"

Franklin continued, "Well, we thought Blakley was totally going to cooperate to move this Committee to the conclusions we all discovered, considering the abundance of information gathered pointing to the CIA, and we even looked at Spector as a man who wanted our forgiveness and would rectify the previous investigations, but no, it wasn't to be! All of us on that Committee were living in a fantasy world. The committee was formed to protect 'the company'-- the CIA-- and like Jim Garrison's prosecution in the sixties, all his witnesses had died left and right, and so had ours.

Blakley turned our Committee into a fiasco. Well, Groden got his uncut Zapruder film introduced as evidence, and the tapes of the patrolman's police radio that had actually recorded more than three bullets fired in Dealey Plaza-- maybe more than seven-- but the committee concluded only four actual shots could be accounted for-- the fourth one coming from the grassy knoll and stipulated it missed Kennedy altogether. And because of those four shots, the first report announced there was a possible conspiracy, but that Lee Harvey Oswald was *still* the lone gunman! Even if every member of the Committee did not agree, it didn't matter.

"We all had to sign our names that we would not divulge any information outside the Committee, and if we did, I for one, like the other attorneys, would be disbarred from the law, never to work again. The same was true for any congressman, senator, or police law enforcement personnel. All of us would lose our jobs. At first, we agreed with the secrecy, but when we were getting closer to uncovering the truth, the funding plug was pulled from Congress. Blakley had the last and only word. He was the only one who came out with our findings and conclusions, and the only one who would write a book about the findings of the House Select Committee on Assassinations. As you well know, the Mafia was implicated in the conspiracy on the November twenty-second murder and the CIA was exonerated-- although Blakley forgot to mention the fact the Mafia, Sam Giancana, Johnny Roselli, Trafficante, all were working under CIA orders!"

"What happened to the investigations of King, Jr. and Bobby?" Modini asked.

"All swept under the rug. Blakley could have blamed the mob on them too! So why waste any more taxpayers' money on the rest of our investigation? Hey! We were just getting started on John Kennedy! What the hell! You and I are two of those taxpayers and all of us continue to allow the CIA to thrive..."

Modini looked up at this tall thin African-American man and added, "It probably didn't help any either whenever I came out with an article agreeing Oswald was the lone gunman."

Franklin just smiled. "Mr. Modini... You're just like anyone else. If you can be used, they'll take advantage of you. But people change, Mr. Modini, when they see the light. The question isn't what you did, or what happened in the past, it's what will happen now, and later. The question is, what are you or I going to do about it?"

Modini looked at the unclassified document of the National Security Action Memorandum No. 273. "Can I hold on to this document for a while?" he asked Franklin.

Franklin nodded. "Keep it, it's yours!" He held out his hand and Modini shook it.

Modini, still skeptical, added, "This doesn't mean I don't believe Oswald wasn't a shooter. I still need more time in my investigation to satisfy myself before I can satisfy anyone else. It does mean I believe the Warren Commission did help coverup the truth of November twenty second. I feel deceived and want answers, not because of a mother's concerns or a wife's threat of deportation, but because Oswald had two daughters and they deserve the truth. As it stands now, Oswald continues to hold the stigma of being a presidential assassin! Richard, do me this one favor. I need Max Slaton to look up a number for me. It's a limo number. I got it earlier today at the airport. I need to know who rented it out for the day."

Franklin accepted the piece of paper Modini gave him.

"I wish you well in your investigation," Franklin said. "I'll be in touch with you soon."

Both men shook hands again and departed, going their separate ways into the darkened streets of Washington, D.C.

Chapter Fourteen

"Micheline"

Later that night the usual stream of traffic filled the Washington D.C. streets. An assortment of cars, limousines, and taxis, arrived periodically in front of The Velvet Fountain Restaurant where prompt valets parked them in a timely manner. The bright lights at the entrance lighted the exterior of the plush restaurant located near the center of Washington D.C.

A taxi arrived, and a valet stepped down to welcome the guests. Judge Henry Kencade and Catherine Rogers exited the vehicle. They had flown in from Madison, Indiana, earlier that day.

Catherine was dressed exquisitely for the occasion in a serene golden outfit, displaying her legs with a cut above the knees. She showed just enough cleavage to command attention.

Her father, the judge, wore a white tuxedo that matched his distinguished white hair. They had arrived in time for their eight o'clock reservations.

* * *

During the same time, in a near by hotel, John Modini sat on a bathroom shower floor, letting the water hit his naked body. He let the water spray over his closed eyes as he rested after a very trying day. He was staying in a cheap, second-rate hotel room. The name of the hotel was inappropriate as well, named the Friendship Inn. It had no room service or complimentary shampoo to boot.

Finally, Modini got out of the shower and dried himself off. He stared at his reflection in the mirror and made up his mind. He would accept Roger Tracy's invitation tonight.

An hour later inside The Velvet Fountain Restaurant, the night life was spirited. The service was first-rate and elegant, where waiters appeared at the snap of a finger, encouraged by the loosely-spent money of its clientele. And one of those people spending money that night was Colonel Roger Tracy.

Tracy sat at a first-class table with two beautiful stewardesses. One was the blonde from the flight Tracy took to Washington that consumed most of the attention. The other was a dark brunette who behaved a little more reserved. The drinks were flowing at their table. This threesome lifted their glasses frequently in a toast, each time as if they were making their first.

The waiter appeared beside Tracy. "Would you and your guests like to order dinner now?" he asked patiently.

Tracy gulped down his Scotch and soda, then took a breath, laughing, "Just give us a few more minutes and we'll be ready!"

"As you wish, sir," the waiter bowed and exited, turning his attention to his other important customers. This restaurant catered not only to the rich, but to the influential politicians and people in government as well. CIA Director William Webster was spotted dining with a group of friends and Senator John Tower.

The waiter headed past one section of the dining area where Judge Kencade and Catherine Rogers were sitting with their party, consisting of two colleagues. As the waiter passed by, the colleagues continued discussing tomorrow's court hearing concerning Judge Kencade and the murder of the prostitute found in the Watergate Hotel Room.

Catherine pretended to be charming as she courteously listened to the conversation. The first attorney, whose name was Birmbaum, expressed the direction Catherine should take. "Now, I really think Catherine has a point, your Honor. I feel that we can wipe this whole slate clean and get rid of this miserable mess. From what I can tell, most of the evidence is circumstantial. The whole process of elimination is in effect here. All charges could be dropped within a couple of days, rest assured!"

Judge Kencade glared at Birmbaum. "And how are you going to do that trick? Do you plan to make the girl's corpse disappear all of a sudden?" he asked sarcastically

The second colleague chuckled and answered him, "Well, after all, what's one more bimbo prostitute!" Catherine, a bit tense, spoke up. "She was a human being...just like you, Jake!"

At 9:15 p.m. the maitre d' spoke exchanged words with John Modini who for the first time in a long while was clean-shaven. He looked like a new person, wearing a pair of slacks and a dark brown corduroy blazer. The maitre d' asked Modini to wait a moment and reappeared with a complementary tie, presenting it to him.

Modini glanced into a wall mirror, adjusted the tie around his neck. When the maitre'd deemed it acceptable, he escorted his guest to the table belonging to Colonel Roger Tracy.

As Modini moved through the restaurant, he spotted Senator John Tower sitting across the room. He wanted to take the opportunity to ask the Senator some questions, but Before Modini could act, Colonel Tracy gestured Modini over.

Modini reluctantly stayed on course, following the maitre'd to the welcoming committee of the Colonel and his two lovely young girls. The second girl, more subdued than the blonde, was pleased by what she saw.

Tracy greeted Modini with an overwhelming shake of the hand. "Hey, buddy, I am having the time of my life! Here, sit...sit down... See who I brought with me." It was apparent Tracy had a bit too many drinks and was obnoxiously loud.

Modini turned his attention to the familiar blonde stewardess he recognized from his plane trip and smiled. "Nice to see you again..."

"Good evening, Mr. Modini, I know we weren't formally introduced. You can call me

144

Missy...and--"

Before she can finish Tracy interrupted, "And I brought you one, too, old buddy. She's a beauty, ain't she now... Her name is..." Tracy tried to remember while Modini looked at this beautiful brown-eyed brunette. She didn't respond or say a word.

Missy felt embarrassed and filled in the word for Tracy. "Micheline!"

Tracy continued, "...Micheline, right! Spreads her wings, just fine, don't ya darlin'! Micheline, meet John Modini..."

Micheline smiled. She was wearing a low cut chiffon gown and raised her glass to Modini, explaining, "He means, I fly, too!" Modini sat down, enamored by her sense of humor.

The waiter approached the table again. "Would you like to order some food now, sir?"

Tracy turned to him with an empty glass in hand. "But of course!" Then ignoring him, he turned back to Modini, "What drink are you having?"

"Bourbon, straight!" Modini was definitely ready for one.

Tracy gave the waiter the sign. "Got that, waiter, and refill all our glasses, pronto!" The waiter just nodded his head and went to get the drinks.

An hour later everyone at Tracy's table had finished dinner. Modini who tried his best to remain polite all evening, decided to take the general conversation into a different direction as Missy and Micheline excused themselves to go to the restroom. "I see Senator Tower is having dinner here tonight..." he mentioned casually, taking a sip of wine.

Tracy, now relaxed, studied Modini. "Yeah, he's having dinner with Bill Webster, CIA director. So what, big deal?"

"Isn't he the Senate's Intelligence Committee Chairman?"

"So Webster is probably asking him for another appropriation of a billion dollars to add to their lucrative bank account, 'the company'. What's your point? This place is known for its wining and dining, wheeling and dealing."

Modini went right to the heart of the issue. "Why are you here in Washington, Tracy? And

145

since when do you hobnob with congressmen?"

Tracy pretended to play along with Modini and gave a mock expression of shock as if he were caught in doing some nasty deed. "Ooh, you mean Senator Fuller? Oh that... It was only a courtesy call. He likes me, what can I tell you?"

Modini didn't buy Tracy's curt answer. "Come on, Tracy, don't snow job me. Why did Fuller meet you at the airport instead of Andrews? And *why* is Fuller meeting with you-- someone who's connected to Naval intelligence?"

Tracy decided to get this over with. "Okay, it has to do with a Congressional hearing I have to appear at tomorrow morning."

"What's so special about it?"

Tracy was a bit intimidated by his question. "Modini... I can't discuss it. Now drop it! Besides, you'll read about it in tomorrow's newspapers."

Modini pushed on. "Tracy, what is such a secret that the press will know tomorrow...but you can't tell me tonight?

Tracy glared at him. The animosity Modini had seen earlier that day had reappeared with vengeance. The liquor didn't help things, either. "Why don't you call your home office at your magazine? They know everything before I do anyway. I thought you'd be the first to be informed on every major story that goes through your magazine!"

Modini was taunted by his remark. "I haven't the faintest idea what you're talking about. Cut the bullshit and tell me!"

Tracy gave Modini an awkward look, "You really don't know, do you? And I thought all those stories you wrote about--" He held up his hand and waved Modini away. "Forget it! If I told you, you would be biased concerning the subject matter. This is too big to fuck up now!"

"Why, because I may know something that isn't the truth-- that I may screw up another medal for you?" Modini wouldn't let it rest. "If I have to, Tracy, I'll go to Senator Fuller myself! We happen to be old acquaintances from way back!"

"I wouldn't if I were you. If he is what you say he is, an acquaintance of yours-- if you approach him on this, he won't be an acquaintance for long!"

Modini took a long look at Tracy. "Are you threatening me?"

Tracy leaned back in his seat. "Just leave well enough alone, Modini, and you won't get hurt! You may not believe this, but I'm telling you this as a friend."

He tried to decide whether Tracy was telling him the truth, when he caught sight of someone walking past his table. It was Catherine Rogers. He recognized her immediately and reacted on impulse, rising from his chair.

Tracy mistakenly thought Modini was offended because of their conversation and stood up, attempting to stop him. "Modini, wait... You're not leaving, are you?"

"Uh... No, not yet." Modini hastily explained. "I'll be back. I'm just going to the men's room!" he said evasively and headed after Catherine Rogers.

Missy and Micheline headed back to the table as Modini passed them. Tracy greeted the girls, smiling, still standing erect, as if everything were normal.

"My... John looked as though he was in a hurry." Missy commented to Tracy on Modini's departure. "Bladder problem?"

Tracy just laughed.

Modini followed Catherine and saw her enter the corridor to the ladies room. Unsure of what to do next, he tried to stall for time. He didn't want to go into the men's room for fear of missing her. He walked over to a rack of pay phones across from the rest rooms. He lifted one receiver and pretended to be making a telephone call.

A few people entered and exited through the restroom doors while he nervously waited. Then, he had second doubts. This wasn't exactly the best way to meet Catherine-- interrupting her during dinner. Sure, he wanted to talk to her, but this certainly wasn't the right time or place. The more he thought about it, the more foolish it sounded.

Just then the door opened from the ladies room, and Catherine reappeared. Modini saw her head for the phones, in his direction, searching in her purse. She pulled out a dollar bill and looked around. She was obviously out of change.

It's now or never, Modini thought, and seized the opportunity. "Need change...Ma'am?" he asked Catherine.

Catherine looked up, almost startled. "Why yes, I..." she then gave Modini a double take as if she recognized him. "...I appreciate it. I never seem to have the right change when it comes to making a phone call."

"No problem." Modini handed her a handful of quarters as she exchanged the currency. He then picked up his phone as if he were planning to place a call. "You should carry one of those calling cards!"

Catherine grinned. "I used to, but it seems as if I take advantage of it and end up crying whenever I see the bill. On top of that, try to memorize all those numbers!" She dialed and spoke with the operator. "Hello? Do I have to call information to make a collect call or can I just go through you? Yes, I'd like to make a collect call to a Michael Bradley in Madison, Indiana... Thank you."

As Catherine waited for her connection, she studied Modini discreetly as he also dialed and he caught her looking at him. "I'm sorry! I didn't mean to stare. It's just that you look familiar. Have we met before?"

Modini smiled and avoided the direct question. "I don't know? It's possible..."

"Excuse me..." Catherine spoke into her phone. "Yes, Michael, it's me. I hear we've been ping ponging all day trying to get in touch. What's the matter? No, it's not going too good but you know how lawyers are. You can't live with them, and you can't live without them-- or is it that you can't kill them?"

Modini's ear caught the last phrase as he was dialing. Catherine noticed he heard her and was embarrassed, but smiled just the same.

Michael Bradley, was in his bed working on some papers. "Catherine, listen to me!" he urgently began.

Modini, meanwhile, had contacted his mother, Marian Modini, in Oregon. "Oh son! It's you. Thank God you called!" his mother said.

Modini was startled by her response. "What is it, Mother?"

"Someone put a bomb in her car!"

"Whose car? What are you talking about?" Modini asked sharply.

"Mary Ann Sweeney's!" his mother said, excited.

Catherine's eyes glanced over to Modini as her ears caught the compelling tone of his voice. But Michael Bradley's voice over the receiver distracted her. "Are you listening?" Bradley asked. "I've got some bad news! I've been with the coroner's office all day trying to get to Karl Hunter's autopsy..."

Modini asked his mother, "Is she all right?"

"Yes," his mother explained. "It was her cousin. She started the car and was ready to drive the both of them to town. Mary Ann hadn't yet gotten to the car, and her cousin was having problems starting it. Luckily the driver's side door was open when the bomb blew her out of the car onto the lawn. She's alive...but in intensive care."

Modini was shocked. "Jesus!" he said loudly, causing Catherine to look over with concern.

Michael Bradley was in mid-sentence, speaking with Catherine. "...Right in the middle of the autopsy, someone from the government came in to stop the procedure and took away Karl's body! Can you believe that! Catherine! Are you there?"

Catherine was silent for a second. "Yes, I'm sorry, Michael. Someone next to me on the phone was having a problem, but I heard you. Someone took Karl's body. Where did they take it?"

Bradley reiterated. "Several government agents came in and just repossessed the body. I don't know where they took it. They just said, 'sew him back up' and then they took him!"

Catherine tried to comprehend all this. "Who? Which men from the government took Karl's body?"

Modini's head swung around as Karl's name was mentioned.

Catherine continued, "...I mean he was a Marine, right... Which branch of government would have authority over his body?"

Modini interrupted his mother, as she was still giving him the details. "Listen, Mother... Thank you for telling me this, but I'll have to call you back. I promise I'll talk to you soon. I have to go now." Modini hung up but still kept the receiver in his hand. He wanted to interrupt Catherine, but knew it wasn't the best time to say anything.

Bradley spoke with Catherine, "I don't know who took Karl's body. I'm going to look into that first thing tomorrow, but that isn't what's important now. This is what I found out-- the coroner's report has been classified as top secret and cannot be released. The coroner knew I was patiently waiting all day and was pissed by the government's interference! He gave me what little evidence he did discover, though. Listen to this, Catherine... At first the authorities said Karl Hunter hung himself, but the autopsy revealed there was a struggle, as if someone else had a hand in it. The coroner discovered a fresh needle mark from an injection on the back side of his left knee. The pathologist said he was taking some medication, and his bodily fluids showed nothing abnormal, but who in their right mind injects himself with medication behind his knee?"

"What was he injected with?" Catherine asked?

Modini, completely overwhelmed by these sudden revelations, suddenly became ill. He doubled over, desperately trying not to vomit as the tears flowed from his eyes. Unable to contain himself any longer, he threw the receiver at the phone cradle, missing it. It fell off and swung like a pendulum as Modini rushed into the men's room.

Catherine was startled by Modini's abrupt behavior. She stared after him in astonishment, half-listening to Bradley on the phone.

"That's it, Catherine," Bradley continued. "We'll never know! Fat chance the government will hand the autopsy report over to us. Someone wants the book closed on this case and that means you and I can't even get a wrongful death suit out of the State of Indiana, thanks to the United States government!"

Inside the empty men's room, Modini found the nearest stall and threw up in a toilet bowl. He emptied his stomach until the taste acid burned its way up his throat. Then he felt his stomach lunge painfully as it tried to clean itself further. He tried to control himself, but to no avail. Tears filled his eyes. He started to weep, overcome with emotion about what he had overheard concerning Karl's body.

Modini's tearful sobs continued until Catherine knocked on the men's room door. She had waited a few moments outside the door, hoping someone would appear, someone who could check on the man, but no one did.

She opened the door and called out. "Sir! Sir! Are you all right?" When she heard no reply, she stepped inside. "I'm sorry to barge in like this, but you looked as though you were very ill..."

Modini exited his bathroom stall, wiping the tears away. "I'm...I'm okay, now," he told her. The sour, salty taste of his own bile was still in his mouth, but he appeared calm and in control of himself again. He went to the sink and threw some water in his face, as Catherine waited for some sort of reply.

Modini saw her reflection in the mirror. He wanted to explain his situation, but decided to continue the charade with her. "Thanks for your concern," he said hiding his turmoil. "But there's nothing anybody can do now." His face was sallow, and beaded with the water that wet his dark hair and gathered on his eyebrows. He could not shake the news about Karl Hunter out of his mind. He gave another explanation for his difficulty. "I just learned that a woman who I met a few days ago in Fort Worth, Texas almost died in a car bombing!"

Catherine was surprised. "A bomb? My God!"

Modini went on, "Yeah, luckily no one was killed, but her cousin was thrown from the car.

151

It was almost a miracle. If her car door hadn't been opened, she would be dead right now!" Modini pulled some paper towels from the dispenser and dried his face and hands.

"How terrible! Who would do such a thing?"

Modini shrugged, "I don't know. I haven't a clue. These ladies are in their fifties and sixties. I can't believe someone actually stooping this low to kill or scare elderly people. I can't explain it!" He put his hands on the wash stand and braced himself, hanging his head, breathing deeply.

Catherine felt the news affected him much than he wanted to admit. Throwing all caution to the wind, Catherine stepped over to him and asked, "Are you sure you're going to be all right?"

Modini just nodded.

"Again, I'm sorry for the intrusion. My name is Catherine Rogers and I'm an attorney. If I can be of any help..." she left the sentence unfinished.

"Thank you... I'll be fine." Modini introduced himself, forcing a smile, "By the way, my name is John Modini!"

Catherine paused a moment, her eyes widening. "That name... It sounds familiar. Are you sure we haven't met before?"

"I won't say yes and I won't say no," Modini evaded, "but I used to work for *Time-Life Magazine* as a photo journalist." He could tell by the way Catherine looked at him that she was impressed. He wanted very much to speak with her, but decided to hold back. "Ahh... Mrs. Rogers, may I be candid with you?"

"Yes, as long as you call me Catherine."

"I overheard your conversation at the phone and I just wanted you to know it's the Secretary of Navy or Naval Intelligence!"

"Excuse me?" Catherine said, not comprehending.

Modini quickly added, "You mentioned a Marine in your phone conversation and what branch of government could take his body."

152

Catherine was surprised. "Right! Oh, yes, thank you very much... That does help a lot."

Suddenly, a gentleman walked into the men's room and stopped in mid stride as he saw Catherine. "Oh... Excuse me..." he politely apologized and reversed his course to walk right back out again.

"Oh, my God!" Catherine exclaimed, realizing where she was. She and Modini both laughed on cue, caught in this embarrassing situation.

"I think we should get out of here before he comes back," Modini suggested.

As Modini exited the restroom ahead of Catherine, the door swung open almost hitting another gentleman, Judge Henry Kencade. "Oh...sorry, sir..." Modini said.

"That's quite all right," Kencade said in his dignified manner, taking the accident as a mistake on his part. But his reply turned to shock and embarrassment as Catherine emerged. "Catie! What were you doing in-- Why were you in there?"

Catherine summoned up all the dignity she could, but could only say, "Oh, hi dad..."

Kencade glared at Modini, then back to his daughter

"Dad, it's not what you're thinking!" Catherine said quickly.

Modini finally found his voice. "It's a pleasure, your honor, you must be Judge Henry Kencade!" Modini offered his hand in recognition.

Kencade's eyes narrowed. "Have we met before? My memory has not been so kind to me lately, so if you'd be so good to excuse me..."

Catherine spoke up, "Father, this is John Modini. He's with *Time Magazine*. He's a photojournalist..."

"Er...was!" Modini corrected, "Not anymore... It wasn't hard to recognize you, Your Honor, you're front page news. Besides, I did a story on you some time back."

This peaked Catherine's interest. "What was the story about.? It was good, I hope?"

"Actually it was a little of both. It was about top judges throughout the country who had the chance to be nominated to the Supreme Court." Modini explained.

Catherine was delighted to hear this. "See dad, someone out there does believe in you."

Kencade didn't know whether to take Modini's last remark as sarcasm or not, so he left it alone. "Catie, we have guests waiting at our table, ready to leave!" He told his daughter.

Modini, still a bit uneasy from all this, took the initiative to set things straight. "Your Honor, please accept my apology for keeping your daughter from your guests..."

Catherine knew this wasn't true but waited for her father's response. "Yes...well, it's nice meeting you, Mr. Modini. If you'll please excuse me..." Turning again to Catherine, he said, "Dear, we do have guests!" Kencade went into the men's room. Catherine waited until her father had gone before she reached out to touch Modini's hand. "I'm sure we've also kept you from your guests as well..."

"Yes, I almost forgot!" Modini excused himself, "It was a pleasure Mrs. Rogers...Catherine. I hope we can meet again in a more pleasant situation."

"I have to say, Mr. Modini," Catherine remarked, glancing at the men's room sign, "No matter what, any situation will be more pleasant than this one."

Modini smiled, and headed back into the restaurant but not before Catherine added, "And thank you for the change!"

John Modini returned to Colonel Tracy's table. "Well, it's about time." Tracy laughed. "The girls were just wondering if there weren't something more interesting happening in the men's room than at our table. They're anxious to party out the night...aren't you girls?"

Missy reacted favorably, but Micheline just studied Modini's response.

"I'm sorry to have to spoil your fun," Modini apologized. "But I've had a long day and something has suddenly come up! Tracy, I need a small favor, if you don't mind." He took out a piece of paper from his wallet and copied the phone number Miss Sweeney gave him, and handed it to Tracy. "If you can help me trace this phone number, or find out anything else about it, I'd appreciate it. The first three digits will be familiar to you anyway."

Tracy looked at the number. "What is it? The prefix is for Raleigh, North Carolina. So?"

"The catch is, it's not the phone number used today. This number is twenty-five years old!"

Tracy put the slip of paper into his pocket. "I'll look into it! But...Modini--"

Modini turned to the women. Micheline appeared especially saddened to see him go. "Ladies, I apologize, please excuse me, but I have to run. Tracy...I'll be in contact with you tomorrow morning. I'm calling it a night. And from what I gather, you have a big day tomorrow, yourself! Thank you for the drinks and dinner!"

At Modini's departure, Tracy was only in half spirits and troubled by all this. He got up and went after Modini cornering him midway to the entrance. "Wait, wait a minute, Modini. Sorry about our little argument earlier, but please, I can't handle the both of 'em. I brought one for you, God damn it! Don't leave the girl stranded here like this!"

Modini half grinned, but his words were sharp, "What's the matter, Colonel, losing your touch? Since when do you care what girl you leave stranded? You're slipping on your own banana peel. It wasn't Karl Hunter who was the juggler, it was you. You were the best at that, remember? Karl was the one who supplied them to you-- whatever you needed, whatever you wanted! Excuse me, Colonel!" Modini turned and headed for the exit.

Tracy returned to his table and sat down, his face pale. Missy asked, "What is it, baby?"

Micheline began gathering up her things. "I believe this is my cue for departure as well. Please... Don't stand up, Colonel."

Tracy stood anyway. He took a wad of bills out of his pocket to offer her some money, but Micheline stopped him. "It's thoughtful of you, but I don't want your money. I'm a big girl now, and I can handle this all by myself. I do appreciate and thank you for a lovely dinner, the drinks and the companionship."

Tracy still offered her money, but she ignored him "You're sure?" he asked.

Micheline was sure. "Yes! Good night. I'll see you soon, Missy, thanks." She kissed her friend on the forehead and departed. Tracy, surprised by this, looked at the money still in hand and sat back down.

Modini motioned for a cab outside the Velvet Fountain Restaurant. As one drove up, a valet stepped forward to open the cab door for him. Modini got in as Micheline rushed out of the entrance. "Wait for me," she yelled to the valet, and handed him a tip before Modini could even react. She slipped into the seat next to him.

Modini was very surprised. "Well, Hello again! Long time no see." he joked. "May I offer to drop you somewhere?"

"Yes, you can. I'm staying at the same hotel as you!"

Modini baffled, "I don't understand. How do you know what hotel I'm staying at?" Micheline leaned back into her seat and smiled. "Trust me!"

The cab pulled away from the Velvet Fountain and Catherine Rogers watched it speed off. As it disappeared into the nighttime traffic, she was joined at the front entrance by her father, Judge Kencade, and their two colleagues. They waited for a valet to summon their cabs.

Not too far away from where the group stood waiting, a man hidden in the shadows watched Catherine's every move. A pair of binoculars focused on Catherine behind the windows of a parked car. Catherine casually watched a valet flag down a cab. She had been under observation for some time now, and she didn't suspect a thing.

The binoculars continued to follow her as her father and friends entered their cab.

* * *

Modini's hotel room, his 'unfriendly' Friendship Inn, was a bit more accommodating now. Micheline had invited herself to his room and, in a few minutes, had begun to strip him of his trousers. She pushed Modini who was facing her, back onto his bed and pulled his pants off. She folded them neatly and hung them over the back of a chair.

Modini, a little apprehensive, watched as this beautiful brown-eyed woman, moved close to him and began massaging his chest. "You're so tense, Mr. Modini!" she purred. "Relax, I'll make you feel more comfortable." She continued to massage Modini, head to toe, applying lotion all over him, poking and prodding. She smiled, looking mischievously into his eyes, as if saying to him, gaze upon my irresistible body, as she slowly stripped down to full nudity.

Micheline poured lotion and oil all over herself and, like a cat on the prowl, she got on all fours and advanced across Modini's body until her eyes met his. Then her hand went down to massage Modini's groin. His eyes closed in pleasure as she continued her foreplay. The ecstasy of this moment was a sweet dream come true for Modini.

Micheline, still on all fours, turned around over his body. As Modini opened his eyes, he was rewarded with a most intriguing view of Micheline's better half. Although she had a beautiful face and hair, this part of her lovely anatomy was displayed most endearingly.

Micheline's hand grasped Modini's the most sensitive part of his body and touched it to her lips. Then as she opened her mouth and proceeded with giving Modini what he craved the most, her derriere descended. It reminded Modini of the metaphor, "If Mohammed can't come to the Mountain, the Mountain will come down to Mohammed and the valley will swallow him up." As far as Modini was concerned, the view of this promising valley was reason enough for all night rejoicing.

* * *

The phone rang after midnight in the hotel room of Judge Henry Kencade. The judge came out of the bathroom with a washcloth from drying off his face and answered it. "Yes?" But there was only silence at the other end. He spoke louder, "Who is this?"

The silence was broken as a man's voice spoke. "Do the right thing tomorrow, or your daughter may wind up as your little prostitute friend!"

Kencade's eyes widened, startled. "Who is this?"

The voice added. "Just think of me as a witness to what you did and will do...a pimp that happened to be around. Or maybe I'm your daughter's last hope!"

The phone clicked dead. Kencade slowly put the receiver down and walked over to sit on the side of his bed. He then lay down, his eyes staring upward at the ceiling.

* * *

At two o'clock in the morning, two bodies rested side by side in John Modini's hotel room. Modini's eyes were closed in sleep while Micheline's were wide open. Her naked body eased carefully from his as she slid out of bed, careful not to disturb him. In the dark, she quietly gathered up her clothing, then entered the bathroom, and turned on the light. Micheline stared at the image of herself in the mirror and started suddenly to weep.

* * *

Simultaneously, Catherine Rogers was also up, sitting at the writing desk in her hotel room, busy checking tomorrow's schedule in her calendar book. She made notes on the court hearing, her flight schedule, then, as a reminder, circled the appointment with Joseph Ziegler at three o'clock at his daughter's institution. She then made a memo to herself to hire Birmbaum's researcher, meet with Michael Bradley between five and five thirty and seek a dossier on John Modini.

Catherine furrowed her brow in deep thought. There was something else she was supposed to do but couldn't remember. She smiled and decided to forget it. It was time to go to bed.

* * *

Micheline emerged from the bathroom into the dark room, and retrieved another item of clothing, a slip that belonged beneath her chiffon gown. She proceeded to slip it on as Modini's voice broke the silence.

"Do you really have to be going now?" Modini's hand reached out for the bed lamp and switched on the light noticing the time.

Micheline quickly responded, "Would you please, turn off the light! Please, I don't like dressing in front of a man."

Modini was a bit critical with his reply. "Oh, but you don't mind <u>undressing</u>? I see!"

"Please, John, don't patronize me!" Micheline snapped back.

He sat up and apologized, "I'm sorry. But don't get me wrong. I get curious when a beautiful and mysterious woman makes love to me and suddenly sneaks off. Don't I get an explanation?" His voice became abrupt. "Or do you have to rush to your next appointment because you haven't met your quota yet?"

Micheline finished donning her slip and glared at him, but would not stoop to his game. "John, if it's any consolation to you. I was just being polite. I didn't think you wanted me to be here when you woke up in the morning..."

"How thoughtful. Since when are you such an expert on reading men's minds?"

Micheline sat on a chair and pulled on her stockings. "I believe all men don't give a second thought to any woman who sleeps with them on the first night. I'm no expert and I'm not blaming you, but that's the way I feel!" Modini just stared at her. She continued, "What I mean is, it's just common courtesy on my part. I was thinking of your privacy. You know what I mean, 'how can I get rid of this woman or bitch' -- whatever you want to call me. As I say, I'm no expert, I wanted you to like me, that's all, John. I like you. Now, go back to sleep!"

Modini, concerned by her explanation, swung out of bed to rummage in his pants, trying to find his wallet. "OK, then, how much do I owe you?"

Micheline was troubled by his offer. "Not a thing," she replied respectfully, "Honest!"

Modini grinned and shook his head. "Oh, I get it! All bought and paid for by the Colonel...my pal! Nice speech, lady!"

Micheline finished dressing. She rose from the chair and approached Modini, now wrapped in a bed sheet. Then, unexpectedly, she slapped him hard across the face. As Modini stood there stunned, she picked up her purse and unlocked the door.

She turned back momentarily, and spoke through her tears. "I deserved all those things you said, but I want you to know I am not a prostitute and I didn't take any money from the Colonel. I never met him before this evening. I went out this evening only as a favor to Missy."

Micheline took a deep breath and continued, "I do want you to know. He did offer me money. He wanted me to find out why you were snooping around Naval Intelligence building in North Carolina."

"He told you this?"

"Yes. He wanted me to find out what you knew?"

Modini paused, frowning. "The big question is how did he know I was at the Navel Intelligence building in the first place."

"I don't know. You'll have to ask him."

"I intend to. Now what about you. Why didn't you try to draw the information out of me?"

Micheline smiled and shook her head. "Funny, but I found it interesting, although you never once spoke a word to me at the dinner table, I-- I liked you! I didn't know how or why, but I wanted you to notice me and like me. Mr. Modini...last night was the first time I've ever gone out of my way for someone. You were only the second man I've ever made love to-- the first was my husband"

Modini looked deeply into her eyes. He knew she was telling the truth.

"He died a year ago of throat cancer!" she stood by the door looking sad and vulnerable.

Modini felt embarrassed by her honesty. Still wrapped in the sheet, he went over to her. He opened the sheet and put his arms around her, wrapping up the both of them. Micheline sobbed as Modini hugged her.

"Either you're a great actress or I owe you one big apology. Either way, you're a good woman, Micheline. You're something else, and I'd like you to accept my apology and to please stay."

Micheline looked up into his eyes, then closed hers and pressed her body and lips to his. As she kissed him, Modini moved his hand underneath her dress.

She stopped, her eyes opened, and she backed away out of his sheet. "I can't, I... Please don't, John! You'll get me hot and bothered and I'll forget what I must do. I have to go now...but, John, I'll stay in touch!" She wiped the tears from her eyes.

"When can I see you again?" Modini asked.

"Tonight, if you'd like," she kissed him again. "Will you still be in town?"

"Sure!"

Micheline opened the door. "I'll leave word at the front desk when I can make it. No need to have dinner out, I'll bring it with me. By the way, John..." her eyes held the desirous look again. "I have to say...you are so beautiful! And not only that, you have a nice butt!"

Modini watched her leave, and he looked to the high heavens, overwhelmed by Micheline's exit line. He closed and locked his door and exclaimed, "Thank you, Lord, Jesus Christ!"

Chapter Fifteen

"To Be Or Not To Be"

It was a little after ten-thirty in the morning as, Henry Kencade and his daughter, Catherine waited impatiently on the steps of The Justice Department in Washington D.C. They were taking a short break as they waited for the court to convene. The Judge had hardly said a word to his daughter all morning. Catherine could see the toll these accusations were taking on him.

Birmbaum, one of their colleagues came out of the building, and motioned to the group it was time to enter. They followed him back into the Justice Department building.

Inside the courtroom, Judge Kencade was in the formal process of being arraigned. A court attendant read the charges concerning the multiple stabbing of one Rita Stebbings at the Watergate Hotel. The panel of judges sat before Kencade and his daughter.

The lead judge, the speaker for the panel asked, "How does the defendant plead?" All eyes were on Henry Kencade, now.

Birmbaum spoke for the group, responding with, "Not guilty, Your Honor!" The speaker allowed the prosecution to proceed.

It was Kencade's second round on the stand that day. Mr. Paxton, the district attorney, took his turn acting as prosecutor, and asked Kencade what occurred during this tragic incident.

Catherine sat stiffly in her chair with her two colleagues by her side, reviewing every word, and nuance the prosecutor said.

"Now, you say when you entered the hotel room you might have had a black out-- that amnesia could have set in for a brief time. You say you have no recollection how you got there, or who brought you there. Is that right?" Mr. Paxton addressed Kencade in a courteous tone.

Kencade, aware of the standard procedure for a witness to respond, was calm and collected as he answered. "It's quite possible, yes...you see, I didn't--"

Mr. Paxton cut him off. "But you say here, you remember approaching Miss Stebbings on the Potomac Bridge, around midnight." The prosecutor fumbled through some pages on a clipboard searching for his notes of the chronology for that night, and maintained his decorum so not to lose his momentum. "What were you doing out there, Mr. Kencade at that time of night? I mean it's hard to believe a man of your age and stature, would be walking the streets at that hour. What was it? Perhaps you were seeking a little salvation?"

Catherine was getting irritated by this line of questioning, though she held her own at this point, knowing her father would eventually tear this idiot apart as long as he remained cool.

Kencade's answer was just a simple, "No..." He would not allow the prosecutor get the best of him.

The Prosecutor acted if he weren't surprised and smiled. "No...Mr. Kencade? I didn't think so. You don't mind if I call you by your surname instead of your Honor... I just don't feel comfortable, concerning the circumstances of this case..."

Kencade looked down at his shoes for a moment then lifted his head high to face the Prosecutor and his daughter as he spoke. "No, I don't care what you people call me!"

The prosecutor moved in quickly for the kill. "But what did you say to Miss Stebbings, when you approached her? What did you call her-- prostitute, call girl, or was it...whore,"he said facetiously, "or did you just offer this little girl a piece of candy?"

Catherine rose to her feet in protest. "I object to this line of questioning! He was taking a walk, for God's sake. He always takes a walk!"

The Judge pounded his gavel on the bench. "Overruled! Have Mrs. Rogers' last words stricken from the court record?" He gave Catherine a scandalous look as did the rest of the panel. "Mr. Paxton, please put a handle on this line of questioning. You may proceed with caution."

The prosecutor hid his smile and turned to Catherine. "Okay, Mrs. Rogers, let's say your client was taking a walk, at twelve midnight-- twelve o'clock a.m.!" He faced Kencade again. "Mr. Kencade, we all, in this courtroom, agree, you were taking this walk. And as a man like you and me," He gave a sharp glance to Catherine as he continued, "even at our age, we all have urges. Don't we?"

Catherine rolled her eyes and squirmed in her chair. Her colleagues urged her to keep still and not overreact.

"And being a top judicial of justice in your state, I realize you have to keep a low profile-- and because of our little weaknesses, we do things we sometimes are not proud of."

Kencade interrupted here, "Maybe *you* do!"

Mr. Paxton's face turned red as a chuckle rolled through the courtroom. He stopped at this remark. "Mr. Kencade, you know the procedure here, you answer my questions when I ask them. Meanwhile, you follow me until I finish my statement or question. Do you understand me, sir?"

Kencade answered with disdain. "Yes, Mr. Paxton, but what I want to know, is it going to be today or tomorrow?"

Catherine turned away, hiding her smile now.

Mr. Paxton addressed the panel. "Your Honor!"

The Judge nodded wearily toward Kencade. "Henry, you know the rules better than I do! Proceed, Mr. Paxton!" he said restraining a grin.

"So when you met this girl, or she met you. You both somehow ended up in the Watergate Hotel. No question about it, isn't that right?" The venom beginning to show,

Another simple "Yes..." came from Kencade.

The prosecutor struck again sharply, "And maybe you had amnesia with your pants down. I don't know, but during the heat of passion, isn't it possible you took that poor girl's life?"

Catherine prepared to break loose again when Birmbaum stood up. "Objection, the prosecution is giving pure conjecture here! The medical report shows no semen from the victim matches the defendant, your Honor. And if the prosecutor will stick to the questions concerning where and how the knife got there, maybe the defendant can give a straight answer to the prosecutor without his own interruptions and crude remarks. That's all I ask, your Honor!"

The lead judge announced "Sustained! You may continue with your questioning Mr. Paxton..."

The prosecutor strutted across the room, planning his next attack. "Thank you, your Honor. I will take the advice." He approached the stand. "Mr. Kencade, you told this court you crossed the street because you thought you saw a woman, Miss Stebbings, being attacked by a man with a knife! The fact is, Mr. Kencade, there was no witness to this so-called attack-- if one ever occurred. Aren't you using this attack as an excuse to explain the presence of the knife in the hotel room...is that correct? Maybe you just couldn't get it up...that could explain no semen!"

Kencade shook his head, refusing to be baited into an angry answer. "I just don't know...sir! I guess... I cannot give you the answer you want."

Jake whispered to Catherine. "What's the matter with your father? He's acting strange, not like himself! This isn't what we discussed last night!"

Catherine, still upset, blurted out, "Tell him! Tell him about the knife!" She turned her attention to the bench. "Your Honor, please! The Prosecutor is trying to confuse him!"

The Prosecutor lifted his arms to the panel, as if to surrender. The lead judge became disturbed by Catherine's outburst and focused on the defense table. "Catherine! Let Hank...er, Mr. Kencade, answer his own questions. Now don't let me have to tell you again, or I'll have to excuse you from this courtroom."

Catherine stared at the panel of judges, then sat back down. Birmbaum rose to add, "I'd like to apologize, your Honor. If it so pleases the court, I'd like to call a recess!" The judge agreed. He picked up the gavel and banged it on the block. "Recess. Lunch, one hour!"

* * *

John Modini walked into a corner cafe on the hill near the capital. Max Slaton and Richard Franklin were waiting for him already indulging in a breakfast of eggs, hash browns, bacon and pancakes. Max got up and hugged Modini. Then Modini shook Franklin's hand. The waitress brought another menu, but Modini just told her he'll take the short stack of pancakes and settled in a seat next to Franklin, across from Max.

Richard got the first word in. "I found Tower's letter in the Report."

Modini nodded. It was good news. "Yeah?"

"It's at the end of the Oswald chronology, and you won't believe this, but they actually say in Tower's letter Oswald didn't date the letter which we know is correct. But, if you look here," he said taking some pages from his briefcase, "you'll see that Connally's letter is dated on your original copy, but the report doesn't let you know either way whether it was, or wasn't dated. I can see now why the commissioner who did this could not put Tower's full letter like Connally's letter into the chronology. Like you say, you would positively notice a discrepancy. You're right. Someone is trying to hide something. If Oswald's chronology is exposed, it will fall like a line of Dominoes. But I still don't get it. Why didn't they just leave the letters out of the Warren Report or just not mention them?"

Modini gave Franklin a pat but sensible answer. "To be safe! They felt anyone who read the Report would think that *they* were being thorough. Also, there's Connally who was the one ally to the conspiracy buffs concerning 'the magic bullet theory.' He spoke out every time he got the chance to refute it and publicly stated he was wounded by a separate bullet. Connally would have definitely brought attention to his letter, had the Commission not included it in the report. They effectively buried it there. In the years that followed, only one person came up with a theory that suggested this letter proved Oswald was chasing Connally and not Kennedy. Here again, no one noticed what the letter could have exposed. So, like Arlen Specter once said, no one will really read the Warren Report, and the ones who do will get lost in the shuffle!"

Franklin asked, "And what of Tower's letter?"

"Here, it was even more deceitful the way it was hidden in the chronology," Modini easily explained again. "They barely even mention it, let alone refer to its importance, but Richard, you found it didn't you? Where? At the end of the chronology! It was lost in this patchwork of their phony timeline based on what Oswald's 'historical diary' had to say. And where is Senator John Tower today?"

Max Slaton spoke up for the first time. "He's the chairman for the Senate Intelligence Committee!"

"From one journalist to one attorney," Modini concluded, "I rest my case, or I should say your case! What do you have for me, Max, and how the hell are you, not in any order of importance?"

Max laughed. "I'm fine, Wop! Good to see you're back with us. Richard said your investigating instincts have aroused the journalist in you. Has the Prodigal Son finally returned?"

Modini shook his head. "Just give me what you got, Max."

Max handed him a sheet of paper. "The limo was acquisitioned by the Pentagon for the day, for the Joint Chief of Staff! There is a rumor out that the Brass plans to crucify some dead war hero..."

Modini decided to put his two bits in as the waitress sets down a stack of three pancakes. "His name wouldn't be Karl Hunter, would it?"

Max responded quickly, "That's him! Modini, you *are* good! How did you know this?"

"Do you know why?" Modini just asked.

"Something about passing government secrets to the Commies a few years ago." Max could only add to the rumor. "You knew him in Nam, didn't you?"

Modini didn't say anything, but Max could see it in his eyes. "Was he a crackpot, John?"

Modini looked at Max and Richard. "No, actually the opposite. He certainly saved many lives over there-- he saved mine."

"Then what's the big secret? Someone must want this rumor out of the bag to spread over Washington," Richard commented grimly.

Modini agreed. "I'm sure it will hit the papers by the *Post* and *Times* by the end of the day." He got up out of his seat, not even touching his pancakes. "Would you fellas excuse me? I have to make an important appointment, and I don't want to miss this. I'll catch you later today..."

Max and Richard exchanged glances. They were more concerned than disappointed as they watched Modini exit.

"I'll get the check this time," Max said.

* * *

One hour later John Modini sipped his coffee in the Sheraton Hotel restaurant. He frequently checked his watch for the time. Colonel Tracy arrived, and, finding Modini, seated himself at his table. Neither one said a word to each other first. Modini just sipped his coffee, staring at him.

Tracy finally broke the ice. "Okay, Modini, you dragged me out of the middle of a hearing. What the fuck do you want? As the waitress approached their table, Tracy snapped at her. "Just coffee, please!"

Modini continued to stare at him. Tracy lowered his tone. "Well, excuse me if I were rude last night, but I wanted a little fun-- is that all right with you?"

Again, Modini took another sip of his coffee, studying him. He put his cup down and stared at it. "I've been checking around this morning and I find out this hearing today has something to do with our friend Karl Hunter!"

"Who told you this?" Tracy flared angrily.

Modini smiled at his friend's irritation. "I still have contacts in this town, Tracy. Friends on the up and up who do things for me occasionally. I put two and two together when I found out about you and the Joint Chief of Staff. I saw him in the limo at the airport."

Tracy didn't say anything, but just gave a guilty look as Modini proceeded. "What I don't get, Tracy, is what are you two, the FBI and Senator Fuller up to? What's the common connection?"

Tracy's attitude changed. He smiled pleasantly. "I don't know where you get your information, Modini, but you are far and away out of line here! I'll tell you one thing though, but you must promise to keep your mouth shut! This is classified stuff."

Modini pretended to be impressed, "All right... You have my word!"

Tracy waited as the waitress poured coffee into their cups and departed before he continued. "You're right, it does concern Karl Hunter, and I've been brought here to go before this hearing to discredit him!"

Modini was puzzled, "To discredit him? Sure...but why?"

Tracy was ready for Modini's question and spoke as though it was a prepared speech. "I have been ordered to dissociate Hunter from the armed forces-- the Marines, to strip him of his stripes, the Medal of Honor, and any other distinguished merits bestowed on him by the Pentagon and by the President."

Modini grew angry and interrupted, completing Tracy's sentence in a way Tracy never intended, "...for his acts of courage and heroism in a time of crisis, under extreme danger, and fire for which he well deserved. God damn you! And you know it!"

Tracy was just as upset. "Shit! Don't you think I know it? I'm not that insensitive. But the fuckhead made one mistake too many! He's not a POW/MIA-- he's a deserter and a traitor!

Modini rolled his eyes. "Oh, here it goes!"

Tracy didn't flinch as he continued. "Not only is he a murderer, not only did he deal drugs in Nam, but here in our U.S. of A. How do you think he's been making his money these last years-

- drugs alone? Fuck no, he's been selling state secrets and military information to the Soviets!"

Even Modini found that too extreme to believe. "The Soviets?"

"See what I mean," Tracy said abruptly. "You can't handle this. Now do you get my drift, Modini?"

Modini shuddered, "Your drift is beginning to stink! I don't believe what I'm hearing!"

"It's true! The evidence so airtight that--"

Modini cut in angrily, "Don't tell me, the CIA has been monitoring him all along, right?"

Tracy was again surprised by Modini's knowledge. "That's right, I don't know how you know and I don't care. The military's position-- *my* position-- is to set an example for the young new recruits who honor themselves as Marines. We can't have our young men and women thinking the worst, especially using Hunter as an example. The Marines only specialize in the best and finest of men, and no Karl Hunter will spoil or discredit his position as an officer in the United States Marine Corps or in any military institution! If war is inevitable, this country will need those young volunteers! Once a Marine always a Marine-- no backing out! Yes, I hate Hunter's guts and I don't deny that, but it's not up to me! Hunter will have a posthumous court-martial, stripped of everything connected with his career in the Marines-- and I'll be damned if I care what you think!"

Modini looked around the room. Tears had formed within the corners of his eyes as he faced Tracy with his calm response. "I can give you the names of two other people who were treated the same way as Hunter has since this all began, and I blame you alone for what you're doing, but what about Conny? Yes, I'm talking about Father Conrad! Do you believe or agree with what your people did to him.? He didn't hurt anyone! He was a Priest, for Christ's sake! He loved--!" The words choked in Modini's throat. "What the hell did Karl do to you, besides save your life? How in God's name did you get picked as judge and jury? Tell me this Colonel, how did a man you say traded secrets with the enemy have the time to rape and murder all those girls around the country, let alone all those in the State of Indiana? How many were there supposed to be-- twenty-three? And if all this is true as you say, then the CIA is an accessory after the fact and should be tried for treason and murder right along side of Hunter! I think, Colonel, you should suggest at this hearing that the Central Intelligence Agency surrender all monitoring equipment, tapes, video, photos-- everything pertaining to Karl Hunter, because I'm sure they have knowledge where all those missing girls are buried. You and whoever are behind all this are making a terrible mistake. And I'm telling you, Tracy, as a friend, both you and the military brass are wrong and will regret it when Hunter is proven innocent!"

Tracy had enough of Modini's speech and got up to depart, but not before he had the last word. "I stand by my own principles, Modini, and I have nothing to hide. I don't have to remind you, twelve men and women sitting on a jury have already convicted him." Tracy threw the morning newspaper down on the table in front of Modini. The front page read *"Jury responds to death of Hunter by giving their verdict-- Guilty!"*

John Modini was stunned by this front page article and looked again to Tracy, "I'd like to be there at the hearing, Tracy!"

Tracy shook his head. "No chance, Modini!"

"Why not! I have a right!"

Tracy looked at Modini's hand gripping his arm. "Your rights stopped when you quit the Marines a long time ago. It's a closed session, military personnel only. They won't let you in the room, let alone in the building! Besides, it'll be all over within a few hours. By then, you can read about it in the evening papers! Sorry, Modini, my hands are tied. I didn't ask to do this. I have my orders. Now, if you will excuse me, I have to be on my way." Tracy started to move off, then as an afterthought added, "Oh, about that phone number of yours-- I'm still having it checked out. Why were you so interested in this number? Why is it so important to you?"

Modini slumped down into his seat. Somehow it seems as if it weren't important anymore. He just responded to Tracy with, "All I can say for the present, is that the person connected with this number may be in danger!"

Tracy thought it over. "Check your message box late this afternoon," he told Modini, "I may have some info for you then. You're staying at the Friendly Inn, right?"

Modini was surprised, "Yes, but how did--"

Tracy grinned as if he were letting him in on a secret. "You're being watched Modini. Don't ask me who or why, 'cause I don't know, but they are watching me, too! To be on the safe side, unless you hear the word 'Hamlet,' don't try to contact me. You remember, 'Operation Hamlet,' don't you, Corporal Modini? Don't forget, you *knew*! And you're in this just as deep as I am... So I'd be careful if I were you!"

Modini didn't say a word, only stared after Tracy as he exited. Modini squeezed his eyes shut as a flashback shook him. He remembered images of a village burning. He saw himself screaming and yelling, but to no avail. Another memory flash: two men in uniform shouting to each other at a Vietnam air base. Their mouths moved, but nothing was heard because of the sound of the aircraft engines starting up next to them. The two men were Hunter and Modini.

Chapter Sixteen

"Double Trouble"

From top of the National Airport Parking Facilities in D.C., a man peered down at three people through a pair of powerful binoculars. Catherine Rogers and her father, Judge Kencade, prepared to board their plane on the airfield and exchanged goodbyes with their colleague, Birmbaum. He seemed happy with their parting and kissed Catherine on the cheek.

The view through the binoculars followed Catherine and Kencade as they headed for their airliner. A fourth man approached Birmbaum on the field with a manila envelope in his hand. Birmbaum pointed, directing him toward the two walking to their plane. The young man raced after them. The binoculars picked him up at the bottom of the staircase leading up to the aircraft entrance. The young man handed Catherine the manila envelope.

At the staircase, Kencade boarded as Catherine received an explanation by the young man. "Mrs. Rogers, I'm the researcher you hired from the law office through Birmbaum. This is the material you asked for. It concerns the background and death of Naval Commander William Bruce Pitzer. The real interesting part is something I never knew. This man Pitzer actually filmed President Kennedy's autopsy on 16 mm film the night of the assassination, November twenty-second. Can you imagine that? They actually have a film on that?"

"No, I can't!" She was shocked by this revelation, but managed to smile at the young man and thanks him again. She climbed the stairs to the plane's entrance.

The man on top of the parking facilities with the binoculars disappeared as Catherine entered the plane.

The airplane became northwest bound, and once in flight, Catherine studied the material provided for her. She read the headline from a November 1966 newspaper:

"Comdr. William B. Pitzer Head of Navy TV Unit Found Dead. Pitzer, a 40-year old assistant head of the Graphics Art Department and Chief of the Educational Television Division of Naval Medical School died unexpectedly in his office at Bethesda Naval Hospital. In an apparent suicide, prior to his retirement, Pitzer shot himself. A bullet hole was in the right temple of his head."

Catherine read on as the researcher added, *"A coincidence followed which may have had some bearing on Pitzer's death. On November fifth, 1966, two things changed radically which appeared in the newspapers throughout the country. President Johnson announced there would be no more committees formed, nor any additional investigations into the death of JFK, and that neither the public nor anyone else would never view the autopsy reports or photos of Kennedy. The coincidence was that Pitzer had photographed and filmed the autopsy of Kennedy at Bethesda Hospital on 16 mm film during the evening of November twenty-second, 1963. The second item in the newspaper that day was the reemergence of former Vice-President Richard Nixon back into the political arena to help campaign for the members of the Republican Party, and to voice his concern against President Johnson and the Vietnam war."*

Catherine felt confused and upset. She stared quietly out her window, then turned to look at her father sitting beside her. Kencade was also very quiet and kept very much to himself. She studied him a bit, trying in her own way to understand what happened today in the courtroom. Though her sympathy for him was easy for him to detect, Kencade turned briefly to her and gave her a look and a smile as if to say, nothing was wrong and everything would be all right.

On Independence Avenue, John Modini lifted a newspaper out of its rack at a magazine stand. The headline read: *"War Hero SOLD Military Secrets to KGB."*

Modini grasped the newspaper in anger as he read on: *"Congressional hearing confirmed today Karl Hunter, a Vietnam war hero awarded the distinguished Medal of Honor, sold top secret information to the Soviets for the past ten years. Hunter, the recently accused serial murderer, had been charged with killing over twenty-five young girls, and was possibly responsible for the*

disappearance of others not yet found."

Modini remembered a Saigon airfield in the year 1969. Hunter conversed with him over the noisy engine of the aircraft next to them. Modini looked beyond Karl Hunter and watched as black vinyl body bags were loaded aboard the aircraft stenciled "Air America."

Modini suddenly felt himself break out in a nervous sweat. The flashback lasted only a split second, but it affected him strongly.

As he arrived at the Friendship Inn, he stopped at the front desk and asked whether there were any messages.

The desk clerk responded, "Yes, one came just a few minutes ago from a...Richard Franklin. He only said he'd call you back."

"Thanks," Modini told him. "I'll be in my room."

Later, Modini checked out the material Franklin gave him at the National Archives. He started to read the full, now declassified top secret memorandum No. 273 report of November 26, 1963, written by McGeorge Bundy, Department of State and NSC files.

Modini's lips deciphered 'NSC,' National Security Council from the headline of 'The White House.' Modini read the memorandum through:

The President (Johnson) has reviewed the discussions of South Vietnam which occurred in Honolulu, and has discussed the matter further with Ambassador Lodge. He directed the following guidance be issued to all concerned:

1. It remains the central object of the United States in South Vietnam to assist the people and government of that country to win their contest against the externally directed and supported communist conspiracy. The test of all U.S. decisions and actions in this area should be the effectiveness of their contribution to this purpose.

2. The objectives of the United States with respect to the withdrawal of U.S. military personnel remain as stated in the White House statement of October 2, 1963.

3. It is a major interest of the United States Government that the present Provisional Government of South Vietnam should be assisted in consolidating itself and in holding and developing increased public support. All U.S. officers should conduct themselves with this objective in view.

4. The President (Johnson) expects that all senior officers of the government will move energetically to insure the full unity of support for established U.S. Policy in South Vietnam. Both in Washington and in the field, it is essential that the government be unified. It is of particular importance that express or implied criticism of officers of other branches be scrupulously avoided in all contacts with the Vietnamese Government and with the press. More specifically, the President (Johnson) approves the following lines of

action developed in the discussions of the Honolulu meeting of November 20.
The offices of the government to which central responsibility is assigned are
indicated in each case.

5. We should concentrate our own efforts, and insofar as possible we
should persuade the government of South Vietnam to concentrate its efforts on
the critical situation in the Mekong Delta. This concentration should include not
only military but political, economic, social, educational, and informational
effort. We should seek to turn the tide not only of battle but of belief, and we
should seek to increase not only the control of hamlets but the productivity of
this area, especially where the proceeds can be held for the advantage of anti-
Communist forces. (Action: The whole country team under the direct
supervision of the Ambassador.)"

Modini reread Part 5, where it said: "*..and we should seek to increase not only the control*
of hamlets..." A sudden flash of a fire explosion tore through to Modini's mind as he read this,
"*but the productivity of this area--*" He stopped abruptly, as in his memory a whole village
exploded into fire and began burning around him. Modini screamed out during this sudden
flashback as the vision of mushrooming fireballs soared into the skies, blackening the air...

Modini caught his breath and was sweating again. He slowly lay back down on his bed. He
forced the ugly images from his mind and tried to concentrate on a more serene time during his
tour of duty. He pulled away a row of stringed beads in long strands from a doorway and recalled
the beautiful Vietnamese girl appearing naked in front of him. But he couldn't rid himself of the
series of haunting images.

Modini shook his head on his bed pillow as tears started, but he made himself sit up and
pick up the memorandum report again. After a few moments he compelled himself to read on:

"6. Programs of military and economic assistance should be maintained at such levels that their magnitude and effectiveness in the eyes of the Vietnamese Government do not fall below levels sustained by the United States in the time of the Diem Government. This does not exclude arrangements for economy on the MAP account with respect to accounting for ammunition, or any other readjustments which are possible as between MAP and other U.S. defense resources. Special attention should be given to the expansion of the import, distribution, and effective use of fertilizer for the Delta. (Action: AID and DOD as appropriate.)

7. Planning should include different levels of possible increased activity, and in each instance there should be estimates of each factor as:

A. Resulting damage to North Vietnam;
B. The plausibility of denial;
C. Possible North Vietnamese retaliation;
D. Other international reaction.

Plans should be submitted promptly for approval by higher authority. (Action: State, DOD, and CIA.)

8. With respect to Laos, a plan should be developed and submitted for approval by higher authority for military operations up to a line up to 50 kilometers inside Laos, together with political plans for minimizing the international hazards of such an enterprise. Since it is agreed that operational

responsibility for such undertakings should pass from CAS to MACV, this plan
should include a redefined method of political guidance for such operations,
since their timing and character can have an intimate relation to the fluctuating
situation in Laos. (Action: State, DOD, and CIA.)

9. It was agreed in Honolulu that the situation in Cambodia is of the
first importance for South Vietnam, and it is therefore, urgent that we should
lose no opportunity to exercise a favorable influence upon that country. In
particular, a plan should be developed using all available evidence and
methods of persuasion for showing the Cambodians that the recent charges
against us are groundless. (Action: State.)

10. In connection with paragraphs 7 and 8 above, it is desired that we
should develop as strong and persuasive a case as possible to demonstrate to
the world the degree to which the Vietcong is controlled, sustained and
supplied from Hanoi, through Laos and other channels. In short, we need a
more contemporary version of the Jordan Report, as powerful and complete as
possible. (Action: Department of State with other agencies as necessary.)

signed by

McGeorge Bundy"

Each page was dated Nov. 26, 1963, of three pages and cc to: Mr. Bundy (his brother), Mr.
Forrestal, Mr. Johnson, and NSC Files.

Modini noticed a fourth page that accidentally stuck to these particular pages that had
nothing to do with this report. Modini tried to peel the fourth piece of paper from the others without
tearing it, and, working slowly, he succeeded.

It was a memo to J. Edgar Hoover on FBI stationary dated January 30, 1960, stating someone in Miami, Florida, used identification cards, military and civil, to acquisition jeeps and trucks for secret covert training and maneuvers with a group of anti-Castro Cubans.

The problem here, the agent pointed out to the director of the FBI, was the identity of the man whose credentials this official was using to acquire these vehicles for military reasons. They belong to a marine by the name of Lee Harvey Oswald who happened to be on the defection list and was supposed to be in Moscow, Russia, as of this date.

Modini stared at this memo, stunned, but not surprised any more as he realized Lee Harvey Oswald wasn't the man who he was supposed to be any more. In fact, maybe, just maybe, there was more than one Oswald running around out there twenty-eight years ago. He stuck the archive material back in his bag as his room phone rang, startling him. The front desk informed Modini a man in military attire requested his presence.

Modini threw on his clothes and approached the front desk. A heavyset lady came from the back office. "What can I do for you," she asked.

Before he can speak up, a man's voice behind Modini interrupted. "Sir, excuse me, are you John Modini?"

He turned around to find a husky looking well-built gentleman in a marine uniform, standing before him who repeated, "Are you John Modini?"

Modini looked at him for a moment before responding, not knowing what to expect. "At one time, it was Corporal Modini of The Marine infantry. Yes...what can I do for you?"

The Marine saluted him, "I have a car outside, I've been asked to escort you to Colonel Roger Tracy, sir!"

"Why isn't he here to meet me, himself?" Modini questioned.

The Marine responded with his orders. "I was assigned to drive you to Andrews Air Force Base. And if you refused or were suspicious, sir, I was to mention the word...*Hamlet!*"

* * *

The law office of Michael Bradley in Madison, Indiana, seemed quiet and deserted as Catherine entered from the lobby. Her briefcase was in one hand and a newspaper in her other. She had been reading the scandalous articles about Karl Hunter.

On her way in, Sherry Keller, her receptionist, asked, "Mrs. Rogers, is there anything wrong?"

Catherine didn't respond. She waved the newspaper, showing the contempt of what she had been reading as she headed down the corridor to Bradley's office.

Once inside, she closed the door behind her and walked behind his mahogany desk that filled most of the room. At one end of the desk sat a statuette of justice, the woman holding the balance scales of the law in her hands.

Catherine threw her newspaper and briefcase on the desk and glared at the statuette. It seemed to be mocking her. With one angry gesture, she wiped it off the desk and onto the floor.

She slumped into Bradley's dark brown leather chair with disbelief regarding the despicable reports she had read. Her head fell into her arms on the desk, as if in defeat, and she started to sob to herself.

A few moments passed when suddenly, but slowly, Catherine's head rose up out of her arms and off the desk to see a file in front of her. The file had John Modini's name on it and there was a paper clipped to it.

She took a tissue from a drawer at the bottom of the desk, blew her nose, and wiped her tears away. Then she examined the note. It was a biography from Michael Bradley's researcher describing the life of John Modini. She opened up the file and found two different profiles, neatly typed. One concentrated on Modini's life from his birth through his Vietnam years, and the other on his career as a Photojournalist with *Time-Life Magazine*. A few of his photos and originally published articles were included.

She leafed through the file quickly, checking out the photos and then started at the beginning of the first profile. She leaned back in the chair, now relaxed, and started to read.

* * *

Meanwhile, the car holding John Modini arrived at Andrews Air Force Base in Maryland. The Marine driver received clearance from another marine guard at the gate and drove onto the facility. John Modini, sat in the back seat and shook his head, wondering what was going on here. When the car passed the main group of buildings, It took a sharp turn and headed to the airfield.

The car drove to the midfield tarmac, where Modini saw the Air Force II aircraft, ready for take off. "I don't get it. Where is Colonel Tracy?" he asked the driver.

The Marine continued to drive right up to the plane, "Sir...my orders were to drive you to the plane and see you board her. That is all!"

Modini looked up at the name, Air Force II, on the side of the aircraft. An expression of surprise tinged with disbelief appeared on his face.

* * *

John Modini had a wide grin on his face. It was a picture of him in a photograph Catherine held in her hand. Modini stood posed in a group photo of his 1st Battalion 10th Marine Division, Second Platoon. Next to him, with his arm around him, was Karl Hunter. Also present in the platoon photo were Daniel "Conny" Conrad, Alex Contos, platoon sergeant, and Corporal Roger Tracy. Their names were listed on the photo among the then twelve remaining members of the unit at the time of photograph.

A note added to this read: "Of the twelve members, three remain alive as the last survivors of this battalion stateside, as of this year, 1988." The three men circled in the photo were Hunter, Tracy, and Modini.

Catherine briefly remembered back to that day in the courtroom, and realized now the unshaven man in dark sunglasses seated in the courtroom might have been John Modini.

182

She continued to read the note concerning the surviving members of the platoon, as it revealed "...two died in Vietnam, after the war in trying to rescue POW/MIA's, and the others died stateside in the last ten years, either by natural causes, or suicide. Most recently, Father Daniel Conrad took his life by throwing himself to his death from a New Hampshire bridge one winter night in early March of '82."

Catherine was stunned, repeating the name, "Father Conrad?" She was surprised not only that was he a priest, but a priest of the Catholic Church who committed suicide!

Catherine continued to turn pages in the file. While reading on, she discovered: "...Modini's photography and journalistic talent concerning his Vietnam stint, and his passion, and sensitivity he put into his work helped gain him stature and earned him respect within the magazine communities with articles and periodicals appearing in Reader's Digest, Playboy, Esquire, and several others including *Life Magazine*, until its demise in 1973.

"Here in photographs, Modini's pictures speak out, without words, describing what our soldiers were experiencing and feeling during the Vietnam war. His articles expressed the controversy stemming from his continued harassment of the critics and the conspiracy theories about the assassination of John F. Kennedy. Modini supported the Warren Report and disputed any other theories involving the FBI, the CIA, the armed forces, the Pentagon, the Secret Service, the Mafia, the doctors both in Parkland and Bethesda, Earl Warren and members of his Commission, the press and Jim Garrison.

"Jim Garrison, as New Orleans district attorney, created the godfather of all conspiracy theories, staged an assassination investigation involving recklessness, cruelty, abuse of power, publicity-mongering, and dishonesty, all on a scale strongly suggesting lunacy leavened by cynicism.

"Though today, as Modini looks back at the Garrison years, he wrote as if he came to admire this man, a man who stands tall despite all the ridicule and abuse the government bestowed on him to this day. And why he asked, should a government do this to a man who still works for the same government as a federal judge in New Orleans? Modini's own belief stuck close to the Warren Commission's conclusions that a crazed Lee Harvey Oswald was the lone assassin. He ridiculed all such committees on the assassination including the Senate and the House Select in the mid and late 1970's as pure hype and sensationalism.

"His disputes continued in the 1980's over the controversy in opening the grave of Lee Harvey Oswald. The story charging Oswald had a double identity, was soon laid to rest. A theory put forward by British author, Michael Eddowes, stated Oswald was actually a Soviet KGB agent on a mission to kill the President! Like Modini predicted, the body exhumed was verified as Lee Harvey Oswald!"

Catherine looked at several more pages. She noticed a newspaper clipping of an article written by the Catholic Diocese describing the investigation in the death of fellow soldier and friend, Father Daniel Conrad. The article described how, with the assistance of journalist John Modini, they discovered Father Conrad committed suicide to protect the Church of accusations spread throughout the newspapers suggesting Conrad in past years had molested countless number of alter boys within the church.

"With the help of Mr. Modini, three years after Father Conrad's death, he was exonerated of all charges. It was hinted someone, or some fraction within the government apparently was involved in framing Father Conrad to keep him from voicing his passionate opinions about the POW/MIA issue."

Catherine was astounded, "My God!" she thought to herself.

An added notation from the researcher revealed more: "It is here where Mr. Modini changed his opinion concerning the views of his own government. He took a one-hundred eighty-degree turn in his thinking. It deliberately appeared as if someone planted false information to destroy Daniel Conrad, a very respected and loved priest in the Diocese. And It was convenient for that same someone to use the rising statistic of molestation within the Catholic Church to frame the man. In addition, it was odd most of Modini's military unit all died in the states. Now, with Karl

Hunter's suicide, this meant only two people were left alive. One is Roger Tracy, a Colonel at the Pentagon, working with Navel Intelligence. The other is John Modini who disappeared this past year. His present whereabouts is unknown. The question now is if John Modini is still with us? Good luck on what you discover." The report was signed by Phillip McCord, the researcher hired by Bradley.

Catherine pondered this information. She looked at the wild smile on Karl Hunter's face in the platoon photo, then compared it to the present day newspaper photo. She Studied Modini's photo, then pressed the intercom button. "Sherry?"

Sherry's voice came over the intercom. "Yes, Mrs. Rogers!"

"Would you try to locate a John Modini?" Catherine asked. "He might be a bit difficult to find but try *Time-Life Magazine*. He was also in D.C. yesterday. Maybe his editor knows what hotel he's staying at. If you get a chance, tell Michael it's important we find him quickly. I'd like to set up a meeting with him. I'll be leaving momentarily. I'm late for my appointment with Mr. Ziegler at the hospital. I'll see Michael between five-thirty and six." Catherine focused on Modini with Hunter's arm around him in the platoon photo, and then her eyes swung to Roger Tracy on Modini's other side.

* * *

John Modini relaxed in comfort in the plush seat of the historical aircraft, Air Force II, as it waited to take off. He passed the time by reading the spy story scandal headlining the newspaper. It featured a prominent picture of Karl Hunter. Overhead, he heard a familiar voice interrupt his concentration.

"May I get you a drink, sir?"

Modini looked up from his newspaper, surprised at the stewardess in front of him. "Micheline?"

The stewardess seemed embarrassed, "Excuse me, sir?"

"Micheline?" Modini called to her again, puzzled at her reply.

"I'm sorry, sir..." the stewardess responded, "I believe you're mistaken. My name is Francine...Francine Baker, and I would like to welcome you aboard Air Force II!"

"I don't get it?" he challenged, "Is this a joke? You're putting me on, aren't you, Micheline?"

The stewardess who called herself Francine continued her business and just smiled. "May I offer you a drink, Mr. Modini?"

Modini was very concerned now. He knew he couldn't be mistaken. "This isn't funny..." he told the woman. "Where are we going? At least you can tell me our destination?"

The stewardess who called herself Francine made an effort to be as polite. "I'm sorry, sir, I'm not allowed to say. Security reasons!"

Modini slapped his knees with both hands in a futile gesture. He made no attempt to mask his anger. "Tell me this, Micheline-- or if you want to be called Francine-- am I being kidnapped?"

Francine smiled, "Nonsense, this is Air Force Two, sir. You weren't smuggled aboard in a duffel bag. You came aboard on your own accord."

"Then why all the secrecy?" Modini asked.

"No secrecy, Mr. Modini." Francine answered courteously, "you'll find out in due time..."

Modini resented the fact he wasn't getting any straight answers. He changed the subject. "What about last night...or are you going to tell me that was your twin sister who told me I was her fuck of a lifetime?"

Francine stopped and gave him a severe look. "Please, Mr. Modini, don't make a scene. I can only offer you a drink. If not, please excuse me!" She went down the aisle without another word.

He impulsively called out to her retreating figure, "Sure, why not, make it Bourbon-- no, two bourbons, straight!" He turned to look out the window into the darkening sky. He didn't know what game they were playing with him and felt annoyed and angry.

A half hour later Air Force II was in flight, northwest bound, flying through a group of billowing clouds. Inside the plane, Francine returned to serve Modini's two drinks to him.

"What, no olives?" he added some sarcasm as he picked up the first drink. "No little sliced lime on the side?" He stared coldly at her as he grabbed up the second drink, and, in one gulp, put it down.

He grabbed the other drink and down it also, but before it reached his mouth, his vision suddenly became blurred. He blinked a couple times but couldn't focus on Francine. His drink slipped from his fingers and dropped to the floor of the plane.

Modini made a desperate grab for the stewardesses' arm, but his fingers wouldn't work properly. "What! Is this...what did you do?" His grip loosened from her; his hand became limp.

Francine leaned down until she was head to head with him and apologized. "I'm sorry..."

"Why?" was the last word Modini said before his body became limp and he passed out.

* * *

Senator Fuller was busy at his desk when he received the word Judge Henry Kencade waited in the outer office, wishing to speak with him. "All right, send him in..." he said to his secretary on the intercom

The door to his office suddenly burst open and Judge Henry Kencade marched in, newspaper in hand. Fuller smiled but didn't rise to greet him, "Hank!"

The first thing Judge Henry Kencade saw when he entered Senator Fuller's office was an oversized window behind his desk showing an incredible view of Indianapolis, Indiana. Historical memorabilia and museum quality collectables filled most of the office, in prominently displayed tables and walls. They were assorted antiques and collectables to remind Fuller's guests of our founding fathers who helped create this country and make America what it is today.

Surrounding the room on three walls of his office, set in expensive golden frames, were the copies of historical texts, the rules and laws under which this country was governed. The Constitution of the United States, The Declaration of Independence, and Lincoln's 'Gettysburg Address' centered on a third wall accompanied by pictures of Lincoln. Other important United States President's pictures were displayed as well: Eisenhower, Nixon, Ford, and Reagan. A small picture frame sat on Fuller's desk with a group shot of his wife, Caroline and Fuller standing with Barbara and George Bush.

Kencade didn't spare any pleasantries and got right to the point, "Don't Hank me, you son of a bitch! What do you mean by not taking my calls!" He threw the newspaper down on the desk. It contained the latest article concerning Karl Hunter's involvement in the spy scandal. "What's with this?"

Fuller, spread his hands innocently. "I don't know what you mean, Hank. Really, I don't!"

"Stop the innocent crap, Gerald!" Kencade erupted. "Did you have anything to do with threatening Catherine's life?"

Fuller narrowed his eyes with concern. "Really, Henry, you're not serious, you know how I feel about Catherine. Has something happened to her?"

"Not yet," Kencade said, his anger lessening, "But believe me, you'll be the first to know...I'll guarantee that!"

Fuller stood and came around the desk to try to comfort his friend. "Now, now... So tell me...what has happened?"

As Fuller put his hand on Kencade's shoulder, Kencade moved away from him. "*No*, you tell *me*! Why am I being set up? And what does Karl Hunter have to do with the Soviets and JFK's murder?"

Fuller's eyes flashed with surprise. "Say, where did you ever hear of such a cornball idea as that? It seems to me, Hunter wasn't more than what-- thirteen years old when Kennedy died. I think you better see someone about these sudden bursts of fantasy, before you start spreading stories like this. People will think you're nuts!"

"There's a tape," Kencade said coolly, interrupting Fuller. "There's a tape, Gerry. Hunter made a tape before he turned himself in. I agree. As you say, it sounds ridiculous, but why did he send it to *me*. But why *after* his death, not before? Don't you think that's odd for him to do that-- and then commit suicide?"

Fuller sighed and confronted his friend face to face. "No, Henry, I don't. He was a nut case from the beginning! You read the papers. I'm as baffled as you are. Besides, who cares if Hunter is dead? He's sealed his own fate for good now. There's nothing left to worry about. Don't you see, you're a hero now? Let it go!"

"I don't want to let it go, Gerry! I want to know the truth, you son of a bitch! My daughter is in danger! Why am I being threatened concerning her activities? *Why*, dammit!"

Fuller tried to calm Kencade. "Henry, please... I don't know," he pleaded. "And believe me, I don't want to know because there's nothing you or I can do about it now! Everything has been taken care of. It's out of our hands, now!"

Kencade stared at him with a frightened look on his face. The reality of Fuller's words finally sank in.

* * *

First, it looked as if a dot sped westward across the flatlands somewhere in Montana State, but from a bird's-eye view overhead, the object was clear. It was actually a gray military car driving along a back road where no signs of civilization could be seen for miles.

Inside the car, in the back seat, Modini awakened from a deep sleep by the shaking of the car hitting the numerous ruts and bumps in the road. Dazed and tired, he sat up straight and looked out the window at his surroundings. What he saw didn't tell him much. Modini didn't say anything, nor did the military officer sitting next to him. He noticed Francine staring at him in the rearview mirror. She was the driver behind the wheel, taking him to his mysterious destination.

At three-thirty central time, in Madison, Indiana, Catherine drove her Honda through the entrance of Glen Ridge Psychiatric and Convalescent Hospital.

She entered the hospital administration office and introduced herself to the head matron, Miss Maxine Hightower. The woman was tall, broad shouldered, with a gracious smile, one who seemed pleased to meet Catherine.

"Ah, we were expecting you, Mrs. Rogers."

"Has Mr. Ziegler arrived yet? I was supposed to meet him here."

Miss Hightower shook her head. "No, I'm sorry. Was he supposed to be here today? Today is not his usual...though I have been instructed to allow you to see Carrie alone. If you'll follow me..." Miss Hightower proceeded to escort Catherine down the corridor.

"I hope this meeting with Carrie will do her some good," Miss Hightower said. "But I don't mind telling you I think nothing may come of it." They finally stopped at a room small enough for a single occupant

Catherine peered into the room through the glass-paneled door. She saw a young girl who appeared to be a mix of half American and half-Vietnamese, staring out her bedside window.

So this is Ziegler's thirteen-year old daughter, Catherine thought to herself. *How pretty and attractive she is.*

The head matron cleared her throat. "I know what you're going to say. Why isn't she in with other children her age? And my professional answer is she won't get along with anyone. Sometimes she throws violent fits and tantrums, and other times--" she allowed her sentence to trail away. "Carrie hasn't spoken one word since she was admitted over six months ago!"

Miss Hightower took out a set of keys and unlocked the door. The women entered the room and quietly approached Carrie, still staring out the window. Miss Hightower whispered to Catherine, "Most of the time we find her at the window-- from the time she wakes up until the time we put her to bed. We think she's waiting for somebody, but God knows who!"

"What about her father?" Catherine asked.

Miss Hightower gave her an odd look. "I'm sorry, Mrs. Rogers, but I'm not allowed to discuss anything concerning her father. My instructions were to allow you access to the girl." Miss Hightower moved closer to get Carrie's attention. "Carrie? There is someone here to see you. A nice lady is here. Her name is Catherine Rogers.

Carrie didn't respond to the head matron's voice. She kept her back to them.

"Can I have a few minutes alone with her?" Catherine asked.

"Just for a few minutes," the head matron said. She glanced at Carrie, debating a moment whether it was a good idea to leave them alone, then left the room.

Catherine watched the door close behind her before facing the young girl. She moved in closer and sat down on her bed. Carrie stood several feet away at the window.

"I hope you don't mind my sitting on your bed," Catherine began gently. She tried to make her voice sound sincere and trustful. "I won't if you don't want me to!"

Carrie didn't move or respond to her words so Catherine continued. "Are you looking at something particular, or maybe waiting for someone? Your daddy hasn't arrived yet. He asked me to see you. He was supposed to meet us here."

Carrie was silent and stared out the window. Catherine became worried when she failed to make any progress with the girl. Carrie's eyes focused out the window as though she had tunnel vision, but there was a small indication she heard the sound of Catherine's voice. Catherine saw her head turn slightly at some of the questions and felt better. At least it's a start, she thought to herself.

* * *

John Modini saw the large military sign as he looked out the window of the government car as it drove across the flatlands. It said 'Government Property. No Trespassing.'

The sign was placed to the side of an entrance way gate. Francine drove up to the padlocked gate and stopped. The Marine officer inside got out and unlocked the gate, swinging it wide open.

There was nothing beyond the fence, just a road, and a wide, empty piece of land that surrounded them, before and after the gate. There was no movement, no sign of life around at all.

Inside the car, alone with Francine, Modini thought he could turn the conversation to his favor. "Okay, Francine, or whoever you are. What kind of game is this? What's going on?"

Francine's eyes flickered from the officer to Modini in her rear view mirror. "Mr. Modini, please keep quiet! Don't talk!"

"You are...Micheline, aren't you?" Modini persisted.

The officer motioned for Francine to continue through. When she did, the officer proceeded to lock the gate and entered the car again. They drove on.

The government car drove down the road on isolated government land for the next three miles, until they reached their destination, a military depot surrounded by a fence with an armed marine guard standing at attention. The guard recognized the card shown to him by the officer in the car, and looked into the vehicle at the three of them. The Marine gave clearance for the car to pass through.

Once the car passed the fence, it entered an area dotted with aluminum quonset huts on either side of a main thoroughfare. The government vehicle stopped at one that read 'Mess Hall.'

"All right, sir," the soldier turned to Modini. "This is where you get out." The soldier got out of the car and held the door open for him.

Francine watched Modini exit from the car through the rearview mirror.

"And what happens here, may I ask?" Modini replied sarcastically. He glanced up at the hut. "Do we all go inside, sit down together and have a nice lunch?"

"Colonel Tracy will fill you in on any necessary info. I'm just the delivery boy, sir!"

As the soldier closed the car door, Francine drove away. The soldier opened the door to the quonset hut and gestured Modini inside.

Modini was escorted through the Mess Hall and into another room in the back of the building, a much smaller one with furnishings that included a cot and a toilet.

Modini examined the lower quality bedroom arrangements and felt he was going further downward in status when it came to accommodations, especially in the past few weeks. "Kind of like the YMCA of the Army, huh?" Modini remarked to his personal guard.

The soldier didn't smile, but continued with his tour. "Sir, this is where you'll stay until further notice. If you are hungry, the mess hall will provide you with the day's menu. A guard will be posted outside your room at all times."

Modini raised his eyebrows questioningly, "Am I a prisoner here?

For the first time, the soldier cracked a smile. "Sir, this is a top secret base! Any civilian caught on its premises without clearance and escort will be shot! Is that clear enough for you, sir?" And then the soldier added, "It's for your own protection, sir."

* * *

With Carrie as her focus, Catherine moved off the bed and slowly approached the thirteen-year old girl, still standing at the window. After spending the past few minutes giving a Reader's Digest biography of herself, Catherine decided to take the risk and try to face her.

Carrie stood immobile, gazing out the window, trying hard to ignore the woman behind her.

As Catherine moved around to the girl's side, her eyes made momentary contact, then Carrie retreated a step, startled. She grasped for a locket secured around her neck, as if it were something dear, something she was afraid would be taken away.

Catherine could see how frightened Carrie was. "Why, sweetheart, you don't have to be afraid," she spoke soothingly to the girl, her eyes smiling. "I'm not going to take a locket from such a pretty girl." She quickly changed the subject. "Say, you must be from Cambodia. You're not Vietnamese at all, are you?"

Carrie actually made eye contact with her as if to say she was right, then looked down.

Catherine continued, "Now, I have to tell you why your father asked me to see you. I'm a defense attorney. I knew the man who your father said...hurt you."

Although still ignored, Catherine stuck with her questioning, trying to treat Carrie with as much respect as possible for a girl her age. "I defended this man because I felt he wasn't getting a fair trial-- although many people would disagree, like your father, because the system found him guilty."

When Catherine mentioned the word 'father,' Carrie's eyes flickered, then returned to the window again.

"I say this, Carrie, because I believe every man deserves a fair trial, no matter whom they are." Catherine could not help think of her father. "Believe me, I should know. I used to be on the other side. I was a staunch prosecutor, and I went after every criminal like a lioness on the prowl, protecting her cubs-- the cubs being the law-abiding citizens of Seattle, Washington. Then one day I realized I became too good for myself. I discovered I'd do almost anything to get a conviction. It became an addiction to me, like a drug."

Catherine lowered her voice. Her emotions came too close to the surface. "But one day, Carrie, I went too far. I convicted a man suspected of being a serial killer who was probably just as bad as your rapist. But this time I was wrong. I made a big mistake, and the wrong man got the death penalty. A few days after he was put to death we had enough evidence to prove he was innocent. And to this day I've never forgiven myself. So, you see, Carrie, I also want what's best for you. And this person who did these awful things to you, deserves to be put away or surely given a death sentence.

"I'm here to help you, Carrie, but I'm also here because I'm still not sure about this man, Karl Hunter. I don't know whether he's this serial killer, or if he's innocent-- or if he's somewhere in between. There are many loose ends, yet I haven't been able to tie together. He's dead now, but I don't know whether it was suicide. Did he take his life or was he killed by someone else? I need for you to tell me what happened to you. I have to hear it from you because I can't let it rest. I want to know whether I'm responsible for an innocent man's death."

Catherine didn't know if what she said was getting through to the girl. "I'm asking you for help, Carrie. Maybe you can help me out with this and we...sort of...can help each other in the process. Will you help me? Please?"

There was still no reaction from Carrie. Catherine sighed and moved back to give the girl some room. "Carrie...if it matters at all, I want you to know this man, Karl Hunter, is dead! So, if he is the man who raped you, he can't hurt you or anyone else anymore."

Catherine stopped behind Carrie as she finished. Carrie's head was bowed. Catherine tilted her head slightly. She saw the light reflecting off a tear next to Carrie's eye. Then she saw more tears sliding down her cheeks.

In the background, behind Catherine, a face peered through the glass window in the door.

Catherine was unaware of the person observing them. She raised her hand to touch Carrie's shoulder, but backed off, having second thoughts. She didn't want to startle the girl. She didn't know how Carrie would react.

Carrie must have sensed something. She deliberately turned around to face the woman. Catherine was on the verge of crying herself, but smiled, trying to restrain the tears. For the first time Carrie acknowledged her presence. They made eye contact and this time it held. And when Catherine saw the tears shining in the eyes of this innocent girl, her heart broke.

Catherine took the initiative and held her arms open. Carrie wavered, then took a small step forward. They went to embrace, when the face in the window distracted Carrie's attention.

It was only a brief moment the man's face appeared at the window in the door. His menacing eyes stared through the glass-panel, looking straight into Carrie's soul. It resembled the form and shape of the face belonging to Karl Hunter. Carrie's eyes widened with terror, and she screamed aloud.

Catherine was startled by the girl's cry, then realized she wasn't responsible for Carrie's reaction. She turned around to see what frightened the child and caught a glimpse of the man's face at the window. In one split second her heart caught in her throat. The face disappeared instantly, but there was no mistaking the features. The face belonged to Karl Hunter-- at least that was

Catherine's first impression, if her eyes weren't playing tricks on her.

Catherine was so stunned, for the first few seconds she was unaware of the screams of the young girl next to her. But Carrie's shrieks jarred Catherine back to reality.

Carrie backed into a corner and clutched her locket tightly to her chest as if it were a magic charm protecting her.

Catherine became frightened, not knowing what had gone wrong. She was torn between running to the door and staying to help the frightened girl.

"Carrie, Carrie, sweetheart, it's all right! I'm here with you," Catherine tried to calm Carrie, but to no avail. *If this girl saw her rapist, Karl Hunter, it was no wonder she became frantic! Karl Hunter is dead-- yet I know what I saw!* She pushed the thoughts from her mind and turned her attention to Carrie. "No one is there! No one can hurt you!" she tried to soothe the hysterical girl.

The door burst open and Miss Hightower rushed into the room, followed by a nurse carrying a hypodermic needle. The nurse paused, staring at the screaming girl.

"Give her the sedative! Now!" Miss Hightower instructed the nurse. Then the matron charged in and held the young girl as she continued to scream and fight her.

The nurse grabbed Carrie's arm and prepared to inject her. Catherine was overwhelmed at what was happening. "Is this really necessary?" she yelled out at the nurse.

The head matron struggled to hold Carrie down, "You better leave the room, Mrs. Rogers!" Miss Hightower ordered, "It won't do any good to interfere!" Catherine wavered. She wanted to stop this, but the matron was insistent. "Now! Mrs. Rogers, outside!" she shouted over Carrie's screams.

The nurse injected the hypodermic needle into Carrie as a shocked and confused Catherine bolted reluctantly from the room.

She waited in the hallway until the girl's screams died down and Miss Hightower emerged from the room. She gave the nurse instructions, then headed Catherine's way.

"Well, Mrs. Rogers?" Miss Hightower said to Catherine, as if expecting a challenge.

"Do you always use drugs and force on your young patients, Miss Hightower?" she shot back in a tremulous voice.

The head matron glared at Catherine, then spoke in clipped words. "I have something to show you, Mrs. Rogers. Follow me." She went past Catherine, heading to her office. Catherine followed. She wanted some answers.

Catherine glanced at the clock in Miss Hightower's office. It was after four-thirty.

"I want you to look at these..." Miss Hightower said, giving her an envelope containing photographs. "I think you'll understand why I do what I have to do." They were pictures taken of Carrie when she was first brought to the hospital six months earlier. The photos were graphic and showed the girl's severe injuries. They graphically showed how bad the young girl was brutalized and beaten and raped.

Catherine felt traumatized by these photos, but forced herself to look at them. Although she viewed many other photos like them in her occupation, these were sickening and turned her stomach. She never could get used to the brutality, and inhuman abuse of young children-- and she thought, never would.

Catherine handed the photos back to Miss Hightower. "I want to apologize for what I said earlier. I know it must have been difficult for Carrie when she first came to the hospital. It's just that I'm not used to seeing pictures like that...of someone still alive who survived such an ordeal."

Miss Hightower slipped the photos back into Carrie's medical file. "That's quite all right," Miss Hightower said, "no need to apologize. We're all used to it here. Most relatives of the patients here only see the worst of our duties. But I have to admit some of the cruelties come from the relatives themselves-- by not visiting their loved ones. Some stick them in here, then forget about them"

"Why do you think she went off like that?" Catherine asked curiously.

The matron put the folder back into a file cabinet and sat down at her desk. "I don't know. Sometimes it's caused by a simple gesture or a word in a sentence. What were you talking about when she went into her fit?"

Catherine shifted uneasily, then rose from her chair. She paced restlessly, as she did in Carrie's room. "Well...it wasn't so much of what I said to her as what her reaction was afterwards. She turned to me, and...I thought for a moment we were ready to connect. She had been crying. I didn't know why. All I could see was...this sweet innocent girl-- and then--"

"And then...what?"

Catherine was very specific as she recalled the scene, reconstructing the event. "Then her attention took a turn, her eyes shifted as if she saw someone else in the room with us, someone frightening to her. Then she screamed. My first reaction was to look to the door."

"Was there anyone there?"

"There was someone...at least I thought--" Catherine gestured broadly with her hand. "I think someone walked by the door-- I don't know..." That was as much as Catherine would tell Miss Hightower. If she told her of seeing a ghost or someone who looked like Karl Hunter, it could only make matters worse.

The head matron mulled it over and shook her head. "I certainly didn't see anyone in the hallway. And no one's allowed in that area of the hospital without authorization from me."

"All right," Catherine remarked, a little unconvinced, "But what about a doctor, or a male intern who may have passed by--"

Miss Hightower cut her off. "Possibly, but I doubt it. No male doctor on this staff will handle Carrie anymore-- she's bitten four of 'em, thus far. Besides, they'd all have to come through me first. No one is allowed in this section, unless I okay it!"

This made Catherine even more confused, "Even if it's Mr. Ziegler?" She sat down in her chair as the matron responded,

"Especially him!"

Catherine frowned in puzzlement. "I see!" she finally said, gathering up her purse. "I'd better be going now."

Miss Hightower walked her to the door. "I'm sorry your visit didn't turn out as well as you planned."

Catherine smiled. "I think I got off to a good start. Maybe I'll have a chance to see Carrie again."

Catherine left the hospital and started her Honda. She slowly circled the building, trying to see whether Carrie was still at her window.

Carrie was there, staring blankly out over the grounds in an almost comatose state. Catherine couldn't even tell whether Carrie was watching her or not.

Catherine headed to the hospital's front gate. As she pulled out onto the main road, another car moved into traffic behind her. The man who had been keeping tabs on Catherine recognized her car and continued to followed her. And Catherine Rogers didn't suspect a thing.

Chapter Seventeen

"The Home Away From Home"

John Modini had been lying on a cot in his room and dozed off. His dreams took him back to a rainy day in a Vietcong village. He was walking with Sergeant Contos and Private First-class Conrad, and Contos explained to him the Lieutenant wanted to speak with him about taking some photographs on their next mission.

The rain came down on them like bullets, hard and pounding. They finally reached their strategic headquarters established in the village.

Contos yelled over the noise of the rain, "The brass wants somebody, and I gave them your name 'cause you're into photography and they want somebody inside. We can't have Dan Rather or Walter Cronkite snooping around on this assignment, but we have to supply photographs, and I said you're our man!"

Modini glanced over to Daniel, lifting his eyebrows. They recognized this was an important meeting. Modini tilted upward into the sky, letting the rain hit his face hard...

Abruptly, Modini's thoughts changed. A beautiful naked Asian girl kissed him on the mouth and Modini awakened, startled from his dream.

He realized where he was and scurried off the cot. He checked his watch. It was already after 6:00 p.m.

Modini's first impulse was to open the door, and as expected, an armed marine with a rifle stood on guard duty. Nonchalantly, Modini addressed him, "Oh, hello. Are you my babysitter for the day?"

The Marine stared ahead at attention.

Modini tried again, "Is there a nice restaurant in the area to grab a bite to eat?" He waited for a reaction, but none came. "No? Then how about sneaking me a pizza, or a carrot to munch on-- anything... You see, I'm a little hungry. I get that way this time of the day. I was told--" Modini stopped. He was getting no reaction from this marine, and was ready to give it up when he noticed the watch on The Marine's arm. Modini didn't want to cause an incident here so he asked, "Do you mind? Can I at least know the time?"

The Marine checked the time and said, "1600 hours!"

Modini smiled, "So you do talk...congratulations! That's 4 p.m." Two marines suddenly appeared in this section of the building and approached them. One of them yelled out, "Attention!" causing Modini's guard to stand ridged.

One of the two marines was the officer who brought Modini into this compound. He approached Modini, "All right, sir, you can come with me, now!"

Modini, still in his sarcastic mood, mocked him, "Come with you now? Fine!"

The clock read 4:02 p.m. as Modini entered the base office of Colonel Roger Tracy. Roger greets him informally, then excused the soldier so they could be alone. The soldier saluted to his superior and closed the door behind him.

The two men left alone in the room, appraised each other without a word. The Colonel grinned, "We got to stop meeting like this, Corporal Modini!" He attempted to lighten the moment.

Modini didn't laugh or smile. "It's not funny, Roger. The fun's over. I'm not impressed with my accommodations, so what the hell is going on here?"

"All right! You want answers? Come with me, I'll show you."

Modini didn't know whether to believe him or not. He followed Tracy outside, onto the base. They walked across the barren ground comprised of a half-dozen quonset huts on this no-name military facility.

Modini surveyed the bleak and empty landscape as they headed down what could be laughingly called the main street. Tracy kept the momentum going, walking at a brisk gait. "Do you know where you are right now, Modini?"

Modini could only guess, "Well...I figured somewhere in the north United States, west but not too west. Maybe midwest, since we are now on mountain standard time and this is an isolated area. It's either North Dakota or Montana. My hunch is...Montana!"

Modini's answer impressed Tracy. "That's correct. You must have been very good in school. You studied your geography!" He sounded too patronizing. The line of shacks ended, and Tracy continued on, heading at a distance from the base down a dirt road into the no-man's land surrounding them.

Modini looked back at the buildings behind him and tried to keep up with Tracy's fast pace. "It wasn't my intention, but yes, I did well."

Tracy continued the game. "Then you know Montana is the third largest state in the country next to Texas and California, don't you?"

Modini played along to see where this was going, "I won't contest it! But then I wouldn't kick Alaska out of bed..."

Tracy grinned. "Very good! Here we have one of the largest states in the nation. Montana is also one of the top three least populated states as well."

"Fine! But what are you getting at, Colonel?" Modini was getting tired of this, let alone walking out to the middle of nowhere.

Tracy now abruptly stopped in his tracks and began examining the lay of the land. "And what do you think the United States military, the Air Force is doing here?"

Modini also came to a halt. There was nothing in front of him but barren land. The military base was a half mile behind them. "Maybe you have nuclear silos stationed in the area-- somewhere out here!" Modini ventured.

The Colonel faced Modini, and in a casual tone told him, "You're standing on one!"

Modini felt uncomfortable and foolishly moved off several steps, as though the ground would suddenly open directly beneath his feet.

Tracy laughed, getting the joke. "Oh, don't worry, this area is still under construction, but there are one hundred and fifty silos spread out-- scattered so to speak-- under this great state of Montana and on through North Dakota and Minnesota!"

They began walking again, and Tracy continued, "North Dakota holds twenty-five hundred nuclear warheads alone in this country. Quite a sum, wouldn't you say, 'Corporal' Modini?"

"Yeah, but it doesn't explain, why I'm here!"

Tracy shook his head, "Ah! Still playing that naive game of yours. Come on, Modini, why don't you grow up for once.!"

Modini confronted the Colonel. He was serious now. "No! *You* grow up, Tracy! Stop playing soldier for one minute and tell me what the fuck this is all about! Kidnapping is a capital offense, and in this army it's a court-martial! Why are you holding a possible gun to your head, bringing me here like this? It's as if I were one of your Vietcong prisoners? My God! Who do you think you are?"

Colonel Tracy had the upper hand then, and glared at Modini as though no civilian had the right to question his motives. Modini backed off a bit. But Modini was still determined to show he wasn't scared of the Colonel. "Are you going to tell me what's happening here, or what?"

Tracy advanced closer to Modini so he could stare him straight in the eyes. "Don't you get it by now, you idiot! It's not who I am or if it's about *me*, Modini! It's who *you* are and what fucking problems *you* are causing! You're walking a very thin line here, and that line has run its course!" Tracy calmed down slightly. "You're a dangerous man, Modini! From this moment on, there's a mine field set before you wherever you go. Are you following me, civilian!"

"I might have to 'follow' you, Colonel," Modini answered. "I don't know where those 'mine fields' are set!" He paused a moment, trying to control his frustration. "At least give me a hint of what the fuck you are talking about!"

Tracy stepped back, examining him with a doubtful eye, then decided to humor him. "What has Hunter told you so far?"

Modini was again thrown off the track. He couldn't follow Tracy's reasoning at all. "What has Hunter got to do with all this?" he asked perplexed.

Tracy exploded at him. "*What* did he tell you about the base?"

Modini looked at Tracy, as if he lost his mind. "Tracy, I-- I haven't spoken with Karl Hunter in over six years!"

Tracy now paced back and forth as if he were an animal prowling his perimeter. "Don't give me that shit. You were at the trial, we knew that! Everyone was checked out months ago...and now this phone number crap!"

Modini changed his strategy, this time switching to the offensive, instead of struggling to defend himself. "Of course I was at the trial, *so what*? Karl Hunter was my friend! I'm sure if Conny were alive today, he'd be there too! I don't see why--"

Tracy cut him off, fuming. "You son of a bitch, you still don't get it, do you.? What did I tell you back at the hotel? You are under surveillance! Why do you think they sent me for God's sake? You think for one minute it was just a coincidence I happened to run into you on that airplane?"

Modini was speechless. He took a deep breath and spoke calmly and rationally. "If you think you can drive me paranoid, it's not going to work! Now, for the last time, I don't know what you are talking about!"

Tense seconds passed. Tracy wasn't giving in.

Modini was hot and tired. "All right, don't believe me...have it your way," he said. Modini turned and walked back, heading in the direction of the base.

Tracy grabbed him and spun him around. "Don't play innocent with me, you fucking bastard! You knew all along! You knew where that phone number would lead!"

Modini made a considerable effort to suppress his anger. "I don't get you, Tracy? What's your involvement? It doesn't make sense! Okay, I admit, the phone number led me to Raleigh and to Naval Intelligence, but what does it have to do with all *this*? And how in the hell does Hunter fit in?" Modini tried to justify the connection between helping Miss Sweeney pursue the source of an old telephone number and the trial of Karl Hunter. He couldn't find the common factor between the two separate circumstances.

Tracy laughed at Modini's bewildered face. "Either you're playing stupid with me, Modini, or you're a Goddamn Laurence Olivier! Which is it? You're trying my patience!"

Modini raised his voice, "And you're trying mine, too! You want to know about this so-called phone number? An innocent woman who couldn't give a fuck about all this, was almost killed because of it-- and I'm trying to find out *why*!"

Tracy nodded and rubbed his jaw in thought. "Now...maybe that's the answer right there," Tracy said steadily, hoping Modini was getting the point, "Maybe it was a warning-- a warning to *you*, Modini!"

"You're making me think you're paranoid, Tracy! You're telling me, it's a warning, and I'm under surveillance-- for *what*? The number is over twenty-five years old, for Christ's sake! Do you know something else I don't? *What's* the big secret?"

"That's just it, Modini, you hit it right on the head!" Tracy felt a little more at ease now to explain. "There are certain people out there who need to keep it that way! Ever since you and I were kids there was always somebody out there trying to stop us from reaching our goals or getting ahead in life. It didn't matter if it were the football coach, or the rival stopping us from getting the girl of our dreams, or the man who beat us out of the job we always wanted, the one we knew was meant for us. It seemed like no man or woman who saw us struggling to get ahead wanted to see us make it. They were always trying to prevent us from reaching our goal. That's just part of the reality of life. It's *no* different *now* as adults, except it's more...dangerous!"

Tracy gestured to the base in the distance. "Take, for instance, the people behind this base. You've probably read somewhere the Air Force is planning to build a vast, deep underground Nuclear Missile Base somewhere in U.S. Well, the plan has been under great scientific study for some time now. It comes before Congress occasionally. But the problem is, we can't wait for the responses of these dickheads every time we need a bill passed for military security-- if you read what I mean, Modini. Then you have some idea of the predicament I'm in right now!"

The closer Modini listened, the more confused he became. One thing was for certain, though. Colonel Roger Tracy had some of the answers he wanted. And Modini would have to play the game to get them. The trouble was the situation was becoming more bizarre than he ever expected.

* * *

At ten minutes after five in the Law Office Building in Madison, Indiana, Michael Bradley compared his watch to the wall clock. He patiently waited for Catherine to arrive for her appointment. Catherine's car approached the building on schedule and entered the underground parking area. Another car followed her, keeping its distance.

As Catherine drove her Honda into a parking stall, the other car, passed by. She took only momentary notice of it as she exited her car. Removing her briefcase from the trunk, she crossed to the garage elevators and pushed the up button. It had been a long and hectic day, and Catherine wasn't feeling well. Her head was feverish, and beads of sweat formed upon her forehead.

Catherine took a tissue from her purse and wiped her brow. Suddenly, she stopped. She thought she heard a faint voice call her name. She wiped her face again uncertain if what she heard was real or not.

Just the same, Catherine glanced around. Standing right behind her was Mr. Joseph Ziegler.

He startled her. "Mr. Ziegler!" She gave a sigh of relief. "Why...I just came from the hospital, I waited for you. I saw your daughter, she--"

"I know, Mrs. Rogers," Ziegler spoke over her lines. "Would you just come with me, please! It's very important!"

"What is so important?" Catherine asked.

Ziegler was very agitated. "It's about that monster, Karl Hunter!"

* * *

Colonel Roger Tracy led John Modini to one of the quonset huts, and together they descended in an elevator deep inside the secret Missile Base in Montana.

"You brought me all the way to Montana to show me the Air Force and Naval Intelligence have an illegal underground nuclear missile base buried out here?" Modini's voice was tense.

Colonel Tracy remained silent. The elevator stopped at the bottom of the shaft and opened, revealing a main corridor leading into the underground base. "Not only that, this underground base provides what we call a *Secure Reserve Force* basing missiles deep underground, making it feasible both technically and militarily to survive a nuclear attack..."

The two men walked slowly through the underground base. He felt the cool breeze of air being circulated by hidden air conditioning systems. He saw a mess hall large enough to hold the House of Congress and the Senate, and bedrooms of one and two for the privileged few, and barracks for the masses.

"What's it all for?" Modini asked flippantly. "So that the high and mighty can come here secretly, huh? Nice of them to live off the taxpayer's money that financed this project, so they can survive a nuclear attack!"

Tracy led Modini past a glass enclosed control center. It looked like a war room, with military personnel sitting at computers and monitoring wall screens.

"This facility has the capability to launch intercontinental ballistic missiles," Tracy said, waving his hands proudly, expressing his joy at celebrating this underground fortress. "This base can be readied in two days for retaliatory strikes. We have placed one-hundred MX missiles in concrete silos sunk into the earth around us. One, mind you, we stood on upstairs."

"Splendid!" Modini said dryly.

Tracy didn't stop here. "There's only one catch though. Congress has put the MX program in political jeopardy!"

Modini burst out with anger at this disheartening thought, "And meanwhile, this secret nuclear base with it's MX program is costing this nation one hundred billion dollars, right? And the poor taxpayers don't know they're shelling their hard-earned money for this, because, in their eyes, it doesn't even exist! Why, even some members of Congress might be unaware of it! Don't the people of this country have the right to decide, for Christ's sake, if they want their country, their land, or their own back yards used for a battleground!"

"This base was built for benefit of the American people," Tracy told him.

"And what do we, the people, get out of it?" Modini continued hypothetically, "War games for the benefit of a few? You and a few military brass-- power hungry moguls-- who have a congressman and a senator working behind closed doors for them. You think you are God Almighty! Shit! Well, fuck you, Colonel and your home away from home down here! I'm fucking tired of you bastards still fighting a losing war! You haven't yet learned a damn thing from Vietnam, have *you*? Now you assholes want to take on the world! Colonel? Fuck Rambo!"

Tracy shook his head and watched Modini as he raved. "That's the point, Corporal Modini. We may have to! Today, ten to fifteen countries, besides ours, including the U.S.S.R. are contracting missile warheads this very minute! We are only trying to protect this country's own backyard, that's all!"

"Yeah, like selling arms to some of these countries who will someday become our enemy. I get the point, Colonel and the people have the right to know the truth and to know where we are heading."

Tracy spoke up sharply, "The people don't have to know shit! In fact, research tells us, they don't <u>want</u> to know!"

Tracy headed down a different corridor. Modini followed close behind him. Modini saw game rooms, bars, and everything you could ask for in living accommodations. They entered a recreation room. It was empty of all personnel.

"Don't you understand how this country survives?" Tracy asked Modini. "The problem with Congress is one matter, but the people--" Tracy laughed, dismissing the thought. "They are incapable of understand the mechanics of how this country works and they don't want to! We do what we have to do, even if it means eliminating those undesirables throughout the world!"

"Does that include Karl Hunter and other innocent people?" Modini asked.

Tracy nodded, "Yes, even some who are innocent. You of all people should know. What do you think your part in 'Operation Hamlet' was all about? Karl Hunter caused trouble! He had to be shut up, because he was going to expose everything. And if Congress found out-- No...*too* much was at stake!"

"Yeah, like all that money and the power to control everyone and everything, all going to waste. How did Hunter find out about all this?"

Tracy stopped at a bowling alley. He ran his hand over a rack of bowling balls. They didn't have any scratches worth noting. "Oh, he knew! Think back, Corporal Modini. Think back to March of '68, to 'Operation Hamlet' and to that man you saw. You know who I'm referring to. That gentleman from Langley. He was someone you forgot to write about in your numerous articles about Vietnam!"

Modini shut his eyes, wanting to forget. But he remembered the incident vividly.

* * *

It was the end of March, the beginning of Spring, 1968. A small Vietcong village was silhouetted in the background of the hard rain pouring down. Three men, soaked from head to toe headed for their command post. Sergeant Alex Contos, Private First-class Daniel Conrad, and John Modini were on their way to be briefed by Lieutenant Brewster, concerning Modini's assignment to take photographs on their next mission.

Sergeant Contos introduced PFC Modini to Lieutenant Brewster. Modini saluted his superior and the Lieutenant returned it. "Son, I have a difficult situation here. The congressmen and senators back home are harping on me to send some pictures stateside for morale reasons. Now our missions are very delicate, and we can't show anything to compromise our situation-- if you get my drift. I promised *Life Magazine* I'd send them some photos, and your Sergeant, here suggested you as my man for the job. Do you think I can trust you to handle this job, Private?"

Modini saluted again, barking out, "Yes, sir!"

Lieutenant Brewster smiled and added, "Fine! We'll give you a camera and film and you'll take shots. Whatever you come up with I'll review and decide which ones will be sent back to the states. Is that understood soldier?"

As Modini answered the Lieutenant, he was interrupted by a radio dispatcher entering the room. "I got it, sir. It's coming in right now!"

The Lieutenant headed out the door. "Follow me, men," he ordered. "This is something you all should hear." The men crowded into the radio dispatch room. Conny and the Sergeant followed Modini in and they heard President Johnson speaking on the radio. He ended his speech with the announcement, "I shall not seek nor will I run for a second term as your President of the United States of America!" The soldiers exchanged glances. The President's decision surprised everyone in the room.

Later that evening, John Modini found some time for himself and wandered through the village. Not many people were left, since the soldiers arrived. When the Americans took over the village, they had commandeered a few huts for their own strategic purposes.

It was raining hard, but at least Modini was alone with his thoughts. He was thinking to himself about the President's announcement. He wondered what was on the minds of the people of

America. He knew there were growing protest and dissension of the Vietnam war stateside. And the word from home was the antiwar movement was growing stronger.

Conny appeared from out of the rain. Modini could see he was totally soaked, although he was wearing a waterproof poncho. "Hey Modini. Corporal Hunter wants to see you."

"I know what he wants," Modini said to Conny. "Care to join us?"

"No...not now," Conny's answer was subdued. "Uh... Maybe I'll buy you a drink later."

"Suit yourself..." Modini wondered why Conny begged off. It usually wasn't like him. Maybe it had something to do with the reason Hunter wanted to see him.

He trudged through the heavy rain to Corporal Hunter's hut. He had no idea what was waiting for him. Not only would it eclipse every experience in his past, but it would overshadow everything to come in his future-- if he got out of this war alive.

Inside Corporal Hunter's dimly lit hut were three American soldiers and one unidentified civilian. The three soldiers were with four young beautiful Vietnamese girls. One of the men, Corporal Tracy, was with a young girl, both in the buff on a table top. Her body was on top of his, using it to massage him.

Modini turned red in embarrassment, understanding why Conny begged off. This was one of the huts they used as a "morale booster." Conny's religious upbringing would cause him to shy from occasions like this. He continued to search the hut and found again, to his embarrassment, two young half-clothed Vietnamese girls in the corner of a room lying in a hammock, with a stoned-out Karl Hunter.

Karl Hunter looked at the civilian, sitting alone at the one available table in the hut, drinking down a bottle of Scotch. The civilian, an American dressed in khaki's, noticed Modini's entrance, then poured another drink from his bottle.

Modini was having second thoughts when Hunter's voice stopped him. "Hey, old buddy, where you think you're goin'?" Hunter tried to sit up between the two girls and grinned a big one. "I've been waiting for you. I've got a present for you. I've saved it just for you, my friend!

Here...which one do you want? He gestured to the girls next to him.

Modini didn't answer. Hunter looked wide-eyed around the room. "I'm <u>stoned</u>, man! Isn't that great!" He stared at Modini oddly, then smiled. "Come on, pick one, anyone... My gift to you!" He waited for Modini's reply, "Well?"

Modini appraised the girl with Tracy who smiled at him. Modini's mind buckled. "I forgot what I came in for," he blurted out to Hunter, avoiding looking at him and the two girls.

Although Hunter was half dazed, he suspected Modini was lying and laughed. "You came in to get laid!" Hunter motioned the two girls out of the hammock and pressured Modini, "What are you waiting for? Take one for Pete's sake!" he said pushing one girl at him. "Here, this one! She's the best looking one-- and she does what she's told."

Hunter climbed out of the hammock and stumbled to Modini. He cautiously backed away, a little frightened.

Hunter became irked. "Modini... Do I have to do everything for you? She'll definitely help relieve you of your tensions-- let alone your virginity..."

Modini felt uneasy. The civilian at the table with his bottle of Scotch was eying him.

The girl Karl chose approached Modini. He saw she had long black hair and was nervous.

Hunter whispered to him, "...And you'll be helping this little filly too. Her cherry hasn't been broken in yet. What a pair you two will make for each other. Now go for it!"

Modini was distracted by Tracy humping away on his girl in the other side of the room.

The girl confronted Modini and touched him. He gave a start, forgetting for the moment she was there. He definitely felt a reaction to her touch, and gazed into her deep, brown eyes.

Her hands unfastened the top of her simple dress, and she let it fall to the floor. Beneath it, she was totally nude.

Modini melted at the sight. The partial light from two half-shuttered windows lit her small body. She smiled at him, and Modini had the impression an angel was looking at him. "Je-sus! You're the most beautiful creature I have ever seen..." he told the Vietnamese girl.

Hunter took a two-second pause from kissing his girl. "You can say anything you want to her," he told Modini. "She doesn't speak English."

Modini was uncomfortable and felt sweat inside his clothes. Heart hammered fast in his chest. The girl innocently took her hand and placed it upon his crotch. Modini didn't expect this. He flinched and backed away. Everything was happening too quickly for him. His mind was spinning, and he closed his eyes.

The Vietnamese girl sensed his reluctance and moved to him slowly. She gently stroked his face and undressed him slowly, sensually. Modini stared into her eyes, hypnotized by them. Although he was still shy and embarrassed to respond, he didn't stop her.

Modini shot a worried glance at Hunter. The girl with him was trying to arouse him with no effect. He tried to get Hunter's attention. "Karl, I don't want to catch anything!"

Hunter looked up at him with his happy-stoned eyes. "Johnny, she's a virgin... Trust me, she's clean."

Tracy chuckled in mid-climax with his girl. "Just fuck her, Modini... I want her next!" He pushed his girl off onto the floor.

Modini turned back to the girl who was undressing him. She gave him a nervous but reassuring smile, then took his hand and escorted him into a side room and over to a bed made of bamboo. She laid him down, still caressing him gently. A row of strand beads covering the entrance way to this room offered the only privacy to them.

"What is your name," Modini asked the girl, but she didn't understand. "My name is John... John Modini..." he said, attempting to communicate with her. She only returned her beautiful smile.

"You have such a pretty face," Modini told her. "And that smile. You could steal every heart in America...my country. I wish you could understand me!" He was frustrated now, gesturing with his hands.

Tracy yelled impatiently, "Hurry up, Modini! I'm getting impatient!"

Modini glared at Tracy with disgust, "Forget it, Roger! I'm not going to let you touch her. She stays with *me*!"

Tracy laughed, "Shit, Oh, God! He's in love with the bitch!"

Modini felt the girl's hand on his cheek. She was concerned about his feelings. The girl's presence overwhelmed him and seemed to put a spell on his thoughts and senses. He reached out and enveloped her in protective tenderness, cradling her head into his arms. He would not let her go or let anyone else have her, for that matter.

Outside the room, the civilian was minding his own business, sitting there drinking his Scotch.

As the Vietnamese girl clung to Modini, she tilted her head up. She noticed tears forming in his eyes and felt Modini shudder as he started to weep.

With a delicate finger, she touched a teardrop on his cheek. Then with a tense and passionate movement, she drew him to her, her tongue licking his tears away. His mouth found hers. Their lips met in a kiss of pure passion, and they each made love for the first time...

* * *

The North Vietcong village disappeared behind them as Karl Hunter and Modini walked out of it. Modini felt both happy and sad, as the men continued their mission.

Suddenly, machine gunfire broke the silence. Modini dived to the ground in fear, then leaped up to run back to the village. But Hunter grabbed him and held him back,

"Hey, hey, hey! It's all right. It's only ours!" Hunter explained to a nervous Modini.

"Wha-- What do you mean?" Modini asked.

Hunter explained, "It's our people!"

"They're shooting up the village?"

Hunter nodded. "They have to! In ten minutes our forces will napalm it!"

Modini couldn't comprehend this, "What do you mean? What about those innocent--?"

Hunter jabbed him in anger. "What's the matter with you! They have to kill 'em. They can't afford to leave these people alive if the NaCong arrive."

Modini stuttered. "You-- you're saying, you approve this?"

Hunter moved right into Modini's face, "Jack, if we leave these people alive, the NaCong will torture them. The Charlies will learn information concerning our whereabouts! Then there goes our mission! You have to understand. It's better for them this way. They won't have to suffer!"

Modini was in a state of shock. He couldn't believe a thing like this was really happening. "Oh my God, Oh God! Those girls-- they're to be slaughtered! My girl, Lea, she's--"

"Yes! Now shut up!" Hunter said harshly.

Modini's shock made him go ballistic, "I just left her! Hunter, I can't let this happen! Don't you see? I've got to tell her!" Modini turned quickly, sprinting toward the village.

Hunter yelled after him, "Jack! Shit!" Hunter took off after him. Hunter tackled him to the ground. As Modini tried to pull free from Hunter, the sound of aircraft engines grew loud and jet planes appeared over the treetops. They flew over the village. The ground shook with explosions. Modini looked up to see the village burning with napalm as he watched in horror.

Hunter shouted into his ear, "I can't let you go back. There's nothing you can do about it now! They're already *dead*, Jack! Believe me, I don't like it any more than you do!"

Modini grabbed his rifle and got to his feet, ready to fight him. "Then for God sakes, why did you let it happen?" he screamed out.

Hunter held him back with his rifle, "I don't have the power to stop it! They had to do it!"

Modini yelled at the top of his lungs, "Who's *they*? God damn it!"

Hunter shook his head. "I can't tell you that, Jack!" he said to Modini.

"What do you mean, Hunter." There was disbelief in his voice. "What do you know? You're supposed to be my friend..."

Hunter knew this, and he tried not to meet Modini's eyes. "Jack, that's what I'm trying to do here, to get it through your thick skull. It's best you don't know what happened here!"

The village blazed in the background and the black smoke billowed into the clear blue sky. He wondered if any of the villagers had escaped the slaughter.

But the strain was too much for Modini to bear. It all came out in words barely coherent, in phrases and sentences mixed with sobs "So why did we jeopardize this village? Why did we even come here? That girl...back there... I loved her, Karl! I even gave her a photo of me, so she'd remember me. And I called her Lea so I would have a name to remember her. I didn't even know her real name. And what about those innocent children playing in the street?"

Hunter stopped him, "It was for morale, Jack! The guys needed it, it boosted yours, didn't it?"

Modini, on this last comment erupted. He took a swing, hitting Hunter on his jaw and knocking him on his ass, "That's for your fucking morale!" Modini said, infuriated.

Hunter looked up to him and adjusted his aching jaw. "I might have deserved that, but if it means anything to ya', I didn't know anything about this until this morning! I just follow orders, just as you do!"

Modini straightened himself up. He wiped his eyes, and asked, "Who gives orders to kill innocent women and children? Karl? Was it that man-- the one in the hut last night? Who was he? Why was he wearing civilian clothes? *Why* was he here?"

Hunter didn't answer, just stared at him. Modini leaned forward and yelled into his face, "*Tell me*, you son of a bitch!"

Hunter shakily stood up. He was hesitant to answer. Then he shrugged his shoulders. "Fuck it... He's CIA!"

Modini was totally confused. "CIA? I don't get it. What are they doing here?"

Hunter started to trek down the trail and Modini followed. "Shit, Jack...why do you think you're here? Why do you think President Johnson sent us, the American Forces, the Fucking Marines, here in the first place-- to protect *our homeland*? Fuck no! The only thing concerning our home front is money-- and for the big shots, it's power! We, you and I, are just small pieces on a big chessboard, doing the fighting for those big honchos back home, and lining their economic pockets-- land, oil, steel, the military industrial complex."

With the wave of his hand, Hunter emphasized this point by indicating the aircraft flying over them after their bombing mission. "And oh, yes, I can't forget those little mind control ingredients we have here in unlimited amounts-- drugs, heroin, cocaine, hashish, you name it! They'll be packing a wallop back in the states for the next ten years, if not sooner. That, my friend, for even the little guy back home, could be a billion dollar industry someday. War, Jack, is the biggest commodity for all nations. You and I are just pawns on that chessboard. We become expendable or replaced-- and the game goes on!"

"What are you saying? This is nothing but one big game?"

Hunter spelled it out for him. "It's all about heroin, man, and cocaine! You know, the stuff that gets you high! It's the market now! The rich get richer, and so forth! That's one reason we're here. It's the CIA's job to keep the market open-- be it ore, copper, uranium, poppy seeds, whatever the interest for the powers that be! I hear Johnson's got a Baltimore College in D.C., growing marijuana for experimental reasons for the President!"

Modini thought this was too incredible to believe. "And who controls the drug trade on the streets once it reaches the states?"

Hunter grinned, "You won't believe this, but the mob does!"

Modini shook his head as if Hunter didn't mean what he said, but Hunter was serious. "It's illegal and they do make a perfect criminal source for distribution!"

"You're saying the Mafia is working for the CIA? You're saying the CIA is here to make sure this war doesn't stop, but continues to waste human lives? So this is nothing but profit sharing at the expense of another country just by invoking the term 'Communism' to rile the people back home! Well, that's just great! We yell 'Communism' is coming to get us, like some deadly disease-- only *we're* the disease!"

Hunter was pleased with Modini's observation. "You got it, to a 'T'. President Johnson sent the CIA here to start the war, and he has a lot at stake here, including his second term. This war had to continue! If it stopped, the rich wouldn't get richer and the powerful couldn't play their big chess games anymore, understand? Meanwhile, I say why not take a piece of that pie while we can? My brother can supply anything we need or want!"

"Your brother?" Modini exclaimed.

Hunter realized he let the cat out of the bag. "Yeah. That man you asked about-- that civilian is my brother. I wasn't supposed to tell you."

Modini couldn't believe he was taking any of this seriously, but quickly figured out why Hunter wasn't bullshitting him. "He's CIA?"

"Yes, but you got to keep your mouth shut about him and about me-- not a word!" Hunter strongly advised. "*You promise?*"

Modini reluctantly agreed, "Yeah, I promise, even if I can't help not believing you."

"Well, you keep believing what you want and you'll avoid trouble."

"Isn't what your brother's doing illegal?" Modini asked.

"As long as it isn't domestic, he's cool," Hunter replied. easily. "Besides he's working for the President of the United States of America, isn't he?"

Modini suddenly remembered why he came in to see him last night, "Yeah, but not if the next president has anything to say about it. I wanted to tell you last night President Johnson announced he isn't running for a second term."

Karl Hunter didn't seem fazed by this and laughed. "A President may come and go every four or eight years, but the CIA is still here with their chessboard. Believe me, no matter who they pick as the next President, we'll still go through the expensive process of electing one as usual. But who ever it is, it's not going to matter. Bob Hope will still keep coming each year to feed us morale and laughs, while men like my brother will keep supplying the girls, the drugs, whatever it takes to keep us happy and in line!"

Karl Hunter put his arm around Modini. "My friend, the next man who leads our country will be manipulated like any of us 'cause he wants what everyone else is grasping for. If it isn't money, it's *power*! Apparently, Johnson's time is up or he can't hack the responsibility anymore. Maybe he feels guilty about something," Hunter smirked. "It doesn't matter anyway. Those who sent us over here will continue to do so, and they'll confirm the next elected President will want what's good for them as well. That means Vietnam will be his first priority, until it wears out it's welcome!"

"If only Mom and Pop back home really knew what their sons are doing over here!" Modini grieved. "What about Communism? Why isn't that a concern?"

"What about it? Jack? There'll always be Communism! To those, it's just another word for hate, and you don't have to fight a war to stop it, especially not this one! John Kennedy found that out! It's all over this God-damned world! It spreads like a venereal disease, there seems to be no cure and you can't stop it!"

"So your brother does his job, and we get killed for it!" Modini added bitterly,

Hunter had to agree, "Yeah, some of us. Hey, we might just get lucky, you know, and get out of here alive. I'll tell you one thing-- what my brother did back there in the village may or might not have saved our lives in your eyes, but if any of what I told you just now gets out, we're both dead! I *mean* it! Keep your mouth shut!"

Modini stared intensely at Karl Hunter, mesmerized by his outspokenness. Roger Tracy came up to them from behind. He interrupted very casually, "Oh, Modini, old buddy, guess what? *I* had your girl! And she was just fine, until someone shot her brains out! Too bad... She had a pussy like--"

Modini swung his rifle around and aimed the barrel at Tracy's forehead. Tracy's face turned white as the blood drained from his face. He held up his hand and backed away. "Whoa...what the fuck are you doing?"

Modini's eyes told a different story, one that even made Hunter nervous. Modini's finger tightened on the trigger of his rifle.

"Don't do it, Jack!" Hunter said, trying to stop him. He knew Modini was so distraught he was capable of doing anything right now.

Tracy was frightened, scared shitless as he wetted his uniform, "What are you doing, buddy?

"*Don't do it*!" Hunter said to Modini. He started to ease toward him. Modini showed Hunter he meant business, and waved him back with the point of his rifle.

Tracy saw Modini was serious about shooting him and blubbered for help, "Hunter! Do something...please! He's crazy!"

Then someone else spoke up, "John, God loves you. He has given you a gift of life and may God forgive the man who gave us this gift to kill." The man who stepped forward to confront Modini was PFC Daniel Conrad. "Please, John, don't waste your gift on this man. He may be pitiful, but he is one of us."

Conrad forced Modini to reconsider. Modini relaxed his grip on the trigger and slowly lowered his rifle. But in a surprising move he swung his weapon and slammed the butt into Tracy's face, knocking him to the ground. His blow drew blood.

"Yes, I've gone crazy, Tracy!" Modini hollered, responding wildly to Tracy's comment. "That's what this fucking war has done to me!"

* * *

John Modini gave himself a mental shake, ridding the thoughts from his mind as he and Colonel Roger Tracy passed through an entrance way opening into a silo. In the center of its launching pad was a nuclear missile. Modini moved to the railing and looked upward to the top of the silo from his position at the bottom of this secret underground military base.

"You're going to kill me, aren't you, Tracy? Modini said as if he were addressing the missile itself.

Tracy came up behind him. "Ah! Remembering the good old days, are ya?" he said perceptively. "You should have killed me when you had the chance, Modini!"

Modini twisted around, his back to the silo missile, to face Tracy. "Tell me, Colonel, what does the President know about your little home away from home out here, or is he in the dark about it?"

Tracy's attitude showed he was unconcerned. "Does it matter? He is the Commander in Chief of the Armed Forces. He does what he's told, and he gets what he wants in his Star Wars program. Everyone is happy!"

Modini realized he was going in circles with this, but continued to humor the man. "You mean everyone is happy as long as you get your money for a program completed years ahead of its time. The Congress or the American people had no choice in the matter! And the people who benefit from this have already bought their way in, haven't they? Who are the people behind all this? Is Senator Fuller involved? Who gave the okay to create this instillation?

Tracy spoke with Modini as if he had no secrets to hide. "How did you get here?" he asked bluntly.

Modini thought about the simplest explanation he could. "You mean, Air Force Two?"

Tracy just smiled. He was his old charming self. "We're always thinking ahead."

Modini wasn't convinced. "I *see*! What makes you so sure he'll be the next President?"

"Oh, he'll be the next President, all right!" Tracy assured him. "When the time comes, the country won't have any choice. The opposition is selected far in advance, and from that, two of 'em are offered to the people to vote for. They usually pick the one we can destroy the best. We can make or break a candidate, but you know that already. It's all politics, Modini! You see, our future is always pre-planned, sometimes not always to a 'T,' but as close as we can get."

"And do the people get to vote?" Modini asked derisively.

"But of course!" Tracy grinned and started to climb an iron-rail staircase leading to the top of the silo. Modini watched him climb, and looked below to the bottom of the silo, then back up again. Tracy stopped midway to see him standing alone. "Well, aren't you coming, Modini?"

221

Modini got the chills and moved to the iron-rail staircase. He started climbing. "If the Vice-President will become the next President, who'll be pushing his button?"

Tracy continued to climb the staircase. "I don't seem to be making myself clear to you. There are powerful people out there, *more* powerful than any President or any military! Sometimes one of them makes it to the White House. Then this country changes-- sometimes for the better or sometimes for the worse. And we have to change with it. You and I are but mice in this giant maze of life. You and I are among the few that might make it out. We're not like all the other mice running around lost out *there,* not knowing what tomorrow will bring!"

Modini caught up with Tracy, pulling him to stop. "All we're asking for...is that...there *will* be a tomorrow!"

Tracy looked down at Modini's hand touching him. His face grew tense. Modini released him and Tracy continued upward.

Modini was right behind him. "This whole nuclear thing has to stop, Roger. It is *insane!* You know it! It's people like you who make it even more dangerous! Some day you might take orders from the wrong man. When that day comes, you better make the right decision or God help you!"

Chapter Eighteen

"Talking War Games"

Michael Bradley sat at Catherine's desk at his law office reviewing some of her files on her computer. The clock read 5:05 p.m. as an unexpected person entered his domain. Bradley's mouth was agape for a second as Judge Henry Kencade strode into the room.

"Howdy-do!" Bradley said sarcastically. "My, my...this is an honor, your Honor!"

The judge was irritated by his sarcastic remark, "Cut the bull, Bradley! I'm supposed to meet Catherine here at five-thirty. Did she tell you?"

Bradley was concerned. "No...and she was due back by five. We have a meeting planned about that front page newspaper article. I'm sure you're aware of what it's about...a deceased client of mine!"

Kencade's mind was elsewhere. He wasn't paying much attention to Bradley's prattle, "If you don't mind, I'll wait in her office."

Bradley leaned forward at his desk, "Sir, this is her office!"

Kencade looked at him oddly and seemed worried about something. "I'll wait in the lounge if you don't mind?"

Bradley walked around his desk to Kencade. "Sir, you may use my-- our office, if you like.

I'll finish my work later. Make yourself at home. Use the phone, relax and I'll have Sherry, if she's still here, bring in some coffee..."

"Thank you very much for the hospitality," Kencade said grudgingly as Bradley left the room.

* * *

Ziegler drove his car across a high bridge, heading north to Gary, Indiana. It was past dusk, and the sky was getting dark. Catherine sat quietly in the passenger seat next to him.

The ride had been quiet so far, and Catherine decided to break the monotony. "I suppose you have your reasons for all this."

Ziegler didn't answer her. Catherine spoke up again, "Mr. Ziegler? I wish you'd talk to me! I rearranged my schedule so we could see your daughter today. I want to help."

"But--" Ziegler shook his head.

"But what?" Catherine tried not to sound irritated. "Mr. Ziegler? I am going to help."

"You said that, Mrs. Rogers," Ziegler spoke impatiently, "You seem to want to help everyone. You want to help me, you want to help Carrie. You even tried to help Karl Hunter. Well, I want to help you. Do you really want to know the truth about Karl Hunter?"

Catherine looked uncomfortably at Ziegler. "I'm sure I don't know what you mean. What do you know about Mr. Hunter?"

Ziegler glanced at Catherine and smiled. "Be patient, Mrs. Rogers, for I will relieve your mind of Karl Hunter forever!"

* * *

Late in the afternoon on the barren grounds of the secret nuclear missile base in Montana, John Modini stood alone atop a pile of dirt that had been dug up earlier. Next to it was the pit the dirt came from. It resembled a grave for someone's burial. He looked up toward Colonel Tracy who was positioned on a hill above him. "Is this where you and I part company, Tracy?" Modini asked.

Tracy stared down on Modini at the open grave site and smiled. He took out a pack of cigarettes and offered one to him.

Modini shrugged his shoulders, "Sure, why not? I don't smoke but what the hell, you only live once, right?"

Tracy threw the pack down to him followed by a lighter. Modini nervously took a cigarette and tried to light it. Succeeding, he asked casually, "About the Iran Contra thing... Bush...he was never out of the loop, was he?"

Tracy laughed now. "Modini, my friend... Bush is the loop! Do you think for one moment the President really knew what happened? Or had the knowledge what was legal or what wasn't! As long as the President was protected, that's all that mattered. That pain in the ass, Nancy, nearly blew everything for us! What the President doesn't know meaning what he didn't need to know..." Tracy looked up, scratching his chin. "That wife of his is the best ally he has! Of course, the Vice-President, who everyone thought of as a wimp, couldn't know either, right?"

Modini nodded his head, "That's what I thought. So North and Casey and McFarlane were all working under Bush? Yeah, why not. Who was Casey to go to for guidance but to a former CIA director? That explains why Senator John Towers, the CIA Senate Intelligence Committee Chairman and Bush's old friend, cleared him out of the loop.

"It's funny, Roger. This somewhat reminds me of the Warren Commission. There was a member representing everyone in government who could possibly be involved in a conspiracy to overthrow the government. There's Gerald Ford who represented J. Edgar Hoover's interests, and the FBI, plus a one-time Johnson ally, Senator Richard Russell. But Russell and Congressman Hale Boggs, were the only Democrats on the commission that refused to sign the Commission report-- why? Of course, they were tricked to signing in the end, but Russell never forgave Johnson-- why? Then there's Allen Dulles for the CIA. Why? The military had a clean bill of health, although most of Oswald's military records mysteriously disappeared, or is that another part of national security? You know what's really funny about all this, Roger. No one within that Commission ever came forward to defend the accused assassin's rights! Oswald who was dead, had no rights! Kinda like Karl Hunter today, don't you think?"

Tracy didn't answer. He puffed on his cigarette.

Modini pretended he was smoking his, nervously, so it would last longer. He continued, "How about this hypothesis, Colonel? Why don't the heads of government, the powers that be, including all the scientists and physicists, sit at one big table and convince-- no, tell each other, 'Hey! You assholes! What we're doing is not going to work! Nobody wins, nobody is better than anyone else, we're all human beings here. We all make human mistakes. We just want to make it through each day. So why screw up what mother nature has given us? Come on, you screwed up human species! Let's all fold up our tents and go to the beach-- instead of hell, which looks like all of us are heading!"

Tracy clapped at Modini's desperate utterances. "Bravo, Bravo...nice speech! But it doesn't work that way. You think for one moment I want my kids to grow up with a nuclear holocaust forecasted? Answer me this! Let's say in the middle east there are two small countries, one friendly and one not so friendly. Both have a good connection with the United States. The friendly one keeps the peace throughout the third world, and the unfriendly one supplies us oil. Let's say, the country who keeps the peace finds out an unfriendly one got themselves a nuclear warhead and threatened to blow their ass off the map! Well...the friendly country now wants our help."

Tracy paced back and forth, gesturing with his cigarette, continuing his scenario. "The unfriendly country has no beef with us, because either we or the Russians supplied the warhead in the first place! But unfortunately, we can't give the friendly country any obvious help because our interference could set off World War III. So, they go to someone else like the Soviet Union or China or another country. This desperate country needs mucho bucks and sells them what they need. The ironic thing is, they may be our own manufactured weapons. Most of the weapons supplied are bought from the U.S.of A. in the first place. Are you following me, Modini...or do you want me to draw you a picture?"

Tracy took one last drag and tossed the butt away. "And so we have two countries who have the knowledge and ability to blow each other off the map-- or anybody they so choose! Now try to step in and cool down these two countries. But trying to get these powers to together is like fixing a toothache in a live Bengal Tiger without novocain, because the unfriendly country has been waiting for the United States to step in. You see, they have a leader, a fanatic who wants to show he can take over the world like Hitler and Napoleon! Or perhaps he's a burned out General who's going to die in six months of cancer or AIDS, and decides the world would be better off going down the tubes with him. Now I ask you, Modini...what do we do?"

Modini calmly thought it over and came to the one solution, "You eliminate the problem! You make the problem impotent, so none of these nuts can get their hands on the trigger."

"Are you suggesting assassination?" Tracy inquired caustically. "That's as old as prostitution. What do you think Vietnam was all about? It hasn't stopped!"

"No," Modini said. "This is no John Wayne movie where the bad guys are licked by the good guys at the end, because John Wayne is dead and there won't be anyone to ride off into the sunset this time. No matter how much money we spend or how many weapons we build, we'll never reach that absolute security in this country! Don't you see? So why would it be any different in any other?"

Tracy gave him a pat answer. "The difference is we have the power!"

"And now, *damn you...*so *does* everyone else!" Modini, not realizing his cigarette was reaching its end, burned his fingers and tossed it to the ground.

Tracy agreed with him, "You're right, and I'm right, but no matter whether you or I agree or disagree; we're just soldiers following orders. Besides it's too late anyway, the unexpected has arrived. The CIA with Naval Intelligence has infiltrated a terrorist group in Tripoli. Somehow a nuclear warhead has slipped into their hands. It's a matter of time before they decide what they'll do with it! Then again, there's something stewing over in North Korea, but that hasn't been confirmed yet."

Modini went ballistic. "*My God*! You people don't stop, do you? You really went and did it this time! You bastards! You fucking son of a bitch!" On a sudden impulse, Modini climbed the hill, coming up to confront him face to face as he did in Vietnam.

Tracy held up his hand, smiled and pointed his finger at him to stay put. "*Not* this time, Modini!" At Tracy's gesture four United States Marines suddenly appeared from behind him with rifles, and took aim at Modini. The clicks from the bolt action of their rifles sounded off in unison, giving notice they meant business.

Modini was scared shitless and immediately halted. Tracy continued where he left off, "I'm sorry, but time is running out and I have to cut our little reunion short! Now, Corporal Modini... I want you to turn around and get back down into that ditch! I mean right *now*!"

Modini, still frightened, hesitated first, but did as he was told. He backed down and placed himself above and at the edge of the ditch.

Tracy appeared pleased. "Turn around, Modini. Do it now or they'll shoot you down without hesitation!"

Modini tried to stay composed as he obeyed Tracy's orders. His heart beat fast. He remained still, all the while aware The Marines' rifles had a bead on him. He took three deep breaths so he wouldn't have an anxiety attack and made the effort to talk himself out of this situation. "Don't do this Tracy, you'll be making a very big mistake!"

"You can't get out of this one, Modini," Tracy responded belligerently. "I have no other choice. If I don't kill you now, then they'll have to kill me-- I won't like that. Then they'll send someone else to hunt you down. So, I'm inclined to like the first option for my own well being, as well as my family's!"

Modini didn't move, but still tried to talk sense to Tracy. "You won't get away with this.

I'm warning you, don't do it! Remember the Domino theory?"

"Yeah, what about it?"

Modini caught his attention and took advantage of it. "One thing leads to another. This-- this situation you're involved in will begin to topple. Then, Colonel, you know the killing won't stop here!"

Tracy wore a weary expression, but humored Modini anyway, "How would your death make a difference when we know Hunter won't be a problem anymore? You're just an assurance, it won't go any further than right here at your grave."

"There's one thing you've forgotten, Colonel. I told you the truth about Hunter. He never gave me the phone number. Someone else did, someone whom you will never know. Hunter never gave me any information! I'm surprised at you, Colonel!"

"What are you getting at, Modini? You're trying my patience!"

Modini, his heart beating faster, tried to remain cool. "Remember, Colonel, I'm a journalist and I work for one of the biggest magazines in the country. And I too, always like to keep one step ahead of the other guy, especially if he's trying to screw me! I think you found out what the phone number meant and tried to play a game of charades with me. I figured my hunches would be right, only I didn't know it had any connection to Hunter until *now,* when you brought me here?"

Tracy interrupted, "You like trying people's patience, don't you?"

Modini didn't stop. "There's a letter, Colonel, awaiting my editor, in case of my death, telling all, including my meetings with you and the General Chief of Staff. That's who you met at the airport, wasn't it, Colonel? And I mention Senator Fuller, and the FBI. It's all there. And the person who gave me the phone number is very much alive-- the same person who hired me to investigate it and is awaiting my confirmation."

Tracy laughed, "Well, big deal, Modini...letters can be traced, stopped. People can be made to believe what they're told to believe, no matter if they decide to hide themselves or not. Haven't you learned that by now? Besides, don't you know that big magazine you used to work for was using you as long as you were writing what they *wanted* you to write? And while you believed in what you were writing, they used you! Who do you think controls your magazine? You've been working for the CIA all these years, and you didn't even know it!" Tracy smirked. "How do you think people like Robert McFarland and Jim Garrison were destroyed? Because people like you were used to spread disinformation. Don't you get it? Karl Hunter became the enemy. Once you decided to investigate Hunter you were through! You became extendible! Now cut your bluffing, Modini, and move to the edge of the pit!" Tracy yelled harshly, "Move it!"

Modini followed Tracy's orders, but wasn't through with him yet. "Am I bluffing, Colonel? Are you going to take that chance? I insured myself by sending my letter to three different people. All it takes is one person to hear of my death or disappearance, and when that letter is opened, the whole world will know what I know-- and they'll know about *you*, Tracy! Your family and your kids will know. Are you going to take that chance?"

Tracy pulled the pistol from his holster and aimed it at Modini's head. "What would they know? There's nothing to convince anyone I've done anything wrong or committed any crime. They'll destroy you as they have McFarlands and the Garrisons of this world or anyone who tries to come up against the U.S. Government, especially Central Intelligence. I'm calling your bluff!"

Modini had nothing to lose, although he knew Tracy was right, he couldn't win-- but that didn't stop him. He was aware The Marines who fixed their rifles on him, had families as well. He appealed to Tracy again. "Is that why you have this secret nuclear missile base out here, because some insane terrorist group will try to call your bluff?"

Tracy stood tall and cocked the hammer of his pistol. Modini's face broke out with beads of sweat. He squeezed his eyes shut, saying a silent prayer before the end came.

Then Tracy pulled the trigger, firing his gun.

There was silence.

Modini's face was shaking from the tension. His eyes suddenly opened wide with terror at the sound of the report. He was still standing, unhurt. Behind him at the top of the hill Tracy held his smoking gun. Modini felt a momentary relief. He had not been shot!

Tracy dropped his arm holding the pistol. "At ease, men." Tracy ordered The Marines. They lowered their rifles. Tracy holstered his gun, and glared at him. "Not today, Modini! Maybe tomorrow, we might try again."

Modini felt a sudden release of tension. His legs suddenly buckled, and he fell down on his knees. Then he leaned down into the grave and puked his guts out.

Chapter Nineteen

"The Killing Fields"

It was a warm evening in Gary, Indiana, and the full moon was hanging high in the sky. Joseph Ziegler drove his car down a dark street and emerged into an abandoned Ghetto area. Many houses and lots were desolate and empty, surrounded by wired fences erected by the authorities.

Ziegler drove past the deserted buildings and deserted low-income high rises and pulled up in front of a chained gate. From what Catherine could see, the dirt road beyond the fence led to the middle of an empty field next to an unlighted warehouse.

Catherine, weary from the journey, was upset at Ziegler for stopping. "Now <u>what</u>, Mr. Ziegler?" she asked him. "Why are we here?"

"This is the end of the line," Ziegler said, getting out of the car before Catherine could respond. Leaving the motor running, he went to the gate and opened the lock on the chain securing it.

Catherine opened the passenger door. "Mr. Ziegler?" she called after him.

After he swung the gate open, he got back into the car. "Close the door, Mrs. Rogers,' he said smiling. He nodded through the windshield at the dark, open field. "The answers you want are over there."

Ziegler eased the car through the gateway and drove down the dirt road. The headlights of his car were the only close illumination in the vicinity. He slowed down near a rocky outcropping along the side of the road and parked the car. "Well, Mrs. Rogers," he said breathlessly, "We're here!"

"And where is here," Catherine asked. She felt apprehensive, her nerves tightening.

Ziegler didn't say a word. He slipped out of the car and closed the door.

"Mr. Ziegler... Mr. Ziegler!" Catherine called. He behaved as though he didn't hear her and leaned against the side of the front fender. Catherine felt her temper rising. How dare he lead her on a wild goose chase. She felt like a fool for trusting him in the first place. She trusted him up to now, but his odd actions made her realize her mistake. She got out of the car and started around the front end when Ziegler turned around suddenly. He reached into his suit pocket and removed a semiautomatic pistol, aiming it at her. Catherine stopped dead in her tracks.

"Don't bother to run, Mrs. Rogers," Ziegler said coolly, "I know every stretch of the area around here, even in the dark, and I'm very good with a gun. I was trained by the best."

"What's going on," was the only thing Catherine could say. She felt her heartbeat hammering in her chest. She was afraid to move an inch.

"Smart lady. I thought you'd be screaming your head off by now. It won't do you any good. So scream if you want. No one will hear you!"

Catherine's white face paled with shock and non-comprehension. "Why are you doing this Mr. Ziegler? What have I done?" There was no answer from the man. He looked around as if his mind were wandering of thoughts other than this moment.

She tried to reason with him. "Mr. Ziegler, you asked me to see your daughter. I did that! Now you bring me here saying it concerns Karl Hunter. What does this God forsaking place have to do with him-- or me?"

Mr. Ziegler didn't respond to Catherine's question. Instead, he moved from the car and gazed up at the empty buildings surrounding them as if reminiscing about another place and time.

The two of them stood in the open field, isolated by their dark surroundings.

"It's kind of dead here, isn't it?" Ziegler said, reading her thoughts. "You know, of course, there are many places like this-- ghettos with hundreds of buildings standing empty like this in every major city throughout the country. They're of no use to anyone-- wasted! There used to be people here-- poor people living here. Oh, yes, some still try to sneak in here to live, but in the end, they are always chased out. The poor unfortunate souls. Can you see them, Mrs. Rogers...coming here in the wintertime to get out of the cold, trying to survive like scabs on bruised knees?" Ziegler stopped rambling and laughed aloud, "Though, if you think of it, a bruised knee can heal-- unless, it becomes infected..."

Catherine tried to make sense of what Ziegler was saying. The thought of being all alone with a disturbed man increased her fear. She became angered for not perceiving his growing irrationality. "Why are we here, Mr. Ziegler?" she asked, trying to keep the tremor out of her voice. "I don't understand what this has to do with any--"

"Bitch!" Ziegler yelled, cutting her off. "Do not, I repeat, do not interrupt me! All this will come to a satisfactory conclusion that will make sense to you, so don't you worry your little head off. One added note-- you can forget about any meetings you had this evening-- just consider them canceled. So relax and listen. You may learn something here. And when I'm through, then you can speak."

With his free hand, he gestured to the nearest section of dilapidated buildings. "In order too understand, Mrs. Rogers, you must first know who owns these buildings, and all this land. Do you know, Mrs. Rogers?" he asked, expecting an answer. Catherine remained silent. Ziegler told her, "Our very own corrupt government, that's who! They own all this property and others similar to it in Pennsylvania, New York, and throughout this country of ours! And you know what? All these years, not once did they try to put a band aid on the bruised knees here! Not one! You can see for yourself how the government moves the poor out and takes away their homes."

Catherine's face was taut with strain. She was trapped with a raving lunatic who was waving a gun wildly. All she could do was listen to him.

"And the rich, they will buy the land and, who knows, someday they'll eventually tear it all down and put up condos or department stores-- something to make a profit! But why? How is this done? The rich can buy and make politicians. And if he's good at it, the politician can keep his position in Congress or the Senate. Who the fucking cares? It certainly isn't the poor that keeps them there. The IRS takes from the poor just the same, but it's the rich who know how to get it back. So the politicians get the government to buy up all this land, and they in turn give it back to the rich."

Catherine wanted to run, to escape from this eccentric madman. But she knew if she attempted to flee, he would gun her down. *I have to be ready to run*, she told herself. *I have to wait for the right chance.*

Ziegler whirled around to face her again. "Have you even wondered, Mrs. Rogers, why the tobacco industry is still where it is and gets away with murder every day of our lives? Just ask any of those forty-yearlong term congressmen. You-- you take a good look at your knees, Mrs. Rogers." Ziegler moved closer to her. "They are both very nice indeed and pretty, aren't they? Not one bruise. I wanted you to see for yourself what state of mind that little girl was in, the one you saw earlier on the video tape in that mental hospital. It's a shame, really, what her mind has done to her this last year. A Band-Aid ain't going to help her one bit, is it?"

Catherine's eyes carefully searched the area, surreptitiously looking for some means of escape. "If I may speak now, Mr. Ziegler," Catherine ventured, "Is that why you brought me all the way here? Because you're upset with the government?"

Ziegler smiled. "No, why should I be, I work for the bastards!" he said laughing again. "My father died for this country and for Cuba-- and for what? The God-damn Bay of Pigs and that John Fucking Kennedy...that's what! I brought you here because I'm trying to tell you how things work in this country."

"You said earlier you were trained to use a gun and trained well," Catherine interjected,

"Did our government train you? Is that what you meant?" Maybe if she could keep him occupied and talking, she could find some way out of this life threatening situation.

Ziegler nodded in agreement, "Yes, ma'am, I was trained to get our country back-- to get Cuba back and to destroy and eliminate Castro! It was all Kennedy's fault we failed!"

"But you're talking about things that happened over twenty-five years ago."

Catherine didn't know what he was hinting at. It was easy for her to pretend to be candid. "But, Mr. Ziegler, isn't it wrong to be upset with Kennedy and worry about the past. None of the former presidents have deposed Castro who still is in control of Cuba. We're ready to elect a president this year. Maybe he'll be able to do something?"

Ziegler appeared surprised by her apparent wisdom. "Yes... And isn't that the shits. You're one smart cookie, lady, I can say that for you!" Ziegler smiled. "Tell me this Mrs. Rogers, how can you defend slime like Karl Hunter and others like him? And why do you suppose we should believe the Bible when it says, 'the meek shall inherit the earth!'"

Catherine almost gave up trying to understand Ziegler's irrational train of thought. His dialogue had become too odd. Was he doing this on purpose or did he really mean what he was saying? Catherine attempted a compelling plea. "Please, Mr. Ziegler, I'm tired! I want to help you, but I don't think I'm the one who can. Maybe you'd better take me back to my office. This has gone too far!"

Ziegler ignored her and rambled on, "All those lovely, lovely girls. I'm sure they would believe. Yes, those girls would!"

Curiosity got the better of Catherine. "The girls...? What girls are you talking about?"

Ziegler had her undivided attention now. "You know what girls I am talking about! You don't fool me, Mrs. Rogers. I'm talking about the ones that slime bucket you defended brought here and raped and killed-- some of 'em right where you're standing!" Ziegler saw Catherine become disturbed by his allegation, and continued to play with her. "Right there, Mrs. Rogers, he did it to them right there. And then, one by one, he murdered them!"

Catherine was startled by his accusation, "Mr. Ziegler, how do you know this?" She saw Ziegler's eyes gleam. "You say Hunter brought the girls here? We knew the prosecution's circumstantial evidence against Karl Hunter could link him to the two murdered girls, but what you're saying isn't possible. None of the bodies were ever found near here or around this area! It isn't possible they could have been murdered here."

Ziegler was excited now, overwhelmed he was now the focus of Catherine's interest. "Rest assured, it is, Mrs. Rogers. I know I can prove to you they were!"

"What do you mean?" Catherine asked cautiously.

"I can prove it, and there are many more than just two! There are twenty-five girls nobody-- no one knows about. I mean the transients-- the young hitchhikers passing through-- all of them buried out here in different places..."

Catherine was taken aback by this. "How-- how do you know all this?"

Ziegler's eyes gleamed again. "Why, I am surprised at you, Mrs. Rogers. Of course, I know! I was here! I was in charge of the distribution!"

"The distribution?" Catherine asked fearfully.

"Yes...the distribution. After each girl was executed. I couldn't take all of them with me, only a select few. I started a new class of girls before his arrest...baby girls bred from the rich. Those few and what I could take from the others, I buried here!"

Catherine backed away slowly from the car. Ziegler was totally insane. "The others?"

"Yes, Mrs. Rogers," Ziegler chuckled, loving every minute of this game. "I thought first it was a nice touch to bring the spoiled rich girls to be buried here, since the rich, as I told you, will inherit all this one day. I thought it appropriate, don't you? But then I thought the Bible said, 'the meek shall inherit the earth,' so I scattered them as well-- what I could anyway, throughout this field--" his voice hardened, "--Just as you will be if you take another step, Mrs. Rogers!"

Ziegler fired a shot off. The bullet struck the ground and kicked up dirt, missing her feet by inches. The sound of the gunfire didn't even echo in the open space they stood in. He raised his gun.

"The next one won't miss! It'll just blow your brains out!" he threatened. "Now come over here!"

Reluctantly, she obeyed as he walked to the back of his car and opened the trunk. He removed a spade-head shovel from inside the trunk and handed it to her. He motioned her back, then took out a flashlight and closed the trunk.

"That way," Ziegler indicated, waving his gun to an area beyond the rocks. He allowed Catherine to walk ahead of him, shining his light on the dirt ground strewn with dried weeds and rotting litter. "Over there..."

They paused before a pile of debris. It was a pile of wood and bricks and crushed stone. Ziegler pointed to a spot with the flashlight. "Start digging," he ordered.

Catherine restrained herself against the urge to swing the shovel at Mr. Ziegler and began digging. She wanted to get away from this crazy man, but knew this wasn't the time. He stood behind her, ten feet away, aiming the gun, preventing her from trying anything.

"What am I doing, Mr. Ziegler," Catherine asked, breathing hard from the exertion, "Digging my own grave?" She knew her tone was sarcastic, but would have said anything to get him talking again.

Ziegler chuckled and watched her as she struggled to scoop out the dirt and rubble from the hole. "Funny, you should say that, Mrs. Rogers. Very funny, indeed."

"This ground is pretty hard," Catherine told him. "I'll be here all night if you want this hole big enough to...to bury something." One part of her mind continued to talk while the other part deliberately made plans, waiting for him to make the fatal mistake and approach closer. Then she'd have a chance to swing the shovel at him.

"Oh, don't worry your pretty little head about such matters." Ziegler moved a little closer now. "In a few minutes, you'll know exactly why I wanted you to--"

Catherine's shovel struck something. She lifted the tool and revealed a section of a green plastic bag buried in the rubble. Ziegler used his flashlight to illuminate Catherine's discovery.

And Catherine screamed and dropped the shovel when the light flickered over a partly decayed and mummified hand. Catherine's shovel had torn through a section of the bag in which a body had been wrapped and buried.   From the look of the clothing on the corpse it had been a young woman, and it had been buried within the past few months.

"You-- you knew...the body was here," Catherine said, her voice stammering, "In this exact spot...."

"Now you know I've been telling you the truth," Ziegler said, driving the point home. "One of the many we killed and scattered in the vicinity. I detected the skepticism in your voice. I had to prove to you I wasn't lying."

Catherine felt as though she would throw up. "No, I guess you weren't lying," she choked out the words.

Ziegler looked sadly at the half-buried body. "Lucky for me I remembered where I put her." Ziegler moved around the corpse and approached Catherine.

She trembled as he stopped next to her. "I don't understand, Mr. Ziegler. You're saying you would...would kill these women and bury them here."

"Here, there, wherever it was prudent. Sometimes I had to take them out of here so they'd be discovered. I'm so sorry your client, Mr. Karl Hunter was accused of some of my murders-- but they did find evidence on the bodies proving the connection." Ziegler then smiled. He seemed to be getting a perverse pleasure of telling this story to Catherine.

"Sorry, Mrs. Rogers. I'd explain if I had the time. Well, in truth, I do have the time-- but you don't. You were getting too close, Mrs. Rogers. Much too close with your questions and investigations. You have become a liability! That's why it is so important to end it here and now."

As Ziegler moved closer, to Catherine, she decided it was time to act. She reached down for the shovel in an inconspicuous manner and was ready to grasp it as a weapon when Ziegler suddenly kicked it out of her hands.

239

The kick was so sudden that her fingers tingled with pain. Before she could react, Ziegler grabbed her by the hair, yanking it forward, forcing her down on her knees.

Catherine felt as though her hair was being pulled out by the roots, but she offered no resistance. It might give him the excuse to murder her right then and there.

"Is this what you did when you raped your own daughter, Mr. Ziegler?" She was filled with so much frustrated anger and hate, she screamed at him.

Ziegler halted his assault, his eyes bulging out. Then he jerked Catherine's hair back, and she cried out in agony. She fell backward to the ground. Ziegler held the barrel of the gun inches from her face. As Catherine opened her mouth to scream again, Ziegler jammed the gun into her mouth and down her throat causing her to choke. He held her head in place with his other hand.

"Now just relax, bitch," he told her. "I promised you I'd relieve your mind of Karl Hunter forever and that's just what I'm going to do!" He gave her a depraved smile and released his hand from her tangled hair. His hand moved caressingly down her body and reached under her skirt. Catherine's eyes flashed in total fear and horror as he yanked her panties down her legs. She remained as still as a stone stature, knowing the slightest protest from her would give Ziegler the excuse to pull the trigger.

Ziegler tore off her underwear and held them up with his free hand and caressed his face with them, smiling to himself. "Nice!"

He tossed the panties aside. "Tell me something, Mrs. Rogers...if I let you live, will you defend and protect me as you did Karl Hunter?" he asked sarcastically. He seemed to take delight in seeing the fear in her eyes.

Catherine, now helplessly trapped, wanted to beg for her life, but the gun in her mouth prevented her. The whimpering sounds emerging from her made Ziegler pause a moment. Then he understood what she was trying to do. "Okay, I'll remove the gun for the moment...only for a moment, Mrs. Rogers, for you to answer my plea for counsel."

Catherine gasped for air and gagged as the barrel was removed, jarring her teeth. Ziegler appeared saddened by her reaction. "Oh, so sorry, Mrs. Rogers, I've made you ill!" He still held the gun inches from her head.

Catherine tried hard to keep from throwing up. Her hand came away from her mouth and there was blood on it. *"You're* the one who is sick, Mister! You need more than a counselor, you need a straight jacket! Why don't you just fuck me and get this over with, you *fucking* bastard!"

Ziegler's face tightened at her fierce statement. His free hand went underneath her skirt and jabbed forward, causing her to cry out in pain.

"Sorry to hear those words coming from that pretty little mouth, Mrs. Rogers," he said coldly, threatening her with his gun again. "I thought you might be a little more cooperative than this!"

Without warning, he swung his weapon, slamming it across her jaw. Catherine grunted in pain. The blow nearly knocked her out as her head exploded in a pinwheel of screaming stars. She thought she lost consciousness for a moment. Maybe she did.

There were noises in the distance. Although her eyes were closed, Catherine was still able to discern Ziegler's voice. But something strange was happening. He wasn't talking to her, but to someone else. There were two voices now. She could hear them arguing. It seemed to continue for a long time. Catherine still couldn't move. She was unaware of the passage of time.

Then a hand touched her cheek. A face drifted in front of her, first in than out of focus. It was a man's face, but it wasn't Ziegler's. The man came closer. His hands grabbed her clothing. Her skirt was pulled aside. Then she felt this man, this stranger, on top of her, forcing himself on her. Catherine felt detached, dazed, as though in a dream. It was as if this savage assault were happening to another person. She made a feeble attempt to struggle against the violation, but was too weak to respond. It was a blessing. Her awareness hovered in and out of consciousness. Finally, she forced her eyes to open and briefly caught a glimpse of the man's familiar face-- and was jolted by what she saw.

Catherine felt a sharp fear cutting through the swirling fog and numbness, a fear more horrifying than she felt by the violation of her body. *Oh, my God! You can't be him!* The thought exploded in her mind. *No! No! It can't be! This isn't really happening!*

Catherine, in her stupor, stared incredibly into the face of Karl Hunter! Although it was dark and the light from the moon caught Hunter's face from the side, there was no mistaking it. The shock was too much for Catherine to take. Seconds later, stars flashed again before her eyes and blackness of unconsciousness engulfed her.

Chapter Twenty

"The Letter...is it Safe?"

There was total darkness for a brief moment. John Modini was asleep, but his dreams took him back to an Asian airfield. It was the same one, the same dream he had frequently.

The day was hazy bright. He was standing on the airfield in Vietnam in the year 1969. Modini's leg was bandaged from his wound.

Hunter stood over him, talking to him. "You're one of the lucky ones! You get to go home alive! Funny, there just might be a God after all. That fucking camera bag saved your life by stopping some of those bullets!"

A door swung open fast. The light fell on Modini, sleeping on his cot, awakening him from his dream. Two men entered the room. Modini's half-opened eyes caught their movement as they grabbed him, then dragged him down a corridor into an empty dark room.

They threw him in onto the floor. A bright light flicked on and burned his eyes. The two men exited the room. Modini looked up to see a figure of a man standing before him, in dark silhouette.

The voice that spoke was not recognizable to Modini. "Mr. Modini...I have a proposition for you. It will buy your life, so to speak. Do you want to listen?"

Modini held up a hand trying to shield the light from his eyes, and tried to discover who the speaking figure was. He had no luck, so he decided to answer in a sarcastic tone, "This better be good, Bub, waking me up like this in the middle of the night! My travel agent is going to hear about these accommodations!"

The man in silhouette turned and spoke with a second man hidden in the darkness. "This guy is an asshole! I thought you said he's ready to cooperate!"

The second man in the shadows came forward, and Modini saw it was Colonel Roger Tracy. He stood next to a table with a VCR and monitor and addressed the silhouetted man. "It's just his nature, sir! Yes, he is an asshole, but he'll cooperate...isn't that right, John?"

Modini was still unable to see the first man. "I'm listening!"

The voice behind the man in the dark was very distinct. "Good! To get to the point! There are two people who we know who might have intercepted information concerning a letter Karl Hunter passed to you or someone in his attorney's office. Colonel Tracy claims you don't have it-- or maybe you do, since he claims you and Hunter were cozy pals..."

"That was a long time ago..." Modini answered. Modini held up his hand, blocking the light from his eyes, still trying to identify the man.

The man's voice deepened, "All I want to know, Mr. Modini is...is it safe?"

Modini looked over to Tracy for some explanation. But there wasn't any. "What's safe? Your guess is as good as mine!"

The man was beginning to get impatient. He motioned Tracy to turn on the VCR machine. "Your friend, Mr. Modini, was in the drug trade out of Nam. After the war, Hunter began a prostitution ring in the United States consisting of Vietnamese and Cambodian girls-- young flesh smuggled into the U.S. of A."

A grainier print, the same pornographic film Catherine Rogers saw in her office, was played for Modini. "As you can see here," the man continued, "It led Mr. Hunter to bigger and better things in porno films!"

244

Asian girls were lined up in the nude and men came forward to pick them, like at a school dance. Karl Hunter took a young Carrie into a staged-like bedroom.

"Oh, speaking of the devil, there's your friend engaging himself...wow! He's having sexual intercourse with a twelve-year-old Vietnamese girl!"

A close-up of Carrie was on screen. Her face looked as though she had been drugged, and her body was tied to the bed.

Modini felt very uncomfortable, trying to straighten up to watch what he didn't want to see or believe. "All right, all right! You made your point with the dirty films!"

The man in silhouette slammed his fist down on the table and yelled at Modini, "We don't want a man like this screwing up and blackmailing the United States government or any military institution! Do you read me, civilian? Now, I need to know about the letter! Is it safe?"

Modini laughed aloud and turned to Tracy. "Hey, Colonel...I thought you said I was Laurence Olivier. This guy's playing Olivier right out of *'Marathon Man'*!"

Before Modini could say anything else, the man came down on him, whacking him across the side of his head with a metal baton. Modini was knocked across the room. The rod slammed onto the table as if to emphasize a point. "If I get one more insubordinate, asinine statement from Mr. Modini, I want you to take him out and have him shot! Is that clear, Colonel?"

Tracy reached down to see to a bleeding Modini trying to get up. "Clear as hell, sir!"

Modini crawled up onto a chair next to the table. He was momentarily stunned. His hand went up and felt the side of his head. Blood came away on his fingers. He tried to shake away the throbbing pain. "I think I'm getting tired of this," he said to Tracy. "Who is this guy who has a hard-on about a letter?"

"This letter contains security matters that might be detrimental to the country-- and we want the letter," Tracy explained. "Do you understand, John? This is your life we're talking about!"

Modini was silent for a moment then acknowledged him. "This letter you speak of...what if I don't have it?"

"Then you won't be of any more use to us...will you?" the man in the dark answered.

Tracy spoke up, "Don't be stupid, Modini, I saved your fucking life out there, and I'm giving you another chance, God-damn it!"

"It's not *enough*, Colonel!" The pain in Modini's head prompted an intrusive flashback to the Asian airfield in 1969, a brief memory of Karl Hunter standing with his wounded self, wearing his marine uniform.

Modini had this image in his mind as he continued to speak with Tracy in the present time, "We all saved each other's lives, didn't we? It's come full circle now. Vietnam is *no* mere blot in my conscience, Colonel!"

Modini couldn't rid himself of the flashback with Hunter standing next to him on the airfield. An Air America airplane in the background started its engines. Modini had his marine gear and bag in hand, ready to be shipped out.

Tracy looked down at the bleeding Modini. "You were the first of us to come home alive! John, you were the sensitive one. Even Conrad was stronger than you, but where is he now? You're just plain soft, aren't you, Modini? But here...I don't get it. You, of all people, still know how to survive! Like Conrad, Hunter is no longer in the picture, but you, Modini, are alive! Don't play around with this anymore!"

Modini hardly heard Tracy talking. He was concentrating about the airfield as the image of Hunter pointed to something on the airstrip.

Modini, in the present, turned to the man in the dark, mimicking the memory of his action, the same way he tilted his head, to see where Hunter was pointing. Hunter indicated body bags filling a corner section of the field. They were laid out in long rows. One by one, the body bags were loaded aboard the same airliner Modini was shipping out on.

Modini told the man, "I'm sorry, I know of no letter. You've wasted your time in bringing me here. Except for the number you and I discussed, Roger...there *is* no other letter!"

The man addressed Tracy who was staring at Modini. "Then it has to be the attorney or the woman!" He shut off the lamp and opened the door.

Modini called out, "What woman are you talking about?"

The man ignored him and spoke with a marine standing outside the door. Modini recognized the marine as the one who brought him to the base. The marine nodded back to the man.

Tracy responded to Modini's question by leaning over him, face to face. "The woman he meant was Hunter's attorney from Washington State, Catherine Rogers!"

Tracy started to leave. "Wait! I know her!" Modini yelled out.

Tracy stopped in his tracks, then turned back to Modini. "What?" he said incredulously.

Modini's mind raced. He saw a possible solution out of this predicament. "If such a letter exists-- and if she has it-- I can get it for you! Is the deal still on?"

Tracy shook his head in disbelief. "Still trying to survive?" he said to Modini. Then he mulled it over. "I'll think it over and get back to you in the morning." Tracy left the room leaving Modini alone on the floor.

Modini, still bleeding and in pain, took a hard, deep breath and slumped to the floor in relief. He just bought himself a little more time. But how much time, he wasn't sure of.

* * *

From the depths of a nightmarish dream, Catherine awoke slowly to the reality of her surroundings. Consciousness came painfully, and in its wake came the dire realization of pain and awareness. It was midnight in the abandoned ghetto on the outskirts of Gary, Indiana.

Her eyes flickered open, and she saw the stars twinkling above in the night sky. The air had become cold and uncomfortable. As far as her limited consciousness could discern, she had no clothes on. They had been pulled off and thrown on the ground next to her.

Catherine raised a trembling hand and touched the side of her face. It was throbbing with pain and was streaked by blood that dried during the past several hours.

Then the grim awareness returned. *My God! I'm alive, I'm still alive...why!*

247

The memories flooded back, the sharp memories of being threatened and brutally violated. A sobbing fury welled up inside her. She wanted to yell out, but stopped herself. She knew there was the possibility of her being murdered at any second, and fought against the impulse.

Catherine's mind filled with jumbled thoughts and emotion. When one became clear, another would take its place. She found it difficult to think properly. It was as if her brain were detached from her body and functioning on some other level.

Something stirred near her head. She heard something small scamper by her ear. Three rats had ventured out of their hiding places to investigate the body in their midst. One of them approached her bare feet cautiously and sniffed at them, then scurried away. The other two were more adventurous and approached her upper torso. Then Catherine felt something on her arm. She forced herself to open her eyes. A rat began an inquiring journey up her arm to her shoulder. Catherine wanted to scream, but her voice froze in her throat. She remained as still as she could.

A sudden noise shattered the night air. The rat climbing toward her face suddenly exploded and disappeared. The sound of rifle fire faded quickly as Catherine heard the bolt from a high-powered rifle slide back and forth.

Catherine squeezed her eyelids tightly. *Oh God,* the thought pierced her mind. *Someone is shooting at me.* Although Catherine was numb and cold, and despite her degraded position, she possessed the self-control to lie still, and not make any sudden moves. She was still naked and helpless and had the possibility of being murdered at any moment. The main thought she kept in mind was that she was alive.

Catherine squeezed her eyes tighter and prayed to herself. Lines from the Bible seemed to drift in front of her and solidify. She recited the comforting lines from the Old Testament, Psalm 23:

> '*The Lord is my shepherd, I shall not want...*'
> *He maketh me to lie down in green pastures, he leadeth me beside the still*

waters. He restoreth my soul: he leadeth me in the paths of righteousness for his name's sake.

Yea, though I walk through the valley of the shadow of death, I will fear no evil: for thou art with me; thy rod and thy staff comfort me.

Thou preparest a table before me in the presence of mine enemies; thou anointest my head with oil, my cup runneth over.

Surely, goodness and mercy shall follow me all the days of my life; and I will dwell in the house of the Lord forever.'

She repeated the lines over and over. Somehow they gave her comfort. Scraping noises intruded upon Catherine's reflections. Not far from her, she heard the sound of a shovel digging in the distance. Then she was suddenly struck by the fearful thought someone might be digging a grave meant for her! Many thoughts swirled through her mind-- being buried alive, for one.

Funny, she wondered, *If I were buried out here, would my body ever be discovered in such a desolate location. Maybe some day when a construction team comes out here to excavate the land to rebuild a new mall or neighborhood, then they'll discover my remains-- and maybe the remains of the other bodies along with mine.* She would become the joke of every law school across the country as the attorney who joined her client's own victims. *God, how ironic.* Catherine fought to focus her thoughts. She was determined to find a way out of this.

Suddenly the shoveling stopped. She listened for any stray sound, but heard nothing. Nearby, came the sound of the car's engine starting. The car drove away into the distance until she couldn't hear it any longer.

Catherine remained still, wondering again if this was a trick. She lay on the ground thinking. *Why did he leave me alive out here...to humiliate me? It doesn't make sense. He knows I can identify him, or...can I? Did he believe I could or would really protect...defend him, this animal? My God! I'm alive, but I don't understand...why?*

249

Then her thoughts shut down again and she drifted in and out of a semi conscious state. At times, she thought she was dreaming or barely awake. She tried hard to focus on a single rational thought, but because of her distorted perception, she lost track of time.

Finally, as her senses returned to her, Catherine felt a growing urgency to do something and not just lie there,

As Catherine's mind cleared, she knew she waited long enough. *If I'm supposed to be killed, I've got to try to make a run for it!* she thought to herself. With an immense effort, she raised herself up in a sitting position. Agonizing pain shot through her body, in every limb and joint. For the first time she felt the cold air on her naked body and shivered. Slowly she rose from off the dirt pile, finding each tiny movement painful.

Catherine covered herself with her arms, more in humiliation than from the cold. She looked around for any of her clothing, finding her ripped and torn skirt and shredded blouse. She slipped them on quickly, without thinking. Her eyes darted in all directions. She was afraid a high-powered rifle had its cross-hairs on her. She remembered what happened to the rat, and coldly put it out of her mind. *I won't think of that now,* she told herself.

Catherine took her bearings. She was still in the middle of the fenced-in field, and searched for the way she had originally come in.

With a quick glance behind her, she headed down the tiny strip of road in the direction of the gate. She moved forward, one step after another, mechanically, not thinking, making her mind blank. She stumbled in the darkness, but the light of the moon showed she was going in the right direction.

Catherine reached the gate and paused. Which way should she go? Should she go back in the direction she came from or head the opposite way? She decided the other way was best.

Catherine staggered out onto the road to find her way out of this jungle of high-rises and darkness.

She tried to force the jumbled thoughts from her mind. She didn't know why these things were happening to her or even how she got this far. Why was she being tortured like this. If they wanted to kill her, why didn't they just do it. She had no answers. In her tortured mental state, Catherine refused to wonder about these questions. Survival was her only thought, and she put all of her concentration into it.

In the distance Catherine saw a lighted area beyond some buildings where the street lights were on. As she marched forward, she felt the fatigue hit her hard. Her body was exhausted, pushed to its limits. But Catherine refused to surrender. She pushed on relentlessly, forcing herself to move on.

Catherine avoided the pools of stagnant water and mud accumulating in different sections of the road, making it difficult to traverse.

She pressed on in the darkness and passed through a one block section of buildings lining one side of the road and a wire fence blocking the other side of the open field. She passed by a wide, stagnant pool surrounded by rough chunks of wood and concrete debris.

She staggered and pitched forward; her strength drained from her knees. She barely caught herself in time. She lay there on her stomach, using every bit of effort to crawl forward. Then she rose to her feet with a determined effort. Suddenly, all the horrors of the evening crashed in on her and she found a release in one long agonizing cry.

Catherine burst into tears and started to cry openly. *Oh, God!* She prayed to herself. *Why me... Why me... Why is this happening to me? Am I in a state of shock! Stop crying!* With great resolve, Catherine forced all thoughts from her mind and raised herself again. She started walking again, one foot in front of the other, making her mind concentrate on each step alone.

As she moved down the narrow roadway, something in the darkness made a roaring sound behind her. She whirled around to see the headlights of a truck swing her way.

Instinctively, she turned away, and started to flee as she heard the growl of the engine behind her. When she turned her head again, the headlights blinded her. She saw the body of the truck, dark and huge, continuing toward her, attempting neither to turn or stop.

Catherine realized she was trapped on this road with nowhere to run. She turned and started running for her life.

"Oh, *my* God! No!" Catherine cried out. The truck headed straight for her. It was determined to run her down.

The next seconds seemed to pass in slow motion. With both sides of the road blocked, Catherine knew she couldn't avoid the charging vehicle.

Acting mostly out of reflex action, she raced to one of the pools of water ahead of her. The truck loomed behind her, closing in fast. But as the truck reached her, Catherine stumbled and tripped, falling into stagnant liquid.

The truck roared by, running over her, leaving her wet but unharmed. Catherine slowly lifted her head from the water, realizing she missed death by inches. It was the depression in the middle of the pool that saved her life.

As she moved to get up, she abruptly touched something blocking her path in the water. It felt like cloth, and for a moment Catherine thought it might be a pile of clothes, but she was wrong. The light from the full moon illuminated the object that caused Catherine to trip. It was the body of Mr. Joseph Ziegler. He was lying sprawled out on his back, dead, his two eyes open and peering up at the sky.

Catherine stifled a scream and scrambled to her feet. She stumbled from the stagnant street pond until her eyes caught the truck in the distance. It turned around at an intersection and was now heading back her way.

Its headlights aimed at Catherine again like the sights on a rifle. *Whoever is driving that truck wants me dead!* Catherine thought.

She turned and ran with one thought on her mind. *I've got to get out of its way!* She heard the truck gaining and chanced a look back. And whom she saw in that momentary glimpse stunned her. The cab light in the truck was on and she recognized the driver behind the wheel. It was none other than Karl Hunter!

The truck approached, accelerating steadily. Catherine knew she couldn't outrun it. She raced ahead and spotted a section of fence ahead of her two feet shorter than the lengths on either side. If she could climb over it, she would be safe.

As she reached out and started climbing, she felt a shock to her hand and let go. She stared at the fence in disbelief. It was electrified!

From high above, Catherine heard an unexpected whirling sound. A police helicopter skimmed overhead, appearing suddenly from behind one of the old buildings.

She looked down from the night sky to see the truck heading for her with its blinding headlights. It slowed and swerved to avoid the debris in the road, but aimed right at her, preparing to crush her into the fence.

Above, the helicopter circled above her and flashed its powerful spotlight onto the road, now blinding the driver of the truck. A police officer in the helicopter spoke over the loudspeaker.

"Halt! You are on government property! Stop your vehicle now!"

The man behind the wheel of the truck, blinded by the helicopter's light, refused to stop. The vehicle stubbornly plowed ahead, then unexpectedly hit a ragged chunk of debris in the road. The driver fought to control the truck, but the front wheel locked, and the momentum made the vehicle skid across the road, angling straight for Catherine.

With seconds to spare, Catherine threw herself out of the path of the truck. The truck smashed into the fence, tearing a gaping hole in it and came to rest, stuck midway through the torn wire barrier before coming to a stop. The electrical lines feeding current to the fence short-circuited, shooting out sparks of electricity. One of the cables fell across the cab of the truck and touched the metal exterior. The person inside the cab, was electrocuted as he tried to open the door.

Catherine raised her head from her prone position to see the death throes of the driver. As incredulous at it seemed, she recognized the face. There could be no doubt now. From her vantage point, the driver of the truck was Karl Hunter!

Stricken by an indescribable panic at the sight of the man's death, Catherine got up and bolted. Half running, half-falling, all she wanted to do was get away. Had she looked back, she would have been a witness to the aftermath of the accident.

The impact broke the truck's gas line, and the volatile liquid spilled through broken lines beneath it. The sparks from the fence ignited the gasoline, and the truck exploded. The explosion shook the still night air as a big orange ball of fire rose into the night.

Flying above the accident scene, the two officers inside the helicopter saw everything below. "Shit!" One of them responded. They were stunned by the smashup which happened before their eyes.

"Oh *my God*! Let's get the hell out of here," the second officer said panicky. "We don't want to be responsible for this!"

Catherine inexplicably watched the helicopter fly from the scene of the accident.

"No, no! Please, come back!" she yelled after them. "Help me! *Please*...help me!" Catherine cried out until she was out of breath, and finally fell back to the ground on her knees in anguish and pain.

Chapter Twenty-One

"And the Bombs Burst in Air"

John Modini sat on his cot in a locked room on the secret military base, contemplating his future, wondering if he had a future. He decided sleeping on it was out of the picture since he wanted to avoid the fear of not waking up. They bandaged his head and treated him with some medicine. All he had to do now was to wait and see what the military was planning for him.

Francine drove through the front gate on the compound in a civilian car, a bright red Studebaker, which stood out prominently on such a bright sunny day. She pulled up in front of a quonset hut fifty yards from the mess hall and waited, checking her wristwatch. She was punctual.

Minutes later, John Modini was escorted out the door and led to the center of the street in handcuffs by two marines. Francine watched as Modini met Colonel Tracy who unlocked his cuffs. He appeared to be giving Modini a lecture and some sound advice.

"That dumping ground out there yesterday could have sealed you up forever! It's a reminder when you leave here it's my job to protect national security. And when you get back to the world out there, thank your lucky stars, Modini. You forget everything what you heard and seen here-- and forget Karl Hunter for both our sakes!"

Modini studied Tracy's face. "Roger...I can't forget! But I'll try on the condition you tell me what was in that letter that could get both Catherine Rogers and myself killed? What is the connection between the letter and Karl Hunter to the phone number? What's the link to all this? Apparently, there is a link, Roger. Otherwise, I wouldn't be here!"

Tracy stared at Modini, then backed away and explained, "The base is part of it. We believe Hunter would expose it to the media, giving the Presidential opposition the ammunition it needed!"

Modini wasn't buying any of this. "What else, Tracy," he asked skeptically. "There's got to be more to it than that! You said yourself the opposition could be bought, and the people manipulated to believe anything. What fuse did Hunter light that caused you to get so nervous?"

"What I can say? What all I know is this. Hunter was ready to expose us-- Naval Intelligence, The CIA-- the works! He had something on all of them! The son of a bitch was trained to work within the intelligent circles after our stint in Nam. You heard about his brother. His brother knew more secrets how this country worked than J. Edgar Hoover did himself. But Hunter wouldn't cooperate when it came time for him to be sent to Russia as a defector in the '70's-- under false pretensions, under a program existing since 1957. He was trained to go to the Soviets to supply the KGB with information the Soviets could play with, some true, some false. It was enough to allow Hunter to infiltrate and to buy time to keep the KGB busy for a few years!"

"What happened?" Modini asked.

"What happened!" Tracy got upset. "The bastard backed out of the program as he was ready to defect, so we sent his double in his place."

Modini interrupted, "Wait a minute -- *his double?*"

Tracy cocked his head, for Modini to walk with him. "Every man who was prepared to defect had a double-- a look-alike-- someone who resembled them physically. Hell, the KGB had theirs, and they've been doing it for years. It soon became the company's policy-- a precaution so they could use him as they please!"

"My God!" Modini was shocked by this revelation. "Did Hunter know this, that he had a double?"

Tracy shook his head. "No, none of them did. Like I said, it was for precaution. Whenever a double was used, the CIA had a babysitter for the real subject. No matter where he went, there was always someone to watch over him and allow the double to do his job. We have the best disinformation organization in the free world, and part of my job right now is to keep it that way! I want you to understand this, Modini, when you leave here!"

Modini's mind was working on another level, attempting to tie up all the loose ends. "What happens to the double when the real agent dies, like Hunter?"

"If they are one of us, they're shipped out of the country to another country, like Honduras or Panama, Guatemala-- you name it, wherever we have a base. The double is sent there for life, or if they become too much of a risk, are eliminated!"

Modini continued, "And the phone number-- what was that used for?"

Tracy saw where Modini was going with this but couldn't believe he was still concerned with this number. He satisfied Modini's curiosity, nonetheless. "The phone number you gave me, as you told me, was no longer in use. But it was active up to the time of the Nixon administration as an emergency code number. If an agent were in trouble or in need of contact, he would use it. All agents knew they had to deny existence of the program, and vice-versa! Deniability from the company was always the policy of the United States Government!"

"Which happens to be out of Raleigh, North Carolina," Modini interjected. "Was all training done there or was some of it done out of Atsugi, Japan?"

Tracy lifted an eyebrow. "Oh, the U-2 program! You are well informed, John. That was a base where some of the agents started their defection training. It was a highly top-secret Marine Base. All defectors were recruited from The Marine Corps. I'm surprised they didn't approach you, since you and Hunter were such buddies. That brother of his was." Tracy glanced at his watch. "I believe you've got enough of the picture to understand why it's most essential to get this letter. That means, Modini, if you don't succeed, both the lady in question along with her attorney friend, Bradley, will be eliminated. And I have no control over what happens once you leave here, so you have three lives, including your own, in a sling right now!"

"Tracy! If this is the truth, I believe we're both being used as pawns. And this letter you mention is more dangerous than you think! We're fucked! Do you realize you and I are the only ones left from our unit in Vietnam? Think about it! How many of us survived over there only to return here to die one by one in some crazy way? Why was Conny driven to suicide? I think Hunter must have been the key."

"Perhaps... Forget him," Tracy said ambiguously. "He's gone...dead...finished!"

Modini stared at Tracy. "You were ordered to eliminate me, weren't you? Believe me, Roger, we are both dead men! We know something from Nam, or they think we do and they want us to be out of the picture because Hunter decided to expose whatever it was." Then a sudden thought struck Modini. "My God! It's his brother! It's probably true! There was a conspiracy!"

"Conspiracy?" Tracy had no idea what Modini was talking about. "My friend," he put his arm around Modini's shoulder, escorted him to Francine's car, "Conspiracy in America today goes hand in hand with mom, apple pie, and our flag waving those stars and stripes in the air."

The two men reached Francine's car. It was provided to escort Modini from this compound. Tracy shook hands with Modini in jest knowing this might be their last meeting together. "This young lady will see you get to your destination. I don't think we'll be seeing each other again-- that's for both our sakes."

Modini got into the passenger seat. "You've got to think positive, Roger," he said.

Tracy shook his head. "I can't guarantee what will happen to you when you accomplish your assignment and find that letter. My responsibility for you ends right here. You owe me one, Corporal Modini. So, goodbye and good luck. You're going to need it!" Tracy saluted him and backed from the car as he nodded to Francine.

As the Studebaker drove off, Modini turned around to see Colonel Tracy standing, watching them.

The Colonel watched the Studebaker until it left the compound and became a speck in the distance, outside the base fence.

"Colonel, the Pentagon is on the phone." It was the Marine who escorted Modini to the compound days before.

"Wait for me in my office. I'll take it there." Tracy replied. The Marine departed after saluting.

Tracy entered his office and picked up the phone. "Colonel Roger Tracy!" He sat down in his desk chair, but heard nothing on the phone. Again, Tracy announced himself, but all he heard was silence.

The Marine Tracy spoke to earlier entered the office.

"We must have lost the call from the Pentagon," Tracy told him.

The Marine stood at attention. "Sir?"

"There was no one on the line when I answered. Did they say who was calling?"

"Let me try to reconnect the call," The Marine offered.

Tracy hung up the receiver and shoved the phone to the other side of the desk.

As The Marine approached the desk, he removed his side arm, pulled back the hammer, and fired it at Colonel Tracy. The sound of the gunshot blasted through the room.

Tracy sat there a moment with an incredulous expression on his face, then his eyes rolled up and he slid sideways off his chair onto the floor, dead.

The Marine held the smoking weapon in his dress gloved hand. He caught the Colonel off guard as planned. Then removing his dress gloves, he slipped the pair onto Tracy's hands and placed the pistol into it. The Marine picked up the phone and dialed out.

"Sir...yes! Colonel Tracy has just committed suicide! Yes, sir! As planned, sir! It is being taken care of as we speak...neat and orderly, sir! Yes, sir!"

* * *

It was half-past eleven o'clock in the morning at Southpoint Central Hospital in Gary,

Indiana, when the Judge Henry Kencade arrived. The elevator doors opened, and Kencade exited onto the seventh floor intensive care unit. He hurried down a corridor past doctors, nurses, in a frantic mood. He stopped to ask directions of an orderly who obliged and directed him by pointing to a nurse's station.

Kencade found the station momentarily deserted, and his frustration mounted. A nurse finally appeared with a chart and noticed the troubled Kencade.

"Excuse me, sir," the nurse said, "Do you need any assistance?"

Kencade approached her anxiously. "I'm Henry Kencade. My daughter, Catherine. She was brought in yesterday, I believe?"

The nurse looked at the patient chart behind the station desk. "Your daughter's name is Kencade?" she asked.

Kencade, trying to remain composed, answered quickly, "I'm sorry, ma'am. Rogers is her married name! She--"

The nurse interrupted, "Just a minute, I'll call the doctor for you." She dialed her station phone.

"She is all right, isn't she? I was told--"

The nurse held one finger up to him. "Dr. Matthews? Yes... Catherine's father is here. Yes..." She hung up the phone. "Mr. Kencade, Dr. Matthews will be with you in a moment. Take a seat please."

Kencade became more fidgety. The minutes he waited seemed like an eternity before Dr. Matthews appeared.

The doctor stretched his hand out to Kencade. "Your Honor! It's a pleasure..."

Kencade cut in, "Tell me, doctor, if she's okay?"

Dr. Matthews lowered his voice. "Follow me, please." He led Kencade down the hall to speak with him in private. "For the present, she is!"

"I don't understand. What do you mean for the present?"

Dr. Matthews tried to be discreet in his explanation. "Sir...this is intensive care. She almost died. Uh...she was bleeding internally when she arrived. She was found lying in the middle of a highway. Apparently, she must have walked for some distance before she received any help."

Dr. Matthews led Kencade to a private room. "We've stopped the bleeding for now. You have a strong daughter in there, sir. I don't know how she did it, but she survived what I believe no other woman could in her condition!"

"Was she able to tell you what happened to her?" Kencade asked.

Dr. Matthews cast his eyes at the floor and then back to Kencade. "Your Honor, your daughter can't speak. Her jaw was broken. We had to wire it shut! It appears...I'm sorry to say...it appears that she was raped and beaten very badly..."

Kencade became so distraught he broke into tears. Dr. Matthews put a hand on his arm. "Can I see her?" Kencade asked, his voice trembling.

"Not right now, sir. She's just come from surgery and is still unconscious. You have to understand what she's been through. We have a police officer outside her door for her protection, waiting to take any statements she will offer. There is nothing you can do for her now. Tomorrow would be a better time to see whether she's better. We'll probably keep her here for the next few weeks. She'll need all the strength and support she can from you to get through this."

Kencade slowly nodded his head in understanding. "So she didn't say anything-- not a word about who did this to her?"

Dr. Matthews shook his head. "She hasn't spoken a word other than your name since she arrived! One thing, though... I talked to the paramedics who brought her in, and they told me...well, they have a feeling she knows who did this to her!"

* * *

On a flat, deserted highway road in Montana State, a red Studebaker raced across the desolate landscape in a northeasterly direction. Francine drove while John Modini outmaneuvered her in the silent game they played on this journey through no-man's-land. Francine avoided all eye contact. Modini did the same from the passenger seat. He kept his eyes focused on the road ahead.

Finally, she spoke. "Are you in charge of the silent department on this trip Mr. Modini?" Francine asked in her most nonchalant voice.

He didn't answer her, and she tried again. "I'm sorry you had to go through this, being brought out here and all...and feel the way you do"

Modini touched the square-cut bandage on the side of his head and shot her a fierce look. "And how would you know how I feel?" he snapped. "And which are you today-- Francine or Micheline? Maybe you could tell me the truth for a change!"

Francine kept her eyes on the road. "I'm both, one and the same." she confessed.

Modini was surprised she admitted it. He hadn't expected her to be so forthright. He saw her eyes shining with tears. "I knew you were Micheline. What I didn't understand is why you denied it."

"No, actually it is Francine. To you, yes, I'm Micheline, I mean-- I'm sorry I lied to you, John, but I never thought you'd run into me like this. I'm telling you this because I want you to know I meant what I said to you the other night. I didn't know you were going to be the passenger on that plane. I thought their business was finished with you."

Francine brushed back her tears. Modini wondered to himself if she were telling the truth or lying to him. He didn't say a word, keeping to himself and looking back to the road.

The car continued on down the empty highway. Several miles away an airborne object flew speedily toward them at a low altitude.

Modini broke the silence this time, "Who is they? Does that include Colonel Tracy?"

Francine shook her head. "No, I didn't know he was here or what this place was, only that it was a secret military base. All I can tell you is I have clearance and work for a group that sponsors the Vice-President!"

Modini gave her a critical look. "You mean, 'of the United States?'"

"Yes, this group wants to make sure--" Francine couldn't continue. Suddenly, the car started to shake as if they encountered an earthquake. A rumbling sound split the air, and they both felt it on ground level. Francine held tightly to the wheel as Modini spun around, reacting quickly to the vibration.

Suddenly, the air exploded with a tumultuous sound like a sonic boom. A blast of wind and sand hit the car like a tidal wave. Francine lost control of the car and the Studebaker slid off the road. Francine drove it off to the side of the highway and stopped short. The two of them were shaken by this circumstance.

Modini peered upward and through a cloud of sand and dust from the road. It blew through and their open car windows. "What the hell was that?" He quickly rolled up his side window. Francine did the same on her side.

They both look outward to see what was happening, but when the wind stopped everything was quiet and settled down. Francine took a breath. "I don't have the faintest idea what it was, but at least it got you to talk to me again!"

Modini stared upward through the windshield again. "Hold it! Quiet! I think it's coming back. It's aircraft of some kind. It's circling back!" He gave Francine a nervous look. "I suggest we get out of the car before this whole front windshield crashes in on us-- like right now, Francine!"

Francine agreed without hesitation. "Good idea!" As they both reached for their doors, a deadly line of machine gunfire hit the road in front of them. Francine went out her door as John went out his, and the machine gun bullets ripped through the center of the car followed by a momentary silence. Francine and Modini scrambled away in opposite directions from the vehicle.

Three beats later, a missile launched from the aircraft made a direct hit on the Studebaker, blowing it to fiery bits.

Modini was running when the impact of the explosion struck him. The shock wave picked him up and threw him through the air, landing in a field off the road.

Modini hit hard and rolled, coming to an abrupt stop. He was a bit stunned and semiconscious. He shook his head and sat up. Moments later, as full consciousness returned to him, he heard the sound of aircraft approaching in the distance. He ducked down and remained still, waiting for it to pass by. As it streaked by overhead and out of sight, Modini shakily got to his knees. He yelled out for Francine, but there was no answer.

Modini crawled out of the field, heading for the burning wreckage of the Studebaker. There was hardly anything left of it. Just chunks of burning and twisted metal and a crater eating up half the road.

He crossed over to the other side of the highway and looked around for Francine. He found her lying limply in a ravine off the side of the road. Her clothes were torn and bloody. She appeared barely alive!

He lifted her head and wiped the blood from her face. "Francine...oh, shit!" He tried to lift her up, but failed. He was weak from the shock he had suffered. They were in immanent danger, and he knew she was too heavy for him to carry.

Francine was dazed, but conscious. "Go, John! Before it's too late..." she told Modini. "Leave now!"

"What are you talking about!" he cried out, "We've got to get you out of here, Francine. I'll try to get you up to the road."

Francine grasped his arm and pleaded with him, "No! John, if you take me off the road, they'll know you're still alive. I'm nothing to them, but they'll come after you." Francine took labored breaths, and her voice fell to a whisper. "They'll hunt you down. They won't stop until they find you!"

Modini held her and watched, straining to stop the tears from his own eyes. "Who? Francine! Who are you talking about?

"Leave me, please! Oh, God! If they find you, John, they'll kill you!"

Modini tried to lift Francine, but surrendered again. He put a finger to her cheek and stroked the hair out of her eyes. "Francine! Who are you? Who are these people you're working for?"

She turned her head from him. "It's too late...please, John... Go! Please forgive me!"

Modini heard the sound of the aircraft again in the distance. The ground beneath them started to rumble. He searched the skies and spotted what he thought was an Air Force F-20 Tiger Shark starting its descent. "Oh, my God!" he said to himself.

Modini tried again to pick up Francine, this time, compelled by the urgency of this deadly situation, he succeeded. He found the strength to carry her a short distance from the road and set her down behind some bushes, hiding them.

The Tiger Shark strafed the area near them with machine gunfire. Modini covered Francine with his body, yelling at her, "God damn it, Francine! You know what that was! It was an F-20 Tiger Shark! They're obsolete! The military isn't supposed to be using this aircraft. Francine! What secrets are you hiding...tell me!"

Francine held Modini's hands tight, gasping for breath as she spoke. "Senator Fuller... I work for him. I'm his mistress!"

Modini shook his head, glancing again at the sky above him, "What's Fuller's connection to all this?" When she didn't answer, he shook her. "*Francine!*"

Francine began coughing blood as she tried to speak. "He's to follow...Vice-President Bush to be...in line as the next President..." More blood appeared. Then her mouth stopped moving and she stopped breathing.

"No... No, Francine... Don't die on me! Not now!" John cried out. "Oh Jeez-us! Help me, God! Francine!" But it was no use speaking to her any more. Her lifeless body had gone limp in his arms.

The Tiger Shark returned and Modini knew it came back for the final kill. It strafed the area, the machine gunfire hitting closer to them. It was as if the aircraft sensed the vicinity in which Modini and Francine were hiding.

The Tiger Shark circled above and zeroed in on them. Modini knew what would happen next, although he didn't want to admit it to himself. A line of bullets strafed the ground in a direct line leading up to them. The last split second, Modini, dived out of the way at the last. Modini picked himself up and ran for dear life, but realized there was nowhere to go.

The aircraft had him in its sights. It locked onto the figure of Modini and descended upon him flying in low for the kill. The Tiger Shark opened fire again, playing with Modini as if he were part of an arcade game.

Modini dodged the strafing line of fire and the Tiger Shark zipped by over him to continue the chase. Another shock wave knocked Modini to the ground as the plane disappeared to circle back far above him.

Modini saw a mountain ridge one hundred yards ahead and made a dash for it. The Tiger Shark swooped down from the same direction. From its position high above the ground, the pilot of the Tiger Shark commanded a bird's eye view of the layout of the land below. The pilot knew if Modini made it past the ridge and to the bridge beyond it, he would lose him. The aircraft made a broad swing, circling again to confront Modini for the final kill.

Modini, exhilarated from the adrenaline rush, reached the ridge and spotted the bridge below him. But to reach it, he had to climb down a steep ledge to get to it. Without any second thoughts, he started climbing down the ledge.

The Tiger Shark launched another missile at the ridge, attempting to take Modini out the easy way.

The missile unexpectedly veered to he right and slammed into the top of the ridge, exploding, blowing a huge chunk of the cliff side away.

Modini reached the bottom and was sheltered by most of the explosion by a protruding overhang of rock. As the smoke and debris from the rocks rained down, Modini slid down the slope the rest of the way and sprinted onto the bridge. He picked himself up and glimpsed the aircraft still in the sky above him. He yelled up to the Tiger Shark in exasperation, "Thanks a lot, motherfucker!"

He raced for the bridge as parts of the cliff, weakened by the blast, continued to fall down upon it, missing him as he bolted across. He knew he might not make it to the other side, but gave it his best shot. He zig-zagged to the center of the bridge before pausing to catch his breath.

Modini heard the sound of water and glanced over the side. Fifty feet below him was a flowing river of rapids. A quick thought crossed Modini's mind. This seemed to be the best escape route if he were to survive at all.

The Tiger Shark made its descent and fired at the bridge, keeping Modini as the target centered in its sights. The bullets struck the bridge and ricocheted, some of them missing Modini by inches. Modini knew his chance for survival plummeted to zero, and made the only decision he could. In one smooth motion, he climbed over the side of the bridge and prepared to jump. It might have been the most insane decision he made in his entire life, but there wasn't any other choice. He was going for it!

The Tiger Shark again targeted the figure on the railing of the bridge. The pilot was low on ammunition but determined to hit his target at all costs, especially now it was in full view. He still had one missile left and pressed the button to launch it.

Modini leaped out from the bridge into the air. He plummeted downward, feet first as the missile struck the bridge, blowing the center part of the roadway to pieces. Modini struck the water and disappeared altogether into the roar and flow of the river rapids below.

High above, portions of metal and concrete, launched into the air in ragged bits and chunks, plunged down, raining the fragments into the moving water. The bridge was structurally sound and remained standing, although it sustained heavy damage.

The Tiger Shark, convinced it accomplished its mission, shot upward and disappeared into the sky and out of sight.

Chapter Twenty-Two

"The Connection"

"On November fifth, 1988, at eight o'clock, George Bush was confirmed as the next President of the United States of America, succeeding Ronald Reagan. Dan Quayle, from the State of Indiana, became his Vice-President. George Bush beat the Democratic candidate, Governor Dukakis of Massachusetts, by a landslide of votes in the tradition of Nixon and McGovern in '72 and Reagan in '80 and '84. It was the first time since 1928 the American voters granted the Republican Party a third consecutive term in the White House. This didn't mean Bush was the most popular candidate. To the voters it meant it was a choice between, an ex-Vice-President, one time considered a wimp who walked away squeaky clean from the Iran-Contra scandal, a former CIA Director who was pitted against a Governor the country thought was ready to release convicts and murderers from prisons if he were elected President.

"This is what the political analysts wanted you to hear and, of course, wasn't true. The media was just as much at fault and gave the public what they thought we, the people, wanted to hear."

Richard Franklin spoke into a pocket recorder as he drove his rented Monte Carlo down Pico street in Los Angeles, California. He turned onto the Avenue of the Stars next to the

Twentieth-Century Fox studios and headed toward the twin towers in Century City. Once this entire complex of buildings, shops, stores and offices used to be the back lot of the Fox studios, before they sold it off to developers.

Franklin added another impression into his recorder before shutting it off. "The election was as simple as that! God help us there will not be a second term!"

Franklin's Monte Carlo drove down a Christmas decorated 'Avenue of the Stars' on a warm bright sunny day, December 19, 1989. The news on the front pages of every newspaper, radio and television station carried the same story-- Manuel Noriega was the scum of the earth and Bush was out to get him.

After crushing his political contenders six months before, dictator General Manuel Antonio Noriega of Panama remained in office defying the United States to act.

It was no wonder he earned the nickname, 'the most hated man in the United States.' Deputy Secretary of State Lawrence Eagleburger charged Noriega amassed a personal treasure of at least $200 million through criminal activities, mostly drug trafficking.

The newspapers uncovered the story Bush authorized three-million dollar covert plan for the CIA to recruit members of the Panamanian Defense Forces for an anti-Noriega revolt. But the word leaked out before the operation got under way, and it had to be abandoned.

Several days later in a village neighborhood in Panama City, during a quiet but festive evening, a family said good night to their neighbors and relatives, wishing them a merry Christmas holiday. The family consisted of four children including a four-month old baby. The child was kissed the last time by the grateful grandparents, and tears of joy were in their eyes as they waved bye to their grandchildren as they walked into the warm, dark night. The children were delighted with the Christmas presents their grandparents gave them and put them next to the Christmas decorations in their house. Then the children sang a Christmas song: *'Oh Come, All Ye Faithful,'* in their language.

As the grandparents walked through the neighborhood from their children's house holding each other's hands, they looked to one another a moment, feeling as if life had been good to them. Suddenly, an explosion behind them shattered their hopes and dreams. They turned around to see an orange-yellow fireball blasting out of a dozen homes.

Their children and grandchildren, all the people who mattered to them, were hit and instantly killed with one strike. The two grandparents tried to rush back, but the blazing fire was so intense. They had to be restrained from getting near to the inferno of houses. They could only fall to their knees and cry out in anguish at the death of their loved ones.

Loud speakers throughout the city announced Noriega was to be placed under house arrest and the bombing would continue until those who know his whereabouts came forward to confess.

Apache attack helicopters appeared on the Panamanian coastline in swarms, like bees around a buzzing beehive. The United States invasion of Panama had begun. It was America's first major post-containment military operation. And it's purpose was to overthrow the dictator of Panama, General Manuel Antonio Noriega.

The city was attacked and bombed relentlessly. Innocent civilians were killed as though this was part of protocol. A war of laser-guided missiles and infrared beams, were launched by stealth fighters appearing out of nowhere, experimenting with their use of new weapons for the first time on a populated city.

It was apparent to everyone, Panama and its people were used, abused and killed as if Murder Incorporated had entered town. Twenty-six thousand U.S. troops were ordered into the country by George Bush, the President of the United States to search for one man. They confronted and actually assassinated Panamanians indiscriminately in the streets for reasons, even today, can't be explained.

A military tank drove over a family car, smashing a family with two children inside and left it for all to witness following the invasion.

December 23, 1989. Five people driving to a relative's home for Christmas were stopped on the highway by American soldiers and all five taken from the car. Each one was told to lay flat on the pavement, then shot to death. Eight Panamanian soldiers under Noriega's rule were arrested and taken into a field. They were tied, hand and foot, and after an interrogation, all were shot as they sat on their knees. Continued use of deadly force became U.S. policy in the weeks to come.

As the media announced the invasion of Panama as if it were a Fourth of July event, another story unfolded in the United States. Dan Rather, Peter Jennings and Tom Brokaw all enthusiastically used Noriega as the front story of every newscast.

And these newscasts were watched by a certain person who sat in a black leather-bound chair, in a darkened family tv room.

Dan Rather announced on CBS news: "Over twenty-thousand soldiers and Marines launched their attack last night in the early morning darkness, by swarms of helicopters..."

On the television screen, viewers saw a Panamanian house surrounded by U.S. Marines demanding the family inside to come out for an arrest. What the U.S. news reporters didn't show were the fires started, one by one, as a U.S. Marine threw fire grenades into the windows of the houses. After each explosion a fire started, and this destruction continued through the Panamanian neighborhoods as families panicked, screamed and ran for their lives.

An old man, cried out, a grandfather pleaded to a soldier as he was taken away, "Why, why is Bush doing this to us? Why isn't your President arrested for doing this to us in our own country? Do you see us in your country doing what Bush is doing to us? My God, we are human beings! There are worse men than Manuel Noriega. At least he was giving us three meals a day. Now we have nothing!"

In America, what was broadcast on the news in the aftermath of the invasion seemed like a Mardi Gras, instead of the reality of what it was-- a massacre of innocent civilians--anywhere from one thousand to two thousand dead. Family members were forced to hunt for their own missing children, husbands, wives and parents, who, as time passed, were never seen again.

At a Hollywood Christmas party in Los Angeles, Richard Franklin stood in the midst of film people from both sides of the camera, actors, directors, and producers.

All were quiet, some sitting in front of a television screen, some standing as they watched. Some were angry and were ready to explode, while others were ignorant and uncaring.

Dan Rather reported, "While American troops take over much of the country of Panama, their chief target Manuel Noriega escaped!"

One of the principals in the room yelled out, "Why wouldn't he? Anybody in their right mind would do the same, especially when our country is breaking international law by illegally invading a foreign country and violating both the U.N. Charter and the Geneva Convention. And for what, to show Bush is not a wimp, that he can kick some butt? Or is it to capture or kidnap Noriega-- is that it?"

An actor taking his cue responded in Bush's defense, "Yeah, like Noriega is such a nice guy. He murders people and is a head of a drug cartel."

The actor smirked, but an elderly screenwriter spoke up with some authority, "Young man, we have no proof Noriega murdered anyone except what our government tells us! This is Noriega's country, not ours! Every country has their murderers, and their drug problems, so why is Noriega any different? President Reagan once said we bought and paid for Panama Canal. That's not true. The French deserted the building of the Panama Canal in 1903. All we did was to take over and finish it in exchange for allowing our military to build a base there and to help safeguard the Americans from any threat of war and keep the peace. If there is a drug problem and it has gotten out of hand, well, you can blame President Bush. It was Bush who, as CIA Director under President Gerald Ford, trained Noriega to be the military commander he is today.

"Carter, during his administration, severed Noriega from American ties within the CIA. The present leaders of this world having no American ties were arranged to be eliminated with someone waiting in the wings to take their places. This can happen in Iraq, Honduras, Vietnam, Guatemala-- yes, even here in Panama. Noriega, either alone or with the help of our own CIA, eliminated the past government of Panama. What happened then?

"Well, the Reagan administration appointed George Bush, the newly elected Vice-

President, as Chairman of the Anti-drug Commission to halt drug trafficking, a terrible burden to our country. But what did Bush do? He put Noriega back on the CIA payroll. It was Bush who appeared in Panama following the sudden and mysterious death of their President and stood next to Noriega, ruling now under the guidance of Bush and the CIA.

"Mind you, young man, under Reagan's administration, the drug trafficking last year in 1988 had tripled in this country. I find Bush stopping the supply of drugs here in Hollywood, alone, a debacle, wouldn't you? And I'm not accusing anyone in this room so don't get all waffled over what I say. I said my piece, and I will not say another word about it. Someone else can have the floor now!"

But no one wanted it. The television had the last word, as pictures of President and Mrs. Bush on holiday at their shoreline mansion in Kennebunkport, Maine, flickered across the screen, speaking to a group of press people. "Mr. Noriega, the drug indicted dictator of Panama... We want to bring him to justice. We want him out, and we want to restore democracy to Panama. So when you read these outrageous charges from a drug related-indicted dictator, discount them. They are total lies!"

Ted Koppel came on the air, continuing to give a retrospective concerning Bush's fight to gain control of the number one hated military dictator and now drug trafficker in the Americas, "...Now belonging in the same fraternity of International villains including Idi Amin, Ayatollah Khomeini, and Muammar Gaddafi, is Manuel Noriega!"

Richard Franklin rose from his chair. A woman in her forties noticed him as he walked out of the room and into the kitchen to make a sandwich.

He picked up a plate from the kitchen table where a sumptuous spread of food was arranged and spread one side of his bread with mustard. Then he applied the sliced turkey and another half dozen varieties of meat.

The woman from the screening room entered and saw the huge sandwich on Franklin's plate. "Merry Christmas!" she said to break the silence.

"And a Merry Christmas to you," Franklin responded, smiling.

"I hope we didn't bore you out there with our political jargon. Not all of us out here are pinheads and bimbos. We do have strong opinions and minds of our own."

"No, no..." Richard quickly cut in, "I enjoyed myself out there. I agreed with much what your friends said. I wonder why I don't see some of the things on the screen instead of all the Rambo crap and Friday the Thirteenth, number two-hundred and three." Franklin now laughed, wiping his mustard hand on a cloth.   He reached out to shake this woman's hand, "My name is Richard Franklin..."

She did the same. "Mine is Kirsten Manderson. Oh, I agree with you, the women want more roles and bigger and larger-than-life characters created for them as well, but there are those who still sweat from the days of the House of Un-American Activities that intimidated the industry for twenty years. We can still feel it whenever we have something to say, and we feel scrutinized by the government every time a studio head says 'no' to this project or that one. Instead, we're stuck with *Happy Days* and *Laverne and Shirley*!"

"I see your point," Franklin said.

Kirsten paused for a moment. "Say, you're that attorney they say worked for the House or Senate Committee for Assassinations on Kennedy and King, aren't you?"

Franklin grinned and nodded, "Word certainly gets around fast!"

Kirsten smiled as well. "Believe me, it's a small world in this industry, where no secrets are kept for long. When an actor is out of a job and needs money, they create a scandal. All they have to do is get someone to call the Inquirer or some trash magazine and they're hot news again. That's how their agents get them back in the limelight. It's a merry-go-round, some get on and some get off. The secret is to stay on."

Franklin found it delightful conversing with this charming and intelligent lady. "And what part of this merry-go-round are you involved in?" he asked jokingly.

Kirsten reached in her purse and handed him a card. "I'm an associate producer and I'm casting a film to start after the holidays."

Franklin was impressed. "I'm somewhat in the business myself."

"Oh?"

"I work for an entertainment law firm."

"That's really interesting! What do you do there?"

"This and that. A lot of legal stuff. I help evaluate a script from the legal angle. I make sure all the I's' are dotted and the T's' are crossed. Maybe you'd like to come by some day to talk about any future projects." In return, he gave her his card.

"I'd like that. But answer me one question, Mr. Franklin."

"Go ahead, shoot away!" Franklin sat down on a kitchen stool and gestured her to sit next to him.

Kirsten pulled up a stool as Franklin bit into his larger-than-life sandwich.

"Well back in 1980 and '81 I was working on an independent production as a lowly production assistant.

Franklin chuckled. I can't picture you as a lowly anything."

Kirsten laughed along with him. Well, I had to start somewhere. My job was to read the submitted scripts and to write a synopsis of the story.

"You were a reader?"

"Yes, a very low paid reader," Kirsten confided. "Well one day I happened to read a script that was-- well, it was different."

"Was it good?"

"To tell you the truth, I couldn't get into it. The subject matter wasn't my cup of tea. It was a political thriller; something I had no personal interest in. I had difficulty reading it. Some of the dialogue and descriptive scenes bothered me. Still, I plowed my way through it and wrote my synopsis."

Kirsten stopped for a moment, reflecting on her thoughts. "You know, I took the job because I needed the money, like everyone does when they try to break into the movies. You take what's given to you, or you don't work, simple as that. Well, the reason I'm bringing this up is, although I thought this script was too wild and crazy at the time, it started to grow on me. You know, like Hitchcock's *Vertigo* did these past two decades. And the script still haunts me to this day. It's been eight years now, and I've been asking myself why ever since."

Franklin's curiosity was showing. "What was in the script that bothered you?"   "Well, at first I looked at the script as a complete fantasy, but then as time passed, what I thought was fantasy became a reality. It began to scare me and gave me the willies. I was grateful my company dropped the project, but when I eventually found out the reason it was no longer in production, reality set in."

Kirsten started to elaborate, "In some way, I felt sorry for the author whom, I have to say, I admired tremendously as a person and even as a screenwriter, someone who had written something important, ahead of its time. I don't even think he knew what he had written, but everyone in Hollywood wanted to be a part of it. Can you believe it, I even heard a rumor Brando wanted to be cast in one of the parts? The next thing I knew, the author decided to split from the Hollywood scene and went back to write for periodicals and magazines. I, meanwhile, kept the script for myself, instead of trashing it, and was astonished every time I picked it up to read."

"What made it so fascinating for you-- a script you supposedly had no interest in?" Franklin asked.

"It was about-- well, in one sentence, what would happen if sometime in the near future, history repeated itself with a similar incident like the Kennedy's assassination. I mean, this script was very visually great for a major motion picture, no doubt about it. The author was very meticulous and described every detail-- how it could be done who did it and how amazingly simple it would be to cover up. He even said it was make believe, because, as everyone who read his script thought, his conspiracy theory was so plausible, it could be mistaken as what really happened in the Kennedy Assassination. His supposition was something a conspiracy theorist could really sink his teeth into!

Franklin was so engrossed in what Kirsten was saying he forgot to chew his sandwich. "I can see why you found his script so intriguing."

"That's not the half of it!" Kirsten continued, "Imagine my surprise when I discovered he really believed in the government's conclusions about the Kennedy Assassination and actually supported the point of view Oswald did it! This guy was playing with conspiracy theories, but by God, Mr. Franklin, this script became real to me, even now.

"Please, call me Richard," he told her. "Mr. Franklin is too formal."

"All right... Richard. Remember when Reagan called Gorbachev 'Satan' and said he ruled over an evil empire? Now Bush is creating the same myth today using Noriega. And people laughed at President Reagan when he told Gorbachev to tear down those walls-- the iron curtain-- but today the rumor is that Reagan may be right. Gorbachev admired Reagan and now Reagan has no more ill feelings for the Soviet Union then he did before. The author of this script opened with the scenario of the Russians and the United States as allies, though it isn't revealed until the very end of the story. There are clever hints all the way through, but you miss them at first because you only think of this story as a fantasy. There's even an American Rock singer singing in the opening scene at a Russian arena."

"You say the author wrote about this stuff back in '81?" Franklin found it a little hard to believe.

Kirsten shook her head. "I discovered the author wrote his first draft in 1977-- about the same time when you were working on the House Select Committee. Now this script bothered me so much that in the mid-eighties, I had my father read it, and he was very much impressed. To my amazement, he wanted to meet the author immediately. Well, by this time I had lost contact with him, although I tried to track him down through the periodicals he wrote, and even through the U.S. Marine Corps, since he was a Vietnam vet. But I had no luck."

"And just who was this screenwriter-- Oliver Stone?" Franklin asked.

277

Kirsten laughed and shook her head. "Oh, Richard, I wish it were as simple as that. Yes, '*Born on the Fourth of July*' was the biggest film this year and even more controversial than '*Platoon.*' But no, the author's name was Modini.

Franklin broke in, "Wait a minute... You...you don't mean John Modini, do you?"

Kirsten's eyes widened, "Yes, John Modini. How did you know? Have you heard of him?"

Franklin laughed loud, "Yes, I met him over a year ago. He and I were working on-- coincidentally-- the Kennedy matter. Then all of a sudden he disappeared. I mean, some people believe he's dead, because nobody knows his whereabouts. And most of his friends have given him up looking for him after all this time. Boy, that is strange!" Then Franklin remembered the question he wanted to ask. So tell me, what did your father want to talk to Mr. Modini about. By the way who is your father-- If you don't mind me prying?"

"No, I don't mind. I feel that I can trust you." Kirsten lowered her voice. "I'll tell you if you promise not to repeat it to anyone."

Franklin nodded with a serious face. "Sure!"

"He used to be CIA."

Franklin's eyebrows lifted, "Did your father tell you why he wanted to see Mr. Modini?" he said, a bit startled.

The audio from the television in the next room mentioned Noriega's name. Some of the guests made loud derogatory comments and were hushed up. Kirsten ignored the distraction and sat up straight on her stool, "My father wouldn't tell me. I can't even tell you his name, but I gathered from his interest it had to do with who covered up the President Kennedy's death and how they did it." she explained. "All my father said to me was Mr. Modini was on to something. So I went back to read the script again and that's when things started falling into place. It became scary. I thought back to when the project was canceled and why!"

Franklin listened intently. He found himself thinking of Modini again after all this time.

"One of the backers on the project had to bail out and he was the largest contributor to the project!"

"Wait a minute," Franklin stopped her. "What was the name of this project? Did they say why the money men bailed out?"

"It doesn't matter," Kirsten told him, "Modini wouldn't divulge the actual screenplay's title, but the original working title was *The Connection.* And months later I found out the man who bailed out of the project was an American living somewhere abroad. First, even Modini didn't know this man's identity. He would get a call in Los Angeles from outside the country through a hookup out of our San Francisco office. Our producers and Modini would talk through a middle man, but eventually the backer wanted to talk to Modini one on one."

A crease appeared between Franklin's eyes. "Did he get many of these calls?"

"He would get these calls periodically and they both became very friendly with each other. Mr. Modini knew he had an ally with this gentleman. Meanwhile, things began to get very interesting. Modini planned to keep as much of his script a secret while trying to bring together the cast and crew for this project. In a surprising move, he spent a month calling Yale University trying to acquire Iris Starling for the female lead

"Oh I remember her, "Franklin said, "She was that actress who starred in several blockbuster movies then decided to put everything on hold for a few years so she could get a college degree."

Kristen nodded, "Yes, she surprised the Hollywood community by that decision. But it was something she always wanted to do. But back to the story, Modini was persistent about hiring Iris for this project and spent every week conversing with her dean as a go-between. After the first few calls, the dean looked forward each week to hearing from him and finally told Modini at the end of the month Miss Starling had expressed an interest in the project and wanted to talk to him the next day. So this woman made arrangements for Mr. Modini to speak to her. Modini was ecstatic. He accomplished what one member of the production crew called his first coup, but within the next few hours, something terrible happened-- which I believe changed the fate of both Iris Starling and Mr. Modini-- and, in turn, devastated our nation. That was the day John Hinckley shot President Reagan and crippled James Brady for life."

Franklin frowned. "Yes, I remember when that assassination attempt happened." He got up from his stool and put his sandwich aside. "Can I get you a drink, cause I need one," he asked Kirsten,

"Yes, I'll have a gin and tonic, please!" Franklin crossed to the small portable bar and started to mix her drink. Kirsten continued with her story. "Modini spent the rest of the day and evening contemplating what to do, especially after it was announced that Hinckley shot Reagan because of love or infatuation for Iris Starling.

"Modini was worried about Iris more than he was for the future of his project and knew he would have to decide whether to tell her about it or ask her to wait until this unexpected publicity in her life subsided. Of course, the crew at my office, at least half of them, thought this would be great publicity for a project just starting up."

Franklin handed Kirsten her gin and tonic as he listened, riveted to her story.

"But, Modini made up his mind after Ted Koppel's 'Night Line' that evening," she resumed. "Can you imagine, they even canceled the Oscars that night! Well, Koppel announced all materials sent in the mail to Iris Starling would be searched and scrutinized by the FBI. Modini realized there was no use sending her a script, because there was no way he would jeopardize the project when he didn't want anyone to know what it was about. So when Koppel mentioned Iris Starling had been placed in an FBI safe house for protection, Modini made up his mind to drop Miss Starling from his intended cast, although he still felt she was perfect for the part. In reality, she didn't know it, but she was already playing the part."

"What do you mean?" Franklin asked.

"The 'Iris' character in the screenplay, along with the leading male character, both become symbolically Lee Harvey Oswald. Can you see Modini explaining her character over the phone to

Iris with the FBI crouched around her call or listening in?"

Franklin shrugged his shoulders. "So what happened when he was supposed to call her? Did he cancel the call?"

Kirsten smiled. "No, he made the call, but decided to be a gentleman about it, and found to his amazement Iris was a lady about it-- a true professional, as well. She actually kept Modini and his call to her private, away from the FBI, perhaps as a courtesy to a future employer-- I don't know, but Iris gave her dean private instructions. The dean knew Modini well enough by now to keep everything confidential."

"The dean told Modini about Iris Starling's predicament, her trials and tribulations with the FBI. She apologized for her absence and told him Iris asked for Modini to send the script through her, so she would pass it along to Miss Starling to read. Modini thanked the dean for this information and explained to her why he couldn't do this, because of the intentional secrecy of the project. He said it was for Iris' protection and for his, and for now, couldn't send any information about the project. That was it. He apologized to Miss Starling on his behalf and thanked the dean for putting the two in contact, but he felt in his heart-- not like some of us-- his project was doomed."

Franklin sighed. "It's a shame he had such strong personal feelings about his script. It seems to me all this need for secrecy was causing more distraction for him than accomplishment."

"More than you think," Kirsten said. Modini's prediction came true a few days later. A call came from San Francisco asking for him. The message was from the backer. He decided he would not finance the film. It would be years later when I found out clues to whom this backer might have been. After that, Modini just put the project back on the shelf and left town."

Franklin, took a sip of his drink, then asked the sixty-four thousand dollar question, "And...? Who was he-- this backer?"

Kirsten took a breath. Her voice became a whisper. "Modini knew his real name, but I didn't. It was always confidential. All I could find out was that he was one of the people close to

Richard Nixon, until the day Nixon said goodbye, waved to a nation, and flew away in that helicopter in August of '74."

Franklin was stunned, "Modini's backer worked for Nixon?"

Kirsten nodded, "In some capacity, very high up. I don't know what job he had, but it was low profile. He apologized to Modini and explained it had to do with Reagan's assassination attempt. And if certain people in the government found out he was participating in Modini's project he would be in deep trouble. He suggested Modini not to abort the project because the people have a right to know, the same thing what my father told me, a right to know the truth.

"Modini was naive and didn't know what the hell the backer was talking about at the time. Then the backer told him he was on the right track and had an important script that should be made into a movie right away! He informed Modini about Reagan's assassination attempt and said not to believe what was in the news or what the government was revealing-- that the Iris Starling story was a facade to hide the real truth.

"The real answer was in Modini's screenplay, and when one realized who had control of the President, day in and day out, he'd get to the truth of the matter. One day, it will be disclosed that an explosive bullet was used to shoot at the President. Now how did someone like Hinckley have in his possession explosive bullets? Think about it. The backer then said he hoped the two of them could meet some day in person and that was it!"

Now Franklin took a breath. "Do you have a copy of Mr. Modini's screenplay?" he asked.

Kirsten reluctantly nodded. "Yes, I can make you a copy from the one I let my father read."

"Would it be possible for me to meet your father?"

"No, I can't. There's no way he'll go for it. He's been out of it since the late fifties, and..." She hesitated, turning it over in her mind. "I'll tell you what, Mr. Franklin-- Richard... You find Mr. Modini! My father definitely wants to meet him. Find him and I'll do my best to set up a

282

meeting."

Franklin wasn't enthusiastic about her suggestion. "What if Mr. Modini is dead?" he said, trying to discourage her.

Kirsten touched his shoulder warmly and briefly as she scooted off her stool. "I don't know what to tell you. I can't promise you anything. But I will get you a copy of *The Connection* as soon as I can. That's a promise."

* * *

In the darkened family room, only the flicker from the television screen lighted up the room. Dan Rather reported on the continued search for Noriega, showing the front page newspaper headlines throughout the country as well as a picture of Noriega in a wanted poster with a one million dollar reward for his capture!

Dan Rather stated, "All things may not be good. One American soldier died today making it sixteen dead so far in the fight to restore freedom."

The person sitting in a black leather-bound chair took the remote and switched to NBC News and Tom Brokaw reporting:

"...And here's more news about the American soldier who died today. It caused grave concern at the White House. President Bush made the announcement earlier today at a news press conference."

Bush appeared at the podium, tight-lipped, angry, and tense as he spoke with the press corps: "If they kill an American Marine, that's real bad! If they threaten and brutalize the wife of an American citizen, sexually threatening the...the...a...the Lieutenant's wife by kicking him in the groin...over and over again, this President is going to do something about it!"

An older woman walked into the doorway of the tv room. The light from the screen gave a silhouetted impression of her face as she interrupted, "What is that man talking about? Is he even making any sense when he speaks out like that? Who's doing what to whom down there anyway?"

The man in the chair said nothing, only responding by pushing the TV remote. As the older woman left the room, A local news reporter came on the tv screen in close-up:

"In other national news tonight, a man who was a heartbeat away in becoming a Supreme Court Justice, Judge Henry Kencade, today officially retired after the acquittal earlier this year in the death of a local Washington prostitute because of a lack of evidence. Senator Gerald Fuller, a staunch supporter of Kencade announced today: 'We are losing a leader from the State of Indiana, one who was destined to become the Republican party's leading candidate as our next Supreme Court appointed judge.' All charges were dropped--"

The hand holding the TV remote shut off the set before the reporter could finish. The room went completely dark.

* * *

The winter season seemed to stand still. It was early March of 1990. The snow remained unmelted, shimmering on the outskirts of the countryside, a hundred miles south of Madison, Indiana.

It was here a quiet convalescent home was reserved for the rich and powerful, those who wish to withdraw from society and from the pressures of every day life. It was here where alcoholic senators, congressmen, and even their lovely wives came to dry out. It was also here where Catherine Rogers' mother, Judge Kencade's wife, committed suicide. And it was here Catherine Rogers resided after her hospitalization from her traumatic ordeal a year and a half-ago. She had been through months of physical therapy and recuperation.

Lately, there was marked progress in her mental and psychological condition and she showed rapid improvement in her rehabilitation. Catherine's doctor explained to Judge Kencade and Michael Bradley the seriousness of Catherine's emotional disorder. She had undergone such an unendurable episode in her life; there was no specific time table for her recovery. She coped one day at a time, and initiated the recovery process at her own pace. In short, it was up to her to make the choice to want to get better.

During the last visits, Kencade and Bradley saw the improvement in her. They saw a little bit of the strength and determination of the old Catherine. They were encouraged. Her physical scars were healed, but her emotional scars ran deep.

On this visit, a nurse helped Catherine into a wheelchair, with the assistance of her father, Judge Kencade. The nurse excused herself and went back to her duties.

Catherine didn't say anything to her father or the nurse. In fact, Catherine had not spoken much since she entered the convalescent home, not because of her injuries, but more so of the fact her attack destroyed her self-esteem, making her more vulnerable and insecure. It became a habit for her to withdraw into her own little world. But gradually she was breaking the habit.

Kencade pushed Catherine's wheelchair to a second floor patio of the convalescent home and stopped short of entering an outdoor balcony. It was a bright day outside, and it was an unusual one. A light fall of snow was coming down, out of a sunlit sky.

"Don't stop here," Catherine told her father, pulling a blanket around her, "I want to go out. I need some fresh air!"

Her father obliged and pushed her out onto the balcony, making faint wheel tracks in the snow. It had been rare for her to speak with him or give him orders until the past few months, so he felt thankful that he could help.

Catherine smiled at the beautiful view as Kencade waited for the right moment to speak. When she finally turned to him, he gave her some good news, "I've been told, Catie, you can leave here in a couple of weeks."

Catherine appeared not to hear her father. She stared out into the distance, seemingly in another world. "Why do you suppose Mother killed herself, dad?" she asked him

Kencade was taken by surprise by Catherine's unexpected question. He became uncomfortable and walked over to the edge of the balcony. He faced the countryside and gazed at the black, leafless trees isolating the property, trying to frame an honest reply for his daughter. "If only I could answer that one myself, dear, I would never have left her in others' care. I didn't know how much she hurt inside. I think she didn't like the world outside and didn't like where it was going."

"You're saying it was because of her work."

"That was only part of it. When we lost your stepbrother in Vietnam in '65, all she did was live for his memory. That's what started it. Remember in the early 70's when your mother was well enough to return home from this place? We were so pleased she found a new focus for her life. She became immersed in her campaign work again and dedicated all her time to reelecting President Nixon to his second term. She thought his trips to China and Russia was the answer to world peace. She had the connections to meet the right people and was convinced she could make a difference.

"Yes... I remember that..." Catherine said.

Well, she did make a difference. And Nixon was reelected. And afterward, when the news of Nixon and Watergate broke, she was devastated. The fact she campaigned so hard for him and believed in him so much, and devoted so much of her time to him, the news became unbearable to her. She blamed Nixon for screwing up the memory of her son."

Kencade crossed back to his daughter and tenderly stroked her hair. Tears appeared in his eyes as he spoke. "I'm sorry if it seemed her energies and love weren't transferred to you, Catie, but she did love you, I do know that. She-- she just couldn't show it. She was always closer to the male side of her family, never to the female side-- especially concerning your Grandmother. She just hated her, and I cannot tell you why."

Catherine listened patiently to her father and finally spoke up, "I know about Mother and her feelings. I've resolved to accept them a long time ago. I always thought of Mother as too strong a woman to have ever wanted to...to kill herself! But life always reveals one's weaknesses. Apparently, Mother hid hers and wouldn't admit them. In a place like this, Mother wasn't aloud to let her idiosyncrasies out. I think she decided it must be better to die and take all her bitterness with her to her grave than to surrender anything and everything to a doctor's medical chart. That's sad, Father... But I now realize she didn't want me to become like her. It was you, dad, who influenced me who gave me your strength and-- yes, even stubbornness. But I am like Mother, Dad. I feel her inside me all the time."

Kencade looked at his daughter, then bent down to kiss her on the forehead. "Yes, Catie, you do-- except you have the mind and the strength and the will to save the world. And some day, I'll wait for you to succeed in doing just that! But no matter, I'll always be proud of my daughter because she is the one person who never wants to give up!"

Catherine grabbed her Father's arm and held on tight, hugging him as he brushed back the tears again. The light snow continued to fall around them, giving them each a quiet comfort and joy that, would be hard to duplicate again in their lifetime.

Chapter Twenty-Three

"Through the Looking Glass, Darkly"

When I was a child, I spake as a child, I understood as a child, I thought as a
child: but when I became a man I put away childish things
For now we see through a glass, darkly: but then face to face: now I know in part;
but then shall I know even as also I am known.

I. Corinthians, Chapt. 13, vs. 11-12

A camera crew filmed the devastation, the destructive aftermath of the fighting in Panama City. They captured in detail how Bush's troops left it, bombed as if it were a city in England in the days of Nazi Germany. The media was just as much to blame. President Bush's words on the subject were issued through the State Department, and by the end of December, with the eventual capture of Noriega, the United Nations had condemned by an overwhelming majority the invasion of Panama as a flagrant violation of international law. Even the mention of this was overlooked by the news media. If any trace of it did appear, it was an afterthought on a news broadcast or hid in the back pages of the major newspapers that supported it-- the *Los Angeles Times*, the *New York Times*, the *Washington Post* and the *Wall Street Journal*.

A mother cried out to the camera crew filming the reaction of the Panamanian people upon finding fifteen mass graves where hundreds to thousands of bodies were hastily dumped following the invasion. The mass graves, hidden for months, were discovered, revealing the murdered bodies of sixty-five percent of the civilians, old and young alike.

As many family members hunted futilely for their relatives, the mother cried out for her daughter, "Your President Bush should pray to God, for what he is doing to my daughter. She no longer wants to live. May his children and the next generation of American children be spared what he is doing to us. He should ask God for forgiveness for all the damage he did to many families down here!"

This is the story America didn't see or hear, or didn't want you to see or hear. Instead, we got Tom Brokaw ending his report one evening with:

"We hear from President Bush tonight, as we end this program, on the high price these young men paid as soldiers. Good-bye."

Bush spoke, "They asked if it was worth it. Every human life is precious, and...and yet, I have to answer, yes! It's been worth it!"

Richard Franklin drove into a Dallas suburb and parked his rented Subaru in front of the home of a gentleman who worked preserving the archives of the JFK Assassination Center in Dallas, Texas.

Jeremy Peters, an expert in computer analysis, was an older man in his mid-sixties, on the heavy side with receding hairline. Peters invited Franklin into his living room where on display was a familiar photo of Oswald with his assassin rifle and revolver supposedly used to kill both Kennedy and Officer J. D. Tippit. It was a picture familiar to the one on the *Life Magazine's* 1964 cover, prior to the release of the Warren Commission Report. The original photo became its Exhibit 134. The picture in the living room wasn't the same picture. Peters handed it to Franklin, and they both sat down on the sofa.

Peters began. "Remember, Marina Oswald, now Mrs. Porter, confessed to taking the picture used on the cover of *Life Magazine*, but when a second picture was discovered, Marina became confused. This *second* photo of Oswald, found soon after the Warren report was completed, was rushed to the commissioners, with the added comment she did not realize it could have been possible. She might have accidentally taken this second photo by tripping over some object as she took the first photo, but could not remember taking it, although the commissioners took her word for it. In fact, for someone, whom Gerald Ford consistently said was a nut and crazy in the head, they believed everything she said-- at least what those who rehearsed her to say. But what can she say about this <u>third</u> picture found ten years later and hidden from the public by both the Senate and House Committees on Assassinations. And how can you explain Roscoe White, a Dallas police officer, had it in his possession?

"There was a rumor that a fourth photo existed in the files at the Dallas Police Department. You see what this means, don't you. I don't think Oswald's wife took these pictures at all! Even if true, Oswald's face in the photos never changes. It looks like the same face attached to the bodies in each of the photos."

Franklin handed the photo back to Peters. "I think Marina was scared shitless by the people protecting her-- the Secret Service or whoever," Franklin remarked, "until her part was done with the Warren Report! Well, she's protesting now, isn't she?"

Peters agreed, "Yes, but again, the media and authorities are all making her look foolish to the public on national television! But getting back to your photo, we know it's not Oswald's body. What's your story on it?"

Franklin stared at the picture on the table. "It was given to us, meaning the House, during our investigation, in the mid-seventies. The Senate had it first, then passed it on to us secretly, with a note attached stating it was in their possession after being stolen from Roscoe White's house! I believe, and always have, the Dallas Police Department or someone in charge, was responsible in getting Oswald killed. If White had this photograph of Oswald all these years, then there was proof of <u>some</u> cover up within the Dallas Police Department itself!"

Peters wasn't surprised. "Well, hell, Franklin! This is one of many incidents where the Dallas Police Department has covered up! What about their protection of Oswald with seventy-five cops surrounding him when he was shot down-- and what about Jack Ruby? Who allowed him in that basement--and how could he pass seventy-five police officers with a gun in hand and fifty newsmen giving their play-by-play to the world? How come the Warren Commissioners can explain Oswald as the lone assassin after he's dead, but can't explain the how and why Ruby shot Oswald-- nor who he was, although he lived to talk four more years? Why didn't the Senate, let alone the House, pursue this third Roscoe White picture? It was significant, and it could have led somewhere!"

Richard Franklin sighed, expressing his concern. "Why do you think I'm here? I disagree totally with the direction Chairman Blakley took, declaring the Mafia the sole link to a possible conspiracy. These were his conclusions not ours! This photo was considered insignificant to the Committee because-- as they put it-- Roscoe White was just an overzealous cop who wanted a souvenir to take home! Some souvenir!" he said with disgust.

"Pursuing White meant linking him to corruption within the Dallas Police Department." Peters said, "and, I also believe, within the CIA, too. One, the House did not want to make waves with the Dallas Police Department. They wanted their cooperation. I know how stupid that sounds, but you've got to remember all these Committees were facades to appease the public and conspiracy buffs. Two, blaming the Mafia would exonerate the CIA, since they always seemed to be the number one suspect. And three, Blakley was brought in to do just that-- which in turn changed the Committee's direction to the Mafia with your tax paying dollars, then to shut down the investigation because Congress felt the poor taxpayer's money was being wasted on something that never could be resolved in the first place!"

"That's true," Franklin said.

Jeremy Peters continued. "One by one you have Johnny Roselli and Sam Giancana all eliminated prior to their appearances before the House Select Committee. And the fact if the investigation did go any further might have found Jack Ruby linked to the Mafia via Chicago and Sam Giancana and-- yes, the Mafia linked to the CIA. But again that would have gotten our Committee back on track again with the number one suspect. You see what I mean, that's why all of a sudden the monies ran out to pursue any investigation into both Kennedy or King because we would have to infer our government agencies probably were involved in this mass conspiracy to eliminate them. The Kennedy and King legacies would have taken us into an era that would not have had a Vietnam War, the Pentagon Papers, an assassin squad to eliminate world leaders on the whim of the American government, a Watergate, nor even Nixon mind you, or a Ford, a Bush, the Iran Contra affair, a Noriega and now what-- a Saddam Hussein?"

"So you strongly believe Kennedy and his policies would have made a big difference?

"I'm not saying our country would have been peaches and cream, but after the cold war and the Cuban Missile Crisis, the Russians cooperated with John F. Kennedy for peace and no more nuclear proliferation. A pact was signed for a possible bright future ahead-- or a chance at one at least-- until the assassination reversed that dream, and changed history in an instant! Who could do such a thing-- certainly not one man-- not Oswald. Only our government could orchestrate a drastic change like that-- a government that needed to take out one man to make that change. It wasn't Oswald who sent us to Vietnam. It wasn't Oswald who broke that treaty with Russia. Russia always cooperated with the United States in areas concerning their Oswald connection, but the people of the United States never knew it. But J. Edgar Hoover knew! Hoover knew Oswald didn't shoot anybody on November 23, the day after the assassination. But, as we all know now, on Sunday November 24, 1963, Hoover, the CIA, the Dallas Police Department, the doctors who witnessed the body and surgery of Kennedy, and the Warren Commission-- *all of them*-- kept their mouths shut in the name of National Security."

"And why do you think they did that?" Franklin asked.

"If Oswald did it, why hide anything from you, me, or the rest of the world? If Oswald was responsible, why keep it a secret? He was just one man with a rifle and gun who changed the history of the world. Why hide it in the name of national security? Why did the Marine Corps destroy his records? Why can the IRS suppress his records of employment and monies he's received? Why can someone say he is Lee Harvey Oswald in one place when the real Oswald is in another place? There's a wolf in sheep's clothing here?"

Jeremy Peters went to his computer and opened a picture of Roscoe White on his screen. "Maybe he can answer all those questions. You know the reason I asked you to come here. You said the reason the HSCA did not pursue this photo of Oswald, now established belonging White, was that it would have led in a direction they wanted to avoid. They then switched to the Mafia theory. Well? You're right, except you still could have utilized this photo in the direction the Committee did pursue, since Ruby and the Mafia could be linked. So too, we have Roscoe White who worked with Ruby, and who can be linked to Oswald by many witnesses and friends. They can also establish White as a connection to Oswald. Rosco White's friends who are alive today, can link Oswald and White together. Roscoe White's widow and son came forward to link Ruby to him-- and, surprisingly, as one of the shooters in Dealey Plaza!"

Franklin's face wrinkled with thought. "Are you serious?"

"Yes, and there's a diary, and I've read it." Peters continued his presentation, "The FBI possessed it but it disappeared somewhere between the transfer of the FBI and CIA. The word deniability will surely be a factor when all this comes out. Don't worry, we have copies, although it will be the word of the widow and son accusing their own husband and father as being part of an assassin squad to kill the President of the United States. Here, read this, these are notes written from the diary by Rosco's widow"

Reaching into his briefcase, Peters handed Franklin a page copied from a hymnbook of sheet music. This page contained the lyrics of 'America the Beautiful.' And written on the top and bottom of the song sheet were the words written by the initials of RAW (Roscoe Anthony White) and read:

Nov. 22, '63. Today is the day. Help me, God.

RAW.

This was inscribed around the title on the top of the page. At the bottom of the page were the words:

America the Beautiful, help me to keep thinking this way so I can complete my job for my country.

RAW.

Peters handed Franklin a second song sheet. "This one was written on a 'Silent Night' song sheet the night of November 23, the day after the assassination..."

Franklin saw the words inscribed:

Jack came by tonight and all he could brag about was the killing of JFK and how he's going to kill Lee tomorrow. God, when does this end?

RAW.

Franklin asked, "Ruby?"

Peters nodded, "Yes."

"That could explain why and how Ruby got into the basement of the Dallas Police Department and shot Oswald."

"Precisely, Mr. Franklin. And remember a car was to be in place to transfer Oswald that morning. The police were not to bring Oswald out until that car was in place. Someone gave the word for Oswald to be transferred, although there were threats and warnings to both the FBI and the Dallas Police Department that Oswald would be a target. They still proceeded with fifty newsmen, as I said, to give the play by play, and seventy-five policemen lined up for Oswald's

294

appearance and transfer. It was for appearance only. It was the signal for Oswald's demise. The car wasn't in place! The order for Oswald's transfer had to be given by either Captain Fritz or Chief Curry. Oswald would have had to stop where the car was supposed to have been and wait, which I'm sure why the officers guarding him were quite nervous."

"Yes, I remember that," Franklin recalled.

"Then there was a car horn that sounded off within the basement of the garage. Again and again the horn sounded. Who honked a horn inside the basement at the precise time of Oswald's appearance? The Warren Commission never did pursue this. Why? Well, the answer was Roscoe White who was a link to Ruby, a link to the Dallas Police Department, a link to the Mafia, and even a link to the CIA. You'll find out he was one of them!"

Richard Franklin still had some doubts. "How does this diary fit in-- and why believe his widow and son?"

Peters was waiting for him to ask. "Exactly! Why would they? Only Roscoe White died mysteriously in an explosive fire following his return from his lunch break in 1971. This was just like all those other mysterious deaths of witnesses who had information crucial to Kennedy's assassination. Do you remember the other officer-- the one who witnessed the German Mauser found originally on the sixth floor of the school depository?"

Franklin remembered. "Roger Craig, the Deputy Sheriff."

"Ah, yes, what was it, about six times they tried to kill this guy. There was an attempt on his life six times! They blew him up in a car, then there was a mysterious fire in his house," Peters commented sarcastically, "and every time it happened, they said he was trying to commit suicide. Well, either he was some dumb cop or he didn't read the policeman's manual on how to commit suicide! All you had to do was put your own gun in your mouth and blow your brains out-- which, of course, Craig did on the seventh try with his shotgun. Somebody either suggested it to him or helped him because he certainly didn't do it on his own. That's what I feel happened to Roscoe White when it was discovered he was collecting souvenirs. Roger Craig's testimony has been preserved on sixteen millimeter film. I believe Mark Lane did that interview with him."

"So where does that leave us at this point?"

Peters explained, "We have White's diary uncovered by his son, Ricky, hidden at his grandfather's home in Paris, Texas. Ricky found it following his grandfather's death in 1982, while cleaning out his father's footlocker. It wasn't until 1985 that Ricky discovered what was in the diary. His mother corroborated this. She had known about it all these years and has given permission to her son to go public. They brought it here. We saw the original and we made copies. I told them not to tell anyone about the copies, especially until we hear what the FBI report has to say. Well, the FBI has misplaced it. It's not to be found I'm sure! One thing is genuine and that's the widow, Geneva White. She worked for Jack Ruby as a 'B' girl-- a 'Rail' girl-- and, as you know, half the Dallas Police Department spent time in Ruby's Carousel Club. Ruby provided his bar and private dancers for Dallas' finest, as perks after hours. Yes, Ruby and Roscoe knew each other and Geneva gave good details about the both of them!"

Franklin speculated himself, "If true, it certainly explains how Ruby kept tabs on where Oswald was, practically minute by minute. If White was who he said he was, then a man with a policeman's outfit could actually walk in and out of a room without calling attention to himself. They would notice him, see him, but would only see he is a cop. He could get evidence, without anyone's knowledge. The Warren Commission mentions police officers without names continually in their report. I wonder if any of those unnamed officers were Roscoe White."

"You said Rosco knew Oswald. Do you think he set him up with the Tippit murder? And since J.D. Tippit was also a Dallas police officer, did the two know each other?"

Again, Jeremy Peters smiled and took out another hymn sheet and holds it up to Franklin. "Ready for 'O Come, O Come, Emanuel?'" The music sheet read:

Nov. 23, '63. Well, everything went according to plan. I also had to kill my fellow officer, J.D. Tippit. But his wife and children will be taken care of. I will see to that.

Each one of us is supposed to get over 100 grand and I will see to it that she gets

his money.

RAW.

Franklin was shocked and just stared back at his host.

Peters in turn just added, "If this is not from Roscoe White's diary then someone wants us to know something through a dead man. Someone who has been dead since 1971, someone who is a police officer but in reality, CIA, infiltrating the Dallas Police Department!"

Franklin shook his head in distaste, but was pleased in this revelation. "Oswald is smeared throughout the Warren Report with plenty of circumstantial evidence to support his as the lone assassin. Even a phony name of Hiddel-- who ordered a 6.5 Mannlicher-Carcano Italian carbine rifle-- may or may not be an alias of Oswald.

Peters was reminded of something. He excused himself for a moment and left the room briefly. He returned with a copy of an affidavit in his hand. "Mr. Franklin, we mentioned Deputy Sheriff Roger Craig earlier. Remember his insistence the rifle found was not the Italian Mannlicher-Carcano-- a 6.5 carbine, said to be the assassination weapon-- but a 7.65 German Mauser? He was an expert gunman. He knew his rifles. Even the District Attorney of Dallas, Henry M. Wade, repeated this information, not only on November twenty-second, but the next day on the twenty-third. He proclaimed at a televised press conference on record, the weapon found on the sixth floor and held by Captain J. Will Fritz was a 7.65 German Mauser. Craig witnessed the discoverers of this weapon, Deputy Sheriff Eugene Boone, Deputy Constable Seymour Weitzman, and another Deputy Sheriff Luke Mooney. They all agreed it was a Mauser!

"Lieutenant J.C. Day of the Dallas Police examined the rifle and Captain Fritz actually picked it up and ejected a live round from the chamber. But when the FBI announced Oswald had purchased an Italian rifle later the next day of the twenty-third, the German rifle suddenly became inconvenient and then disappeared. Where?" Peters then handed Franklin the affidavit and concluded. "This should speak for itself."

Franklin read the affidavit:

Affidavit of Seymour Weitzman

Affidavit in Any Fact

The State of Texas,

County of Dallas"

Before me, Mary Rattan, a Notary Public in and for said County, State of Texas, on this day personally appeared Seymour Weitzman, W/M, 2802 Oates Drive, DA 76624. Bus. Robie Love, RI 11433.

Who, after being by me duly sworn, on oath deposes and says: Yesterday, November 22, 1963, I was standing on the corner of Main and Houston, and as the President passed and made his turn going west towards Stemmons, I walked casually around. At this time my partner was behind me and asked me something. I looked back at him and heard three shots. I ran in a Northwest direction and scaled a fence where we thought the shots came from..."

Here, Franklin stopped a moment to give his opinion concerning the last sentence. "I take it, when he means the direction he ran, it was toward the grassy knoll?"

Peters just winked at him, letting him read on:

...Then someone said they thought the shots came from the old Texas Building.

Again Franklin stopped. "Ha! The phony secret service plant!" Franklin continued to read:

I immediately ran to the Texas Building and started looking inside. At this time Captain Fritz arrived and ordered all of the sixth floor sealed off and searched. I was working with Deputy S. Boone of the Sheriff's Department and helping in the search. We were in the northwest corner of the sixth floor when Deputy Boone and myself spotted the rifle about the same time. This rifle was a 7.65 Mauser bolt action equipped with a 4/18 scope, a thick leather brownish-black sling on it. The rifle was between some boxes near the stairway. The time the rifle was found was 1:22 P.M. Captain Fritz took charge of the rifle and ejected one live round from the chamber. I then went back to the office after this."

(S) Seymour Weitzman
Subscribed and sworn to before me this 23 day of November A.D. 1963.

(S) Mary Rattan, MARY RATTAN
Notary Public, Dallas County, Texas

Peters told Franklin to keep the copy and added, "You won't find this affidavit in the Warren Report, but if you can find volume 24, the Commission published it on page 228 under 'Rumors and Speculations!'"

Jeremy Peters escorted Richard Franklin to his car and handed him a book entitled, *On the Trail of the Assassins.*

Franklin's eyes questioned the validity of it, and Peters assured him, "It's Jim Garrison's new book. Read it. We finally realize how and why Garrison stayed out of the limelight all these years. You'll be glad he's back to raise up a little storm again. There's talk about making a movie out of it. Maybe, it'll turn out better than Mark Lane's book, *'Executive Action,'*" he laughed, shaking Franklin's hand. "Thanks for coming, it's been a pleasure talking to you. Incidentally, is it true you campaigned in Washington for Ted Kennedy for President?"

Franklin grinned, "Yes, sir, twice. In 1980 and '84."

Peters felt sympathetic, "Do you know the truth about the Chappaquiddick affair?"

Franklin sighed at this. "Only that he'll never be able to run again for President."

"Do this... Look to Richard Nixon for your answers, young man. You'll find out why the Kennedys seemed cursed. Nixon was the one who gained the most from both Chappaquiddick, Robert's and John's assassination and Ted's stupidity. With every one of these brothers, you'll find out Nixon's hand was in the till. When the people realize Watergate had everything to do with the Kennedy's demise, you and everyone will understand Nixon's own destruction. One example you can examine after you satisfy yourself with JFK-- ask yourself why Ted Kennedy forfeited the presidency by telling a lie to the country he didn't need to tell about his involvement in the Chappaquiddick incident-- and, in this case, who the idiot was who gave him the advice he took!"

"To this day, Mr. Franklin, both the sheriff's and police department's investigators and experts can't find any evidence Ted Kennedy was ever inside that car when it went into the water! Explain that one! Nixon had a spy in the Kennedy administration, a senator who was supposed to be a Kennedy advocate, but a close associate to Nixon and BeBe Ribozo. Hah! There's a name for you! Who the hell is BeBe Ribozo? Why isn't anyone writing about him? When Kennedy and Nixon ran against each other in 1960, they made a pact with each other. Joseph P. Kennedy, the father, had a lot of dirt on Nixon-- I mean 'Tricky Dick' or 'Mr. Clean-cut Dick'-- whichever you pick. Nixon was screwed and Joseph planned to drop the bomb, but John stopped it. He told his father this presidential race would be clean. Jack went to Nixon and made a deal with him. Nixon agreed, knowing what Kennedy's father could do to him. Jack Kennedy proposed if Nixon laid off the Roman Catholic controversy, he'd call off his dad. Nixon agreed and Nixon lost-- and Nixon never forgot!"

Franklin hung on every word. Peters stopped to take a breath. "At the time, the committee chairman for JFK was Lawrence O'Brien. After JFK's assassination and Joe's death, O'Brien was in charge of Nixon's dirty little secrets, which grew larger as the years passed-- even when the Kennedys found out about his assassin squad he set up while Vice-President in the Eisenhower administration. All this was given to Bobby Kennedy's campaign, with O'Brien holding the purse strings as Bobby's chairman for President, if Nixon decided to run again in '68. This time, though, after years of blaming himself for his brother's death because of the Mafia ties, Bobby Kennedy's own investigation into his brother's death, revealed the government's involvement. Bobby decided to seek justice, to bring the truth before the American people and to stop the Vietnam war. To do this meant he had to run for the office of President of the United States.

"Johnson, knowing he was already politically dead, decided not to seek office for a second term. That left Richard Nixon alone to run against the Democrats. By June of 1968 and the night Bobby was to be assassinated, it was decided Bobby would be the Democratic candidate for president. This meant Nixon would be campaigning against another Kennedy, something he did not want to face, knowing he might have to repeat those words he sadly spoke with the media in 1962: 'You won't have Nixon to kick around any more!'

"But there was no need for Mr. Dick Nixon to worry. He had been told since 1963 he would be the next president. He shouldn't surrender now-- Johnson's out, and before the night was out so will be Robert Kennedy.

"While Bobby was speaking at the Ambassador Hotel in Los Angeles, Larry O'Brien was on his way to meet Howard Hughes who like everyone else, thought Kennedy would take the nomination and the presidency. Mr. Hughes offered a substantial contribution to Bobby's campaign fund." Jeremy Peters laughed at what he was planning to say. "Howard Hughes wanted the presidency to be a part of his future strategy. He even gave contributions to every candidate, including Nixon! He wanted the presidency in and out of his pocket. Nixon did win the presidency as he was told, but against Hubert Humphrey, and by a close margin similar to his race against

JFK. So, Nixon continued to make history and, coincidentally, O'Brien went to work for Howard Hughes.

"Now coming full circle, O'Brien found out from Hughes his one time right hand man and attorney, Robert Maheu was the conduit between the mob and the CIA to rid Fidel Castro from that island called Cuba, ninety miles off the coast of Miami Beach. And so began in January, 1960, under the orders of then Vice-President Nixon, what became a fiasco for President Kennedy one year later-- the Bay of Pigs! Eisenhower was sick in his last year in office, we don't know whether <u>he</u> even knew what plot Nixon was hatching."

Richard Franklin filled in the blanks, "So Johnny Roselli meets E. Howard Hunt, Frank Sturgis, etc., etc..."

Peters nodded, "Exactly, except it continued on and on without the Kennedys' knowledge down the line, and it wasn't until the missile crisis woke up President Kennedy and made him realize what the country and the people meant to him and what he had to do. He took his job as president seriously and saw right through Alice's looking glass, witnessing the truth. He started cleaning house in the White House as well as the government. He sought world peace, and soon he was the most popular President, let alone person, in the world. I don't have to tell you it's all recorded for posterity for future generations to witness. The world loved him and his first Lady.

"O'Brien told Hughes what dirty little secrets the Kennedys had on Nixon all these years. Hughes, always looking ahead, now had Nixon sewn his pocket, come 1972. The Republican and Democratic conventions were getting ready for a full swing with Nixon to run this time against George McGovern. Lawrence O'Brien who left Hughes to pursue another career, was asked to chair the Democratic convention. It was here Hughes decided he wanted Nixon to stay in his pocket and made a call to him. He told Nixon what evidence his former employee had that could knock him right out of the race. Ironically, Nixon, in 1972, would become the most popular President, elected by the largest landslide in the history of the Presidency.

"Nixon made a call to his old cronies, E. Howard Hunt, Frank Sturgis who later would be known as 'the Plumbers'-- in reality, his group out of the CIA! You see, they also had a lot to lose if the illegal activities they had carried out over the years were ever discovered. It could harm the future existence of a certain agency John F. Kennedy said, just prior to his death, that he was going to splinter into a thousand pieces. Nine years later in a hotel in Washington, D.C., Watergate was born. Now the CIA had an agenda, but way before this, Nixon's agenda was to stop Ted Kennedy in '72 and this started in early '69. It was Nixon's first coup by the end of the first six months of his Presidency, hatched over the holidays in Key Biscayne, Florida, by a senator close to the Kennedys, a newly elected president and a mysterious fellow by the name of BeBe Ribozo."

Chapter Twenty-Four

"Nixon and Hidden Agendas"

Michael Bradley heard the news report broadcast over his car radio. "The breakup of Communism throughout Eastern Europe continued as the Cold War looks as though it's ending with the Soviet Union no longer considered the 'evil empire' our last President, Ronald Reagan, so eloquently named it in his first term. Who would think those prolific words of Reagan in his second term would come true."

The voice of Reagan repeated his famous speech, "...Mr. Gorbachev will you tear down that wall!"

A commentator followed, "President Bush must be ecstatic about all this. I don't mean the good news of the breakup of the Soviet Union, but the fact Bush needs to find a new evil force to keep the military and U.S. Intelligence Agency on the payroll and to keep their appropriations in billions of dollars from being cut. The question is why didn't the CIA see this coming? In other news, one of two bodies found last week in Northern Idaho's Priest River was now identified as Colonel Roger Tracy--" Bradley adjusted the car radio, switching stations to another channel, until he heard the music of Fleetwood Mac and he drove outside the city perimeter and into the bright, sun-filled morning countryside, heading to a convalescent home.

The home was preparing the release of a special recuperative resident.

Catherine Rogers sat into a wheelchair for the last time. When Michael Bradley arrived, he tried to take over for the nurse and prepared to handle the chair.

Judge Kencade became perturbed by all this. "Bradley, let the nurse handle the chair. Why don't you take Catherine's things to the car and put them in the trunk?"

Bradley gave the judge a dirty look. The two of them didn't like each other, but Bradley did as he was told for Catherine's sake.

Catherine smiled up at Bradley. "Thanks for being here today," she told him as he picked up her suitcases. He smiled and took her luggage down the hall. Catherine waited for him to exit into the elevator before turning to her father and speaking her mind. "Father, you shouldn't treat Michael that way-- as if he were some dog. He's my friend and he's done a lot for me!"

Kencade let out his feelings quickly, "If it weren't for him bringing you into this in the first place, this would never have happened and you would never have been here! No! I don't like the guy! I never did! He'll always be a two-bit attorney in my book!"

"Dad, that's not true. Michael is my best friend, and I respect him very much."

"Time to go,' the nurse said, preventing a protest from her father. She pushed Catherine down the corridor of the convalescent hospital as Kencade followed.

Catherine continued to defend her friend. "Remember, dad... Michael wasn't the one who brought me out here from Seattle. It was the rumors about the case. It was you, Dad! You're my father, and I love you, but right now, during times like these, I don't know whether I have any respect for you!"

Kencade, upset by Catherine's attitude, confronted her once and for all. "You're saying your father is some corrupt old judge who can be bought and paid for? That he's somehow losing his faculties, and Karl Hunter's suicide is somehow my fault?"

Catherine stopped the nurse from pushing her wheelchair. "Please, nurse...could you excuse us for a moment? she asked her. Just for a minute?"

The nurse regarded both the Judge and his daughter. "I'll be back in a few minutes," she told them. She headed down the hallway and when she was out of sight, Catherine got out of her chair to confront her father face to face. "No, father, I *don't* believe it-- any of it! But I do somehow believe Gerry Fuller has you into something so deep it's hard for you to crawl out of it! Just tell me the truth, Dad. Were you railroading Karl Hunter?"

Kencade was silent here, wanting to tell her off for blasting him like this, but something told him to be cautious. He decided it would be better to explain it, instead. "All right! I admit, maybe there's something wrong here, but it's not what you think. Gerry asked me to do this favor for him and try this proceeding. It seemed a sure, open and shut case.

"A terrible thing happened in our own community and it spread like an epidemic throughout our neighboring states. Young girls in their twenties were being murdered by a serial killer. All the evidence pointed to Hunter. How and where Gerry got it. I didn't know, and I didn't care. I just wanted this guy put away for good, but Gerry was persistent in demanding the death penalty before the trial even started."

"What were you supposed to get in return for this favor?" Catherine asked her father.

"Gerry said it would help my chances to get the newly elected President to put me on the top of the list for my appointment to the Supreme Court. But under the circumstances, although the charges against me were dropped for killing that prostitute, I asked to have my name withdrawn. I want you to understand, Catie. They fed me evidence and made me believe Hunter was guilty. Although the evidence was circumstantial, I convinced myself he was guilty, beyond a doubt! But I had <u>no</u> idea it would go this far and end with Karl Hunter taking his life. If it were my fault, then I'm the one who has to live with it."

Catherine decided it was the time to make a shocking revelation. "Dad, maybe not. Maybe the man who committed suicide was not Karl Hunter!"

Kencade looked at her strangely as if to ask 'what are you saying?' Then Catherine told him what was on her mind. "Dad, I believe Karl Hunter was the man who raped me!"

306

Kencade was unwilling to believe her statement. He thought he didn't hear his daughter correctly. "Dear? I don't think I understood what you just said?"

Catherine pulled no punches. "I'm saying, Karl Hunter didn't commit suicide! He did not die! He was the one who raped me and tried to kill me! Don't ask me how or why, I just know it was him!"

Kencade became worried about his daughter. He glanced around to see whether anyone was watching or listening to their conversation. He played up to her as he took her hand and tried to set her back into the wheelchair. "Catherine," he said sympathetically, "even if you believe this person who attacked you was Karl Hunter, then who was the man whose body they found hanging in the prison cell? And, if Hunter were alive and free, why would he want to kill you? You were defending him!"

Catherine spoke up candidly as if she had proof. "Because I know where the bodies are buried!"

Kencade put his hand to his mouth in embarrassment so not to let on his concern for her mental state, "Bodies, Catherine?"

"He did it...he *did* kill those girls, dad! And there's lots more! I'm sure I know where some of the bodies are. Mr. Ziegler, the man whose daughter I told you about, took me to this place--"

Her father interrupted her. "Why didn't you tell any of this to the police?"

"I couldn't. I told them about Mr. Ziegler and the man who tried to kill me." Catherine settled down, but she was still agitated. "I didn't want them to think I was crazy because the police found no body, not Joseph Ziegler, nor the person in the truck-- the man whom I thought was Hunter. The police deny their patrol helicopter was in the area, or what I said ever happened. And...and you know I wasn't in any shape to...to follow up on this. You're the only one I've told this to-- about Hunter and the bodies!"

"Let's keep it that way," Kencade told her, trying to calm her down, "Just between the two of us for now,"

But Catherine was persistent, "You <u>must</u> believe me, Dad! A truck tried to kill me. And Hunter was the man driving it!"

Kencade didn't know what to do or say. He was afraid for Catherine's state of mind because he wanted her out of this place and at home with him. He decided to appease her. "What is it you want me to do, Catherine?"

"I want you to get a court order to authorize an exhumation of Karl Hunter's grave!" Catherine told him,

"You want me to do WHAT?" He exploded. Kencade felt Catherine's demand was absurd.

Before he could say another word, Catherine explained, "If Hunter's not in his grave, then we have proof, right! And then it's a whole new ball game!"

Michael Bradley appeared now from the elevator, interrupting the two of them,

"Hey, what is it with you two? You hate to leave this wonderful place or what? The car is waiting in the loading zone with nobody to load! What new ball game are you talking about?"

Catherine brightened, an idea forming in her mind. "Michael, you're going to help father!"

A puzzled look came over Bradley's face, "I'm going to help *who*?"

Kencade responded, "Shut up, counselor, I'll explain later. For now, let's just get her out of here!"

Bradley agreed, "Anything you say...your Honor!" and then yelled for the nurse.

* * *

The dark silhouetted figure sat in the leather-bound reclining chair and watched Richard Milhous Nixon interviewed on the PBS channel. The interviewer inquired into Nixon's relationship with George Bush and asked how far back they went.

Nixon answered, "Well, George and I go back to 1952. His father, you know, was in the

Senate. When campaigning in Texas, George became my advance man there-- a go-go person. I don't think President Bush ever knew this, but Eisenhower told me he thought George had some potential back then."

The interviewer asked, "He was your man in Texas?"

Nixon nodded, "That's right. He was a comer!"

* * *

It was a hot summer night in New York City when Richard Franklin, briefcase in hand, walked toward the sound of a sudden burst of machine gunfire. Franklin was unafraid as he proceeded with caution, turning onto one of the side streets of Harlem.

Suddenly, a man appeared from the shadows and stopped him from going any farther. The man, an African American, was carrying a megaphone in one hand. "Can I help you, Sir?"

Franklin showed him his card. "I'm here to see a Mr. McBerny. He's expecting me."

In the background behind the man, not thirty feet away, machine gunfire exploded in the night air again. Franklin saw the yellow flames spurting from several automatic rifles carried by two running men. Agonizing screams faded away into the night. Suddenly another voice, using a megaphone, yelled the word, "Cut!"

The man confronting Franklin took his own megaphone and yelled to the crowd behind him. "Okay, folks, that's lunch! One hour! And that means," he paused to look at his watch, "be in your places, gentlemen, here at one-thirty a.m. sharp!" He turned back to address Franklin. "As you can see, we're filming late tonight. My name is George Denham. I'm second A.D. here. So, you're here to see Mr. McBerny? If you'll follow me now, I can take you to him."

Franklin thanked him and looked around the movie set he walked onto. "I take it the neighborhood isn't sleeping tonight from all this noise!"

George responded, "On the contrary, they think this is an event! They're all out here working with us as extras or they're spectators. No, they love it. It's not every day a black community gets a black film crew with a black cast. That's, of course, with the exception of Judd Nelson who plays a cop. But it's an event when a black writer, director, and producers all shoot a major studio movie in their own back yard!"

George and Franklin crossed into a warehouse-like setting, where tables were set up for the cast, crew, and extras to eat their midnight'lunch.' They were a curious group, dressed as pimps and mobsters and other street people. The black actors and crew lined up to receive their hot meals, though it was a quarter to one in the morning.

George tapped a black gentleman on the shoulder, as he was giving orders to someone. The gentleman turned around, and George introduced Mr. McBerny to Franklin.

"Ah, the man from Washington!" McBerny said warmly, inferring the nation's capital. "Pleased to meet you, Mr. Franklin. Let's go into my production office where we can converse in private." McBerny led Franklin to one of the mobile trailers, and they went inside.

"Well, what brings you here, Mr. Franklin?" McBerny asked after they were comfortably seated. "I got your message telling me you might stop by this evening."

Franklin reached into his briefcase and brought out a script. "I have a favor to ask of you. I'd like you to read this."

McBerny looked at the title. "*The Connection*," he read aloud. "Yours?"

"No, not mine," Franklin replied, "but I thought it was important enough to bring it to you in person."

McBerny gave him a weary look. "You're aware I receive a half-dozen scripts a week, including some by friends and acquaintances."

"Since you're in the movie industry, I expected as much. But this script is something special. I think you'd be very interested in it."

"And why is that?" McBerny asked skeptically.

"Because it deals with a subject I know you're interested in." Franklin explained.

"And that is...?" McBerny left the sentence open.

"A fictional account of the Kennedy assassination conspiracy, one that takes place in the future! It says a lot..."

McBerny took a deep breath. "You sure know how to get someone's attention."

"I thought it would. Do you mind if I leave the script with you?"

"I'd prefer that. I'll be able to read it after I finish shooting this movie. I'm on a tight schedule." McBerny held the script in his hand. He was doing his best to resist the temptation to open it and flip through the pages. "I'd like to do something with some bite, something for the mass audience, but I haven't found the right story to dramatize yet-- one with all the right elements. If the script is good enough for feature film material, I'll consider it as the next project."

"Well, you won't be disappointed with this one," Franklin assured him.

"You said it wasn't yours. Was it written by a friend?"

"You can say that. As a matter of fact, I'm trying to contact him now-- in case you're interested in buying it from him."

"He doesn't know your letting people read his scripts?" McBerny asked, puzzled.

"You're the only one I'm allowing to read it. Besides, I've had no luck hunting him down, yet. I don't know whether he's dead or alive."

"If this is true, how do you know he hasn't shown this script to other producers or production companies."

"Oh, he has, in the past, but he wasn't able to interest anyone in it because of the subject matter. But I heard about your interest through others. They said you're involved in themes like this."

Franklin reached out to tap the script in McBerny's hand. "I read it. This script is actually the answer to our own conclusions from the House Select Committee-- not Blakley's-- but the staff who did the investigations then forced all of us to keep our mouths shut! If the conspiracy theories in this script were exposed to the public, we could prompt an investigation, not only in the Kennedy assassination, but ultimately expose those who were behind Martin Luther King's death. And we know who they are, don't we?" Franklin gave McBerny a knowing look.

McBerny sighed. Well, I hope I can help you. That's assuming the movie I'm working on now is a big success. If it pulls in the bucks, the Warner's Studio will let us do anything we want. Like I said, both my partner and I wanted to break into the white market for our next film, to make something different from an all black film." McBerny smiled. "If this white guy has written something good, then we might have a chance. But something worries me. You say you're looking for him. What happens if you don't find him? How do we get the rights?"

Franklin nodded. "I've thought about that. If you decide to commit, I can get permission from a family member. There shouldn't be a problem, especially if the standard money is offered."

McBerny smiled, "Money is no object if we feel we have a hit on our hands. But that's only speculation now." There was a long pause as McBerny looked at the script in his hands. Then he came to a decision. "I'll tell you what, I'm here for another week, then I'm heading back to my office at the Burbank Studios in Hollywood. My partner and I will read the script and meet with you in two or three weeks. Does that sound all right with you?"

"You have a deal." Franklin smiled in agreement, and McBerny shook his hand, "This just might be the next project my partner and I are looking for!"

* * *

The television set in the darkened room continued to broadcast the images of Nixon. The interviewer asked whether he believed Lee Harvey Oswald acted alone.

Nixon smiled as he answered. "I was asked that same question in France in 1978 and I spent three hours speaking on the subject. I really don't know...and I refuse to read the new books and see the new docudramas. I don't believe docudramas are any good anyway, but that's another matter. I don't think much of tv!"

"Do you think John Kennedy was responsible for the assassination attempts on Castro's life?" the interviewer pressed. "Did you see any information while you were President to suggest his attempts to kill Castro inspired Castro to kill him?"

Nixon closed his eyes and answered, as if this question bothered him. "No! No," he emphatically stated, "I have never seen any information of that type. All I know is what I read in books, newspaper articles, and what I have seen, a modest amount, on tv!" Nixon smiled.

The woman sitting on the couch within the darkened room responded to Nixon's last statement, speaking to the person in the leather-bound chair. "Tricky Dick just contradicted himself! First, he said he didn't read any books or newspaper articles on the subject, lambasting television, saying he didn't even watch it. Then he reversed himself on the second question saying he got his information from those exact areas he so despises! In other words, he avoided both questions by giving us an anomaly."

The interviewer proceeded, discussing Kennedy. "Both you and John Kennedy rose together as senators and during that period until the 1960 race. You must have gathered material about Kennedy's character and so on, yet it never came out in view of the closeness of the election, why not?"

Nixon answered. "I think we thought it to be counterproductive. I'm sure he would have done virtually anything to win, knowing it would be a very close election! It was my view then, and has been my view since, that engaging in criticism in a candidate's personal life is counterproductive. I don't like to do it, and I also think it hurts! That's what prevailed when I met with my advisors! I'm certain the idea was raised because it was no secret!"

The interviewer added, "Look what happened to Gary Hart!"

"Well, Gary Hart-- that was a different situation," Nixon answered. The media is always looking for dirt to expose. Let's say today a homeless family would not make the evening news, but a politician sleeping with another man's wife would be news. The media would never have gone after Kennedy back then as they did with Hart now, even if Hart was closer to the media than most politicians. The media couldn't resist a story like that and so...they blew it up! The media in 1960 would not have played an aggressive role in chasing Kennedy!"

"Could you, Mr. Nixon," the interviewer aggressively asked, "have taken the election if someone set out to expose Kennedy and his playboy image?"

Nixon replied. "No, the people would not have tolerated it back then. The media liked Kennedy a lot, and even if the media knew Kennedy's background as a ladies man, they liked him too much to expose him. And besides, back then the issues were the agenda, both a liberal Democrat and a conservative republican, as I was-- we agreed on most issues. And you know that was the last election where most of the American people came out to the polls to vote. It hasn't been the same since."

The interviewer again asked, "Are you saying you sacrificed the election by not exposing Kennedy, like Gary Hart, when you could have been the President of the United States because it was considered negative campaigning-- that you didn't believe in it?"

"No, I'm not saying we could have used that or not, or that information to the contrary was necessary, I'm saying it was not an issue!" Nixon told him.

The woman got up from the couch, upset, and prepared to exit the room. "I'm going to bed, dear, I don't think I can take how Dick Nixon was such a pal to Kennedy, or that his strategy to become president in 1960 was protecting Kennedy's image from exposure as a ladies man! Especially when he destroyed so many lives to get himself into position as a congressman and senator. Everyone just loved him when he destroyed half the population's minds with the Vietnam war and Watergate. I cannot believe this same man who despised the Kennedy family is now telling us he sacrificed the 1960 election because he wanted to play fair in the campaign! 'It was not an issue!' What does that mean?" She kissed the person who sat in the chair.

The man in the chair spoke, "Good night, mother..." and turned his attention back to the tv.

The interviewer on the television screen asked Nixon, "You would have sent troops into Vietnam would you not, had you won the election in 1960?"

"Yeah!" Nixon said. "Ah... I would have certainly sent troops into Vietnam, had I been elected, but I wouldn't have had to do it because I would never have joined in a conspiracy that resulted in the assassination of Diem. If Diem had not been assassinated, I do not believe it would have been necessary for troops to go to Vietnam. The second point is, if I had survived Watergate in 1972, or if it hadn't occurred, I believe it could have been possible to get Congress to provide the funds that were necessary to see that the South Vietnamese received as much aid as the Russians were supplying to the north. Assuming there would not be a Watergate, and I was in position, there's no question that South Vietnam would be a free and independent country today, .and a very prosperous one instead of a poor one that it is..."

Tears fell from the eyes of the person in the chair, the person now recognizing his mistakes as he had a flashback to Saigon on the tarmac with the transport Air America plane. Karl Hunter escorted John Modini to the aircraft then pointed out the body bags being shipped aboard along with Modini.

Then a quick, sudden flash to the memory of Father Daniel Conrad. It was an image in Modini's mind of Conny as he jumped off the bridge, falling to his death in the river below.

The tears continued as John Modini started to sob. In the background on the television set, the interviewer asked Richard Nixon a speculative question about John Kennedy. "If he would have lived, do you suppose we could have had the turmoil we had in the 1960's? Would he have stayed so long in the Vietnam War and so on?"

Nixon answered, "I know there has been a lot of speculation that he might have discontinued the support of South Vietnamese and would have wound out the war. I don't agree. John Kennedy was a very strong person and was very persuasive person-- oh, except for his, what I consider his mistake in knocking off the second air strike of the Bay of Pigs. He took strong action for example in the Cuban confrontation. I think John Kennedy has distinguished himself from Johnson in that he would not have gone as far as making Vietnam a policy of gradualism. He would have taken a strong stand to bring the war to an end soon, and he would not have escalated it as Johnson did-- at least that's my judgment, knowing the man as I did!"

The interviewer still persisted with the original point, "And so you think the turmoil that followed might not have existed or taken place-- that the culture revolution of the United States during the 60's might have been avoided?"

Nixon smiled as he answered. "That's another subject. I think the culture revolution had a life of its own. I think it was very unfortunate because I don't happen to be a man of the 60's of that respect!"

Here, Modini lifted his head up and his body was jolted in a sudden reaction as a series of unexpected images flashed through his mind. They were an assortment of shocking scenes: JFK's and Bobby's assassination, King's assassination, The Beatles singing *She Loves you, yah, yah, yah*, a village in Vietnam being Napalmed, a Vietnamese child shot, The Doors singing *Light my Fire*, more Napalming, a young naked Cambodian girl running for her life, a heroin needle poised above an arm of a rock singer, body bags shipped aboard Air America, POW's and MIA's stating they do exist, a Vietnamese Buddhist burning in the street, and Modini realizing he was shot by a sniper in Nam. All these thoughts flickered within his brain.

Nixon was still on the television in the background: "...To give Kennedy and Johnson his due, I think Kennedy would have taken a stronger position on Vietnam than Johnson did. I do think he would not have let it drag on because he was a decisive kind of person, and he thought he had enough public support I think Kennedy however would not have bitten the bullet on civil rights which Johnson did! Just as I was the only one that could have gone to China when I did in 1972, Johnson was the only one that could have brought about the passage of the Civil Rights of 1964!" Nixon sat back and smiled as he concluded: "So, we give both men credit where it's due!"

* * *

A few days later, John Modini was sound asleep when the phone rang. His mother answered the call, "This is Mrs. O'Leary speaking. Yes, I know. It's because of my son's disappearance I'm using my late second husband's name-- not Modini. Too many reporters and inquiries, you can understand."

Modini awakened from his sleep. He listened to his mother's conversation.

"Who did you say is calling?" she asked.

Richard Franklin was phoning from an office phone in the twin towers in Los Angeles. "My name is Richard Franklin. I'm an attorney in Los Angeles. I met your son in Washington, D.C., a couple of years ago. In fact, Mrs. O'Leary, I was one of the last ones to see your son alive the day he disappeared. When you faxed some information about Oswald to my friend in D.C., I was the one who got the fax to him. Yes, that's true. Well, I'm calling you, Mrs. O'Leary, because I'm aware from those in D.C. about your concern for your son. Believe me, I've been searching for him myself, since I urgently need his help. He and I were working on a matter of importance I think he'd want to know about if he were still alive. Right now, I need to get permission from you to allow me to show a project of his to some people. It's a screenplay John wrote between his return from Vietnam and the late 70's. Would it be all right to do that, Mrs. O'Leary?"

Modini's mother glanced in the direction of her son's bedroom, where he watched and listened, but didn't say anything. She hesitated, then came up with an answer, "Mr. Franklin, I do not mind if you do that. But only if you call his partner and get permission. John has a partner in Santa Barbara, California. He has left all his manuscripts and writings in his charge in case of death. His name is Dr. Robert Doreen, and if it is unlisted, you can call my sister. She lives in Santa Barbara. I'll give you her number."

Franklin grabbed for a pen in his pocket. "Just a minute, Mrs. O'Leary, I'll write this down. He scribbled down the number she gave him, and he thanked her. Mrs. O'Leary received the phone number of Franklin, as well, before hanging up.

There was a noise from behind her. She turned around to see her son yawning from his sleep as he appeared in the kitchen in shorts.

"Who called?" Modini asked.

"Someone named Richard Franklin," his mother told him. "He said it was urgent he get in touch with you. It has something to do with selling your script."

"If Mr. Franklin calls again, and I expect he will, have him come here to Salem," Modini told his mother. "But don't let him know I'm here. Convince him you need to see him about the matter. He'll need your signature because that's what Dr. Doreen will tell him. You'll tell him you'll give the signature only to him and only in person!"

* * *

Michael Bradley set up a VCR projector in his conference room of his law office to show a video to a couple of staff members. As he finished plugging in the cables, he looked at his watch.

Two new colleagues had since joined the firm. One of them, Thomas Sanders, an investigator, asked whether Catherine Rogers would be present for this presentation?

"She will." Bradley responded. "She asked for this, and I have to say you put a damn good presentation together! I'll wait a few more minutes."

The second colleague, a new attorney on staff, Jennifer Tamura, an Asian woman, was excited and spoke from her chair, "I was just as surprised what we came up with as you were. If the people knew the facts about our President, or should I say 'Presidents,' especially the Republicans, I can't believe they still let these cover ups go to this day! There's no way we can trust Bush now, a man who was once the head of the CIA! I'm ashamed of our congressmen and our senators, especially the ones who know about this," she shook her head. "Why do they condone it? Why?"

Thomas Sanders glanced at his watch. "If they were aware of the cover ups and spoke out, they'd be afraid! 'We the people' wouldn't continue to vote for them, and I wouldn't blame them. It takes a man with plenty of guts to confront all the deceptions that have exhausted the credibility of our nation over the past years. Do you know of any man who represents our country as a congressman or senator with those credentials?"

Before Jennifer could reply, Catherine rushed into the room. "Sorry for being late...traffic. she apologized, taking off her coat and seating herself at the table. Michael Bradley gave her a weary look and smiled, forgoing any comment. He started the VCR projection. Thomas nodded his greeting to Catherine as he turned off the room lights.

As the room went dark, Catherine said, "Oh, just like in the movies-- any popcorn?" The others groaned at this remark.

The words on the screen came toward them, framed in bold letters, the title read: "The Cold War." A narration started over the pictures and archival footage on the screen.

"The main target of the United States in the cold war was Communism," the unseen narrator explained. "In the 1940's and '50's, the CIA began training Russian, Ukrainian, Bulgarian and other exiles for operations throughout eastern Europe. These exiles were all staunchly anti-Soviet and rapidly anti-Communist.

"Unfortunately, many of these same exiles actively fought alongside the Germans during the Nazi occupation, supported the Holocaust, and still openly advocated fascism. Thousands of them were considered war criminals under official policy. But the CIA and the State Department decided the past was past and the *Red Threat* justified bringing many of these men into the U.S. intelligence services and defense industries.

"Nazi spy networks, like the infamous *Gehlen Organization* and its leader, SS General Reinhard Gehlen, were assimilated, first by Army Intelligence, and later by the CIA.

"In the 1950's these operations, code named Rusty, Paperclip, Bloodstone and others, were a major state secret, because they were a flagrant violation of international law and the Nuremberg Principles. Even today, very little is known about these programs, and the government continues to stonewall researchers' Freedom of Information Act (FOIA) requests for documents.

"Once in the United States, the fascist exiles were often employed by defense contractors as executives and security experts. From these positions, they joined the American far right in pushing the U.S. into preparations for all-out war with the Soviet Union or any nation they considered Communist.

"In 1955, The National Security Council Order 54-12 created a group within the council to

319

consolidate the supervision of all exile and anti-Communist operations. This would be known as Group 54-12. Among its members were its chairman, then Vice-President Richard Nixon, CIA Chief Allen Dulles and his deputy Director General Charles Cabell, and C.D. Jackson, a propaganda expert who, as head of the CIA's funding conduit known as the 'Committee For a Free Europe,' was also the CIA's paymaster for the various exile groups!"

The word Cuba in big letters swept across the screen showing the island ninety miles off the coast of Miami. It revealed a picturesque view of the country as it was in 1959. There were various shots, from the religious communities to its bathing beauties and gambling casinos in the vacation spot of the world, Havana. A voice over continued with section two: "Cuba."

"In 1959, the focus shifted to Cuba, in what would be the newly-Communist nation ninety miles off the Florida coast. Wealthy Cubans settled en masse in Miami and led the call for the restoration of a 'free' Cuba.

"But pre-Castro Cuba was hardly 'free!' Rather, Cuba was a prime source of revenue for large corporations like United Fruit, which could maximize profits by using cheap labor and avoiding U.S. health and safety codes. It was also the center of preparations for major oil operations throughout the Caribbean.

"Havana also had the CIA's largest base in the Western hemisphere. And it was the Mecca for the Mafia's dream city, a criminal playground for every hood and entertainer throughout the United States, from which the Marcello, Trafficante and Lansky syndicate ran gambling, drug smuggling, and money laundering operations.

"These business, crime and intelligence, would walk hand in hand over the years as interests overlapped more often than not. Meanwhile, the average Cuban was poor, hungry, and illiterate.

"Starting in 1959, Castro's new dictatorship expelled those corporations, the Mafia and the CIA. And so the committee that formed the 54-12 group went into effect, led by Vice-President Nixon. It began in 1955 with Guatemala's change of government to suit the United States direction in foreign policy. Here Nixon, planned in late January of 1960, an invasion of Cuba by a secret army of Cuban exiles and American mercenaries with CIA backing.

"But Nixon lost the 1960 election to Kennedy before the year long coup in Cuba could start. Under JFK the invasion took on a new light. Staged at the Bay of Pigs, this became the greatest disaster in the CIA's history.

"As they successfully done earlier several times in other countries since 1955, the agency planned a quick assault on the island designed to appear as though it was initiated by Cuban exiles acting on their own.

"Kennedy denied air support to the operation since it was illegal and against the Geneva Convention and policies of the United Nations. Kennedy also feared the use of American planes would make it obvious to the Communist world the invasion had been coordinated by the United States. Whether the operation would have succeeded with such support is debatable, but the absence of air cover did make the invasion brigade sitting ducks for the Cuban military.

"In hindsight, it looked as though the CIA had two agendas on their mind; either succeed as they planned or embarrass the new President for possible impeachment. The CIA opted for the latter. Instead of a quick, clean, deniable operation installing a friendly government, more than a hundred Cubans and mercenaries were killed, and over a thousand more were taken prisoner. It was a domestic and foreign policy catastrophe. The CIA officers involved in the raid placed the blame for the disaster entirely on Kennedy.

"What these CIA officers did not expect was what happened next, Kennedy came forward and took public responsibility for the failure, while inside the corridors of the White House, he in turn blamed the agency, believing they lied to him, trying to force him into an all-out invasion of Cuba.

"Kennedy here, removed the CIA's leadership, forcing out its longtime head, Allen Dulles, and two of his top deputies, General Cabell and Richard Bissell who headed the Bay of Pigs operation."

Section Three of the movie began with the title words, *"The Mafia and Covert Operations,"* crossing the screen from right to left, and showed the new administration's progress in the coming months: the introduction of the Peace Corps and the Green Berets, the new space program, the down side of the continued cold war confrontation and the Cuban Missile Crisis. The voice over continued:

"The firing of CIA Deputy Richard Bissell further alienated another group of covert operatives-- the Mafia hit-men, used by Bissell since August of 1960 in assassination attempts against Castro. These attempts continued until Bissell's removal by the new president.

"And the Kennedy administration was prosecuting the CIA's Mafia friends like never before. They declared open war on organized crime. Because war was declared in the months before Dallas, these mobsters were recorded by the FBI discussing the death of one or both of the Kennedy brothers. One conversation mentioned putting a hit on the Attorney General, Robert Kennedy. Then the exchange turned to John Kennedy when one Mafia kingpin suggests, 'Why cut off the tail? When you can cut off the head, automatically the tail will fall off!'

"But meanwhile, the covert operations didn't stop Kennedy. First, he simply tried to seize control over them not knowing the Mafia's involvement. Both JFK and his brother, Robert, the Attorney General, were still enamored of special operations. It was John Kennedy who created the Green Berets, and in June of 1961, Kennedy issued National Security Action Memoranda 55 and 57, designed to limit the CIA's independence and improve the President's control over all covert operations.

"The Cuban Missile Crisis pushed the split even further. While the CIA and the Pentagon pressed for another invasion, JFK's solution was a promise never to invade Cuba, in exchange for the withdrawal of Soviet missiles.

"From that point forward, Kennedy began working toward the breakup of not only anti-Castro operations, but the CIA itself, even speaking of breaking the Agency into a thousand pieces and scattering it to the winds.

"JFK still tried to appease the Cuban exile community with promises Castro would one day be deposed, but to the Bay of Pigs veterans, he became a liar who was as much an enemy to their cause as Castro himself.

"JFK now had enemies who were well-versed in removing heads of State. Group 54-12 did not dissolve when Nixon lost the election, it prospered in the coming years.

"And, one by one, remove them they did. Besides Guatemala, in the previous years prior to the assassination, the CIA staged coups in Bolivia, Argentina, Peru, Ecuador, Peru again, the Dominican Republic, Brazil, Honduras, Burma, Togo, Iraq, Syria, the Congo, Laos, and South Vietnam. It was here in South Vietnam in the second week of November, 1963, President Ngo Dihn Diem and his brother, Ngo Dinh Nhu, was assassinated, foreshadowing what was yet to come in Dallas, Texas. The Kennedy assassination and Vietnam became synonymous, linked in historical accounts for all time.

"Vietnam was another turning point of conflict between the CIA and JFK. Kennedy's last important act was the signing of National Security Action Memorandum 263, moving toward the withdrawal of American troops from Vietnam. Over in Saigon the CIA was openly defying White House and State Department policy, and many at the Pentagon were adamantly opposed to JFK's policies. NSAM 263 was countermanded by the newly sworn-in President, Johnson, before JFK was even buried."

The film presentation came to a conclusion, and Bradley turned the lights in the boardroom on. It was quiet as the four of them in the room assessed what they just saw. Catherine awaited an open discussion.

It was Jennifer who spoke up first. "Wow! This is some strong documentary, don't you agree? I think this 'Executive Action' order discovered in the Pentagon papers came from this Group 54-12 to be used in Dallas on November 22, 1963. And was still controlled by Cabell and Dulles who still had some control within the CIA, even after being fired by Kennedy. It is an established fact both General Cabell and Nixon were in Dallas on the day, or at least the night before Kennedy arrived. And Cabell's brother was the mayor of Dallas at the time. He was responsible for arranging the route of the motorcade through Dealey Plaza. That is a bit spooky! Of course, Nixon could be considered innocent as an angel in all this, but I don't know. This is some coincidence, wouldn't you say? And what about Allen Dulles, becoming one of the Warren Commissioners? I mean, the man was fired by Kennedy and now he's supposed to be investigating his death? Half the commissioners were connected to Nixon somehow, and as you know, one of them, Gerald Ford, became his Vice-President, then President, and the biggest advocate for Oswald, insisting to this day no one but Oswald could have killed the president. And he is still considered the most honest of all our twentieth century presidents. What national poll did that one?"

Michael Bradley stood up at the front of the boardroom table and asked, "So what do you all suggest, where do we go from here?"

Thomas, looked to the others before speaking, then added as if on cue, "I'll give you my suggestion. If Catherine's tape is for real, I think we should go for it. I'd love to see what's written in that letter. Aren't any of you curious to see what our country has been hiding for all these years? We want the truth about our country's crime of the century, and I don't mean Kennedy's death, but the fact Oswald didn't do it! That's the crime!"

"But are we prepared to be scrutinized by the media and the government like the Mark Lanes and the Jim Garrisons have in these last twenty-seven years?" Bradley asked. And are we prepared for the law firm to be ridiculed and attacked to the point of bankruptcy? Are you prepared to no longer be practicing law-- period!"

Jennifer interrupted. "But, Michael, we can bring this out gradually. No one is aware of Hunter's tape and letter except, maybe Mrs. Roger's father. And we all know he doesn't believe the tape anyway. I think Mrs. Rogers is right by--"

Catherine held up her hand and stopped her. "Please, if we're going to work together, please call me Catherine. You make me sound old, calling me Mrs. Rogers."

Bradley smiled at her comment. He was more relaxed as he turned his attention back to

Jennifer.

Jennifer continued. "Thank you, Catherine, I'll do that. I feel Catherine's suggestion about getting this out in the open should start by exhuming the body in Karl Hunter's grave!"

"But Jennifer, that's one thing we can't do!" Bradley strongly protested, "The military and Pentagon refuse to allow exhumation at Arlington Cemetery!"

This fact didn't stop Jennifer. "Isn't it curious to any of you that a committee was formed to discredit Hunter as a Marine and war hero? This means no Marine guard salute or honor or burial in Arlington Cemetery. But when an autopsy was suggested by this law firm on its own client, the government steps in and seals the autopsy records, then buries him in the ground where he was originally banned!"

"I get what you're saying, Jennifer," Bradley said, "but where are we going on this?"

"If we're going to be scrutinized, as you say by the media and government, I think we should get a sneak preview if what Catherine said is buried out there in that field in Gary! If any of those bodies are discovered, wouldn't it be a revelation and a spark to the media? Look at how many troubled parents would be interested. We would be blessed in getting this out into the open, right? Then the media and the people would be behind us, enough so we could move forward with the exhumation of Karl Hunter-- a client *we* believe did not murder those victims! At least, we should be assured the real Karl Hunter is buried there!"

"But Jennifer," Thomas asked, "what if it is the real Karl Hunter buried in Arlington? That's maybe what Michael is talking about, the ridicule that might come of it. Look what happened when they exhumed Oswald's body? And for that matter, what if there are no bodies in that field in Gary?"

Catherine now stood up. "That's the chance we have to take, won't we? You keep forgetting we have a two fold question here! Either Karl Hunter is buried there, and he is an innocent man-- which would satisfy Michael and me for defending him, or another person is buried there and the real Hunter is still out and about. I know what I witnessed. I've had two years of therapy to think about this and to relive it. I want to prove it one way or another. If we do decide to move forward, I'll go all the way with you on this matter. If we fail, well, we'll decide what to do when we cross that bridge. I want to go along with Jennifer's plan!"

Jennifer smiled at Catherine and nodded her thanks.

Thomas took a deep breath, "I'm game if you guys are. This will be some experiment!"

Michael Bradley proceeded to Catherine, put one arm around her and gestured to the other members of his staff. "Catherine, I present to you your team. They are here at your, and for your, command."

Her two colleagues came forward to greet Catherine. Jennifer actually hugged her with tears in her eyes. Bradley stood back, proud of Catherine.

Thomas made an announcement once things were calmed down. "I want you all to know. I have something here that is unbelievable, but as Jennifer spoke of a coincidence before, this is certainly a coincidence in timing. This was in yesterday's Dallas Morning News front page." Thomas slapped a newspaper onto the boardroom table. The front page headline read:

New JFK Theory Outlined. Midland resident presents an unsubstantiated claim his father carried out orders to kill President.

Next to the headline and story was a picture of 29-year old Ricky Don White who offered his account Monday outside the JFK Assassination Information Center concerning...

A diary he found, written by his father Roscoe Anthony White, a diary his son now says has since disappeared after providing it to the FBI two years ago.

Chapter Twenty-Five

"Hooray for Hollywood...!"

When Richard Franklin approached the Burbank Studios drive-on gate, the one nearest the Water Tower, he noticed a well-dressed gentleman described to him as Dr. Robert Doreen standing to the side of the guard house waiting.

Franklin stopped his car and leaned out the window. "Excuse me, are you Dr. Doreen?"

"Yes I am," Dr. Doreen responded.

"I'm Richard Franklin. It looks as though we're attending to the same meeting. Are you waiting for someone?"

"No," Dr. Doreen indicated the guard shack, "I was waiting for a phone call so I could be allowed in."

"Why don't you hop into my car and I'll drive you on the lot."

"Thanks," Franklin unlocked his passenger door and Dr. Doreen got into the car. Franklin checked his watch. "It's early enough. Maybe we can have lunch together before the meeting starts."

"Good Idea."

"Besides," Franklin added, "there are a few things I'd like to talk to you about."

Franklin received a pass at the gate and drove onto the lot. After finding a parking spot, both men began walking through one of Hollywood's magic kingdoms of film making.

Franklin and Dr. Doreen rounded a building and paused at portion of the studio known as the back lot. In this small area, there were streets and buildings of every nationality. This was where they filmed practically every city of the world for either Warner Brothers or the Columbia Studios.

"Follow me," Franklin said, "I've got to show you something." He walked down the sidewalk and stopped in front of the facade of a corner store. Next to them was a junction of buildings imitating a modern city intersection. "I remember I stood here, at this spot, back in 1981 when Ridley Scott was filming one of my favorite movies of all time, *Bladerunner*-- remember that movie?"

Dr. Doreen was impressed, "Yes, my wife and I are big fans of Harrison Ford."

"Of course, the street was all dressed up and modified for the future look, but I still remember it as if it were yesterday."

A couple of television actors walked by, and Dr. Doreen recognized them. He grabbed Franklin's arm. Look at them! You know who they are!

"Yes. They're from that tv medical show. I think the exterior hospital set is at the end of that street."

"They took me by surprise. I'm going to keep my eyes open from now on."

Franklin smiled, "You'll be seeing a lot of actors where we're going."

In the middle of lunch in the Warner commissary Franklin raised a question. "So tell me, Dr. Doreen, what type of doctor are you.

"I'm a heart specialist," Dr. Doreen modestly acknowledged, "I have my own practice."

Franklin laughed, "You must be a good one if you were friends of Mr. Modini. How did you two meet and become his partner?" Dr. Doreen was momentarily distracted as he recognized a popular television actress carrying her food tray to a table of friends. "It actually was very simple," Dr. Doreen explained, tearing his eyes away. "When John came to Los Angeles in the mid-70's,

328

he began writing for a newspaper. We met almost immediately. I was in my internship, and he needed a quick examination that snowballed into a two-hour ordeal, and next thing we knew; we became close friends. John met Dr. Jules Stein at a dinner party also around this time. In those days, Dr. Stein was the chairman of MCA Universal. Well, Stein's biggest client was Alfred Hitchcock. This was the same year when Steven Spielberg's film, *Jaws* made such a splash--" here Dr. Doreen laughed at himself. "I just made a pun, didn't I?

Franklin laughed, and Dr. Doreen continued, "Well, John impressed him and was invited to Stein's office one day on the top of the-- Universal calls it, the Black Tower. Stein asked John what would he like to do, and John told him he'd like to help rewrite the problem script for Hitchcock. You see, Alfred Hitchcock was planning a movie at the time called *The Short Night*. The script had some problems and, as things go, the studio was looking for writers to polish the script-- at least make it workable as a feature film. To my surprise, Stein introduced John to Mr. Hitchcock and they met a few times after that. John expressed his willingness to work on Hitchcock's script, but Dr. Stein confided with John that Mr. Hitchcock would never make *The Short Night*. Stein and Universal were only placating the director, since Hitchcock didn't have the health to start production. Stein asked John to write his own script. Upon completion, he would have Lew Wasserman take a look at it."

Franklin shook his head, impressed, "Wow, I never knew this. It's hard to believe the same John Modini I knew was wheeling and dealing in Hollywood like this. I thought he was a regular reporter."

"The ironic part was that the Alfred Hitchcock story came out only after the director's death. It was discovered Hitchcock had enough stock to own a third of the Studio. Hitchcock could have produced any movie he wanted to without any interference, but his last project was derailed by the people working for him."

"That was a shame. Theoretically, his last movie might have been '*The Short Night*.'"

"Yes, but it never got off the ground." Dr. Doreen shook his head.

"That was a lost opportunity."

The story gets better," Dr. Doreen continued, "as I said before, Lew Wasserman was to read John Modini's new script--"

"One moment," Franklin interrupted, "You mean Lew Wasserman, the man who today has replaced Dr. Jules Stein as chairman?"

Dr. Doreen nodded, "Right, and it was here John Modini came to me with the script, which became *The Connection*, and why you and I are here today meeting for the first time. Isn't life amazing when a manuscript can bring two people together after all these years because someone shows an interest in a project that has so much potential going for it!"

Franklin grinned, "Potential? My ass! I'm surprised this script wasn't made into a movie a long time ago! Did Mr. Modini ever show it to Dr. Jules Stein or Wasserman?"

"No," was the plain answer from Dr. Doreen. "To be honest with you, John never mentioned Stein, or any of what I just told you. He respected Dr. Stein so much for befriending him he didn't want to show Dr. Stein anything until he knew he had something strong. To be honest with you, Mr. Franklin, John actually didn't know what he had-- and he thought he had to have the great American Novel before showing anything to Dr. Stein. At the dinner for the AFI tribute, Stein, prior to his death, ran into John and asked him where he had been and where the script was. Then came Reagan's assassination attempt in 1981, and John put the script on the shelf. I have another half a dozen scripts of his in Santa Barbara, and most are better than this one, but John never followed up on them."

Franklin was surprised by this revelation. "Really? Then tell me, why did someone like Mr. Modini who wrote steadily over the years and originally believed a conspiracy within the Kennedy assassination was a figment of a troubled person's imagination, wrote something like this? How can a person who believed Oswald acted alone write something completely opposite and then claim it's a conspiracy!"

Dr. Doreen thought for a moment, trying to frame an explanation, "I'm not sure, since I'm not a psychiatrist, but I know he liked people and trusted them. I tried to warn him repeatedly he'd get burned, but he continued trusting people just the same. And I know all those people who believed the conspiracy buffs or theorists troubled him, so I think he wrote this fictitious piece of work with this in mind. So if there were a conspiracy to assassinate the President-- and not just Kennedy, but any President-- this would show how it could be done."

"Well, I think Mr. Modini came up with something substantial," Franklin said, "because the points it makes shreds the accuracy of the Warren Commission report."

A black gentleman approached the table. It was George Denham, the second assistant director, who Franklin had met in New York's Harlem. "Mr. Franklin, it's good to see you again, Mr. McBerny is in his office and is expecting you when you finish up with your lunch. I'll be glad to escort you there whenever you're ready."

* * *

Richard Franklin and Dr. Doreen entered McBerny's office and were introduced to his partner, Mr. Wilkerson. They both sat down as both partners explained their position at the studio and bragged about their first film publicized in Hollywood as a potential hit for the studio. The producers knew it would establish them as key players allowing more black films to go into production. They'd be considered the forerunners in the black community who started many black directors, like Spike Lee, on their way.

It was the fact that both producers were eager to please the white audience as well, to get their attendance and money at the box office like any good businessmen.

McBerny and Mr. Wilkerson were enthusiastic and proceeded to explain to Franklin and Dr. Doreen the script *The Connection,* had everything needed to make this their next successful project. Dr. Doreen and Franklin were as pleased as could be from such good news. After all these years, Modini's script might have a chance to go before the cameras.

Mr. Wilkerson, a big man, got right to the point. "Are we going to have any problems with the author of this screenplay? I hear he passed on. Can we get the complete rights to this, I mean?"

Franklin faced the question squarely. "Mr. Wilkerson, that's why I've brought Dr. Robert Doreen to this meeting. He has full authorization to sell this project and is the partner of the author!"

Wilkerson looked over to Doreen. "Is that correct, Dr. Doreen?"

Dr. Doreen smiled, "Yes, I can speak for the author and I can make the decision for the screenplay. As long as I get the author's mother to sign the paperwork. The only thing is--"

"Yes?" Wilkerson waited for the shoe to drop.

"The thing is, Modini's mother requests to sign the papers in person!"

McBerny shrugged, "Well, we'll fly her down, if that's what it takes!"

"It's not as simple as that," Dr. Doreen added. "She doesn't want to leave her home or make any trips these days."

McBerny's eyes widened. "You mean she wants us to fly down and witness signing the paperwork?"

"I believe I can make it easy on you, if you don't mind," Dr. Doreen said. "If I may suggest...Mr. Franklin is an attorney-- he could fly up and get her signature."

Mr. Wilkerson smiled, "Splendid! That shouldn't be a problem, would it, Mr. Franklin?"

Franklin, surprised by this, answered back. "It would be a pleasure, Mr. Wilkerson"

"Good! When we get all the legal papers out of the way, we'll be able to proceed." Mr. Wilkerson explained, "We have a deal with Warner Brothers Studio, a *carte blanche* contract for a five-year deal. Once we get the green light to go, then we can start on our follow-up project. Not to mention, the other studios in town are courting us as well. So in a sense, we have complete control to make any films for the future of our company."

This final statement was a comfort for Dr. Robert Doreen to hear. He now felt confident McBerny and Mr. Wilkerson would finally get John Modini's project off the ground, one that had been a jinx for him all these years.

Richard Franklin grabbed a newspaper from the magazine shop and tucked it under his arm as he picked up his carry-on bag and headed for his plane at the Burbank Airport.

Aboard his flight, Franklin opened the *Times* to a headline reading: "Journal on JFK Killing Called Hoax. Anachronisms Cast Doubt on Supposed Diary of Ex-Dallas Policeman."

Franklin read the story: "A Houston private investigator on Thursday released copies of a diary in which a former Dallas Policeman agonized about killing President John F. Kennedy under CIA orders."

Franklin's finger moved down the page.

"But a former CIA operative who examined the original document early Thursday told reporters the new evidence was a 'very clumsy fabrication' at best. The private investigator contends the journal could belong to Roscoe Anthony White, a former Marine in 1957 with Lee Harvey Oswald and a Dallas Police officer who died in a mysterious fire in 1971."

Franklin was not surprised by what he was expecting to see printed:

"Mr. John Stockwell, the former CIA operative said he doubts the diary's authenticity because each entry for a fourteen-year period beginning in 1957 was written with the same felt tip pen, a model that did not exist in 1957. Mr. Stockwell who served in the CIA from 1964 to 1977, called the document a hoax. He pointed out one entry, dated shortly before Mr. White's death in September of 1971, refers to the Watergate burglary. The break-in at the Washington headquarters of the National Democratic Committee occurred June 17, 1972.

"The co-director of the JFK Assassination Information Center in Dallas announced, 'It's an embarrassment and could impede further research on the assassination.' Ricky White, the son of the man who he accused last month of the November twenty-second, 1963, assassination believes the journal which the CIA says is a hoax is not the one he publicized back in 1988 when he first contacted the FBI and believes it was this agency that has stolen the original journal. Geneva

White, the widow of Roscoe White, confirms her son is correct in what he states about his father and says she overheard a conversation between Jack Ruby, whom she worked for at the time as one of his dancers, and her husband, plotting Oswald's death. It was disclosed Oswald was to be killed during the extensive media coverage after the assassination, and Oswald would have never fired a shot! Mrs. White said the day of the assassination she and her three-year-old son, Ricky, were spirited out of Dallas for their protection. Mrs. White also stated Ruby caught her listening in on one of their conversations when she overheard her husband speak of an affair he was having with a girl who worked at Jagaer-Chiles-Stovall Company. This company was contracted by the U.S. military, and Oswald worked there shortly after his arrival from the Soviet Union. Ruby suggested Geneva may have to be killed for what she has overheard, but instead her husband agreed with his wife, to take four sessions of electroshock to erase her memory of the meetings and to save the lives of herself and her family. It wasn't until her son found his father's diary in a footlocker in 1982 and confronted her about his father, that the memories returned to her and she told him it was true. A spokesman from the CIA stated this was a farce, denying any CIA involvement in the Kennedy assassination and chalked it up as an attempt to make money or a movie deal."

* * *

John Modini watched the television screen as two brief news items appeared. One Item inferred one of President Bush's sons, Jeb, may have ties to the S&L scandal, and the other was a banker in Atlanta, Georgia was causing a controversy by stating the order to transfer funds through an Italian bank to brokerage a drug deal connected to the Contras came from the White House. The BCCI representative said he was being made a scapegoat.

Switching to local news, Modini listened to a reporter introducing Mark Lane as a Washington D.C. lawyer and author of the book *Rush to Judgment*, published in 1966 who had studied the assassination over the years.

"Mr. White's story may have some validity," Mark Lane said. "Everything he says is consistent with the evidence we know to be true!"

The reporter filled the TV screen to add, "Mr. Lane who campaigned for Mr. Kennedy in New York during the 1960 Presidential race and served in the New York State legislature, spent years studying the Kennedy assassination. Evidence convinced him the Warren Commission's findings are false.

"In other national news on Capital Hill today, while the S&L scandal proceeded on the Senate floor, in the House, a fifteen-year old girl from Kuwait told the members of Congress what she witnessed in a hospital. Iraqi soldiers, on orders of Saddam Hussein, took newly born babies and threw them to the cold floor and stomped on them until they were dead!

"Members of Congress were shocked and appalled as the fifteen-year old girl continued to say Iraqi soldiers not only took these newly-born babies from their cribs as their mothers cried out for mercy, but also from incubators. Some soldiers put them on stove burners, letting each child suffer before they would die. This brave girl then wept before Congress, as did some of its members.

"President Bush, angered by Hussein's bullying military tactics and continued buildup on the Kuwaiti border, appears on television this evening to make a plea to both the American people and Congress, to have Congress pass a bill to allow U.S. military involvement, as one commentator puts it, 'to stop Hussein from crossing the border into Kuwait, to jeopardize the Middle East peace accord, and from stopping countries like Iraq from barbaric tactics as these to our innocent children. If we just sit back and allow these types of atrocities to continue, one day it could mean it could happen to our own children right here in America!'"

Even Modini was in tears as he watched this event reported on Capital Hill followed by Bush's reaction. Just as this news item ended, a special news bulletin interrupted the local news live from Gary, Indiana. The viewers were shown a closed Ghetto and slum district of the city where an excavation was being conducted in a field. Bulldozers were digging up dirt behind a reporter who was trying to speak over all the noise surrounding him. Vehicles from the police and coroner's department moved in with a dozen ambulances following.

John Modini, his back to the television, was ready to leave the room when he heard the reporter announce the name of Catherine Rogers.

"A defense attorney, Catherine Rogers, from the State of Washington, convinced Gary, Indiana to excavate bodies of murdered victims by serial killer Karl Hunter. Hunter, a client of the Rogers and Bradley Law Firm. Karl Hunter committed suicide two years ago on the eve of his conviction. The area where the excavation is taking place had been condemned by the State for the last ten years. The property was controlled by a government agency allowing the city counsel to redevelop it at a future date. Presently, we cannot answer or confirm what agency of the government controls this land within this underdeveloped area. We do have information that two bodies of young girls have been discovered thus far, and it is alleged nineteen to twenty-five young girls are expected to be recovered if Mrs. Rogers' information is accurate. The two unidentified girls found so far has already convinced the coroner's office to proceed with the investigation. This is Lyle Acker for WPWS news, Gary, Indiana."

Another newscaster from his desk added, "We will keep you informed throughout the day on the progress of the excavation."

* * *

Judge Henry Kencade watched the same news broadcast with a colleague, another judge in his old chambers in the courthouse. He shook his head in disgust, and spoke with his friend. "Sam, I told my daughter if she found only one child in that excavation, I would help her to get Hunter's excavation okayed at Arlington. I'll need your assistance to get through some red tape!"

Sam took his robe off and hung it up on a hanger. He smiled at his retired friend. "Hank, you know I'll do what I can, even if they blow smoke up my flabby little ass!"

"Sam, it won't be smoke they'll blow up your ass," Kencade said soberly. "Expect to carry a fire extinguisher!" They both chuckled at his remark.

336

In his Indianapolis office, Senator Gerald Fuller was on the phone with his Miami friend. "Don't worry, Rogers is not hurting us. This will only validate our standing with Karl Hunter's guilt. The people will compliment us for protecting society from scum like him. I have no idea what is in the mind of this woman! I can only speculate she is digging her own grave because if Hunter is tied to anything they find out there, it can only guarantee my reelection! My biggest concern right now is my President! I've got to get those guys in Washington to pass that bill so George can play chess with Hussein in the desert gulf! No, no...not play golf with... It's a metaphor! He wants to go to war against Saddam Hussein! Yes...all right. I'll call you tomorrow," Fuller hung up the phone and laughed to himself. "Yeah, he wants to play golf with Saddam in the Desert Pro-Am!" he laughed again, "I got to remember that one..."

* * *

Marian O'Leary, a.k.a. Mrs. Modini, answered a knock on the door. She opened it to see an African American man gazing at the scenery surrounding her home.

Richard Franklin turned around to smile at the small woman whom he came to see.

"You must be Mr. Richard Franklin," she quietly announced.

"Yes... Yes, I am. Thank you for allowing me to see you."

"Please... Come inside." Marion held the door open as he entered. She escorted him to the back room.

Franklin saw someone with his back to him, sitting in the leather-bound chair and excused himself. "I'm sorry, Mrs. Modini-- I mean, O'Leary, I didn't know you had company!"

John Modini rose from the chair and confronted Franklin. "Hello, Richard!" he remarked anxiously

Franklin was startled at his appearance, jumping at the sight of him. He then began to laugh,

337

blurting out, "I knew it!" He threw his arms around Modini and patted him on the back. "I had the feeling you were still alive!"

An hour later, both Richard Franklin and John Modini sat down to dinner served by Mrs. O'Leary. She served them fresh meat loaf and macaroni with hot buttered cornbread. Modini took the opportunity to explain how he survived his ordeal, and how he was bedridden for months afterward. A Montana farm couple helped him recuperate and kept his secret from the authorities all this time. He explained to Franklin if he allowed himself to come out into the open, he would surely be signing his own death warrant.

Franklin also filled him in on what was happening to him. He told Modini the reason he was there-- the producers wanted to buy his screenplay, *The Connection*.

Modini shook his head, "I wrote that thing back in the late '70's. No studio will ever make that into a film," he said disparagingly. "I stepped over the line of credibility when I wrote that."

"That's right, Mr. Modini!" Franklin snapped back, "You did step over the line! The same line the House Select Committee stepped over when it came to the real conclusion-- a conclusion never to be divulged to the public. We got Blakley's conspiracy conclusions and to this day nobody is doing anything about it! This movie will open a can of worms," Franklin continued, "and these producers are serious. Their first film is predicted to be a top sell at the box office in its first week out, and the producers want to do *The Connection* next!"

Modini shrugged, "Well, it sounds good, almost too good to be true. I hope you're right, but could bet you a million dollars it won't happen. Who knows, maybe our country might wake up, change its attitude, and see the light. But I'm that cynical to believe it won't."

"You've got to give it a chance, though," Franklin told him. "It isn't every day a studio wants to make a movie from a script you wrote!"

Both men laughed and shook hands for luck. Franklin then got down to business. "You and I may have perfect timing. Remember Kirsten Manderson? You and she worked together back in 1981. She and I met at a Christmas party. Her father has always wanted to meet you-- he's

CIA." His eyes lit up, but Modini's didn't. Franklin continued, "We've got to meet with her father, and only you can make that a reality. He wants to talk to you-- and don't be alarmed. He's okay. Kirsten can easily set up the meeting! She'll be happy to know you are still alive! And believe you me, so am I, brother!"

Modini was hesitant. "Now, wait a minute! As long as you understand my circumstances. I'll talk to Kirsten about this but only if all of us agree to keep the fact I'm alive a secret. I'm sure her father will agree with this, if he is who you say he is. I'll do it because I trust you, Franklin-- and you believe in Kirsten." Modini stopped speaking. His face turned white.

Franklin became concerned. "What? I agree with you. I trust Kirsten!"

Modini shook his head. "No, not that! It just dawned on me-- with Roger Tracy's body found in a river in Idaho, everyone in my platoon in Vietnam who survived and returned to the states is now dead. Karl Hunter and I always thought it strange some of our buddies died from friendly fire, not from the enemy."

"Do you mean to tell me all those who did survive there and returned home have also died," Franklin asked.

Modini slowly nodded. "Now, I'm wondering if that friendly fire was really friendly. As of now, officially I'm dead! Everyone in my platoon is dead! Let's make sure we keep it that way!"

Chapter Twenty-Six

"The Death List"

Thomas Sanders walked into Michael Bradley's office with a folder in his hand and waited for him to finish preparing an affidavit on his computer. Michael looked up for a second to see who wanted his attention. "What's up?" he asked, continuing to type away.

Thomas put the folder on his desk quietly, "Well...it's a death list!" he responded awkwardly.

Michael stopped after completing a sentence. "A what?"

Thomas gave a mischievous grin. "A death list! It's all the people, or at least the ones recorded who died between the time of JFK's assassination and the Senate and House Select Committees investigation of the '70's up to today. All of them were either witnesses or had information concerning that fateful day in Dallas, or had evidence pertaining to Oswald, Ruby, and those who may be responsible for the assassination!"

Michael picked up the folder and opened it up. His eyes opened when he saw pages of names listed. "My God, this looks like a holocaust list," he said. "There's at least one hundred and fifty names!"

"Like I said, those are the only ones recorded," Thomas explained. "There are probably more unaccounted for..."

Michael looked over the list again and asked, "What are the asterisks for?"

Thomas went down the line. "Well, the <u>one</u> asterisk is for those who died before the Warren Commission came out. They either testified or never made it to testify before the Commission. In either event, they died prior to the release of the Warren Report. The <u>two</u> asterisks mean those who were witnesses or those with information interviewed by Mark Lane and Jim Garrison prior to Garrison taking Clay Shaw to court. That was the only official record Kennedy's assassination ever went to trial to date. The *three* asterisks identify those who didn't make it to the House Select Committee when they reopened both Kennedy's and Martin Luther King Jr.'s case in the late '70's, mainly between that and the Frank Church hearings in 1975-76."

Michael noticed two asterisks next to Dorothy Kilgallen's name, including her job description as a Washington D.C. columnist and the circumstances of her death. "What the-- Why would Dorothy Kilgallen's name be mentioned here? I'm sure she must have known the Kennedy brothers, let alone the family, but it doesn't mean she had--"

Thomas interrupted, "Actually, this is one of the simple ones to explain. Apparently, Dorothy Kilgallen went to Dallas to interview Jack Ruby just prior to his death. What he couldn't tell the Warren Commission--or from Ruby's point of view, what the Warren Commission didn't want to hear-- he told Dorothy. She came back to D.C. with the biggest bombshell that threatened to rock the corridors of our government, but her story suddenly disappeared. Her interview with Ruby disappeared and within days she was dead of some mysterious drug overdose!"

Michael was tongue-tied for the moment. He picked out the name of Deputy Sheriff Roger D. Craig of Dallas. "What can you tell me about Sheriff Craig," he asked.

Thomas was flustered at this one. "This guy was something else! I saw an interview with him years ago. He made the interview to get the information he had on record because he knew someone was trying to kill him. Someone had tried five or six times before they succeeded. He was in the book depository when they found the rifle. Craig swore the alleged Oswald rifle, the Italian

Mannlicher, was not the rifle they found-- it was a German Mauser. Craig was found dead with a shotgun wound to the head, supposedly a suicide!"

Michael's face drained of color when he spotted William Pitzer's name. "Pitzer! His name is familiar, but it says he died in 1966, also with a gunshot to the head. A suicide? I think his name passed through our office sometime in the last two years, I'm sure I've seen it somewhere. It says he was a commander at Bethesda Naval Hospital in Washington. What's the connection?"

Thomas smiled. "Maybe his name is familiar because Karl Hunter mentioned his name on the tape."

Michael remembered. "Yes, that's right. Catherine had one of our paralegals get research on him. Pitzer was the one who actually took pictures and filmed the Kennedy autopsy the night of the assassination. My God! What did he see? And what did he know?"

"There is a witness who can answer that. He saw the photos and film after Pitzer had the negative photographic images processed. He said what the Warren Commission stated as fact in their report was, in fact, totally the opposite and false."

Thomas glanced around the empty room. "By the way," he asked, "Where is Catherine now?"

* * *

Catherine Rogers drove her Honda Prelude into the parking lot of the Glen Ridge Hospital, the same mental institution where she first met Carrie two years earlier.

As she parked in the visitor's section, she glanced up at the window where she remembered a little thirteen-year-old girl stared out for hours. There was no one at the window now. *She's fifteen years old now,* Catherine thought to herself. *I wonder what condition she's in now. Has she been cared for? All I know is that she's still here!*

Catherine entered the hospital and discovered the head nurse, Miss Maxine Hightower, was now an administrator of this section of the hospital. Her office was decorated like an attorney's office, one that was doing very well. It had an interior of mahogany and leather. Maxine's new title had changed to 'Head Chief of Staff.'

"It's nice to see you again, Mrs. Rogers." Miss Hightower stood to greet Catherine. She seemed not to have changed in the past two years. She picked up the morning's newspaper from her desk. "I've been reading about you all week. I see they've found nineteen bodies so far in this excavation you're putting the State of Indiana through. I admire your guts-- considering what you've undergone yourself!"

Catherine raised her eyebrow. Miss Hightower continued; trying to be as tactful as she could. "I read the other article about you, the one in the newspaper two years ago."

"Thank you, Miss Hightower," Catherine said, reluctantly touching on a subject she would rather avoid. "I wouldn't want anyone to go through what I went through. I know first hand how a girl of eleven or twelve could be as traumatized as Carrie was."

Maxine came over to sit near Catherine. It was a gesture to show she was less of a professional and more of a friend. "I assure you, Mrs. Rogers," she confided, "you'll be surprised how Carrie has healed these past two years. She still doesn't communicate with any of us-- the adult faculty, but she did make a connection...a link to other troubled minds of the younger children here."

"She's talking to the other children?" Catherine was surprised.

"Yes, She's turned herself into a mother hen, a figure for those unfortunate, especially the unstable ones. She's their guardian angel, so to speak. I can't explain it, but you saw how she just stood at her bedroom window waiting! I've thought about it often. I believe the person she was waiting, and praying for-- be it imaginary or real-- was her guardian angel. Her involvement allowed her to open up and interact with the other kids her age. She became just that herself-- a guardian angel looking after others."

There was skepticism in Catherine's voice. "You're not serious about what you just said, are you? I mean--"

Maxine cut in. "Mrs. Rogers, it's only a theory I have and I think it's a good one to go on. A great change has occurred in Carrie since the last time you saw her."

"But surely, Miss Hightower," Catherine challenged, "isn't it possible Carrie was only waiting for her father to return? And then when Mr. Zieg--"

Miss Hightower interrupted. "I hope you didn't have any impression her father was returning for her!"

Catherine was pleasantly surprised. "No. I mean, yes, at first I did. Her father sent me to see her. It was the same day you and I met here, don't you remember?"

Miss Hightower shook her head. "Mrs. Rogers, Carrie's father is dead!"

Catherine took a breath and tried to remain calm, "I know, I was there that night. I was taken by gunpoint to Gary, Indiana. I was assaulted and raped by two men, one of them was Mr. Ziegler, her father! Later that night, I found his body. He was presumably killed by the man who raped me-- the one I saw <u>here</u> at this hospital, during my first visit, peering into Carrie's room. That was the reason Carrie screamed her head off, you do remember that, Miss Hightower?"

Miss Hightower was silent for the moment. Then her attitude changed from personable to professional. "Excuse me, Mrs. Rogers. I don't know who you think Carrie's father is or was, but Carrie's father is not Mr. Ziegler. I've never met the man, and as far as I know he never came around this hospital when I wasn't here. Believe me, when I was on duty I would have known about it! I knew only of him from the phone calls and the correspondence I would get in the mail. Secondly, Mrs. Rogers..." Maxine held up her hand, preventing her from speaking, "Carrie's father was already dead. He died years ago in the Vietnam war, so Carrie couldn't be waiting for her father.

"But Ziegler told me <u>he</u> was Carrie's father. Why did he lie to me?

"I don't know. Perhaps he wanted to help Carrie. Perhaps he thought if you talked to her, you could reach her? I have no idea."

"You say you've never actually met him?" Catherine pressed.

"That's right. He never came to this hospital to visit Carrie. Nor do I know whether Carrie has knowledge of his existence. He said in one of his letters he was the one in charge of sending us the monthly check to pay for her hospital costs. He was the one who dealt with the financial matters of her case."

Catherine could not believe what she was told, but was relieved just the same to know Ziegler was not Carrie's real father. "But if this is true, how did Carrie come into the care of this hospital?"

"Carrie was brought into here by the Catholic Church," Miss Hightower freely explained, "by two nuns, and a Mother Superior."

"And how was Carrie's progress monitored. Did someone come in to check on her progress?"

Miss Hightower nodded. "A priest from Our Lady of Lourdes periodically came in to check on her, though never to see her. He met with me, and I kept him updated on the girl's progress."

"Do you remember this priest's name?" Catherine asked.

"No, not offhand," Miss Hightower told her, "but I can look it up for you."

"Please. It's very important to me," Catherine said anxiously.

Miss Hightower got up and opened her file cabinet. She rifled through a series of files until she found the right one. "Here it is. I found her file" She opened it up and started looking through the papers.

Then a sudden thought struck Catherine. It was as if she had given herself a mental slap. "Her file..." she called out to Maxine, "If Ziegler isn't her real father, then her name isn't Carrie Ziegler... That's what I thought all this time. What a fool I've been."

"You weren't much of a fool, Miss Rogers," Miss Hightower confided. "When Mr. Ziegler set up the meeting between you and Carrie, he gave instructions not to release her last name-- even if you asked. I discretely avoided the subject."

"Then what is Carrie's last name listed in her file?"

Miss Hightower indicated the file in her hand. "Modini... Her full name is Carrie Modini!"

Catherine's face turned white with shock. She stood up, cutting Maxine off, "Wait, wait! Wait a minute. You said, Modini! You're telling me the name of Carrie's father was Modini?"

"Yes. Right here! It says 'John Modini.' He's listed as the father. Is something wrong?"

Catherine couldn't answer. She was too stunned to find the right words. This sudden information was too incredible for her to believe all at once. A whole new set of questions begged for answers.

Miss Hightower, oblivious to Catherine's astonishment, flipped though Carrie's file and found the page she was looking for. "Here it is. The information you wanted about the priest who visited us. The priest's name is Father Conrad."

Catherine's breath caught again. "Father *Daniel* Conrad?" She remembered the name from the file she had on John Modini.

Miss Hightower was surprised. "Yes, how did you know?"

Catherine quickly shook her head. "I--I did some research, earlier..." she said, knowing full well the excuse sounded flimsy. She knew she had to wait until later to untangle this predicament. But right now she knew what she had to do next. "Would it be all right if I could see Carrie now?" she asked.

Miss Hightower took Catherine to the hospital common room where they looked through the glass window set in the double doors. Inside, they witnessed a fifteen-year-old Carrie taking care of the little children, entertaining them by reading a book. She had just finished a story. She put her book down and joined in playing games with the children. Another nurse was there, as well, rocking a child to sleep. She smiled at Miss Hightower through the door.

When the two women entered the room, another wide-eyed child wandered up to them with a book and patiently waited, ready to be read to. Carrie suddenly noticed Catherine and Miss

Hightower.

Catherine took a few steps toward Carrie. "Hello, Carrie," she said softly, as not to frighten her, "Do you remember me? My name is Catherine."

Carrie remained frozen as Catherine approached her. Then Carrie grabbed for her locket around her neck, holding onto it tightly, as if it could afford her protection. She moved back against the wall and slid down to a squatting position.

"I-- I don't know whether she remembers me or not," Catherine said to Miss Hightower. "Would it be possible to spend a few minutes with her?"

"I don't think it would be a good idea," Miss Hightower replied, noticing the young girl's reaction. "Maybe we'd better go now."

Catherine watched the assistant nurse shepherd the rest of the children out of the room. "All I'm asking for is two minutes-- two minutes alone with her."

Miss Hightower shook her head. "You see how she reacted when she saw you."

"Of course I did," Catherine replied sharply. "But she recognizes me. I don't think she's really afraid of me."

Miss Hightower pursed her lips and looked at Carrie. There was a look of curiosity on her face, not fear. Then Miss Hightower decided to give Catherine the benefit of her doubt. "I'll just wait outside the door for you." She went out and closed the door behind her and peered through the glass window.

"Hello, Carrie..." Catherine approached Carrie very slowly. When she saw the girl get nervous, she stopped. She saw Carrie still clutched her little locket around her neck.

Catherine continued to cross the room. "There's nothing to be frightened by, Carrie. It's only me, Catherine..."

The girl was apprehensive as Catherine knelt down next to her. Catherine's heart went out to the girl. She wanted to touch her, to comfort her, but thought better of it, knowing the possible consequences. She tried to establish a connection with the teenager. "Well, Carrie! I see you still have your locket. Do you remember me? I was here along time ago--"

Before she could finish, Carrie nodded her head in response to say she did remember.

Catherine smiled and proceeded cautiously, not wanting to frighten the child, "I apologize for taking so long to see you again, but I've been in a hospital...like you. I was very sick, but now I'm well again. I came by to see how you were doing, and to tell you I want to help you find a new home if there is any way possible..."

Carrie stared at Catherine in a shy, puppy dog way, not saying a word, but she was listening intently.

"Now you can think about this before making any decisions, but--" here she put her hand gently on the girl's shoulder. "I'd like to know if you'd like to come and live with me?"

For a moment it looked as though Carrie would say something, but she lowered her eyes, deep in thought.

"I'll be back soon," Catherine tried to encourage her. "In the mean time, you can think about what I've said. Okay? When you're fully well and if you want to come and live with me, you can let Miss Hightower know." She took out one of her business cards from her purse and wrote down her home telephone number. "Carrie... I want you to have this, just in case. If you ever want to talk to me, here's my phone number. You can call me anytime." Carrie watched as Catherine set her card down on a table.

Catherine knew her time was up. Reluctantly she stood up and moved to the door. "I'll talk to you real soon," she promised, and exited the room.

As she stepped into the hall and the door closed behind her, Catherine looked back through the glass window and saw Carrie pick up the card.

Miss Hightower was waiting near by. They walked down the corridor together. "I want you to protect that girl with your life, Miss Hightower!" Catherine told her straight out.

They headed to the front entrance. "Mrs. Rogers, I hope you don't get the wrong impression about our work here at the hospital," Miss Hightower replied. "We don't treat our patients like--"

Catherine cut her off. "No, I don't mean that. I'm sure you're a decent administrator. You have a good staff, and Carrie seems to be recuperating. What I meant to say, Miss Hightower, is that you and Carrie may be in danger! Now listen to me! You have to get your security to keep a constant eye on that girl in there! I believe the reason she's here is to keep her from identifying someone!"

Miss Hightower gave Catherine an inexplicable look, "Who? Why would you say such a thing?"

Catherine took a picture from her purse and presented it to Miss Hightower. "Can you identify this man?"

"Yes, that's Father Daniel Conrad," she replied. Then she saw the dumbfounded expression on Catherine's face. "What's wrong?"

"No, this photo is not Father Conrad," Catherine said, her voice striking a serious tone. "The real Father Conrad died in 1982 when he committed suicide by jumping from a bridge in New Hampshire!"

Miss Hightower was disturbed and bewildered by this information. "I don't understand. Then who is this man in the photo?"

"This is the man who I told you I saw when I was here two years ago. Carrie saw him and screamed. This is the man who raped me and tried to kill me that night! This man is Karl Hunter, but Karl Hunter supposedly committed suicide in the State Prison up in Fort Wayne days before my rape, so until I find out what's happening here, I want that girl protected, is that understood?"

Miss Hightower listened patiently, but stood her ground, "I understand your concern, Mrs. Rogers, but Carrie already is in good hands. Believe me, nothing will happen to her as long as I'm here!"

Catherine nodded, "Good!" She gave Miss Hightower a business card. "I want you to call me at any time if anything suspicious happens concerning our little girl. I definitely will be in touch with you soon!"

* * *

Richard Franklin was in flight aboard a Delta airliner heading for Scottsdale, Arizona. He finished a story in the U.S.A. Today newspaper concerning President Bush's January fifteenth deadline for Desert Storm. The article reported American soldiers were undoubtedly heading for a confrontation with Saddam Hussein.

Franklin folded the newspaper and set it down beside him, then opened his briefcase. He took out a legal tablet with names and a set of pictures on it. Franklin stared at a photograph, one showing a distinguished man, an exhibit from the House Select Committee on Assassinations and wrote down on the next line the names, *David Atlee Phillips*. Then he added next to Phillips name, *the CIA, and Castro.*

He looked at another photograph and wrote down the name *Charles Nicoletti*. Next to his name he wrote *Giancana, Chicago Mafia and Castro.*

A third photograph, and this time he wrote the name *Frank Sturgis.* A photo with the name E. Howard Hunt was provided, linking it with Sturgis. He wrote next to their names, *the CIA, Castro and Watergate.*

Franklin picked up another photograph. As he was writing down the name *George DeMohrenschildt*, Franklin lifted his head feeling someone watching him. He glanced around him throughout the plane, but no one appeared to react suspiciously to him. Everything seemed normal. He understood now what people meant when they might be a little paranoid. Franklin laughed off this sudden feeling and then penciled in a line next to George DeMohrenschildt's name, *Bush, Oswald and the CIA.*

* * *

Catherine walked into Michael Bradley's office and saw him examining the "death list." He had a 'who's who' documentation book beside him. "Hello, Michael," she said, breaking the

350

silence.

He glanced up. "Who is George DeMohrenschildt?" he answered with a question. "I can't find anything about him except he's Russian and did business around the world for Texas Oil."

Catherine gave him a perplexed look. "Why are you so concerned with George De...somebody?"

Michael tapped the list with his pen, "Well, Thomas brought in this death list earlier today. Some of the names Karl Hunter mentions on his tape, like your William Pitzer and George DeMohrenschildt, and others with Italian names, were killed with a gunshot wounds to the head. Their death certificates described them as suicides. For instance, both Pitzer and DeMohrenschildt died the same way, and both were mentioned by Hunter. And both were somehow connected, as Thomas suggests, to Kennedy's assassination. How? Why? There's nothing stating Pitzer filmed Kennedy's autopsy, yet there are witnesses who claim they were there now stating the autopsy was filmed. But why didn't the Warren Commission never mentioned this or--"

"Were they ever aware of it?" Catherine finished his sentence. "Michael, we've got to move! I have to check Dad's status on Arlington. We need to start excavating the grave of Karl Hunter now. And it's essential we find out if John Modini is still alive or dead."

Sherry Keller, stepped into the office. "Sorry to interrupt," the secretary said, "but Tom wants you to see something in the boardroom. He says you've got to see it to believe it!"

Catherine looked at Michael and shrugged. Now was as good a time as any. They went into the boardroom and saw Thomas Sanders stationed in front of the television broadcasting the CNN News. An anchor reported from the front entrance of the Capitol in Washington D.C. where a news event was breaking:

"It is in our estimation and surprise the little fifteen-year old Kuwaiti girl who identified herself only as Nayirah and spoke before the House of Representatives about the atrocities the Iraqis were doing to the Kuwaitis newly born infants in these last weeks, was not who she represented herself to be..."

Catherine watched from the doorway as CNN ran footage of the girl speaking before Congress. Her voice broke with emotion describing the horrific incident at a hospital in Kuwait City where she said she was working as a volunteer.

"...Iraqi soldiers burst into the hospital with guns and took infants from their incubators, letting them die on the cold floor!" she recounted. "A friend was almost drowned in a swimming pool by being dunked by an Iraqi soldier. Then they pulled his fingernails out and applied electroshock to private parts of his body!"

The anchor appeared again. "These words from a teenage girl who caused the White House to pressure Congress to pass a bill to stop Iraq from entering Kuwait, appear now not to be true and the whole event that happened before Congress might have been staged or been a hoax! A correspondent from one of our sister networks recently discovered whom this fifteen-year old girl really was. She said she was vacationing in Kuwait with her mother when the Iraqi soldiers invaded, but she also said she was volunteering in a Kuwaiti hospital when said this incident happened. Now we discover the teenager who calls herself Nayirah, is actually the daughter of the Kuwaiti Ambassador who lives right here in Washington D.C.! It looks as though his daughter was used to get Congress and the Senate to pass the bill for sending our U.S. forces to fight President Bush's war against Saddam Hussein. Both the State Department and President Bush refused to comment until a complete investigation has taken place."

The anchor proceeded. "In other news from Capitol Hill, the President's problems don't stop with Saddam Hussein, but continue in his own back yard. It is now official. Since 1985, Washington has engaged itself in a massive cover up, desperately trying to hide the true dimensions of the savings and loan debacle! Both aided and abetted the thrift industry and its hired-hand accountants, appraisers and attorneys. Key figures on both sides of the parties, included names such as Charles Keating, Donald Regan, David Stockman, Alan Cranston, and William Proxmire. And Bush's own Secretary of State, James Baker, has refused to face reality that American taxpayers will have to pay a cleanup bill that could exceed $500 billion dollars by the year 2020! The S & L cover up still continues today. This is CNN News at the Capitol!"

"Now wasn't that special!" Thomas remarked in a Dana Carvey accent. He followed this by confronting Michael with a wink, adding seriously, "If Bush has an agenda, he's either learned a lot from his mentor, Tricky Dick Nixon, or he was able to manipulate the public by his skills as the CIA director, wouldn't you say?"

"Except someone from the media just caught him!" Catherine spoke up.

Thomas finally noticed her standing in the doorway. "Oh, hello Catherine, it's always a pleasure to see you," then added sardonically, "Did Michael show you our 'death list,' yet?"

Chapter Twenty-Seven

"The Bagman of Scottsdale"

John Modini sat down at a coffee shop in an air-conditioned Holiday Inn and sipped a hot cup of coffee. He still enjoyed it, although it was late fall and the ninety-degree weather was still prevalent, considering this was Scottsdale, Arizona.

Modini glanced at his watch, and told the waitress in a few minutes he would place his order. He was expecting someone to join him for a late breakfast. A few minutes later Richard Franklin entered, briefcase in hand, and saw Modini reading the U.S.A. Today paper. Nervously, he sat down next to him.

Modini set his paper down and shook Franklin's hand, "Nice to see you again. Are you okay?"

Franklin returned a small smile. "Nervous a little, I guess, but I'll be fine. Everything is set. We meet in Suite 702 on the seventh floor. There's a connecting suite that will be unlocked ten minutes prior to our meeting. We enter on our own accord and go to the back bedroom where our friend will meet with us! We have one hour before it's time. Have you ordered anything? I'm not very hungry!"

Modini indicated the waitress a few tables down. "She'll be taking our order soon.

Everything should be okay."

Franklin looked at Modini awkwardly, wanting to say something. Modini recognized his discomfort and broke the tension, "Well, what is it?"

Franklin struggled to get out what he wanted to say, "I believe I have some bad news!"

"Well, I'm waiting with baited breath," Modini said sarcastically. "Don't tell me there's a problem with the meeting I don't know about!"

Franklin shook his head. "No, nothing like that. No, it's just that I-- I may owe you that million dollars you wanted to bet me!"

Modini's mind raced along, trying to grasp what Franklin was trying to say, then it dawned on him. "You mean about the movie-- my script? It's not going through with Warner Brothers?" Modini leaned back in his seat and sighed. "I'm not surprised!"

Franklin tried to explain, "Of course, it's supposed to go, but this company run by McBerny and Wilkerson won't return my calls, and there's no written agreement nor contract yet. I'm being ignored, for one thing, but I did get an assistant to give me a partial answer. The studio told these guys they hired them as black producers to make predominantly black films for the black market, not to delve into the white market! Besides this, I'm told Warner Brothers is not in the market for political films today!"

Modini's eyes opened wide to this news. "Have you read U.S.A. Today recently?" he asked.

"I've read it but, did I miss something?" Franklin asked.

Modini proceeded to show him where it was announced Oliver Stone was making the movie, *JFK* based on Jim Garrison's novel, "*On the Trail of Assassins*," for Warner Brothers Studios.

Franklin was surprised by the article. "You're kidding, I just read that book. But why would Oliver Stone be making this film? I mean, what a switch from Vietnam to this! How in the hell did Warner Brothers get involved when I was told--"

Modini cut in with an easy answer, "One, Oliver Stone can make anything he wants, at any studio he wants, he's the number one filmmaker in Hollywood today. Two, *Time Warner* is, I believe, the book's publisher. Hence, the reason *Warner Brothers* is doing it is that Oliver Stone is marketable and has a good track record. And three, remember the document you gave me a few years ago in D.C. about reversing the policy and direction of the Vietnam war?"

Franklin nodded and Modini proceeded. "Well, Oliver Stone agreed with you. Kennedy was killed because he would not allow our country to expand the Vietnam War. So, there's the Vietnam War angle. Someone, like you, Mr. Franklin, on the House Select Committee gave Mr. Stone the same information as you gave me. Stone has the power to do what he wants to do. I, on the other hand, can be buried easily. Who am I-- nobody!"

Franklin saw Modini's point, but didn't agree. "Mr. Modini, don't sell yourself short. Power is knowledge and it's how you convey that knowledge to the American people-- to make them wake them up and make them listen. Yes, Mr. Stone has power, and I'm sure it will prove itself well in his motion picture. I'm sure he'll have every Tom, Dick and Harry in the conspiracy world helping him to the truth of the matter. Mr. Stone would immerse himself in eighteen months or less of planning to put this movie together. Do you realize the knowledge *you* possess, the sacrifices *you've* made, in not just the last few years, but your whole life? If I'm not mistaken, God has given you a gift. You may think at this stage it's a curse, but no, sir! God has saved you and kept your life going, to this very day. And where is that, you say? Well, let me tell you! Right now, someone wants to see you, to talk to you as I did-- just like that man from the Nixon administration who first wanted to finance your project. Garrison's book gave us reason to believe there was a conspiracy, but it's not going to close any wounds about who had our President killed."

Modini nodded in agreement as Franklin continued, "If anything, it is only going to cause more anger on both sides of the coin. An alarm will be set off and that's what Garrison's book-- and now to be a film-- will do to the public. But that alarm could be shut off when it begins to ring too loudly. I mean there are people in the government who will do the same to the movie as they did to all our hearings and committees formed and paid for by you and me and the taxpayers of this country. Our money will be wasted to protect *one* entity, those who protect the interest of the Central Intelligence Agency of the United States of America. It is they who truly control the outcome of what affects our 'America the Beautiful!' No matter what Stone does, they'll pounce on him as they did Garrison!"

Modini stared at Franklin. "That doesn't surprise me one bit," he said gloomily. "I don't feel like waiting here. Let's go now."

Following a quiet elevator ride, John Modini and Richard Franklin unlocked a seventh floor room of the hotel. They entered, sat down in the comfort of their surroundings and they waited.

* * *

In Miami, Florida the Miami Police Department was as busy as ever. It was a humid day, and the sweat was noticeable on Jennifer Tamura's yellow culottes dress as she entered the precinct. The desk officer made a call, hung up and winked at her, "He's expecting you, go right on up. Follow the yellow stripe on the floor."

Jennifer saw a four-color stripe system leading on up the staircase. She ascended the stairs following the yellow one, heading for the office of Raymond Corrigan.

Captain Corrigan was now in charge of the precinct's detective division. He was grayer in his years, though he never slowed down in his dedication to his work. He looked up through the window of the glass case partition of his office to see an attractive Asian woman heading his way. He decided to greet her in person, knowing the lechers in his department were drooling at her as she passed them to get to his office.

Jennifer, the confident woman she was, nodded to the officers with, "Nice to see all of you working so hard today, boys!" She overheard one of the officers whisper to another, "I'd love to lick the sweat off this one!"

She laughed to herself as a wolf-whistle followed, and the voice of Corrigan yelled out,

357

"That's enough, you guys, it's shower time! Hello, Miss Tamura, come into my office. I promise you, no handcuffs." They both laughed.

Corrigan allowed her to enter first, adding, "I can't blame the men. You are indeed a gorgeous creature. Please have a seat."

"Thank you," Jennifer said to him as she seated herself. Corrigan opened a small refrigerator and offered her a soft drink. She chose Perrier water and took a sip. "I'd like to know what you thought of the material and the tape Michael Bradley sent you?"

"I thought it was very interesting," Corrigan said, "and I'm pleased to see your firm was doing its homework. You appear to be serious in taking on the government. It's been tried before, and each time the government shuts it down. I know you're doing this with the deepest secrecy, and I, for one, support you and will help as much as I can, but I won't be surprised when Bradley's office decides not to dig any deeper. I hear that you have some new evidence," he said casually

Jennifer acknowledged there was. "I haven't seen it nor do I know where it is, but it may tie the CIA to the hit on Kennedy. A deceased client of ours provided this information and the tape we gave you!"

"Well, the question is, what can I do to help you-- using the little resources I have?" Corrigan asked her.

Jennifer provided a sheet of names, including those of Frank Sturgis and Johnny Roselli. "If there are any acquaintances or relatives of the people on this list still alive, we'd like to talk to them. I'd appreciate any help on this."

Corrigan nodded, "I can't promise or guarantee you anything...but I'll try!"

"That's all we can ask," Jennifer smiled.

* * *

Franklin was nervous as he sat in the suite, waiting with Modini to speak with their guest. Both kept silent until Franklin got to his feet and stretched as if announcing, "Let's do it!"

358

Modini stood, taking a deep breath. "I can tell you're nervous," he said to Franklin, "Well, it just caught up with me."

Both men went to the door and Modini followed Franklin into the connecting suite.

Modini proceeded to close the door behind them. Once inside, they looked around. Modini said, "Back bedroom!" As quiet as it was in the room, they continued to proceed with their instructions.

They entered the bedroom. Everything looked normal. The bed was tidy, as if no one slept in it, and the room was immaculate.

Franklin noticed two comfortable chairs sitting side by side facing the wall at the south corner of the room, and sitting in a third cushioned chair was a gentleman. His arms were folded, and his legs crossed.

The man smiled, but didn't stand to greet them. He waved to the two empty chairs. "Sit, please!"

Before they did, Franklin spoke up, "You're Kirsten's father, so I'll imagine you go by her name, Mr. Manderson?" He offered his hand in greetings, and the gentleman reciprocated by reaching out to shake it. Franklin introduced himself.

"Nice to meet you, Mr. Franklin. You can call me George if you like...and you must be Mr. Modini..."

Modini quickly shook his hand and made himself comfortable in his chair.

Franklin slowly sat down in his. "Thank you for seeing us, sir."

"Let me say, first, my reason for agreeing to this meeting was because of John Modini and my daughter's trust in you, Mr. Franklin. Now, if I may, I will state the ground rules before we begin. Since the situation of my past background is of a highly confidential nature and-- to put it melodramatically, shrouded with secrecy-- I can only say so much. I can tell you this, though, I no longer work for the CIA and was not present in the 'Company' at the time of Kennedy's death; so I have no knowledge of that period. But I know, Mr. Franklin, you have some questions you want to ask me. Don't be surprised if I can't answer you. But first things first.

"I will start with you, Mr. Modini, and ask you a few questions concerning your screenplay. You may, in return, ask me anything you feel is necessary if you like," Mr. Manderson assured him. "You are not in any way obligated to answer my questions, nor am I to you. If everything is satisfactory with my rules, I will begin."

Modini nodded along with Franklin and asked, "Sure, what would you like to know, Mr. Manderson...George?"

Manderson smiled. "Well, I read your screenplay *The Connection,* I believe, ten years ago. I feel then as I do now, it would make a very good movie. Kirsten told me you gave up on it and shelved it. That was a pity!"

"Well, it wasn't as if I shelved it once," Modini interjected. "I can tell you I shelved it a half dozen times! The industry, as a whole, was afraid of this type of film, although it was fictitious and was set in the future, there was something in it that hit a nerve. And to be honest, this is what it was supposed to do, but I didn't think it would affect as many people as it did. I was also influenced by the Francis Ford Coppola film, *The Conversation,* in 1974, which dealt with paranoia at the time of the Watergate scandal. The movie industry might have felt the same with my screenplay! Maybe my screenplay might have seemed to some people all too real."

"Where did you get your ideas from?" Manderson asked. "I was surprised the information you presented in the setup and conclusion of your story. I don't know who did what in 1963, but I feel your outline of the events you wrote years ago can very well happen today! You wrote this in '76, or in the late 70's, and the information you had back then was remarkable-- remarkable as in the sense of its accuracy!

"The CIA protagonist in your script, the gentleman known by the name of the 'Scorpion,' for instance, was realistically depicted. Amazingly, in reality, there was an actual CIA operative who became a renegade within the Intelligence circles. He broke from the agency and became a freelance assassin-- an operative causing problems for the CIA. A contract was implemented to silence him.

Apparently, he had a fetish for killing young girls, usually Asian, upon completion of a job. He liked to strangle them after making love to them. I guess the term today would be a serial killer. So you can say there was a _real_ serial killer within the inner circles of the CIA. This is something not too surprising, after all the types of people they've incorporated these past years. How, Mr. Modini, did you ever come up with this character? Did you do some type of research? Your information is amazingly perceptive."

Modini smiled, "To be honest with you, Mr. Manderson, as I've told Mr. Franklin, most of it came to me in a dream one night. I was having problems in developing a story for my first time at screenwriting. I took the advice of a director friend and one night I had this terrible nightmare. I woke up and immediately wrote down one word, thinking it would help me remember it once I woke up. Well, it did! With that, I put together all the thoughts and feelings from my dream and it all fell into place exactly as it was portrayed in my script. Then I incorporated a Kennedy conspiracy theory as it might happen several years in the future, as you say today, and that was about it!"

"It is difficult for me to believe your entire screenplay was founded on a dream, Mr. Modini," Manderson said skeptically. "The details you depicted--" he stopped, tangling with this thought. "What was the one word you wrote down?"

Franklin was intrigued, and curious to hear his reply.

Modini smiled and said, "Shark!"

Franklin couldn't believe it. "You got all that in a screenplay based on the word 'shark'?"

Modini nodded turning from Franklin to Mr. Manderson, "Yes, the fact 'shark' was from 1975 to the 80's the biggest villain in screen history until Darth Vader was introduced to the public in the movie _Star Wars._ I thought of Steven Spielberg's _Jaws._ I made the hired assassin, a human shark on land, both terrifying and evil, controlled by what I call the _Jaws_ of government, a faction within, manipulating destiny and swallowing up the innocent!"

"I see you added a biblical point of view in its outcome!" Manderson said.

Franklin agreed.

Modini shook his head. "Well, I can't help it if people read too much into this! If you read it that way, then I wasn't aware of it's true implications. Maybe I wrote this screenplay subconsciously, and it came out that way. I did my basic background research like all good writers, but that's the truth of the matter."

Manderson leaned forward. "I want you to know, Mr. Modini, you definitely have something here, something better than a dream. The facts you present in your script, although framed in a fictional story, are something the American people have the right to know. Without saying too much, I think you know what I am talking about, so I'll leave it at that. If at any time you need me to guide or help you with this project, I'm at your service, all you need to do is contact Kirsten if you need my help."

Franklin looked over to Modini who pretended he knew what it meant, but in reality was a bit confused.

"Thank you," Modini said to Manderson. "I really appreciate that. I definitely will keep you in mind. Mr. Manderson, I have a question concerning Oliver Stone. I hear he's planning to make *JFK*, a movie based on Jim Garrison's book, *'On the Trail--'*"

Manderson interrupted, "Like I said, I was not around when Kennedy was hit, so what Garrison says had no bearing on what I think. Though I agree with you, Garrison's story should be told. Most people know of one side...the side of those who tried to destroy him. I say 'tried' because today he's a federal judge, so he must have won a few battles to get this far! He may have something to say, and Oliver Stone surely has become a powerful man to present the printed word on that big screen for millions of people to conjecture.

"You, however, get to the point and tell it like it is. You cut through the fat and tell how and who began the cover up. I'm sure when Stone's movie is made there will be much speculation. There is another question on my mind. How, may I ask, did you come to that conclusion, since your recent articles take a detour from what you presented in *The Connection*?"

Modini shrugged. "Again, as I told Mr. Franklin, if I were to conspire against the United States and take out the President, I would find someone I could trust or use to get close to the man. And how obvious can you get but to use the obvious. If the CIA can infiltrate the Dallas Police Department, which I'm sure they did, then they can infiltrate anyone! Simple, who controlled Kennedy alive and dead?"

Manderson smiled as well, "Are you surprised?"

Modini looked a bit puzzled.

Changing the subject Manderson asked, "How did you happen to come to work for *Time-Life*?"

Modini's concern grew. It was as if Manderson knew something he held as a secret all these years. "Actually," Modini started, as if to confess, "I got the job through a friend. It was a vet I went through Vietnam with. Well, his brother had a connection to the magazine."

"Really!" Manderson regarded him keenly, not giving anything away, as if to say 'this is interesting.'

Franklin didn't know where this conversation was going. He patiently crossed his legs and relaxed, letting the other two talk it out.

"This vet friend of yours-- his brother wouldn't happen to be with intelligence, would he?" Manderson asked.

Modini's eyes widened with alarm as if to wonder how he knew this. Franklin waited for Modini to give some type of answer, but nothing came out of him. Manderson saw he struck a nerve. "Don't worry, Mr. Modini. It was only a guess!"

"But how can you guess something like that?" Modini asked.

Manderson answered matter-of-factly. "As long as I know I was right, everything falls into place!"

Franklin was confounded. "What do you mean? I'm afraid I'm lost."

Manderson explained. "The day you went to work for *Time-Life* magazine, Mr. Modini, someone kept their eye on you. They knew what you did, where you vacationed, what you wrote, what you ate, drank and how you pissed, and where you were at all times on your assignments. Someone thinks you know something-- something you must never divulge or write. And there was always someone guiding you in what stories to write. Isn't that correct?"

Modini reluctantly nodded. "I picked my own stories, but now, as I look back, you're somewhat correct. Are you hinting at what I said earlier about the CIA's infiltration of the Dallas Police-- or any corporation?"

Manderson smiled. "Even better than that. In the early years of the CIA, they became major stockholders for Henry Luce and his *Time Magazine*. Soon, *Time* would branch itself out into other fields of endeavor. Why do you think *Time* took over defunct *Life Magazine*?"

Franklin attempted to answer this. "Other than making money you mean?"

Modini contemplated what Manderson was trying to tell them and then it dawned on him. "Oh, my God! You mean the 'Zapruder Film!' *Life* owned it, now *Time* has it! Wow! And that means they control--"

Manderson interrupted. "They say the more you live each day; the more you learn. Now what did you say about Oliver Stone and this movie he's supposed to make? What studio is behind the Garrison story Stone plans to do?"

Franklin was startled, "Son of a bit--Excuse me. You're saying Warner Brothers, the studio that rejected Modini's project, is going ahead with this Oliver Stone movie?"

Manderson again interjected. "*Time-Life* owned and operated under *Time Warner*, right?"

"Why would Stone put himself in this position when he could film this movie anywhere?" Franklin inquired.

Manderson looked at Modini. "If Mr. Modini knew he was scrutinized by the magazine he worked for, do you think he'd taken the job?"

"Not if he knew it in advance, probably no!" Franklin replied. Modini didn't saying anything but let Franklin continue. "So you're saying Mr. Stone doesn't know what he is getting into?"

"Not only that, when Stone announced he was going to film his next project, the Garrison book-- which I wouldn't be surprised they owned-- I'm sure Warner's Studio went out and sought Mr. Stone and offered him all the money he needed to back him. Not because they wanted to make the film, mind you, but to stop anyone else from making it. Like you said, he's big enough and powerful enough to make his film anywhere in the world. Here, they have some element of control-- to the point of deciding how to release this movie once it's completed."

"You mean Oliver Stone, unaware of this, eventually will make his film, no matter how great, factual, or nonfactual, it may be," Modini said angrily, "and he might never see it released at the end?"

Manderson nodded. "That will remain to be seen, won't it? Your film is still unable to go isn't it? You've written a powerful political statement with an exciting adventure story. It's box office! But your film, no matter how good or marketable it is, hasn't been made. So you tell me!"

Franklin shook his head, "I see now why that company I was dealing with at Warners wouldn't return my calls. Someone at Warners intimidated and manipulated them, I'm sure." He pondered this as Manderson sat back quietly for a moment in his chair, viewing the two men before him. "So the way I see it, in the Kennedy Assassination, we have one main cover up to start with that blows up into a complete government sweep under the rug. It does make sense that those who controlled Mr. Kennedy's body alive also controlled his body upon his death."

George Manderson moved on, "Mr. Franklin, you had some questions you wanted to ask me. Kirsten tells me you're an entertainment lawyer at present, but you worked with the H.S.C.A. on Kennedy and Martin Luther King, Jr."

Franklin was pleased by the recognition. "That's correct, sir!" He opened his briefcase to the photos.

Manderson looked over to Modini, giving him a clear-cut stare and proceeded. "All right, this is what you two can do. You can ask any question you like or show me what you like. I see you have photographs. As I said up front, I'll answer what I can, but don't be disappointed in the areas I can't touch upon because of my connection to Central Intelligence. There are certain boundaries I cannot cross. Again, keep in mind I have no knowledge of Kennedy's assassination, since I was no longer living in the country then, nor working for the agency! Regarding the photographs, please do not mention any names, simply show me each photograph and if it is someone I can identify, I will just remain silent. If it's someone I can't, I'll say no, is this understood?"

Both Franklin and Modini nodded in agreement.

Manderson gave them a wide grin. "Now, if all what I have said is clear to you, then you may proceed with your informal inquisition!"

Franklin glanced to Modini to see whether he'd like to speak, but Modini relaxed and allowed Franklin the floor. Franklin took his notes and photographs out in order from his briefcase nervously and assured Manderson, "I want you to know we're not wired or recording anything here."

Manderson smiled. "I realize this. It's only a precaution for us in this room. I feel it is better to do it the way I suggest."

Franklin kept his cool and poise as he settled his nervousness. "Mr. Manderson, how long were you with the Central Intelligence Agency and when did you join?"

Manderson crossed his legs. "I left the Agency after ten years in 1958. Prior to what we know today, the CIA was called the OSS and headed by my mentor, William Donovan. When World War II ended and the Cold War started, President Truman decided to give the OSS legitimacy and formed the CIA in 1947. I joined it at its infancy, and for the next ten years I did my best to serve our country."

"Can you tell me what you did for the agency during that time?" Franklin asked.

Manderson's response was blunt. "I'm sorry, I cannot."

"Can you tell me what you do now, what is your business today?"

Again smiling, Manderson answered him. "Yes, today I am into diamonds and mining. I brokerage both, out of the country."

Franklin shuffled through his notes from his pages of material, trying to figure in his list of names how to use them with the photographs.

Modini saw that Franklin needed a few moments to find what he was looking for and decided to respond, asking a simple question, "Did you like working for the CIA?"

Manderson was eager to answer. "Yes, Mr. Modini, for a while there it was a very patriotic thing to do. It was exciting to be a part of a company securing the safety of this country from the Cold War and enemies abroad. During the war Donovan had been a hero of mine."

Modini, a bit stumped at this most positive answer. It prompted him to ask the most oblivious question, "Then why, Mr. Manderson-- what made you leave it?"

Franklin was busy rearranging his photographs to be presented, when he stopped, waiting to hear Mr. Manderson's reply. "I left the Agency because it wasn't the vision of Bill Donovan anymore, a spy network used for intelligence and gathering of information. Instead, it was turning radical, too far right, and used, or I should say abused, for purposes of assassinations and of taking over countries. This soon became standard policy for the 'Company...'"

Franklin was intrigued at this revelation. It took his mind off his material for the moment. Manderson continued, "It was determined to take over as many countries as possible, to manipulate and change their governments, and once succeeding, would then add American military bases with advisors for training purposes. This showed the U.S. was there to protect and serve, but by the controlling auspices of the CIA.!"

Franklin and Modini were both amazed at Manderson's disclosure. Franklin jumped in. "You mean to say the CIA implemented a plan of assassination if, let's say any of these countries-- let's say for instance, Guatemala, didn't want to play along?"

Manderson was silent for a moment as Modini studied him, then spoke again. "What I can say is, a country that refuses to cooperate can be bought, or elections can be stacked in favor of the opposition, usually a CIA candidate, like recently Noriega and the Panama controversy. Noriega was CIA until he took what he learned from them and the U.S. advisors and turned it around for his own advantage. He took over Panama and made a deal to fulfill President Carter's contract to keep the Panama Canal, discharging previous U.S. Policy. Your President Bush, however, who was also CIA, is now planning to get rid of a malignancy that could ruin him today if ever their *Connection* ever came out tying him to the Iran Contra scandal. The Iran Contra fiasco has been transformed into what is known now as the BCCI scandal. It hasn't stopped!

"Bush finally got Noriega even when the election did not work. Noriega was way ahead of what the CIA was trying to do. An assassination would have been a final solution, but in this enlightened age where there are individuals and groups who scrutinize and monitor our government policies, it was impractical. So instead, the CIA manipulated the media to their own ends and made Noriega this evil monster where people in this country would not have blamed Bush if assassination really became a factor. Believe me it almost did come to that. And it will be for another CIA appointee. Saddam Hussein, when Desert Storm begins!

"And the outcome to Noriega? Well, they cooked up some drug charge, whether true or not, and actually went in to kidnap this Panamanian leader. He surrendered, which was smart, on the international news so he wouldn't be killed. Then he was flown to Miami, where they locked him up for national security reasons-- which, incidentally, were illegal. Now Panama's elections work out for the benefit of the U.S. government, although the new president and Vice-President are CIA appointees. The drugs still prosper through these new leaders, still bred by U.S. policy. You see, if one thing doesn't work, they go to the next step of implementation."

"Until that final solution," Franklin finished, "the order for 'Executive Action!' What's the difference between what the CIA has done and is still doing from what the Mafia does?"

Manderson smiled. "I can only say, that's a good question. During World War II, the OSS used Lucky Luciano and the Mafia. I'm sure their methods rubbed off in many ways into the CIA. That's why I left the agency. We were no longer an organization any more. To me, power and destruction were their policy, something I did not want anything to do with or be a part of!"

Modini straightened up in his chair, "Is this for real?" he looked to both Franklin and Manderson.

Manderson added, "You have to realize it isn't a fact-finding-- let's steal secrets-- organization anymore! The CIA is out there to take over as many countries they can. There is not one thing they will allow to stand in their way. The American people were supposed to believe Communism was the real threat to the world. Where is it now? Look what has happened to the Soviet Union! Where is the Berlin Wall?" Manderson chuckled, "It is now pieces of rock in someone's back pocket or a doorstop in homes. And some of us got lucky and bought a piece of it as a souvenir! Communism is not what you think. It has now turned into, what some consider, into the CIA itself! And that, my friends, is the threat we have surrounding us now, because countries today will not be threatened by the CIA. The Cia, once friend, now foe, now threatens us and our own self preservation!"

Franklin was concerned. "And what of the threat of Saddam Hussein and this deadline of Desert Storm?"

Manderson laughed, "Oh that? It's a smoke screen, a facade. You tell me, what is the single most concern of our government in the Middle East?"

Modini, with a blank stare, answered calmly, "Oil!" Manderson answered right back. "Exactly!"

"But then we have the crazy fool syndrome that may or may not have nuclear capabilities." Modini suggested.

Manderson again laughed, "So what if he has? Don't you think the CIA and your President know this? Hell, they are in bed together, for God sakes! If he has the nuclear warheads, they probably have 'made in USA' written all over them. There's no benefit to Hussein to use such tactics. The worst he could do is to blow all its oil fields. It's a game, a chess game and America's fighting forces will make Bush the hero of the day and get him a second term.

369

"Don't kid yourself. Bush has got so many problems here in this country to tackle. The Iran Contra scandal is still there to haunt him, and now this BCCI situation threatens to blow up in his face. He even has a son who's connected to the S&L with half his administration involved. And then there's the POW/MIA matter which won't go away."

Modini's eyes closed to this comment. In his mind he heard the echo of Father Daniel Conrad's voice. "We can't leave them over there! We have to get them out. The President must go along with the agreement. The Vietnamese government will not let them go until it's implemented. Do you understand the consequences if the United States Congress ignores this?"

Modini suddenly snapped back out of it. He spoke up. "What of the POW/MIA matter, Mr. Manderson?"

Franklin, surprised, looked over to Modini, then to Manderson, now silent for a brief moment before answering him. "There is a little man in Texas who's concerned with this subject and is doing everything he can to bring the matter to light, but simultaneously does not want to jeopardize any chances to bring our men home. So Congress and the President are playing some mind game with this man, Ross Perot, to pacify him for now. He originally made a deal with Reagan, then Reagan got shot. Perot had been getting the run-around ever since, as are all those American families who have lost their loved ones. Only those people like Ross Perot and a few Green Berets who use their own money, time and expertise to track the MIA's, to get them out of Vietnam, are the ones who succeed. Oh yes, you'll see one pop up every few years, as time passes. It is the Vietnam government's way of letting those know in America, if you want your boys back, pay up! I see, Mr. Modini, you are impressed with what I say?"

Modini was more than impressed. "I know about Nixon's offer of one billion dollars to get all our men back, but after Watergate, Ford did not implement it, and then Congress refused to pass such a bill. In their opinion, we do not pay ransom money to the enemy, neglecting the fact of former President Nixon's promise. Today, Congress pretends the MIA's don't exist! Someone will have to pay the price someday! Apparently our Congress has no conscience! I take it this Ross

Perot character knows what's inside Bush's dark and secret closet?"

Manderson agreed. "Come election time, that man could destroy Bush's second term! Only time will tell. He can actually participate in the President's board game with America's future or stack it in his favor!"

Franklin was curious about what Manderson said. "Sir, I'm puzzled. I have to wonder, if you're not still with the CIA, the way you talk certainly sounds like it!"

Manderson smiled and agreed, "You're right, Mr. Franklin, one does not actually leave the Central Intelligence Agency. You're always on call to do something for them, be it an errand or passing a message from one contact to another. Because of my age now I'm no longer active."

"Well then, sir, after 1958 when you retired so to speak from the company, what did you do when you were still inactive?"

"I was a bagman, Mr. Franklin!" Manderson stated in a matter of fact way.

Modini was taken aback. Franklin was careful in the way he tried to respond. "Mr. Manderson, a bagman, to me, is a Mafia term used to give money to one source or another for payment in illegal or threatening situations, be it a shop owner used for protection or police corruption and government graft! Are you telling us you were in such a category?"

Manderson answered bluntly. "I was a bagman for Castro!"

Modini again reacted, but tried to keep his cool as he interjected, "You mean, Fidel Castro? You gave him money?"

Manderson nodded. "Sometimes... Sometimes it was guns, whatever he needed!"

"You're saying you and the CIA put Castro where he is as dictator of Cuba?" Modini asked. "Why? I mean, I knew the Mafia wanted him there, but--"

Manderson cut him off as Franklin became nervous. "I have no knowledge of the Mafia's participation. They were working for an entire secret entity within the company. I know their participation in trying to take Castro out has been disclosed. What have I been trying to tell you in our conversation about our foreign policy? What did I say was the main agenda for the CIA? What was the United States' interest in Cuba? What happened?" Manderson posed all these questions for the two men.

Modini could only say, "My God!"

Franklin was a bit excited. "I think I can guess what you mean. Besides U.S. stakes, the mob wanted their casinos and prostitution business back in order and the drug trafficking to continue. But this didn't happen, did it? And you say the CIA put him where he is. Why did he change?"

"I believe, like the Kennedys," Manderson speculated, "Castro never knew of the involvement of the mob's participation in putting him into power, as I did not know either at the time. No one knew! It wasn't until years later did I find out. And I believe to this day Nixon knew! He had to, he was the one who implemented not only our desire to control Cuba but the aftermath! He created the Bay of Pigs!"

"Yes, you're right," Franklin elaborated, "When Kennedy won the election, Castro by then was a Communist. He thought Nixon would be the next President. Then Kennedy was lied to by the three men he would ultimately fire-- Dulles, Cabell and Bissell-- after the invasion. Nixon knew all this and kept his mouth shut...still, all these years!"

Manderson did not say anything more. He kept silent as did Modini. Franklin saw an opening to change the subject. He took out his photographs "If you don't mind, I'll show you these photographs and, as you requested, I won't mention any names unless you do not identify them..."

Manderson nodded in agreement and Franklin handed the first photograph to him to study. The photo was of Charles Nicoletti. Manderson looked at it and handed it back, shaking his head no. The same for the second of Johnny Roselli and the third, Sam Giancana, all no. The next two photos Franklin didn't bother handing to Manderson. Instead, he held both up in each hand as Modini tried to see them as well.

The two photos are of Santos Trafficante and Carlos Marcello. Again, a shake of the head no! Franklin placed the photos together in a pile on the floor next to his briefcase. "Though you don't know any of these people, you may know of them. I would like to ask whether you have ever seen these people in person. Or were in the same room and recognize one, but didn't want to know who they were at the time?" Again, the same answer is no.

Though not frustrated by this, Franklin proceeded with the next group of pictures, this time beginning with the photo of Frank Sturgis. Manderson handed it right back to Franklin without a sound, a word, or a nod one way or the other.

Modini noticed this as Franklin asked, "You know him?" Manderson did not respond.

Modini asked, "Mr. Manderson, did you know this man during your days with the CIA or after?" Manderson did not respond one way or the other. Modini turned to Franklin and the photos, "Give him the next photo!"

Franklin handed Manderson a photograph of E. Howard Hunt. Again, Manderson handed back the photo quickly with no response. Franklin looked at Modini who asked, "These two gentlemen you witnessed-- were you working with them, the two of them, when you were a bagman for Castro?"

Manderson did not respond. He sat silently. The next photograph was of a distinguished gentleman, a movie star type from the '40's. He returned the photo to Franklin with no response.

Franklin took out a piece of paper, tore it in two and wrote a name on each piece. As he did this, he gave some background to what he needed to know. "Sir, in the late seventies we interviewed this man for the House Select Committee. With the assistance and cooperation of the CIA, this was their man they provided us at the time. He went by the name of David Ward, though we found out later this was not his name, although this session of investigation was behind closed doors. He lied to the Committee. I'm not concerned why, because he was CIA. They all are in denial, because that's the name of the game. But another informant came forward and told us he was known to him by this name. I believe used as a code for this man and for other men like him."

Franklin handed Manderson the first piece of paper with the words 'the Bishop' on it.

Manderson looked at it but was unfamiliar with it. He stated a simple, "No!" Franklin handed the second piece of paper with the name David Atlee Phillips written on it. Manderson handed it right back with no response.

Here Franklin straightened up, looked over to Modini and winked, then turned back to Manderson with a sign of awe and a comment, "I see..." Franklin handed the photo of Phillps to Modini, "You see this gentleman? He was known only to anti-Castro and Cuban Rebels being trained for the Bay of Pigs invasion as 'The Bishop.'"

"This was the man in charge who gave orders. The informant who came forward recognized the man who said his name was David Ward, as 'The Bishop,' a.k.a. this name here..." Franklin pointed to the name on the second piece of paper. "This informant was one of the Cuban Rebels who were trained by the CIA for the invasion and testified he was the one giving the orders to all involved. No one could jump including the men training them unless it came from the mouth of this man!" he pointed at Phillips' picture. "He also said this man, 'the Bishop,' told them Bobby Kennedy promised the Cuban Rebels upon their invasion; the President would supply them the navy and air power. Of course, this was never true, but it was the incentive of the CIA to make them believe it, so they trusted the U.S.A. And they still believe to this day Kennedy let them down. President Kennedy, with a sudden surprise, took the blame which the CIA had told them all along, and came up smelling like a rose to the Cubans. Little did these rebels know Kennedy would fire those responsible in high command, the Director of the CIA, his deputy director and the controller for the Bay of Pigs!"

Franklin handed over a newspaper clipping of Roscoe A. White. Manderson shook his head no. The next photograph was of a man named George DeMohrenschildt. Again, Manderson couldn't identify him nor knew him, but Franklin had a question. "This man has been investigated in three areas. Since you have no knowledge of him, I would like your expertise in answering a question. Let's say this was a man of Russian descent who worked for Russian Intelligence during World War II. But in 1942 he offered his services to U.S. Intelligence. He was refused at first because his brother was an associate to Adolph Hitler, but after the war he convinced the now newly Truman-appointed CIA that he, DeMohrenschildt, could be useful to them after all and did some undercover work for them. Is this scenario possible?"

Manderson didn't mince words. "Of course it's possible! In fact, the more foreign they are, getting from one country to another with the language barrier, the more power. If the CIA can use them, you bet they would!"

Franklin was satisfied. "All right. What if this man represents himself to the European and South American countries as an agent for oil coteries of Texas, but also in reality was CIA.?"

Manderson wasn't phased by this line of questioning and gave a brisk answer, "Well...that's simple isn't it? This gentleman was working, you said, undercover. What a convenient way to walk in an open door of an opposing side or enemy to get information. Oil is a prominent factor of power in this world as what we discussed earlier, isn't it?" He looked over to Modini who seemed to be in the dark where this conversation was taking them.

Franklin agreed with him, but wanted a more elaborate answer "Right!"

Manderson added, "Doesn't it make sense to use the oil companies as a front when entering a covert situation?"

"Sure, except the oil coteries would have to know, wouldn't they? What if a situation came up where someone covering their ass in Berlin or Communist country wanted to make a check on this agent for legitimacy?"

Manderson cut in, "But, of course, the oil cartels and CIA have carte blanche to each other. If one scratches the other's back the other follows, all they do is make a call. How do you think George Bush became the CIA Director?" he laughed. "Now they're one and the same. Small world, we have here...isn't it?"

Modini was beginning to see where Franklin may be taking this conversation. "Do you think this DeMohrenschildt character would be a good candidate for the CIA?"

Manderson acknowledged, "I would say he would be a perfect candidate for the

'Company,' let alone any intelligence agency for that matter. Where does this DeMohrenschildt fellow fit into your scenario here?"

Franklin wasn't going to mention anything further on the subject and was surprised Manderson asked, but felt somewhat obligated to answer him. "Well, you've heard the recent news about the LSD experiments the CIA was conducting during the early '50's. One agent committed suicide because of an injection he got from another agent, the babysitter, or controller of the experiment?"

Manderson heard of it and nodded. Franklin continued. "Well, I have been investigating the suicide tendencies within the CIA, and I find it has run rampant over the last thirty years. It was either suicide or dying of some disease. Now it's the AIDS epidemic. You do agree, sir, the CIA has been experimenting and developing chemical drugs, and germ warfare. I mean, they can invent a deadly disease if they wanted, right? They're preparing for Desert Storm right now, as we speak as if Saddam Hussein already had germ warfare planned. So is the United States prepared to use it if it comes to that?"

Manderson didn't comment, but listened as Franklin continued, "You see, sir, most of our witnesses for the House Select Committee on JFK had died like Mr. Garrison's witnesses had, before he went to trial. A lot of them were gunshot wounds to the head or were possibly injected with something that gave them a heart attack or a disease difficult to detect.

"To get back to George DeMohrenschildt, he was a top priority for the House in our investigation on the assassination, not because he had been CIA, not because of his ties to the oil coteries in Houston, but because of his association with Lee Harvey Oswald in Dallas! He was Russian! How convenient for DeMohrenschildt to befriend someone like Oswald. Why? Was it to reminisce about old times? No, they never knew each other until Oswald's arrival back in the U.S. Was it comradeship because DeMohrenschildt missed his old country, the good old U.S.S.R? I doubt it, he never wanted or cared about his country if he were working under the auspices of the CIA. This leaves us with two options, either the CIA was curious about this so-called defector they allowed back into this country as the Warren Commission admits without scrutiny, or option

number two, DeMohrenschildt was a CIA babysitter, a plant to know Oswald's whereabouts at all

times, so Oswald could be used for some purpose in the not so distant future!

"We recall during the Garrison period that was exactly what he said concerning Clay Shaw

of New Orleans, except the judge wouldn't allow Garrison's evidence to prove Shaw was a front

for the CIA. But now, six years after the trial and Shaw's own mysterious death, Richard Helms,

ex-CIA Director for both Johnson and Nixon, at the Church hearings in '75, lets it slip Clay Shaw

was CIA!

Here was a man, Shaw who may or may not be the CIA babysitter for Oswald in his time in

New Orleans where Oswald worked for an ex-FBI agent by the name of Guy Banister in the

middle of town where all the intelligence agencies house themselves. We have witnesses still alive

today who can state both Oswald and Shaw spent time together. Meanwhile, in Dallas, Marina was

being wined and dined and taken care of by the DeMohrenschildts. Why? Why would such a

mannered couple as the DeMohrenschildts want to have anything to do with what Gerald Ford, our

future President said in the Warren Commission, are a couple of nut cases? This was why the

House wanted to speak with George DeMohrenschildt. And he was contacted to appear in

Washington before the HSCA in March of 1977, but backed out because of illness. He said he had

been injected by some drug that was slowly killing him. He suggested to the Committee to send

someone from the HSCA to Dallas to interview him at his home. This was when someone in our

government was trying to shut the HSCA down. So the afternoon before the set date,

DeMohrenschildt was found dead, killed by a blast to his face from a 20-gauge double-barrel

shotgun. Gruesome, huh! There goes another witness, and another what-- suicide? Like I say, the

statistics for suicide within the CIA are very high!

"We did find one thing, though that was curious at the time, and is more so today. I should

say two things! One, the Dallas County Hospital report confirmed George DeMohrenschildt was

injected with some strange drug they could not identify, and he had been sick for five months prior to his death. And two, most curious, especially today-- It's funny you should mention George Bush's name earlier. Well, in Mr. DeMohrenschildt's address book they found the address and the telephone number of the ex-CIA Director and our future President, George Bush!" Franklin finished his story.

Manderson was silent a moment before saying one word, "Interesting."

Franklin knew time was a factor and politely told Manderson, "Since we don't want to take too much of your time, I have one more photograph, and I don't even know the identify of this man," he handed Manderson the photograph, a picture of a man showing no foreground and no background included around the large, heavyset figure. "Someone, maybe a technician in photography, removed the foreground and background out of this photo. Very peculiar, wouldn't you say to have all surroundings removed around the figure of an unidentifiable man in the center of the photo?"

Manderson handed the photograph back to Franklin with a 'no' attached to whom he was, but asked, "How is this person connected to your inquiries, and whose possession did this photo come into contact with in the beginning? Maybe your answer is there."

Modini looked at the photograph for the first time and laughed, "Oh, isn't this the man, some ex-CIA and LAPD investigator tracked down in Europe to expose as an assassin of JFK. I wrote a mock story on this. McDonald was his name, I believe. I mean the cop, not the photo of this man. I believe he called this guy...Paul-- no, Saul. It was a code name he used. Boy, I haven't seen this in years, but here it is, definitely noticeable, especially since the foreground and background as you say, are missing. It never dawned on me to consider the foreground or background elements when I saw this picture years ago-- after I returned from Nam. In fact, this McDonald person had worked as Barry Goldwater's head security during the '64 presidential campaign."

Franklin listened with interest to what Modini said. "It even gets more murky and stranger," Franklin told him. "Besides the fact there's no fingerprints on the so-called Oswald rifle, J. Edgar Hoover at the FBI wrote a memo explaining, he knew the next day on November twenty-third, the day after Kennedy's assassination Oswald was *not* the assassin of President Kennedy, and this was the picture that convinced Hoover to write this memo. But eight months later the Warren Commission and Hoover both agree Oswald was just that-- the lone assassin!"

Modini leaned in closer to Manderson.

"Now my question to you, sir. Yes, you're right, Mr. Manderson, the answer is in the picture. And where did it come from in the first place, and why all the subterfuge? The CIA sent this photograph to Hoover and told him they had audio tapes and film and photos of Lee Harvey Oswald in Mexico at the Cuban and Russian Embassies when Oswald tried to get a Visa-- first to Cuba, then back to the Soviet Union. This is serious business. Here, they have in custody in Dallas, a man named Lee Harvey Oswald who just returned from the Soviet Union who supposedly murdered the President of the United States, so Hoover asked for confirmation on the tapes, the files, and any photos of this Oswald in Mexico.

"Here we quickly have the CIA and FBI assisting each other! That was strange in itself! The problem was the audio tapes, the files, or video, or whatever, are not of Oswald. And mysteriously, all of them were accidentally erased, all except this photo. This was the man that the CIA office in Mexico said was Lee Harvey Oswald. Does this photograph look to you, Mr. Manderson, like the same man who Dallas, Texas had in custody? Of course not!"

Manderson smiled and shook his head "no" as Franklin proceeded. "Well, good, because all these years everyone still thinks Oswald was in Mexico trying to get back to the Soviet Union. The Warren Commission asked to see all the above, but that's when everything was mysteriously erased except for this picture! What Hoover now found to his embarrassment was Oswald was on the FBI payroll as an informant. He now had to keep this information from slipping out. So the FBI and CIA tracked each other to see who had the most discriminating evidence on the other. This photo made it to the Warren Commission, showing a strange man with no name except Oswald's name attached. There was one stipulation before the Warren Commission could get this photograph-- and that Central Intelligence demanded, of which the Commission agreed to-- and this was that the foreground and background had to be eliminated before anyone could see it! This they did, and this was what you see now and what the HSCA would see as well, though the public didn't know this was the Oswald depicted by the CIA to be the one in Mexico City of September 1963. Why, if there were no significance to him or identification attached to Kennedy's assassination, would it matter to the CIA what was surrounding this man? To this day, no one can identify him except, like Mr. Modini says, this Mr. McDonald fellow!"

Manderson turned his head to gaze at the simple paintings on the walls, then suggested, "To me the only explanation would be a facility or person also that appears next to him they did not want someone to see. They may be protecting themselves because the picture could have been shot at the office of Central Intelligence in Mexico City, if-- mind you-- this actually was shot in Mexico."

Franklin interrupted, "What do you mean?"

"Well, are you certain the picture was taken in 1963?"

Richard Franklin acknowledged it was, and Manderson followed up. "Well, I said I'm sure it would have to be a facility or person connected to Central Intelligence they were protecting. You said the photo was taken at either the Cuban or Soviet Union Embassies. There's no reason to hide this fact unless someone else was in the photo as well that might be recognized. All they had to do was eliminate this certain person and that would explain it, but this doesn't seem to be the case here. It's the area he's standing in that they don't want you to see or identify, which makes me think its possible someone within the company's organization wanted Hoover to know they needed to find and investigate this man. Oswald wasn't the assassin, and by finding this man, they could find a key to their problem. Remember, you said everything that could positively identify this the man in Mexico City who, in the CIA's opinion, was Oswald-- was erased. Why didn't they eliminate the photograph as well and then say on top of it that it *was* Oswald?"

"Maybe the CIA didn't know what Oswald looked like, especially those agents in Mexico City," Modini said.

Manderson smiled at his remark, "Yes, but why, as Richard said, the subterfuge? There was no need, except to hide what may incriminate them or prove someone sent the photo to the FBI. So, Hoover saw something in the photo other than this gentleman pictured here! It convinced him about the real Oswald!"

Franklin glanced at the fake Oswald photo. "You mean, if this photo wasn't taken in Mexico City and was forwarded to expose the deception to begin with, then Hoover had the CIA in the palm of his hands?"

Manderson followed up, "Yes, until the CIA blackmails Hoover with Oswald's informant connection to the FBI."

Modini exploded. "What you guys are saying is this picture could have been taken on the day of the assassination for all that matters, in Dealey Plaza itself!"

Franklin expressed surprise at Modini's outburst, but Manderson grinned and acknowledged. "That's something the CIA would not want anyone to see or know if that were the explanation. But, we will never know, will we, unless this gentleman ever comes forward and exposes the truth"

"And the fact this McDonald, if he were to be believed, was told by the man in this picture he was in Dealey Plaza on November 22, 1963!" Franklin added.

Franklin was nearly finished with his questioning. Modini had another question to ask Manderson. "In those last years with the agency, were you aware of a group of Marines being trained to defect for the Soviet Union by Naval Intelligence between 1957 and 1963?"

"Yes, I was aware of this group," Manderson admitted. "About forty-four men total, were trained and taught the Russian language. I have no idea how many ever returned, but--"

Modini broke in, "Sir, have any of them ever returned?

"Oh! I see what you're getting at. It was possible, yes, especially when no one had ever heard from the other forty three, if he were one that is!"

Modini elaborated the fact. "Gary Powers who was shot down in his U-2 over the Soviet

Union, stated, until his death in '86 in a Los Angeles helicopter accident that Oswald-- since he was a trained radar expert out of Atsugi, Japan, where the U-2's were tracked-- Powers believed Oswald provided the Soviets information about the U-2 and its distance of flight, and was responsible for his, Powers, capture in 1960.

Manderson looked at the two of them and made up his mind to divulge information never reported before about that international incident. "I doubt that very much. Let me tell you why. If Oswald was an agent for Naval Intelligence and passed those kinds of secrets to the Soviets, whether he was a double agent or defector, Oswald would have been a dead man before he could ever make it back to the U.S.A. and no one would care.

"The other reason was there were many denials being spread around concerning the U-2, including our own President announcing to the American people Gary Powers was dead after being shot down. Now, I'm not saying Eisenhower was lying to the world, he definitely didn't tell us the truth, but it was also possible this was what Intelligence wanted him to know. So he stated it as fact. Then the Soviets surprised-- I should say, embarrassed-- Eisenhower by proving Powers was alive, captured and under interrogation by the KGB at that very moment! What Powers did not know, and possibly the Eisenhower administration did not know, was the moment Powers took flight on his mission, a second plane, an E.C.M. aircraft similar to the U-2 also took off simultaneously.

"The E.C.M., or the Electronic Counter Measures, had a special purpose. It was to fly along at a distance from the U-2, and its operator, using 'the Raven' as a code name, would jam the radar from the space covering any reconnaissance over the Soviet Union between the U-2 and the Russians. What happened that day with Powers was this: the E.C.M. aircraft malfunctioned and never got off the ground, and so Powers never knew he had no protection. He took it for granted and no one from Atsugi or wherever called him back because he was to be undercover so to speak. And I'm sure, to his death, Powers never knew this!"

Modini wasn't surprised. But right now he thought of something else. "Can you tell me then what NRO represents?"

Manderson was a bit stunned to hear him mention those three letters in that order. "How, Mr. Modini do you know about NRO?"

Modini nonchalantly stated, "I don't, I just know someone who once worked for it. Do you know what it stands for?"

"I wouldn't mess with it if I were you," Manderson warned Modini. "It means, 'National Reconnaissance Organization' and it was developed sometime after I left the agency-- I believe sometime between the Johnson and Nixon administration. I left the agency because of letters like NRO. This is a secret outlet protecting other agencies from bad publicity. I'll put it another way, they make people disappear..." he snapped his fingers, "..like that!"

"What do you mean?" Modini asked.

"I mean, if they determined the enemy to be you or me, we would suddenly disappear," Manderson explained. "So I wouldn't mention the NRO if I were you, even as a joke! It's like President Johnson said once about his administration: 'That we're now running a murder incorporated from the White House!' In truth he *wasn't* joking!"

Chapter Twenty-Eight

"Making One Disappear"

White flakes of snow floated from the dusky sky and fell upon a middle-aged gentleman walking down a residential sidewalk in Salem, Oregon. As he approached the front door of Marian O'Leary's house, he saw the front porch all bright and decorated with Christmas lights. He rang the doorbell and waited.

The door opened, and Mrs. O'Leary asked, "Yes, what can I do for you?" The gentleman courteously took off his hat and showed her some identification. "Ma'am, my name is Derek Brown. I'm an investigator from Chicago, and I've been hired by the Bradley Law Firm out of Madison, Indiana to find your son."

Marian, calm and cool, smiled, "Would you like to step out of the cold?"

"I don't mind at all," Derek said. Marian closed the door behind him as he entered the house.

* * *

The year 1990 came to an end and Catherine Rogers joined her father, Henry Kencade, for the Christmas Eve celebration in a small town restaurant in Madison's trendy downtown area. As she seated herself at the table, Michael Bradley came into the restaurant to join them. He brushed off the snow as he took off his coat, heading for Kencade's table, "Good evening. Merry Christmas Judge. How are you?"

Kencade wasn't pleased to see him. "I'm fine!" he said curtly.

Catherine kissed Bradley on the cheek and then kissed her dad. "Now, I have my two favorite people joining me for some holiday spirit," she laughed. "Get it Dad, it's a little joke-- holiday spirit. We're having drinks in your favorite restaurant!"

Kencade got it and pretended to smile for her. Catherine brought out a couple of wrapped gifts from a department store bag and gave one to Bradley, putting the other one back into the bag. "Merry Christmas, Michael!"

Bradley was surprised, but was more concerned with the other gift she put aside. "Aren't you going to give the other one to your father?"

Catherine laughed again, realizing the mystery of the other gift. "Oh, no, father has his gifts already under the tree. This one is for a special friend. You remember, I've told you about Carrie, the young girl at the hospital. I'm planning to see whether she will be able to spend Christmas with us..."

The barmaid served drinks around the table and everyone lifted their glasses to a toast. When they finished, Judge Kencade made an important announcement.

"I want to say I received confirmation today allowing Karl Hunter's exhumation for late Spring of 1991." Catherine, now in tears, stood up and kissed her father and hugged him. This made the evening extra special as the new year approached. They all stood up now and gathered to toasted the holidays.

* * *

Thomas Sanders stood by with Bradley and Catherine in the law firm's conference room as the latter two settled in their chairs to face the television screen. They watched the President of the

United States make his entrance on Capital Hill for his State of the Union address. The event was presented live, the scene switching from the Speaker of the House, Thomas Foley, and the Senate President, Dan Quayle, to President George Bush making his way to the podium. Several members of Congress and the Senate patted his back and shook hands as he moved down the aisle. Applause and a standing ovation followed The President to the lectern.

As the three watched, Thomas commented on George Bush to his two-person audience in the room, "Oh boy, here he comes, the wimp who made it to the White House, the forty-first president of the United States, a man who walked into the Oval Office about as easily as Gerry Ford, who was the last Republican to hold the highest office in the country and wasn't even elected!"

Thomas continued, now that he had their attention. "Let me fill you in about the background of Mr. Bush-- Mr. George Herbert Walker Bush. First, we turn the clock back to 1944. Known as the Tom Cruise of World War II, they say Bush was the youngest Air Force pilot in the Naval Air Reserve. He got out of the war by bailing out of his plane. And listen to this-- he survived four tortuous hours in the Pacific Ocean until a submarine picked him up! He received the Distinguished Flying Cross and three air medals and was an acknowledged hero.

"But that depends which of the many biographies you read. It seems this Tom Cruise character has a half dozen stories to tell when it comes to his heroism. It changed whenever he ran for political office from his first Senate race, to Congress then changed again drastically when he ran for President both in 1980 and 1988. There were those who dispute his actions when he bailed out of his plane. Remember he was *the* pilot. No one will ever know the truth about his two crewmen who were reported missing or dead. You see, it was the pilot's responsibility to get his men out of the plane.

"Other squadrons said he could be called a survivor, but not a hero. There are other soldiers and fliers who spent up to as much as twelve days in open waters before they were ever discovered compared to Bush and his four tortuous hours. By the 1980's they settled his war record with the sentence, 'Bush saw a considerable amount of hazardous action...' Quite a change from war hero, although the Bush machine would again take it out of mothballs to use it against Dukakis. He followed the war by heading to Yale University, hitting the fraternities, getting elected to Phi Beta Kappa and becoming a member of the exclusive 'Skull and Bones' society.

"He married his wife, Barbara, in 1946, and instead of following in his father's Wall Street banking business in Connecticut, Bush took off for the State of Texas and got himself into the oil business. His father, of course, was the director of the company he started with, and by 1954 he had his own company. By 1964 he decided to run for Senator, like his father, the Senator of the State of Connecticut, but lost to Democrat Senator Yarborough. He bid for the House of Representatives in 1966 and was elected as the first Congressman in history from Houston for two terms. As an oil man himself, you can imagine whom his constituents were.

"In 1970, on the advice of President Nixon, Bush ran a second time for the Senate, but lost again, this time out to Democrat Lloyd Bentsen, Jr. whose popularity in the State of Texas out-shined the oil industry who contributed and supported Bush as did a secret slush fund that came from out of the White House. My, my! Following this loss, Nixon offered Bush several high posts in his administration and Bush became the chief spokesman for the policies of the Nixon administration.

"With no experience in diplomacy and foreign affairs, and a position headed earlier by such illustrious men as Adlai Stevenson and Arthur Goldberg, Nixon, with the help of Secretary of State Henry Kissinger, appointed Bush to the United Nations as it's permanent representative of the United States. There was also talk of his candidacy as Nixon's Vice-President in 1972, but was offered the chairmanship of the Republican National Committee.

"George Bush was definitely Nixon's man and the most trusted since he was but one of the handful who defended him to the very end in August of 1974. Besides the fact history now shows Alexander Haig had a hand in Nixon's resignation as President, there was also another trusted friend of President Nixon who had the power of persuasion. George Bush on August 7,

1974 handed Nixon a letter to step down. And Nixon did!

"Then under the Ford administration, Bush took the newly appointed Ambassadorship to China, but was recalled immediately to Washington to head the Central Intelligence Agency. This was after Gerald Ford fired William Colby in 1975 for exposing what the 'Company,' quotes..." here Thomas gestured by wiggling two of his fingers on each hand, "...did not want the Senate Committee hearings to know but did anyway!

"Incidentally, here's a sidelight for you. After going to Yale University and investigating the records there, I discovered Gerald Ford, like Bush, was also a member of a fraternity, Delta Kappa Epsilon. And I also found most of the Warren Commissioners, especially the Assistant Counsel, including David Belin and Arlen Spector as well as Bush, were all Phi Beta Kappa. If that isn't a coincidence! Ford's first political experience was with the young Republicans in a campaign to clean up corruption in local government! Ha, Ha! Also, everyone should know this-- Ford was the favorite candidate in 1960 to be Nixon's Vice-President, but eventually lost to Henry Cabot Lodge!

"Starting in May 1979, Bush announced his candidacy for President and was determined to embarrass President Carter. He would succeed behind closed doors. Before running, Bush knew if he were to win in 1980 he would have to surrender his position as President of the Trilateral Commission, consisting of a group of the most powerful people who actually are the ones that make or break this country. But one year later, to the month, a movie actor, and former Governor of California changed all that when he picked up a microphone and shouted Bush off the dais and put him on hold for the next eight years. Once elected, Ronald Reagan was the one who would change and bolster the Republican Party back to the forefront of the nation. But this would only last 69 days into his administration. Reagan was shot down by Hinkley, but you didn't have to worry. Vice-President Bush was waiting in the wings!

"Luckily for Bush, his best friend, James Baker, was appointed Reagan's Chief of Staff, which made it affordable to know everything and anything concerning what happens in the White

House and he had *carte blanche* whenever he wanted to see the President. This meant Bush had access to all Reagan's departments and materials, including all briefings with the Intelligence agencies. Like Nixon, he now had the power and an open door to the President and all his policies. This was George Bush before he would find his way to the highest position in the country, the position that had been waiting for him all along. This was the same George Bush the entire country called a wimp, the man no one really knew, except for those who planted him in the White House in the first place and knew what was truly happening behind those closed doors."

Thomas looked back at the television set, concentrating on Bush making his way to the podium while shaking hands with both Foley and Quayle. As the people and noise settled down, the Speaker of the House announced, "The President of the United States," and the pandemonium started again.

Thomas walked to the doorway, annoyed. "I've had enough of this. I leave you two with your President."

As he exited the room Sherry, the secretary, bumped into him. "Excuse me, Mr. Sanders. You have a long distance call from Jennifer in Miami."

* * *

Catherine and Bradley sat in the conference room watching the State of the Union Address as Bush addressed the nation, "One year ago the Panamanian people lived in fear under the thumb of a Dictator. Today, Democracy is restored. Panama is free!" The audience yelled out and applauded in unison.

Bradley turned to Catherine, with a glum look, "I wonder if that million dollar bounty he put on Noriega was paid for by Bush or *us*, the taxpayers? And who got it? Who was the lucky lottery winner? Noriega's mouth is closed as long as he's imprisoned under lock and key of our sunny city of Miami."

Thomas Sanders returned to the room, his eyes focusing on the snowstorm outside the window. "Speaking of Miami that was Jennifer. She called from the hottest spot in America, right now, and said her tan is darker-- as if she needed one, if you know my meaning! She called to report she had a meeting set up with some retired Mafia kingpin, but there's one condition!"

"And what is the punch line?" Bradley asked, his brow creasing in curiosity.

Thomas glanced over to Catherine, "This guy wants you, alone, Catherine -- right there for the interview or there's no deal!"

This condition surprised Catherine. Bradley asked, "Why is it necessary for Catherine to be there? What has Catherine got to do with this?"

"I don't know," Thomas answered, "that's what Jennifer said was the deal. We take it or leave it!"

"Then we leave it!" Bradley exclaimed angrily.

Thomas became frustrated. "We can't do that," Thomas became annoyed, "This is a great opportunity. It's one we can't pass up! How often do you get to sit down with a Mafia kingpin and talk about who whacked who in the Kennedy assassination?"

"Okay, okay," Bradley said, "I get your point, but it doesn't matter! Catherine is not going to--"

Catherine stood up, "Tell Jennifer I'll be there to meet with this gentleman-- but on one condition!"

Bradley cut in, "I think you're rushing things, Catherine! We don't know anything about this person! What's this hood's name?"

"No names were mentioned," Thomas explained, "Captain Corrigan set it up. They want this under a shroud of secrecy. What's your condition, Catherine?"

Catherine's reply was clear and firm, "I want Captain Corrigan present with me at the meeting!"

Thomas nodded, "Okay, I'll tell them what you want! I'm only the middle man here!" he smiled and quickly exited.

A few days later in Miami, on a Friday afternoon, Captain Raymond Corrigan spoke on his office phone to Michael Bradley and assured him he would be there at the meeting with Catherine. "Mr. Bradley, you don't have to worry about these guys. They're no longer in business. It's not as though they're going out and plugging somebody every night. It's more like shuffleboard, horseshoes and bingo at their age. So you just leave it to me. Catherine will be all right!"

Bradley was still skeptical. "I don't care what you say. I still think it's dangerous. But I'll put aside my worries for now. I'm holding you responsible for Catherine's safety."

"I know you are," Corrigan's voice came over the phone, "so I'll take extra precautions."

"Thank you, Captain Corrigan. We'll talk again soon." Bradley hung up the phone and looked out his office window. In Madison, Indiana, a cold blizzard forecast came true. It was dark and snowing.

A tanned Jennifer walked into Bradley's office as he hung up with Corrigan. Bradley tried to be pleasant, although he was not a happy camper, concerned with the danger Catherine might face. "Is everything okay with you?" he said to Jennifer, pretending to be unconcerned.

Jennifer smiled, "Hey, the sun down there is just gorgeous, as you can see by my tan. I envy Catherine. I really wanted to be there with her. I did find out a name of the man she'll be meeting. His name is Costalanno."

"Hmmm," Bradley said, drawing a finger across his lip. "The name doesn't ring a bell. I'm concerned about this so-called interview."

Jennifer put a reassuring hand on Bradley's shoulder. "I'm sure Catherine will do fine. That girl is one smart woman if you don't already know that! She can take care of herself."

* * *

A Northwest plane on a late afternoon flight schedule glided down from the sky and came in for a smooth landing at the Miami Beach airport. Catherine exited from the arrival gate, carry-on bag in one hand and attaché case in the other. She searched the milling crowd, and spotted Captain Corrigan of the Miami Police Department when he waved.

"Mrs. Catherine Rogers..." Corrigan shook her hand.

"How do you do, Captain Corrigan."

"I'd like you to meet Henry Crocker." Corrigan said, waving to the uniformed police officer next to him.

"How do you do, Mr..." Catherine shook hands with the officer.

"Please call me Henry, Mrs. Rogers," the officer suggested. He made an all out effort to be polite.

Catherine eyed Corrigan wearily. "Is he supposed to be one of my bodyguards?" Catherine asked.

"Yep. Henry's going to be looking after you tonight. He volunteered for this assignment. Technically, he's off duty, but he's earning extra brownie points in my book." Corrigan reached for her bag.

"No thanks, I'll carry it."

"Your attaché case too?"

Catherine nodded. "Hey, it's the 90's. Women can do that!"

"Well, I hope your flight was okay?" Corrigan guided her from the arrival area. Henry followed close behind.

"All right, I guess," Catherine said. "At least I survived the landing. For me, it's the worst part of the trip." She brushed away the gloomy thoughts and smiled, "Thank you again for the offer to pick me up."

"Service with a smile, ma'am," Corrigan said, winking to his fellow officer. "Baggage claim is that way." The three of them headed through the crowded lounge.

When they reached the baggage turnstile, Catherine was pleased to see the luggage coming off the conveyer belt. After retrieving Catherine's bags, they all headed for the door.

As the three exited through the terminal exit and onto the sidewalk, they were unaware another gentleman observing them. The man was athletic looking, with a severe blond crewcut. He carried a plain overnight bag like any other passenger. He spotted Catherine exiting the arrival gate and kept a low profile, blending into the crowd, continually keeping the woman in sight.

Nervously he reached into his jacket pocket and removed a pack of cigarettes. He was ready to take one out when he saw the no smoking sign posted on the wall. He jammed them back into his pocket and waited.

The man pretended to check his watch until Catherine departed the terminal with her escorts. Then he went to a bank of empty pay phones and dialed a number.

"She's here at the airport. Yeah...with two men from the MPD," the man spoke with a low voice into the receiver. He listened to the reply. "No problem. Everything is going according to plan. We know where she's staying and everything is arranged. It will seem like a little accident!" He hung up, picked up his overnight bag and left the building.

* * *

Catherine had an early dinner with Corrigan in a small beach-side cafe. They found a comfortable table near a window framing the low-hanging sun. Corrigan told Henry he needed to speak with Catherine alone and should meet him back at the table in a half hour.

Corrigan ordered cold iced tea for the both of them and casually briefed her on the scheduled agenda for her meeting the next day.

"A Miami Police Department officer will be with you at all times," Corrigan told her. "It's Henry's shift tonight. He'll be the one camped outside your hotel room door. Your Mr. Bradley must think very highly of you. He's asked us to take every precaution for your safety!"

"Well, thank you." Catherine blushed, somewhat embarrassed by Corrigan's personal attention. She wondered if he weren't being extra nice for some other obvious reason. "You really shouldn't have gone through the trouble. I don't think this is necessary, but I know how persuasive Michael can be once he puts his mind to something. I consider Michael my best friend and big brother, if you know what I mean."

"I believe I do," Corrigan smiled, "Some of my own officers feel that way about their partners. They protect each other as if they were a family! I wish all of them did that!"

Even with the air conditioning on, Catherine felt the heat and humidity within the restaurant. She took a sip of her cold iced tea drink, then voiced the main question on her mind. "Captain Corrigan, why are you doing this? Why are you helping us?"

Corrigan reached into his pocket and handed her a tape of the recording he and his ex-partner made on November ninth, 1963. "I believe, Mrs. Rogers, our government deliberately covered up President Kennedy's assassination."

Catherine was astonished, yet impressed by his statement. Corrigan must have seen the hint of skepticism in her eyes, because he continued to explain. "I'm not a conspiracy buff or theorist, I'm just a cop-- a good one, if I should be so modest," he laughed at his own expense, but then turned serious. "But someone, either FBI, or Secret Service, did not want the Warren Commission to get our tape! I believe if Kennedy had made his scheduled trip to Miami on the eighteenth of November, it would have been our city shrouded with the dark cloud instead of Dallas. If not Oswald, then some other poor sap would have been the pawn blamed for the President's assassination here in Miami, I'm sure of that!"

"Why do you believe that?" Catherine asked.

Corrigan took a sip of his tea, "The thing that bothers me is that most of the time President Kennedy was in Dallas, he was never fully protected by the Secret Service, or even the local police. Now here, in this city, if we didn't see our President getting the protection he deserved, we'd be all over him like leeches. If we had known in advance what was on this tape, every one of us here in the Miami Police Department would have never taken a day off-- like many police officers did that day in Dallas. Given a choice, some of us would have worked for nothing!"

"So you're saying there was a plot to assassinate Kennedy here in Miami before it fell through and was switched to Dallas."

"I'm speaking from hindsight now, but you'll believe it when you listen to this tape recording. Someone deliberately kept the seal of full protection away from the President, and both the FBI and Secret Service knew of this tape five weeks prior to Dallas! You would think they'd be doubly concerned in protecting him." He gestured to the tape in front of Catherine, "Just listen to it and you'll see what I mean!"

Catherine slipped the tape into her purse. "I'll do that, Mr. Corrigan. As soon as possible."

After dinner, they made small talk until officer Henry Crocker returned. Then they drove Catherine to her hotel, a nice high-rise near the beach. They escorted Catherine to her hotel room.

Catherine unlocked her Hotel room and went inside. It was more spacious than she imagined it would be, with a bathroom off to one side and double doors leading to a balcony overlooking the ocean. There were two dressers, a night stand and a color tv with a cable box. The air-conditioner was on high and it was colder than Catherine expected.

Corrigan and Henry entered with her suitcases and put them on the luggage rack. She tossed her attaché case on the bed and put her carry-on bag on the dresser.

"I'll see you bright and early tomorrow morning, Catherine," Corrigan said.

"Yes, I know. Good night. And good night to you, Henry."

The officer gave her a weary smile and jokingly saluted her. He had the pleasure of standing guard in the corridor outside her room all night.

"Are you going to be all right?" she asked Henry as he was ready to exit.

"No problem. I'll get a chair and some magazines. Good night, Mrs. Rogers."

"Catherine... Call me Catherine." She closed and locked her door after they left. At last, she had some time alone to herself. She was worried about the meeting tomorrow with Mr. Costalanno, and she wanted to review the questions she would ask him.

The yellow-orange light from the setting sun filtered through the curtains covering the double doors to the balcony. Catherine shivered again. She threw her purse on the bed and crossed to the balcony doors. Holding one of the curtains aside, unlatched the hooks and pushed one of the doors open. She felt the hot, humid air on her face as she stepped out on the balcony.

The balcony deck was small, about four feet by eight feet long with fancy wrought iron railings. From her vantage point eleven stories above the ground, she had a bird's-eye view of the beach and Atlantic Ocean.

A movement caught Catherine's eyes on the balcony next to her. The neighboring balcony was separated by ten feet of space. A man sat in an aluminum beach chair having a smoke. She could hardly avoid seeing him. He looked older than she, and had a nice physique and a blond crewcut.

"I hope my smoking doesn't bother you, ma'am," he gave her a friendly smile, "but it's not allowed to smoke in the rooms-- with the fire detectors and all."

Catherine smiled and shook her head, then casually turned and looked out at the view again. By the tone of his voice she knew he wanted to open a friendly conversation, but right now she wasn't interested. She lingered a few moments more and went back inside before he had another chance to speak with her.

Catherine closed the door and latched it. Sitting on her bed she thumbed the combination on her attaché case and opened it. Inside were file folders, notes, and an assortment of pencils and pens. She removed a yellow legal pad with a list of questions she intended to review. Maybe she could add a few more to the list before tomorrow. She removed one of several silver metal pens and clicked it. She briefly scanned the reminders she had made, then rubbed her eyes and sighed.

Work, work...always work. I don't have to do this now, she told herself. *I'm entitled to a break. It can wait until later.* She tossed the legal pad and pen back into her attaché case.

On an impulse, she got up from the bed and turned on the television. She was promptly rewarded with an annoying commercial. She fiddled with the channels, but had no better results.

She decided to leave it on the CNN channel. *So much for that.*

She turned from the set. It had been a long day, and Catherine felt drained. The thought of a warm luxuriant soak in the tub would feel good about now. She went into the bathroom, put the stopper in the bathtub drain and turned on the water. Catherine poured in the complementary bath oil and bubble bath into her bath water, then slipped off her suit jacket. A sharp noise attracted her attention. Did it come from the other room?

She left the bathroom and glanced at the television set where CNN was covering the Desert Storm war in Iraq. Several shots of videotaped SCUD missiles traveled through the dark night sky and exploded in the air and on the ground. She tossed the jacket on her bed next to her purse and turned up the sound to listen to the commentator reporting the news.

A warm breeze filtered in from the balcony doors, fluttered the curtains of the balcony deck. A man's silhouette from outside the balcony withdrew. Catherine wasn't aware of it at all. She didn't notice the small broken pieces of window glass beneath the curtains.

As Catherine started unbuttoning her blouse, her eyes remained riveted to the incredible and disturbing sights of the Desert Storm war. She listened to the reporter's voice as the videotapes continued. "...Not only are the bombs bursting in midair as our flag definitely stands and waves over Kuwait, but it looks as though it was the Forth of July instead of January of 1991. A magnificent sight if there ever was one, but a sight that means only death and destruction as the result when it's ended and done with..."

Catherine paused and shook her head pitifully, wondering what political forces had been set in motion to make it come to all this-- sending our troops overseas to protect the resources of another country. It was as if America had fallen into this obligatory plan of attack as if it had no option. As she returned to unbuttoning her blouse, a sudden thought struck her. *The bath water!* She hurried back into the bathroom to turn it off.

The hot water misted up the mirror and turned the bathroom into a sauna. She turned the faucet off and went back into the bedroom to retrieve her suitcase. She opened it and took out her

397

navy blue terry cloth robe, her toothbrush and toothpaste, then went back into the bathroom to undress.

Behind her, the curtain continued to billow. Had Catherine looked down, she would have seen a pair of shoes poking out from under the drapery. Whoever the intruder was, he was now hiding in the room.

After taking off her clothes and slipping on her robe, Catherine grabbed her toothpaste and toothbrush. She still had an aftertaste of artificial sweetener from her tea with Corrigan and wanted to get rid of it.

She wiped the mist from the mirror and started to brush her teeth. Her thoughts went back to the images she saw on the television. The flashes of light from the streaking missiles across the sky, and the tanks in the desert. An American flag rippling in the wind, billowing back and forth...billowing like the curtains over her balcony doors.

Catherine stopped brushing her teeth as the sudden realization hit her. Toothbrush in hand, Catherine shot out of her bathroom and froze in mid stride. Her eyes caught the movement of the curtains billowing from the sea breeze on her balcony deck.

But I locked those balcony doors! She took a closer look. The doors were, indeed, shut. Then her eyes fell to the broken glass on the carpet.

Before Catherine had a chance to react there was a movement behind her. There was no sound, no warning. In one horrifying second, someone stepped up behind her and threw a wire garrote around her neck-- and luckily upon her hand as her toothbrush was ready to enter her mouth.

No... No... This can't be happening, the thought flashed like lightening through Catherine's mind. *Oh, God!* she shrieked silently. *Not again... Please no...!*

The cord tightened around her throat and around her hand holding the toothbrush. It was the only thing preventing her breath from being completely cut off. Her mouth opened to scream, but choked on her toothpaste.

Her assailant pulled hard on the rope. Catherine felt a ring of fire blazing around the sides of her neck. Her other hand with the toothbrush was trapped, caught by the fixed cord. She clawed at the wire with her other hand, but it was too taut for her fingers to grasp.

Catherine's vision started to fade as a million stars burst in front of her eyes. Instinctively, she fought back. She dropped her free hand from her neck, and her arm flailed out, jabbing, swinging, trying to hit anything behind her. She felt it connect-- once...twice... Did she hit his arm? His head? She didn't know. The only thing she was certain of was the pressure on her neck didn't change. She was being strangled to death!

The man didn't expect her to struggle and was forced to use more strength than he thought he needed. He braced himself and pulled hard on the wire garrote, lifting her up off the floor.

Catherine was helpless, panic stricken and tried another tactic. This time she desperately flailed out with both her legs, twisting and kicking them to put the two of them off balance.

They both fell hard to the floor. Catherine felt the pressure disappear from her neck, but the pain made her feel as though she was being decapitated. The hand that once held the toothbrush was throbbing with pain.

She took a deep rasping breath into her burning lungs and began coughing so hard she found it difficult to raise herself off the floor. *I've got to get away,* her mind screamed.

Heart pounding and mind reeling, Catherine pushed herself off the floor and started crawling to the door. She had to find some way to warn the police officer in the hallway.

Where is Henry! Doesn't he realize what is happening to me!

Her arms and legs wouldn't respond as fast as she wanted them to. She tried to escape from this killer as fast as she could, but every movement she made seemed to happen in slow motion.

As Catherine made a desperate lunge at the door, she stumbled and fell. Her attacker took advantage of the situation and again threw the looped cord over her head.

For the second time, she felt the deadly noose tighten around her neck. *I'm going to die,*

399

Catherine thought. *He's going to kill me and there's nothing I can do.*

The assailant pulled her to her feet and dragged her onto the bed, still fighting and struggling. Catherine blinked the tears from her eyes and caught a glimpse of her attacker in the mirror above the dresser. She recognized him immediately as the neighbor with the blond crewcut from the balcony next door.

The assailant pulled her to her feet and dragged her onto the bed, still fighting and struggling. The television in the room blared, showing additional Desert Storm combat footage. This time, instead of SCUD missiles being fired, American tanks were racing through the desert, while others were firing their large caliber rounds. The noise on the television created a bizarre counterpoint to the attack happening to Catherine.

I can't let him kill me! **I won't** *let him kill me!* Catherine tried to summon up every bit of strength within her terror-stricken body to fight back. But her attacker was too strong. She was driven face down on the bed and her head hit the edge of her opened attaché case. The sharp impact on her scalp seemed to focus Catherine's perception of her deadly predicament.

Oh, God... The pain... My head... I must have cracked it open on the edge of my briefcase ... And with that split-second realization, Catherine knew she had a chance.

Her hand swung up, and she thrust it into her open briefcase. It pushed the legal pad aside, and her fingers closed upon one of her pens. She grabbed it and yanked it upward, twisting her wrist. The metal point struck the man's wrist, and he cried out in surprise. Her attacker released his garrote and examined his hand and saw the blood trickling from his wound.

Catherine let out an anguished gasp, finally getting some air into her tortured lungs.

The crewcut man was enraged now. He grabbed the pen from Catherine's grasp, flinging it aside. Then he made a fist and socked her across the face with an angry, impulsive gesture, slamming her across the room and into the wall.

Catherine let out a loud, though strangled scream and somehow remained on her feet. She was in pain and fought for breath. *Oh, God...* Her single thought was to get to the door and alert

Officer Henry outside in the corridor.

As she bolted for the door, Crewcut lunged after her, grabbing her foot from behind, tripping her.

They both fell hard against the door. Stationed outside, Officer Henry Crocker responded. He took his eyes from the magazine and glanced at Catherine's door. The sound was brief and nothing important enough to alert or concern him. His eyes reverted back to the article he was reading.

This time Catherine's attacker was determined to finish her off.

The garrote again looped around her neck-- the biting pain came again. There was no response from Henry outside, as Crewcut now picked her up and threw her again on the bed, his knee aiming at her backbone.

Catherine's adrenaline-driven fear now turned more to anger as she noticed the open briefcase next to her. She took one deep breath and used her last ounce of strength to give her body a convulsive twist. Catherine grabbed the briefcase handle with her free hand and put every bit of effort into this unexpected movement, hoping it wouldn't be her last. She swung the briefcase as hard as she could and let go.

Everything inside, all of her papers, notes, pencils-- everything-- exploded in the air as it flew across the room and hit the door.

Officer Henry Crocker heard the noise again, but this time his curiosity was kindled. He got up from his chair and knocked on the door. When there was no response, he pressed his ear to the door. All he could hear were the noises from Desert Storm on the television set.

"Mrs. Rogers... Mrs. Rogers... Is everything all right?" he inquired. When Catherine didn't answer, he shrugged and went back to his chair and magazine.

Inside the room, Crewcut grabbed Catherine and pulled her off the bed. Catherine opened her mouth to yell for help, or make some type of noise, but the pain in her throat made her gasp.

Her attacker changed his tactics and started dragging her over to the double doors of the balcony.

Catherine continued to struggle. *What is he doing? Why doesn't he let go of me?*

Crewcut jerked open the balcony doors and proceeded to pull her over the threshold. Then the terrifying realization hit Catherine. *He wants to throw me off the balcony!* She redoubled her efforts and tried to break free from her attacker's grip.

Crewcut's legs buckled, and they stumbled into the curtains covering the double balcony doors. The momentum carried the two of them forward, onto the outside deck.

Outside, from the balcony, the sky had turned a bright orange as the sun started to set on the horizon. With Catherine's pulling and the man's pushing, half of the curtains tore loose from the rods and enveloped them. They hit the railing with such an impact, both lost their balance, and were flung over the side.

Catherine managed to fling out her hand and hung for dear life from the railing. Below her, entangled and hanging onto the curtains was her assailant. The curtains, stretched from the broken glass doors, had snagged and caught between the doors and the railing. Catherine squeezed her eyes and held on. She was fearful of summoning any strength to scream, for if she did, she was sure she would surely fall to her death.

Two apartments over on the same floor of the hotel, an elderly couple was having cocktails when they heard the crash of the balcony doors. They witnessed from their balcony two figures now hanging in mid air eleven floors off the ground.

Irene Wymer, the better half of this couple in their sixties, was the first to react as she stared in disbelief at Catherine and her attacker struggling on the balcony.

"Do something, Vern," his wife shouted. "That woman is being attacked!"

"Right," her husband quickly replied. He went inside to the phone and started dialing. "Who should I call? The police or the hotel manager?"

"No, stupid! I'll do that," his wife told him. "Go over there and help that woman. Try and stop that man!"

Vern gulped, "Me?"

Irene gave him a stern look. Vern nodded and ran out the door. As he headed down the corridor, he was astonished and relieved simultaneously to see a policeman, especially when one needs one, sitting right outside the door for which he was headed.

Officer Henry Crocker stood up as the hotel guest approached. "What's wrong?" he asked.

"What's wrong?" the man asked incredulously. "There's a woman and a man hanging out there-- on the balcony!"

Officer Henry Crocker wasted no time. He threw himself at the door, attempting to break it open.

Meanwhile, on the balcony outside her hotel room, Catherine was fighting for her life. Her assailant now was trying to climb upward over the tangled curtains to reach her again, in an obvious attempt to save himself and ultimately throw her to her death.

Catherine wouldn't let go of the railing. She held on to it as tight as she could. But nonetheless she did not have the strength to pull herself up either.

The more Crewcut tried to scale the damaged curtains, the more they tore. The attacker ignored the ripping, and was determined to reach his intended victim no matter the cost. He proceeded to grab for her from below, relentlessly committed to finish the job he started.

Catherine reeled from her attacker's hand of death and stared down into his intense eyes. Fear and determination were etched on his evil face. Catherine screamed with what voice she had left. "Help! Help me! Someone!"

The blood from the man's wound, already splattered across her cheek and neck, now stained her ankles. And every time her attacker's hand would close upon her feet, Catherine would flail her legs and kick him away from her.

The curtains continued to tear with each blow the attacker received. Finally, Crewcut reached out and seized Catherine's blue robe in his grip and started to pull her downward to him

Behind them, in the hotel room, the door broke open.

Officer Henry Crocker crashed into the room, losing his footing, landing onto the carpeted floor.

Crewcut continued yanking Catherine's blue robe as he heard the noise from inside the room. He knew he had only moments to finish his deadly assignment. As the curtain ripped apart, with one savage burst of strength, Crewcut pulled Catherine down, pulling her from the railing.

Catherine would have plummeted straight down to her death as he planned if she hadn't clutched the arm that suddenly reached out for her, grabbing her....the arm belonging to Officer Henry Crocker. Catherine looked up to her rescuer and held firmly to his arm as Henry peered down at her assailant, desperately trying to pull Catherine from the balcony.

But the sudden rending of fabric from the curtain got the best of him. Henry watched as Crewcut made an unsuccessful attempt to grasp to the torn section of drapery. But his weight was too much of a strain for the cloth to bear. The remnants of the tangled curtain finally tore loose from the balcony deck, severing the assassin from the building.

Catherine and Henry heard his scream as he flew like a bird, spiraling downward with the portion of torn curtain, eventually falling eleven stories to his death.

Henry Crocker stood there, stunned, holding tight to Catherine, too shocked for the moment to peer down to see what was the inevitable sight.

Catherine, too, saw and heard everything. She was frozen to the spot, clinging to Henry's hands.

With strength he didn't know he had, Henry pulled Catherine up and over the balcony railing and onto the deck.

Catherine refused to release him, although she was on firm ground again. She found it difficult to convince herself that the attack had ended. Finally, her bloody hand went to her bruised throat as she felt the fiery pain. She knew she was lucky to be alive. Then all at once something snapped within her. Tears filled her eyes, and she started to sob and tremble violently in officer Henry Crocker's arms.

It was three hours after the incident and Catherine sat on the examining table at the hospital emergency ward. She shuttered to herself, thinking what might have happened if Officer Crocker had not been there for her, or if the elderly couple had not reacted.

Captain Corrigan offered her a hot cup of chocolate. He ordered it earlier after she was examined by the doctor for her cuts and bruises. Catherine took the chocolate with a bandaged hand and took a sip. Corrigan touched her shoulder. "It's all over with, Catherine," he tried to comfort her. "I'm just glad you came through this all in one piece." Corrigan glanced at officer Henry Crocker who was also present, nodding to him.

"I just wish I would have acted sooner," Henry told Catherine.

She could see he was overwhelmed by guilt. He was on shift to protect her, and he felt he let her down. She reached out and touched his shoulder. "You saved my life, Henry," she assured him. "I'm alive right now because of you."

"I wish I could have stopped him before he..." Henry let the sentence trail off, still shaken.

Catherine touched the bandages around her throat. They itched more than they hurt. She wasn't suffering too much because of the medication the doctor had given her. There was a small bandage on her hand where the garrote had drawn blood from her palm.

"It wasn't your fault, Henry. As far as I'm concerned, you got there in time," she managed a little smile. "I'm still alive, aren't I?"

Henry smiled and nodded, but Catherine felt he was just humoring her. They both knew she had been seconds from death.

"Is something wrong, Captain," Henry asked.

"I don't like things like this happening in my own back yard," Corrigan said.

Catherine stared at the floor. "I guess Bradley was right when he asked for protection for me. You would think the mob would warn me or threaten me away, not put out a contract on me."

She shook her head in disbelief.

"That's not the case here," Corrigan said.

"What do you mean?"

"I'd say what happened here today was not intimidation or a threat. Somebody wanted you dead! And to tell you the truth, I don't think organized crime is involved here."

Catherine frowned, "Why do you say that?"

"My gut feeling was that someone *wants* us to think organized crime was involved, and to keep you from your meeting," Corrigan explained. "That's my opinion! I guess what I'm saying is maybe you should wait until I can find out more about this man who wanted to kill you."

Henry spoke with Corrigan. "Have they identified Catherine's assailant, yet?"

"No, not yet," Corrigan replied. "He had nothing on him except a wallet with a fake I.D. There was nothing else in his room but a travel bag. It looks to me like a professional job."

Catherine took another sip of hot chocolate. "So you think the people who asked to see me, weren't responsible for what happened here tonight?"

Corrigan nodded his head. He seemed to know something that she didn't.

Catherine lifted an eyebrow, "Why?"

Corrigan pursed his lips. "It's only my gut feeling. The Mafia, Costa Nostra, mob, whatever you want to call them, wouldn't announce they want to see you, have me and MPD know about it, then attempt to kill you once you've arrived. They don't work that way."

"And what way do they work?" Catherine asked.

"If they wanted to kill you, they wouldn't need to send for you! Someone else knew in advance you'd be coming down here. They planned to kill you and blame your death on the people you're meeting. That's the only thing that makes sense to me!"

Catherine sighed and put her cup down. "I think it's time I get some sleep," she told Corrigan. "I'm planning to get up early tomorrow."

Corrigan was surprised, "You aren't serious about going to that meeting tomorrow, are you. Especially after this?"

"I wouldn't miss this meeting for the world. Nothing will keep me away!"

Corrigan shrugged, "Well, it's your choice. If you feel up to it. But you may change your mind tomorrow. Give me a call either way." He motioned to Henry it was time to go.

"We'll check you into another room at the hotel," Corrigan said to Catherine.

"And I'm still spending the night outside your door," Henry told her.

"Thank you, Henry. You can if you wish. I don't think anything more will happen to me tonight. I'm going along with your gut feeling, Captain Corrigan," she shook his hand good night, "but I'm telling you right now, I still want to make that meeting tomorrow."

Chapter Twenty-Nine

"The Actress, the Socialite, and the Voice As the Go-between"

Michael Bradley hung up his phone, working late as usual in his office. He looked up to see Jennifer and Thomas who were sitting on the couch. Concern was written on their faces.

Bradley gave them the news, "Someone tried to kill Catherine tonight. And with a policeman stationed outside her hotel room!"

"Is she all right?" Thomas asked, concerned.

Bradley nodded, "And she's still going to the meeting tomorrow? I can't believe it!"

Thomas cut him off, "You're not going to stop her are you?"

Bradley took a deep breath, making up his mind. "I...I'm going to take the first plane out tomorrow morning. Jenny, you'll have to take care of my cases in court. Get them changed, switched, postponed, whatever you can do. Thomas, you're in charge of the office until I get back. I want you here on call for the next twenty-four hours, is that understood?"

The two of them agreed. "No problem!" Thomas said. Jenny grimly nodded.

Bradley closed his briefcase, then paused and shook his head. "No one can stop Catherine when she sets her mind to do something!" Then he went out the door.

Captain Corrigan stopped his car in front of the hotel, blocking the morning city traffic. He put his police light on top of his unmarked car as a couple of traffic cops got out to direct the street traffic to an alternate destination. A third officer remained in the car. Another police officer brought Catherine out the hotel's main entrance as Corrigan waited with the back car door open. He stepped forward and proceeded to escort her into the car. He got in and sat beside her.

One officer took over the driver's seat as a follow-up police car arrived. The two policemen entered it and followed Corrigan's car as an escort.

Inside the car, rushing through traffic, Corrigan told her, "I was right about last night. I don't think we'll have any problems concerning our meeting today. Meanwhile, your Mr. Bradley is flying down this morning. He should be here before noon."

"I suppose you told him about last night." Catherine asked. She still had the bandages on her throat.

Corrigan stopped her, "I know what you're going to say and I know what you're thinking-- believe me! For our sake I had to. I promised I'd call him if anything out of the ordinary happened. And last night was certainly not ordinary! Besides, I was up half the night trying to get some information concerning your assassin!"

"Did you find out who he was?" Catherine looked at Corrigan for an explanation.

Corrigan clenched his jaw, "Well, not exactly. He had no I.D. on him except a piece of paper with a phone number and the word 'Bishop' written on it. Does that word mean anything to you?"

Catherine shook her head no. "And did you find out anything about this number or whom this 'bishop' is?"

"We don't know." Corrigan shrugged. "The person on the other line didn't even say boo, let alone hello! And when we traced the call, we found the number no longer exists!"

"How can that be?"

"I have a team working on it," Corrigan said, "but I'm sure the number was unlisted and requested that way. In the end, we'll trace it to some motel room, maybe and the person or persons will be long gone!"

The cars drove down MacArthur Street, heading south on the coast of Miami Beach, an elite area. It was a neighborhood of seclusion, where privacy was one of the main perks for those lucky enough to be so wealthy.

The cars slowly approached a secured entrance way gate. A security guard sitting in a booth greeted the two police cars, both stopping at his request. It was not unlike Elvis Presley's Memphis entrance, but here the wrought-iron gate was electrified.

The officer driving Corrigan's car commented, "Who are we visiting? This looks like the Presidential compound?"

Corrigan laughed, "No, I think it's Oliver North's. He's the one who can afford the luxury of an electric fence these days, bought and paid for by the U.S. Government-- meaning the taxpayer!"

The security guard, a large man, approached the driver's side but was motioned by the officer to the back seat as Corrigan rolled down his window, "I'm Captain Raymond Corrigan with the MPD. We have an appointment with a Mr. Costalanno..."

The guard excused himself and returned with a clipboard. "It says here a woman with the name of Catherine Kencade is to be a part of your party. Is that you, madam?"

Corrigan was a bit baffled and exchanged glances with Catherine. She grabbed Corrigan's arm to stop him from saying anything, "That's correct. That's my maiden name!"

"May I see some I.D. please," the guard asked politely. He checked her driver's license, then handed it back. "Please be patient. I'll be right back." He went into the booth to make a call.

He soon returned and explained to Corrigan his car alone would be allowed to enter the compound and the second follow-up police car would have to remain on the outside the gate. He also asked the police officer driving Corrigan's car to remain in it until they got back. Corrigan agreed with the terms, but sent the follow-up car back to the station, and had his car drive through the security gate.

"Now entering 'Fort Knox," Corrigan's driver said sarcastically.

As they drove to their destination, Catherine turned to Corrigan, "How do you suppose they got my maiden name? I only go by Rogers."

Corrigan didn't even know himself. "If these people want to know whom someone is, they have friends in high places. They can find out where you live and where you like to eat and when you sleep! I wish, sometimes, I can gather information as fast as these people can!"

"What do you mean by people in high places? Like Congressmen...Senators?" Catherine asked.

Corrigan acknowledged her with a nod and added, "Even some police officers and judges -- anyone who likes to take a bribe"

Catherine narrowed her eyes. "My father is a judge! And he has never taken a bribe in his life!"

Corrigan did a double take, "So, you're that Kencade! Your father could have been appointed to the Supreme Court! Wow! Now I know why they wanted to see you and why this Bradley fellow thinks you're so hot and heavy! I definitely thought something shady when your father's case in D.C. was dropped suddenly. It looked to me like a set up!"

Catherine was embarrassed, but still adamant. "Yes, that's what it was, but it can't be proven. My father doesn't remember. He received a concussion from a hit and run accident prior to the incident."

The car slowed to a stop. "This is it, the front entrance," the driver informed Catherine and Captain Corrigan. He motioned to two men waiting for them at the entrance way. "Sir, the goon squad awaits your pleasure..."

Corrigan looked up at them and laughed, "All right, Mrs. Rogers, let's do it!"

Captain Corrigan and Catherine were escorted to a pool-side terrace, overlooking the

Atlantic Ocean. Here, a little old man sat, a Sicilian from the old country. He made America his new home these past sixty years, and planned to make it his final resting place.

To Catherine, he looked like someone who couldn't harm anyone. He wasn't the image of an Al Capone or someone who presided over "Murder Incorporated"-- just a little old man with a jolly smile.

He got up to greet Catherine and kissed her hand. He made no reference to the bandage around her neck. Then he shook Corrigan's hand as if they were old friends, although Corrigan never met him before and knew of him through newspaper articles.

Mr. Costalanno, now approaching ninety, sat back down in his chair and insisted the two of them do the same. Then he excused, what the driver referred to earlier, the goon squad. He told his guests he prepared delicious salmon fettuccine for lunch to be served later. For several pleasant minutes they discussed the weather, the Miami Dolphins, Desert Storm and the fact his grandson was stationed over there. "Now, how might I be of help to you two, on this beautiful day, if I may inquire to your business at hand?" he said graciously.

Corrigan glanced over to Catherine before explaining, "I'm here, Mr. Costalanno, as an observer only. The questions Catherine would like to ask are presented by the Bradley law Firm in Madison, Indiana."

Costalanno smiled as he waited for Catherine's questions. He saw she was a little nervous. "My dear lady...there's nothing to be nervous about. So proceed. Ask me anything. I'll try to be of help to you. Remember one thing, if I get out of line, you can kick my wobbly little ass!"

Even Catherine laughed at this and started to loosen up. She admired how this little old Sicilian put her at ease and allowed her to gain her confidence back from the initial intimidation. "Thank you, Mr. Costalanno," Catherine said awkwardly. "I'm guilty of prejudgment. I thought of you as, I guess, someone more like John Dillinger, carrying a gun and holster at your side."

Costalanno smiled and opened his robe to a sleeveless t-shirt and bathing trunks covering a wrinkled, scrawny body. "Well, as you can see, *no* gat! I carry no gun! I'm what you see here,

412

Mrs. Rogers, now you know. What other people say can influence you to believe anything. This is what you get from newspapers and folk tales. I'm certainly no saint, but you can trust me!"

"All right!" Catherine forced a wide grin. "Let's talk about who killed, or was responsible, for the deaths of Sam Giancana and Johnny Roselli, if I may be blunt, for starters?"

Costalanno, surprised at first, stared at her for a long moment. She finally realized he would not answer her and was surprised and then shocked. He got up from his seat and approached Corrigan. Then he squeezed Corrigan's arm and quietly asked, "Mr. Corrigan...would you be so kind as leaving the two of us here alone. You may amuse yourself by exploring my house. That is if you don't mind?"

Corrigan understood what Costalanno meant. "Is this going to be all right for you?" he asked Catherine.

Catherine hesitated, unsure how to reply.

Then Costalanno reminded Corrigan. "I wouldn't worry, Mr. Corrigan. You know she could kick my ass if I got out of line."

Catherine laughed again at this strange, little man. "I'm an attorney, Captain. He knows this. It's an attorney-client thing. He knows what he tells me could never be used inside a courtroom. I'll be all right..."

Costalanno rang a tiny bell on the table. A Cuban servant appeared and Costalanno spoke with him. "Get this gentleman a drink or whatever he wants and make him comfortable in the house. We're going to have a conclave out here and I do not want to be disturbed. I'll call you in a bit." Then he addressed the Captain. "I'm sorry for the inconvenience, Mr. Corrigan."

Costalanno addressed Catherine. "Would you like a drink as well, my dear?"

"Just coffee, please!" she responded conscientiously.

Costalanno then told the Cuban to attend to Corrigan, and they both disappeared into the house.

Costalanno gestured to a table where drinks were set out. He told Catherine her choice of coffee and orange juice was on the table, and she could help herself. She did this, pouring a cup of coffee with a little cream. He poured himself a glass of orange juice.

Catherine sat back down in her chair with her cup of coffee, "Now, Mr. Costalanno, about that question I asked you? You're a smart man, and I give you much credit."

"What I have or haven't learned, my dear, came from a smart man by the name of Meyer Lansky. Does his name ring any bells?"

Catherine nodded, "From what I've read and what I'm told, he was the true brains behind organized crime?"

Costalanno acknowledged this fact and smiled in remembrance. "When he gave his word, he meant it. No one fooled with Lansky. The FBI could never get him. They tried but failed each time. Lansky was a gentleman. What I learned from the man was why I have survived so long today, but my days are numbered now. Sometimes I think I lived too long. Maybe there is some truth to this Ponce de Leon fellow after all and his discovery of the fountain of youth here in our sunshine state of Florida," he laughed, "but as I say, my days are numbered. I know this. All my friends are dead, and our organization is in the legitimate businesses now. We even make movies, good ones! 'Superman' with Brando. We financed that one. It would never have been made without Brando. The deal was you put him in it. We would finance the picture! That's how we make movies in Hollywood. Brando got what he wanted, the studio got their deal and profit, and we got ours. Like Meyer Lansky said not so long ago, we're bigger than U.S. Steel! Well, we now work along side U.S. Steel, the oil industries and our government of the United States. And we pay taxes just like you. The only difference is our businesses are more disciplined than your average company, but we are legit and still growing everyday!"

"But wasn't Lansky skimming money in illegal gambling?" Catherine asked.

Costalanno explained, "If he did, it was his own money or his share from those he allowed to muscle in on his territory. Havana for one, Vegas another, all legit! He was always a man with his word. He loved America and was a top advocate in telling people gambling was not good for the human heart, it was a disease and he would kick people out who abused it.

"No, there was a demand for it and you can say Lansky was a Robin Hood who wanted to steal from the rich and give to the poor, but he didn't even steal from the rich either, because he always had a legitimate casino running. The dice were always checked before use. He never allowed crooked tables, and he fired anyone who tried it in any of his hotels. He was fair to everyone. He never wanted to hurt no one. He respected the lives of this country's government officials and institutions, and this even meant John F. Kennedy!"

"I'm assuming you're questioning me concerning his assassination. Lansky had no beefs with Kennedy. He always thought he was only doing his job. Lansky didn't believe in eliminating his opposition. He never thought of Kennedy as his opposition. For one, he always felt presidents come and go, it was only a matter of time who we could put into office who could be beneficial to us. And we always had someone who benefited from the money in our pockets. Believe me, ma'am, we've had many presidents in our pockets, beginning with McKinley. We groom and build their egos, make them congressmen, senators, and prepare for when it's time for them to be put in that position to control not just the country, but even to influence the rest of the world!

"We're no different from what the military installations and institutions do in this United States! You have the Rockefellers and Rothschilds who control this country as well. How do you think Nelson Rockefeller ever became the Vice-President of the United States? Just think, if anything in 1975 happened to President Gerald Ford, like that time this Manson girl, Squeaky Fromme took a potshot at him, yours truly would have been 'President Mr. Rockefeller'-- imagine that! Only in America!

"You ask me who or how Giancana was killed. Now ask yourself, Catherine Kencade, why wasn't Vice-President Rockefeller's death probed? This man who once was a heartbeat away from the presidency, a man who died in the saddle with his twenty-four-year old secretary from a heart attack. They certainly shut that one up! I bet you his wife wasn't happy about her beloved husband ridin' that saddle off into the sunset, never to return!" Costalanno suddenly laughed at his crude joke while Catherine stared at him in total confusion. He then realized she didn't get the joke, "I'm sorry, ma'am, I just said a joke. 'Happy!' Rockefeller's wife's nickname was 'Happy.' I just realized what I said!"

Catherine smiled courteously, now getting the meaning of it.

"Now about Johnny Roselli and Sam?" Costalanno continued, "Well, let me see... Where are you going with this, Miss Kencade? I hope you don't mind my calling you by your birth name." He sipped his orange juice.

Catherine took a sip of her coffee then set it down and straightened her chair to confront Costalanno. "Mr. Costalanno, you can call me anything you want, far as that goes. I just want to get this straight. If I am out of line here, you can tell me to go to hell, sir! I am a believer in the truth and justice for all. I am an attorney who is not in the business for greed or prestige. I'm just a servant for the people. Only one other person ever said that while I've lived on this earth, and he was assassinated! I was too young to vote and my folks voted Republican, but if anyone on this earth ever gave me a challenge in life, it was John F. Kennedy. A client of mine died with information concerning his assassination. He knew he would be killed and took the secret with him to his grave. Was he protecting something or someone? We may never know. He prepared to give my father enough information to examine, but somehow it got into my hands instead. I think he believed my father was a part of this so-called conspiracy or cover up. I don't believe this. My father would never betray his country, though my client wasn't a saint, either! The fact is, he could have exposed my father and he didn't, and was killed for it. He warned me about his impending death and told me if he died, I was to believe it a suicide. Later with information he had supplied me, I eventually realized the position he had put me in to seek out the truth and the fact I'm here here with you right now, proves it."

Costalanno sat there patiently listening. He lighted up a Cuban cigar and asked, "Did you? Did you find out what you needed from this information your client provided?"

Catherine was silent for a moment, scanning the ocean and blue sky before returning to answer. "I haven't at this time. The information is in safekeeping for now. To investigate further, I have to take certain precautions. Any evidence I may uncover might be destructive to the national security of our country. I don't know whether you heard about my incident last night where I was almost killed. My thoughts at the time when I almost met my maker were of you, Mr. Costalanno. I thought you brought me down here to have me killed!"

Costalanno took a long puff on his cigar and blew it out into the warm breeze now cooling them. "My dear lady, I do know about your ordeal last night and I, wondering the same thing, was concerned for your safety." He gestured to the bandages around her throat. "That is the reason for all this precaution. Is this matter still bothering you in your thoughts now? What can I say or do to convince you I am not the one to be worried about?"

Catherine gave a weary smile. "Mr. Costalanno, I don't believe you tried to kill me. Captain Corrigan had convinced me of that as you have already. You have a certain charm that can mesmerize anyone, but I know, sir, there is a rattlesnake hiding under that exterior of yours. You can suddenly strike at any moment you desire. You see, I studied the psychology of power. And that is your strength. Apparently your Meyer Lansky had it, and so did Santos Trafficante.

"He and Carlos Marcello both lived to be a ripe old age before, during and after the in-house investigation on Kennedy's assassination. But Sam Giancana and Johnny Roselli were not so lucky! Why? This has disturbed me ever since the chairman of that committee stated a conspiracy did happen but put the blame on Mafia ties-- but not Trafficante or Marcello because there were no indictments! I know how the courts work, Mr. Costalanno, and I'm sure the behind closed door routine was for immunity purposes so no one could ever prosecute these two gentlemen. What do you suppose they said? What would Santos Trafficante say to that Committee that would give him the confidence he could walk right out of that room and live out the rest of his life in peace? What? Is it possible he said he could give them Sam and Johnny?"

Costalanno puffed again on his cigar, his eyes chillingly riveting her through the smoke. "What does your client say about this, about our role we played in this information you possess?"

417

Catherine looked at him a moment as if debating how to answer. "Well, he did mention, Johnny Roselli's name. He was attached to a man within the CIA in the assassination plots against Castro. The man was a CIA operative named Harvey. Roselli was working for Santos Trafficante and Jack Ruby met Santos through Giancana. I was hoping you could tell me who killed Giancana and Roselli and why. Was it Trafficante and Marcello?"

Costalanno put his cigar down, confronting Catherine, steely-eyed. "Let me tell you something now, that no one knows to this day, not even the organization. Yes, everyone was looking over their shoulder thinking the family did it. Which one? New York, New Jersey, Miami, New Orleans, or Giancana's replacement in Chicago, who? And the FBI, the police, they didn't give a rat's ass, so it's forgotten. Years pass, people die, and yesterday you almost joined them. Why would we want to kill you? To expose us? For what? What did we do?

"Yes, there were those in the family who wanted those Kennedy brothers dead, but how stupid do you think Trafficante and Marcello were, to cook up some way to whack the President. Hell, they knew if the President ever were killed, who'd you think they would blame? Shit, yes! That Bobby Kennedy would have come down here with both barrels shootin'! There's no way Marcello or Trafficante, no matter how much they hated Kennedy, would ever have his blood on their hands for Bobby, Hoover, or even the Warren Commission to find!

"I can tell you this much, Miss Kencade, someone prior to Sam Giancana's appearance before the House Select Committee, put a hit on him. Believe me it wasn't us! Why would we want to hit Sam, if Sam were responsible to organize the hit on Kennedy? It would only be because of his association with one man, and this man made the same rounds here in Miami with us, Lansky and Trafficante and in New Orleans, Carlos Marcello and with Giancana's man in Dallas you mentioned earlier. It was the same man that Sam could get released from prison with a snap of a finger!"

"After this person's involvement concerning a late-forties murder of a Teamster's Union rep, and this person's arrest, Sam just made a call to his friend, then Congressman Richard

Milhous Nixon who in turn made a call to the head of the FBI, J. Edgar Hoover, to release an informant of his by the name of Jack Rubenstein, who Sam would then send to Dallas, Texas, to represent him in the South. Here, he would be called 'Jack Ruby' and he would be on call at all times.

"Sam sent his boy from Chicago, Charlie Nicoletti, periodically whenever he needed to check up on Ruby. Meanwhile, this man making the rounds was in contact with Nicoletti concerning Sam's involvement with the CIA in getting rid of Castro. Yes, Nicoletti was a suspect connected to Sam's death. The police say it was our hit since it was our signature for his silence, but we knew Sam was no stoolie and Nicoletti loved Sam like a father. He'd kill himself before lifting a finger on Sam! This left one man, the one who made the rounds, the man who could easily walk into Sam's apartment and share a taste of spaghetti! A man who could easily walk into our circles of the organization and the inner circles of the Central Intelligence Agency, the man you speak of through your client!"

Catherine grasped all this, then finished Costalanno's thought, "Johnny Roselli? Mr. Costalanno, are you saying the CIA or someone within the intelligence circles had Roselli hit Mr. Giancana?"

Costalanno picked up his cigar and saw it had gone out. He relit it, puffing it a few times before answering her question. "Well, it surely wasn't us, and Roselli was their liaison to us, wasn't he? And your client, if he has any knowledge to what you say, does mention him, doesn't he?"

"Who then killed Mr. Roselli?" Catherine asked.

Costalanno winked at her and smiled, "Does it really matter now who did him in? He had such a horrible death, cut up in pieces and stuffed in an oil drum, then thrown into the Atlantic right here in our own sunshine state. By this time, there were many people who wanted Roselli dead, including Nicoletti and someone from the House Select Committee who wanted his big mouth shut forever. Someone threw Roselli a bone too many he couldn't stop from collecting. Roselli was a loud mouth and always wanting the limelight.

"Bugsy Segal had the same problem but Roselli knew where all the bodies were buried, let alone those still alive. Someone shut him up and someone wanted us down here to know about it. They say we have a signature whenever one of our own is found murdered, who's signature do you think was represented and tied to Johnny Roselli? Whose body parts were stuffed in a drum that once held a greasy liquid substance known as oil? Tell me who then hit Charlie Nicoletti in 1977 and then six FBI men prior to their appearance before the House Select Committee? What ties do they have that contributed to JFK's demise, and why did Hoover squash any rumors that Oswald worked as an informant for his 'FBI'?"

Catherine questioned his last statement. "What do you mean, what was their involvement? This Nicoletti person, he was what?"

Costalanno gave Catherine a sad look. "The government we have in this country is all screwed up! Don't get me wrong, Miss Kencade, I love this country, but they call us Sicilians in the movies, Murder Incorporated. They got that Brando fellow stuffing tissue in his mouth mumbling, 'I got a proposition you can't refuse,' yet we send our young kids to fight someone else's war! Why? For what? So America can have a monopoly on the oil market, and we can introduce the next generation of kids to a new type of drug that can waste and kill them faster than we already have? I should talk, we helped them on the latter and like everything else in this country. It got out of hand and now five and six-year old kids are on crack. If we're not helping to put our kids six feet under before adulthood, then we're frying their little brains for future generations. This I do not like! This I stop! This I tell you because you're a good woman, Miss Kencade. This I tell you because I feel you can make a difference. This I tell you because I will die soon. Please, someday you will ask your heart to forgive me."

Costalanno now smiled, his jolly face reassuring her again. He proceeded with his explanation. "Chuck Nicoletti knows more about the Kennedy hit because he was there, but *no* House or Senate Committee cared enough or was concerned enough to ask him to appear before them. He knew everything about Watergate, about Nixon and his plumbers, about Hoffa. Now here was an idiot! All Hoffa had to do was keep his big mouth shut and live the rest of his days being husband and grandfather to his grand kids, but no, he didn't know when to quit, he wanted everything! Bobby Kennedy sends him to prison and once Bobby's hit and out of the game. Guess who comes forward to pardon Hoffa, our friend and now president, Mr. Nixon! Only in America! Isn't life wonderful, but Hoffa, once he was out, didn't take orders! The stipulation for his freedom was to avoid the Teamsters, the union that got him in trouble with Sam in the first place. That fucked up idiot-- excuse my French, ma'am-- but Hoffa was just that!"

Catherine was confused, "Then you're saying Hoffa put the contract out on JFK?"

Costalanno became upset as if he weren't communicating correctly with Catherine. "No!" he pounded his fist on the table to make a point. "Listen carefully, Jimmy Hoffa could not find himself out of a paper bag, let alone put out a contract! His way of putting out a contract was to do it himself, to put a bomb in Bobby's home to kill everyone, his wife, Ethel, and those ten Catholic kids of his, he was crazy! No, it was Sam, he took the contract for the organization and Hoffa was to remain mute to keep from controversy. It was Sam who made the contacts in the beginning. It was his show. He's the one who made deals with the father, Joseph P. Kennedy, the son of a bitch if there ever was one! And I say that for JFK's sake as well because he had to sell out his own son to get the presidency. Sam got to be a bit too big for his own britches to see the light on the other side. Joseph P. made an arrangement for a deal, through old blue eyes--Frank Sinatra-- with Sam.

"Sam controlled Virginia and Chicago in the state elections for the presidency. Of course, Nixon had this in his pocket. He knew if he couldn't completely control the Texas electorate, he had Virginia to sandbag. But the old man had a trump card, a marker to cash in, so to speak, from the old days. A New York family, the name I won't mention here, put out a contract on the old man and got Sam to reverse the contract from New York and to snap up the state of Virginia and the Chicago votes in exchange for getting Bobby Kennedy off the Senate Crime Commission and off our backs! Next thing, we see Sam make this miracle a reality, with no more Bobby on the Senate

Committee!"

"The old man makes Bobby JFK's campaign manager. What Sam didn't know was somewhere in making this deal through old blue eyes, he didn't pay much attention to what was said between the lines in Sinatra's conversation, a part of the deal neither Jack Kennedy nor Bobby knew. This secret deal was made through their old man. So, what happens? Everything works out for the Kennedy boys, the old man got his son elected and the now newly elected President appoints his baby brother as the new Attorney General of the United States. And what was the first order of business in the new year? How many of us will go to the pen! Hoffa went ballistic! All of us, one by one, were marked. Bobby was cleaning up Dodge City!

"We see our miracle disappear before us, and the families are all looking at Sam who never thought for once Nixon would lose the election, and if he did, Kennedy was to be in his pocket! Why do you think Nixon never contested the election? Nixon was thinking, 'why the switch,' but knew how it could have been done since Sam controlled it! Only Nixon got the knife in the back, something Sam would soon regret, but would make it up for Nixon next time."

Catherine poured another cup of coffee. "You mean it was that close of an election? Nixon could have won the election by a sudden switch of a small group of delegates?"

Costalanno snapped his finger. "One snap of a finger could have turned the tide of that election! Of course, now, Sam was mad as hell and wouldn't have this as a burden to carry within the family for the next four years, so he makes a call to Sinatra and meets with him. Frank reminds Sam in his angry stupor and stubbornness that Jack and Bobby are never to know what transpired, and the deal they made was to remain a secret between Sam and Frank. Sam tells Sinatra he better tell the old man to put a stop on his boys, or he'll do something about it himself. Sinatra passed this news to the old man, but the old man had a stroke after the Kennedy brothers found out what their father had done. I believe the way they found out was through Sam's intimidation and jealousy in Jack's extracurricular activities with the ladies.

"Again, Sam called Sinatra to ask about this broad or that broad and he heard about this

Judith Campbell who was a wife to some low life movie actor that Sinatra set up with JFK in Vegas. Sam makes arrangements to meet this woman through Sinatra, and they date, but Sam's eyes were on one lady in Vegas and that was, of course, Phyllis McGuire. But he's got an idea. He can use this Campbell chick as an intimidation link to the President. The information was passed on, and that was how Jack found out what his father did. Jack and Bobby were angry, and the father never set foot in or visited the White House. Then he had a stroke! I believe Sam got a kick out of screwing the women JFK had, and now was getting back at him."

Catherine questioned this. "Why use her to get to the President when he has Mr. Sinatra?"

Costalanno smiled, "Well that would soon end because of Hoover's blackmailing schemes. It's like the old story of Samson and Delilah. Sam was like King Huaron sending Delilah off to seduce the man, to weaken the power he possessed no matter what the cost would be! When it came to Marilyn Monroe, Sam went too far. If Kennedy had her, he had to have her too! Sam makes a call to Frank and says he wants to meet the movie star. Frank makes arrangements with Peter Lawford to bring Marilyn up to the Cal-Neva Lodge that Frank and Sam secretly co-owned at the time.

"Here, Marilyn was introduced to Sam, a big mistake, not knowing why she was being exploited. I believe that Frank and Kennedy's brother-in-law did not know what would transpire over that weekend either, but Sam's plan was to make it with Monroe one way or another. Monroe wasn't too impressed with Sam, but she'll do anything for Sinatra and wanted to please her host. Sam had to get her plastered to make his move on her. It was easy to do with a pill-popping lush she was, but this turned out to be a sexual assault and this was not good. Distraught as she already was, Marilyn Monroe would be dead two days later!"

Catherine was shocked at this statement. "My God, do you know what you just said! He raped her?"

Costalanno stood up and walked over to the end of his terrace at the rail and looked out into the ocean, "Miss Kencade, I haven't told you anything, remember! I'm just giving you some advice to take back to that Bradley Law Firm you're working for. You see, the day Monroe died, Sam got a message to those Kennedy boys that morning. The message was he could have or take away anything those Kennedys desired to possess-- that he, Sam, could give and take away whenever he so chose. They, the Kennedy brothers, did not have a monopoly on this country. But wait! Then came the missile crisis and for the next year it looked like Kennedy would have a monopoly on not just this country but the world. Jack Kennedy was planning to control the board game now, until what Sam did next... Well, you know the rest!" Costalanno didn't finish his sentence.

Catherine watched her host standing by the rail. "So Giancana put out the contract to hit the President of the United States?" she said tentatively.

Costalanno turned around to face his guest and nonchalantly told her, "No, not quite. He did not put out a contract-- he was offered a part in it. He had the contract for his team and had his shooters. They accomplished their part, but there were together three other sets of teams, beside Sam's!"

Catherine took a deep breath, "There were *four* sets of shooters out there that day in Dealey Plaza? Who...who were the others?"

Costalanno walked slowly over to the table where Catherine sat, his hands stuck deep in his robe pockets. "Miss Kencade, I told you what Meyer Lansky once said, 'We're as big as U.S. Steel.' Sam could never have made a move on his part without the others in total agreement, and I am not talking about the others in our family organization. This could never have come off without the cooperation of our much larger family, the United States Government. Why do you think there was such confusion on the murder of the century? You think little old Lee Harvey Oswald could do all the damage that eventually changed the course of history? If you believe that then I have some swamp land down the road I can sell you dirt cheap!

"No, ma'am. You'll have to investigate further to know the full truth about that fateful day in Dallas, Texas. It shouldn't be difficult since the House Select Committee quickly shut down after Santos made his private appearance before them!"

"Why did it have to go that far?" Catherine asked, "I mean what about Hoffa and the fact tape recording devices linked to him were discovered in Marilyn Monroe's home as late as 1978. There were rumors of the Kennedy brothers pairing off with the actress. You could have destroyed the presidency just with that piece of information. Instead, Bobby sends Hoffa to prison and he runs for the presidency in 1968. Those tapes must not have proven anything that could sabotage the Kennedy brothers, or I would imagine Hoffa would never have gone to prison. What went wrong? Why didn't Hoffa use the tapes for blackmail?"

Costalanno was annoyed, mostly because he was getting tired and was hungry, but he looked at Catherine as if she were a champion horse he wanted to please, "Actually, you can blame your Mr. Hoover for those rumors concerning Bobby and Marilyn Monroe's fictitious romance. And then you have a few idiots out there who still live with the memory of this icon actress, pretending to be involved with her, saying she left her dying secrets with them-- like the idiot Norman Mailer who writes more about the mysterious and fictitious Marilyn than the abused little girl she really was. The fact was Hoffa went to prison for Sam! Once Sam was dead Hoffa wanted the teamsters back! Other than what most people think today there was more discriminative evidence on Sam on these tapes than there was anything else. Like I told you before, two days earlier Sam had raped Marilyn and someone had to come in to shut her up!

"Months later he again played King Huaron to that Campbell woman's Delilah and sent her off again to seduce Samson at the White House. But this time this Delilah was carrying a child, except whose child it was, was anyone's guess! I suspect it was Sam's, and he wanted to continue this charade of deceit and power. But it didn't work, and Sam ended up taking Delilah to get an abortion. Now, if it were Kennedy's kid, Sam definitely would have gotten a blood test to prove whose it was before the abortion to use later. Again, that poor Campbell broad was used as one of Sam's ugly jokes that proved to backfire. I'm sure Delilah weakened the strength of Samson for a time, but only a short time because he would become stronger than ever. When his downfall finally came, Sam paid off the Mexican government, hid there until he was brought back to the states to testify under government protection, and was murdered to look as though it were from us, under government protection. So you figure it out, Miss Kencade who whacked who with the Feds protecting Sam on the eve before testifying before the House Select Committee? How about we go and eat something, I'm famished!"

As the two joined Corrigan at a table serving salmon fettuccine, Catherine still was curious, "Then what happened to James Hoffa? Why did he suddenly disappear? What was his connection.?"

Costalanno laughed, "You don't give up do you? Well, I'll tell you this, if Nixon wasn't so obsessed with the Kennedy family as he was, he'd still have remained President, and no doubt become one of the greatest ones. If Hoffa would have done the same and accepted Nixon's pardon and stayed put and kept his mouth shut he'd still be alive today, but both those two men had obsessions that wouldn't quit! I imagine Hoffa made enemies real quick with both Giancana and the U.S. Government when he exploited the fact he would open a can of worms concerning the Kennedy matter. So I imagine Johnny Roselli got his orders from one or the other and if it came from Sam, I suppose Charlie Nicoletti was commissioned for the job, to make Hoffa disappear. And those eighteen minutes missing on Nixon's tapes for historical preservation would have unsettled many those who call themselves a member of the Republican party." Costalanno looked over to Corrigan and gave him a sly wink.

Catherine looked to Corrigan who took a bite of a piece of salmon as if to say 'don't mind me.' She turned her eyes to her food. She wasn't really hungry from their conversation, but being polite she took a bite of her fettuccine. She suddenly broke out with a smile. "My, this is excellent! Mmmm..."

Costalanno was happy by this and let the two guests know this was a mixture of his own special sauce with his mother's old recipe, "...may God let her soul rest in peace!"

Corrigan became curious as well. "Mind if I ask you something off the record, Mr.

426

Costalanno? That is, I'm putting this puzzle together. May I ask whether you know what were on those missing eighteen minutes of tape? I know they consist of two separate tapes-- one with five minutes and the other thirteen minutes erased!"

Costalanno didn't mind. "Off the record, those eighteen minutes are not necessarily erased. Nixon's tapes might have been deleted, but there is a copy out there preserved for safekeeping. And I'm sure the Republican Party would not want to know what exists on it nor the United States Government for that matter. But let's say we always had a mutual friend to the President who was close to the subject at hand. In fact, he didn't live too far from here. He used to dine here at this table often, right where you sit, Captain Corrigan. You must remember, Mr. Bebe Rebozo, I'm sure?"

Costalanno smiled as Corrigan understood the point he was making. "You see, sir, the White House was never too far from my own front door. As it was on the West Coast, San Clemente was minutes from our LaCosta front door. It's why we continue to exist. Yes, we still have family feuds but we handle our own."

Costalanno smiled at Catherine and then winked his charming eye at her. He added, "We all prosper when we work together, don't we? That is what gives this country its strength, when all of us work toward the same goal anything is possible. For any poor simple immigrant who wants to make it here in this country-- no matter what color, race or creed-- that's the American way. The CIA needed us, and we used them as well!"

* * *

When Corrigan and Catherine exited through Costalanno's gate, they saw Michael Bradley on the other side, patiently waiting. The car stopped next to him. Catherine jumped out and hugged her friend. His eyes were moist with tears to see she was fine.

"It went well, Michael," Catherine said, "I now understand why there are so many pieces of the puzzle missing." They hugged again, and then both got into Corrigan's car and drove off.

427

Inside the estate, Costalanno sat in his deck chair watching the sky turn to dusk. He admired the colorful reds, grays and oranges reflecting on top of the ocean, and watched the sun slowly melt into it. He sat there in deep thought and as he did, a figure approached him from the back. Someone spoke softly to him, someone he knew so well, but he didn't react to the voice or acknowledge the man's presence. Costalanno knew exactly what the man was planning to say and he listened, but his mind was on the sunset.

"What did you tell her?" A man moved closer to the deck chair, waiting for Costalanno's answer.

Costalanno held his cigar in hand. He lifted it to his mouth and took a puff before he gave his response. "I told Miss Kencade enough for her to lead you to what you want. I'm sure I've given her all or enough reasons to go that extra step. But I want you to promise me, and I want your word on it, to find out who was responsible for last night's attempt on Miss Kencade's life. I do not want anything to happen to her, is *that* understood?"

The man moved around so Costalanno could see him. Costalanno looked up at the man and waited for his reply.

"You have my word, sir!" he bent down to take Costalanno's hand, then kissed his ring. And Costalanno peered into the man's face, to stare into his eyes. It was the Italian gentleman who associated with Senator Fuller earlier. The same man Judge Henry Kencade would never "forget."

Chapter Thirty

"The Man Who Knew Too Much"

In Atlanta, Georgia, the twenty-four-hour news station brought the country and the world full coverage of the Desert Storm war. It was reported Saddam Hussein tuned in for strategic information to use against our U.S. troops. Meanwhile, the networks bombarded the airwaves with constant repetition of air strikes of scud missiles. They said you couldn't tell the real explosions from the barrage of explosions from the Nintendo games controlling the hawkish minds of our youth on TV screens throughout the country.

At war's end, thirty days later to be exact, CNN's number one news commentator, Bernard Shaw was a nervous as he prepared himself that evening for an interview with a former President of the United States. He was to be the first African-American news commentator to interview Richard Milhous Nixon. And it was a major coup for the independent network, the same network that provided most of the feed to the commercial networks while the war against Hussein waged.

Nixon was definitely in form this evening and wasn't as nervous as his interviewer. He prepared to answer everything and anything Shaw threw at him. There was one particular question which started simply, but would throw some people watching the interview into a total loop.

Bernard Shaw was halfway through his interview, and in a more comfortable, when he asked Mr. Nixon about President Bush's ties to him, and Bush's decision concerning what effect the result of Desert Storm would have on the country. Nixon puffed himself up when it came to taking responsibility for bringing Bush under his wing and into the political arena in 1967. He let Shaw know Bush eventually came aboard to join his staff and became his spokesman for his policies. This position was culminated by Nixon's endorsement of George Bush as Ambassador to the United Nations. And in 1973 Bush became the Chairman of the Republican National Committee. But when it came to Bush's involvement with Desert Storm, Nixon's face changed visibly, not wanting to contradict a present commander in chief's policy and was diplomatic about his position.

Bernard Shaw wasn't ready to let Nixon off the hook so easily, and asked the question in a different way. "Mr. President, if you were in the place of the President and was in charge of the situation, how would you have handled the war with Iraq?"

Nixon proceeded to answer this question with the utmost enthusiasm and expertise in foreign affairs and foreign policy. "If I were the President, mind you-- and this was my administration-- my position would never have been to send American soldiers over there or gotten them involved. The problem here was not this country, or that country did this or did that, the problem was with Saddam Hussein. And there is only one solution to a problem like that-- I would have had him assassinated!"

These last words echoed as it was broadcast throughout the world. One particular television set on in Los Angeles belonged to Richard Franklin, whose jaw had just hit the floor of his living room. He was amazed, trying to listen to more of Nixon's commentary, and simultaneously dial the phone.

"Are you watching the Shaw/Nixon interview on CNN?" Franklin stuttered into his phone, "Did you hear what he just said? Yes! I think Nixon must think his secret policies are now open for discussion! I bet you a million to one the CIA has just taken a shit and I'm sure it already hit the fan!"

* * *

The next day in his Los Angeles office on the fourteenth floor of the twin towers in Century City, Richard Franklin spoke into his own pocket tape recorder as he followed a transcript of the Warren Commission:

"This is a tape recording of Oswald's famous debate on August twenty-first, 1963, over a New Orleans radio broadcast with WDSU commentators Bill Stuckern and Bill Slatter against Carlos Brinquier, the Cuban exile who had staged a public confrontation with Oswald, and his Fair Play for Cuba leaflets he passed out on Canal Street. Oswald was arrested and taken to jail, following a confrontation and assault. But instead of asking to see a lawyer, he demanded an interview with an FBI agent. One week later Oswald hired two day-laborers and passed out 'Hands Off Cuba' leaflets outside the International Trade Mart where WDSU-TV cameras happen to film the event."

Here, Franklin stopped and mentioned the name, "Clay Shaw." Then he continued, "TV Cameras, Oswald's notoriety and then this debate on radio," he said writing 'International Trade Mart' next to Clay Shaw's name. "Is there a connection--here?"

He turned on a small cassette recorder and heard Oswald's voice from the Oswald tapes. "...I and several other of my members had a demonstration in front of the International Trade Mart..."

Again, Franklin wrote down the name, "Clay Shaw-- Controller-- ITM."

The Oswald tapes continue with Stuckey and Ed Butler, an anti-Communist propagandist opening the debate as they both produce newspaper clippings that exposed Oswald in his 1959 attempt to renounce his American citizenship. Oswald denied this exposure, but asked, "During those two weeks (as I arrived in Russia) I was, of course, with the knowledge of the American Embassy, getting this permission (to enter and reside) At no time was I out of contact with the American Embassy."

431

Bill Slatter, the radio commentator from WDSU News asked, "I'm curious to know just how you supported yourself during the three years that you lived in the Soviet Union. Did you have a government subsidy?"

Franklin followed the transcript closely. Curiously, he noticed an error in what the Warren Commission transcribed in Oswald's answered statement than what Oswald actually said.

He stopped the tape recorder and read the Commission's Exhibit #3, Oswald's answer: "...I worked in Russia. I was <u>not</u> under the protection of the-- that is to say I was not under protection of the American government..."

Franklin repeated the word 'not' in his recorder and wrote it down adding a question mark.

Oswald's voice now took over as the tapes continued with his recorded answer, "Well, as I uh, well, I will answer that ques...uh, question directly then, since you will not rest until you get your answer. I worked in Russia. I was under, uh, the protection of the uh...of the uh...that is to say, I was not under protection of uh...the American Government. But that is, I was at all times considered an American citizen..."

Franklin stopped the Oswald tape and continued to remark on the Commission's Exhibit #3. "Is this a Warren Commission error or were they now putting words into the mouth of Oswald like John Modini now suggests? Oswald's Russia chronology is a Warren Report facade! Here, a simple word 'not' is slipped into a transcript to make it look as if he were stammering or making a Freudian slip, or is this just hiding Oswald's slip of the tongue? Either way the word not alters the meaning of his statement and dismisses Exhibit #3!"

Franklin deliberated further. "If Oswald was not an agent or an informant for the FBI, why is his 'Hands Off Cuba-Fair Play for Cuba' leaflets stamped with the same address in New Orleans that housed no such committee, but did house a detective agency of Guy Banister who used to head the Chicago FBI office! Ties to Sam Giancana, maybe?"

Again, Franklin jotted down the fact Oswald refused a lawyer when he was arrested at the International Trade Mart, but instead asked for an interview with an FBI agent. Into his pocket recorder he stated, "It is Warren Commissioner Gerald Ford who insisted that Oswald's 'Commitment to Communism' be listed as motivation for murder. Ford also was liaison to FBI director J. Edgar Hoover, who the day after the assassination knew Oswald was not the assassin! How and why was Gerald Ford able to obtain classified transcripts of Warren Commission meetings, print them word for word in his book 'Portrait of the Assassin,' and reap the publishing profits without being charged with violating federal secrecy acts?"

Franklin started to pace the room. "Why did Ford and other Commissioners hide the fact from the public that a secret meeting happened in January of 1964 stating through top Texas officials in Dallas that Oswald was an FBI informant? And why did Ford and Allan Dulles, once heads of the CIA, and Warren himself, refuse to take Jack Ruby to Washington when he pleaded to them his life was in danger and that he would provide the information, the real reason behind Oswald's death? How could Ruby pass through seventy Dallas Police officers on the morning of November twenty-fourth, 1963?"

Franklin reviewed all these questions in his mind. "As the Kennedy's suspected assassin, Oswald, was led out of the city jail in Dallas to be transferred to the county jail he was handcuffed to Dallas detective, James R. Leavell and lead Oswald to a waiting police car. Amazingly, it was a car that was not there to begin with. This gave Jack Ruby the opportunity to push through the crowd, pistol in hand, and shove it into Oswald's stomach, pulling the trigger. Talk about lack of proper timing! Yet, Ruby is a unique witness to the Warren Commission. Leavell testified if the car had been placed where it should have been where he, Leavell, was told it would be by Captain Fritz, then the car would have been sitting directly upon the spot where Ruby was standing when he fired the shot!

"This was only one incident in the strange circumstances of Jack Ruby's killing of Oswald. He was directly involved in the chain of events-- not just a witness or someone who knew one or possibly two of the participants. One example was Officer Tippit. He was the officer, the Warren Commission theorizes who was killed by Oswald based on one of fifteen witnesses who

433

identified him as the assassin.

Kennedy, Tippit, Oswald-- all were dead! If there were a conspiracy to the assassination, potentially, Jack Ruby had the most revealing testimony of all. But it wasn't discovered until seven months later when the Warren Commissioners finally confronted him in a Dallas jail cell. Ford and Warren joined Lee Rankin, head counsel who urged the Commission not to question him-- that did not make sense from what was just explained. And Ruby kept hinting reasons he needed to be brought to Washington, D.C. and out of the custody of the Dallas Police Department. He said if not, he would die. And that's exactly what happened, didn't it."

Franklin proceeded to switch from the Oswald tapes to the Ruby transcript, and recorded this in his pocket recorder: "This is inside the Dallas Police Department where Chief Justice Warren, Ford and Rankin would interview Jack Ruby. Joining them from the Commission was the assistant counsel, Joseph Ball, and Arlen Spector-- this man was everywhere! Also present was a who's who of the Texas legal establishment: two Special Counsel to the Attorney General of Texas, the Texas Court of Inquiry, Robert Storey and Leon Jaworski. This was the same Jaworski who replaced Spiro Agnew as Vice-President after his resignation in 1973 and then nominated Gerald Ford to replace *him*. Nixon appointed Leon Jaworski as Special Watergate Prosecutor in the 70's and then it got real sticky! Wow! It's a small world isn't it?"

Franklin wrote on, listing the characters that boggled the mind. He wondered why all these people gathered around a man who was not suspect that already was convicted of this crime and was not denying he was responsible.

"Where was the conflict of interest here? We also have local law enforcement there as well: Jim Bowie, Assistant D.A. without his Bowie knife-- must be an ancestor; Joe Tonahill, Ruby's lawyer who Jack repeatedly explained he had no desire for Tonahill to be his counsel, and repeatedly wanted him to leave throughout this meeting; Joe Decker, Sheriff of Dallas County; and Elmer W. Moore, Special Agent of the U.S. Secret Service. Why was he there-- to protect the Commissioners and all those Texas law enforcement officers? Inside what-- Ruby must have had a courtyard for a cell. And why did this Secret Service agent, prior to the meeting, have an interrogation with Ruby and, at the meeting was allowed to interrupt the Commissioners questioning of him? How was Warren able to get any information from a man who hinted constantly he couldn't talk with a bus load of people in the same room?"

"Chief Justice Warren was responsible for assembling the facts of the crime of the century and had the power of the President of the United States and the Supreme Court to subpoena anyone he wanted, but chose not to comply with Ruby's best wishes-- which could have changed the result of the Warren Report. Instead, Warren pretended to act powerless in front of a man who may have all the answers. A man who would have talked if the Commissioners did their job. Instead, they continued to make a mockery of their own report. Senator Russell opposed Warren when he-- Warren-- refused earlier the power of subpoena, thus the Commission then voted itself the power to Subpoena."

Franklin turned on another tape deck and heard Ruby speak to Earl Warren:

Ruby: "Is there any way to get me to Washington?"

Warren: "I beg your pardon?"

Ruby: "Is there any way of you getting me to Washington?"

Warren: "I don't know of any. I will be glad to talk to your counsel about what the situation is, Mr. Ruby, when we get an opportunity to talk."

Ruby: "I don't think I will get a fair representation with my counsel, Joe Tonahill, I don't think so. I would like to request that I go to Washington, and you allow me to take all the tests (lie detector and any truth serum) that I have to take. It's very important!"

Tonahill: "Jack, will you tell him why you don't think you will get a fair representation?"

Ruby: "Because I have been over this for the longest time to get the lie detector test...somebody has been holding it back for me."

Warren: "Mr. Ruby, I might say to you that the lateness of this thing is not due to your counsel. He wrote me, I think close to two months ago and told me that you would be glad to testify and take, I believe he said, any test. I'm sure of that, but he said you would be glad to testify before the Commission. And I thanked him for the letter, but we have been so busy that this is the first time we have had an opportunity to do it! But there has been no delay, as far as I know, on the part of Mr. Tonahill in bringing about this meeting. It was our own delay due to the pressures we had on us at the time."

Franklin turned off the tape and asked himself, "The pressures, Mr. Warren, that threatened to expose the fact both Oswald and Ruby were informants for the FBI. Hoover provided you with the Ruby information, and you have top Texas officials providing you with the Oswald ties since January, and here it is June?"

He shook his head and picked up the Ruby Transcript. He leafed through it and stopped at page 191 of Volume 5 of the report. He read where Ruby met with a Dallas policeman thirty-six hours prior to the Oswald hit. This officer suggested someone who could get to Oswald, to kill him, would be a good idea. Ruby knew the officer who made this suggestion because he was having an affair with one of Ruby's employees.

Franklin reacted to this information intensely and turned on the Ruby tape to this part of the transcript. Ruby's voice again took precedence: "...I heard someone honk a horn very loudly, and I stopped. There was a police officer sitting in a car. He sat with this young lady that works in my club (The Carousel) ...and they were very much carried away, and I was carried away! And he had a few beers, and it's so bad about those places open (most bars were closed because of the death of JFK), and I was a great guy to close; and I remained with them (the officer and the girl) ...did I tell you this part of it? I didn't tell you this part because at the time I thought a lot of...(the name of this person is never mentioned) police officer, and either it slipped my mind in telling this, or it was more or less a reason for leaving it out, because I felt I didn't want to involve them in anything because it was supposed to be a secret that he was going with this young lady. He had marital problems. I don't know if that is why I didn't tell you that, anyway, I did leave it out. And they talked, and they carried on, and they thought I was the greatest guy in the world, and he stated they should cut this guy (meaning Oswald) inch by inch into ribbons and so on..."

Franklin spoke into his recorder. "Now Attorney Joe Tonahill mentions here, 'This is the thing that started Jack in the shooting,' stating that a Dallas police officer motivated Ruby to kill Oswald. Ruby was not questioned further on this by the Commission!" Franklin asked himself, "Why?" He then smiled, "This Dallas Police Officer wouldn't happen to be the one and the same person who was attached to the underworld and to the CIA--the same man who was in the Marine Corps together with Oswald--the same man who confessed to a priest in 1971 he helped murder his fellow officer Tippit and JFK as he lay dying after a mysterious fire?

"This man wouldn't be Roscoe White, would it? And this same police officer wouldn't suggest if all was said and true these Commissioners believe this explanation-- this officer was grieving over this fellow officer to suggest Ruby or someone needs to hit Oswald for what he did or didn't do, since a court of law would eventually find this out? Or was it that Oswald's mouth needed to be shut, for he truly was a man who knew too much?"

The recorder continued to play with Earl Warren's voice asking the pertinent question: "Did you know Lee Harvey Oswald prior to this shooting?"

Ruby: "That is why I want to take the lie detector test. Just saying no isn't sufficient."

Warren: "I will afford you that opportunity."

Ruby: "All right..."

Warren: "I will afford you that opportunity. You can't do both of them at one time?"

Ruby: "Gentlemen! My life is in danger here...not with my guilty plea of execution! Do I sound sober enough to you as I say this?"

Warren: "You do! You sound entirely sober..."

Ruby: "From the moment I started my testimony, have I sounded as though, with the exception of becoming emotional, have I sounded as though I made sense, what I was speaking about?"

Warren: "You have indeed, I understood everything you have said. If I haven't, it's my fault."

Ruby: "Then I follow this up! I may not live tomorrow to give any further testimony. The reason why I add this to this, since you assure me that I have been speaking sense by then, I might be speaking sense by following what I have said, and the only thing I want to get out to the public, and I can't say it here, is with authenticity, with sincerity of the truth of everything and, why my act was committed. But it can't be said here! It can be said, it's got to be said amongst people of the highest authority that would give me the benefit of the doubt. And following that, immediately give me a lie detector test after I do make the statement. Chairman Warren-- if you felt that your life was in danger at the moment, how would you feel? Wouldn't you be reluctant to go on speaking, even though you request me to do so?"

Warren: "I think I might have some reluctance if I was in your position, yes, I think I would. I think I would figure it out very carefully as to whether it would endanger me or not? If you think that anything that I'm asking you is endangering you in any way, shape, or form, I want you to feel absolutely free to say that the interview is over."

Franklin sarcastically remarked to the tape recorder, "I bet you would like this over with, Mr. Warren!"

Ruby: "What happens then? I didn't accomplish anything."

Warren: "No, nothing has been accomplished."

Ruby: "Well, then you won't follow up with anything further?"

Warren: "There wouldn't be anything to follow up if you hadn't completed your statement..."

Ruby: "You said you have the power to do what you want to do, is that correct?"

Warren: "Exactly!"

Ruby: "Without any limitations?"

Warren: "Within the purview of the Executive Order which establishes the Commission. We have the right to take testimony of anyone we want in this whole situation, and we have the right, if we so choose to do it, to verify that statement in any way that we wish to do it."

Ruby: "But you don't have a right to take a prisoner back with you when you want to?"

Warren: "No, we have the power to subpoena witnesses to Washington if we want to do it, but we have taken the testimony of two-hundred or three-hundred people, I would imagine, here in Dallas without going to Washington."

Ruby: "Yes, but those people aren't Jack Ruby!"

Warren: "No, they weren't."

Ruby: "They weren't!"

Franklin shut off the Ruby tape and commented into his own recorder, "There was a dozen people in this Dallas County Jail. Ruby is reluctant to talk and was giving complete warning and clues he did not want to speak in front of all or some of these people in the room. It's like the feeling I had when I visited a movie set one day, and an actress was ready to do a nude scene for the camera. She started to feel uncomfortable with fifty crew members and extras standing around, waiting for her performance. So the director solved the problem by clearing the set and the shot was completed in a comfortable manner. Why didn't Warren who has the power to take Ruby to Washington-- which we can see he was definitely avoiding-- just clear the set? If the police were in on Oswald's demise, it would certainly be difficult to talk in these surroundings!"

Ruby: "When are you going back to Washington?"

Warren: "I am going back very shortly after we finish this hearing-- I am going to have some lunch."

Ruby: "If you request me to go back to Washington with you right now that couldn't be done, could it?"

Warren: "No, it could not be done. It could not be done. There are a good many things involved in that, Mr. Ruby."

Ruby: "What are they?"

Franklin said, "This guy, I have to hand it to him, is persistent!"

Warren: "Well, the public attention that it would attract, and the people who would be around! We have no place there for you to be safe when we take you out, and we are not law enforcement officers."

Franklin became upset. "Oh spare me, Mr. Warren! You're just a poor old Supreme Court Judge responsible for the crime of the century, and you're so helpless to do anything that might ruin the status quo of your report!"

Warren: "...and it isn't our responsibility to go into anything of that kind, and certainly it couldn't be done on a moment's notice this way!"

Franklin angrily shut the tape recorder off. "Ruby constantly pleaded to go to Washington and volunteered information the Commission is not even asking, wanting them to wake up. He asked Warren if he were in his place right now, would he feel comfortable if he felt his life were in danger? This next statement he made was very convoluted, but again tried to tell Warren he had more to say in this transcript than meets the eye-- that possibly there was a plot. He is asking in so many ways for a private meeting. Did he get it?"

Franklin took a deep breath and turned on the Ruby tape:

Ruby: "...But I am certain -- I don't recall definitely, but I do know my motive for doing it, and certainly it was not to gain publicity, take a chance of being mortally wounded as I said before, and who else could have timed it so perfectly by seconds? If it were timed that way, then someone in the police department is guilty of giving me information when Lee Harvey Oswald was coming down."

Franklin again hit the pause button. "No, I guess not! Mr. Ruby, in trying to cooperate the only way he could, didn't get the help he needed or asked for. He was ignored! In fact, he wouldn't even get his lie detector test. He would die right there in his own jail cell as he predicted. What bothers me was that Ruby requested to be interviewed in private, and no matter who left, I have a feeling this secret service agent, Elmer W. Moore, wouldn't leave the room-- even when it was noted he had already interviewed him earlier. He apparently bothered Ruby by his presence along with Tonahill who Ruby again did not consider to be his lawyer. If Moore were not part of the investigation any longer, why was he there and why did he question Ruby in the presence of the Commission's own investigation as Ruby continued to plead?"

The Ruby tape continued, this time asking Special Secret Agent Moore where he fit in here: "Where do you stand, Moore?"

Moore: "Well, I am assigned to the Commission, Jack."

Ruby: "The President assigned you?"

Moore: "No, my chief did, and I am not involved in the investigation. I am more of a security officer!"

Ruby: (to the Commission): "Boys, I am in a tough spot, I tell you that!"

Moore: "You recall when I talked to you, there were certain things I asked you not to tell me at the time, and I respect your position on that and asked you not to tell me certain things."

Franklin hit the pause button again and thought about what he heard. "What certain things? Why was he now admonishing Ruby here in the first place? And why did Sheriff Decker tell Moore earlier, 'his body is responsible to you! His body is responsible to you!'? Why was his presence needed now at the official Commission inquiry? Certainly not for protection with all the security available to him in that jail cell?"

Franklin then turned on the Oswald tapes. Oswald was questioned by WDSU News reporter: "Oswald, I'm curious about your personal background. If you could tell us something about where you came from, your education and your career to date, we'd be interested..."

Oswald: "I'd be very happy to. I was born in New Orleans in 1939. For a short length of time during my childhood, I lived in Texas and in New York. During my junior high school days, I attended Beauregard Junior High School. I attended that school for two years. Then I went to Warren Eastern High School for over a year. Then my family and I moved to Texas where we have many relatives, and I continued my schooling there. Then I entered the United States Marine Corps in 1956. I spent three years in the United States Marine Corps, starting as a private, working my way up through the ranks to the position of buck sergeant, and I served honorably; having been discharged. Then I went back to work in Texas and have recently arrived in New Orleans with my family, with my wife and my child."

Franklin said, "Oswald leaves out a pertinent part of his life here-- three years in the U.S.S.R.!"

Oswald was then questioned with: "What particular event in your life made you decide that the Fair Play for Cuba Committee had the correct answer about the, about Cuban-U.S. relations?"

Oswald: "Well, of course, Americans, in general, have only begun to notice Cuba since the Cuba Revolution. That is very true. I think...uh, I became acquainted with it at about the same time as everybody else in 1960...uh, I always felt that the Cubans were being pushed into the Soviet bloc by American policy. I still feel that way. Our policy, if it had been handled differently--and many others much more informed than I have said the same thing-- if that situation had been handled differently, we would not have the big problem of Castro's Cuba now, the big international political problem. Although I feel that it's a just and a right development in Cuba, still, we could be on much friendlier relations with Cuba. And had the government of the United States, its government agencies -- particularly certain covert, uh, covert, uh, undercover agencies like the now defunct CIA..."

Franklin smiled and said, "Yes, Lee Harvey Oswald, don't get too technical here. We don't want Gerald Ford, nor Arlen Spector to recognize the fact you're the same Oswald who wrote the unintelligible 'Historic Diary.' Or the same nut case who shot at General Walker, the man who was fired by the President of the United States for treason-- and who worked for the John Birch Society and was responsible in passing out leaflets stating: 'Kennedy wanted for treason.' And Ruby stated this same group wanted him and Earl Warren dead! My God-- who was Oswald working for? There was no Fair Play for Cuba Committee existing!"

Oswald answered the questioner how the CIA was now defunct: "Well, its leadership is now defunct, Allen Dulles is now defunct...that, I believe that without all that meddling, with a little bit different handling of the situation, uh, Cuba would not be the problem it is today."

Franklin again asked, "Dulles was the man who established the CIA who began as director in 1947 and was fired by the President of the United States after the Bay of Pigs in 1961! Who is Oswald for? Apparently not Castro! If anything, he was playing the same game or on the same team as the CIA! It was as if he were a schizophrenic playing both sides. Was that what his job was in the U.S.S.R., playing both sides of the coin? Oswald definitely was an anomaly!"

Franklin shut off everything and crossed to his couch. He was tired from reviewing all the material. He stretched out and decided to take a nap. As he again closed his eyes he remembered Nixon's words to Bernard Shaw concerning his thoughts on what he would do to Saddam Hussein if he were Commander-In-Chief. Franklin whispered them to himself as he fell asleep, "I would have had him assassinated!"

* * *

The winter season came to a close in Miami, and the city readied itself for the last rush of college students swarming in for their spring break.

Captain Raymond Corrigan was not concerned because his Miami Police Department lab came up with an important clue-- a telephone number. They discovered an imprint of it on a scrap of paper in the hotel room belonging to the assassin who tried to kill Catherine. For the crime lab, it was more in line like the Sherlock Holmes method of analyzing a piece of paper for the imprint of the number. They were successful, however, the lab could only decipher seven digits. Several calls eliminated it as a local number. Since they needed three more digits for the area code, a staff systematically called each county, city, district and state the original number might originate from. They narrowed their search by eliminating Alaska and Hawaii and the State of Florida. The West Coast would be a last resort, as was the Midwest, so they concentrated mainly on the East Coast, around Virginia, New York, Maryland, the D.C. District, and New Orleans. Eventually, they hit pay dirt in the state of Indiana.

Captain Corrigan wanted to be the first to give Catherine Rogers the news, whether good or bad. They discovered the right number, which was good news, but the bad news was the identity of the person at the other end of the line.

When Captain Corrigan called the Bradley Law Firm in Madison, Indiana, Sherry Keller answered the phone. It was 8:30 a.m. in this time zone and the law firm was almost empty at the time. Sherry told Corrigan both Bradley and Catherine weren't in, and were not expected back soon.

"Is there someone else there I can talk to?" Corrigan asked. "This is too important to leave a message."

"One moment," Sherry said, "I'll find someone..."

She found Thomas Sanders using a slide projector in the conference room. "Thomas..."

"Just a second, Sherry?" Thomas answered.

Before Sherry could explain about the phone call, her attention was diverted to the screen, a large sheet of white paper taped to the wall. Thomas set up a slide projector and projected a slide of the grassy knoll fence in Dealey Plaza on it. Thomas clicked the button, and the slide was replaced by a blow up of some bushes overlooking Elm street, the street of Kennedy's motorcade route. Near the bottom of the frame was an image resembling a helmet and holding what looked like a long stick.

"Sherry, do you think that looked like a man with a rifle?"

Sherry stared at the photo. "I'm not sure...it looked like a bush or a bunch of leaves to me."

Thomas took his ruler and pointed to the area where the rifle was. A marker at the end of the ruler drew on the paper screen the outline of the rifle and the shape of a man's helmet, supposedly on the man's head.

Sherry was amazed. "You're right, it did look like a person with a long stick or rifle!"

Thomas seemed satisfied. "Thank you! Now, what was it you wanted to ask me?"

"There's an important long distance call for Catherine." Sherry told him. "And they don't want to leave a message."

Thomas turned off the slide projector. "Everyone's in court today. Jennifer's got a trial and Michael is giving depositions."

"It's Captain Corrigan. He wants to speak with someone if Michael or Catherine isn't available."

Thomas grabbed for the desk phone, hitting one of the blinking lines. "Thomas Sanders here...what can I do for you, Captain Corrigan?"

"I take it Catherine isn't available," Captain Corrigan said. He sounded disappointed.

"If it's important, I can reach her quickly enough," Thomas replied.

"I have news concerning the phone number we were trying to decode. We've got it."

Thomas grabbed a pencil and paper, ready to write. "And who does the number belong to?"

"The phone number belongs to a residence. It's the phone number of Gerald Fuller...Senator Gerald Fuller."

Chapter Thirty-One

"The Body in the Grave"

Judge Henry Kencade was in the den of his house, mixing a night cap, a gin and tonic, at his bar, before heading off to bed. While shaking the mixer, he noticed the time. He set it down and quickly walked over to turn on the television set.

Two news anchors introduced the evening news broadcast. "From CNN headline news, the top story tonight: Born on the twenty-ninth of September, 1925, Senator John Goodwin Tower, the Fort Worth Senator from the State of Texas, died suddenly today in a mysterious commuter plane crash near Brunswick, Georgia.

'Tower was an expert on military and national security affairs from 1961 to 1985 when he retired. He was appointed Chairman of the Armed Services Committee in his last years. After becoming a consultant to the weapons industry, he was asked in 1987 to chair the Commission that investigated Ronald Reagan's role in the Iran Contra scandal. He criticized Reagan as President, but nonetheless took his friend, then Vice-President George Bush, out of the loop.

"In January of 1989, after Bush took office, the newly elected President nominated his long time friend for Secretary of Defense. This ended in rejection from both the Senate and the House. Senator Tower was humiliated by the publicity of rumors he was a womanizer and a heavy drinker, casting him as morally unfit for the post! Instead, President Bush appointed him to the Foreign Intelligence Advisory Board which he chaired until his death. His colleagues are expected to honor him on the Senate Floor tomorrow morning!"

"In other news, film director Oliver Stone, whose controversial films include the Oscar-winning titles *Platoon* and *Born on the Fourth of July*, now has a new controversy brewing before his next film can reach the big screen. This continued harassment from the government was announced by Stone involving the making of his newest film, *JFK*, currently in production and scheduled to shoot in Dealey Plaza in Dallas, Texas. This feature film, produced under the auspices of the Warner Brothers Studio, now has another twist to it. Although he tried to keep the film under wraps, and shoot in secret, Stone has been furious over recent leaks to the media about his story.

"Reels of film have been missing from the production. And now the secretive screenplay under lock and key these past months has also been stolen. Stone feels the government is doing everything in its power to sabotage his film. No one knows whether this is a publicity stunt for the *JFK* production or an excuse to blame outside factors for the problems in completing his film. Could this be a sneak preview or an advanced warning that Hollywood's new wonder king may have a box office bomb come this Christmas season, and that our Oliver will do anything to leave us with no *Stone unturned*?"

The female broadcaster laughed at her male colleague's intended pun as she continued on with other news. "In the State of Indiana, a former judge, Henry Kencade, one time a nominee for the Supreme Court, has been instrumental in getting permission to exhume the body of Vietnam war hero and convicted serial killer, Karl Hunter, at Arlington National cemetery tomorrow afternoon. It's one law firm's concern to discover whether the body in the grave may or may not be the same man who committed suicide in his prison cell in 1988. Henry Kencade, now retired, along with two present colleagues in the State of Indiana and the District of Columbia, fought the United States military establishment to open the grave site at Arlington Cemetery honoring our war heroes and Presidents of the United States. The U.S. military states this is another way to desecrate our country's war heroes who've been laid to rest. These are men who have died in battles to preserve this country's Constitution. It has not been made clear to us why this exhumation is to occur. Hunter was never intended to be buried at Arlington until a protest of Vietnam War Veterans took precedence and petitioned the government. In the news and around the world next on--"

Henry Kencade turned the television off and stared blankly at the set. He took another sip of his gin and tonic. The telephone suddenly rang shaking Kencade out of his stupor. He set his drink on the bar and then answered the ringing phone.

The voice on the other end swore. "You know what you are digging into, you son of a bitch? Your own grave, that's what!"

Kencade startled asked, "Who is this speaking, hello, hello?" The other end of the line was disconnected. Kencade stared at the phone and was furious. He set the receiver back down on its base and again the phone rang, startling him. He quickly picked it back up, "Who is this, who is calling?"

There was only silence on the other end, then a voice answered. "Before you ever see death knocking at your door, Judge, you'll see your daughter buried first!" The caller hung up. Kencade's eyes widened with terror like the night before his court hearing in D.C. as he remembered the past events in 1988. Kencade then dialed 911 and asked the police department to come to his home to put a wire tap on all incoming calls. He wanted to get to the bottom of this once and for all.

* * *

On Sunday, the next day, a television crew along with the other members of the press gathered around a yellow taped perimeter surrounding a grave site. This one was in Arlington Cemetery. It was drizzling, and an examination tent was set up to exhume the body of Karl Hunter.

Judge Kencade and Catherine Rogers were to one side next to a roped-off area for them as they watched the coffin being lifted from the grave site.

Michael Bradley kept the press informed on the developments, but mainly made sure no one came near Catherine.

As a newscaster gave a report of the scene in front of a television camera near the Arlington Cemetery entrance, a black limo drove by, then slowed down as it neared the perimeter of the grave site.

"I believe we may have trouble!" a voice said inside the limo, as if speaking to himself. The car slowed to a stop as the back seat tinted window slid down to identify Senator Gerald Fuller. He spoke on his car phone as he watched what was happening at the exhumation. "The body, for Christ's sake! It's actually being exhumed this very minute...as we speak!"

In sunny Miami, Florida, on a penthouse balcony of the Fountainbleau Hotel, the man of Italian descent spoke with Senator Fuller on the other end of the line. "Well, well, well! Now it seems to be you who are in the panic mode at present. What can they find...notta! Nothing, right? So quit your sweating and squawking! I'm telling you this for your own good!"

The drizzle became a light rainfall now, outside the black limo. Inside, Fuller's voice intensified. "That fucking cunt! She...she is *not* dumb! I know her! She...she'll come up with something and start putting two and two together! If the lid comes off this one, *everything* will go to pieces! It will begin to crumble, and if it reaches certain people in the government, my career will be over! God *DAMN IT!* This nation...if ever the people find out they've been betrayed after all these years; our country will never be the same! The people would never trust us, let alone feel safe to live in their own country! My God, I'm afraid we may have a Goddamn revolution on our hands!"

On the balcony of the Fountainbleau Hotel, the man of Italian descent continued to calm the Senator down as he observed two naked teenage girls sitting in a Jacuzzi, in his penthouse apartment. "Believe me, Senator, there's nothing to worry about! Besides, there are officials much higher than yourself in D.C., experts who work with us, in positions you wouldn't imagine to dispute things you so worry yourself with. If it still bothers you, your friend Judge Kencade can be written off any time. After all he had undergone, who knows, he could have a sudden seizure. And his daughter, that attorney, well... If she gets out of hand, she'll meet with a nice little accident down the road. But for now, let's see how far she wants to play. Hell, Senator, she doesn't know who her opponents are yet!" he said smugly. He turned back to the Atlantic and laughed, then added one last chilling touch. "Senator, you should be glad they are not digging up Kennedy there in Arlington. Won't they be surprised what they'd find if that ever happened! Think about it, a President with a skull made of ninety-percent plaster of Paris, among other things... Good-bye, Senator!"

Inside the black limo at Arlington, Senator Fuller held the phone in his hand with a stunned look on his face. He quickly woke from his deep thought. A flash of lightening and a crash of thunder came from outside. Fuller fumbled with the phone, then hung up. He looked out at the grave site and rolled up the car window as it started raining hard, ordering the driver to move on.

Two pathologists and a dental hygienist inside a portable tent, hastily erected for the occasion, were conducting a preliminary examination of the body. When they opened the plain metal coffin, the body of Karl Hunter appeared to be well preserved. Photographs were taken, and someone with a video camera was directed where to shoot at specific areas of the body. Both Kencade and Catherine sat outside in a chair huddled together under an umbrella waiting nervously while Bradley continued to speak out to the media, getting drenched in the process. Jennifer was thoughtful enough to rush to his side with an umbrella.

A news reporter suddenly gestured at the tent catching Bradley and Jennifer's attention. The two pathologists and the dental hygienist exited the tent together. They conferred with an awaiting colleague, then approached Kencade and Catherine.

Catherine was nervous as she stood, noticing they had a glum look on their faces. The dental hygienist handed her the dental charts to look at. "There's no doubt about it...it's him, it's Karl Hunter!"

Catherine took the news hard. She hoped for some type of startling revelation to turn their investigation around or provide proof a conspiracy existed. She was still haunted by the man who attacked her-- the man with the face of Karl Hunter, or at least someone who resembled him. Now it was established the real Karl Hunter was in that coffin. There would be no more speculation he was really alive. Catherine's thoughts swirled in her mind as she tried to sort them out.

As the rain turned into a downpour, umbrellas opened over the scene. The press and camera crews rushed forward to get the story. They followed Catherine and Judge Kencade who walked beside the doctors to exit the cemetery. The press gathered around the doctors as they stopped to give them an informal press conference. Catherine continued to walk away, refusing to answer any questions. Kencade accompanied her, repeating to the reporters, "No comment! No comment at this time!"

An outsider stood in the background watching the proceedings from a distance. John Modini, wearing dark glasses, discretely moved from the crowd going in the opposite direction and headed to Michael Bradley who reluctantly decided to stay behind. Modini approached Bradley who didn't seem to recognize him. "Mr. Bradley! May I have a word with you?"

Bradley didn't want to see anyone right now. "Please, I really don't need this. I've already said what I told you people already. There will be a formal press conference in a day or two, once the examination is complete. If you want a one-on-one, you'll have to make arrangements with my office for an appointment. As you can see, it's all over for now..."

Modini cut in. "Mr. Bradley, I don't know whether you recognize me. My name is John Modini. We met in '88 at--"

Now it was Bradley's turn to react. He blinked and stood staring at the man before him.

"Are you all right," Modini asked.

Bradley smiled and relaxed, then found his voice. "Sorry! My God! We thought you were dead! We've been looking everywhere for you!"

Modini reluctantly nodded, "I think we better find a safe place to talk. I believe our lives are in danger!"

The men left the cemetery and sat down in a small cafe. Modini filled in Bradley with his missing years. He explained his connection to Hunter, the investigations that had taken him across the country leading up to the odd coincidence in the death of Karl Hunter and, in some ways, its connection to Lee Harvey Oswald.

So he told Bradley he was thrown into a loop when he learned Catherine staged Hunter's exhumation.

Bradley, however, was a bit amazed about the facts he revealed about Hunter and Oswald when Modini was supposedly one of the foremost authorities on Oswald's guilt as the sole assassin. Modini laughed, "Hey, I can make mistakes, too, like anyone else. I was as much duped as anyone with the government's broad plan for spreading misinformation!"

Bradley acknowledged Modini's sincerity, "Yes, Mr. Modini, but you actually were allowed to preach it in your periodicals and newspaper articles to the world!"

Modini knew of his guilt and had a hard time acknowledging it. He asked Bradley, "Didn't you ever write a false report or involve yourself in a breach of contract or a deposition that you felt wasn't trustworthy? Have you ever gone before a judge in court and stretched the truth for your client's case?"

"All right, all right! You're killing me!" Bradley, held his hand up to stop. "I have only to say, no comment! You win!"

Modini tried to compose himself. "The only difference here is I believed in what I wrote all those years! I'm just sorry I was so naive! I've also got to say I've never met an attorney I've ever liked."

"Well, I forgive you that one," Bradley smiled. "About Karl Hunter's exhumation, you'll have to talk with Catherine to find out why she staged this-- what the media will call an exhibition. I suspect my clientele will dwindle off for the next few months and my law firm will take a dive."

Modini disagreed. "No, no, no... Don't push this aside. Like I said, I don't know why Catherine Rogers did what she did, but I'm glad she did it. I mean, I knew Karl hunter's body would be there, it would have to be him, no doubt. But what was Catherine thinking, why did you go along with her? Hell, you got me here out of hiding. That means there'll be others, and I mean what I said when I told you I believe all of us-- you, me, Catherine-- are in grave danger. If word is out that I'm alive, I'm as good as dead...again!" he made a weak joke.

Bradley was quiet as he realized Modini risked his life to be here, knowing what he already discovered these past months. "Mr. Modini--!"

Modini cut in, "You can call me Jack or John-- either one is fine."

Bradley continued, "All right, Jack then, if you don't mind. Catherine thinks you're on a hit list, or were on a hit list since all of us gave you up for dead..."

"What type of hit list?" Modini asked.

"She can give you more theory and detail," Bradley said, "but she thinks after Hunter's death there were two or three of you left alive in your platoon from the Vietnam War. I know it sounds crazy, but one of my ex-staff members who did research for Catherine discovered the fact most of your unit was killed either while you were over there or when you returned to the States. It's a fact, isn't it, the ones who did return to the states are now all dead, including the most recent death of Roger Tracy. You were the last one to 'die,' and now you have risen again from the grave. I think this has something to do with what Catherine was trying to find out at the cemetery today."

Modini reared back. "This was done because of me?"

Bradley explained. "Not exactly, but it did tell us all members of your Platoon did not die of natural causes. No, Jack, I have to tell you something I thought I wouldn't have to repeat to anyone. To be blunt with you, I'm sure it would be hard for Catherine to tell you this part of it. You see, the time you disappeared off the face of the earth was the time Catherine ordered our office to find you. She wanted to save your life. Don't ask me why, because I have no idea, but it did have something to do with Karl Hunter."

Modini listened to Bradley and wondered why Catherine was involving him in this investigation. He got the answer.

Bradley cleared his throat, "What I'm trying to say, Jack, was...she was brutally raped that night, the day you disappeared. She believes to this day Karl Hunter was the one who raped her! Crazy, right? Insane, isn't it?" Modini could see Bradley was embarrassed to disclose the fact.

He was upset to learn Catherine was raped, but wasn't surprised with Bradley's last revelation. "No, Michael ...insane, yes! But not so crazy as you think. Catherine may have the answer to a puzzle I've had a problem putting together"

Bradley's eyes narrowed. "You say you believe Catherine, even after today?"

Modini stared past Bradley and thought aloud. "I see that piece of the puzzle now. Catherine may be the person who could possibly clear this mystery up. She was a witness to what I need. That's why she had this exhumation. It all makes sense!"

Bradley was even more confused. "I'm glad you can make sense of it, it's killing me!"

Modini smiled, "You'll have to get a meeting set up with her. That is, if she'll talk to me."

Bradley looked at him strangely. "Oh, she'll talk to you. You may be just what the doctor ordered! How can I get in touch with you?"

"I'll call you at your office in Madison tomorrow morning around eleven a.m. if that's okay?"

"Sounds good," Bradley said. And upon that agreement, he nodded and shook hands with John Modini. Then they left the cafe, each going their separate ways.

* * *

A high-rise apartment complex became the focus of attention for Catherine Rogers in the early evening in Washington D.C. She observed the building as she sat in the back seat of a yellow cab parked on the street. The blue sky darkened, and some of the lights came on in the building. *Well, It's now or never,* she thought to herself.

Catherine got out of the cab. She was dressed as if she wanted to be mistaken as a man, wearing a heavy coat, jeans, sporting boots and a western cowboy hat. She paid the cab driver and asked him to stick around a few minutes in case her party wasn't in.

Catherine studied the building a few minutes more before approaching it on foot. She paused a moment, took out her beige Motorola cellular phone from her purse and dialed a number written down on a piece of paper. The phone rang, and a voice recorder came on the other end. The voice of Max Slaton announced he wasn't in and to leave a name and number for him to return this call.

Catherine hesitated to say anything at first, but quickly took a breath and spoke up, "My name is Catherine Rogers. I got your number from Richard Franklin who tried to reach John Modini from Los Angeles. I'm calling from my Cellular phone. My number is--"

She was interrupted suddenly by the real voice of Max Slaton, "Where are you calling from?" he quickly asked her.

"Is this Max Slaton?" Catherine nervously asked.

"Yes, this is he..." Max answered, "now, where are you calling from?"

"Well, actually I'm right outside the lobby of your apartment complex!"

The line was silent. Then Max made his request, "I would appreciate it very much if you would see me in person. I'm on the fourteenth floor, room 1402."

Uneasy at first, Catherine yielded to his offer, knowing this meeting was inevitable. "Is Mr. Modini there with you?"

There was no answer, only a click on the other end of the line letting her know she had been disconnected. Catherine went into the building.

A knock at the door signaled Max Slaton to check his peep hole. He peered through it and saw Catherine Rogers standing alone on the other side of the door. This time she was not wearing her western cowboy hat. Instead, she held it nervously in her hands.

The door opened and Max allowed Catherine to enter. "You weren't followed, I presume?"

Catherine put her hat back on her head. "I usually never wear a get-up like this. And I tried to take precautions before making this trip here. Besides, I think whoever is following me wants what I have in Madison, not here in D.C."

Catherine took her hat off again as a voice came from a bedroom, "And what would that be, Mrs. Rogers?"

Catherine, still nervous, turned around to confront the man entering from the back bedroom. She was apprehensive, but smiled just the same, "Mr. Modini? Is that you?"

John Modini nodded, accepting her recognition of him. She was caught off guard as what to do next. Being the professional person she was, Catherine stuck her arm out to shake his hand, but Modini didn't respond. For Modini's part, he was so tense, he couldn't move and stared at Catherine's hand.

Catherine felt like an idiot with her arm sticking out, so she took the initiative. She stepped forward and reached for his hand. Modini finally recognized her gesture and shook her hand.

Catherine blinked, and tried to find the right words. "I'm so glad you're alive, Mr. Modini!"

Modini acknowledged this, "So am I, Mrs. Rogers. And I'm sure my mother feels the same as you do!"

"Oh, your mother, yes," Catherine broke into a smile. "I'm sure she would be. Do...do you realize how many people out there think you're dead right now?"

Modini grinned back. "Yes, I do, Mrs. Rogers-- and I hope they continue to think that way for now!"

Catherine was a bit surprised by his reply. "Oh, you do? Uh, ah...Catherine... You can call me Catherine if you'd like!"

"And you can call me John...since that's the name you've always known me by..."

Max was getting tired of this back and forth getting acquainted routine. "I don't know what you two will do or talk about, but I'm going to leave you alone while I go to the nearest bar. My place is all yours."

Catherine stopped him from departing. "Mr. Slaton, please don't leave on my account. I have a cab waiting for me downstairs. I was thinking, John... If you would like to join me, we could drive out to the Lincoln Memorial. We could talk and get a bit of exercise, too, if...if that's all right with you?"

Modini thought it was a good idea. "All right. Max, why don't you stay put. That way you can stick by the phone."

The taxi driver watched as he saw his customer exit the building with her friend, John Modini. The two of them got into his cab.

"Thank you for waiting," Catherine told the cab driver.

"Where to, Miss?" the cabbie asked

"Somewhere romantic," Catherine said jokingly. "Can you take us to the Lincoln Memorial?"

"You're kidding, right?" the cab driver responded.

Catherine became embarrassed. "No, I...unless you're trying to tell us it's not safe at this time of the evening?"

The driver laughed, "No, I didn't mean it that way! It's just a cliché. Whenever people come to Washington, I can take them anywhere they want-- but the Lincoln Memorial is not the most romantic place to go, if you know what I mean."

Catherine and Modini laughed, and the taxi took off into the night. Immediately after it pulled away, a car parked a block away started its engine. The lights turned on, and it moved out in the direction of the taxicab.

A short time later they arrived at the Lincoln Memorial. Modini and Catherine dismissed the taxi, and they walked up the broad stone stairs. Once at the top they took a brief look around at the giant figure of Lincoln and the carved words of his Getteysberg Address on the wall. They didn't start any serious talk until they decided to sit on the top steps. From their position they looked down over the great sweep of stairs below them and had a marvelous view of the Washington Monument in the distance, lit up for the night, against the sky of stars above.

"I'm glad we finally got together," Catherine confessed, "Michael told me you were going to pick the time and place for our meeting, and I could hardly wait. So much has happened since the last time we talked. Why didn't you tell me who you were and that you and Karl Hunter were friends?"

Modini was quiet for the moment, then followed up. "To tell you the truth, I felt, at the time, it was no one's business. I didn't want anyone to know I was investigating Hunter's background, and I didn't trust anyone for that matter. Hell, I didn't even know who you were until I saw on the news and they said you were Judge Kencade's daughter. It was about what happened here."

Catherine looked into Modini's eyes. "What do you know about my father?"

Modini was almost afraid to answer. "Well, only who he is and what he did in the public eye. I've only met him once, besides the last time you and I met."

"You mean in Washington, at that restaurant?"

Modini nodded and hesitantly added, "Yes... And that weekend in 1967 in Santa Barbara!"

Catherine again stared at him strangely, trying to make sense of what he was saying. With a growing realization, fragments of her memory started to return. She tilted her head awkwardly as she finally recalled their previous encounter. "You mean, you're him? That spring when we were just kids?"

Modini grinned broadly, "Oh so you <u>do</u> remember that day? I didn't think you'd ever figure that one out!"

"Oh, I remember? Oh, God, do I!" Catherine shifted uneasily. "I wasn't the best person to be around then. Many personal things were happening in my life. I remember you were that skinny kid. And I...I was very mean to you..."

Modini nodded silently in agreement.

Catherine gave a hopeful smile. "Can you accept my apology after all these twenty-odd years?"

Modini now laughed, surprising her. "I'll accept anything after that day. It was one of the worst days I've ever experienced, believe me! I didn't think you were mean, though. I thought--

you want to know what I really thought-- I thought you were the prettiest girl I'd ever seen. I even committed your name to memory. It was a shame you turned out to be such a brat!"

Catherine put a hand over her face as she blushed in embarrassment, "A brat!"

"Yes," Modini repeated, "a spoiled thirteen-year old brat who, like me, didn't want to be where she was at that time! Someone who was used to getting anything she wanted and having her own way! If you didn't want to get to know me that was your problem, not mine!"

Catherine looked at Modini, shaking her head at his brashness. "You're not modest, are you?"

They stared at each other unemotionally, for a few seconds, and then, as if on cue, they both burst into laughter. As the laughter trailed off, Catherine asked, "All right, if I were a brat, what was your problem that day? You could have pursued me if you had any guts!"

"That's it!" Modini pointed a finger at her. "You hit it right there on the button. I had no guts! I was a spineless person looking for company. Looking for someone to talk to. There were things happening in my life, too! Like many guys my age, I had one big worry on my mind-- was I going to be drafted or not?"

Catherine was silent, not knowing whether Modini was kidding her or not. Either way it was a sticky subject to pursue so she tried to be diplomatic about his statement. "I don't think you were spineless, John. Anyone who travels to a foreign country and fights for their own country, no matter what the reason, is a hero in my eyes.

She paused awkwardly as painful memories returned. She gazed out into the night sky, past the Washington Monument. "My... My brother was killed in Vietnam when I was eleven. I'll never forget that...and I still don't understand why we were over there in the first place! I saw what it did to my mother. And I saw what it did to the young men, no older than yourself, and the burden they had to bear when they returned to the states! To this day I believe war is a room filled with misunderstood men with power! No, John-- You might have been confused maybe, scared yes, but not spineless! I don't think you could never be that!"

459

Modini looked at her, trying to hold back his own tears. Her words conjured up deep memories of his own past, preventing him from responding. He took her hand and squeezed it, then released it quickly, to show his thanks.

Modini stood up and wiped the tears from his eyes. "Let's take a walk," he suggested, "I need to tell you something!"

The two of them descended the memorial stairs. Catherine endured the silence until they reached the bottom step, then spoke up. "I can now say I, sort of, saw the Lincoln Memorial. Was it a first for you, too?"

Modini nodded, then changed the subject to something she said earlier in Max Slaton's apartment. "You mentioned the fact no one followed you to me because what they need from you is not here, but in Madison. What did you mean by that?"

Catherine stopped at the bottom step. Modini knew by her expression something concerned her. "Mr. Modini...John! I came to see you tonight because I had to know you were really alive. I don't know whether any of this is a coincidence or if it's just destiny working its way through our lives. I know I made a big blunder today, exhuming Hunter's coffin. I feel as though I were Geraldo Rivera opening Al Capone's safe in Chicago and finding what-- an empty bottle? I embarrassed many people today that mean a lot to me. My family and friends took a great risk for me, and I blew it!"

Modini smiled and looked into Catherine's eyes. They darted everywhere but to him. "Hey," Modini said confidently, "don't beat yourself up about what you did or had to do. I'm glad you did it. We wouldn't be here right now talking this very minute if you hadn't done what you wanted!"

Catherine was stumped. "You're glad...why?"

Modini guided her in the direction of the Washington Monument and answered her while they walked. "You said something about destiny. I don't believe in coincidence. A coincidence is something I feel is done on purpose." He glanced up at the night sky and the stars overhead. "Do you believe in God?" he asked searchingly.

Catherine was caught off guard, "I guess so. Either that or I'm crazy, constantly talking to myself. I guess it's probably God I'm talking to."

Modini smiled his best smile for her, "I believe God is working in us always. He's working through you and me to get to the truth!"

"You mean about Karl Hunter?"

"Well, first I thought that, but no-- God has used Karl Hunter for you and me to seek the truth. I truly believe what you did today helped us put a piece of a puzzle together that may explain an important event in the history of our country."

Catherine blinked, wondering where this conversation was heading, "So...you believe Karl was innocent?"

Modini nodded his head. "Yes, what Michael told me today finally makes sense to me."

"Michael told you what happened to me and why I wanted the exhumation?"

Modini nodded again, "Yes! And I'm glad you went through with it!"

Catherine was lost for words and embarrassed. "But...but I'm afraid it only made me look crazy or delusional! I thought I saw Karl Hunter less than a week after his death. This man, whomever he was...actually raped me...and tried to kill me, John! Apparently, this man was not the real Karl Hunter, and my obsession proved me wrong. What I saw or thought I saw then tells me I'd better keep my mouth shut or I'll find myself back in the hospital. On top of that, there's a chance I'll be disbarred from ever practicing law again. Right now, I'm being mocked by the media. Who will ever want me as an attorney after this?"

Modini and Catherine continued to walk.

"Catherine, what was the urgency that brought you to me? I, too, couldn't wait to see you. That says something about what I feel. But I had a reason to see you. What, may I ask, is yours?"

"There are two things I need to understand. If you believe in Karl Hunter's innocence, then the first thing I must ask is if you're aware of the strange phenomenon concerning the men you served with in Vietnam. I'm talking about the mysterious deaths of those who died there and those who returned. My investigation revealed some of the men in your platoon picked for special assignment never returned from their mission-- and those that did, were supposedly casualties. But while researching Father Daniel Conrad, a member of your platoon, we recently discovered some of those men who died were actually victims of friendly fire."

Modini didn't say anything to refute Catherine. It made him feel guilty, and he didn't want to respond. He allowed her to continue, knowing he was hiding something from her, and it was painful to be reminded of the fact. Modini had a momentary flashback-- images of the airfield and the body bags being loaded aboard a transport plane. Again, Karl Hunter was there, explaining to him the significance of the body bags-- knowledge Modini possessed to this day, but continued to keep a secret.

Catherine saw she hit a raw nerve. She proceeded to explain tactfully. "But I don't think 'friendly fire' was an accident-- that's what friendly fire is, right? I mean, our own military killed your men, something that wasn't in the original report. It wasn't until Father Conrad came forward and demanded the truth, that our military brass had to admit it was friendly fire. In reality, I believe it wasn't friendly at all, but someone who <u>deliberately</u> wanted the men in your platoon to die and not return home! I'm still searching for the reason. Now my second question. Tell me, John, about Father Daniel Conrad. Is he alive or dead today?" She knew the answer to that. She wanted to hear what Modini had to say.

Modini was surprised and irritated by her question. "Do you want to dig his body up as well? I was there, in New Hampshire, when they buried him! It was in early '82...late winter."

Catherine studied Modini's sorrowful eyes and saw the pain within, the loss that came from losing a good friend. "I wanted to know whether you knew if Father Conrad was dead? And you certainly agree Karl Hunter is buried out there in Arlington. And recently, the body of Colonel Roger Tracy was found in Priest River in Northern Idaho, supposedly after he committed suicide..."

"Yes, what's your point?" Modini wanted to end this conversation.

Catherine tried to explain before he got upset. "Well, *you*, John, are now considered *dead*! Ever since you were reported missing, everyone assumed you to be dead. That makes it a very odd coincidence every one of you in your platoon was killed, in one way or another. You just told me you don't believe in coincidences. Maybe you can explain it to me!"

Modini thought about it and then gave his own opinion. "No, what's happening is not a coincidence. Do you know why I disappeared? There's a reason! Yes, I believe somebody wants me dead. And the only way I'll find out who it is and why they're after me is to stay low! I thought, first, Roger Tracy was involved, but now I think he was just used to track the rest of us down for elimination. They thought I was dead, so they eliminated the final person, which turned out to be Tracy himself. He made the big mistake of trusting the people he worked for when, in actuality, he was a pawn used by them. He was ordered to discredit Hunter, which was not hard to do since they hated each other's guts."

"Who was Tracy working for?" Catherine asked.

Modini gave an impromptu answer, "Naval Intelligence!"

Catherine didn't say anything, mulling this over.

Modini felt like this was his cue to proceed with his original question, the one he wanted to ask. "What's the matter! Are you concerned with the letter Hunter provided you before he died?"

Catherine was caught off guard. "How do you know about that?" she asked him abruptly.

"That's why I'm here, Catherine. There are people out there who are searching for a certain letter. At first, they thought I had it, and when I didn't cooperate, they attempted to kill me. These people will do anything to get this letter, and that means they *know* you or Michael Bradley must have it! I'm sure you're being watched at every turn, and that's why Max Slaton asked you whether or not you were followed! I knew immediately what you meant when you made that statement earlier. Listen to me, Catherine," Modini pleaded, "Your life is in grave danger and I'm here to help you!"

Catherine became frightened by the intensity of Modini's revelation. "John, how...how am I to know I can trust you? You could easily be one of them?"

Modini was dumbfounded, never thinking for a minute he had to prove himself. "For one, Catherine," he told her, "you're still alive, aren't you?"

Catherine backed away, her suspicions growing. "Yeah, but I haven't told you anything yet. Maybe you're waiting until I tell you something you want to know!" Modini was making her nervous now.

Modini, too, was on the defensive. He stepped away from her as well. "Okay, Catherine, if it makes it easier for you, I'll prove it to you. I'm not here for what you think, I'm not working for anyone, I just want the truth to come out, that's all-- and to save your life. You want to be suspicious of me? Fine! Then I'm going to leave. I'll go my separate way, and you can go yours. If you want to talk to me, ask Michael Bradley to call me. I'll leave word with him tomorrow where and when he can find me."

Modini turned and walked away.

"Stop!" Catherine yelled out.

Modini stopped and swung around to face her. She stepped forward and asked, "Mr. Modini...John! I need to know something from you-- just one more thing!"

Modini didn't say a word. He lifted his arms in the air as if to say, what?

"John, do you have a daughter?"

Modini stared at her a long moment before answering. He knew it was a serious question. "Not to my knowledge. Why do you ask?"

Catherine chose her words carefully. She didn't want to offend Modini. She wanted to get the information from him. "Was there any-- I mean, did you have any experience or relationship in Vietnam or Cambodia that could possibly explain why I'm asking you this question?"

Modini remembered his first experience with the Vietnamese girl whom he saw once and never saw again. He felt that it could not be possible. He knew she was dead. None the less, the doubt was planted in his mind. He asked, "How old is this girl?"

Catherine thought quickly, "Well, I met her in 1988, when she turned thirteen. She was supposedly raped by Karl Hunter six months earlier. The name given to her when she was submitted to the hospital, was Carrie Modini, the same as yours!"

Modini smiled now to himself. "Modini, huh? Funny, there's your coincidence after all!" he said flippantly. "I wish I could say she was mine, but that makes her birth to be in '75 or so... I left in '69, so I'm sorry to say she isn't mine!"

Catherine was disappointed by his answer. "I see, Mr. Modini, but can you explain this. Why does a half-American, half-Cambodian girl, raped by Karl Hunter, have *your* given name? What if I were to tell you Carrie was placed in the care of a mental hospital, and sponsored by the Catholic Church?"

Modini gave a careless shrug. It didn't mean anything to him.

Catherine continued, "...sponsored by a Father Daniel Conrad. He was the one who registered her for observation and care, six months prior to my introduction to her in 1988-- a man you say died in 1982!"

Modini was stunned by this information. Catherine sensed his alarm and asked sarcastically, "I would say that is a remarkable coincidence, wouldn't you, Mr. Modini?"

Modini nodded in silence and then told her, "I don't have any answers for you." He tried to put together some type of explanation. "It couldn't have been Conny, because I know he's dead. Could It have been someone posing as Conny? I don't know! I'm hearing this for the first time. Maybe I can look into it later. There has to be an answer to this.

"Do you know of any way of finding out?"

No, not at this time." Modini was flustered. "Right now, the most important thing for us to do is to lie low and avoid drawing attention. I'll have to look into this thing about Conny-- Father Conrad later. Remember, Catherine, I'm dead! No one, besides you and Mr. Bradley, are to know this! Until we meet again, I suggest you be very cautious yourself, especially if you insist on keeping Hunter's letter in your possession. I'm seriously reminding you, your life is in danger! If I were you, I'd destroy the letter or give it up to the authorities. If you don't, whoever is after it will get to you, eventually."

Modini started to leave, but Catherine stopped him again, "John! There are two letters! One contained a tape recorded by Karl Hunter, the other was written by-- in Hunter's words-- a man known only as Mister X. This second letter, written in 1963, hasn't been opened. Hunter told me if his death looked like a suicide, I was to go to the post office and pick it up. It was addressed to my father. All I can say for now, is that's it's in safekeeping."

"What did Karl say on the tape?" Modini asked.

Catherine approached him again. She was hesitant to answer, but knew he had to know the truth. "Hunter left a tape with my father. He said in it that my father should have this material, and if he were an honest judge he would know what to do with it."

"What is your father's involvement in all this?"

Catherine's voice faltered. "I-- I don't know. My father doesn't want any part of it. He thinks Hunter was a nut case, and after today, I'm sure he must think the same of his daughter!"

"What if I told you what you did today was the only thing that made any sense. You said that it was Karl Hunter who raped you. You could identify him! You even said you saw him twice-- although he's dead and buried in Arlington. Yes, I knew Karl would be there in his coffin, but you said you saw him alive. By uncovering the bodies of those murdered victims, you proved that they were buried by the man responsible who you said you saw alive.

Catherine did not understand. "But why? Why do you say you believe me? Are you saying this to me out of pity?"

Modini snapped back, "I don't know what Karl wrote or said to you or your father. You may think me crazy for what I'm about to say, but here goes. There are two ways of looking at this! If the real Karl Hunter did kill himself in his prison cell, it was because he was protecting someone. Why? I *knew* Karl! He would have been shouting his innocence in that courtroom, if something weren't preventing him from doing so. Then again, if the man killed in that cell wasn't Hunter, then the real Hunter might have died in Gary, Indiana, as you claimed.

"But you said you knew it would be Karl Hunter in the grave," Catherine stated bluntly. "It sounds as though you're confused, saying there were two of them!"

Modini nodded, "That's what I'm saying, yes!"

"But that's absurd! Even my father could poke holes in that theory!" exclaimed Catherine.

Modini agreed with her. "I said you might not believe me. Do you remember the last time we met here in Washington, at the Velvet Fountain? You were on the phone, and you were told that someone within the government appropriated Karl's body. The autopsy was halted, and no one had access to the cause of death. The autopsy was to be done by the military and the autopsy report sealed. Well, someone wanted to verify the other Karl Hunter was accounted for and eventually, you did that for them. You did say Hunter's body was left at the scene following your ordeal in Gary, Indiana. And what did the authorities find?"

"Nothing! No body was discovered. But I *know* I saw--"

"--Yes I know-- Karl Hunter!" Modini finished. "That's correct, so what does that mean? Now two bodies have disappeared. Two bodies we know to be Karl Hunter's! Problem solved, both bodies are accounted for-- made to vanish in the public eye. Then the real Hunter is finally given permission to be buried in Arlington Cemetery after a nationwide protest of Vietnam Veterans!"

Catherine followed the scenario but was skeptical. "You're saying Karl Hunter was somehow a victim of the wrong man syndrome. You were there in court! Was that the real Karl Hunter you knew, or not?"

"Yes, it was! I believe it was Karl you were defending, and that he knew *he* was the wrong man in the wrong place. But you said yourself, you thought at one time he was trying to protect something or someone. I knew that last day in court it was Karl. Never once while I was in that courtroom did he, in all those weeks, ever try to grant me recognition. It was almost as if he were

467

protecting me. He always protected me, since we've known each other, and now I know why. Finally that last day before they took him out of the courtroom, he turned to me. You were talking to Bradley at the time. Karl let me know for the first time he knew I was there. He smiled at me. And now I'll tell you the real reason he either committed suicide or was killed. If he did kill himself, it was to let people know the *real* killer was still out there. He wasn't the serial killer you thought he was. He was being set up-- framed because of the information he had-- and allowed you to possess-- in that letter!"

"So everything that's happened so far was because someone wants the information in that letter?" Catherine asked.

"That's right," Modini replied, "And now for the crazy part. I believe this trial was a facade, and I'm not saying this to belittle the serial killings of these girls. This was a tragedy, one that was to rile up the country-- and that's what it did. Until we meet again, I'm leaving you with one thought-- and you, Michael Bradley and your father will have plenty of thinking to do before you make your next move. I believe the real reason everything happened, including Karl Hunter's death, has something to do with, or is connected in some way to Lee Harvey Oswald!"

"Oh Jesus!" were the only words from Catherine's mouth.

Her loud exclamation surprised Modini. "What?"

"The letters!" Catherine exclaimed, "Hunter's tape mentions November twenty-second, 1963. My God, how do you know this?"

Modini put his hands on her shoulders. "Calm down, Catherine! I *didn't* know! It was a lucky guess..."

Catherine gave a sarcastic laugh, "Yeah, right. A coincidence, as you say." Catherine moved away from him again, refusing to trust him. She felt he was playing a game of cat and mouse with her and she didn't like it. The tears welled up in her eyes. "I don't believe it. He isn't involved! Yet, in some way, I do think he was being used!" she said to herself.

Modini didn't know what she meant. "Please, don't be afraid. Now who do you believe

468

isn't involved, and who's being used?"

Catherine gave Modini a fierce look, "My father! Why would Hunter give this information to him-- through me?"

Modini remained silent for the moment, trying to rationalize all this himself. He came up with the only explanation he could. "I believe, Catherine. As I said before, Karl was protecting someone or something, and he knew he would die. Your father was a respectable judge, a top ranking one and well respected throughout the country. He would have made a great Supreme Court Justice. Hunter must have known this and wanted the truth to come out after he was dead, knowing your father would have a guilty conscience if he tried to avoid it. Catherine, he believed enough in you to hand the information over to you instead. He must have trusted you to do something courageous. I have to say, so far you made a good start with his exhumation. You proved that the real Karl Hunter was in the coffin. It was he because it was supposed to be him, remember. It was the same with Lee Harvey Oswald back when his grave was exhumed."

Catherine said candidly. "Yes, and your magazine articles positively embarrassed the heck out of those involved in that wild goose chase-- as it's embarrassing me now! I'm the laughing stock on the news!"

Modini was a bit embarrassed himself. "I must confess, there was more to the story than what I told. Like you and Hunter, there were people out there who never made an appearance to the Warren Commission because they had seen Oswald in one place when he was in another. For instance, he was supposed to be in Mexico City, in September 1963, when someone was with him in Austin, Texas. Also in 1960 and 1961, he was seen here, in the United States, when he was a defector in Moscow. Oswald was in different places simultaneously! You, however, say you saw Karl Hunter when you knew he was dead. Someone out there wants you to look crazy no matter what you did or proved, as long as you believed that!

"What I didn't write about in those articles was the fact Marina Oswald allowed the exhumation to be filmed and was to be the sole owner of that property. When Oswald was examined by the pathologists, it was discovered, like in your case with Hunter, it was undoubtedly the real Lee Harvey Oswald. When the gentlemen who originally embalmed Oswald back in November, 1963, got their turn to examine him, they came to another conclusion. Yes, they both agreed it was Oswald all right, and would later report it wasn't the same person who was buried that November day.

"This person grew two inches taller, they said, and there was no sign of a craniotomy they performed. His head had no visible scars! From the dental records and his Marine file it *was* Oswald, but not the one they had buried in 1963!"

"This was in 1981, right?" Catherine asked. "Why would these two morticians say this or lie about it?"

"Well, it all stems from the documentation of the film that was shot, Modini continued, "in addition to the eyewitnesses who saw the grave and the position of the coffin. You have to know this, the coffin itself was set in a cement-sealed vault. The only way someone could get to Oswald would be to smash through the cement to get to the original coffin. Now if nature were involved, then the only destruction or damage made to the coffin could have been done by an earthquake-- but then again how often have you ever heard of an earthquake happening in Dallas, Texas?" Modini raised his eyebrows questioningly.

Catherine was shocked, "Are you saying someone broke into Oswald's grave?"

Modini explained, "I'm just as startled as you. The reason I'm saying this is because of a document declassified in 1975 written by a Warren Commission lawyer back in 1964. I believe Slawson was his name. This is how early this story goes back because Oswald's mother asked for an exhumation in 1967, to see whether it really was her son buried there. That's scary enough."

"But then how did she get this idea in 1967?" Catherine asked.

"Well, since 1978-79 a British author, Eddowes, I believe his name, has been speculating Oswald was a double substituted in Russia and sent here to hit Kennedy. I don't buy that idea-- I never did-- but the more I study it, the more I continue coming up with more Oswalds popping up everywhere prior to the assassination! The Warren Commission's excuse was that every person who spoke with the Committee or a member of the Committee had to be mistaken since the Committee's proof was Oswald couldn't have been in one location when he was where they-- the Commission-- already decided he was in order for their chronology to make sense! Instead of accepting these witnesses versions and investigating the fact there were more than one Oswald, the Committee refused to ask who kept popping up in the wrong place and at the same time? Didn't the Warren Commission want to investigate the possibility of a double? Getting back to Slawson, that Commission lawyer, why did he write this classified report at the time stating the CIA wanted to dig up Oswald in 1964 to see whether he had a scar on his wrist because he supposedly tried to commit suicide his first month in Moscow?"

Catherine interrupted, "Oswald tried to commit suicide-- in Russia?"

"That's the story and it's a long one, and I don't have time to explain, but in one sentence, he did it so he wouldn't be deported back to the U.S. This British man, Eddowes, felt it might have been then when the Russians-- the KGB, whoever-- wanted to make a switch. Marina wouldn't know whether that was the real Oswald, or a trained Russian she married or not!"

Catherine was wide-eyed, "I'm mostly shocked, hearing this coming from you after reading some of your articles! This is totally opposite of what you've always said you believed in! You've always supported the theory Oswald was the lone gunman."

Modini nodded, grim and somber. "I'm not going to apologize, because there's many people out there who need to do a lot of explaining, including Robert Blakley who chaired the House Select Committee and formed its final report-- and who by now has the declassified information to pursue an investigation. If it weren't for people like Richard Franklin whose dedication and research he's put into this investigation, these facts would be buried forever. Unfortunately, it's a shame for the House Select Committee to have all this information dropped in the hands of a Blakley just to let it all fall apart. There is no excuse for Congress or the Senate to form committees to seek the truth and then have one of their own sabotage the investigation. I can

471

see why they would have done it. It might reveal fingers getting caught in the cookie jar. Maybe it would reveal some secrets that would rock the foundation of this country of ours."

Modini pointed to the Washington Monument, lit up against the night sky, and asked, "This America the beautiful! Hell, give me any day, 'your tired, your poor!' Let's see what our leaders are really doing to them! The people certainly won't like it when they find out the rain that falls on them from our leaders is really piss after all!"

Catherine felt distracted with his histrionics, but what he said earlier intrigued her. "John, I can see you're serious and mean what you say. You honestly believe Karl Hunter might have had a double-- or Oswald was more than one person?"

"Now I do," Modini said, attempting to calm down. "I'm sorry, I thought maybe I lost you-- that you'd walk away thinking me crazy.

Catherine felt a little uneasy. She asked, "What was the condition of Oswald's grave when they exhumed him?"

"Oswald's grave had been tampered with. The cement vault was broken apart, and Oswald's own coffin was in pieces. The two men who had embalmed Oswald made sure whenever the day came to reopen his coffin, his body would be preserved. Instead, the body was practically mummified. Prior to all this, there were political reasons and government people trying to stop the exhumation. It wasn't until Marina Oswald joined forces with Eddowes that the order for exhumation was finally granted in October 1981."

"Was Oswald's mother present at his exhumation?"

"No, it was held just months after Marguerite Oswald's death. The funny thing about all this was, she always wanted her son exhumed, but the one person who tried to stop it was Oswald's own brother, Robert. That I'll never understand! I mean, you wanted to know whether the man you were defending was Karl Hunter or not-- to exonerate the person who wasn't guilty. Why wouldn't Oswald's brother want him exonerated if it weren't him? And why did he keep proclaiming his brother's guilt to this day when his mother fought for his innocence all these years."

"Wait a minute," Catherine interrupted. "Didn't Oswald have a second brother-- a half-brother?"

"Yes, he did. And Oswald's own half-brother agreed with their mother of the difference in Lee Harvey Oswald, not only in appearance but the way he talked and the manner he approached them! History books tell us Robert Hauptman was involved in the Lindbergh baby kidnapping. Hauptman's wife had spent every day of her life proclaiming her husband's innocence! Now, Marina is out there defending Oswald as the same pawn Lee himself proclaimed to be back in November, 1963."

"And your gut instinct says Karl Hunter, too, was a pawn in this whole situation," she said, considering his theory.

"Listen, Catherine. Karl Hunter didn't kill anyone unless it was in the line of duty! Something happened in Vietnam to the two of us that'll never be forgotten! I can't talk about it now, but I may have to some day! All I can say is, we both were involved with a situation we couldn't stop. I, for one, was not told about it until after the fact-- and Hunter who *was* told, would not participate. So I think I knew him well enough to know he could never have killed those young girls!"

Modini's words stirred a disturbing thought in Catherine's mind. "What if I told you about a video tape I saw. It was a tape showing Karl Hunter having sexual intercourse with a twelve-year old Cambodian girl here in the states?"

Modini stiffened. "If it's the one I'm thinking about, then I saw the same tape. It's sickening, but again that's why I'm here, Catherine. I don't think the man in the tape was Karl."

"Are you sure -- really sure?"

"Do you think that was the real Oswald on the front cover of *Life Magazine*, or a composite of him? The video I saw was grainy, and I felt it was done deliberately as a performance for someone. That man *knew* he was being video taped. He glanced at the camera more often than I

473

expected showing his face — am I right?"

Catherine nodded, "Now that you mention it, you're right."

"Plain room, one bed. The tape starts when he walks the girl in through the door? Then he cuffs her to the bed and takes off his belt?"

"Yes, I guess we did see the same video," she shuttered.

"That *wasn't* Karl. He could never do that-- allow a camera into his private life!"

Catherine shifted gears and resumed her role as attorney. "Yes, but this tape was produced to sell for profit. Maybe he was paid well for his...well, participation."

Modini shook his head, "No way! The Karl Hunter I knew would never have put himself into a position that could someday backfire and come back to blackmail him or convict him! No, Karl was too smart for that!"

By the way he talked, Catherine knew Modini believed what he said. If what he said was true, then there was more to this case than she had ever believed possible. Somehow, the frankness in Modini's voice dispelled Catherine's fears. Was it something in Modini's personality, maybe a part of his journalistic integrity that made her see him in a new light? Whatever it was, she had a feeling she could trust this man. They both shared something in common. The belief that Karl Hunter was innocent.

Catherine took a deep breath of the chill night air and felt more composed now. It was getting late and she didn't want to leave him, but she knew she would have to at any moment. "That little girl you saw in that tape..." she began.

"Yeah... What about her," Modini asked.

"She's the girl I was telling you about, the one with your name, under the care of Father Daniel Conrad!"

Modini shook his head. "I don't know what this all means. You and I will have to look into this-- check out this Catholic Church and the hospital records. But first things first! There was another reason I wanted to see you. Do you think you can set up a meeting with me and your father?"

"My father?" Catherine was surprised by his request. "Why do you want to see him?"

"There are a few important things I'd like to discuss with him. It's very important to me." He steered away from giving any specific reason. "Maybe Michael Bradley and Richard Franklin can be of some help."

"Yes...I think I can arrange...something."

"Good! Then at least we've accomplished something today." Modini checked his watch. "It's getting late."

"Yes, I know. I think its time we get back."

"By the way," Modini asked, "why did Richard call you instead of Max Slaton to find me?"

Catherine decided to play it coy, "I-- I guess it must be a conspiracy!" she said facetiously. Then she noticed he wasn't laughing and dropped the attempt at being cute. "Well, I can have a sense of humor you know! All right, once I knew from Michael you were alive, We had hired a private detective through Bradley's law firm sometime ago to find you. Richard Franklin's name came up and is attached to our file. I made a call to Franklin, and he knew you were here to see me, so you can blame him if you want!"

Modini grinned, "I will!" Then he raised his eyebrow and gave her a sidelong glance. "So you can be a clever one when you want to?"

"I guess so."

"Will you set up a meeting with your father?"

"Yes, I can arrange it."

Modini felt relieved. "Once you do that, I'll let Michael know the location. Meanwhile, I'm going to meet a mutual friend of ours."

"And who might that be?"

Now it was Modini's turn to play with her. "Oh, come now! You remember there was a certain Congressman-- now Senator-- who was at my aunt and uncle's party that spring of 1967?"

Catherine felt her face go hot. She hoped he didn't notice. "You mean, Gerry Fuller? John, you must know he's a part of all this. I believe it was Fuller who got my father into this mess in the first place. Not only that, but I believe there's a connection between Fuller and Hunter's prosecution!"

Modini hardly reacted. "This doesn't surprise me..."

"John, I don't think you understand what Fuller is capable of doing!"

Modini looked at Catherine closely. "Believe me, Catherine, I know the type of person Fuller is and what he is capable of doing. I'm not afraid of him or anyone anymore. If he knows anything about me at all, I'm sure he'll have a coronary the next time he sees me."

"You're planning to see Senator Fuller?"

"I'm thinking about it. Maybe I'll go to his office for a surprise visit." He glanced up and down the street. "We'd better find you a taxi."

"I'll take care of it," she told him. "Let's head for the next corner." She took out her cellular phone and punched in a number for her taxi.

Modini and Catherine waited at the corner after she gave the dispatcher the names of the cross streets.

"So how am I going to find you -- or will I always have to go through a third party?"

"Hey... Remember, I'm supposed to be dead! I'll keep in touch." A few minutes later the taxi arrived. "Chow!" he said as he helped her into the cab. Modini waited and watched the taxi pull away. Then he moved down the street and disappeared into the darkness.

Chapter Thirty-two

"The Confrontation"

John Modini, dressed impeccably in a suit, his hair a bit longer and wearing sunglasses now, walked up a staircase leading to the dome of the Capital. He nervously straightened his tie as he entered the building.

Modini had been watched through binoculars by a man hidden in the same car that followed Catherine and him a few nights before. This man grabbed a walkie talkie on the passenger seat next to him and spoke into it. "This is Cobra Two calling Cobra One, copy."

Seconds later, Cobra One copied, "Roger! What is it?"

Cobra Two followed through with an update, "I've followed our man to the Capital Building and still have no clue who this guy is? Copy!"

Cobra One asked, "Who do you think he's seeing there? Copy!"

Cobra Two sounded even more confused. "I haven't the faintest idea. Is the Senate in session today? Copy!"

"I suppose so. I'd get your ass in there and find out why he's there or who he is seeing. Copy!" Cobra One responded.

"Should I pick him up and drag him in for questioning, just to scare him? Copy!" Cobra

Two asked.

"Hell, no! Cobra One shouted back, "Stay away from him until we have the package. No one is to know or be suspicious, do you read? Copy!"

"Roger, I'm right on it and out!" Cobra Two set the walkie talkie back down and released his safety belt, and exited his car.

Modini entered the Capitol building and headed down one of the halls. He had been given the directions to Senator Fuller's office and had no problem finding it. But when he walked into the open office, he found no secretary. He continued on, cruising through a doorway into a much bigger room where he saw a man sitting at his desk using a lap top. Modini, reluctant to interrupt him, waited for the man to look up.

The man's fingers paused a moment. Here, Modini found the opportunity to knock on the open door. The man looked up, bit startled. It was Senator Gerald Fuller.

"Who are you and how did you get in here?" he barked, embarrassed at someone appearing unannounced.

"I'm sorry, sir," Modini apologized, "but your door was open and there was no secretary or anyone for that matter to speak of in the outer office!"

Fuller clenched his jaw and calmed down. "She must have headed off to the little girl's room. Just the same you should wait in her office.

As Modini complied with Fuller's suggestion by backing out of the Senator's office, Fuller asked, "Do you have an appointment?"

Modini stopped to answer, "No."

"Well, who the hell are you anyway?" Fuller growled. "What are you doing here and why the dark glasses indoors?"

Modini took his dark glasses off and approached in a gentlemanly manner. "I suppose you don't remember me, but we met when I was just a kid. It was in Santa Barbara, California, at my aunt and uncle's home way back in the Spring of 1967. You were a Congressman then...my name's John Modini!"

The Senator sat back and started to think, trying to remember, still not sure. "John Modini?"

"As I recall, Judge Henry Kencade and his daughter were also present that day," Modini reminded him.

This disclosure jogged Fuller's memory, and he smiled. "Why, yes," he snapped his fingers, "I do seem to remember."

They shook hands. "But you must excuse me," Fuller said, "I was trying to figure how I knew your name more recently than that, and it just dawned on me you're the journalist who wrote those articles on the Vietnam War-- am I right?"

Modini nodded in agreement. Fuller shook his finger at him. "Oh my! Don't tell me you're that kid who was the president of his school, somewhere in Oregon, wasn't it?"

"President of my Senior class." Modini said, getting flustered. "That was the confusion."

Fuller moved out from behind his desk and shook Modini's hand in an overwhelming greeting, "And there was some confusion about you being drafted...but I must definitely say you did and became quite a photo journalist at that, receiving the Pulitzer. I read your articles. I didn't know you were the same youngster, otherwise, I'd have had you here with me years ago. So how did you find your tour of duty in Vietnam?"

"I was shot, Senator," Modini replied, with a bit of humility. "I came home with a lot of casualties. A plane with all body bags and just me! It was the only way out of there at the time. A friend got me on the first transport out and that was it!"

Fuller, feeling a bit embarrassed, expressed his sympathy. "Sorry to hear that, son. God must have loved you to spare you like that. I see he's given you the courage and humility you carry to this day!"

Modini unfolded his sunglasses and slipped them on, this time to hide the tears forming in his eyes. "I'm sure, sir, God must have loved those men as well who made that trip back with me to the states!"

Fuller was perplexed a moment then realized what Modini meant. "The body bags you mean? Oh, yes, I'm sure you're right. I didn't mean any disrespect to our boys who died for our country. They're all heroes as far as I am concerned!"

Modini nodded without a word. Fuller gestured to Modini to sit on a nearby sofa. "Please sit down. So tell me, what can I do for you?"

Modini remained standing, framing his thoughts as diplomatically as he could. But before he could speak, Fuller became troubled by his sunglasses.

"The sunshine is outside, Mr. Modini. Is there a reason for the dark glasses in my office? I always like to see the eyes of the people I talk to-- and that goes for my constituents as well. I always meet them eye to eye. That way I can tell whether I'm being lied to or not!" he laughed. "The truth is in the eyes, Son. The eyes reach through to the soul of a man!"

Modini took off his dark glasses, folded them, and put them into his jacket. "I agree, Senator...the eyes do reflect the soul of the man."

Fuller slapped him on the back and gestured Modini to the couch as he pulled up a chair. "Good, then we still see eye to eye, don't we? I just said a pun, get it?" he laughed again. "Now tell me, are your folks still living? And how are George and Julia doing these days?"

They were unavoidable questions, and Modini answered them. "Well, sir... My mother is doing all right. My father deserted us when I was a kid. He died soon after Bobby Kennedy's death that summer of '68. Uncle George died in the mid-seventies and Aunt Julia passed away last year. I didn't get to see much of them. My life has been up and down these last few years."

Fuller's smile slowly faded. He was embarrassed and gave Modini his sympathy and condolences, then added, "I am ashamed to say I didn't maintain much correspondence with your aunt and uncle as I should have. You know your Uncle George was an original contributor to my campaign as Congressman. I owed your uncle a lot. I must say that to you."

Modini was surprised, "No, I didn't know that, sir..."

There was an awkward silence, then Fuller asked again, "Well, what can I do for you, John, after all these years?"

Before Modini could reply, a red light within the Senator's office blinked and a buzzing sound was heard. Fuller glanced at the light "Please hold that thought. I'll just be a moment..."

Modini, thinking it was some type of emergency alarm quickly stood with him. Fuller put his hand on Modini's shoulder. "Don't be alarmed son. It's just the Senate calling for my vote. They need me right now. The Central Intelligence Agency is asking us to pass a badly needed appropriation bill."

Modini frowned at this. "Senator! I think the CIA has enough money as it is!" he said impulsively.

Fuller smiled, "It is more than just money, son. When our Intelligence Agencies need power to-- let's say, move a mountain-- they need to get our okay, simple as that. Then it's up to us to either stop them from moving that mountain or allow them to continue."

Modini played the part of the reporter, looking for the angles. "How about you, Senator? Which side are you on?"

"Excuse me, son." Fuller walked into his secretary's office, tactfully avoiding Modini's question. Fuller's secretary was at her desk. They exchanged a few words. Then she asked him for his signature on a notation pad. As he was ready to sign, he turned back to Modini in his office. "Why don't you come with me and see for yourself...come see how our government works, Mr. Modini, please!"

Modini nodded, "I'd like that very much."

Fuller proceeded to sign his secretary's paper. "John, this is Madeleine, my personal secretary, I don't know what I'd do without her!"

Madeleine blushed, "Oh, sir!"

Modini noticed it wasn't her sexual attractiveness that kept her job here. Maybe Fuller's wife made the decision who would work for her husband.

Fuller continued the introduction, "Madeleine, this is an old friend of mine, a vet and a hero of the Vietnam War, John Modini. We will return momentarily, could you please order us some lunch? We'll have it in my office. Anything is fine...fruit salad and some sandwiches. Is that okay with you, John?"

Modini shrugged, caught off guard. "I wasn't planning to stay for lunch, but it's okay with me." The two of them left the office and walked down a corridor, one of the huge ornate hallway of the Capital.

The man known as Cobra Two had entered the Capitol building a few minutes earlier. He scouted around for any sign of John Modini and kept a low profile as he checked down several corridors. He paused at a corridor corner for a few seconds to get his bearings, when Modini and the Senator walked past him. His quarry was in such a deep conversation with the Senator that he hardly noticed the man called Cobra Two. He continued to watch them as they headed for the Senate chamber.

Another Senator approached Fuller before he entered the Senate chamber. Cobra Two took the opportunity to pretend to be a visiting tourist. He asked a security guard whom Fuller was, and the security guard smiled and told him. Cobra Two thanked him and used this cue to head away the direction Fuller was going in.

Cobra Two headed down the hallway, searching for Senator Fuller's office. Maybe there he could find out whom his quarry was.

The Senator from Michigan who confronted Fuller at the Senate chamber entrance told the distinguished Senator from Indianapolis his vote would make or break the appropriation bill on the floor. Fuller advised his colleague to oblige him by keeping company with his guest, John Modini.

They introduced each other.

"I'm Wesley Martin, Senator from Michigan."

"Pleased to meet you, Senator. I'm John Modini," he said confidently.

"My pleasure!" Senator Martin said pompously. "Stick with me kid and watch how the magic wand works." The three men entered the Senate chamber from the hall to see the grand view of one of the most exciting and most beautiful sight before their eyes, the Senate floor of the Capital. Senator Martin held up a hand to stop Modini as they watched a discussion on the floor below. Fuller headed to his seat on the floor, shaking hands and nodding to the other Senators.

Senator Fuller had been a Senator for twenty years now, and his peers gave him recognition as one of them. Fuller had started as a Congressman in 1964 and became a Senator in 1974 during the second term of Richard Milhous Nixon.

Fuller smiled and waved, while the President of the Senate, his distinguished colleague from the State of Indiana and the Vice-President of the United States, Dan Quayle, banged his gavel for attention and to quiet the Senate floor.

Arlen Spector, the Senator from Pennsylvania, had the floor as the President announced the distinguished Senator and his colleague from the State of Indiana, Gerald Fuller. Senator Spector then proceeded with the count and the votes of the issue at hand as Senator Fuller and everyone seated themselves.

With the majority nay and yea votes now behind them, the final decision on the present bill was to be made by Quayle himself. As the President of the Senate, it was his responsibility to break the tie in situations like this.

Senator Martin explained this in a whisper to Modini, "...and Quayle will vote definitely as Bush wants him to, so it is all in the hands of Gerald to make or break the majority. You see the nays lead the vote to empower the Central Intelligence's appropriation or not..."

Modini interrupted hastily. "You mean if Fuller says nay the CIA will not get what they want?"

Senator Martin gave Modini a serious look and answered sternly. "That's right! Spector heads a committee for the CIA's needs. But watch now as Fuller's power takes precedence on the floor."

Arlen Spector spoke out and asked for Senator Fuller's vote. Fuller stood at his seat and recognized the President of the Senate and then nodded to the Speaker of the floor.

Meanwhile, Cobra Two had entered the office of Gerald Fuller and found it empty as Modini did earlier. He crossed to the desk to see whether there was an appointment book available. He had only a few moments when Senator Fuller's secretary walked in from Senator Fuller's office.

"May I help you, sir?" Madeleine said.

Cobra Two turned around, prepared to pretend he was a constituent of the Senator.

"Yes! My name is Hardings. There were supposed to be some papers for me. This concerns a donation to Senator Fuller's campaign fund." Cobra Two said in a businesslike manner. "I was supposed to get the address for his campaign headquarters."

"Just a moment, "Madeleine said, opening a drawer on her desk.

"I spotted the Senator on his way to the floor and I was told his secretary would provide me with the information." Cobra Two lied.

She handed him a business card with the information on it. "All campaign contributions are being handled through his office in Indianapolis. .

"Thank you very much," Cobra Two said, placing the card in his wallet. As he was ready to depart, he paused at the door and spoke again to the secretary. "Ma'am, I was curious. The young gentleman with the Senator looked familiar. His name escapes me at the moment."

Madeleine smiled pleasantly, "Yes, he is quite striking isn't he. I believe the Senator said he was a war hero in Vietnam, a Mr. Modini!" The name shocked Cobra Two who hid his reaction from the secretary.

"Thanks again," he told her and quickly disappeared out the door.

In the Senate chamber, Senator Fuller stood on a quiet Senate floor and announced, "To all my distinguished colleagues of the Senate, my vote as you all know, is always with the respect of our President of the United States. He can count me in for his support. My vote is an affirmative yea!"

Half of the Senate floor was engulfed in an uproar. Senators applauded and cheered simultaneously. The gavel from the Senate President banged, but went unheard as he tried to control the floor for his vote to break the tie.

John Modini tired fast of all this hoopla. He didn't feel like watching politics in action anymore. He excused himself from Senator Martin, who himself was one of the rowdy crowd, applauding and whistling for approval.

"Please tell the Senator I will meet him in his office!" Modini told him. The Senator from Michigan nodded in acknowledgment and continued his whistling and noise making as Quayle quieted the floor down.

Modini headed out into the corridor, witnessing some of the Democratic Senators leaving as well. One of them was Senator Edward Kennedy of Massachusetts.

Modini stopped in his tracks as if he saw a ghost. He watched in awe as the Senator passed by, unable to say a word. Senator Kennedy was a man who was more respected, as much as he was disrespected around the world. He was one who had suffered more tragedies in his lifetime that would have defeated stronger men. But this man could still control today's government. He was still influential enough to make things move and advance for the Democratic Party. The world powers and critics said he came from America's own royal family. Good or bad, he was now the head of the Kennedy clan.

Modini finally composed himself and smiled, heading back to Fuller's office. "Richard Franklin would be proud of me now, as a coward yes, but proud none the less..." he muttered to himself.

Cobra Two watched from the entrance as Modini passed by. He took one long look at Modini and then headed for the Capitol exit.

Modini entered Fuller's secretary's office and made himself comfortable in a seat near her desk. Madeleine walked in with papers and books piled high in her arms from Fuller's office. Modini got up to help.

"Thank you, Mr. Modini. They were getting pretty heavy," she said. Can you put them on the file cabinet?

"Sure thing." Modini set them down where she suggested.

"So how did the vote go?"

Modini smiled and answered cordially, "You know the answer, if you work for the man."

Madeleine looked at him fondly as if to appreciate the diplomatic compliment. "You're right. When the Senator wants something bad enough, he gets what he wants!" She sorted through the books and added, "He's a good man. I think he'd make a great President some day!"

Modini found her statement hard to accept, but replied anyway. "I see. I suppose you want to be there by his side if he ever goes in that direction. Do *you* think he is heading that way?"

Madeleine gave a generous smile. "I hope so. Yes, it would be wonderful to be a part of it. Wouldn't you want to take part in helping our country?"

Modini looked at the photo of Abraham Lincoln in the center wall of Fuller's office and commented, "I would have done almost anything to have worked with him!"

Madeleine, busily putting the books and papers in order didn't realize he was speaking of Lincoln and thought he was speaking of Fuller. "Well, why don't you ask the Senator for a job?" she suggested in a friendly way. "He seems to admire you and thinks highly of you. If I were you, I'd give it a shot!"

Modini turned from Lincoln's portrait, realized Madeleine's error and discreetly corrected her. "Who, me? No, sir-- ma'am. I'm the last person who the Senator needs right now. I'm just a writer searching for a story."

"You could help write speeches for the Senator, "Madeleine recommended. "He'll need all the help he can get if he runs for high office. No, you seem to be a bright man, Mr. Modini. For instance, people have already taken notice of you. Just minutes ago, a man came in here, a constituent of the Senator's and knew immediately you were someone famous!"

Modini straightened like a marionette. He suddenly felt a shiver of apprehension. He walked casually back into Madeleine's office. "What man are you talking about?" he asked, his curiosity getting the better of him.

Madeleine was a bit startled at Modini's question. Then she smiled and explained. "Oh, he was one of the Senator's future contributors, I gave him the information he needed and he left."

Modini felt his heart pounding in his ears. He had a feeling something was terribly wrong. "Yes, but what did you tell him about me?"

Madeleine stepped up on a chair to put a book onto a shelf. "Only who you were, your name, what the Senator had said about you being a war hero and all." Madeleine said offhandedly. "He just said he recognized you, but didn't know your name! I must say, you certainly made an impression on him."

Modini looked to the door as if it were time for him to depart. "I bet *I* did!" he said, trying to keep the sarcasm out of his voice.

Madeleine agreed, "Yes, you did!"

Modini moved to the door. It was time for him to leave. But before he reached it, Senator Fuller charged into the office, clapping his hands in exultation and putting his arm around Modini. "That was politics, son, and I relish every moment I get out there! Just think, every time we speak on the Senate floor, we're making history. Good or bad, we make it happen! Isn't it exciting? I'm so hungry I could eat a horse!" He turned to Madeleine. "Have the sandwiches arrived?"

"They should be here in a few minutes," she said.

Fuller, still with his arm around Modini, escorted him into his office. "Let's talk, son, let's get down to your business!"

Modini sat down on the Senator's couch and suddenly felt overwhelmed with conflicting emotions. He wanted to sit and talk to Fuller one-on-one, but he could not suppress the panic rising within him. He put his head in his hands and ran his fingers through his hair in despair.

"What's wrong, John," Fuller asked, "is something troubling you?" Fuller stopped and leaned up against the end of his desk.

Modini looked up to Fuller and responded. "You can say that, sir! I just realized there must be a lot more of you involved than I imagined!"

"Involved, John? What do you mean, son?" Fuller was bewildered at Modini's remark.

Modini shook his head, "How many of them are there, Senator? How many good old boys are there like you in the Senate and Congress, in our United Sates Government who cheat and lie to the people of this country, the ones who pay your salary, sir!"

Fuller became disturbed at Modini's outburst and confronted him. "Do you know what you just said, son! Are you out of your right mind coming into *my* office, and saying that to me? You accuse *me*!" Fuller thumped his chest to make a point. "The people have elected me term after term! Hell, I'm an institution for God's sake! I shake, rattle and roll for my constituents. They elected me and they can throw me out of office any time they tire of me! You hear that, son? So don't give me any of your pompous attitude."

Modini looked up at him despairingly. "I know. I know, sir, but your constituents aren't the people who are starving and constantly in need of a job out there!"

Fuller cut in, "I get my people jobs, I get the poor off unemployment, there's places to go for a meal! I don't let my people starve out there!"

Modini stood up to face Fuller eye to eye, "Senator, you say that as if you were God yourself! But there are starving people out there, families who are sleeping in their cars, and homeless people living on the streets. Things are so bad we have rock singers trying to save farmers from getting their land taken away by bankers! Your coup here today was to give the CIA what they wanted-- more money to carry on their unbridled ways. Tell me, Senator, did you know our distinguished late Senator John Tower from Texas!"

Fuller drew himself up solemnly, "I'm proud to say he was not only a great Senator but one of my closest friends!"

Modini nodded his head, "That figures! Does that mean, you're going to fill Tower's shoes or is that job going to Arlen Spector?"

Fuller was angry and started to pace. He didn't know what to make of this man whom he had earlier taken a liking to.

Madeleine stepped in to see whether everything was all right. "Senator?" she inquired discretely.

"Leave us alone," Fuller suddenly barked at her, "We're not to be disturbed."

"Then I suggest you hold your conversation down to a dull roar. I'm sure they can hear you clear to the Senate floor!" She closed his door behind her.

Fuller faced Modini and answered his question. "You asked me whether I would fill Senator Tower's shoes. If I'm appointed to this position, that's the President's decision. I will jump to fulfill my duties for my country as you did in Vietnam. If the Senate decides to ask me to chair any position, I will oblige my fellow Senators if I feel it's to benefit this-- *our* country. Meanwhile, I will do everything I can for my state and my constituents-- everything I was elected to do, do you understand, soldier? You do what you're told!" He stopped in his tracks, trying to control his emotions with difficulty.

Modini looked at him pathetically, "Sir, I do understand a couple things. One, your constituents you speak so highly of are both the rich and corrupt--"

Fuller interrupted, "How *dare* you!"

Modini stopped him, "Just let me finish, will you Senator? Secondly, I know about the secret military base in Montana. I know you are a part of that. In fact, I can tell you I might have walked into your special quarters, sat on your bed under hundreds of feet of ground. I witnessed the silos there as well. I know about and met your mistress, sir. Now what was her name..." Modini pretended to think. "Oh yes. Francine Baker! Did you know she had a twin sister, too-- Micheline-- or was she one person pretending to be two? No matter! Before she died she told me everything, Senator."

Modini watched Fuller's face turn beet red from anger, but this time it was mixed with fear and embarrassment. Modini continued, "She was an attractive girl, Senator. What a waste it was for the government to have her killed. I bet you weren't too happy when you got the word of her demise! Believe me, I certainly wasn't, since I was supposed to be killed along with her!"

Fuller walked over and slapped Modini in the face. And Modini took it like a soldier, unflinching. He was shaken for a moment, but continued on, "I know about the MIA/POW cover up, Senator. How many of you are in on that one? And I'm not just talking about Vietnam but the Korean War as well! How many of our men were left out in the cold? How much did our government do to get those who were alive and captured by the Russians, back to our side? What was the real reason General MacArthur was fired by Truman? Using National Security reasons, did both Truman and Eisenhower ignore the pleas from General MacArthur to save those men?"

"So, you pretended to be an expert on the MIA issue, eh?" Fuller said sarcastically.

"I know about Richard Nixon's deal he made with the North Vietnamese government," Modini told him, "He wanted to get back all our men who didn't return in 1973. It was the four billion dollar deal-- or was it a ransom Nixon would pay? After Watergate and the resignation of Nixon, the Congress, the Senate and the new appointed President, Gerald Ford-- all pretended Nixon's deal didn't exist, so henceforth, no prisoners were returned. Why? Many of those in my platoon didn't survive the Vietnam War. But one of those who did, made it back and fought to shed light on the issue. He became a Catholic Priest, and he committed suicide for nothing-- at least I thought-- until I realized he was not only speaking to the church but to all of us to stop the government from hiding the truth-- the truth you helped to shield, Senator!"

"I shielded nothing, young man-- *nothing*!" Inwardly, Fuller was seething from Modini's comments, but still let him speak.

"I hear there are secret organizations Father Conrad was aware of-- Green Berets and certain ex-Marines who were trying to do what they could and bring back those men. I hear of a man from Texas named Ross Perot is secretly trying to bring back the MIA/POW's. First, he confronted Nixon who made the deal, then he confronted Reagan about it."

"I was there! I know what happened!"

Modini folded his arms. "Then you also remember when Reagan announced that one of his first priorities as the incoming President was to investigate the POW/MIA matter, to assure we could finally bring those men home. Then suddenly the issue was dropped. All of you who run this country didn't want any embarrassment! Our own government pretended the POW/MIA issue didn't exist! Hey, it worked during the Korean War with the Russians! All you needed was the shield of National Security to keep everything neat and quiet, and soon it would just go away. All of us were expendable! Pawns! It reminded me of the time the House closed the Select Committee down so quickly after phase one of the Kennedy assassination investigation was ready to break. Martin Luther King and Bobby Kennedy's assassination were never pursued in detail. Question after question still isn't answered! Why?"

Senator Fuller remained silent. He moved around his desk to sit in his chair, staring at Modini.

Modini moved in front of the desk. "I was told once that George Bush would be the front runner for the Republican Party in 1980, Congress stopped all appropriations to the House Select Committee to continue their investigation on the Kennedy matter. They knew President Carter would be shoved out of office. But Reagan surprised everyone, didn't he? He made you and all the others nervous at first because his fight was with big business. That scared you, didn't it, Senator? Things began to look worse because our own government was about to be scrutinized again and possibly exposed as allowing the Kennedy assassination cover up to continue all these years! Were you afraid, sir of the embarrassment that the people would take up arms, like our forefathers in the American Revolution and start wiping out the corruption and dishonesty of our so called leaders hiding behind patriotic symbols like our Liberty Bell or Constitution of the United States?"

Senator Fuller sat silently, listening to Modini's accusations. He could have interrupted a dozen times, but didn't. It seemed as if all the fight had gone out of him.

Modini lifted his hands and gestured to his surroundings, to the building they now stand in. "I can't believe I'm even saying this to you, Senator. All this has been building up within me, killing me these last few years, I thought I could control it, but now...now I can't take it any longer! I, too, wasn't supposed to return from Nam. If it weren't for one man who put me on that one transport back to the States, I wouldn't be alive today! And now all of us who did return are dead, even me, Senator! Right now, I'm supposed to be dead! Everyone thinks I died out there, two thousand miles away, with Francine Baker, your mistress! Only you and a handful of people know I'm alive right now. Maybe you presumed all along I was dead and thought I was a ghost when I walked in here today."

"Listen to me good, son! Our government is not in the business of killing its own people!" Fuller said in a shaky voice.

"Let me guess," Modini said abruptly, "Was Ronald Reagan supposed to be killed in 1981 and Bush thrust into office in a quick transition of power, or was Reagan just to be frightened off. Or does it even matter? Either way, Reagan's priorities were suddenly canceled, weren't they? Then there were those of you in government who made it look as if the First Lady was evil incarnate who in actuality, was the finest woman any man could have had as a wife and first lady. All she did for the next eight years was to protect her husband from the corruption surrounding him and keep the image of this country from cracking!"

"Meanwhile, Ross Perot is on his own fighting crusade to bring back our missing soldiers whose families have constantly been in turmoil over the years. Committees are formed and sabotaged. The MIA groups get no answers, and the Assassination investigations go nowhere! Do you remember that night back in 1967, Senator, when we were talking about Jim Garrison? You said he was the scum of the earth. But you were wrong. All Garrison was trying to do was to heal the nation, bring us together, to relieve us of the pain we the people and our country were living with then. I know I sure felt the loss, Senator. I had lost my own father as a child. I didn't know he was dead or alive, so, I grew up fast. John Kennedy became my father figure, and I'm sure many have felt the same way. So, when Kennedy was killed I felt my father left me again. I hated Lee Harvey Oswald for what he did, I applauded Jack Ruby for shooting him, but soon I was ashamed in my own feelings and wanted to know *why*. And the more I realized there was no reason our government had to hide any involvement in his assassination, the more the government tried to hide or bury the facts. I followed Jim Garrison's investigations and saw all the ridicule heaped upon him. But that still was no excuse to try to destroy a man who only wanted to get to the truth and heal our nation...is it? I have to admit; I blame myself."

"The truth has been brought out countless times!" Fuller argued. "What's the matter son? Are you telling me all those reports and all those conclusions over the past twenty-five years are wrong?"

Modini's voice hardened, "This is America! As a reporter I had the right to search and to investigate the facts like anyone else. The Warren Commission certainly didn't. I'm not the only one who found information after information falsified in the official Warren Report. Stupid me for not looking at it earlier! Before my investigations, I helped the cover up more by discrediting those who found discrepancy after discrepancy! Many things in the report were lies! Then there's your fellow Senator Arlen Spector, the man behind the magic bullet theory. I'd loved to know his constituents. Funny isn't it? We've almost come full circle. As we speak, a movie about Jim Garrison is being made. And after all these years he'll finally be able to tell his side of the story. But this time, Senator, the machine of the government will have to bring out the heavy ammunition, not just to discredit Garrison again, but to discredit the man who's making the film, the man who threatened to expose some of the truths about the Vietnam War. It's the Pentagon Papers again, but now everyone will know seven members of a Commission, and a dozen or so attorneys spent six to eight months, not investigating Kennedy's assassination, but exposing one man as an evil little degenerate who alo*ne* changed the course of history. This is contrary to the fact where hundreds of real investigators, journalists and law enforcement officers have dedicated their whole life in exposing the truth and uncovering new information these last twenty-eight years."

Fuller sat in his chair as Modini continued to stand, speaking his mind. Modini waited for him to lash out at him for all his accusations and for his abuse of office. Instead, Senator Fuller calmly asked, "All said and done, how are you going to prove this?"

Modini put all his cards on the table. "I know about you and Catherine Kencade, sir. I saw you two that night in my Uncle and Aunt's house in Spring of 1967! What's the country going to say when it learns you took advantage of a thirteen-year old child when you were a Congressman?"

For a full moment Fuller looked at him in shock. Then the realization hit him. "What would you like me to do?" he asked resignedly.

Modini could see the blood draining from Fuller's face, trying to find some way out of this dilemma and accepting the fact there wasn't any. He stared at Fuller, half-expecting him to throw him out of the office. He slowly sat back down thinking now how pitiful the Senator looked. Instead of exposing this man, he now had the conflicting emotion of wanting to help him. He finally found the courage to say what he came in here for.

"Senator, sir? It would benefit us all if you did one of two things. If you are serious in what you say, then you could go out there, you could expose everything you--"

Fuller interrupted. "I could be impeached if I do what you're saying."

"If it comes to that you would become a hero going out of the Senate with your chin up, at least!"

"Hardly a good choice. What's the other alternative?" Fuller asked.

Modini buried his head in his hands again for a moment then told it like it was. "If you don't tell what you know, then you'll need to resign or forget running for a next term!"

This last statement frightened Fuller. "If I did that I'd be a dead man before you know it!"

And Modini saw the fear in his eyes. "Then the other alternative is to expose the others who are in on this, even if we have to rebuild the trust in the American system again from scratch!"

Suddenly, Madeleine screamed in the outer office. The office door exploded inward, and two Federal Marshals barged into the room. "Senator are you all right?" one of the Marshals demanded.

The Senator acted quickly, perceiving a way out. He backed from Modini, pointing at him as if the Marshals were here for him and yelled, "This man-- he tried to blackmail me! Please officers..."

The second Federal Marshal asked, "Is this man John Modini, sir?"

"Yes, yes..." Fuller yelled out, "he threatened me!"

The Marshal proceeded to say, "Mr. Modini, you are under arrest. I advise you to put your arms behind your head, don't move until my partner can secure handcuffs onto your wrists! You are being taken into custody!"

Modini stepped back. "Why am I being arrested-- and how in God's name do you know I'm John Modini?"

Marshal approached pulling his gun from his holster. "Take another step and you're a dead man," he threatened, "Now put your hands behind your head and do as you're told!"

The other Federal Marshal, a heavily set man, came forward with handcuffs.

"What's the charge?" Modini demanded an answer

"First-degree murder was all we knew!" the first Marshal told him.

"Murder?" repeated Modini, incredulously.

"Now hands behind your back, sir. I don't want to use this!" the Marshal said as he cocked back the hammer of his revolver.

The second man grabbed for Modini's arm and twisted it around, slapping one side of the handcuffs on his wrist.

The cuff bit into Modini's flesh. "Hey, not so rough!" Modini yelled, twisting around from the pain. The second Marshall was too close to Modini when he fastened the cuff. Modini's involuntary action threw him off balance, and he fell backwards into his partner. The gun flew from his hand and hit the floor.

As the Marshal dived after it, the second man reached for his gun. Modini's instincts kicked in. The threat of danger and possible death snapped Modini's reflexes into action. He side stepped the second Marshal, kneed him in the groin and jumped for the open door.

The First Marshal spun around, his gun in hand, and fired, accidentally, hitting his partner, in the back. As the man fell to the floor with a shoulder wound, Modini ducked out of his line of fire. He ran past Madeleine who started screaming when the shots were fired and headed out into the hallway.

Feeling the rhythm of his own pounding blood, Modini escaped into the corridor of the Capital as more bullets were fired after him. The sounds of the shots echoed eerily down the corridor carrying the explosive noises in every direction.

Modini now found himself running for his life again. *All this for a man supposed to be dead,* he ironically thought to himself.

Modini raced through the Capital corridor as security personnel were alerted.

Modini saw one security guard come around a corner, followed by others. In the face of sudden jeopardy, he found the strength of insane desperation. He slowed down knowing any hurried movement could hurt his escape. The two guards from the front entrance headed his way. Without hesitation, without reflection, he yelled out, pointing in the direction of Fuller's office. "Two men... there!" He kept his other wrist with the handcuffs still attached hidden behind his back.

The security officers sprinted past him, barely acknowledging his existence. A Marshal appeared from Fuller's office with gun in hand ready to shoot at Modini past the running security personnel. The two guards halted, guns drawn and aimed at the Federal Marshal.

"Drop it! Drop your gun, *now!*" ordered the lead security man.

"Get down! He's escaping," the Marshal cried out.

Then one of the security team members fired his gun. The bullet struck the wall next to the Marshal, and he ducked back inside Fuller's office. He yelled out for them to stop shooting, but confusion reined.

Modini continued walking away in a steady pace from the commotion. With hand in his pocket, he joined a crowd of people moving to the exit. He blended in with them until he passed through the doors to the outside. Without looking back, he headed a distance from the Capitol Building. He mingled with the other men and women on the sidewalk and disappeared among them, leaving no trace for the authorities to follow.

Chapter Thirty-Three

"The Dragon: To Protect and Serve"

It was early evening in a south Chicago suburb. The commuter train passed by on an elevated trestle as Thomas Sanders crossed the street underneath it, and walked to a modest looking home. The spring air had a bit of a chill in it, left over from the aftermath of the winter season.

Thomas Sanders was investigating a lead tied to his 'death list' he put together for Bradley. The gentleman he was visiting, had invited him over. He was a technician who once worked for Bethesda Naval Hospital back in the time of the Kennedy assassination. Now retired, he was willing to speak out about his friend, William Pitzer's death.

The man who came to the door was a short, skinny man who looked as if he were a constant smoker and a fondness for bourbon and gin.

"Excuse me, sir," Thomas said, looking at this thin, silver-haired gentleman. "Are you Charlie Gant?

The man nodded, "Are you Thomas Sanders, the gentleman who called from the Bradley Law Firm a couple of days ago?

"Yes I am," Thomas said as he shook his hand. The two of them entered the house. Charlie suggested they talk in the kitchen over a cup of coffee his wife prepared. The TV set was on the news channel, and as they passed it, John Modini's face filled the screen. Thomas didn't notice this because the sound had been muted upon his arrival.

Thomas took off his coat to get more comfortable, and the two men stopped and entered the kitchen.

"Please, Mr. Sanders, let me take care of your jacket," Charlie offered. "I must ask how you happened to find me?"

"Please call me Thomas." He gave Charlie Gant his coat and sat down at the kitchen table. "I did plenty of research. To be honest with you, I was reading David Lifton's book and was amazed about all the medical records during and after Kennedy's autopsy. It all seems to be a shell game concerning both the medical papers, the photos, and even Kennedy's original coffin with the medical doctors, advisors and technicians acting as con artists. No offense to you, Mr. Gant, but it seems strange to me-- maybe to you, too-- for a doctor do his first autopsy in his career on the President of the United States, then the next morning burn the original autopsy report because he realized he made a mistake. He thought the Parkland Hospital doctors in Dallas had done a tracheotomy on the President, then found out they thought it was a frontal shot through the president's throat."

Charlie listened to Thomas as he put the coffee mugs on the table and poured the coffee. Thomas continued.

"Then there was the condition of Kennedy's head when he was first brought in with hardly any brain left, and half his skull gone. Where did the brain of the President go? This tells me, Mr. Gant, that someone had already messed with the President's head, so to speak! Well, anyway, I decided to find out who was still alive that day and was not accounted for. Lifton did a good job in interviewing everyone, including the Marines who were in charge of Kennedy's coffin. Or maybe I should say coffins, since one Marine says one thing while another says he participated with a second group of Marines. They all say they were sworn to secrecy! You see, while Bobby and Jackie Kennedy were escorting a coffin containing what they thought was JFK's body, another group of Marines had already put Kennedy into the autopsy room prior to Jackie's arrival to Bethesda from the airport. Who the hell was in that coffin if Kennedy's body were already on the slab with doctors, military officials, and camera crew filming the event?"

Charlie shrugged his shoulders, "I know it sounds unbelievable, Thomas, and I can't explain that day. I can only tell you what I saw the next day!"

"Well, I realize this." Thomas added hastily. "Your name came to me as I was writing a report on Naval Commander William Pitzer. You spoke, I recall, after the death of Pitzer. You thought Mr. Pitzer would never have committed suicide, but you never gave a reason. You hinted his death was, well...mysterious!"

Charlie took a slow sip of his coffee. "Thomas, I have to be blunt with you. I don't know whether any of what David Lifton reported in his book is true or not, except it was a very scary time. Everyone was on alert as if a war were ready to break out. President Johnson expected a retaliatory attack from the Soviet Union. This fellow Lifton was right when he said everyone in Bethesda was sworn to secrecy. Our careers were on the line, including a court-martial if any of us said one word about anything happening at Bethesda, including William Pitzer's death in 1966!"

"Why then-- and why Pitzer?" Thomas asked.

Charlie replied, "That's the funny part. Pitzer was planning to retire. He had a month to go and was even offered a job at a major television news station. He was interviewed a lot then and told me what he knew about the camera and the fact his biggest coup was shooting Kennedy's autopsy. He had been offered more than his share of television gigs. Next thing you know, he's dead! He was found in his own office with his head blown practically off. One thing was strange for sure, Pitzer was left handed, but they say he shot himself in the right temple! How did that bullet hole make it through at that angle? His wife and family couldn't see their husband and father ever again. They couldn't even bury him! His body was taken-- I don't know whether it was Naval Intelligence or not-- but the government suddenly made his body disappear. His wife couldn't get his wedding band, let alone any information other than it was a suicide. And because he did this in a military and government establishment, they had full ownership of the body for National Security reasons. I've never heard of this, especially since we were in the middle of the Vietnam War and thousands of our men were coming home in body bags to their families!"

Thomas could see Charlie was getting nervous. He stopped to get a grip on himself and grabbed for a cigarette from his shirt pocket. Before he lighted up, he asked, "I hope you don't mind?"

Thomas nodded, and Charlie lighted up. He took a long puff before proceeding, "Now, let me tell you what happened that day, the day after Kennedy's death. It was the twenty-third. I was walking by Bill Pitzer's editing room, and I peered in to see how he was. He invited me to come in and asked whether I could keep a secret. He wanted to show me some photos and film he was developing and been working on all night. He told about all the top brass that had been in and out of Bethesda in the last twenty-four hours. Now mind you, Thomas, this was before anyone got their hands on what Pitzer was doing. I saw photos of Kennedy's head blown away. The damage was so severe that you couldn't identify him."

"That's what I've discovered from some of the reports I've read," Thomas told him.

Charlie took another drag on his cigarette. "The Warren Commission totally lied about the film of an autopsy in their report! Someone, if it weren't Earl Warren, established no one was ever to see the real pictures that were taken, because what I read in the report about Kennedy didn't match the Kennedy pictures I saw that day! I was horrified, sir! They asked Bill to take a picture of the President's brain, and all Bill could see was bits and pieces of what was left of a brain that you could fill a specimen jar with-- if that tells you anything. Someone was surely putting one over on all of us because either the bullet that killed the President blew the President's head off, or someone else had. Like you said, someone in the beginning had already messed with the President's head before he got to Bethesda. And I mean someone other than Parkland must have given Kennedy a premature autopsy because of what I saw! I don't see how anyone could have done anything to him other than start over from scratch and rebuild his head because there was practically nothing left of it, I'm tellin' ya!" Charlie's eyes were moist as he finished.

Thomas leaned forward. "Are you telling me the truth, and not exaggerating?"

"That's...that is God's honest truth, sir! And I know Bill did not commit suicide because if he were alive today he'd have those Commission members' heads on straight about the truth. I think that's why he was killed! Because, I'm sure Bill was upset with the lies going out about everything! First, the autopsy, and second, he felt pretty bad about the burden those two little girls were probably goin' through since he was a family man himself!"

Thomas knitted his brow. "What two little girls are you talking about, Mr. Sanders?" Thomas realized Charlie might not know how old he was. "I have to tell you I wasn't even born until 1969," Thomas explained. "Do you mean Caroline and John, Jr?"

"Well, I'm sure those two children, too," Charlie acknowledged, "but no. I mean the two girls that Lee and Marina Oswald had. They didn't know whether their father was really the assassin or not, did they? Our government contends that he was--the same government of whose country they lived in. But what if Oswald *didn't* do those things and everything including the autopsy was one big lie? Then that means every President from Johnson on would have to be blamed for allowing this cover up to continue, wouldn't they?"

Thomas gave Charlie a startled look and thought about it for a moment, then asked, "What if every President were lied to? Or what if they didn't want to know any of the details so they could continue with their business!"

Charlie smiled, "If that were the case, I'd feel sorry for anyone who wants to be President because if they don't rectify a mistake as this it certainly will come back to bite 'em again. It's a matter of time, but hell will freeze over before we get another man like Kennedy into office. I think it was Carter who was the last President who made a dent with the House Select Committee whose semi-conclusion found a verdict of conspiracy. I say 'semi' because the government didn't pursue it. That's a strange one! Now look what's happening today, some idiot almost assassinated a Senator right in our own Capital building. What's next, the White House?"

502

Thomas was shocked, "Are you serious? When did this happen?"

"Hell, grab your socks, a cup of Java and some of my darling wife's cookies she just made. Follow me, I'll show ya. It's been everywhere on the boob tube!" Charlie took a sip of his coffee and one last drag on his cigarette before putting it out.

The two men went into the TV room, and Charlie picked up the remote control. The sound returned over a game show, and he switched channels to the twenty-four-hour news station.

A commercial ended and a news broadcaster read the headlines, "How billions were stolen around the world is today's topic. This refers to the 'Bank of Credit and Commerce International' or what is also known as the BCCI scandal now linking to Saudi Arabian and American Intelligence operations known to be the Riyadh Connection. It looks as though this scandal is growing like a cancer and may become a tumor when President Bush runs for a second term, which incidentally, is not so far away."

Charlie clicked the remote to flip through the news stations. He stopped at WGN Chicago, as John Modini's face flashed on the screen.

Thomas dropped his cookie on the floor. "Holy shit!" he exclaimed aloud. "Excuse me, but I think I know this guy! Turn up the volume!"

He shut his mouth as Charlie turned up the sound. The men listened to a female news reporter. "Today, John Modini, thought once as missing, reappeared today in Washington and attempted to assassinate Senator Gerald Fuller in the Capital Building while the Senate was in session. Luckily, two Federal Marshals confronted Modini and stopped him. Modini fought with one of the Marshals, shooting him in the back. This was followed by an amazing chase through the main halls of the Capital itself where, in the confusion, John Modini escaped.

"How Modini could enter the Capital with a gun was not fully explained, since the security in most Federal buildings would detect it. The Federal officer, Brian Seccombe who was wounded, was in critical condition as he was rushed to the hospital, the name being withheld for security reasons."

"That means she hasn't the faintest idea," Charlie said. "They always say that when they don't have the information."

The news broadcaster continued her report. "Modini is wanted for the murder of a young flight attendant, Francine Baker, and for questioning in Colonel Roger Tracy's mysterious suicide!"

Charlie spoke up again, "There, see, again another mysterious suicide but this time he's a military officer, this sounds weird to me, Mr. Sanders!"

Thomas, still staring at the TV, added ironically, "And you don't know the half of it!" Thomas rushed into the kitchen to grab his coat, appearing again to Charlie. "I hate to cut this short, I can't explain now, Mr. Gant, but believe me, I will keep in touch. It's very important I get back to Madison immediately!" Thomas took something from his wallet, "Meanwhile, here's my card. If there's anything else you might remember that could help me, don't hesitate to call. Sorry, but I've got to run!"

* * *

Early the next morning as the sun rose in Los Angeles at the Riviera Golf Course in Century City, the Golfers were already playing on the courses. They refused to wait until the air warmed up and ignored the bit of dew still on the greens.

Richard Franklin was there that morning, but not to play golf. He was there to meet someone. He checked his watch and frowned. For once he was early. He strolled to the Riviera Clubhouse.

Several men came out of the door. It was a case of Franklin being in the right place at the right time. By chance, he noticed the black celebrity O.J. Simpson in a foursome with three white men heading for their tee-off.

Franklin yelled out, "The Juice!" getting O.J.'s attention briefly. O.J. nodded, showing his charismatic smile and continued on.

504

Franklin's momentary excitement made him grin, then quickly faded. He caught sight of Dean Martin, putting alone on a near by practice green. Franklin was reminded briefly of the recent death of Dean's son.

Outside the main clubhouse, Franklin reached into his pocket and fiddled with some change. He deposited the right amount into the *Times* newspaper vending machine, and removed a morning newspaper.

The paper opened to the headline reading *"Modini Wanted for Murder." "Modini, a fugitive on the run...armed and dangerous!"*

Richard Franklin was so stunned he couldn't say anything for the first few moments. "You're fucking joking!" he said aloud in disbelief. "This is not happening!" Franklin headed quickly to the coffee shop.

Dr. Robert Doreen came from another direction of the Riviera and met Franklin as he arrived at the coffee shop. Doreen was in a sullen mood, but tried to smile as he approached Franklin. "Richard Franklin!" he said aloud.

Franklin turned around to meet Doreen. "Dr. Doreen, nice to see you again."

"Thanks for coming on such a short notice." Doreen shook Franklin's hand and saw he had a newspaper. "I see you've heard the news! Let's grab some coffee, I have a half hour before I tee off...you play golf?"

Franklin shook his head no and showed Doreen the front page news. "I just found out about this! Of all the days I don't catch the news, this happens. I just don't understand it! Why is the news media so one-sided? You and I know Modini didn't do this!"

Dr. Doreen agreed. "I know! It's been on the tv, all last night. The government has convinced the media John is some type of assassin, and they're out to kill him! I mean not just them, but they got the FBI and every police department in the country out to get him! And to shoot to kill!"

The two men seated themselves. Franklin gave their order to the waitress, "Two coffees, please!" Dr. Doreen asked for an English muffin while Franklin agreed to a Danish roll. Franklin spoke up to say, "I'm really angry about this. I'm considering putting a press conference together and blow the whistle on this whole thing. That's the least I can do."

"No, I would wait if I were you until you hear from Modini." Dr. Doreen suggested. "Let's get all the facts first. We'll listen to his side of the story and ask him what should be done. I like your idea, but it might take a ninety-degree dive, and the next thing you know they will be using you to entrap him. No, I think you should play it cool and wait for now."

Franklin was hesitant, but agreed, "You might be right." He tried to hold his emotions in check.

After the waitress served them their coffees, Dr. Doreen finally got around to business. "The reason I asked to see you, Mr. Franklin, is about a friend of mine who's having problems concerning an ad campaign he is in charge with. Well, I won't say 'problems,' but it's very strange. Because of our association with John Modini's project at Warner Brothers Studio last year, I felt the need to ask you a pertinent question concerning the same subject matter. It's because I know your reasons for wanting Modini's script made into a feature film. My friend is in charge of getting movie billboards up here in the major cities throughout Southern California. One of his clients is Warner Brothers. The studio you and I dealt with."

Dr. Doreen took a sip of his coffee and continued, "This friend of mine is responsible for putting the Oliver Stone movie *JFK* out, and the deadline is fall with final marketing to be finished by Thanksgiving week. My friend has a contract with the studio and much of his money tied into this. Now someone from the studio is telling him to hold everything back, that they may not even release the film and to prepare for their February release of the new Bruce Willis film, *The Last Boy Scout,* to move it up to replace *JFK's* release date in late December!"

Franklin narrowed his eyes, "Did they tell your friend the reason?"

Instead of answering, Dr. Doreen instead asked him a question. "Mr. Franklin, do you know who a 'Mr. James Garrison' is?"

Franklin was surprised by this question, but now understood why this movie was made-- because of people like Dr. Doreen who didn't know where truth and fiction finally met. So he smiled at him and explained, "Well, Dr. Doreen, the movie of *JFK* is not about Kennedy, only about his assassination and the following six-year aftermath in searching for the truth. At the time James Garrison was the District Attorney of New Orleans who became the only prosecutor in history so far to bring a man to trial associated with the assassination of Kennedy-- a man by the name of Clay Shaw. He was in charge of the International Trade Mart Center, and a man of influence in New Orleans. He was charged with conspiracy in the murder of John F. Kennedy which culminated in a courtroom trial in 1969. They said Shaw was linked to both Oswald and the CIA, but none of the accusations stuck. The judge dropped all charges, acquitting him!"

Dr. Doreen nodded, "I remember that verdict."

"In 1974, Clay Shaw mysteriously died and his body disappeared, but a year later Richard Helms, a former CIA director for both Presidents Johnson and Nixon, admitted at the Frank Church hearings that Shaw did have links with the CIA. And the mystery still continues today. That's what the film *JFK* is about. This is Garrison's point of view of what happened to him during those six years, not the Government nor the media's point of view. This is his side of the story based on his novel, *On the Trail of the Assassins!*"

Dr. Doreen reflected upon this, remarking. "I see! I now understand why my friend is having this problem. It was the mention of this Garrison name that prompted the Warner Brothers Studios to pull the picture!"

Franklin was not surprised, but pretended to be. "You're kidding! They're planning to pull the picture?"

"So far, that's what they're saying. My friend is on hold for now and is to prepare to cancel all ads and billboards. I'll keep you posted if anything develops-- positive or negative."

"Please do," Franklin said. "And thank you for telling me this information. It confirms certain points Mr. Modini and I have recently discovered!"

507

Dr. Doreen stood up. "We'll keep each other posted if John calls either one of us. I'll be there for him if he needs my help. I know you'll do the same. Well, my golf partners are waiting for me to tee off. Thanks for seeing me!" he shook Franklin's hand. "Stay in touch!" Doreen slipped on his golf gloves, smiled and nodded goodbye as he departed.

* * *

In Taos, New Mexico on a Pueblo Indian reservation, tourists were allowed by invitation by the Indian community to be guided within their compound to relive their cultural history and tribal customs of this national treasure. It was not unlike the Universal Studios tour. It was established to make money. It was also to help continue to preserve their heritage.

The Pueblo Indians of Taos were the forefront of the revolts against Spanish domination, and in 1847 joined Mexican settlers in their last rebellion-- this time against the fledgling American government.

Ironically, located on one side of this Native American reservation was a secret government facility housing a group of scientists and ex-military personnel whose job it was to filter out any domestic and foreign elements that could be either illegal or a detriment to the government of the United States. Their job was to weed out the unscrupulous individuals who were undermining our government from within.

This secret project also tracked down the human targets who might be working in various capacities associated with the U.S. Government. These included both men and women who worked within the White House and the Pentagon as well as the Central Intelligence Agency.

A top secret protocol existed deep within our government, hidden from the general public and known to only a few authorized personnel. It's purpose was to find these people who were following their own agendas and stop them.

The people in this secret compound worked for a man whose pseudonym was known only as the Dragon. Working out of Kirkland Air Force Base in Albuquerque, New Mexico, this special agent took direct orders from the White House. He reported to only two sources in the government, a man from within the Pentagon and the President of the United States. And his orders came from them, as well.

At the highest level, this agent's objective was to provide crucial and damaging information to the President of the United States unquestioningly, and fulfill any mission he was assigned. The directive existed primarily to rid the White House or Pentagon of any cancer festering within it's domain-- to monitor those in power who abuse their position and authority. If the President had to remove a staff member or a Cabinet member from their post, a secret and private message was sent to the agent known as the Dragon.

This agent would then give orders to investigate the assigned individual, using sophisticated computers and surveillance equipment, include satellite technology, to document any misbehavior or wrong doings. If the evidence warranted it, the offending person was requested to resign, avoiding any government scandal that might be attributed to the President or the White House. This clandestine procedure was kept secret from the American people, allowing the President to conduct business without embarrassment.

The biggest problem this secret network faced involved the CIA. If CIA operatives were conducting domestic espionage or illegal assignments within the United States, and the threat of revelation would harm the Presidency, then those operatives were tracked down through a state-of-the-art computer system linking dozens of databases.

This system, deemed unconstitutional because it infringed on the privacy of individuals, outstripped any equipment the CIA had access to. Again, if the CIA agents were pushing the envelope, they would be arrested quietly, so not to embarrass the public.

On this day, the Kirkland Air Force Base, received an ultra-urgent message addressed to the Taos' Base Commander. The message was for his eyes only: *Locate the Dragon.*

A big tanned man, an ex-Colonel and Green Beret in civilian clothes, entered a secure computer room in an isolated section of the air force base where several people were working.

He sat down at a special cordoned off keyboard and entered an encrypted code identifying himself as the Dragon.

He glanced around the room, waiting for a link to the Pentagon to be established. There were only three individuals of the support crew working in this top secret computer room, searching, downloading and categorizing files.

The Base Commander notified the ex-Colonel, and he was on-line within two minutes. A phone next to his console beeped as a call was placed through from the Pentagon.

"Hello," he said flatly, putting the receiver to his ear.

A female's voice answered. "Hello. Sorry to disturb you, but we have an incident here at the Pentagon. Priority one!" There was a trace of nervousness in her tone.

"Can you elaborate."

"Of course," the female voice replied. "We have two men under observation as we speak. They attempted to enter a restricted area of the Pentagon. Instead of having them arrested, we allowed them in. Their I.D.'s were sophisticated enough to get them this far-- that's what makes it so unusual. We called you immediately. How shall we handle this situation?"

"Let them proceed to their destination," The Dragon told her. "I want to know what they're going after." he stared at the screen. Why the phony credentials? Either way these intruders were foreign and didn't belong there. He reassured the female operative, "We'll have them stopped and arrested in the end, if necessary...but the main thing is to find out what they want!"

* * *

John Modini joined a group of tourists visiting the Vietnam War Memorial in Washington. He wore a pair of dark frame sunglasses and was again, wearing a beard to blend into the crowd. It was his new disguise, since the front page photos in all the newspapers showed six composite shots of him. The pictures circulated of him were enhanced and sharp, made from surveillance cameras when Modini arrived and exited the Capitol Building.

Modini waited until he was alone, then ran his finger down the Vietnam Memorial Wall, checking out names from his unit. He stopped at the name of his Sergeant. "Alex Contos," he said aloud.

Earlier, he had noticed how the Veterans honored Corporal Daniel Conrad with a special plaque for his participation and help in tracking down POW/MIA's dismissed as dead since the end of the war. Tears came in earnest to Modini's eyes. He took off his sunglasses, embarrassed. He reached up to dab the wetness away and shield his eyes.

A voice behind called to him in a whisper, using his nickname and mother's former name. "Jack O'Leary!"

Modini responded to the name. It was a code used by his contact-- and he knew whom his contact was. He wiped his eyes and slipped his sunglasses back on, then turned around to greet Michael Bradley.

They shook each other's hands. Modini was nervous. "Thanks for coming!"

Bradley nodded, "I thought it wise not to inform Catherine about this. I want you to know she's worried sick about you. What did you do to her, put some kind of spell over her?"

Modini shrugged his shoulders.

Bradley got to the point. "I'm going to drive you to a car on the outskirts of D.C. After I return the rental to the airport, I'll take the next flight to Madison." He gave Modini a slip of paper. "You'll drive to this address, where my associate, Thomas Sanders, will put you up in a safe house until all this dies down. If you're ready, let's get out of here!"

Modini turned again to the wall to give silent notice as if he were in a Catholic Church, by motioning with his hand the sign of the cross. Then they left the memorial passing the tourists who were still arriving to make their own pilgrimage.

* * *

A group of half a dozen FBI men in one of the conference rooms at the Washington FBI building, reviewed the surveillance video from that day's surveillance tapes in the Capitol Building. The tapes showed Modini strolling casually in the hallway to Senator Fuller's office. The time and date were printed at the bottom of the screen, and the people in the video moved in the standard jump-cut manner in frozen motion, frame by frame.

"Look at that," FBI agent Huxley said, his mouth gaping. "I can't believe it. Do you see what I see?"

Another agent responded, "The first camera picked him up coming in and the second had him in sight as he headed for Fuller's office. What's so unusual about that? The images are clearer and sharper on the subject than we'd ever hoped for?"

Huxley, responded, "That's just what I mean! Look at that guy, our big-time killer! He strolls into the building without setting off any security alarms. Take a closer look at the pictures. It doesn't seem to me as though he's carrying any concealed weapons."

The second FBI man, agent Robie leaned forward and scrutinized the scene. "You're right. The internal metal detectors would have been sounding by now."

The FBI agents watched Modini, go into Fuller's office. There was a time lapse, and he came out escorted by Senator Fuller. They walked down the hall and turned the corner. Robie took the cassette out and slipped another one into the VCR. This one showed Modini and Fuller heading down the corridor to the Senate chamber.

Agent Huxley, the one who seemed to be leading the inquiry shot an order to a third man in the room, agent Blandings. "Get the Senator of Michigan and request his presence at FBI headquarters the minute he is free today! Tell him it is essential he be here. There are some questions that--" He stopped momentarily as he spotted something odd on the screen monitor. "Whoa! Stop! There, go back a frame or two!"

Robie, the agent in charge of the video, slowly reversed two frames and freezes it. The lead agent took note. "Well, well, look what we have here. I wonder what *he's* doing there in the Capital

Building?" The monitor showed a man in the corridor facing the camera, watching both Fuller and Modini heading to the Caucus Room.

Huxley asked, "Do any of you recognize this guy?"

Blandings spoke up, "If it's the same man I'm thinking of, he's CIA!"

"That's right! I recognized him, too!" The lead agent then pointed to two of his men. "Blandings... Maxwell... Put a surveillance team together immediately. Find out what he's up to. I want to know whether there's a connection to our man, Modini, and this guy!" he said pointing sharply at the man frozen on the television.

The other agents as they grumbled and reluctantly rose to pursue their assignments.

"I want this one bad!" Huxley reminded them. The last thing he saw when he left the room was the face of Cobra Two staring at him silently from the monitor screen.

* * *

In Taos, New Mexico, the Indians were restless in their compound as a crowd of tourists gathered around to watch the young and old natives painted up and dressed in their native attire. They performed a custom rain dance before the crowd and for their community. They had undergone a long dry spell and needed water for their land.

The people in the government building near by them were having their own set of problems. The Dragon was called back to his phone at his computer base. Fans kept the warehouse cool as he grabbed a cup of natural water from a container reading *Pure Cascade* mountain water.

Before answering his call, he gulped the cup of water down and wiped his mouth with his sleeve. He looked at others in the room, each at their own individual keyboards. They were busy at work as usual. He contacted the Pentagon again. "I read you!" the Dragon responded to the same woman on line who spoke with him earlier.

"I think, sir, we have a problem!" the woman said.

The Dragon smiled, "Honey, there's nothing we can't handle! What's the problem?"

She told him about the two men they were keeping tabs on, "After refusing entrance at their destination, Section Eleven! The two proceeded to enter 'Darth Vader's' office!"

The Dragon was a bit surprised. "You're kidding! The only thing I can do for now is place someone on their tail. Continue to deny access to Section Eleven and string them along until our men make contact. Do not, I repeat, do *not* arrest them. I want to see how far they'll go and what they're up to. Thanks for the update. I'll keep in touch."

He hung up the phone and checked the computer. It confirmed what he already knew: 'Darth Vader's' office was the Commander of the Joint Chiefs of Staff.

The Dragon turned to another colleague on the nearest keyboard. "Hey, Tony... What are you working on?" he asked.

His colleague finished typing and looked up. "I'm typing out a speech for the Secretary of State. He's giving it tomorrow night at some classy dinner in London before the Prime Minister at the Middle East Conference..."

"Then find out where Dick is. Tell him we need two men for a tail at the Pentagon-- not to bite the tail but to find out what they're up to. I want them to get back to me as soon as they can." The Dragon sat back in his chair, considering his options. "Tell him not to use the FBI, or they'll have to report to the director. This is classified. I want a couple of NSA men to do the tail. Call the Director of the FBI and have him put someone on the trail of the Commander of the Joint Chiefs of Staff. We have to find out whom and what he's dealing with."

Tony rose out of his seat. The Dragon yelled after him. "And keep everything above board here, nobody has done anything wrong yet, we just want to keep it that way." The Dragon shut off his computer. "That's all. I'm outta here!"

The Dragon exited the computer room, knowing he had to stay on top of this one.

Chapter Thirty-four

"Read My Lips"

Anita Hill, a reserved woman and a specialist in commercial law, appeared on a C-SPAN tv news screen. She was interrogated by Senator Arlen Spector before a fourteen member Senate subcommittee investigating allegations against George Bush's Supreme Court nominee, Clarence Thomas, of having sexually harassed her when she worked for him in the early 80's. The problem facing Clarence Thomas, a respected African-American law professor from the University of Oklahoma, considered a replacement for retiring Thurgood Marshall, was that he was unfit for the nomination because of his sexist attitude toward women, especially African-American women.

Anita Hill once admired this man she had worked for and was recommended by him for tenure and advancement. Still, the Republican Senate embarrassed her for several days, with the exception of the democratic side, including the Chairman, Joseph R. Biden Jr., a Democrat from Delaware. The Democrats tried their best to keep her reputation intact once she was forced to come forward into the public eye, and now before the Senate Judiciary Committee.

On this day, Miss Hill described how Mr. Thomas would use a pornographic movie to brag about his sexual prowess by comparing himself to one of the characters. Arlen Spector asked Miss Hill, quote, "Who, Miss Hill, is this actor or character you said Mr. Thomas repeatedly mentioned?"

Miss Hill averted her eyes from Mr. Thomas, sitting stoically, his white wife beside him, then answered Senator Spector, "I believe the name he used was 'Long Dong Silver'..."

Senator Edward Kennedy's eyes rolled upwards in a mixture of astonishment and embarrassment on the panel. Bush's allies, besides Spector, were Orrin Hatch and Strom Thurmond of the Republican Party, zeroed in on Miss Hill with a vengeance. They were agreeing with President Bush's determination to discredit Anita Hill. Despite the hearing that happened and the aftermath, the fact remained there was supposed to be a promise of confidentiality at this inquiry. And despite the character defamation Anita Hill endured on television and in print, including Arlen Spector's continued assertion that Hill was a perjurer, she always said she would still testify if she had to repeat it all over.

* * *

Judge Henry Kencade spent most of his free days watching these hearings and the eventual confirmation of Clarence Thomas to the Supreme Court by a vote of fifty-two to forty-eight. He was relieved it wasn't him.

Kencade also watched an interview with the outgoing and first black Supreme Court Justice, Thurgood Marshall who sided with Anita Hill and commented, "President Bush is making a mistake by his nomination of Thomas. If it's the colored barrier he is so concerned about, there are much better black folk out there that would make a better Supreme Court Judge than Clarence Thomas ever could!" Kencade was also irked by Thomas' remark before the Judiciary Committee characterizing the hearings as a 'high-tech lynching for an 'uppity' black'.

But Thomas' nomination was inevitable, as commentators across the country had a field day reporting the event: *Thomas' nomination was confirmed on October 15, even after refusing to submit to a polygraph exam and categorically denying Anita Hill's charges, the Senate confirmed Clarence Thomas to the Supreme Court in the second narrowest approval margin for any*

516

nominee in history."

"The Republican senators followed the hearings by citing Hill as a 'scorned woman' willing to perjure herself to get revenge! What we also saw was how easy it was for them to tear down the character of an African-American woman before the world. The senators made certain any attempts to contradict the nominee were to fail while allowing him to refuse to answer those charges against him. Here, President Bush, like in Desert Storm, won another battle-- not the war, just a battle, though this was what it seemed for now. A man from the State of Texas in Bush's own backyard soon changed all that. This man became a well known figure throughout every household across the country, as the man who challenged the President-- his name, Ross Perot."

Two other news events would eventually become the cause of President Bush's downfall. First, the saga of the BCCI scandal continued to develop. It was like connecting dots of a picture puzzle from one dot to the next. This time the most recent dot connected the Central Intelligence agency to the BCCI. As one news anchor reported, *"The CIA has become a law unto itself, unchecked by scrutiny from Congress and the public and the media! The Central Intelligence Agency's involvement in both the Bank of Credit and Commerce International scandal, and the Iran-Contra affair was guilty in slanting their reports to serve their political ends. The connections were explored as committees set up five congressional hearings taking note of alleged fraud!"*

Following the path of the dots, we now draw the line from the CIA dot to the next dot of the puzzle to what appeared to be George Bush! So now the question is how is George Bush and the BCCI connected. Who knew when? Documents written by the House Armed Services Committee Chairman, Leslie Aspen, focus attention on George Bush's office as Vice-President in 1984. The documents implied the BCCI financed activities backed by the then Vice-President, activities involved in the Iran-Contra affair!

Although the public and media would not know this Richard Franklin had reason to follow the second news-breaking event which caused a big headache in the White House. It started as a nationally televised preview on Thanksgiving day 1991. A film released soon changed all the rules. It was narrated by Martin Sheen and was followed by the actual last minute release of the controversial movie on December 21, 1991, of Oliver Stones' explosive three-hour epic, *JFK*!

As the new year 1992 opened, the controversy would increase throughout the year from every political figure to the deathbed of real life character actor Kevin Costner would play on screen, Jim Garrison who would eventually die on October 21, 1992.

The controversy continued through the twenty-ninth anniversary of Kennedy's assassination, with a stopover between on the House and Senate floors with Oliver Stone's request to those in power to release the Kennedy files. They were hidden away all these years by the Intelligence circles, the FBI and the Warren Commission. Stone wanted to open all the files to the public, seeking justice where justice was due. This caused George Bush to consider a way of accommodating the people as well as his future voters and simultaneously, keeping a lid on it. Bush found a way to do both at the same time.

Both *Time* and *Newsweek* magazine critics gave the film *JFK* the best reviews of the year, although in a section next to the review in *Time Magazine*, a writer for the government's point of view called it pure fantasy. Thus began the smear campaign against the motion picture. Every government official was now an expert in derailing and crying foul at Oliver Stone's film, using every aspect of the media to destroy his credibility.

After *JFK* and Stone were nominated for the Academy Award, Stone lost to another director and film, like Orson Welles' *Citizen Kane* had been nominated in 1941 and Frank Capra's *Mr. Smith Goes to Washington* nominated in 1939.

Jack Valenti, the President of the motion picture rating board, and who had once worked in the White House under President Lyndon Johnson, had this to say about Oliver Stone's film after the Academy Awards were over. "*My own rebuttal to Mr. Stone comes down to this: I was there, and he wasn't!*"

Oliver Stone's reply: "*Jack Valenti is a former government official who never did anything to get the files released!"*

Richard Franklin took all this in, recording every event as one political figure after another came out in the open to comment on the film, including Gerald Ford, John Connally, President Nixon, and the CIA directors such as Helms, Colby and Webster.

Arlen Spector, worried about his credibility to hang on to his Senate seat, began an about face, agreeing to allow the release of the files for the people to get this whole conspiracy theory out of their system. He thought the public had to see for themselves he was right all along, and the Warren Commission had done its job! Soon, Warren Commission advocate Dan Rather from CBS turned an about-face, knowing his ratings could take the greatest dive of his career if he criticized Stone's film.

John Modini sat in his safe house somewhere in the State of Indiana, witnessing one of the most extraordinary events on television. It was from the mouth of the ex-CIA director and present Commander in Chief of the United States who was traveling abroad.

After the release of the movie *JFK* and the demand by Oliver Stone for the government to release the files, reporters approached George Bush on a stop in Australia and asked him this question: *"What do you think now with the release of Mr. Stone's film gaining all this attention, and as a former CIA Director, did you discover any improprieties within the Central Intelligence files concerning their involvement in JFK's assassination? And sir, do you feel the government files closed to the public until the year 2039 should now finally be released?"*

Modini got out of his chair and paced back and forth nervously, listening closely to Bush's answer, since he heard the same question asked before at the Church Hearings in 1976. He accepted this future President's word, then the acting CIA Director. George Bush's answer, upon replacing Director William Colby, fired from the agency by President Ford, was a simple, *"I've gone over the CIA thoroughly with a clean-tooth comb and found no evidence in the files or anywhere connecting the CIA to the thirty-fifth President's assassination!"*

But that was then, this was now! President Bush gave his straight-laced answer in front of millions watching around the world. "As CIA Director I was so busy during that period I never had the time nor opportunity, let alone desire or concern, to take a look at the files concerning the Kennedy matter--"

Modini abruptly stopped his pacing to think about what the President of the United States said. "Holy Shit!" he said to himself, and shut up to hear the rest of Bush's reply to the reporters.

"--And about Mr. Stone's film, well... Isn't Elvis Presley supposed to be alive? I'm sure that film will make a good movie and should be coming out soon!" Bush laughed and chuckled at his own joke as he walked away from a dumbfounded press corps.

"My God!" Modini commented, "This is the President of the United States.! Hell! I wonder if he's uttered one true comment to the American people since the day he came into government!"

Modini continued to pace back and forth in front of the television, too upset to think straight. He turned off the tube and tried to wrack his brain for some answer to why the news media never question the answer. "Why do the people who ask the questions accept what a public figure gives for answers? It's like a film actor who's lying through his press agents' teeth about everything, including who they really are! Well, hell, why not? That's why they're actors, aren't they? They're never themselves, only figments of our imagination, playing a variety of roles."

The telephone rang interrupting Modini's open thoughts. He answered the phone, discovering it is Richard Franklin calling from Los Angeles. "Oh, hello Richard... Hell, yes, I'm going completely bananas here! Yes, I just heard it! I mean nothing these guys say from now on will be believed, you know that! Soon it's going to be Oliver Stone against the government, period. And in the end he'll lose. So why don't we let Oliver Stone do his thing for now until it runs out of steam! At least for now the country now is rallying around him. Maybe he can help open some doors for us. Maybe those hunting me will pull off and eventually chase Stone because he is hot right now, hot as a brick! Let him fight our windmills! Tell me, Richard, something is bothering me. When Bush went before Frank Church in the Senate hearings, why didn't Church's Committee pressure him to prove he wasn't covering up for the CIA? Why? Dammit! Why have these committees in the first place if you don't investigate, but pacify the witnesses? Why waste everyone's time and money? I don't get it?"

Franklin, on the other end, smiled with rye amusement. "Maybe Bush was too new to the agency?" he suggested. "I mean maybe the hearings thought Bush was actually trying to cooperate at the time-- you know Frank Church was quite popular as a Senator during this period, and as a Democrat he was well liked on both sides. Though he did make waves, he still wanted to please everyone. His main interest was trying to clean up the corruption within the CIA and FBI, getting the public to trust government again, after a rash of assassinations and a corrupt President was ousted out of office. I think he opened a can of worms and that's why the House Select Committee was formed-- hold it! Wait a minute!" Ho--ly smoke!"

"What? What is it?" Modini asked.

Franklin finally replied, "Can you hold on a sec-- You may have hit on something just now -- hold on, I'll be back!"

Modini was confused, "What, what did I say?"

Franklin searched in his bookcase for a book of law, looking through one after another until finding the one he needed concerning the Church Hearings. He opened it and checked the members of the committee: Frank Church, the Chairman and Democratic Senator from the State of Idaho. He continued down the page until he found what he was looking for. Franklin walked back to his phone and picked it up to ask Modini, "Are you still there?" He heard Modini mumbling in the background and grinned. "Guess what? Guess who I found in the Church Hearings?"

"Uh, Arlen Spector?" Modini guessed. "Big deal!"

Again, Franklin grinned. "No, you won't believe this, but when you said you wondered why the Church Hearings treated Bush with kid gloves-- well, guess who was heading the Republican side of the Committee? You got to remember until you start connecting the dots who other than Johnson benefited after Kennedy's demise?"

"Well, Spector would have only been counsel, so--" Modini continued to think openly. "Of course, It would have been Nixon and Ford! It wouldn't be Rockefeller, because he headed Ford's Commission-- we're talking Republican here! A Republican? It has to be Republican, ah-- not, don't tell me! Ah..."

There was silence on the line as Franklin waited for an answer. Then Modini said, "You're kidding me-- you're not kidding me, oh, my God! Don't tell me it was Senator Fuller?"

Franklin laughed aloud, "You're hotter than a pancake-- it's even one better than that! The Republican Party and the Texan oil men benefited the most. Do you know what they both have in common, besides Nixon and Bush?" Franklin looked at the picture in his book. "It was Bush's best buddy from Texas, Senator John Goodwin Tower!"

* * *

Former President Richard Milhous Nixon held a circuit of interviews across the country in a week to debunk Oliver Stone's movie *JFK*. Ted Koppel on Night Line and Larry King on *Larry King Live* on CNN, asked Nixon, "What was the reason you were in Dallas, Texas, at the time of Kennedy's arrival on November 22, 1963?"

Nixon had two different pat answers for each interview. The first time, on *Larry King Live*, King asked Mr. Nixon the question, but did not get an answer. So King diplomatically turned the question around by already putting Nixon in Dallas and making a straight statement in the form a question he had to answer.

Richard Franklin explained the details of this interview as he led a seminar on the UCLA College campus regarding the reaction of the former leaders of the United States Government to Oliver Stone's film. He stood behind a lectern and spoke from the theater stage to the students in the audience. He set up a slide and film presentation for his lecture.

It was an idea he got from Modini to keep the fires burning within the youth movement, and what Franklin explained, "...Is uncalled-for in the furor over Oliver Stone's movie, *JFK!* It helps us to open our minds to those who are brainwashed to believe Oswald was the lone assassin when every one of us has our own thoughts, our own ways of getting to the truth of the matter! Look, all you future lawyers out there, all you journalists-- how much time would you need to investigate Kennedy's assassination-- two days?

The students laughed at his last statement. Franklin grinned too, "I didn't think so. Well...then how about four months, or even eight months? Do you think eight months is time enough to solve the crime of the century? That's all President Johnson gave those seven commissioners in the Warren Commission, just eight months. It wasn't enough time to revise their report if any new information surfaced, *Notta*!

"So now we have the twenty-ninth anniversary coming up and an abundance of new information over the years from researchers, investigators, pathologists, senators, congressmen, all who have come forward with their own knowledge and facts. But no...the Government stuck with that eight-month investigation as the official report. President Johnson forced the House, the Senate, and the Dallas Police Department to individually shut down their scheduled investigations. And on top of that, our Government still hides a bulk of that Commission's information in boxes of files the public can't see until the year 2039!

"If Oswald did it, then what is there to hide? If there isn't anything to hide, then open the archives! Open the FBI files, especially the ones concerning the CIA. Open the files on the Rockefeller and Church Hearings. The files in the House Select Committee, in which I was involved in, should also be open. I had to take an oath to remain silent, and I would have been disbarred if I spoke out!"

"What about the files in the Dallas Police Department? We can't forget those either! I never knew one man like Oswald could be so popular and have so many files throughout the country that can't be released. These are files that you, you and you..." Franklin pointed to members of the audience, "...and your parents and neighbors paid for as taxpayers!"

Franklin crossed the stage, playing to the audience. "The government officials of our

523

country are calling Mr. Stone's film the twisted truth! That's funny. For twenty-nine years critics across the nation called the Warren Commission the same thing, except they left out the word truth! David Belin, the lead counsel, along with Lee Rankin for the Warren Commission says 'Stone's film would make Adolph Hitler proud!' Again, that's funny since a lot of us on the House Select Committee thought Belin's tactics in suppressing evidence within the Warren and Rockefeller Commissions were right out of Hitler's regime. He switched exhibit letters to match the wrong jacket, claiming it to be Oswald's, after it was established one found near the scene of the crime in Officer Tippit's murder was not Oswald's. Then there were the bullets at this same site. The officer in charge confiscated five bullets in all which were later entered as evidence to have matched Oswald's pistol-- the same one that was supposed to have killed Tippit! However, these bullets turned out not to be the same ones the officer had confiscated in the first place-- because he always marked his evidence with his own initials. The exhibit bullets Belin had before the Commission was not marked at all by the officer's initials! The same bullets that Belin said matched Oswald's pistol. This was one of the greatest shell games this attorney played to convict a dead man in the crime of the century!

"So, you tell me *who* investigated the Warren Commission's report? Nobody, because we took the word of our own government, because no one believed they would lie to us, right? But then why should anyone get upset if someone like you or me or Oliver Stone or a Jim Garrison tried to challenge it? This is America! We the people have that right, don't we? Before I conclude, I want you to see how former President Nixon avoided a question on a talk show everyone wanted answered, but continued to avoid.

"The interviewer was Larry King. Oliver Stone announced, before his film was released, 'the establishment and press are trying to kill my film before it can even be seen and they're saying the film can't be trusted!'

"In my opinion Larry King said it like it is! He said, 'the film critics are raving and the historians are raving mad!' Now, I present King's recent interview with Nixon-- keep in mind now,

Larry King had not mentioned either the movie *JFK* or Oliver Stone."

The lights dimmed, and the film started. The image of Larry King was projected on a white screen on the auditorium stage interviewing Richard Nixon. Larry King started with a statement. "On the day you flew out of Dallas-- you were attending a convention-- Pepsi Cola?"

The view from Nixon's back showed him nodding his head yes. King proceeded, slowly getting to the point.

"Your law firm represented Pepsi Cola?"

"That's right!" Nixon replied

"Do we know that whole story?" Larry King countered.

Nixon sat thinking a moment almost in a stupor before speaking. "I am not one of those who saw the motion picture. Ah, but...his credibility was questioned in my mind, when I read a piece by it's producer Oliver Stone in which he made the statement. Ah, that President Johnson in 1965 sent the first combat troops to Vietnam...well, now that wasn't true!"

To Larry King's surprise, Nixon forced a smile and proceeded to answer a question he was never asked: "President Kennedy sent the first troops, sixteen-thousand, to Vietnam when he was President-- which I think, incidentally, was the right thing to do. I supported it at the time and there were four-hundred casualties while he was President! So, I would say if anyone who was that ah, ah...off base is not perhaps the *best*..." King tried to interject here, but Nixon raised his voice to finish his thought and to make his point. "...*expert* as to whether there was a conspiracy or not!" Nixon closed his eyes, completing the statement.

"That aside-- did you believe the Warren Commission?" Larry King asked.

Nixon again carefully considered his thoughts before speaking. "I didn't study it carefully. Ah...I have...never questioned it before and I don't question it now! Ah...a lot is being written, but the reason I don't is that nothing is going to happen as a result! If I thought it to be useful to try to dig into it, I would do so."

"Are you surprised that seventy-five percent of the American public don't accept it?"

Nixon shook his head. "Not at all surprised because ah, we..." Nixon smiled again, now stuttering to get his words out: "...that...we... people think usually that there is a conspiracy about...about almost everything... In fact there's a conspiracy about the Lincoln assassination, still. You know the stories that are out! Ah, but in this case I know the people don't believe that, but I don't see a useful purpose to getting into that. I don't...I don't think it's going to be useful to the Kennedy family to constantly raise that up again, so I am not going to get into that!"

King quickly jumped into this. "And you agree to keep the files closed then for a...another twenty-three years, I guess."

"Ah, keeping the files closed is another matter." Nixon responded. "Ah...I see no reason to keep the files closed unless there is a national security problem involved...ah...and I can't see any national security involved, because for example, if Cuba were involved or some other foreign power...ah...that has all changed. I think at the present time I see no reason to keep the files closed!"

The interview ended, and the auditorium lights came back on.

Franklin asked, "All right, can you tell me any misconstrued statements made by Mr. Nixon within this short piece of film?"

Hands were raised from the students demanding to ask questions.

Franklin pointed to a young lady in the back row, and she stood to answer. "Well, I don't want to say President Nixon was wrong in the things he said because he was there and I wasn't, but I did find it odd he sidestepped the original question put to him. I say this because I saw *Night Line* the other night and Ted Koppel asked him the same question, 'Why was he in Dallas on the day of Kennedy's assassination?' and again, like here, he skirted the issue. Koppel continued to ask that question, but to no avail. Nixon refused to answer him until Koppel was so annoyed he finally gave up!"

Franklin nodded, "Good observation!" He pointing to a male student in front this time.

The student stood up and smiled, "My observation, Mr. Franklin, is either Nixon is giving

526

us a new history lesson or all our books have misinformation. He opened up a textbook. "It says here there were advisors sent over to South Vietnam to train Vietnamese for combat and it was Eisenhower and Nixon's administration who sent those soldiers there. There's nothing here saying Kennedy sent combat troops. When Kennedy became president, he added more advisors, establishing the Green Berets. I know, because my father was one of those Green Berets President Kennedy sent as an advisor to Vietnam. Also, it says here Johnson sent the first combat troops when he started the war in Vietnam in March of 1964. By then Kennedy was dead and 1,000 advisors had come home on orders by Kennedy at Christmas time, 1963!"

Franklin applauded the student. "Well, if you're so correct and if the textbooks suggested this, maybe we should debate President Nixon on this issue!" The whole auditorium burst into laughter.

"Let me read to you what Nixon wrote in his autobiography after the Bay of Pigs happened in April of 1961, less than seventy-five days in office. Kennedy had met with Eisenhower at Camp David to discuss the issue with the former President including the misinformation given to him by the CIA. Dean Rusk informed the U.N. Ambassador Adlei Stevenson they had been duped. Whatever was discussed, those involved were either resigned or were fired.

"It was here at the height of the disaster John Kennedy made a call to Richard Nixon. Now why, after conferring with Eisenhower, did Kennedy need to speak with the ex-Vice-President? Was it because Eisenhower didn't know the facts of the plan concerning the Bay of Pigs-- but Nixon did? It didn't make sense that Kennedy, the leader of the Free World, would have to confer with the man who was the former Vice-President-- unless this V.P. was running his own show-- which he did, following Eisenhower's illness in his last year in the White House.

Franklin referred to his notes. "This is what Nixon described from his point of view: 'My daughter Tricia had taken the call and left me a note by our hallway telephone. It read: *JFK called.* I knew it! It wouldn't be long before he would get into trouble and have to call on you for help!'"

Franklin continued to read Nixon's text describing his meeting with the President: "He

(Kennedy) jumped up from his chair and paced back and forth in front of his desk. His anger and frustration poured out in a profane barrage, 'I was assured by every son of a bitch I checked with all the military experts and the CIA-- that the plan would succeed...' Everything had been going so well for him. A few days earlier he stood high in the polls, and the press was overwhelmingly favorable. Now he was in deep trouble, and he felt the innocent victim of bad advice from men whom he trusted. It suddenly struck me how alone he must feel, how wronged, yet how responsible. It was not entirely his fault, but nonetheless, it was his inescapable responsibility."

Franklin looked up to his student audience and commented, "How profound of Mr. Nixon, wouldn't you say? Kenneth O'Donnell, Kennedy's best friend and Chief of Staff, wrote on the night after the disaster that he and Press Secretary Pierre Salinger were up until 4 a.m. talking and discussing the agreement to dispatch B-26's from Nicaragua to give cover to the men on the beaches. He agreed that six unmarked jets from the aircraft carrier Essex could cover the B-26's. This too, the CIA would eventually screw up as well. Castro would have a resounding victory after six days of fighting, capturing 1,150 of the enemy. O'Donnell wrote, 'Jack was during all this, close to tears.'"

"To Theodore Sorensen, his special assistant, he admitted: 'How could I have been so far off base? All my life I've known better than to depend on the experts. How could I have been so stupid to let them go ahead?'"

Franklin addressed the students again, "Like I said--how profound Mr. Nixon was, not by his part in this fiasco, but the fact he knew damn well why he was having this meeting with the President in the first place. But you and I will never know because Nixon never divulged to anyone the truth of his participation in that episode. But the big surprise was yet to come, especially for Richard Nixon. Kennedy came forward at a press conference shortly afterward with this to say: 'There's an old saying that victory has a hundred fathers and defeat is an orphan. I'm the responsible officer of the government.'"

"A press release followed emphasizing what Mr. Nixon had called the President's 'inescapable responsibility'. President Kennedy stated from the beginning that as President he bore sole responsibility. He had stated it on every occasion and restated it then. 'The President is strongly opposed to anyone within or without the administration attempting to shift the responsibility!'"

Franklin stopped for a moment of silence then added, "This last statement is something that Mr. Nixon later could have gotten advice from, concerning his Waterloo-- his Watergate; but this too, we will never get President Nixon to admit. It is said that if you look down the elevator shaft at Watergate, Dealey Plaza appears at the bottom. Does our present President Bush offer apologies or blame concerning the scandals that continue to pile up within his administration, beginning with the hostage situation in Iran? Remember who was CIA before Carter came into office-- the Iran-Contra affair spun from that. And what about the continued controversy of the POW/MIA concern in Vietnam? Neither Ford nor Nixon did anything about it. And Reagan either couldn't or was sidetracked. Is Bush doing anything about that?"

A student, a tall black man, raised his hand, "Mr. Franklin, what do you want from all this? Why are you complaining and raising these issues, spending your life this way? What can come from this?" He looked around, embarrassed for asking this question, as the auditorium became filled with a murmur of disapproval.

Franklin quieted the students. That question is a good one," he told him. "It's a shame I never asked that question of myself. All right! I'll tell you, and this is for you who are black and white, purple, and yellow, red white, and blue-- all the colors of the world. My President was murdered! *Your* President was murdered! When I was a child, he was the first white man who treated our African-Americans as equals.

"He asked Martin Luther King, Jr. what he could do to help before he became President of the United States and during his term in office allowed Mr. King in the White House. Martin Luther King, Jr. was the man to march on Washington. He tried to stop the South and the Ku Klux Klan from killing us, destroying us as human beings. He fought J. Edgar Hoover to do his job.

You, as a black man, know what that means to our people-- to a people who are now accepted as equal.

"Until we know the truth about Kennedy's murder, can we find the truth of his brother Bobby and to our brother Martin Luther King, Jr.'s murder! Until we solve these issues within our own country, the race issue will always be used to continue the upheaval in dividing us as people. God forbid it be another holocaust of a Nazi-Germany or what is happening in our third world countries. Until we can tackle that race barrier, we can't focus on those words of our beloved sixteenth President Abraham Lincoln: 'That we the people are all created equal!'"

The students started to clap, several at first, and then more of them joined in. Soon the auditorium was filled with the majority of students giving Franklin a standing ovation. The respect and admiration brought tears to Franklin's eyes, trying to smile in gratitude. At least the students here were listening to him. It was a start.

* * *

Oliver Stone spoke on the Senate floor before both Houses of Congress and broadcast by the television and news media throughout the world. Citing his movie *JFK*, Stone took another step by making a case to open all the Kennedy files-- á la 'Mr. Stone goes to Washington.'

In other news a commentator announced, "*Jackson Stephens capitalized on his campaign donation and his friendship with President Bush's son, George W. Bush, Jr., to get BCCI funding of a Harken Energy offshore oil project in Bahrain. The President's son is a Harken board member. Facing death threats, Maschur Rahman has paid a heavy price for being the first to testify about bank corruption.*

"There was a memorial today for the wife of Senator Gerald Fuller of Indiana. Caroline Fuller was one of the victims of the TransAmerica plane crash last week which killed one hundred and thirty-one passengers and crew. Mrs. Fuller and Martha Mitchell who also died in a plane crash in the 1970's, were outspoken advocates against their husbands' involvement with Nixon

and his administration."

* * *

A government car drove up to the front of Marian O'Leary's house in Salem, Oregon. Two men exited the car. They approached the front porch and stopped. The FBI agent named Jack Clayton, signaled to his partner, Ken Gordon, to take the back side of the house as he proceeded up the steps.

Mrs. O'Leary answered the loud knocking on the door with a curious smile. "Yes, may I help you?"

The man showed her his FBI credentials. "I'm Mr. Clayton from the FBI.

Mrs. O'Leary patiently waited for what came next. And the FBI man waited for her to respond. She stood there as this crude FBI man chomped on a wad of gum.

This irritated her. "Yes?" she said again, as if to comment 'so what.'

"Ma'am, you're probably aware why we are here..."

Mrs. O'Leary played dumb, "No, I really don't know why you're here. You tell me!"

Suddenly from behind her, she heard Gordon's voice in her own house, "He's not here, no one is here." This scared Mrs. O'Leary out of her wits, causing her to cry out.

She turned around and screamed at her intruder. "How dare you come in here like this!" She grabbed a cleaning broom and came out swinging. She hit the second FBI agent in the side of the head. "Now, get out, all of you...coming here like this, scaring an old lady-- get out!" She took another shot at the FBI agent that ran past them out the front door.

FBI agent Clayton grabbed the broom. "We're here for your son, Mrs. O'Leary! Are you going to cooperate with us, or are you willing to be arrested for obstructing justice?"

This comment made Mrs. O'Leary angrier. "Who is obstructing whom here? You can dig up the late J. Edgar Hoover and bring him here for all I care, and you'll find nothing! Besides, the government has already interfered with my life as it is, coming here to announce my son's death.

531

Now you two come here and break into my house--"

Gordon appeared again in the doorway. He held a picture frame up to Mrs. O'Leary showing an eight by ten snapshot of her son, John Modini, in uniform with beard. "Is this your son, ma'am?"

Mrs. O'Leary grabbed for the frame as the agent stepped back onto the porch. She followed him out the door. "You give me that back this minute!"

Gordon taunted her with the frame, holding it over her head as she continued to jump for it. "This is evidence, ma'am-- your sweet son is alive and well-- he staged his own death and now he's wanted for attempting to murder a Senator and shooting a Federal Marshal in cold blood!"

Mrs. O'Leary took another shot at the agent, this time by kicking him in the groin. He released the picture. It fell to the porch, cracking the frame. Gordon grabbed himself with both hands as his face turned red and he fell to his knees in pain. Clayton joined them on the front porch.

Mrs. O'Leary turned to Clayton who held up his hands in embarrassment, shouting, "Please, ma'am I give up! You've got me! We'll get your son one way or another, dead or alive, Mrs. O'Leary! It's no skin off our nose!" He chomped away on his cud. "You could be the one to save his life if you'd help us!"

Mrs. O'Leary went inside her house, and grabbed the door. "If my son did what you say he did and you have witnesses to that fact then you better in God's name prove it!" Then she slammed the door on both FBI men. Clayton shook his head as he glanced at this partner, still curled up in pain.

* * *

Catherine Rogers appeared at Caroline Fuller's well-attended funeral. As the minister gave the eulogy, her attention shifted from the minister to Senator Fuller who stared silently at his wife's coffin, an empty look on his face. Fuller lifted his head at the end of the sermon, and became aware

532

of Catherine's presence. Fuller looked at her and nodded to her in recognition.

Catherine's eyes met his and stared back at him, silent and emotionless.

* * *

Catherine Rogers climbed the staircase of the capital in Indianapolis and passed through security checkpoints. Once inside, she asked for directions to Senator Fuller's office. Fuller expected his guest and was in his private bathroom primping himself for her arrival.

Madeline, his secretary informed him by intercom Catherine had arrived. He looked at himself in the mirror momentarily, knowing he aged these last years, at least in appearance and told his secretary he'd be right in. He combed and brushed his hair, adding a squirt of breath freshener into his mouth. Then he straightened and tightened his tie and exited into his office.

Fuller's secretary stood beside Catherine as they waited for his entrance.

"My...my, Mrs. Rogers," Fuller said in his most polite manner. He was surprised to see what a lovely woman she had become. He approached and took her hand. "It is nice to see you. Won't you please have a seat on the couch?"

Catherine gave him a polite nod, but didn't speak. He led her a few steps then turned to his secretary. "You may take your lunch now, Madeline..."

Fuller waited for his secretary to leave the room before speaking with Catherine again. "I want to thank you for attending Caroline's funeral. It is so good to see you after all this time, Catie. It must have been at your mother's funeral since we last saw each other. Is that right?"

Catherine stared at him tolerantly, nodding he was correct, as Fuller sat down beside her on the couch.

She responded in a businesslike tone. "Senator, do you mind if you conduct yourself behind your desk? If not, maybe I should find a single chair. I'd like this meeting to be proper and above board." Then on his look she added emphatically, "I am not one of your floozy girlfriends, Senator!"

533

The Senator looked at Catherine oddly. Then his temper flared, and he slapped her across the face. Her hand went to her face as she stared at him in shock. He stood up, towering over her. "How *dare* you speak to me in that condescending tone, offending me like that! Who do you think you are?"

The slap caught Catherine off guard, but she was in control of herself. She wasn't ready to let Fuller get the upper hand of this situation. She rose from the couch and answered him. "I *know* who I am, Senator-- who the hell do you think *you* are?"

Fuller glared at her in disgust, knowing what he wanted to do to her.

Catherine backed off, but refused to let her guard down. "Now, Senator-- do you want me to leave or do you want to talk business!"

Fuller hesitated a moment, then crossed to his desk and sat down in his leather mahogany chair. "What is it that brings you here, after all these years?" his voice was tight with suppressed anger.

Catherine sat straight in the plush chair in front of his desk. "That's much better. Now we get to the point. I know you had something to do with framing my father with that Watergate hotel murder. You can deny all you want-- but I couldn't believe you'd let it go as far as it did. My father's future is over with now. I know that, and I can't prove that you were directly involved, but I do have evidence to show that you collaborated to frame Karl Hunter, and might be responsible for his death."

Fuller was planning to say something when Catherine stopped him. "No! Senator, you can say what ever you want when I'm through. But before you do, you're going to want to hear this! It's about a little matter that happened down in Miami earlier this year, around the time of Desert Storm. The Miami Police Department will back me up on this. Captain Corrigan and I have traced your phone number and found it tied to this matter. I will not discuss it in this room, in case you're bugging your own office."

Fuller swiveled from her in his chair, a gesture of uncaring authority.

534

Catherine continued, "Senator, you could be arrested anytime I give the word. I also have some other little tidbits, but I don't want to bore you to death with all that unless you force me to."

Fuller's eyes swung to hers. He wasn't ready to say what was really on his mind. "What is it that you want from me...money? My resignation?" he asked calmly.

Catherine was impressed by his reply. "Well...that would be good for the finale, but what I need from you is to call off the dogs on John Modini and exonerate Karl Hunter. Unless you have proof on the contrary, Senator, there is another Karl Hunter out there who committed those crimes. And if you don't help me, I'm going to prove you had the real Karl Hunter killed!"

Fuller smiled as he protested. He, too, was good at playing the cat and mouse game. "You, my dear, are much mistaken here! You come in here and threaten me with innuendo. Where is this so called evidence that will make me believe this incredible story."

"Test me, Senator. I'd love to have the authorities see my evidence."

"But I had nothing to do with Karl Hunter's death! Ah...yes, I admit I had something on that murderer. But he would have gotten the gas chamber just the same! Besides, what would my reason be for having Hunter killed; knowing he would die anyway?"

Catherine rose from her chair. "Senator, I think you know the answer to that...just as I do?" she said sarcastically. "Hunter told me things. He told me I should get involved as much as I could. He provided incredible information, which my investigations collaborated..." She was bluffing her way through this and hoped Fuller couldn't tell. "He hoped it might help his case. It concerned facts you and your cronies wanted so badly."

"It would be a shame if...something would happen to you before you could use this information." Fuller hinted subtly.

"Of course you could try to stop it, but If anything were to happen to me the information will still get out." Catherine stood up and headed for the door. "Besides, what's it to you now...you're going to resign anyway..."

Senator Fuller glared at her. His mouth was a straight line, his eyes very hard. He didn't like being threatened, but now he felt trapped.

"Good bye Senator," Catherine added. "Remember, you have by the end of the day to call off the dogs or your career won't be worth a plug nickel when it comes time to memorialize you!"

Fuller quickly stood up to get Catherine's attention, raising his voice. "Catherine, stop!" She paused at the door, hearing the tension in his command.

Fuller groped for words. "Think what you're doing-- this...this situation is too big for either one of us! It won't matter what I do. It's totally out of my hands now. Before I could do what you wanted, I'd be a dead man-- don't you see? Modini is already a dead man if he isn't already! The only reason you're still alive is that my...friends don't know what you know, but that won't matter...they'll find out eventually." He was almost pleading with her now. "What will it matter then if all of us are dead and buried? Life would go on as it did before, but you won't be alive! We have to live while we can, Catherine, we have so little time left as it is..."

Catherine nodded. She knew he was frightened, but still could detect the touch of sincerity in his voice. "I suggest then, Senator, you'd better start saving our country before those who you work for destroy it for us! Because if you don't, I'm going to do everything I can to bring you down! I'm sure you can get help. Not all Senators are as corrupt as you...I pray!"

She opened the door and walked out, slamming it behind her, and paused a moment to settle her nerves. She closed her eyes and took a deep breath. Her heart was palpitating in her chest. She caught his secretary looking at her from behind her desk. She straightened up and walked out of his office without saying a word. Despite the mixed emotions inside her, she felt a personal pride in what she accomplished.

* * *

"The words of the Kennedy era in the days of Camelot sounded different from the words Eisenhower used in the previous administration: 'I don't believe you can change the hearts and minds of men with laws and decisions.' By May, 1961, thirty days following the Bay of Pigs failure, a Greyhound Bus carrying Freedom Riders testing racism and segregation in the Southern States was set afire by angry whites in Anniston, Alabama. And this was only the beginning. No one knew or expected what terrible events would happen next in the following months. John F. Kennedy had already appointed black people to his staff: Andrew Hatcher, an associate press secretary in the White House, and Robert L. Weaver, chairman of the Housing and Home Finance Agency. President Kennedy had also noticed no black cadets in the Inauguration Day Parade. He gave instructions for the admission of blacks to the academy. But the action of the Freedom Fighters spoke a thousand words, and blazed across the nation more than any of the presidential appointments. Over thirty years ago the Kennedy brothers could not stand watching the constant harassment on national television, showing police dogs attacking and fire hoses spraying people in the black communities of this nation's southern states. Martin Luther King Jr., himself, came to see more in Kennedy's 'ability to respond to creative pressure' than mere political calculation and crisis management. Kennedy frankly acknowledged he responded to mass demands, but this was so, according to what King states: 'because he thought it was right to do so.' This is the secret of the deep affection he evoked. He was responsive, sensitive, humble before the people, but bold on their behalf!'"

Richard Franklin listened with tears in his eyes to these words broadcast on his car radio, as he drove to an important appointment. He tried to keep his eyes clear for the road, and wiped them as the broadcast continued.

He heard a speech given by JFK five months prior to his Dallas visit. It was recorded on June 11, 1963, and televised from the White House: "This nation was founded by the men of many nations and backgrounds. It was founded on the principle that all men are created equal, and that the rights of every man are diminished when the rights of one man are threatened. It ought to be possible for American consumers of any color to receive equal service in places of public accommodation, such as hotels and restaurants and theaters and retail stores, without being forced to report to demonstrations in the street. And it ought to be possible for American citizens of any color to register to vote in a free election without interference or fear of reprisal."

Suddenly, in a blinding flash through Franklin's thoughts, he pictured the bullets, one by one, take down Medgar Evers, John F. Kennedy, Malcolm X, Martin Luther King, Jr. and Robert F. Kennedy. He blinked and opened his eyes wide to realize he was driving through war-torn South Central Los Angeles, and saw the aftermath of the Rodney King riots.

All Franklin could do was voice his fears aloud, "Will there be more of this to come? Racism never left our nation! The Reagan Era hid the facade beneath some carpet! Did it just happen to resurface? No, it's always been here. We shut a blind eye to it for the present...and only God can help us now!"

The radio broadcast continued. "Congress has been trudging in the direction of unsealing records of the investigation into President John F. Kennedy's assassination, as have the Senate who has considered taking a similar step. The pace, meanwhile, hasn't picked up. The wheels turn slowly on the records of the Warren Commission appointed by Lyndon B. Johnson, and the Rockefeller and Church Commissions which focused on questions the Warren Report either didn't raise or left unanswered. Congressional interest in the matter developed after director Oliver Stone's controversial motion picture, *JFK* came out last year, depicting a grand, high-level conspiracy to cover up the circumstances surrounding Kennedy's death. The Warren Commission concluded that Lee Harvey Oswald was the lone assassin acting alone."

* * *

John Modini jumped out of his seat and yelled at the television set, scaring Thomas Sanders. They were watching a report about the Kennedy Assassination on a news broadcast. "When is it ever going to dawn on these people to read the Warren Report? Nothing in that report says or can say, Oswald did it. It is only their *theory*! They can only say *alleged* assassin! When is the news media ever going to get that into their mind for God's sake?"

"Ask Dan Rather," Thomas Sanders laughed. He was resting his head and arms at the kitchen counter, watching the tv. "I've never seen such a one-sided, one-dimensional news anchor in all my life."

Modini shook his head, "Why blame Dan Rather?"

"Because he continued to lie to the American people. He always tells the government's version!"

Modini was very irritated. "Well, Thomas-- a few years ago I was of the same opinion as Dan Rather, remember? I, too, believed Oswald Killed Kennedy."

The news commentary continued: "...A House investigation agreed Oswald was the killer..."

"Yeah, tell that to Franklin!" Modini said to the screen.

"...But the House concluded that audio tape evidence raised reasonable questions about another gunman. With moviegoers' interest aroused, the public started putting pressure on the government to end the secrecy. The most immediate confrontation may lie in the oval office where officials in the Justice Department are advising President Bush to veto the legislation. His advisers' dubious rationale is the materials are part of the executive branch's decision-making process and thus should be under direct control of the executive branch!"

Thomas Sanders walked from around the kitchen counter and confronted Modini. "So what does that mean?"

Modini flopped down in his chair. "It means the law relates back to President Johnson's law he made back in 1964, that the President is the only one to have the power to release any of this information. That's one of the reasons Robert Kennedy decided ultimately to run for the office of the Presidency when he did. He knew as President and being the brother of John Kennedy he would have the power to open all files. Those close to Bobby said, those first years after his brother's assassination, he blamed himself, thinking the Mafia angle was tied into his brother's death, and that he, the Attorney General, was the instigator of the outcome. But as the years passed, Bobby had plenty of time and opportunity to investigate behind the scenes like James Garrison did.

But Garrison got caught. Meanwhile, Bobby discovered the truth and decided he had to clean up Dodge. Well, you can figure the rest!"

"You mean the answer was always there? The fact before JFK's death he was going to clean Dodge-- including the CIA?" Thomas Sanders asked.

Modini nodded, "Unfortunately...but no one can do anything with that faction of our government. Every President has brought in a new director who says the CIA needs to clean up their act. But what happens? Another scandal erupts, another new director or a new President. Nothing ever changes, does it? And so, if President Bush passes a law allowing us to see these files, we still won't be able to see them because someone other than the President controls them! Meaning when files do come out, you may see some and you won't see others. And the ones you do see, you won't be able to read because they'll be heavily censored!"

Sanders interrupted. "Why? Why do they want to hide this information from the public?"

Modini smiled, "That's the government's standard operating procedure. Don't let the public see any classified material-- important or not. Just remind yourself of Fawn Hall and Oliver North. The Attorney General warned North of the State Department coming to raid his secret little war room and headquarters. On go the shredding machines, there goes Fawn Hall leaving the premises with documents hidden inside her underwear! Now this is priceless. North got what-- a six to twelve hour warning from the Attorney General himself? Mind you, he was the investigator! Now Bush himself can take all his time between now and the election to make the decision of which documents to release. Meanwhile the CIA, knowing what Congress and the Senate are up to, especially with their liaisons in each House informing them daily, get each document-- thousands, maybe hundreds of thousands of pages of information-- and black out everything they think is important. You think the CIA will hand out material to the public that puts them or the government in a bad light? Hell no! Most likely, they destroyed all that sensitive material years ago! Bush will tell the CIA he'll get a time table from those in charge of the Commission and CIA files, when to announce his forced decision! You know the CIA already is on top of this since the election is in

November, but Bush will be the one to empower it, and the next President will have to go along with it or the whole process will begin again."

"I guess that mean's we won't be seeing any of these papers soon," Thomas said bleakly.

"It'll be the year 2001 when the materials start to be released. No matter what, we don't win anything, all we'll get is blacked out paper with a word or two...maybe one sentence to read on a page. Will there be enough to find a conspiracy? I doubt it! That's why all our government leaders are cooperating so reasonably. They know they're complying with 'we the people' and they worry, too, about the November election. And on the other hand, they also appease the CIA who in the end will give you nothing anyway!"

Thomas Sanders shook his head, exasperated. "Then what you're saying is, this is a waste of time-- a circle going nowhere?"

Modini threw his arms up in disgust. "What can I tell you?"

"Well, we do have Karl Hunter's letter. Oh, incidentally, I got all the witnesses' statements from the Dallas Police Department."

"Good!"

"And as I was going through those statements, I found an odd coincidence. You'll find this interesting. I think it was early on the day of the assassination, November 22, 1963, a name came up that wouldn't mean anything then, but would later. A Houston oil man witnessed a member of organized crime enter a building near Dealey Plaza. He was identified as a Mafia bagman by police agencies, and his name was Jim Braden. He was connected to the New Orleans Mafia boss, Carlos Marcello, and was arrested immediately for suspicious behavior minutes after JFK was assassinated. Then he was released. It wasn't Jim Braden's name I was shocked and surprised with; it was the name of the Houston oil man that informed the police who reported the incident."

Modini looked at Thomas, waiting for a punch line. "It's right here, hidden among the many witnesses who came forward that day. It was a telephone call to the Dallas Police Department from the one and only, George Herbert Walker Bush!"

Modini turned around, again back to Sanders, giving him a double take. He was so astounded he couldn't say anything.

Chapter Thirty-Five

"The Awakening"

Late one evening, Lieutenant Colonel Donald Casson, a former Green Beret out of Fort Bragg, North Carolina, watched a talk show program hosting several conspiracy theorists and investigators discussing Oliver Stone's movie. They discussed the footage from the real events that happened the day of Kennedy's assassination in Dallas.

Mark Lane, Robert Groden, David Lifton, Josh Thompson were all on a dais arguing, yet agreeing with the commentator it was a conspiracy. Also on the dais was one of Lee Harvey Oswald's friends from New Orleans who connected Clay Shaw to Oswald and Ruby and the latter two with Roscoe White, who he claimed was a shooter in Dealey Plaza that day.

Lieutenant Colonel Casson, wasn't interested one way or another in what was said and overlooked their opinions until the end of the program. It was announced an organized list would be provided of those who died since the Warren Commission was created whose deaths were connected to the assassination of President Kennedy.

The names were familiar and not so familiar, but it was the 1966 death of William B. Pitzer that caused an explosive reaction from the former Green Beret. Casson swore and grabbed for a piece of paper and wrote down the information from the screen. He immediately dialed the phone.

His wife came into the room to see what all the commotion was about. All she saw were names scrolling on the television screen. Seeing nothing unusual, she went back into the kitchen.

Casson called the television station broadcasting the talk show and asked if he could come down to the station to take a look at the broadcast again. He got the run-around first, but he was finally connected to someone with authority to get his request okayed.

* * *

In downtown Miami it was a hot, scorching mid-afternoon when Captain Corrigan came out of a Jewish deli with the mayor of the city and a fellow officer. They shook hands as Corrigan thanked the mayor for lunch, then departed. Corrigan and the officer headed to a parked unmarked police car.

A man in a yellow Camaro watched the two men crossing the street. He dialed a number on his cellular phone. The two officers passed. Corrigan picked his teeth with a toothpick.

The man watched as they entered the unmarked car. He spoke with the party on the other line as if he were playing a game of chess. "To Bishop... Knight is on the move..."

Corrigan's car passed the yellow Camaro. The man spoke into the receiver, adding, "Bishop now takes Knight, putting Queen into check!"

An ambulance parked near a city park while both paramedics were seated inside their cool, air-conditioned cab eating their lunch. An emergency call came over their radio. They dropped their lunch in their lunch boxes and started the ambulance. The medic on the passenger side commented, "Let's part the sea, partner!"

He sounded the siren, and the ambulance sped straight down the street, dividing the cars in front of them. The ambulance driver said, "I love the sound of panicky drivers in mid-afternoon traffic...the power, the power!"

The medic on the passenger side followed a map and said to the driver, "Turn here!" They drove into downtown traffic, their siren chasing everyone on the road to one side or the other.

Corrigan got an emergency call on his radio to get to an address a few blocks from his present location as fast as he could, "A 7ll emergency, an officer is in trouble!"

"Should we make some music?" Corrigan's driver asked.

Corrigan nodded. He threw a police light on the roof of their unmarked car as the driver switched on the siren. They took off down the road.

Within two blocks of each other, the ambulance, heading west, spotted a speeding police car traveling north. Instead of slowing down, the ambulance driver accelerated his engine to speed up as if to beat the police car at the intersection.

Corrigan's driver and fellow officer didn't hear or notice the ambulance until the last second. He swore loudly as he turned his wheel to swerve away, but was too late. The police car plowed into the rear of the ambulance with a thunderous crash and spun around. It flipped over and slid sideways striking two other cars parked on the street.

The ambulance was knocked off center from its path on the road and careened off at an angle, T-boning into the back of a parked car. The vehicle flipped the ambulance over on its side, and it crashed into the sidewalk immediately killing two innocent bystanders. The ambulance came to rest near the entrance way of an outlet store.

The people on the street raced to the police car to help. Several burly men pulled the door open and worked to free the officers from the wreckage. As they worked, the car's gas tank, damaged from the accident, leaked gasoline in a pool around the site.

As two men dragged away one of the men from the unmarked car, a spark from the debris ignited the gasoline. The car suddenly was enveloped in flames and seconds later exploded in a ball of fire.

* * *

Catherine was in her Honda driving home when she heard the report of the accident on the radio. It had made the national news. Arriving at her father's home, she raced into the house.

Judge Kencade finished making himself a cocktail as Catherine rushed into the room and switched on the television set. She used the remote control as a pistol until reaching a news station detailing the Miami story.

Judge Kencade entered the room to see what his daughter was up to. "What's going on, Catie?" he asked after he saw his daughter's pale face.

"Dad, we've got to talk!" Their attention was drawn to the screen by a female newscaster giving a remote report.

"...One of the officers is dead and the other is in critical condition," The newswoman stated solemnly. "One of them is reported to be the captain of the Miami Police Department, but for now no information about the names are confirmed until their families are informed of this tragedy. The police have already begun a preliminary investigation into the matter."

Catherine switched channels, stopping as a witness was interviewed. Still upset, Catherine swore to herself, "Damn, damn! Damn me!"

"What's wrong, Catie? What are you blaming yourself for?" Kencade calmly asked his daughter.

Catherine switched off the TV set and threw the remote down. Her eyes were wet with tears. "One of those police officers, I believe, is Captain Corrigan. If he's dead, it will be my fault. It's still my fault even if it's the other officer...my God! What have I done?"

Kencade became concerned. "How could an accident that happened in Miami be your fault?" he asked her.

Catherine shuddered deeply. "*Daddy!* This was *no* accident! If Captain Corrigan is one of those men, maybe John Modini is right. This is *no* coincidence! Corrigan has evidence, father, that can destroy Senator Gerald Fuller's career. I saw your friend Gerald the other day in Indianapolis and told him about the evidence--!"

Kencade stiffened and paled. "You did *what*?"

Catherine continued, "Yes, father, I confronted him about everything. I told him Corrigan has evidence on him, and now this happens! Father, we've got to talk. I'm in trouble, and I'm not going to be able to handle this if Corrigan is dead!"

Kencade shook his head. "What are you up to, girl? What does this Captain Corrigan have to do with anything concerning you, for God's sake? I want to know Catherine." Suddenly the realization hit him. "Did you have anything to do with that matter at the Capital?"

"No, father. But I know John Modini was trying to help me. Did you know Senator Fuller tried to have me killed! That's what Corrigan found out! Now Modini is being hunted down and set up! Does this sound familiar to you, dad--? Isn't this what they did to Karl Hunter? Isn't this what they did to *you*?"

Kencade exploded in a blaze of anger, pounding his fist in his hand. "For God's sake, Catherine! Are you truly out of your mind? I thought with all that happened, you were through with this nonsense!"

Catherine passed a hand across her face and covered her eyes as they brimmed with tears. She calmed herself, making an effort to regain her composure. She looked searchingly at her father, feeling the anger deep inside her. "No! Not by a long shot! God forbid, father, he's a Senator of the United States of America! I'm going to expose the man for what he really is...and, by God, you're going to help me!"

"Now listen, Catie--"

"No! There's something I want you to do," Catherine said firmly.

"But I--"

Catherine cut him off. "This is very important, dad. I asked Judge Spencer to allow us to use your old chambers at the court house. When I can arrange it, I'll take you there to meet John Modini! I want you to hear what he has to say about Karl Hunter!"

Judge Kencade tried to comprehend what his daughter said. "I'm going to do what?"

"You heard me! We're going to get to the bottom of this once and for all!"

As Catherine approached her father and touched his arm Kencade's anger reached the boiling point. He broke from her, turning away.

"Father," she pleaded, "you know your life...your career was destroyed by Fuller...a man who supposedly was your friend!"

Kencade exploded in a sudden, savage response. "I don't give a flying hang about my life or career anymore-- it's over-- finished! It's done with...you hear me! They can bury me tomorrow if they want...for all I care!" He pointed an angry finger at her. "It's *you*, Catie! It's *you* I worry about! It has always been you, dear! I don't know how I can get it through that thick head of yours!"

Catherine looked searchingly at him. "Don't you think I know this, daddy? You're all I've got left!" Catherine paused a moment, considering something her father had said. "You just admitted twice...you said *'they.'* If *'they'* want! *'They'* can bury you! That's what I mean, father. They won't get away with anything as long as I have the means to stop them. I'm not going to let your career-- your life be wasted after all you've done in your career. You're a builder, father. And no one-- *no one* will cut you down like Gerry Fuller did! He used you and then just spit you out as if he were the Devil incarnate himself. Is that the person you want to represent our state and our country for our future generations? We can only pray we'll never see the likes of that scum bag again! I don't want those men out there like Fuller whose gain is exclusively for the rich! My God, you can turn on the television every day and hear it constantly from the person on the street...'the rich get richer, the poor get poorer.' And the people are right! Unless *we* the people do something about it, nothing's going to change!"

Catherine let her arms drop to her side. Her father looked at her awed, not wanting her to stop. She did continue, knowing how to take advantage when she had the floor.

"I should know what I'm talking about. As an attorney, I have to deal with this situation every day. There are clients who ask for help because they can't afford an attorney. And I can take *pro-bono* only so much! But who's going to protect the common man or the employee who blows the whistle on big business or a major company? I've handled cases in both the government and big business where those in authority abuse their power-- similar to Senator Fuller. Most of the time the little guy is helpless compared to the overwhelming forces he's fighting. I've seen first hand what happens when the average guy tries to fight for what he believes in. The powers that be amass their forces. They can crush any opposition. They can wrongfully terminate an employee by false accusations and, if they have the right means, they can destroy him by making him a nonentity, going so far as assuring he can't be employed elsewhere, or can't even get paid for unemployment!"

Kencade was surprised by his daughter's opinion and the way she expressed it. He let her have her say without any comment from himself.

"You said '*they*!'" Catherine repeated. "'They' have the power to destroy the person who wants to feed his kids and to have a little dignity with his family and his friends! *Who,* father who protects them? Yes, *you* do, and judges like you across the country who make a courtroom safe and fair from lies, corruption, and graft. Yes, and safe for me too. And that's why I came back here, father, to give Karl Hunter a fair chance! I want Mr. Modini to help you to see what can be fixed. I want to be right, father, but...if I *am* right that means you were wrong, so maybe, just maybe, you can rectify this. And if it turns out I *am* wrong and you were right, I'll be the first to shout it from the mountain tops and proclaim it to the world! Please, dad! Let's work together to resolve this!"

Kencade looked at his daughter a long moment and then smiled at her. Catherine laughed at her father's change of mood, knowing she had won him over.

"That was a very fine closing argument, Catie," Kencade told her.

"I hope some of it or part of it made sense."

"Catie... Catie... You're as sane as the man in the moon." His daughter laughed again, and Kencade felt very proud.

"Don't you see, dad?" Catherine added a last thought, "Don't you see the irony of all this? Either way it goes, *you* win!"

Lieutenant Colonel Donald Casson knew the layout of Fort Bragg in North Carolina. He saluted the Marine guard upon entering the main gate and proceeded to drive to the General's headquarters. General Peterson's secretary greeted him. She informed him the General wished to see him in the officer's quarters of the commissary over lunch.

In the commissary, Casson, dressed in civvies, saluted General Peterson who returned the salute. The two men seated themselves for lunch. The menu was excellent: prime rib, potatoes au gratin, green beans and sliced carrots. By the middle of the meal they had finished with family chit chat and finally got down to business.

General Peterson studied Casson and asked him to explain in detail the matter they discussed over the phone. Other than this, Casson told the General his story, beginning calmly with all the red tape he had to go through to get information about a fellow Green Beret stationed with him at Fort Bragg back in the 1960's.

Casson spoke frankly, "Sir, I imagine you were much younger than we at the time maybe to remember any of what I'm ready to tell you, or maybe I'm wrong and you've been made aware of the circumstances concerning what happened here at the base. It was during the early sixties, late 1963. May I ask you before I begin if you ever heard of 'Operation Eagle' sir?"

"No, I don't believe I ever heard of 'Operation Eagle,'" General Peterson replied.

Casson studied the General who seemed sincere about not knowing the meaning, so he proceeded with his story. "Sir, all I can say is-- and this is hard for me-- after the assassination of President Kennedy, Fort Bragg was a very busy colony. Some of us Green Berets, Sir...would be ordered for briefings in the CIA building. We were on alert because of President Johnson' was worried of a possible attack from the Soviet Union. There was always the assumption the Soviets were involved in Kennedy's assassination. Johnson kept reminding us he would be next if we didn't prepare to do our job. I don't know how to explain this, but the oddest thing occurred here, General. The CIA had this top secret building, and the funny thing, sir, is that inside this building the CIA built a miniature mock setup of Dealey Plaza-- I mean, wouldn't you think that a bit strange, General-- right here, at Fort Bragg, after the assassination?"

General Peterson nodded, agreeing. He continued to listen to what Casson had to say, but Casson became cautious, wondering if he should continue. The General felt the pressure now to speak. "Well is that all, Lieutenant Colonel?"

Casson decided to add another element to the story, but not enough to divulge anything that may jeopardize his main concern here. "Well, no, sir! A group of us Green Berets, sir, were being briefed and eventually trained by CIA instructors on the tactics of terrorism and assassinations!"

"Interesting...to say the least!" General Peterson nodded.

Casson, still nervous, grinned and added, "I thought so, too, sir!"

General Peterson considered this for a moment and then explained his own thoughts about the matter. "To tell you the truth Casson, I don't know where you're going with this-- but at the time you say there was a full alert, I could only speculate the CIA had reason to create this mock setup. You say you witnessed this model and suspected it for purposes of possibly trying to investigate the Kennedy assassination. I hardly think they were going to wait to see what conclusions the Warren Commission came up with. I don't find it strange or anything to be troubled with. They...they were concerned about their President as any institution of the government was."

Casson felt uneasy about the General's dismissal of his observation. "Sir, for one, at the time there was no Warren Commission and for another, neither Congress, the Senate or even the FBI had a program or committee to investigate this. Johnson had informed every institution in Washington to keep hands off the Kennedy assassination once he formed the Warren Commission. And yes, I do agree with your opinion, Sir. But why *here* at Fort Bragg when the CIA has no jurisdiction to be doing such a thing domestically. And sir...why involve us?"

There was a touch of annoyance in General Peterson's voice. "Lieutenant Colonel, what is the point in all this? And what is it you want of me?"

Casson saw he wasn't getting through to him. No matter what he said, General Peterson had some type of pat answer. "Sir, I would like to apologize in taking up your valuable time. I know what that entails, so I don't want to take anymore than I have already. I felt that I had to tell someone of my concerns. Please, forget we even had this discussion--"

As Casson started to rise from his chair, General Peterson stopped him. "Hold on, Casson, I didn't say I wouldn't help you out. I'll examine this matter if you want me to. You came here for a reason. Tell me what you want."

Casson stared into the General's eyes, hoping he could trust the man. "If you're sincere, sir... I'm...I'm having trouble cutting through the red tape. I can't seem to locate a fellow Green Beret. He doesn't seem to be on file or any list. When I called the Pentagon, a spokesman told me the person's name I'd given them never existed in the military. General, I have to prove this man did exist! He was a Green Beret stationed with me right here at Fort Bragg!"

"Do you have those papers with you, Lieutenant Colonel?" General Peterson asked.

Casson took them out of his inside jacket. The General read the information, then asked Casson, "Are these copies?" Casson nodded they were. The General stood up from his lunch table and motioned for Casson to follow him.

The two men walked to the General's headquarters and into his office. General Peterson spoke with his adjutant. "I want you to bring me all the files pertaining to the men who served at the base between 1963 and--" he looked over to Casson to fill the hole.

Casson quickly took the cue, "1966, sir!" The adjutant wrote all this down.

The General added, "And bring me a list of all Green Berets who served here at the base in the same year," he turned to address Casson again. "Did he serve in Vietnam?"

"As far as I know, Sir." Casson replied, "We all did, at least a couple times. Some of us came home that Christmas after Kennedy announced a thousand of us would be coming home every six months. But after Kennedy was gone, those of us that came home went right back in March of '64."

552

The General motioned to his adjutant to get on with his request and he left the room as ordered. "Susan," he called his secretary into the room. Get me the Commander of the Joint Chiefs of Staff at the Pentagon on the phone." General Peterson turned to Casson. "See, we got everything covered. It won't be long now before we get some answers. If you'd like to wait, please take a seat, Lieutenant Colonel!"

Casson accepted General's invitation, he sat down on the General's couch. He was somewhat gratified by this accomplishment. He took a deep breath to relieve his nervousness.

A few minutes later the phone rang on the General's desk. His secretary put through the call from the Commander of the Joint Chiefs of Staff who returned the call from the White House. General Peterson hit the button to connect him to the call. Casson sat comfortably on the couch as the General politely greeted his caller.

"Hello, Commander, how are you? Well, good...fine, just fine, I hate to bother you, since you are in a briefing with the President, but I have a little matter I need to dig into. I know if I go right to the top, I can get quick results." The General winked at Casson. "Yes...well, all I need Commander is a search on..." He read from Casson's papers, "a former Captain, a Green Beret. Yes, sir. Here at Fort Bragg. Oh, I suspect around the early to mid-sixties. His name was Randell Clarke. Yes, with an 'E' Yes, sir! Well, no sir, I don't believe he is MIA or dead." He looked to Casson for guidance who shrugged his shoulders in the negative. The General added, "There's no record here, sir. That's why I need the info. Yes, I will Sir, I appreciate this, Commander. Please give my best to the President. Thank you and goodbye."

General Peterson put his phone down and smiled at Casson. "He's having someone at the Pentagon fax the information over to us. While we wait, how about taking a short walk? We can look over your old stomping grounds."

Casson stood at attention and was happy for the suggestion. "Thank you, sir!"

General Peterson and Casson took a brief stroll on the grounds, conversing about old times, comparing the Old Fort Bragg to the new one. They watched a formation of Marines, all newly

553

inducted, marching and drilling. Their Sergeant gave their Commander a show. It affected a teary-eyed Casson whose memories were reawakened.

"Incidentally, Lieutenant Colonel," General Peterson asked as a curious afterthought, "what was 'Operation Eagle?'"

Casson knew by now the General must be in the dark about what he had told him earlier. "General, you must have an inkling somewhat of the meaning to that. You must know what the code for 'Eagle' means?"

The General caught on quick. "You mean 'Eagle' is the Commander in Chief of the armed forces-- the President..."

Casson nodded in the positive.

The General, meanwhile, became quiet as his face turned red. "I see..." was his only remark.

Casson shot him a quick glance. "Do you, Sir?"

Chapter Thirty-Six

"The Fig Tree"

It was an early, quiet evening in Madison, Indiana. The city Court House closed for the evening and happy hour was almost over. The general population that wasn't drinking headed to the homestead. The days were growing longer as the spring season ended, giving a sneak peek at the summer months around the corner.

The 1992 Presidential campaign was in full swing. The rumor was that Texas Republican Ross Perot would give George Bush a run for his money by becoming a third party candidate for President. This decision might cause a possible split within the Republican Party, putting a big dent into their upcoming August convention.

The Democrats, however, were counting on a small time governor from Arkansas to head their list, one who managed to take his state from the bottom of the heap twelve years earlier, and brought it to the top. William Jefferson Clinton would become the Democrat front runner in the run for the White House.

However, the fact remained the state of Indiana was proud to be the home state of the former Vice-President of the United States, Dan Quayle, a definite contender to follow George Bush for the Republican party's next candidate for President.

The evening skies darkened over Madison's State Court House. Inside, the darkened hallways echoed with the sound of footsteps as two silhouetted figures walked down a corridor leading to Judge Lucas Spencer's chambers. It previously belonged to Judge Henry Kencade for over thirty odd years before Spencer acquired it upon Kencade's absence from the bench. For the first time since his retirement, Kencade was ready to enter it again.

Catherine removed a key from her purse and unlocked the door into Spencer's chambers. Kencade followed his daughter into the darkened room. "I thought you said he was here," he said to his daughter.

Catherine called out, "Michael?"

Someone within in the darkened room stirred. The man sat quietly in the judge's chair behind his desk, waiting.

As Kencade reached out to hit the light switch, there was a muffled cry from Catherine. As the fluorescents flickered into life overhead and flooded the room, Kencade recognized Michael Bradley sitting in the Judge's chair holding a sign. He had prepared for their entrance. The sign read: *"You are being bugged!"*

Kencade looked at Bradley stunned, then turned to his daughter, now surprised by her present predicament.

John Modini had seized Catherine from behind, his hand over her mouth preventing her from calling out.

Kencade didn't get this at all. His anger took over. "What's going on here?"

Modini turned a frightened Catherine around to him, whispering to her, "Tell your father to act as if he is visiting Judge Spencer," he indicated the sign. "Do you understand what Michael is saying?"

She nodded her head.

Modini whispered again. "I'm going to let you go now..."

Catherine took a deep breath in relief when Modini released his grip on her. She looked to

Bradley, whose finger was on his lips gesturing to not say a word.

Bradley disguised his voice to sound like Judge Spencer who responded to Kencade's question, "Why...why good evening Henry. I'm glad you could come," he pointed to the sign he held.

Catherine took her father into her confidence, whispering to him what Modini asked her to. Troubled by this charade, he nonetheless played along. "Joseph! It is nice to see you again." Kencade watched Modini motioning him to continue, reluctantly he continued.

"Ah... Thanks for meeting me on such short notice." As Kencade continued to speak, Bradley motioned them to the other door Modini held open.

"Let's go inside, shall we?" Bradley tried not to break up from giving what he thought was a bad imitation of Judge Spencer.

The door lead into the courtroom, the same room where four years ago Karl Hunter had his trial. Modini closed the door behind them as they turned on the lights.

Bradley couldn't hold it in. He burst out laughing from his amateur theatrics. So did Catherine. "Congratulation on your fine performance, Michael," she said suppressing a giggle.

Kencade did not find any of this remotely amusing. "I do not see the humor here!" he said, annoyed. "We are in a court of law, if you people don't mind!"

Catherine went to her father and kissed him. "Father you were great. You played it like a pro! Now let's lighten up. We're here among friends!"

The courtroom was brightly lit as the three watched Modini walk over to the witness stand. He addressed his comments to them. "It's nice meeting you again, your Honor...Mrs. Rogers-- Catherine. I'm sorry for the secrecy, but I felt this was the safest place to meet. No one would ever look for us here, of all places, and it seemed the most suitable place-- especially for what needs to be said here tonight." Modini sat down in the chair within the witness box.

Kencade was not pleased by Modini's approach. "What's the meaning of this cloak and dagger routine?"

557

Modini did his best to conceal his nervousness before the former judge. He tried to express himself in a calm manner out of respect for the old man: "It's more than just cloak and dagger, sir. Haven't you noticed? These last few years you and your daughter haven't led a normal life...together or separately! I certainly know I haven't! You think digging up someone's grave is normal? Hell, right now I'm supposed to be resurrected from the dead, if you haven't heard, but I don't plan to give these people any satisfaction myself until I know it's safe! And you know what? I don't think it's ever going to be safe for any of us, if we don't work out something here together...tonight!"

"I haven't the faintest idea what you mean?" Kencade was stupefied by Modini's remark. He could hardly believe the words he heard from this strange, radical character in the witness stand. "Who the hell are you and what do you want from us?"

Michael Bradley confronted Kencade for the first time to gain control of the courtroom. "Your Honor... Would you please shut up and just listen for once!"

Catherine tried to keep this cozy group's temperature from rising. "Father! You'll have a chance to respond." She turned to the others. "It's important to set the ground rules. Mr. Modini is here to provide us with information on the background of our deceased client, Karl Hunter-- and why in recent months it has affected our daily lives. In return, I expect, he would like us to provide him with what material Mr. Hunter left behind following his death. I'm sure all of us can be of some help to each other. Mr. Modini is in a situation for which I can't blame him, since I know the circumstances of his situation. And I want to make it clear to Mr. Modini...if he decides to give himself up to the authorities, the Bradley Law Firm will provide you with counsel. Now that I said this, Mr. Modini, lets get on with business. Michael told us you have reason to believe our lives are in danger-- including my father's!"

Everyone looked at Kencade. Modini quietly responded, "That's correct, and I asked to meet you here because I believe Bradley's office is bugged. Besides what I found in your former chambers, Judge, I'm sure these bugging devices and wiretaps were planted here prior to Hunter's trial. Once you're bugged, sir, you stay bugged! Apparently, those responsible don't believe in cleaning up. Is there a reason your office should be widely opened to certain groups of people with such devices? Did you have certain information that could be used for their purposes?"

"Not to my knowledge, no." Kencade answered, "but again, you were in that same room as well, weren't you? How do I know you didn't plant them yourself?" He stopped in mid-speech as Catherine's look kept him from continuing his next thought.

Modini smiled at Kencade's accusation. "Wasn't the conviction of Karl Hunter very important to <u>certain</u> people, your Honor, people outside this court?" Modini continued, emphasizing his point, "Someone who was close to you-- perhaps a friend?"

Catherine wondered why her father didn't respond. "Tell him, father? We have to trust each other here!"

Modini interjected, "Not so fast, Catherine...I wouldn't trust anyone just yet! Oh, but you'd better worry, Judge-- your friend controlling others in high places also have friends in even higher positions he has to deal with. These friends have such a tight rein over that he can't budge an inch without their knowledge!"

Kencade didn't buy any of this. "If you have something to say, mister, come out with it! Just what are you accusing me of?"

Modini again responded, "Judge! Don't get me wrong. I'm on your side. I'm a little tired myself." Modini gave a weary sigh. "*My life*, sir-- I haven't any at the present! All I'm saying is that I, too, am just a pawn to them as you are! We are all expendable! I'm sure you've realized this by now. We're being set up and used for their own purposes until they get the information they're looking for-- or in this case, to stop those from going public with it."

Catherine cleared her throat, "And what would that information be, Mr. Modini?"

Modini looked at all three in the courtroom and decided to test the waters. "One of us in this room has something that must be very critical to the institution of our United States government and to the people who govern it. I think it must be highly volatile for national security purposes because I was almost killed for it. My kidnapers thought I had it. After I convinced them I didn't, they tried to kill me anyway."

Modini knew he was being flippant and didn't care about it. "They thought they succeeded, but they found out I was alive when I resurfaced in Washington D.C.-- first with your excavation stunt, which I thought was genius, and second with that incident at the Capital. That's where my cover was blown. Someone wants to stop me before I get to the one who has the information I'm seeking."

"And what information are you seeking, Mr. Modini?" Catherine asked.

"From what I gather so far, it's in the form of a letter or document."

Bradley stepped forward, "And you think one of us has this document or whatever it is? What reason would we have for withholding it?"

"What I'm saying, Mr. Bradley, is they already know who has it?" Modini turned his attention to Catherine and looked straight into her eyes, "And they will go so far as to kill to stop it from resurfacing again!"

Catherine assumed his words were meant for her and responded, "If you're right, Mr. Modini, and I have this particular 'something' these people want, do you think for one moment I'd just hand it over to them? Or even *you*, for that matter?" How do I know you're not one of them, yourself?"

Modini smiled, solemnly amused. "Remember, Mrs. Rogers, what I asked on the evening of our last meeting? It was about the reason you exhumed Karl Hunter's body?"

Bradley looked at Catherine, unaware of this fact until now.

Catherine felt embarrassed in front of the others. "Yes, I do remember," she said reluctantly.

"Why, Mrs. Rogers? Why did you think Karl Hunter wasn't in the coffin?" Modini spoke with Catherine, but looked at Kencade.

Kencade cut in angrily, just as Modini expected. "She doesn't have to answer to you! God damn you! What is the point to all this?"

Catherine ignored her father and answered Modini's question. "Because there was a man who fits the description of Karl Hunter who raped me and tried to kill me! There, I said it, father! It's true! I had no doubt at the time it was him!"

Modini stood up slowly in the witness box and confronted the judge, proceeding to set him up. "Sir...your Honor, what your daughter confessed is the point of what I'm planning to reveal. I have evidence Karl Hunter had been working for a U.S. Government Intelligence Agency, Naval Intelligence-- and *that* agency had created another agent to double him. This agency was acquisitioned not only to double Hunter, but to double some of their other agents. I believe there was the possibility Karl Hunter didn't know himself he was doubled. His double was to use you as a pawn, Judge, and to discredit the real Karl Hunter any way he could!"

Kencade protested. "This is preposterous! I'm not going to take any more of this bull crap!" He walked up to the witness box.

Catherine moved after him and grabbed his arm. "Father! *Please!* Let's find a seat!" She guided him to the prosecution table where she made him sit in one of the chairs.

Kencade continued his complaint. "Mind you, young man...I know many influential people in Washington who are honest men and women who are most respected by their peers in the political arena..."

Modini rested both hands on the witness box and respectfully honored Kencade's protest. "I know you do, sir, but one of those you trusted could have gotten himself mixed up in a barrel of rotten apples, couldn't he? In fact, one of those rotten apples got you into a lot of trouble. You had to abandon your nomination to the Supreme Court and retire, isn't that right, sir? You can believe me or not, but I'm here to help. I need your cooperation, or else we can all kiss our asses goodbye once we leave this courtroom! People out there won't care what happens to us once we disappear, but we have to let them know that we do care what happens to them!"

Kencade wore a contemptuous expression. "What is it, Mr. Modini," he asked sharply, "what is your connection with Karl Hunter?"

Catherine took the floor, "I'll answer that, Mr. Modini." She turned to her father. "Dad, John Modini is the journalist from *Time-Life*, you met in D.C. four years ago at the Velvet Fountain, the night before our court hearing?"

Kencade waved his hand, "Yes, yes...so?"

Catherine continued. "He was in Vietnam with Hunter. They go back to the late '60's, early '70's, serving in the same platoon. Modini was fired by his publisher during the Hunter trial and disappeared following our first meeting at the Velvet Fountain. Modini was assumed dead until this year." Catherine turned and grinned at him. "You see, Mr. Modini, I know all about you. Michael and I have a complete dossier on you at the office, including a report how you saved the reputation of another vet and friend, Father Conrad!"

Modini returned an ironic smile. "A complete file, Catherine? Did you forget already-- that Spring of '67?"

Catherine remembered. "Father, you won't believe this, but you met John Modini back in 1967. Remember mother's best friend in Santa Barbara, Julia, and her husband, George?"

Kencade stared at Modini trying to remember, but it didn't register.

"John Modini was their nephew. And you met him that night. I remember Gerry and Caroline Fuller was there. You do remember Julia, right?"

Kencade agreed, "Yes, sure I do, but I'm sorry, son, if I don't remember you. It's been a long time. Julia and George were wonderful people. Recently, I was told your Aunt Julia passed away. I'm sorry to hear that. Catherine's mother and she were practically sisters. Caroline Fuller, Catherine's mother and Julia were all in the same sorority at college. She was a good woman!"

Modini remained quiet until Kencade finished speaking. "I have to say; I was telling you the truth in D.C. about following your career. I admired you very much, your Honor. To tell you the truth, Karl Hunter spoke well of you one time and I had the feeling he was an admirer of yours as well."

Now everyone's attention shifted to the courtroom door. Thomas Sanders and Jennifer Tamura entered from the hallway entrance. "I apologize for being late," Thomas said, ushering in Jennifer and closing the door.

Modini was encouraged by their arrival. "No, you're just in time," he said, the nervousness going out of his voice.

Jennifer hesitated a second. After hearing about John Modini for the past two years, it took her a few moments to work up the courage. Then she walked up to the witness box and cordially shook Modini's hand. "It's a pleasure to meet you, Mr. Modini," she replied in her most businesslike manner, then rejoined Thomas.

Modini addressed everyone. "Since all of you are here, what is important now is to put this whole case in perspective. I'll need all your cooperation, help and expertise in this court of law. Then we just might find the answers we need and resolve some differences."

Catherine found herself nodding to Modini, hinting to him he'll have no trouble getting her cooperation. She appreciated Modini's change of manner, his take charge attitude. For the first time she became aware of his aggressive nature. Catherine walked over to her father and straightened his tie. "Help him, dad. He's trying to help you. Can't you see that now?"

Michael Bradley spoke up. "I'm willing to help out," he told Modini. "What do you want us to do?"

Modini touched his index finger to his forehead and saluted Bradley and Thomas, nodding to them in gratitude, "Well...I hope you're not embarrassed by this, but I'd like you all to take your place in this courtroom as if it were in session. I'm planning to conduct a murder trial!"

Modini came out from the witness box and crossed to the table to shake the judge's hand. "Please be patient with me a little longer, sir. I'll soon make my case. Please, your Honor, would you take your position behind the bench, sir!"

Kencade didn't know what to make of this. He thought of protesting again, but decided to go along with his daughter's wishes. He looked to his daughter for guidance, waiting for any cue of how to respond. Catherine's eyes urged him to play along. Catherine kissed her father, sending him up behind the bench. Reluctantly, Kencade obliged, placating his daughter's wishes.

Modini continued with his requests. "Mr. Bradley, would you play yourself along with Mrs. Rogers."

"Catherine," she said correcting him. "Just call me Catherine!"

Modini proceeded. "Catherine...and Mr. Bradley, please take your usual places at the defense table! I'll play the prosecutor and act as a witness. Jennifer, you'll take my side as assistant prosecutor. Please take your seats. Is everyone with me so far?"

Each individual took their places, while Thomas felt left out in the cold. "What about me," he asked Modini, "aren't I a part of this, too? I'm the investigator here, remember, I can play anything!"

Modini grinned at the investigator's eagerness. He picked up the attaché case he brought with him earlier and took out some paperwork and set it down at the prosecutor's table. "No, Tom, you're going to be the essential person of all. Your place will be in the witness box, so get to it!"

Thomas surprised everyone by jumping over the gate dividing the main courtroom in half from the spectators seats. As he landed on the other side and spun around, he cracked up. "I've always wanted to do that and get away with it!" He sat down in the witness box.

Kencade took his place, and everyone gave the judge their full attention. He was reluctant at first, because everyone was watching him, but then he picked up his gavel. He was ready to call the court to order when he saw Thomas sitting in the witness box

Thomas smiled, waiting for something to happen, but the room was silent. Then he noticed everyone in the room was standing, staring at him. He pointed to himself, and Bradley nodded his head. Thomas, now red-faced, quickly stood up as well.

Kencade, on cue, pounded the mallet down on the block.

Thomas shrugged. "Okay, I'm an amateur at this sort of thing," he explained apologetically.

"Quiet!" Kencade yelled out. Thomas was embarrassed and kept his mouth zipped. Kencade felt comfortable slipping back in his role. "Court will now come to order."

"...The Honorable Judge Henry Kencade presiding!" Modini added.

The Judge glared down at Modini for a silent moment. "You may all take your seats." As they did, Kencade announced, "The prosecution will bring forth their case before the court." He addressed Modini, "Mr. Prosecutor, you may come forward or you may state your case from your table. Either way you have the floor."

Modini stood and decided to stay at the table with Jennifer at his side. "Thank you, your Honor! What we have here," he gestured to Catherine and Bradley, "are two attorneys for the defense who defended their client, Karl Hunter, who they felt was innocent. It didn't matter though because the odds had stacked up considerably against them because the residing Judge..." here he indicated Kencade, "...feels in his heart, as do I, the Prosecutor, with all the evidence before us, that the defendant is guilty as hell-- hypothetically speaking!"

Kencade said nothing, but listened with inquisitiveness, wondering what point Modini was trying to make.

Modini proceeded with his opening statement, "Now the Judge has the right, like anyone else in this courtroom, to his own feelings or opinions as long as he keeps them to himself-- except, unfortunately, the judge in Hunter's case was always one step ahead of everyone. Someone outside this courtroom was providing information and evidence about Hunter secretly to him. No one knew of course, not the defense, nor the twelve member jury. The prosecution also received information from their private source, not known to this judge. Now the people behind the scenes were being very cautious in feeding information that would eventually destroy Hunter, the defendant before you, Judge, and the media as well. It didn't matter if the information was true or not, it made good copy! This courtroom became a daily soap opera for public satisfaction."

The others watched Modini as he paced back and forth in front of them.

"Am I happy? Of course! I am the prosecutor. Everything is going my way! Hey, why not?" Modini said sarcastically. "I'm a hero on national television and the judge-- well, he didn't know his source was brainwashing him with false information. He only thought he was taking one of the biggest scum bags off the streets, like a hero in this daily soap opera! But, *oh*, those poorly misinformed defense attorneys and jury members. Or were they? You can bet yourselves, your Honor, Mr. Bradley and defense...that if anything failed on my part, the prosecution side, the Honorable Judge would stick with the rules, allowing the burden of circumstantial evidence to insinuate Hunter was guilty — which it did in the end. However, something unexpected happened. Someone threw a monkey wrench into the works. We suddenly find out the defense came up with a secret weapon, a very commendable one, I should say, from Seattle, Washington!" Modini looked over to Catherine and gave her a smile. She returned it.

Kencade listened patiently while the prosecution's case was presented against the defendant. He clearly gave moody glances on and off, during the proceedings but tried to conceal it with a pensive look.

"Well, as I said," Modini gestured to the empty jury box, "you can bet there was tampering happening within the jury. So you have a jury, you have the judge and the prosecution all updated to assure Hunter was not only found guilty, but would also get the death penalty! They all had information before the fact. Plus, you have the media who have already convicted him! Case closed, right?"

Modini moved from his table, past the others to position himself in front of the empty jury box.

"We, I'm sorry to say, are all fallible people, used and abused at one time or another. We're not perfect, are we? We can and do make mistakes causing the system to break down." Modini turned back to look up at Kencade. "Your Honor, don't get me wrong here, I believe you thought Karl Hunter was guilty. Just like your daughter thought Hunter's body wasn't inside his grave this spring. And I'm sure, Karl Hunter knew what was happening in this courtroom, but nobody got to hear his side of it, did they? The point is in this courtroom you both faced a dilemma and you both believed in the end you were *right* in what you did!"

Modini faced Jennifer as he continued. "Of course, what I've said could just be speculation. I'd have had to prove all the things I said ever happened, right? That means Jennifer and I also have to prove what the truth is and share that truth with the defense."

Modini turned around to confront Kencade again. "Now, in a normal murder case, arriving at the answer is a straightforward process, isn't that right, your Honor?"

"That's correct..." Kencade agreed.

Modini then turned to Catherine and Bradley who watched attentively in their places. "The two of you may interject anytime if ever I'm off track..."

Catherine grinned. "You're doing just fine. No complaints so far!"

Modini clapped his hands together hard causing Thomas to jump in the witness box, "Are you with me, Tom? I'm not boring you, am I?" Thomas waved his hand and shook his head in acknowledgment.

Modini proceeded, turning back to Kencade, "Okay, now...to begin this process, your Honor, the police need to start an investigation in a normal murder case, let's say legal searches." Modini confronted Bradley and Catherine in his examination. "There are things you lawyers have to do as well, get a court order from a judge and so forth. Isn't that what an officer of the law has to do before just breaking into someone's home? But the police, the same law enforcers, now have to follow this process or they're breaking the law, isn't that right? How am I doing, Tom?"

"Fine, Mr. Modini," Thomas said, "you're doing all right from here!"

"Good, I needed your support for what I'm planning to explain." Modini paced from the jury box to his table. "So what's the next step? The police! They now begin to build their case for the prosecution." He pointed to Thomas. "He works with them collecting evidence. Then they start with the victim's family and friends. They check his history, his background to find out if he had any enemies. They list them and decide who among them had a sufficient motive to kill the victim. The next step is evaluating whether they had the opportunity and motive. Where were they at the time of the murder? And, of course, if they have alibis. Could there have been a professional killer involved? Had any great amounts of money appeared or disappeared on bank statements within a certain time frame before and after a murder?"

Modini tried to list the possibilities, so all can grasp what he was getting at. "Finally we get down to the matter of means. Did the victim's enemies have access to the weapon that killed him and expertise to use it? Mind you, Karl Hunter certainly had the expertise being a Vietnam veteran. He was a Marine, a war hero for Pete's sake! He was an expert with a rifle and packed a .38 caliber pistol wherever he went!"

Bradley's face turned grim as he heard Modini opening a good case against Hunter instead of for him. He exchanged looks with Catherine, and she whispered, "What can I tell you-- he's the prosecution!"

Catherine watched her father. Judge Kencade appeared attentive but irritated by Modini's speech making.

Modini stopped short at the defense table, raising his voice. "Surprisingly, the person I have just described also characterizes *another* Marine who had the same expertise back in 1963-- that man being Lee Harvey Oswald!"

The courtroom became silent as this point sunk in. Modini's eyes scanned the room. He had their attention.

"Let me take a minute to detail a few interesting comparisons between Oswald and Hunter. On the day of Kennedy's assassination in Dallas, what were Oswald's motives, his opportunities at the time? Could Oswald-- now think about it-- could he have known Kennedy would be riding in an open car, knowing rain was a factor in his drive through downtown Dallas, let alone know the type of protection the Secret Service was providing? Did Oswald have the knowledge this open car would be driving right in front of his work place? Did he know the original route was changed the night before, but not reported or announced until that morning in the newspapers? Hell, as far as anyone was concerned everyone including Kennedy and Connally thought the morning was just an open parade. Kennedy didn't know what streets he'd be driving through, because he was now in the hands of Dallas, Texas, and his own secret service! Did Oswald all of a sudden decide 'hey, I have a rifle, I work at the school depository, there's lots of windows, I can pick the President off and no one will know the difference! Yeah, that's the ticket! I'll even leave my rifle there as a sort of calling card. I'll even make things look complicated by shooting through the trees at an angle down Elm street instead of straight on at the President when he comes towards me on Houston Avenue. It doesn't matter though my rifle is so old the sights aren't lined right, nor easy enough to work the bolt and aim accurately.'" Modini frowned thoughtfully, dropping the sarcasm.

"Ladies and Gentlemen, your Honor, it sounds as though many things must have been going through Oswald's mind, doesn't it. A lot of crazy things! And here's another crazy thing to consider could he, Oswald, like Hunter, have been in different locations with different people simultaneously?"

Though Kencade was tempted to admonish Modini for not keeping to the main points, he let him speak. He wanted to find out where Modini was going with this.

Modini approached the bench, counting on his fingers. "Motive, opportunity and the means! All three essentials in any murder investigation! If you have all three you should have no problem in convicting the guilty party! If you have only one, you have no case! Yes, all this could have happened and Karl Hunter could be the killer that this courtroom and the media strongly convicted-- if it were a normal murder case! But, this wasn't a normal murder case, was it, your Honor? Not unless Karl Hunter was *two* different people!"

Bradley stood up, requesting to speak. Modini gave him the floor. "Mr. Modini, I know you mentioned something before about Oswald and Hunter. Am I hearing you right? If not, correct me, please. You're saying Karl Hunter, like Lee Harvey Oswald, the man who killed the President, could have had a double?"

Modini answered quickly. "Yes, Michael, that's what I'm saying, except-- concerning Oswald-- I'd say he was *alleged* to have killed JFK. The Warren Commission showed no proof he was the assassin. Like everything else, it's only speculation and circumstantial evidence! Isn't that right, Mr. Sanders?"

"Yes, sir, Mr. Modini, that's correct!" Thomas acknowledged.

Michael Bradley still played devil's advocate. "And you're saying Hunter had a double, too? Mr. Modini, aren't we going a bit out of bounds here?"

"No, I don't think so. There is enough evidence to suggest Hunter did have a double. Catherine may be the first to agree."

Catherine stood up to protest but was stopped short as Modini pressed on with his reasoning. "A few minutes ago Catherine said she was sure it was Hunter who…who attacked her and tried to kill her. She was so sure; she even believed he wasn't in his own coffin! I believe, like Lee Harvey Oswald, Karl Hunter had a double as well. And I keep bringing up the name Oswald because there is a connection between the two!"

Judge Kencade reached the end of his patience. He stood up behind his bench in protest. "That's it! This is absurd! What are you driving at, son? This is pure insanity, and I feel sorry for you! I allowed you to ramble on and speak your mind, but that was a mistake! I will have *no* more of this mumble, jumble!"

"I've heard other people use those same words," Modini yelled back. "Why can't the issue be addressed if there's sufficient evidence to work with? Why is the Kennedy assassination taboo when someone comes up with evidence contrary to the Warren Report?"

Kencade pounded his gavel hard, getting the attention of everyone. "I've had enough of this, Modini! You're supposed to be presenting facts about Karl Hunter and instead, you rant and rave about conspiracies and the Kennedy Assassination and Oswald. Where is your so-called evidence?"

Catherine, got to her feet and tried to calm her father, "Wait a minute! Father, listen to me, this man formerly wrote the Bible against these conspiracy theories. He must have spent over a decade dispelling them! It was his articles that helped convince the Rockefeller Commission in '75 to close the book on the subject. Then at the Church Hearings he persuaded us to believe the government's word and even predicted Oswald would be in the grave when they opened the casket-- as he told me Karl Hunter would be in his. At least let's find out why he's changed his opinions! He told me the real Karl Hunter was not the one who attacked me four years ago. He understood Hunter better than anyone who appeared at his trial. And this is what's sad. I know it's too late now, but for some reason I want Mr. Modini to be right, no matter how insane he may sound. I need to believe him so I can get my life back. I've experienced something I wouldn't want anyone to go through!" Catherine began to break now, a sob filling her throat. She was all worked up and unable to restrain her emotions or to continue with her thoughts.

Judge Kencade watched his daughter turn her head away and weep. All the anger seemed to drain from him. He set his gavel down slowly and looked at Modini who now spoke from his heart.

"Sir, all of you in this courtroom, everything that Mrs. Roger's-- Catherine, just said is true. Catherine says I wrote the Bible to prove Oswald was the lone assassin and the conspiracy buffs were nuts or just plain wrong. That's not exactly true. My problem is the same as most people in this country. Like you, your Honor, I believed our government could never lie to us, so maybe I can relate to Saul who changed his name to Paul and wrote a section of The New Testament where he changes from hunting down the followers of Jesus Christ to following him and even dying for him in the process. He was a devout Jew who turned to Christianity! I guess you can say that was a good way of trying to say I disbelieve the Warren Commission and have switched to the other side. Everything I have written, no longer means a hill of beans to me. But the real sad fact is-- and I can only describe it to you from the perspective of the Holy Bible-- I loved my country and believed in my government and all the principles our forefathers created, and I was proud to be a part of it!" Modini let out a deep sigh and walked to the front of his table.

"With your permission, I'd like to give you an example from the Book of Mark in The New Testament where Mark talks about the Fig Tree. I believe this incident occurred at the peak of our Lord Jesus Christ's popularity. He was greeted with love and admiration as he journeyed to

Jerusalem, a week before he was crucified on the cross at Calvary. But something happened to upset Jesus before his entrance to the city. I'm not a preacher and may not have everything straight here, but like the Warren Commission, you can check it out in The New Testament yourself. But this is what I saw in Mark's version. Mark was a disciple of Peter after the crucifixion and ascension of Jesus into heaven. In fact, no other disciple ever explained this story of the fig tree in such detail as Mark did. Jesus the Christ woke up on one of the greatest days of his life. The people couldn't get enough of him. Jesus rode on a donkey as he ended his historic journey to the entrance of Jerusalem. I believe he hadn't eaten anything all day, because before entering the city, he stopped and saw on a hill in the distance what looked like a bountiful fig tree."

The courtroom suddenly went quiet as those listening forgot where they were for the moment. They became mesmerized as Modini continued with his Bible story.

"This fig tree stood between the outskirts of Jerusalem and its entrance. Now as Jesus approached the fig tree, something strange started to happen. Jesus noticed the closer he approached the tree; the less beautiful it became. And when it came time to pick a fig for his empty stomach, Jesus discovered all the figs were either picked or spoiled. Nothing edible was left on the tree. The fig tree was cursed by Jesus. And later, upon his second return to it from his Father's temple in the city, he found the tree had eventually deteriorated before him.

So this first time Jesus turned away from the tree and continued into Jerusalem on the donkey where he appeared at the house of worship. This is where he took out his rage and cursed the church members and tax collectors, lifting and overthrowing tables one by one as he walked through, shouting out his wrath! Suddenly, no greater anger in Jesus was ever witnessed as it was on that day, before or since! So what happened? Why did Jesus explode as he did, going so far as to scare his own disciples? The answer was, because of the fig tree! Now why, you ask? Mark was the one to let us in on Jesus Christ's thoughts. Christ was letting us know, through Mark, something the other disciples missed. The grand entrance to Jerusalem was symbolically represented by Jesus' discovery of that beautiful fig tree. And the fig tree represented the house of worship, the church, the synagogue, the cathedral of Jerusalem. Jesus went in there and discovered there were no figs, and the leaves withered. Instead, there was corruption and sin happening inside this house of his father. People were buying and selling, collecting taxes, doing everything but what this house was meant for, the worship of God the Father! Now think folks, what Mark was saying. Look what's happening to our country today. Is this the type of country you want for your children and great grandchildren? Let me tell you there are fig trees throughout the world waiting to be picked, but if Jesus Christ came down today and made the same entrance on a donkey or in a taxicab ride to Washington, D.C., he would find that fig tree standing where the White House has always stood. And again he would find no figs, and again his wrath would come forth, but this time the tables he would be overturning would be corruption, graft, sin, drugs, taxes, war, Iran-Contra, Watergate, oil, fraud, CIA, assassins!" Modini leaned against the table as he reached the conclusion.

"I could go on but I think you get the point. Jesus would get to the bottom of it all, by finding the man responsible, probably hiding under one of the overturned tables. And once found, Jesus in his rage would take his wrath out on him-- be it Bush or whoever-- and kick his wimpy little ass. Then everyone would say 'Amen!'" Modini turned to Judge Kencade.

"Your Honor...it shouldn't be such a shock to any of us to hear of today's big corporations stealing from the general public. If you have the money or the power you can get away with murder. The same goes for the government. Those in power think they are above the law. If a politician sleeps with a male page or an underage girl, it is not considered unusual. You've all heard the stories. Look down at the tidal basin in front of the Jefferson Memorial. That's where a stripper named Fannie Fox went swimming in the nude one night on a drunken spree with Wilbur Mills, the House Ways and Means Chairman! Look, there's Gary Hart's not-so-secret little hideaway for his affairs! Oh, how about over there on the right of the Lincoln Memorial. You can see where some burglars broke into the Democratic National Headquarters in a hotel called Watergate! Those burglars were actually CIA agents who worked under the strict orders of the Republican President

573

of the United States, Richard Nixon, whose chairman of the Republican National Committee is now our present commander and chief of the United States of America today. We forget the Pentagon papers shocked a nation, or the CIA was hiring professional assassins, or J. Edgar Hoover was a bigger threat to civil liberty than the Communists ever were, or politicians were taking bags of cash on Capital Hill or Southern Police chiefs were enforcing Jim Crow laws with killer dogs and fire hoses. But there was a man who tried to be honest with the American people, by trying to be honest with himself, one who did help the black man, a man who wanted to build our youth by helping him create a new frontier. He saved us from a missile crisis, something that could have been a nuclear holocaust. He made a mistake because he was only human, he never thought himself as a God which some people today may say he was. Year after year, his enemies did anything to dig up any scandalous dirt, imaginary or real, to destroy their image of him. He, however, thought only of himself as a servant of the people and would not take a dime from the taxpayers to represent them as their President. And yes, he may have slept with a future gangster's moll and certainly it is possible to have slept with Marilyn Monroe, but then again he was only human.

"The strange and sad thing in the end was that four little children would not have their father, Caroline and John-John for one and June and little Rachel for another, but for millions of children who grew up during that period who didn't have a father, looked to that man in the White House to be a father figure to them. They, too, would be shattered by that missing piece of their life when he was gone. Many people over the years are still working today to find the truth of what really happened on November 22, 1963...a tragedy that continues to tear this country apart!"

Modini put a hand to his chin, trying to recollect his past emotions. "I look back on this, your Honor, and say, though Mr. Kennedy's moral values can be questioned and scrutinized, there is no doubt he loved his beloved Jackie and his two children, and we saw their love for him as well. There is no doubt through the eyes of both Jackie and Marina Oswald they saw their beloved husbands, opposites of each other, shot down and taken away from them-- used and abused, sir. Those in power purposefully changed the course of history and reversed Kennedy's new frontier.

Peace was Kennedy's agenda, not war! He wanted, like Bobby, for all races and colors to work together and live as one. He wanted us to resist adversity, and that's why some of us had to go to a war-- a war none of us, once there, ever understood. And when the American soldiers returned, there was no self respect, nor esteem for what we did. *We* were considered the enemy. What kind of country does this to its citizens? Some soldiers left there in Nam never had an identity except as a number on a body bag or one as a MIA or POW?

"I wish my friend Richard Franklin were here today. He could go on about the African-American. He could inform you better on Kennedy and Martin Luther King than I ever could, and he has made his livelihood on this subject. No, there are more important people out there that can make a case. Oliver Stone, the film director, tried to get to the truth, to the heart of the matter. Maybe, just maybe, we can bring our country back together again, at least back on a track. I'm sorry if I got off the track, but what we have here is a fatal flaw in our system of our government concerning the investigation and prosecution of my friend and fellow human being, Karl Hunter! Our system, both in law and government, failed him!"

Modini crossed to the defense table to confront Catherine. "Even *you*, Catherine, thought so, didn't you? Or you wouldn't have made that trip from Seattle, Washington, four years ago to find out for yourself. Whatever reason is none of my business! But for *whatever* reason, Catherine, you found a defect in the law, and-- being the perfectionist you are-- you wanted to correct it! It was a flaw not unlike the Warren Commission's investigation of Lee Harvey Oswald. Therefore, like in Karl Hunter's case, they proceeded backwards. They assume he was guilty and then find evidence to support it. Some of the government's critics discovered it. Some were attorneys like yourself."

Modini turned from Bradley and Catherine to Jennifer. "I've discovered, in both cases, they took a single suspect, one who had neither the motive nor the means, and constructed the facts in a fashion to make it look like Hunter had the motive and means..." he turned to Kencade on this point, "...and that *you,* of all people, your Honor, *knew this!*"

Kencade was planning to comment, but Catherine shot him a warning glance.

575

Modini anticipated this, and he emphasized his next words. "<u>Not</u> unlike Justice Earl Warren's findings in the case of Lee Harvey Oswald. Although Oswald never got a trial, Warren knew the result was always going to be finding Oswald guilty! That's what President Johnson wanted and that's what he got, because Johnson convinced Mr. Warren it was a possible revenge plot set up by the Soviet Union or retaliation of Castro's Cuba. You see, you have the missile crisis on one hand and the Bay of Pigs on the other! Perfect, right?"

Modini continued to address his accusations to Kencade. "Someone, Sir, approached you before the trial of Karl Hunter started. Someone had to make sure you were the appointed judge for the case and then put the fix in. It was like President Johnson controlling the strings of the Chief Justice in Oswald's case. And we all know who the person was who had you in his pocket."

Catherine became upset at Modini's accusations. She didn't like what she was hearing. Modini continued, unaware he was agitating both father and daughter.

"Here we have a State Senator, a close friend of yours, Gerald Fuller of the United States Senate pulling your strings, Judge, thinking he's doing you a favor in saving the taxpayers a long trial by quickly trying Hunter, convicting him and executing him! It would be an open and shut case, over with a snap of the finger, and you would get an added bonus at the end of the trial. Only it wasn't for your benefit, your Honor! It was Senator Fuller's own gain that was important here. He, like Johnson, had other hidden motives. You just had to know what you were going to get out of this in the end. Only you, your Honor, can ever admit what that was. In hindsight, you can see the wrong man was sent to his death, sir!"

Kencade had enough. He pointed his finger at Modini. "Now, *Just* hold on *here*, Mister Modini! Who the hell do you think you are coming off like that! You have no right at all--"

"I believe I *do* have the right, your Honor!" Modini turned around and walked to the bench. "Damn it, sir, I *do* have! If anything of what I just said is true, please believe me, you don't want to hide it any longer. The sooner the truth comes out; the better we can begin to trust each other. I mean it! We *all* need each other now! Time is running out!" Modini took in a deep breath.

"Now, I don't know whether this will work, but we have to get an autopsy report on a Colonel Roger Tracy who was in my unit in Nam and was a Naval Intelligence Agent."

"And what will that prove?" Kencade asked.

Modini answered sharply, "One, that he didn't commit suicide, and two, foul play might have been involved. Then I could open a whole new can of worms by testifying of his knowledge concerning the doubling of agents in the Intelligence circles. We could subpoena and question those who were under his command at a secret nuclear base in the State of Montana-- a base I was kidnapped and brought to against my will. We must investigate those officials above Tracy, including the Commander of the Joint Chiefs of Staff who have a connection to both Colonel Tracy and Senator Fuller. I think I can prove, based on the autopsy report alone, Tracy died the same day I left this secret base, and that it wasn't a suicide. Colonel Tracy was as stable and sane when I left him, as stable as any of you in this room. I'll prove Karl Hunter was used in some capacity by those in the Intelligence community. Something must have happened or spooked Hunter into not wanting to play their game anymore. For some reason, he wanted out of it at the last minute!"

Modini turned to confront everyone, walking back to Jennifer's side at his table. "They were training Hunter to defect to Russia, acting as a decoy to give the Soviets fake, as well as real, information to confuse them while American Intelligence continued with their secret business. Hunter was to become our agent to spread disinformation as a defector. This is nothing new. The Russians have been and are doing the same thing as we speak. Sounds a bit like a game of chess, doesn't it? Well, in a sense it is. That's how the Intelligence agencies in our government worked during the cold war. Neither the KGB nor the CIA has ever trusted each other. There is still a KGB even if you don't believe it since perestroika and glasnost. They still exist, yet we continue to play the game. I have a phone number given to me four years ago. It goes back to 1963, your Honor, to be precise."

Modini walked up to the bench and handed a piece of paper to Kencade. Kencade took a look at the paper with the number, then passed it back to Modini. "So what does this mean?"

Modini answered cautiously, "Well, your Honor, it's a funny thing, it was actually a coincidence. Somehow in the end this phone number made a connection to all I've been explaining. If I hadn't investigated the incidents behind this simple little telephone number from start to finish, which took me these past four years, I don't think I would be here, making these statements to you now. Thank God, there were those critics out there who never stopped questioning the government's part in a cover up! Hell, I never wanted to believe there was a conspiracy to hide the truth, but whenever I got close to finding one piece out of a huge jigsaw puzzle with a thousand confusing pieces, there was always someone high up in government who would cause that piece to vanish or disappear before it was ready to fit in with the others.

"Your Honor, let's put some of those pieces that still exist out into the open. It's always thought that the American people at the time of Kennedy's assassination were strongly suspicious of Vice-President Johnson! Johnson, however, knew this and was approached by those he knew were responsible for the President's murder by telling him to create a commission. Now, mind you, Johnson was the number one suspect. That meant the Democratic party was not very popular going into the new year, so many members from the party jumped ship to the Republican side, including one person destined to become a future President, Ronald Reagan! Then in 1973, following Watergate, and his stint as Secretary of the Treasury in Nixon's administration, John B. Connally, a witness to the Kennedy assassination himself who still carried shrapnel within him from the bullet that struck him that November day in Dallas, jumped ship on the advice of ex-President Richard Nixon. Nixon's offer? Nixon said he could make Connally a future Presidential Candidate as a Republican!

"Okay, I know this is getting complicated, but this is how it all fits in with Johnson's forming the Warren Commission. The people who advised Johnson-- whose main concern was 'what do the American people really think of him' and how to get rid of Bobby Kennedy once he used him to get elected in 1964-- recommended him to ask for support from the Republican Party, to call upon the head of the party to put this Presidential commission together. Enter Nixon who, incidentally, was secretly being groomed as the next Republican candidate as President. Nixon would always be waiting in the wings. Looking back, we can see the people who murdered President Kennedy had an agenda, and the Republican Party gained tremendously in Presidential candidates in the next thirty years.

"Once both Kennedy brothers and the Reverend Martin Luther King, Jr. were out of the way in 1968, the following three elections of '72, '76 and 1980 marked the end for Edward Kennedy. With the latter two years, Nixon knew Gerald Ford had no chance in hell to win the presidential election, because of the bad rap the Republican Party got because of Watergate and the repercussions Ford had from pardoning him. Nixon feared Edward Kennedy's chances were high for the Democratic nomination, so he brought out his secret weapon, John Connally, to run as a Vice-Presidential candidate for Ford in '76, and then as President in 1980. Nixon's strategy was to split the favorable Democratic party. What a coup, right? Except something God-awful happened in Texas. The Hunt brothers destroyed any chances for Connally to even run for dog catcher. There was no conspiracy here, it was just one of those things that got in the way of Nixon's strategy. You see, the Hunt brothers hated Connally and everything he stood for and they were suspicious of bribery on Connally's behalf. These were the seeds of deception planted by another Texan on the road to the White House by the name of George Herbert Walker Bush, Nixon's protégé. Nixon would have one agenda, beside wanting to put the Republican Party back on top from his Watergate fiasco. His biggest concern was to confirm Ted Kennedy was again out of the picture! Well, Nixon got his wish at last. Kennedy was definitely out for both elections while a Democratic peanut farmer from Georgia and a Republican movie star took over the White House for the next twelve years.

"All right, let's back up here to Johnson forming the Warren Commission. Everyone's agenda now was to put Oswald in the spotlight and keep Ruby as far from that spotlight as they could. And they did just that! Nixon must have helped a lot with the adjustments within the Commission because every Republican on it was connected one way or another to Nixon and

Nelson Rockefeller. We will get to him a bit later.

"Nixon's attorney, David Belin, was Lee Rankin's second counsel for the Warren Commission and soon would be the head counsel to the Rockefeller Commission in '75. His staff would include Arlen Spector out of Philadelphia, now Senator from Pennsylvania. Now who'd ever think he'd run for office! There was the Chief Justice, Earl Warren himself, a personal friend of Nixon from California. I'll remind you again, Johnson forced him into playing his role by scaring him into believing a world conflict existed with the Russians that might lead to a nuclear confrontation. I'm sure Nixon himself had a hand doing his duty for his country for all concern.

"We also have Allan Dulles! What was his part in getting picked as a commissioner, especially after he was fired from his job as head of the CIA after the Bay of Pigs? Well, Mr. Nixon chaired a secret group while in the Eisenhower administration, using a small entity within the CIA to assassinate world leaders. Dulles headed this group within his own organization in which the Bay of Pigs was part of it. To protect both the future of the Republican Party and the CIA's part in this secret group, both men had an agenda to hide certain facts, one of them that may even have included the CIA's involvement in Kennedy's own assassination. This made it definitely necessary to plant the ex-director of the CIA into the Warren Commission to conduct the investigation to focus on one individual, Lee Harvey Oswald!

"Now, you have the President of the United States ordering all investigations shut down from the Senate to Congress to the Dallas Police Department by forming a commission that would become a smoke screen for the next year to detour a possible American Revolution in this country. And there was Gerald Ford, an old colleague of Nixon who's friendship went back to their Congressman years together. I'm sure it was easy for Ford to participate, It is certainly thought provoking. Ford is a man who has been recently polled as the most honest of this century's Presidents, yet he has constantly lied to the American public since the beginning, not just within the Warren Commission but to gain the nomination as the Vice-President of the U.S. When Vice-President Agnew had to resign from Nixon's administration, Ford's lie became a trail of lies, beginning with a book he wrote about Oswald after the Warren Report. Then there was possible evidence H.R. Haldeman, Nixon's Chief of Staff, was hiding Nixon's involvement in Watergate five days after the June 1972 break in, and that Ford himself knew it. For Gerald Ford was the man in government who literally became the man who knew too much! How convenient for him and Nixon! Now this alone would be a call for an impeachment of a President and would have totally destroyed the Republican Party if it were known their non-elected replacement for President was just a facade to hide the real criminal maneuvers of Richard Nixon!

"We get to Rockefeller's nomination as Vice-President to Ford's administration. He had his New York pipeline to the oil men in Texas. He also had his hatred for the Kennedy family. He ran for the presidency in 1960 on the Republican ticket, losing to-- then supporting-- Nixon against Kennedy. I believe his commission in 1975 was a smoke screen for the CIA's involvement in assassinating political foreign leaders as well as our own President in Dallas.

"Between 1960 to 1972, Nelson Rockefeller was Nixon's man in New York as George Bush would be in Texas. And *pow*! Ford's next coup, besides, pardoning Nixon, was his appointment of a Houston oil man as the CIA director to his administration, George Bush. Bush had a great impact in putting Mr. Nixon into the White House in 1968 with the Murchinson and Hunt brothers-- the same oil men who were enemies of the Kennedy administration. This man who would become Nixon's devoted spokesperson throughout the world and ambassador to China, the chairman of the Republican Party's reelection committee, and who one day would become the President of the United States, was George Herbert Walker Bush! The die was now cast. How?

"Well, you see how easy the pieces of the puzzle can fall into place when you use a chronology like the one Ford and Arlen Spector used on Lee Harvey Oswald in the Warren Report? Except neither those two men ever knew him, nor the truth of whom the real Oswald was, as we, the people of America, do not know for certain the real Nixon, the real Gerald Ford, the real Arlen Spector, or unfortunately, our President, Mr. Bush! A facade? Yes, of course! You can blame this partly on our own media. They helped to sell them to the American people! Their excuses will

581

always be, 'Who knew? The government wouldn't lie!' Nor would the Walter Cronkites and the Dan Rathers of the news media, would they? There were many reporters who didn't do their homework or stopped further investigation because their jobs were at stake!"

Kencade listened with patience, though stunned. He asked Mr. Modini, "Do you really believe all this rubbish you continue to spill out of your mouth?"

Modini sat at the end of his table looking at everyone. He lifted both arms up in disdain. "I don't want to believe this either. There's no need for any of us to believe it or not, your Honor. The facts happen to exist! They have always been there in front of us all this time. No one ever cared, or should I say *dared* to take a look! I could continue and tell you there is a great connection with J. Edgar Hoover as the middle man between Presidents Johnson and Nixon. All three men had a connection with Sam Giancana and Sam's man in Dallas, Jack Ruby. Recently on national television, Johnson's mistress revealed Johnson knew Ruby. So, Ruby, a nobody bar keeper in Dallas, certainly knew what he was talking about when he told a group of reporters on camera that his involvement would never be exposed concerning Oswald's demise because too many people who were controlling the event would never allow it to come to light! And how high are these people he spoke about, the reporters asked. Ruby's response was 'as high as you can go!' Is this all just a coincidence or what?"

Modini finished this last statement, turned to Catherine Rogers and winked. Then he waved the piece of paper with the phone number in the air to remind Kencade. "On this piece of paper, your Honor the first three digits are the area code for Raleigh, North Carolina. The rest of the number, I've discovered, belongs to Naval Intelligence, where back in the late 50's, it was given to Marines training to defect to the Soviet Union. This number is the same number dialed back in 1963, the last call ever made by Lee Harvey Oswald before his death."

"You're implying Oswald was one of these trained Marines?" Catherine responded.

Modini sincerely nodded. "Yes, Catherine. I think he was. That could explain one reason Oswald did what he did in Russia to the point of faking a suicide to assure he wouldn't be deported back. And when he returned to this nation with a Russian wife, there were no repercussions-- no CIA or FBI surveillance or concern. It was as if he were coming back from vacation. This was when America's cold war enemy was the U.S.S.R. Now come on, who's pulling the wool over whose eyes? Or then again was there surveillance? And if so, those concerned had to know about Oswald before, during and after. Someone in Intelligence had to monitor him all the way to Fort Worth, then New Orleans, then to Dallas. How did the CIA-- within hours of the assassination-- have data on him as quick as they did, including his recent visits to the Russian and Cuban Embassies in Mexico City? This is if we're talking about the real Oswald. There was evidence of someone posing as Oswald at those embassies-- J. Edgar Hoover himself knew that the day after the assassination! Hoover also knew someone was using Oswald's credentials in 1960 while he was trucked off to Minsk. It was something that would eventually open the door to the Bay of Pigs affair-- and I mean Richard Nixon's 'Bay of Pigs' just one year before Kennedy's inauguration!

"So what does this, you ask me, have to do with Karl Hunter? Well, Roger Tracy, the Colonel I was telling you about earlier, connected the number to Karl Hunter. I couldn't believe it. This blew me away because the Colonel had no idea I was talking about Oswald at the time."

Chapter Thirty-Seven

"Defector, Spy or Double Agent?"

Either make the tree good, and the fruit good;

Or else make the tree corrupt, and its fruit

corrupt: For the tree is known by his fruit!"

Matthew 12:33

It was late evening in Madison, Indiana, and the city courthouse was closed, but in the main courtroom, a strange presentation was taking place.

John Modini paced the courtroom floor, taking center stage, playing the part of prosecutor before an assembled group of people. Judge Kencade was at the bench. His daughter, Catherine Rogers, sat at the defense table next to Michael Bradley.

Catherine's colleagues, Jennifer Tamura and Thomas Sanders, were also present to witness Modini's unconventional performance.

Modini had assigned them different parts to play to explain his remarkable theory about Karl Hunter. Under Modini's urging, the key people had resumed the same roles they had in the trial of Karl Hunter.

Modini observed the reactions of the group as he explained how Colonel Roger Tracy had connected the phone number in his own personal investigation of Lee Harvey Oswald to Karl Hunter, his friend. Modini suggested Karl Hunter, like Oswald, could have had a double posing as him. By the expressions on their faces, he had piqued their interest.

Bradley interrupted here to clarify a point. "You're saying Karl Hunter, like Lee Harvey Oswald, was to be used in the same manner, to pretend to defect, but actually spy for this country as a double agent?"

Modini nodded, "Yes, you could say that, but not only was Hunter a double agent, but he was *literally* doubled! What Oswald didn't know when he returned to the United States was someone had already been using his identity here while he was away in Russia, during and after. There was a look-alike portraying him, some critics say, trained by Naval Intelligence here in the states. How else would they know how Oswald ticked *if* they hadn't plucked him right out of the Marine Corps, studied him in Russian and trained him themselves?"

Kencade was tiring of this. "Catherine!"

Michael Bradley interrupted him, sticking to his thoughts. "*If*...a big if! If what you're saying is close to the truth, then how do we know it was the real Oswald in Russia?"

Modini pointed to Bradley. "That's just it, Michael, you hit it on the button. We don't know anything. That's the charade in all this. The CIA and the FBI would have destroyed all materials connecting them to Oswald including their Mafia Connection and the Kennedy assassination file with the autopsy reports, and so on. That's why Oliver Stone, who's trying to bring these files to the surface, will find nothing! Remember, Allan Dulles, fired from the CIA by JFK after the Bay of Pigs, was also there as a member of the Warren Commission! Convenient, right? Once Oswald was eliminated, they would have to get rid of his double because they couldn't afford having him running around. How and what they did to him was only a matter of time and place. This way there is no connection, except by hearsay. If a reporter or writer wants to go to Russia today to dig into the KGB files on Oswald, what will they find? The CIA gave strict orders to the KGB to keep the lid on it.

"But it'll never be forgotten because all anybody has to do, is view the Zapruder film. The evidence is right there. There isn't anything magic about it. I'm sure the world has by now witnessed the film repeatedly, especially in the recent movie *'JFK!'*

"Without Stone's movie, the Zapruder film stood alone in its many interpretations. The numerous lies and the government's deception the government jumped right out of the screen into our laps. It's *all* there for anyone to see! Oswald alone *couldn't* have pulled the trigger of the rifle that killed John F. Kennedy. And like Oswald, Karl Hunter had a double he had *no* knowledge of and did not know about until the day he died. They used Hunter's double to discredit him! He didn't know what was happening or what was in store for him when they finally arrested him and brought him to trial!

"Meanwhile, Hunter's double was used to discredit you, Judge Kencade...and in the end your daughter as well!"

Modini turned to Catherine. "You, Catherine, kept a secret, knowing if you disclosed this fantastic theory of yours, you too would be discredited. But you know, in your heart what I am saying makes sense to you."

Modini looked up at Kencade sitting unemotional at the bench. "Sir, you now can say you were not to blame for the death of Hunter or the corruption in this courtroom, nor the mysterious death of the young lady you were charged with. Her real murderer, hired by our own government, is still out there somewhere. Maybe it was Hunter's double setting you up, using your daughter to prove the ultimate irony in all this. Sad isn't it?"

Catherine spoke out to Modini. "This 'Colonel,' you speak of, John. Is he the Roger Tracy who was a member of your unit in Vietnam?"

"Yes," Modini admitted she was correct. "Then you know about the FBI investigation-- the posthumous court martial and the way our military is manipulating the people to believe this cover up? This is the real Karl Hunter they're talking about!"

"Only what I read in the papers, John," Catherine conceded. "Nothing about a cover up. But I understand how one can see it from your point of view. How do you get anyone, let alone this country to believe what you've told us."

Michael Bradley took some papers out of his briefcase. "Mr. Modini, I may have some bad news about Colonel Tracy, concerning the evidence you suggested." Bradley looked over a letter from the State Department and read it to Modini. "It says here, speaking to the Bradley Law Firm, 'Sorry to inform you, but the body of Colonel Roger Tracy has been placed on non-clearance status for reasons of National Security by the orders of Naval Intelligence. No autopsy reports will be forthcoming...' and so forth! You see, Mr. Modini, no matter how hard you try to bring this evidence out, you'll lose in the end!"

Modini walked over and took the letter from Bradley. "How did you come by this-- I mean investigating Roger Tracy and asking to see the autopsy reports?"

Bradley exchanged a guilty look with Catherine. "Well, you'll have to ask Catherine about that, Mr. Modini. It was her idea. But if she doesn't mind, I can speak for her." Catherine gave him a nod and Bradley continued. "Four years ago, she had a hunch, after reading about your platoon being eliminated one by one. She set up an investigation in which she intended to find you before you became the last little Indian on the list, ala 'and then there were none.' Her hunch was right and she found you. And in my investigations, I confirmed this fact about the Colonel."

Modini gave back the letter to Bradley, giving Catherine a respectful look, then asked, "What else did you people find?"

Thomas Sanders stood up in the witness box to give his testimony. "Mr. Modini, we were on the same track as you have been, call it coincidence, or what have you, but you have confirmed to us some of the same facts. Mr. Bradley and Mrs. Rogers needed to know you were not one of them?"

Modini was confused by this, "Excuse me, one of whom? Who is 'them?'"

Jennifer responded from her place at the prosecution table. "We don't know, Mr. Modini.

587

That's why we thought it was important to talk to you tonight. Now I'll say this, since you've passed in my book," she glanced over to Bradley who didn't stop her. "We've gotten threatening phone calls, Mr. Modini, and we, like you, are convinced Catherine's life is in danger if we pursue this matter any further."

Modini was still a bit confused. "You mean to tell me your investigation into Karl Hunter's death has resulted in threats to back off by someone, I presume, within the government?"

Jennifer moved around the table and approached Bradley and Catherine, "No, Mr. Modini, not Hunter's death, but John Kennedy's. Tom and I came aboard as investigators for the Bradley Firm, to help Catherine find out what the Kennedy assassination had in common with Karl Hunter. You gave us part of the answer."

Modini stood back, astounded by this and shook his head with realization. "So there is such a letter from Karl Hunter after all, and you have it, don't you?"

Catherine gave Modini the same look she gave him the night of their walk from the Lincoln Memorial. "Now, John, do you believe in coincidence?"

"If you have this letter, Catherine," Modini expressed concern, "these people know you have it. Why haven't they tried to get it?"

"Believe me, they have tried," Catherine answered. She threw a quick glance to her father, "As long as I haven't brought it into the open, all of us are safe. I believe that's what they are waiting for."

"What does it say," Modini asked significantly, "is it written by Karl?"

Catherine looked at Bradley and shook her head, "No, I have no idea what Hunter was up to or why he wanted me to have it. What I do know is that it wasn't written by Karl. It was written not long after the Kennedy assassination. Hunter told me if I read it, my life would be in danger. So, I'm afraid he does have something that could shake this country-- and as you have stated so elegantly before us-- there is something here people will kill for. I'm afraid for me. I'm afraid for my father. As Bradley stated, I was afraid Karl's and Tracy's death would complicate things, so you are obviously next in line to be killed."

"Hear, hear!" Kencade announced from his bench. Both Modini and Catherine looked up. "Mr. Modini! Would you please end this floor show so I can go home and get some sleep! I don't know what all these amateur theatrics will prove?"

"I think with this letter we may have something here," Modini acknowledged his concern. "It's something that could get Congress and the Senate all shook up. But first we need to dig into Colonel Roger Tracy's records. We may not see his autopsy report for now, but maybe I can talk to his wife and family. Maybe if they put up a big enough stink something might rattle the cage and attract media attention. Meanwhile, I know Roger Tracy did not drown in any water and he did not commit suicide-- at least not by his hand. And we have another added bonus here, National Security can't help hide the fact of a person's death they have no jurisdiction over. There was also a question of the woman found near Colonel Tracy's body. Maybe we can check for witnesses around the Priest River in Idaho..."

Bradley looked in his files and brought out a newspaper clipping. "A Miss Francine Pierce, it says here, drowned. She was an airline stewardess!"

Modini glanced at Bradley's paper. "Yes, that was her." He agreed with the article. "You have to take my word Miss Pierce didn't drown. If her body were autopsied you'd find wounds on her body caused by a weapon from a Tiger Shark Aircraft, now obsolete from the United States Air Force. I know this as fact because I was with her when she died. And I'm sure, your Honor, that's a good reason for those who would rather see me dead right now! I suggest, while I try to contact Tracy's wife, you people try to claim Miss Pierce's body. If you can, get your own pathologist there with you as fast as you can before her body suddenly disappears! Even if you have to dig her up as you did Hunter, get someone you can trust. Your Honor, this is a chance for you to pull some more strings, if you wouldn't mind helping us? We shouldn't hesitate a minute on this, because we've got to gain control of this situation. Mr. Bradley, I'd wake some people up tonight or we'll be knee-deep in horse manure if we fail!"

Bradley agreed, "I think you're right!"

"If you don't mind, Mr. Modini," Kencade asked, "How did a man as you get to write for such a highly respected magazine? Is it your vivid imagination or just luck?"

Modini turned to the bench as he answered the question. "Mr. Kencade, your Honor, if all people out there in this world were like you-- no disrespect intended-- then we are in deep trouble here. But there's a consensus that says most of the people today believe there was a conspiracy to murder President Kennedy! It took a movie of high technology and research to reach the masses to get that consensus. You can believe me or not, sir, and not even bother to lift a finger to find out what is false or what is truth yourself.

"But I want you to realize one thing, your Honor, many people have been killed for that word, 'truth,' sir. Karl Hunter who stood at this same bench and convicted by you, was not a serial killer and did not kill those girls. And if you were involved with Senator Fuller in any way to set up and cover up this tragedy, then this deep horse manure we're stuck in at this very moment has just risen up to your nostrils! Here's a chance, your Honor, to do something about this past mistake-- and this isn't just about Karl Hunter! It's about our country!"

Catherine called out to her father, "Dad, remember, the cassette and letter from Karl were in your name. He wanted you to be the one to do something, knowing you were the one sending him to death. He was trapped, dad. He wouldn't even defend himself on the stand! Why? Who was he protecting, certainly not himself! But knowing what would happen to him, he trusted you! That must mean something, after all!"

Kencade sat back down and pondered his daughter's words, knowing she was right. He thought about the strange instances that caused his descent from the bench and unexpected retirement. The only bit of hope he had left was knowing his daughter was a fighter for the truth, and would not stop until she found it. But he was afraid this would happen! He knew his stubborn streak kept her from accomplishing her goal, seeking the truth to the very end. He looked at Modini standing before him, asking for his help and advice, something that he was supposed to be good at.

590

But giving it here and now was not so easy.

"First, Mr. Modini," Kencade contemplated his reply, "I do not think you are so much out of order here. I'm a curmudgeon, as I'm sure Mr. Bradley can attest to. Often, though the years as a judge, I have seen and heard many wild things throughout my years, but I have learned to be impartial. Some of those things you've brought to my attention tonight have been incidents my daughter has questioned and that have also gone through my mind. I imagine other officials and lawyers have pondered one idea or another-- their views, concerning the Kennedy matter. In the end, all it is really just a theory. The time runs out, and you realize it is only a theory and it's time to go back to work. You move on with your life. I understand your feelings, son. I had those same feelings at one time or another, but you've got to let go, get back to the mainstream-- get back to reality here."

Modini cracked here, the anger boiling up inside him. He refused to let Kencade continue to let himself turn his back on this. "*Reality*! Judge? God damn you, there are people who are dead because of this. Are you going to forget about them? Just move on, get back to the mainstream? This is *it*! Wake up! I avoided the assassination stories all my life! I turned my back then as you have right now! I was sick to death of it. I thought I had read everything there was to know. I told Thomas the other day I was no different from Dan Rather! My theory on Kennedy's assassination was this: after the statute of limitations was up and everyone involved in the conspiracy was finally dead, if somebody didn't write a book for five mill, then there was no conspiracy! But do you know what, sir? I'm sure you already know this. There is no statute of limitations on an unsolved murder, it remains open for investigation until it is solved!

"During all this time your Honor, one thing has always bothered me...why didn't Kennedy's murder have the same importance and priority as did Nixon's Watergate scandal? Explain that one to me! How a President of the United States get caught, threatened with impeachment, and forced from office in such a short period of time is amazing! But when it comes down to a President's murder, in a matter of months, Johnson, the new President, gets the right to appoint his *own* commission, his *own* time limit, to make his *own* conclusions. And when it's completed on time-- that is, prior to election time-- the facts of the murder and investigations are shelved for the next 75 years in the name of National Security! Why in God's name did the President who is supposed to be a servant of the people, have the unquestioned right to begin and end an investigation. Suddenly, he became judge, jury and executioner of a murder case!"

Modini paused a few seconds, suddenly overwhelmed by weakness. He took several breaths to recover, then continued.

"Years later, when Ford became President, a man not elected by the people, he pardoned Nixon, the man who abused the power of his administration. After the Watergate scandal broke and the smoking gun came to light, President Nixon was brought down to his knees on national television by a group of Senators and lawyers who went by the book, all because the poor fool was a paranoid and a crooked son of a bitch, something everyone seemed to have known already! Where were these Senators and Congressmen when it came to investigate our thirty-fifth President's death? Johnson certainly was allowed to pull the strings that got him elected President of the United States. How convenient for him!"

Kencade retorted. "Mr. Modini, if you have evidence that is contrary to the Warren Report, or something that is directly connected to this conspiracy you speak of, then, by *God*, why don't you take it to the Attorney General himself and let him handle it?"

Modini gave Kencade a weary look. "Because, your Honor, we the people do not elect the Attorney General. As you know, it is an appointed office. Right now, I don't know who to trust any more. There's many powerful people out there and I'm sure the President isn't the only one who wants to keep a lid on this!"

Kencade chuckled at this. "Then why trust me?"

Modini, showing his fatigue, sat down at the defense table. He was aware Catherine was also waiting for his answer. "Your Honor, I don't know. Maybe, because I trust your daughter. Maybe it's because Karl Hunter left this important material to you. If it is what I think it is, it may be the possible smoking gun!"

"And if it is?" Catherine questioned.

"Then I'm just as guilty...as anyone!"

Catherine was stunned by Modini's admission. "I don't understand?"

Modini lapsed into a blank stare for a moment. In a split-second flashback, he saw himself with Hunter at the Saigon base and the body bags. The image and the emotion overwhelmed him as he relived this event again.

Bradley spoke with Modini. "We've got a problem!"

In his trance, Modini heard the voice of Bradley coming out of Hunter's mouth. The room started to swirl and darken. Suddenly, he felt his consciousness slipping away and the sensation of himself falling.

Blackness. Then voices. Modini snapped awake with a feeling of nauseousness. He found himself on the floor from having passed out.

Bradley spoke with him, trying to revive him. "Mr. Modini, is everything okay? John, are you all right?"

Modini seemed embarrassed by not knowing what had happened. He tried to get up while Bradley advised against it. "Just keep still for the moment and catch your breath."

Catherine rushed forward with a wet handkerchief, courtesy of the drinking fountain out in the hall. She compressed the wet cloth onto his forehead.

Modini looked up to her as if to ask the same question she now asked him, "What happened?"

Thomas thought he knew the answer. "I believe it's a lack of nourishment. I suspect the poor guy hasn't eaten a thing in the last few days. I know he's been nervous about being here tonight!"

Modini responded. "All I could hear was Michael's voice but it was coming out of Karl Hunter's mouth."

Bradley, fascinated, asked, "What do you mean, Karl Hunter? Where?"

Modini shook his head and grabbed the edge of the defense table to brace himself. Bradley and Catherine helped him. "Oh, it's just a dream I keep having over and over. We're both at a military base in Saigon. It's just a reminder."

"A reminder of what?" Catherine was curious.

Modini gave her a sober look. "You don't want to know!"

Now it was Michael Bradley's turn to be curious. "What was it I thought Karl said?"

"He said-- or you did, 'We've got a problem...'"

"I did say that just before you hit the deck here!"

"Why?"

"Well, you were discussing the details of what evidence we can provide, and whom we can or can't trust, which is no one in Washington at present. It dawned on me we can't go to anyone in this administration, because it may lead back to you-know-who in the White House. But now I may have an idea."

Kencade interrupted, emerging from the judge's chambers with two vodka tonics in hand. "Is Mr. Modini all right? Here, I brought you this. You probably need one!" He handed one of the glasses to Modini, but Catherine intercepted it, taking it from him.

"What Mr. Modini needs is a good hot meal, not a drink!" Catherine told her father.

Modini's hand shook. He was dying to get that drink from her and did just that. "Let me be the judge of that!" He took the glass from her and gulped two sips down, "Thanks, your Honor, I needed this!" Modini finished off the rest of the vodka tonic. "Now, Mr. Bradley, what was your idea?"

Catherine backed away as her father took a drink. "Well, you two are on your own. What time is it anyway?"

Bradley looked at his watch. "It's near midnight. Wow! How time flies when you're having fun! You're going to like this idea, the elections are in November and that means Bush is in or out, right! With H. Ross Perot now a possibility of running for president, we can approach him, right? And I happened to know someone who can help us. And if the Democratic party picks William Clinton as their candidate for President, I have a friend in Little Rock that has close ties to both Clinton and his wife. I'm sure he'll be campaigning for them, I'll check up on it. You see, Catherine-- everyone-- nothing is so impossible. We just find a way to fit in and make it work..."

Modini liked the idea. "Mr. Bradley, you're a genius. Not only that, it'll give us the time to put all this material together. We'll find out what it is and give both Perot and Clinton a push to oust Bush, because if we have four more years of Bush, *we* could be in that horse manure without a chance in hell to get anything out in the open. If Oliver Stone joins the same league as Jim Garrison, Lee Oswald, his mother, his wife, Marina and everyone connected to Gerald Ford's vocabulary of nut cases out there, then we have to turn this around. That means the media must be turned around in their thinking as well! I mean, let's get real! The government has never entered a confessional, have they? We take them for granted at face value?"

"Why don't you tell it like it really is, Mr. Modini," Thomas spoke up, voicing his own opinion. We will be up to our nostrils into horse shit if Bush is reelected in November!"

"I think, Tom," Jennifer said, "that's the difference between you and Mr. Modini. He's a gentleman." She gave Modini a quick kiss on the cheek. "I'll do what ever is asked of me, whatever is involved. It was a pleasure to meet you!" She started to gather up her things. "If you need me, I'll be in my office at nine,' she told Catherine. "I'm going to hit the old bed springs! Goodnight, you guys!"

As Jennifer departed, Catherine spoke up, "Thanks for coming tonight, Jennifer."

Thomas yelled out after her, "Hey, wait up, I'm taking you home, remember? See you people tomorrow, it won't be nine a.m. though!"

"Don't forget those summons tomorrow, Tom," Bradley countered. "They've got to be delivered before five p.m.!"

Thomas hollered back, "I haven't forgotten! I haven't let you down yet, have I?"

Michael Bradley responded humorously, "There's always a first time!"

Modini looked over to Kencade as Catherine prepared to leave. "Sir, do you still think it wise to go to the Attorney General?"

Kencade swallowed a sip of his drink. "Whatever you do, son, you better have something concrete to back what you are trying to spill out there or else they'll pack you off to a loony farm!"

"He knows that, dad," Catherine said tactfully, "This is what he's saying."

Modini responded earnestly to Kencade's statement, "With your help, Judge and your daughter's help, I'll survive!"

"Mr. Modini, you keep forgetting, there is a prosecutor out there waiting for me to make some stupid move, so he can then grab me by the gonads and hang me again for that murder in Washington." Kencade glanced down at his drink, swirling his ice in the glass. "Besides, even I feel that your story is farfetched. I don't see how could I be of any help. I'd be an anchor around your foot as you walk the plank!"

"Sir...If this letter is what I think it is, I'm not worried. Don't forget, I'm wanted for murder, too. In fact, to the world right now, I'm responsible for Colonel Tracy's death and Francine's death-- whatever her real name was-- and God knows how many others they want to tie me to! I damn well *know* now how Karl Hunter felt when he was at the end of his rope, but if I'm supposed to die for something I'm not responsible for, I'm going to make sure the government comes down with me! I'm not going to be like Richard Nixon who continued to lie to this country so he could keep his pension. Those were Nixon's choices no matter what Alexander Haig said. He had three of them! One, he could fight those impeachment charges and lose, and that meant losing his pension, too, along with the Presidential perks and privileges for the rest of his ruined life. Two, resign and get a pension and those Presidential treats, but be forced to stay out of politics forever. Or three, commit suicide, because if he didn't, he and his family would suffer the consequences. If Nixon went down, the CIA would follow and the CIA wouldn't allow that to happen! That's been proven year after year. So you tell me, Judge, which decision would you have made if you knew it would affect your life, your family, and your country?"

"I see your point," Kencade said.

"Funny, isn't it, sir, when it comes right down to it, Nixon finished taking all three. I thought he was telling the truth, and he would go out fighting. That's the Nixon I remember, but it just goes to show, we didn't really know the man, did we? He allowed his ally, the CIA, to set him up as well as Woodward and Bernstein. Well, in a way, Richard Nixon was a lot like the tragic figure of Richard III in Shakespeare. After all, what Tricky Dick did to get where he was going included ruining the lives of Alger Hess and Charlie Chaplin and Helen Gahagan and any of his opposition by stirring up a phony red scare of communism in this country. It came down to this, it was one of his men who tripped him up, be it someone in the CIA or an Alexander Haig, no matter! The change would only continue to benefit those controlling the strings. I want to cut those strings, sir. And you can help me by exposing this letter of Karl Hunter's!"

"I understand what you're saying, John," Catherine said in a concerned voice, "but maybe father's right. They could come down on him hard now with this letter! Are you sure you want to risk it?

Modini wanted to confide in Catherine, but still hid some of his private thoughts, thinking this wasn't the time or place to reveal them. "Many people have been killed because of this letter. Now you and I can stop it!" he looked at Bradley who agreed. Modini then added, "I feel I *am* a guilty party to it-- just as guilty even today for keeping my mouth shut all these years!"

"Why?" Bradley interjected, "There's no connection here to you, John. Never once did Karl Hunter ever mention you, to either Catherine or myself at any time. Besides, this tape cassette he left behind, doesn't mention you, either. The letter was written before Vietnam. You can't blame yourself for anything from his perspective."

Modini's eyes grew moist. He was too overwhelmed with guilt, letting the words and the tears spill out. "That's because Karl always tried to protect me all these years! Don't you understand? As long as I kept my mouth shut, I would be a nonentity. I got the opportunity to write for publications thinking I could help support the veterans who came back as these monsters to American society. Yes, I thought I could help, instead I just continued to hide the lie. You certainly heard stories of corruption in war, the horror stories from the Lieutenant Calley trial after the My Lai massacre and inquiry. Then there were the lies of Oliver North-- a person who actually is no different from me. To tell you the truth, I didn't act on the lies. I only hid them. That's why Roger Tracy suddenly popped up after all these years to seek me out. Why? Because *he* was a part of it, too! What he didn't realize at the time, though, I was onto something else-- something not connected to the reasons he thought. And then he was killed for it! I was supposed to be killed for it, too, but Tracy spared me. That son of a bitch spared me, can you believe that? This is a man I almost killed in Nam, someone I've hated all my life and he...he spared my life. We were both set up for the wrong reasons. Whatever those reasons were, no matter how falsely presented to him...are in your letter, I'm sure!"

Catherine put her arm around Modini, consoling him. "Then you must understand my concern, John. I must remain a nonentity as well. Karl stipulated in his tape that my life would be in danger once I revealed what is in the letter!"

Kencade stepped forward, lines of worry creasing his brow. "If you are correct about this Colonel Tracy incident and he was murdered as you say, these people know you are alive. They may just be using you to get to my daughter!"

"I'm sure you're right, sir," Modini agreed. "That's why we took precaution here tonight. I don't want your daughter to be in any danger, but I needed you to know the reasons why! They have your daughter monitored day and night, either through you, sir, or through the Bradley Law Firm...it's that simple! In the end, they'll get to her one way or another. That's why it's imperative to get to that letter." He turned to Catherine and spoke in a restrained voice. "Catherine... When the time comes, you will have to bring the letter out into the open..." Modini noticed the Judge wasn't comfortable with this suggestion,

Bradley's concern for Catherine came out. "I don't know, Mr. Modini, if these people do exist as you say. Wouldn't that mean Catherine becomes bait for them? They might kill her!"

"That is why we will figure out a plan to put the game in our ballpark and let them play with us on our terms."

Kencade looked at these two men oddly, "You both will do *what* with my daughter?"

Bradley tried to calm the Judge, "Mr. Kencade... Catherine won't do anything she isn't comfortable with."

Kencade slammed his drink down on the table. He wasn't happy with any of this. "Look, I don't see this as you people do. First, my daughter brings home a recording of this man, Hunter who states something about Jack Ruby's involvement with Kennedy's assassination. Now you, Mr. Modini, come up with this Oswald connection. Big deal! It's over with, the past is the past! Let it go! If this letter is as dangerous as you say, why don't you just burn it and be rid of it?"

"All right, dad," Catherine answered, trying to calm her father down. "That'll be one option, but first we still have to get the letter, don't we?"

Modini was still disturbed by Kencade's attitude. "You still don't get it, do you, sir? You can help us, or you can go right on telling people the past is past-- but not quite! It's not as simple as you put it. Every government official, no matter whom they are, can interfere, or put a damper on the election process, even if they weren't even born when JFK was killed. The Senator Kerry's and John Glenn's of this country, even the Kennedy family members in government positions, have an obligation if they will represent us in government, to bring the truth out into the open-- no matter how harmful it could mean to their constituents or to themselves. So, sure, they'll be the ones to agree with you, sir, but you know the country thrives on such corruption and this letter can possibly be the answer to bring all this into perspective. Look at film director, Oliver Stone. He has the people's interest now. And yes, it'll all die down when nothing comes from it. I don't see any government official doing anything, except pretending to appease the people.

"You know what I did yesterday, your Honor? I called Congressman Conyers in Washington. He chairs the seat on the subcommittee to decide whether to open the Kennedy files.

He commended Mr. Stone on his fight for truth and justice. It looked real good for television, but the fact here, sir, is that Mr. Conyers was only acting, like a character in one of Oliver Stone's own movies. He seemed sincere, but is he? You see, he wants to be reelected as much as the others who also sit on that subcommittee. We know Fuller's office is against the Committee. Why? Well, I did hear from Conyers' office. An advisor to Mr. Conyers didn't want to hear any new evidence I may have concerning Kennedy's assassination, or about Oswald, or about anything! Do you know why, your Honor? He didn't care! I could have been JFK's assassin confessing, and it wouldn't have mattered. He told me if I provided any information, he didn't want to hear it or see it because he didn't want to make further waves with the remaining Warren Commissioners and existing staff members. Well, la de da for those poor souls who still feel they own the Bible to the final conclusions of JFK's murder! What's the whole point of having a subcommittee, if not to question what most of the people in this nation feel is a cover up! Your Honor, the Warren Commission is the cover up! Maybe not inadvertently to some, but it is, just the same! It's unfair to those who think they are getting their money's worth from their leaders. The poor, the unemployed folk out there, get pissed on every day as they work their asses off to get their dignity back as a human being. There are those in America dying of starvation in our own streets, while big businesses continue to thrive, and the high and mighty get away with bloody murder! If I can clear some names, be it Oswald or Karl Hunter, I'm going for it! Karl is the real hero here! He fought the real war out there for his country, and the same people who sent him to Vietnam killed him right here, Judge, in your fucking courtroom! And like it or not, that's *why* you're going to help us to stop them, sir!"

Michael Bradley, inside, said to himself, "Yes!"

Catherine was wide-eyed, surprised at Modini's sudden intensity. She might have also found a missing piece to this puzzle.

"John... The night we talked at The Lincoln Memorial -- I told you about Karl Hunter's tape and the sealed letter, written by a man known only as Mister X."

"That's right," Modini answered. "What about it?"

"What you said here tonight made me wonder-- I mean to say I'm aware you and Karl were very good friends. Do you know whom this Mister X is-- the one Karl spoke of?"

Modini grimaced at Catherine and nodded awkwardly. "I think so. That's why I said I felt just as guilty as anyone! So, your Honor, I too have my demons to cast out! May God ever forgive me!"

"But why? You were just a kid in those days?" Bradley said, not understanding.

"Besides, Karl said this Mister X is dead!" Catherine added.

"From what you've told me so far, Catherine, I believe Mister X is-- or was-- Karl's older brother, a member of the CIA! One of his jobs was to make sure the Vietnam War would keep going. Big businesses, like the pipeline from the Rockefellers in New York to the Texas oil men, had too much at stake for it to end.

"Then there was the military industrial complex which Stone's movie centers on. Those stories you heard about innocent Vietnamese women and children being slaughtered were just a small part of it-- part of a grand scale cover up! What would you do if you were one of these poor villages invaded by big bad America? The Russians were supplying one side, Ho Chi Min in the North, and we were supplying the South. It came to the point where everyone was being used in this war, even the dead! Nobody, once there, knew why or what we were fighting for! Just that it meant everything to the goodwill of America. Imagine, a small piece of land no bigger than the State of California ripped this country apart for ten years, and we're still suffering from the aftermath!"

Bradley interrupted, "John, what do you mean by 'even the dead were being used?'"

Modini felt his face heat up and the shame that came with it. "Yes, I'm coming to that. I met Karl's brother in Nam. One of his jobs was keeping our soldiers morale alive. He supplied the men with everything they possibly could want on a silver platter-- things they couldn't get in the states-- women, all the Asian women you could want, even drugs to mellow them out-- you name it! And throw in Mom's hot apple pie. But who needs apple pie once you're hooked on the drugs supplied to you? Vietnam was a hot bed in the black market for whatever you needed. Someone was making a fortune with the stuff so much, someone had the bright idea on a much grander scale of bringing it to the streets of downtown U.S. of A. Wasn't it obvious looking back now to those days of free love into the '60's and early '70's that this country of ours had a bad drug problem? Well, the way Karl's brother handled it, once the way of getting it here became obvious, was very simple!"

Modini told them of the recurring dream he had on the Asian airfield in Saigon. It was his last recollection of the place, and he remembered it vividly. He was on crutches, ready to board Air America, a CIA operated airliner. Karl Hunter stood next to him staring with sadness at the surreal sight before their eyes. From Modini's point of view he saw, the body bags of dead American soldiers loaded into the plane as hundreds more waited their turn near by. They were laid out on a staging area next to the airstrip to be shipped out by additional planes. Modini took one last look at the body bags then turned to shake the hand of Karl Hunter.

"I'm going to miss you, brother," Hunter said, earnestly, "I'm happy for you that you're the first to go home..." He stopped to steal a glance at the cargo next to them, "...*alive* from our platoon-- and not in one of those body bags." He now laughed as an afterthought came to mind, "Incidentally, John, do you know what else is being shipped home with you?"

Modini was naive and hadn't a clue, until Hunter took out a rolled joint, opened Modini's front jacket pocket and stashed it inside. Modini was shocked, "You're kidding? My God, you're not kidding! Why?"

Hunter shrugged his shoulders. "Why not? Hey, if you can brain-dead the soldiers to believe they are fighting a war over here in Nam, someone back home thinks we can do the same there and make a lot of money doin' it!"

Modini had his suspicions-- he heard the rumors, but now couldn't believe his friend was confirming it. "But those bodies-- someone's going to ask questions about the bodies, the missing—"

"No, not to worry," Hunter interrupted calmly. "Everything has been worked out to the max at the other end. Half of the bags are labeled with names of the dead, the other half, with the missing or unidentified. Some of those bags will have markers so those on the other end know what to expect."

"What do you mean by the missing?" Modini asked.

Hunter explained. "Well, let's put it this way, if someone is missing in action or captured, we don't know whether they are alive or dead at this point. We just label the soldier's name with the marker."

"Although there is no body to be accounted for?" Modini interjected angrily. "What happens if one of these supposedly dead soldiers appears later on?"

Hunter shook his head and laughed, "That's a good question. I'm sure the government will come up with some explanation by then. Who cares anyway? It'll be some idiot's clerical error by then. Why someone's loved one suddenly appears alive and is coming home will be of no concern to anyone but the family, and they'll just chalk it up as a miracle. Meanwhile, my friend, you and I have to keep our mouths shut about all this or we may find ourselves joining this body bag brigade as well!"

Modini finished telling his story of his dream-- in reality, his nightmare, to the people in the courtroom.

Bradley asked Modini for clarification. "You're telling us that drugs were being transported on that plane bound for America in body bags?"

Modini nodded. He felt drained of all emotion.

"The CIA was involved?" Catherine sounded dubious, "And they had total immunity, even when shipping what ever they wanted in and out of the country?"

Modini, looked at the three of them, now understanding why he was so naive. "Really, is it all that shocking? If you think back on it, you realize it took us years to believe what was happening to our country. Especially the turmoil in 1968 with the riots. After the assassinations, instead of the civil rights movement in jeopardy, the law enforcement now used attack dogs and hoses on the white folks. This was when no one trusted the government. And the beginning of what could have been the next American Revolution started to come to a boil after Johnson took over when Kennedy was shot! You had every drug from hashish, heroin to cocaine monopolizing the country while the American people watched on the tube, day after day, the growing Vietnam War. It drove the people and the government against each other!

"Meanwhile, the two men who were trying to stop the war, Martin Luther King Jr. and Bobby Kennedy, were both killed. Nobody wants to believe something like this could happen within our own government. And I'm not asking you to. Our government is great, always remember that. Whether you believe our politicians as they lie to you on the tube or not, this is the best country to live! Why complain? *But* somebody *was* responsible! You can blame President Johnson or big business, the CIA, or whoever, but it came down to someone in our own government that was responsible! I didn't ask to go to Vietnam...and neither did thousands of other young men!"

Kencade was alarmed by Modini's revelation, but understood his predicament. "Is this what Catherine's letter is all about?"

Modini quietly dispelled this rumor. "I don't know, sir. It's very well possible, yes, but something bothers me. There has to be more to it. Karl possessed a lot of information, more than what I have told you. There's also the POW/MIA issue. He came to my defense when I was trying to clear accusations of our friend, Father Daniel Conrad's death. Father Conrad was secretly helping to get financing together to bring back POW's left over in Vietnam. He learned that one mission in Laos, which was to take place to secretly rescue American prisoners was, in actuality, an assassin squad ordered to eliminate any Americans sighted alive! Father Conrad discovered the orders came from Washington to sabotage any U.S. covert actions to save any POW's/MIA's. Hunter's brother might have had some involvement with this as well. I don't know. But somehow the information Karl's brother possessed might have been a safeguard upon his own death. This letter was then passed on to Karl."

Catherine was still puzzled and concerned. "But why didn't Hunter come out with this sooner? Why tell me about it in the first place? Why give it to me at all? It was addressed to my father."

Modini didn't know the answer to this, but could only speculate. "Maybe he thought you were a good judge of character. Maybe he thought you would make your father understand once you made a decision to go forward. Maybe he's still trying to protect someone. I don't know."

Catherine stared at Modini in a curious way. "Hunter must have really loved you-- I mean, to do what he did, to keep you as far at a distance from all this...whatever it was that was eating him alive."

Modini covered his eyes with his hands. "It's the letter. Whatever is there will be the clue to what we need to know. I believe Hunter would have wanted us to resolve all this by exposing the letter." Modini looked now at Kencade. "Otherwise, Judge, he'd have it destroyed himself, don't you think? He might have thought you'd use your own discretion, your power within the court system."

Catherine put her hands to Modini's cheeks, lifting his face until her eyes stared into his. "I'll go along with you on this, John," she told him, "but I'm not going to ask Michael or father to get involved. I was almost killed myself and I don't want those I love to have--"

"Hey, wait a damn minute here," Bradley cut her off, "don't you count me out of this! I put a lot of time and money into this so far and no one is dropping me like a hot potato. I'm in this all the way, and as your own father pointed out, I brought you into this quagmire, whether you agreed or not!" He got up behind the defense table and began packing his things into his briefcase. "I'm on it right now! Within twenty-four hours, I'll have a pathologist confirming the body of Francine Pierce. I'll put out a story that your body has been recently recovered, if I have to dig up a cadaver myself. I'll make that call to my friend in Little Rock. Then Mr. John Modini, you can toss in the dice to start the game! I say we wait until our next meeting, then we'll decide what to do about the letter. Well, it's getting late. Goodnight all. "Bradley hustled up the aisle of the courtroom.

Modini stopped him. "Bradley! The game started the day Hunter died! Be careful!"

"Don't worry about me! I'm going to be there at the finish!" Bradley exited into the corridor.

Modini swung around to Judge Kencade who was still pondering all this. "Your Honor...whatever you decide to do is fine with me, but you need to know one other matter. Francine Pierce, the girl I mentioned earlier, I told you I knew her. I was with her when she died. Her body may have been discovered with Colonel Tracy, but believe me, the Colonel was alive when I left him that day. Francine died in my arms, sir. She told me she was Senator Fuller's mistress. If you were aware of this fact but were covering up for your friend...I understand. You seem to be hiding something within you. I could see it in your eyes all evening. But you should know this...Fuller is expected to be on a future ticket as the President's recommendation as a candidate for the Vice-Presidency. I'm sure it was Karl Hunter who must have sabotaged his original plans back in '88 when another Indianian by the name of Quayle replaced him. And you, sir, were cut off and replaced by Clarence Thomas even at the President's expense of Anita Hill. As they say in government anyone is expendable. There's no telling what power they control to make you or me or anyone disappear off the face of the earth if they want you to. Life goes on, sir, and people soon forget!"

Kencade thought about what Modini said, his mind wrestling with the new information. The fact of the matter was that Kencade's anger was getting the best of him, but he wouldn't unleash it here in front of his daughter, nor at Modini upon his revelations. Instead, he remained quiet and acknowledged, "I'll consider what you said here tonight, Mr. Modini. I'll give it some thought, make some calls and get back to you on this. Does that seem fair to you?"

Modini agreed. "Yes, sir, it does."

Kencade smiled at Catherine, then took the last sip of his drink. "Come, daughter...let's go home and go to bed. These are late hours for me!" Kencade took the two glasses back into Spencer's chamber to wash and put away.

Catherine put her hand on Modini's arm. "What are you going to do now?"

Modini stared down at the courtroom floor, trying to avoid eye contact with Catherine. "I'll walk out of here and head down main street...and I'll just disappear again into the night."

Catherine felt touched and saddened. She forced a smile. "Why do that when you can come home with us? We have plenty of room."

Modini looked up into her eyes. "I can't! We can't be seen together now. I'll wait until you're gone before I leave this building. You can do something for me though."

Kencade waited at Spencer's door for Catherine. "Ready when you are, Catie!" he yelled out.

"Be there in a minute, dad!" Catherine responded. She waited to hear Modini's request.

"Call Richard Franklin sometime tomorrow, he's in L.A. Leave word it's time we need his help. He'll understand."

"I will," she told Modini. "Mr. Franklin and I know each other by now. We're pals. Besides, I owe him one. Good night!" Catherine grabbed her coat and joined her father. They disappeared into Spencer's chambers. Modini sat down alone in the empty courtroom.

Modini waited a minute, then came out into the courthouse corridor and climbed a staircase all the way to the roof. He unlatched the door to the roof and stepped out beneath the starry sky. He walked onto the tarpapered surface until he reached the edge. A parked car started its engine in the street below. Modini watched as Kencade's car departed the premises. After it disappeared into the night, he watched and waited in silent, scanning the empty street below. Finally, another car a block away started it's engine and drove off into the street, its lights off, following same route of Kencade's car.

Modini waited several minutes before leaving. He left the U.S. Courthouse as he said he would, out a side entrance, walking up Madison's main street and into the darkness beyond.

Chapter Thirty-Eight

"Senator Fuller's Requiem"

Richard Franklin drove through Penn Center, the birthplace of the nation in Philadelphia, Pennsylvania. It was named after William Penn, one of our forefathers of our country, and was home of the Unknown Soldiers of the American Revolution. One thing of particular interest to Franklin was the John F. Kennedy Stadium, site of the Army Navy football game. On this rainy Spring day, he drove into a charming residential area where chestnut trees in full bloom lined block after block.

Franklin drove to a colonial-type structured home and parked in front of it. He stared at the house a long moment. With leather briefcase in hand, he exited his car, and walked to the front door. He rang the doorbell and waited.

A girl sixteen years old with short cropped blonde hair answered it, "Yes, can I help you?" she said in a terse tone. She was dressed in her Catholic school uniform

Franklin gave her an innocent smile. "Is this the residence of Mrs. Roger Tracy?" he asked.

The girl stared at him rudely and asked, "Why aren't you in uniform, mister?"

Franklin smiled. "I'm not in the service, ma'am..."

"Then state your business," the young girl demanded. "Why are you here?"

Franklin politely explained, "I'm here to see Mrs. Roger Tracy about her husband..."

"My father is dead!" the young girl said bluntly.

He nodded with respect, "I realize this, miss."

The girl stared at him a moment and then turned and yelled out in a disrespectful manner, "Mother! There's a black man at our door and he's not from the military!"

Franklin bit his lip. He thought he heard it all. A blonde boy, fourteen, now came to the door to view their intruder. He was more cordial,

"Hello... My mom will be here presently," he said stiffly. His older sister crossed her eyes, giving him a dirty look and then ran away back into the house. The fourteen-year old smiled and stared at him and spoke up again. "My name is Gregory. What's yours?"

"My name is Franklin," he responded, "And it's a pleasure to meet you."

A woman's voice came from inside. "Get away from the door, Gregory!" Gregory did what he was told, and Mrs. Roger Tracy appeared before Franklin. "Yes, what is it now? I've had it up to here with you military brass sneaking around asking questions I can't answer! Unless you have good news for me concerning my husband's pension checks, I have nothing further to say!"

Franklin patiently waited for her to vent her anger before responding. "Mrs. Tracy, I'm not here from the military. I'm here as a request of a Mr. John Modini. Do you know him?"

Mrs. Tracy didn't seem to react except to ask tactlessly, "If you're not from the military, why am I even talking to you?"

Before she could slam the door in Franklin's face, he stopped it with his hand. "Ma'am! It's about your husband's death! There is reason to believe he did not commit suicide!"

Mrs. Tracy stopped pushing the door, then slowly opened it. "I know he didn't commit suicide! So, who are you and what is it you want?" she demanded.

A few minutes later Franklin sat in the Tracy's living room. The children were playing Scrabble in the room next to them with the tv on. He explained whom John Modini was and the relation he was to her husband. He told her Modini was the last person to see him alive the day he died.

Mrs. Tracy was encouraged and laughed through her anger. "I knew he didn't commit suicide!" she said, repeating herself. "I thought they were just trying to spare me because of the woman he was found with!"

"Mr. Modini feels your husband might not have been with this woman at the time of his death. He explained to me how she was killed and how she died in his arms. As I said before, Modini left your husband earlier at the Air Force Base in Montana, not Idaho!"

Mrs. Tracy was bewildered. "I don't understand! "Why would the military go out of their way to do something like this?" Then there was another reason she found it difficult to believe Franklin. "Why isn't Mr. Modini here himself?"

"Modini would be here, speaking with you now, except for the fact he was at present in a safe house in protective custody," Franklin told her. "I'm sorry, but I can't give specific details. But the military, or maybe your husband's Intelligence Agency would like to get their hands on him because he knows the truth about Tracy and the people involved in his death. I can't elaborate any further, but you can see Mr. Modini if you help us!"

"If all this mystery surrounding my husband is true, how can I possibly help?" Mrs. Tracy asked.

Franklin realized the impossibility of getting the military, let alone Naval Intelligence, to let anyone view her husband's body. "I'm aware they haven't released his body to your custody. Maybe... Maybe you can convince the newspaper and television media that an outside pathologist should be brought in. It might speed up those pension checks so pertinent to you. The least it can do is shake them up."

Mrs. Tracy carefully thought it over. "It makes sense, except...it doesn't matter anymore." She held up her hand. "You see my wedding finger, Mr. Franklin?" Franklin smiled and nodded as she showed him her diamond wedding band. "I asked his superiors if I could at least slip my wedding ring onto his finger before they buried him. Of course, this was my way of trying to see how my husband died, knowing a shotgun to the head theory wouldn't hold water with me. But I had persistence with the military, Mr. Franklin. Imagine trying to raise two children, trying to explain to them why they could not see their father again. I mean for God's sake! I thought they had to at least give me the dignity to view the body so I could confirm it was my husband, but no! Family and God come second and third when it comes to his life in the military. Not only do they have jurisdiction over his body and possessions but those bastards authorized his cremation as well! And I, nor anyone else, couldn't do anything about it!"

Franklin was lost for words, but was not surprised. "About the girl, Miss Pierce," he asked as an afterthought. "Did you know what had become of her or how she was associated with your husband?"

"At first, I didn't care...after all I had experienced..." Mrs. Tracy whispered. "All the red tape became a barrier for me, blocking me from getting any answers. But I felt I had the right to know! The military, in their true self-deprecating and insensitive way, told me flat out I had no rights when it came to the military or when National Security is involved. All the information was considered classified! So your guess is as good as mine, Mr. Franklin!"

Franklin nodded grimly. "First your husband's body, then his records were detained because of National Security. I assume that will explain why no one will be able to see Francine Pierce."

Mrs. Tracy was now in tears. "All I wanted was what we deserved, a family funeral with my folks and our children able to say goodbye to their father-- not to some empty box! But the military had no respect for them!"

Mrs. Tracy was distraught and wiped her tears away with her hands. Franklin offered her his handkerchief. "Here...use this... It's clean."

She thanked him and took the handkerchief to wipe away the rest of her tears. "I'm sorry, Mr. Franklin, for not being of any use to you...you see, there is nothing I can do to help!"

Franklin leaned back to contemplate the present situation. He glanced into the other room at Tracy's two young children who were arguing over a word in their game of Scrabble. He decided to give it one last try. "Maybe you can still help, Mrs. Tracy. May I call you soon when it's time for me and my friends to come forward with the information we're gathering? You could be of help if you would join us, ma'am, support us in our cause, so to speak. I would appreciate it, and I know Mr. Modini certainly would."

Mrs. Tracy reached out to shake his hand. "If I can be of some help, Mr. Franklin, I will be there."

* * *

An American Airliner touched down in Little Rock, Arkansas on a late Spring evening in June. Michael Bradley left the plane and took a cab to the law firm of Powell, Leland, Vincent and Eisenbaum. Mr. Frank Vincent was expecting him and waited for him at their appointed time and rendezvous. Bradley entered his office, and they greeted each other. "Good to see you again, Michael!" Vincent offered Bradley some Bourbon to mix with the 7-Up brought in for the meeting. Their discussion got under way.

* * *

Jennifer Tamura, wearing a matching olive green lady's pantsuit, walked through the hallway offices of the Bradley law firm and entered Michael Bradley's office with some legal papers for him to sign. She was surprised to find Catherine sitting behind the desk instead of Bradley. "I'm sorry, Catherine," she excused herself, "I thought Michael was back by now. I won't disturb you."

"No need! You're not disturbing anything." Catherine motioned Jennifer back into the office. "Is there anything I can be of help with?"

"Well, do you know where Michael went last night? It's not like him to be late for the morning conference."

Catherine shook her head. "To tell you the truth I don't know whether he'll be in today. Come in and sit a moment." Jennifer sat down on the chair next to the desk. Catherine continued. "I know he left last night on the six o'clock flight to Little Rock to meet with Frank Vincent. I guess this was his contact in the Clinton organization. I'll be leaving on a flight to Miami this afternoon, so you'll have to keep the ship afloat until one of us is back.

Jennifer, winced as she felt the burden of responsibility rest firmly on her shoulders. She forced a smile and rose from her chair.

Catherine couldn't help notice there was something else on her mind. "Meanwhile, Jennifer... Is there something I can do for you?" she shot her colleague an inquiring glance.

Jennifer shrugged it off. "I'm sure it can wait. It's nothing to get excited over." Then she stopped, and changed her mind. "Do you mind, Catherine, if I ask you a personal question?"

Catherine was both surprised and curious. "Ah...well, no. Be my guest," she now laughed. "As long as it isn't *too* personal. Go ahead, shoot!"

Jennifer returned to her chair and took a few moments to frame her question, hoping it wouldn't sound too offensive, "Catherine, if I may ask, well... I don't know what your relation is to Michael-- if you're just friends, partners or what. I don't care, in that respect, but...I did notice there was a sort of um...tension between you...well, whenever you're around John Modini."

A crease formed on Catherine's brow. "Tension? What kind of tension?"

Jennifer stared at a corner of the room as she brushed aside a strand of hair from her face. "Well, I guess I mean um...sexual tension." She winced at her outspoken statement. "Now I may be way off here, but this is just my opinion, just one girl to another, telling you what my eyes see and instincts are telling me-- but I may be wrong, of course," she finished quickly.

Catherine blushed and gave a short laugh. Jennifer was relieved at Catherine's reaction. "Jennifer, do you have a...romantic interest in Michael?"

Jennifer stopped her. "Oh, no! That isn't what I'm saying. What I mean is, if I'm right about you and Mr. Modini, then I suggest you do something about it when all this is over with, otherwise...uh...otherwise Catherine, if you don't, I'm ready to jump all over him myself!" she finally confessed and took a deep breath. "I'm serious! He's what every female-blooded human being out there should want in a man-- at least what I want in a man! I'm sorry if I'm blunt about this, but this is something I want to know!"

Catherine became flustered and practically speechless. "I'm amazed at you, Jennifer! I never thought anyone would take notice of anything I felt or thought, let alone this. I'll be the first to admit I've thought about John Modini a few times, but a serious relationship has never been on my mind. If you have feelings for Mr. Modini, that's something you should allow Mr. Modini in on...don't you think?"

Jennifer grinned and got up out of her chair. "Whatever, Mrs. Rogers, whatever you say. I apologize if I embarrassed you!"

Catherine shook her head "No, no, not at all, I'm glad you took the initiative to tell me this. It reminds me I'm still a woman and it's nice to hear that from someone else once in awhile. Since we're on the subject, I thought you and Thomas had something going romantically."

Jennifer's eyes widened. Her face turned red from embarrassment. "I guess you don't know then," she said, astonished at Catherine's comment.

Catherine was baffled. "What?"

"That Tom is gay!" Jennifer said simply.

Catherine responded, dumbstruck, "Oh!" She tried to smile comfortably, adding, "How nice!"

Jennifer smiled with her, but before returning to her desk she asked, "About Miami-- anything I should be aware?"

"No, it isn't business." Catherine told her. "I'm going to pop in and visit our mutual friend, Captain Corrigan. He's still in the hospital, but he's well enough to see visitors. I owe him and his family that!"

Jennifer walked over and kissed Catherine on the cheek like the one Catherine gave Modini. "Give a kiss for me to our friend in Miami as well!"

Catherine was surprised by Jennifer's concern. "I think I may just do that!" she said to herself and brightened with a big grin.

* * *

At the airport in Little Rock, Arkansas, Michael Bradley wished Frank Vincent luck on the Presidential election and thanked him for the meeting and for his hospitality. Bradley departed to his flight, suitcases in hand. He was pleased everything turned out so well as it did. Vincent told him he would do everything he could to help Franklin if Clinton made it to the White House.

* * *

Catherine Rogers' flight into Miami landed on schedule. This time, without any police formalities or protection, she grabbed a cab and headed to the Metropolitan Hospital. Once inside, Catherine was escorted by a MPD officer to a hospital room. The hospital staff explained to her the patient had been taken off the critical list.

A uniformed police officer stood guard outside the hospital room door and opened the door for Catherine after checking her identification. She entered the room and saw Captain Raymond Corrigan, awake, resting in bed. He had bandages on his face and body, and an I.V. tube was attached to his arm. She could see some bruises on his face. Corrigan looked up and saw her. He was very pleased to see her.

She crossed to his bedside and kissed him on the forehead, telling him, "This is from both Jennifer and myself." She tried to wipe her tears away. "I'm sorry if I didn't bring any flowers, I wasn't thinking! My mind has been totally out of whack these last few weeks!"

Corrigan smiled and winked at her. His lively spirit never left him. "I never expected to see you so soon. Your being here is enough of a gift to me. I'm sorry if I look a mess, but you should have seen me a few days ago!" It hurt as he laughed.

Catherine tried not to choke up. "I'm...sorry about the officer who died in the accident. When I heard the news, I thought it was you at first."

He nodded. "Sorry about the misinformation. Believe me this was just a tragic accident-- nothing more. My boys investigated the accident thoroughly. There was no plot or plan in the works."

"Well, I don't think so," Catherine informed him and told Corrigan about her confrontation with Gerald Fuller, and her belief that her meeting with the Senator might have been the trigger to set this incident off.

He understood what she said. "It does seem strange, but I'm inclined to believe it was just a tragic coincidence. The news must have come as a shock to you!"

"For the first time I was scared about what I should do." Catherine told him candidly.

"I want you to do nothing now." Corrigan said, calming her down. "Time will tell you soon enough what you should or shouldn't do. And whatever decision you do make, I'll be there for you."

Catherine wiped a tear away and forced a smile. "Thank you!" she said, glancing at the doorway. "I see, Captain, you have the police force out there guarding your door!"

"It wasn't my idea."

"It reminds me of the tradition within the force where police officers have to protect each other."

Corrigan took a breath and watched Catherine's mouth as she spoke. "My, Catherine, you have a beautiful smile that would knock any man over!" he said tactfully changing the subject. She blushed as he pursued a more personal question. "Why haven't you remarried? You're one beautiful woman! Why hasn't someone scooped you up by now?"

"I think it's because of my work," Catherine confessed, "Or it could be because of my intimidation. Men get turned off by it, but that's to be expected in my line of work."

"But, Catherine, don't you want to make a family for yourself some day and have kids running around the house, Christmas tree gatherings, or Easter egg hunts?"

Catherine laughed, "Raymond, I get your point! Are you proposing?"

Now Corrigan laughed, "Well, no...but if you'll beg my pardon, I would at a drop of a hat. Only my wife would think it to be a little crowded in our house, and the state of Florida frowns on encouraging that kind of lifestyle-- especially from one of their top police officials!"

Catherine paused a moment, then responded wistfully. "Well, I do want children, sir. And since you brought it up, I'm in the process now of adopting a young girl who turned sixteen this year. She is a Cambodian, half American. Her American father, now dead, brought her into this country when she was between eight and eleven and placed her in the protection of the Catholic Church. She just turned thirteen when I met her back in 1988." There was an awkward pause.

Corrigan saw something was troubling her and changed the subject, "I take it her father must have been an American soldier held over from the war?"

Catherine was surprised by his unexpected comment. "I always supposed it was a mail order situation-- but you may have something there. If she were born in 1975, the 'war' was over by then and all the American troops were back in this country."

Corrigan raised his eyebrows questioningly. "So you have no idea of the background of her mother or father?"

"Oh, yes..." Catherine responded quickly, "At least I thought I did. You see, the Catholic Church was responsible for her in the states and they have the records. I found out about her while-- you remember the case trial I was working on in Indiana?"

"Yes, I remember..." Corrigan said.

"Yes, the serial killer case four years ago. My father was the court-ordered judge on the case. He--" Suddenly Catherine's face went pale. She stopped, suddenly jolted by a new thought. "Oh my God! It can't be!" she exclaimed aloud.

"What is it?" Corrigan watched her struggle with her thoughts and words as she turned to him.

"Captain, you might have given me the answer! *Oh, God!* I think I know Carrie's secret..."

* * *

The mainstream news stories in July of 1992 featured Bill Clinton nominated as the Democratic candidate for President, while references of the Iran-Contra affair came back to haunt George Bush. But the big headline was an astonishing one. H. Ross Perot withdrew from the race altogether as the third party Independent candidate for President by stating "Someone in the Bush camp has threatened the life of my daughter." The Texan believed the threat may have come from the Central Intelligence Agency itself. The Agencies' response was "Perot's allegations were "pure poppycock! The next thing he'll be saying is his daughter will soon be abducted by a UFO, and he'll blame that one on us, too!"

The critics within the political arena accused Mr. Perot of either grandstanding or creating a publicity stunt for attention. "*Is this the man you want to be the next President of the United States? Is Perot a nut case or what?*" The man was wasting millions on his campaign drive, but Perot's supporters were saying "*at least it was his money and not the taxpayers' he's spending.*"

The voice of the news media pushed the drive for Bill Clinton for President, even with his extracurricular activities: "*Bill Clinton continues to lead in the polls for the race for the Presidency. Only time, will tell whether Perot's supporters will turn to the Democratic candidate or lead themselves back into the Republican Party and the Bush camp.*"

The phone rang in the den of Henry Kencade's house in Madison, Indiana. The judge took his time in answering it. It was early in the evening, and his mind was more on watching Cary Grant and Jean Arthur in a Howard Hawks' movie, *Only Angels have Wings,* on the cable channel. Cary Grant in a comical scene from this 1939 adventure poured ice water on Rita Hayworth and soaked her. It was here where Grant actually said the famous line everyone loved to imitate. Twice Grant repeated, "Judy, Judy!" to Hayworth's character in this classic.

Kencade, watched this, a smile on his face, something that usually never occurred concerning the man, but the smile suddenly changed when the constant ring of his phone didn't stop.

Kencade took his tv remote and pressed the mute button and answered the phone. "Hello!"

There was no response from the other end, which irritated him. Again he repeated, "Hello? Is someone on this line? If you're there, why don't you have the guts to come out with--"

The voice on the other end interrupted him. "Guts, You say, Judge!"

Kencade heard a voice now that was familiar to him four years ago. He heard it the night before his Washington D.C. Grand Jury hearing. Kencade listened again to the voice he could not forget, as if it were the Devil on the other end of the line.

"*Guts* is what you will see one day all over the pavement, Judge," the voice continued, "In front of your cozy little home that stands in your small but comfortable little town. But first, you will witness what we'll do to your precious daughter before it's time for you to make the late evening news!"

Kencade shouted into his phone, "You don't scare me anymore, punk! Take a hike before I have you arrested!" He hung up the phone. It immediately rang back. Kencade answered it and listened, this time not saying a word.

"This is for you, Judge. Your daughter is dead! She is *dead!*" The mysterious caller hung up. Kencade slowly put the phone down and reflected a moment before making his next move.

He dialed a number and spoke into the phone. "This is Judge Henry Kencade. I wish to speak with Senator Fuller, please..."

Fuller soon responded, "Yes, Hank... It's been a long time. What can I do for you?"

Kencade's voice was very tense. "Gerald...we need to talk! Right away." He listened a moment. "Fine! I'll drive up tonight..."

Kencade hung up the phone and reached underneath his desk where he retrieved a hidden key. He unlocked the desk drawer and took out a black box. Inside was a blue steel .38 caliber revolver with brown wood hand grips. Six bullets were lined up in a side compartment. One by one he deliberately loaded all the bullets into the gun's chamber.

Closing the desk drawer, Kencade crossed the room to turn off the television set and grabbed his coat. He put the gun in his coat pocket and exited out a side door entrance into his garage where he drove off in his Monte Carlo.

* * *

As the first full month of summer concluded, John Modini stood next to a newspaper stand and waited. A newspaper truck drove up to dump the late edition. Modini watched the man open the bundle and put the newspapers on the stand. Modini picked one up and read the headlines:

"*A body was found early this morning floating in the Priest River. It was tentatively identified as Pulitzer-prize winning writer, John Modini, a photojournalist who was reported missing back in 1988, but was rumored alive earlier this year.*

This discovery links him to two other bodies found in the same location in the Priest Lake area of Northern Idaho just this last year. The Washington Gazette reported earlier this year that John Modini was responsible for shooting a Federal Marshal in the Capitol Building in Washington D.C. in an altercation with Gerald Fuller of Indiana.

Senator Fuller could not be reached for comment. An investigation is pending to find out if a possible impostor could have impersonated Modini and if he had anything to do with the deaths of the two bodies found earlier in the Priest River.

This story gets more involved as Mr. Modini was not only linked to Colonel Roger Tracy of Naval Intelligence, one of the two bodies discovered, but also to serial killer, Karl Hunter who committed suicide four years ago at the state prison in Fort Wayne. All three men were assigned to the same platoon unit in Vietnam in 1968-1970.

Colonel Tracy, found in a similar manner as Modini, was reported at the time to be a suicide. In a strange twist of fate, it was announced today his widow wants a separate

620

investigation concerning her husband's death, independent of the government's findings. Mrs.
Roger Tracy stated, 'a coverup under the aegis of National Security.'

John Modini's death will not be official until a full autopsy has taken place. Modini's
career as a photojournalist began during his tour of duty in Vietnam. It was here that his
experience during the war with a camera garnered him a Pulitzer-prize in photojournalism."

Modini turned the pages of *The Washington Gazette*, reading the story to its conclusion,
then gave twenty-five cents to the man at the newsstand. He smiled as he folded the newspaper, then
slapped it against his knee in exhilaration. He walked into an alley, disappearing back into the
shadows as he did continually over the last four years.

* * *

Judge Kencade, taking more precautions than necessary, drove his car off the commercial
road into a nearby residential area near Senator Fuller's office. He sat in his car for a moment
putting his thoughts together and considered everything he was planning to do.

Kencade opened the glove compartment and took out a pad and a pen. He wrote a short
letter to Catherine, as if it were his last. He headed it: 'If I will be arrested,' and put the letter back
in the glove compartment. He checked his coat pocket, patting the revolver gently with his hand,
then exited his car.

Kencade walked four blocks to Fuller's state capital building in Indianapolis, Indiana. As
he neared it, he heard a police siren in the distance, coming his way.

Nervously, he paused as the siren of a police car approached. He closed his eyes and froze
where he was. He didn't turn until the noise of the siren passed him by and disappeared in the
distance. He took a deep breath of relief again and opened his eyes. He had taken that first step
forward, reminding himself of that night in Washington, D.C., after his visit at the Lincoln
Memorial. His thoughts were of the girl being attacked and of her attacker, the man with the knife.
A hired killer, maybe, one who makes a living by murder, he thought. That man was just a small

621

part of a much larger society of hired assassins, constantly going about their job as a public service for those who want things to stay the way they are or change them to suit their own purposes.

Henry Kencade continued to stroll to the Indianapolis capitol building, thinking about his confrontation with Fuller. Kencade was planning to assure the one person with such power to change things in this world that he would never be able to abuse that power ever again.

He entered the capital building with the permission of a security guard who had been waiting for him. The guard recognized and greeted him with a hearty welcome. "It is good to see you again, your Honor. It's been a long time, hasn't it? He's still upstairs. He hasn't budged. He's been waiting for your arrival..."

The Judge gave the guard a grandfatherly smile and shook his hand, thanking him. As Kencade walked past the security apparatus, the alarm went off. The security guard turned it off and smiled, inquiring, "What do you have on you, Judge...a gun?"

Kencade laughed, "Oh, I'm sorry, I have some metal shrapnel in my leg from the war in Europe! You might have heard of it-- World War II?" Kencade started to take off his coat. "If you'd like to search me, of course, I'll--"

The guard just waved him on. "No need to, your Honor. I was given orders not to delay you, and not to keep the Senator from waiting!"

Kencade nodded and buttoned his coat again. He entered an open elevator on the lobby floor. When the doors closed, Kencade turned his back on the camera next to the ceiling and took out his gun. Closing his eyes again, he took a deep breath. It was too easy for him to get into the building and past the security check. He felt sorry for the security guard who would have to account for his improper inspection procedure when Kencade completed his objective. He checked the gun over. It was loaded and ready. Once satisfied, he put the gun back in his coat pocket and faced the elevator door. As the bell rang signaling the elevator's arrival at the Senator's floor, the doors slowly opened.

Kencade was perspiring as he entered the corridor to Fuller's office. There was no aid or

622

secretary on duty at the main information desk since it was after hours. He knew just the two of them would be at this meeting. He walked past the desk right to the opened door of Fuller's office. There were no lights on inside the room.

That's odd, Kencade wondered. *If Fuller was expecting me, he should at least put some lights on.* The situation made the Judge more nervous than he was.

He heard the voice of Fuller speaking within his mind. It was from their previous confrontation: *"Everything has been taken care of. It's out of our hands now!"*

Kencade entered the darkened office, passing the secretary's desk, and opened another door leading down a hallway to Fuller's inner office where he should be waiting.

The door to Fuller's office was opened. It too, was dark. Something was not right. He felt the cold sweat of fear now. The faint light in the room came from the office buildings from across the way, through the Senator's picture view window. He nervously took out the gun.

Something is very wrong here, Kencade thought. He slowly continued on, feeling as if someone were watching his every move, wondering if maybe he was walking into some trap.

Kencade noticed Fuller sitting in his leather chair, turned so he could look out his window. Kencade also saw the figure of himself reflected in the window as he approached Fuller's desk. The Senator's voice spoke from the darkness.

"Come in Hank," Fuller welcomed the Judge. "Don't get shy on me, now!"

This startled Kencade as much as the shadow behind him did. "Gerry? Fuller didn't answer. He approached the desk, curious to why Fuller didn't follow through. "Gerry? Is there someone else in this room with us?" Fuller didn't answer him.

Kencade again repeated, "Gerry!" This time he waited with his gun drawn in response.

Fuller again spoke out. "How's Catherine doing these days. I just wanted you to know, pal, if I go down, you'll go down with me, too. And that includes your precious daughter. Well, I want you to hear it from me, I already went down on her a long time ago. She was cherry when it happened. Oh, you don't believe me? Then be my guest. Why not use my phone? Call her and ask her yourself!"

Kencade stood there motionless stunned by what he heard. Fuller's voice came again from the darkness. "Her career is on the line, Hank, and I can crush it any time I say!"

Kencade, in a fit of madness, rushed forward and swung the leather chair around to face the Senator directly. And Kencade stepped back in horror, his eyes wide with fear.

There was a gun in the Senator's hand and a bullet hole at his temple. Blood covered the side of his face. It ran down the chair, forming a small pool of blood on the carpet. There's certainly no way Fuller could have just spoken with him since he had been dead for some time. *He must have been killed between the time I talked to him and the time I got here,* Kencade thought. Kencade tried to understand how the Senator's voice could speak on cue. And as he moved back from the desk, the voice of Fuller spoke out with the words repeating: "Come in Hank, don't get shy on me, now. By the way, how's Catherine doing these days?"

Kencade stepped forward, cutting off the Senator's voice. Then he got down on his knees in the dark he felt the rug beneath him, setting his gun down momentarily. He finally found what he was looking for. He felt a wire stretching across the floor from one end of the room to the door. He followed it led to the top of cabinet behind the Senator's desk where a recorder was rigged to switch on and off and play the tape on an endless loop.

Kencade ripped out the tape and put it into the Senator's ashtray. He lighted a match and set the tape on fire. It started to burn, casting flickering orange light into the shadowy room. Suddenly, Fuller's desk phone rang. Kencade didn't want to answer it so he let it ring. Then he remembered the security guard.

Kencade picked up the phone and listened. The voice on the other end was a familiar one, the same mysterious male voice from his home telephone earlier today. The voice repeated, "I hope you enjoyed my little joke, Judge! I had Fuller record his words earlier. I convinced him it would be better off blackmailing you than killing you-- then I changed my mind. I warned you what would happen if you continued to pursue the Hunter case. You better say your prayers, Judge! Your time has just run out. So has your daughter's! The next time you see her she'll be dead!" The person on the other end hung up.

Kencade's thoughts were a jumble. Obviously, this was an elaborate setup to frame him again. Whoever it was must have been monitoring Kencade's calls or had him under observation. No one else, beside himself, knew he was meeting the Senator.

Kencade quickly dialed a number. When they answered, Kencade almost shouted, "Bradley, is that you?"

"Yes, it is Mr. Kencade," Michael Bradley said.

The Judge closed his eyes in relief, "Bradley, where's Catherine? What the...why is she there? Well, never mind. When is she going to return? Listen to me! You've got to find her Bradley, and stay with her. Her life is in danger. You've got to get protection for her no matter what, they will kill her. I can't explain it right now, you've got to believe me. If anything happens to her, I'll never be able to forgive myself. I know all these years you never thought much of me, Bradley, but I'm willing now to work with your friend, Mr.--

Michael cut him off before he mentioned Modini's name, realizing there might be a security breach. "Ahh... *Mr. O'Leary*, I see!" He hoped Kencade would catch on to why he did that.

Kencade continued, "I need to see him tonight, Michael, please...this is an emergency!"

Michael Bradley listened carefully to Kencade with his eyes closed and became just as frightened. Kencade never had called him by his first name before. And Bradley never heard the judge speak with such panic in all the years he knew him. Bradley tried to calm the Judge down by cautioning him, "Don't worry, Sir, Catherine is in good hands right now. I don't think we should say anything more over the phone, if you know what I mean. So, I'd better get that call into Seattle now, and then I'll set up a meeting between you and Jack O'Leary. Yes! I will! Don't worry, sir...I love your daughter, too!" Bradley hung up his phone. As he lifted his hand from the receiver, he noticed it shaking like a leaf.

Something serious was happening in the law office of Michael Bradley and Jennifer Tamura, and Jennifer couldn't put her finger on it. When she had arrived for work in the morning, Michael Bradley was already there having a private meeting with Thomas Sanders. She continued getting her paperwork in order until Bradley asked her to join them in his office.

"What's up?" she asked as her boss closed the door.

"In just a few minutes, you'll have your answer," Bradley replied mysteriously. So she and Thomas Sanders sat on his sofa and watched Bradley nervously play with his pen. The men were obviously waiting for something, but Jennifer didn't know what. She made herself comfortable and passed the time making mental plans for her weekend.

Shortly before nine-thirty, Sherry buzzed the intercom. "I have a phone call for you, Mr. Bradley. It's Mrs. Rogers."

"Thank you, Sherry," Bradley replied. He pressed the button on his speakerphone so everyone could hear. "Hello, Catherine?"

Her voice came from the speakerphone, both apprehensive and strained. "Michael, there's something important I've got to talk to you about."

"What is it?"

"It concerns what we talked about before-- about the letters Hunter gave us. I've been doing a lot of thinking. I think the time is right to release the information to the public."

"What are you talking about? You said you were going to keep it in a safe place."

"Well, that's just it. It's doing us no good under lock and key. Karl Hunter's letter is the key to solving this whole problem."

"What do you mean?"

"If I bring the information to your law offices, we can determine exactly what we have. There, we'll be able to examine, document and study it. I'm sure Hunter had plenty to say about the people he was involved with."

Michael's voice wavered, "I don't think it's a good idea, Catherine."

"Why not? Once we see what's in the letter, we can do follow-up with research or release it to the media. Either way, we start the ball rolling."

There was a desperate edge to Bradley's voice, "I have a great idea. Why don't we get together when you're back in town so we can talk about it."

"No, Michael," she countered, "We can't afford to wait until the time is right. Tomorrow night I'll go to the terminal to get the package. Then we can make things happen ourselves instead of waiting for things to happen to us."

"You're making a hasty decision. You should leave the package where it is! It's too risky to bring it here now."

"Good-bye, Michael. I'll be back in town tomorrow, and I'll see you with the info tomorrow night!" She hung up.

Michael Bradley turned off the speaker phone and motioned them out of the room. He followed them out and led them into the conference room. "Well, what do you think."

Jennifer felt very uncomfortable. She felt that Catherine had compromised their efforts by instigating a course of action not approved by everyone. "I...I have to agree with you, Mr. Bradley," Jennifer told him candidly. "She shouldn't take it upon herself to act without thinking through the consequences."

Bradley seemed pleased. "Would you please explain your opinion a little more clearly?"

"Well...what if someone found out about this call. What if your phones were bugged, or Catherine's line tapped from wherever she was calling from, for heaven's sake!"

"That's just what we're hoping for, Jennifer!" Bradley chuckled and shared a conspiratorial glance with Thomas. "As a matter of fact, I *know* my office is bugged. We just set the mouse trap!"

It was then that Jennifer knew Bradley had been play-acting, planning something. And she knew it was something big.

Chapter Thirty-Nine

"The Cheese in the Mousetrap"

In Taos, New Mexico, an urgent message came through on the computer, coded to Dragon, stating: "Investigation continuing concerning the two unknown men in the Pentagon whose identities are still in question. The men who had a brief meeting with the Commander of the Joint Chiefs of Staff, then left the Pentagon, and made arrangements to fly too a small city in Indiana called Madison." The computer monitor displayed: "Need status if possible drug deal goes down. Haven't a clue why Madison needs instructions for us to proceed if illegal maneuvers happen. Staking out city Greyhound bus terminal with two FBI agents at your request."

In Madison, Indiana, two men sat inside a dark van with binoculars staring at the two unidentified men they were ordered to observe. FBI agent William Rutland, was irked by his assignment, "I don't get it, why are we stuck here in small town America? This doesn't make any sense? It can't be a drug deal. If it were, the Dragon's orders would be to get DEA here on this one..."

Phyllip Shayne, his partner, disagreed. "Yeah, unless these guys do something out of the ordinary like passing a nuclear device or top secret materials to an agent of the North Korean government. Until then we keep a low profile!" His binoculars panned over to their two prey, the people they had under observation. They were two plainclothes men seated in their parked vehicle, a tan Dodge Dart, as if waiting for something to happen.

Rutland argued, "I tell you this isn't a drug deal going down, you'll see! I haven't seen shit so far that these guys have done anything to get excited about!"

Again, Shayne retorted, "I don't know what else it could be!" Then something caught his eye through the binoculars. "Wait a minute, who's that?" The two men responded to a third subject exiting his parked Bentley next to the phone booth. The agent observed the men were also watching this man.

It was Michael Bradley who headed for the phone booth and entered it.

The agent adjusted his binoculars on the men in the Dodge and caught one of them exiting on the passenger side of the vehicle. The man closed the door and stood next to it. Shayne peered through he binoculars and watched the man stare at the phone booth.

Shayne lowered his binoculars and told his partner, "I think this guy in the Bentley may be the contact they've been waiting for, except nothing is happening. The guy in the Bentley just got out and went into a phone booth. Our man is standing by the car watching him!" Rutland took the binoculars to see for himself.

* * *

Catherine Rogers sat in her hotel room where she had spent the last few days in hiding. The hotel was on the same street as the bus terminal, four blocks away. The phone rang in her room, and she picked it up quickly, not waiting for a second ring, "Michael?" She had expected his call. She let him speak and became very tense as he explained his instructions. "Michael! I can't go through with this!" Catherine suddenly exclaimed, "I'm worried! Dad...he's been missing two days now! What if they have him?"

"Don't worry about your father!" Bradley told her, "The old goat can take care of himself!"

Catherine, angry and upset now, disagreed, "No, Michael...you *don't* understand! Senator Fuller is dead. The authorities discovered his body today, and dad's voice is on Fuller's answering machine Friday evening as the last person he was to meet with. Now my father has disappeared!" She started to cry.

 Bradley became alarmed by the Senator's death. "Senator Fuller is dead?"

William Rutland still had Bradley under observation. He turned his binoculars and swung them around to their prey, staring at the man who stood next to the passenger side of the car. The man got back into his Dodge and turned his ignition on. It departed and drove slowly from the phone booth.

The agent handed the binoculars back to his partner and started up their van. "Well, Phil, there goes your drug theory and contact. They've just left the premises!" Shayne saw their prey's Dodge Dart go around the block. His partner backed up their van and moved out to follow behind.

* * *

"I'm scared, Michael!" Catherine cried into her phone. Bradley's silence told her all she needed to know. Finally, she heard his response.

"And you're saying I'm not, Catie?" She heard Bradley take a nervous breath, "We all are, now you know what Karl went through. Now John Modini is risking his life *again*...and for what? He's proven we were right about Karl, and now he wants to save not only our lives, but the future of this country...so there is a lot at stake! Trust me, I know you, Catie...you'll be fine!"

Catherine felt ashamed by allowing Bradley to say the things she already knew. She took a deep breath, wiping her tears away.

Bradley's concern called out to her, "I love you, Catherine!"

Catherine smiled knowing he meant what he said. Then she cleared her throat, "How much time before I have to enter the terminal?"

Bradley gave a sigh of relief. "That's my girl. Give me ten minutes and you're on your own..."

Catherine carefully thought this over, knowing what she was expected to do.

Bradley's voice asked calmly, "Are you still there, Catherine?" She forced a grin and told him, "Yes, I'm just wiping my tears... I love you, too, Michael! God Bless you!" Never having said those words to anyone in years, she quickly hung up her phone. She took out her makeup kit from her purse and nervously put on some makeup to hide the redness of her eyes. She followed this up with a quick powder to her flush cheeks. She quickly exited the hotel.

Once on the street, Catherine looked at her target in front of her, the Greyhound Bus terminal. She couldn't help feel afraid.

A dispatcher at police central for 911 received an urgent call. An unidentified person reported he had placed a bomb inside the Madison Greyhound terminal, and it was set to go off in fifteen minutes. The woman dispatcher glanced at her clock. It read: 8:50 p.m.

The dispatcher alerted the necessary departments, including the bomb squad. She traced the call and discovered the caller had made the threatening call from a phone booth two blocks from the bus terminal.

* * *

The van carrying the two FBI agents followed the Dodge Dart another block until it stopped and parked again. The men in the van found this strange as they watched their two targets get out of the Dodge and head to the phone booth.

FBI agent Shayne had a smile on his face. "Well, well, well...I should have put a wager on my instincts after all!"

Rutland parked the van on the side of the road. "Why, what are they up to?"

Shayne shook his head, "I don't get it...they're going back to subject three in the phone booth, but they aren't carrying any valise or briefcase to make any transactions."

"Maybe they are paying by check and the other has secret information on microfilm,"

Rutland said sarcastically.

Shayne had a bad feeling. "No...it's got to be something else. The guy in the phone booth is crossing the street pretending he doesn't know them. *They* seem to know him. They're showing him something, maybe a badge? No, wait, he's acting as if he doesn't know them as he walks away but--" The sound of gunfire interrupted the agent's commentary. "--they-- holy *shit!* My God! They just popped him!"

"What?" Rutland exclaimed, confused, "They just shot your supposed contact?"

"It's a hit, for Christ's sake, it's a God-damned hit!" Shayne gave the binoculars over to his partner to see for himself.

His partner peered through the binoculars as he watched the two men rifle through Michael Bradley's clothes, searching for his wallet. They took his credit cards and money, then tossed the wallet out into the middle of the street. "Who the hell are these guys? They are making it look like a robbery and holdup. You're right, it's a hit! We've got to do something!"

"Without Dragon's approval we can't do shit!"

"Wake him up if you have to! Whoever these guys are, they just violated the perimeter of both the Pentagon and committed murder right before our eyes! What the fuck is going on here?"

* * *

The man known as Dragon was making love to his attractive wife when his beeper on his night stand went off. He was within his secured home, outside Santa Fe, New Mexico. The Dragon walked nude to the kitchen area to make his call, knowing his beeper wasn't to go off unless it was an emergency or a political crisis of some kind.

"This better be good!" he spoke sharply into the phone.

The voice on the other end came from the Kirkland Air Force Base in Albuquerque, "A 'Code Red,' sir! They told me you better get down here! 'Code Red' is what they told me to say. They gave no further details, sir!"

The Dragon's jaw tightened. "Thank you," he told his caller. "I'll be there in sixty minutes."

* * *

Catherine crossed the street and entered the bus terminal. It was busy at this time of night, and she looked around nervously, suspicious of everyone around her, including those just passing by. She became aware now, more than anytime before, the type of people who permanently existed here-- the homeless, the bums, the transients. Some were sleeping on the benches while others were squatting in the corner.

She moved slowly through the terminal where travelers waited for their time of departure. A teenage mother carrying her baby in one hand and a suitcase in the other, exited to a call for her bus. Her grandparents kissed her goodbye.

Catherine tried to calm herself, acting as detached as possible. She accidentally brushed up against a bum, lying on a bench in a womb-like position, momentarily disturbing him. "Oh... excuse me... I'm terribly sorry," she said to him.

He groaned in discomfort but paid no attention to the disturbance. Catherine looked at him as if she felt sorry for him and then moved on, knowing time was a factor here. She headed to the locker area. When she reached the lockers, she rummaged through her purse, making the motions as though looking for something. She periodically glanced at the terminal clock for her cue. The time was 8:59 p.m. She counted the seconds before moving to any particular locker. She had the overwhelming suspicion she was being watched. She had to wait for the second hand to reach the number twelve on the clock before she could continue any further.

Catherine had a right to feel nervous. She was under observation and pressure. From the building across the street, the cross-hairs of a telescopic rifle were centered on her. The rifle was strategically placed, with a full view of the lockers, through the tall sections of glass window panes. They had followed Catherine as she strolled through the bus terminal from the entrance.

633

Catherine checked the clock. It was time. She moved to a particular locker.

The sniper followed her in the cross-hairs, his finger near the trigger, waiting for the right time to fire.

Catherine opened the locker with her key and stood there, letting the seconds pass. Then slowly, as not to attract attention, she moved to the locker next to it and opened that one.

The cross-hairs followed her as she went to a third locker and inserted a key. Then to another...and another. She continued this diversion until a dozen lockers stood open in a row in full view of anyone watching.

The cross-hairs examined each open locker then swung back to Catherine, never able to see what she was doing in front of them, nor whether she was retrieving anything from them.

Upon finishing this charade with the lockers, Catherine returned to each locker again, this time shutting and re-locking them.

Police and fire truck sirens disturbed the night air approaching in the distance. The cross-hairs never left their sight of Catherine's head or torso as she turned to see the commotion happening outside the building.

The two FBI agents in the van who earlier saw Michael Bradley shot down in cold blood, now watched the chaos developing in front of the bus terminal. From their viewpoint, they had the ringside seat as the police cars arrived, sirens screaming, followed by the bomb squad and two fire trucks.

"What's going on here," Shayne asked.

"I don't know, but we'd better find out, and fast!" Rutland said. He picked up the cellular car phone and dialed a special code number. He described what they were witnessing and asked whether they should overrule their noninterference policy.

"No," the voice at the other end asserted. "Just follow your two targets and see what happens. You are not to intervene in any way!"

Rutland told his partner what their orders were. Shayne wasn't happy. "Then we'd better keep them in sight. They're heading for the terminal. Let's go."

The two special agents drove their van closer to the commotion in the street ahead.

The security officers supplied by the local authorities responded professionally. Upon entering the terminal, the officers fanned out quickly and escorted the waiting people and travelers from the premises. The bomb squad rushed through the doors with their masked, protective gear and carrying their equipment. They pushed into the terminal and spread out, searching for the signs of any bomb.

The police, meanwhile, helped security by hurrying the people quickly and safely out of the building. The fire department and firemen prepared their equipment for the anticipated operation.

The cross-hairs of the telescopic rifle never left Catherine and followed her as two outfitted members of the bomb squad, in mask and protective gear, approached her. The sniper behind the telescopic sight observed the men motion for her to leave, as one member offered to escort her to safety.

Meanwhile, the two Federal agents entered the terminal and saw Catherine and one of the bomb squad men approaching. The first man took out his badge and stopped her. "I'm sorry, Mrs. Rogers. You're going to have to come with us!"

Catherine halted in her tracks and suddenly went pale. She grabbed a hold of the bomb squad member's arm and squeezed it, as if becoming faint. This action concealed the motion of slipping a key into his hand. It went unnoticed by the two Federal agents. Then she went limp and fainted to the floor.

The masked bomb squad member held onto her as the cross-hairs of the rifle sights panned from her onto him. The person holding Catherine waved to another passing squad member for his help. "You! I need you to help this woman out of here and get her to an ambulance quickly. She's fainted, and--" he turned to the two agents, "--I recommend the both of you get the hell out of here! There's a bomb in here ready to go off at any moment! Now move it!"

The second bomb squad man picked up Catherine and carried her to the entrance. The two men followed behind trying to get his attention. "We'll take possession of the lady, if you don't mind. We're Federal agents!"

The bomb squad man ignored him until the first Federal agent yanked out a 9mm Beretta pistol with an attached silencer as he flashed his badge. The man stopped and yelled angrily through his protective mask into the agent's face, "Are you *nuts?* We have less than two minutes before a bomb goes off here! We have a responsibility to get these people to safety. Now get the hell out of here, or I'll be picking up pieces of your flesh and bones off this God-damn floor; myself!"

The agents didn't budge. They were too stunned to move.

"Are you deaf! Now outta my way!"

As the man pushed past him, the first Federal agent chambered the pistol, put the weapon to the back of the man's head and pulled the trigger. The gun fired silently, and the man fell to the floor dead, dropping Catherine.

Catherine managed to break her fall when she hit the floor, since she pretended to be unconscious. She started to get up when the agent shoved the gun into her face. She froze in place as he gave her a smug smile.

"There was no bomb...isn't that right, Mrs. Rogers? This was just a ruse!" Now, get your ass up off the floor or I'll kill you right here!" he said harshly. He grabbed Catherine and hauled her to her feet, keeping the gun aimed at her head.

Catherine tried to compose herself, "I--I don't know what you're talking about," she stammered.

"Don't you, Mrs. Rogers?" The second man grabbed her by the hair. "You're under arrest!" He yanked her hair, and she screamed out in pain.

The old bum, disturbed earlier by Catherine, now staggered to her and the two Federal agents. The second man told the bum, "Go away old man, unless you want to get hurt!"

The bum stopped in a drunken stupor in front of the group, blocking the line of sight of the sniper across the street, still keeping the sights trained on Catherine. From his point of view, the sniper could not see what was happening. The bum appeared to be blocking Catherine and talking to the two agents.

The bum, in fact, had a revolver in his hand and pointed it at the two agents.

"Let her go," the bum said.

Catherine was jolted by the realization who this person was. His features had been successfully hidden behind the dirt and grime and fake facial hair. "Daddy?" she asked bewildered.

"Lower the gun, now!" Henry Kencade ordered the first agent to move the gun from Catherine's head. "Nobody will be arrested here, Gentlemen!" Kencade quickly turned to the second man. "Now before somebody gets hurt here, Mister, you and I and Wyatt Earp here, with his long tall gun, will take a walk out that front door, without a fuss...is that understood? Now, I'll take that gun if you don't mind!"

The first agent with the silencer refused to play by the Judge's rules, "You're not going to shoot anybody old man. Now I suggest you put that gun down before I have to put a big fat hole in--"

Kencade didn't hesitate to fire, hitting the Federal agent in his hand, causing the man's weapon to clatter to the bus terminal floor.

The noise of the gunshot went off like a miniature explosion, echoing throughout the bus terminal. Panic ensued as everyone, including the bomb squad members, the police, and the customers hit the floor, mistaking it for the planted bomb. Several people in the room screamed and started fleeing. The two Federal agents knew Kencade meant business, and slowly backed away.

Kencade, his temper rising, yelled to them, "Now move it!" He moved closer to his daughter without taking an eye off them. "Catie! There's a car waiting for you at the side entrance. Take it, get out now! The keys are inside, now go!"

As Catherine faced her father, the cross hairs from the sniper's rifle fell on her again.

"Dad! I'm not leaving you!"

Kencade shouted at her, "Go! Damn it! Do as I tell you!"

The cross hairs of the telescopic rifle slid over to Kencade now, again in the line of fire. Catherine was shielded by her father as he started to push her toward the door. The sniper squeezed the trigger and fired. The bullet hit Kencade in the back and the impact brought him down.

Most of the people who witnessed this scene panicked and ran for the exits. Catherine, before exiting through the side entrance saw her father fall. "Daddy!" she screamed. Another bullet hit the glass door inches from her head. She threw herself to one side and hugged the wall.

The two Federal agents saw their chance. The first man retrieved his gun from the floor, and both agents began firing at Catherine.

One of the bomb squad members rushed her, throwing her to the floor. More bullets, fired by the sniper, sprayed the terminal, missing the two of them. As the bomb squad member and Catherine tried to move to cover, the building shook with an earsplitting blast as a real bomb exploded at the other end of the terminal. The explosion was set off in an unoccupied area of the terminal, but it was close enough to kill one of the agents instantly.

There was an eerie silence after the blast. The lights were out in half the terminal and the few that were still on flickered from lack of power. Catherine moved through the dissipating smoke from the explosion and reached her father.

"Daddy...Daddy...are you all right?" she asked, tears filling her eyes.

"Catie..." Kencade tried to speak through his pain. "Catie...you have to go..."

"Oh, Daddy, noooo," she sobbed.

One of the bomb squad members crawled to Catherine and tossed a smoke bomb into the center of the terminal to the locker area. This caused a bigger smoke screen than the original blast. Then he shoved a protective gas mask in Catherine's hand. "Put this on and get to the car outside..." he pulled her off her father and forced her away. "Get out of here, Catherine! I'll handle this!" His voice was muffled, but she understood every word.

Another member of the bomb squad sprinted up and grabbed Catherine before she could reply. She reluctantly went with him but couldn't take her eyes off her father, lying there on the floor. Her eyes never left him until she was hustled out the side entrance.

The remaining bomb squad member reached down to Kencade to check for any signs of life. He felt no pulse and realized Kencade was dead. He took a key from his own pocket that Catherine slipped to him earlier and glanced at the number. He walked into the smoke screen around the lockers and pulled a flashlight from his uniform. He snapped on the light and headed straight to the locker with the matching number. He opened it up and retrieved the material inside, then moved back to Kencade's body.

Catherine was shoved into the car by the second bomb squad member who dragged her out of the terminal. He entered the car with her, closed the door and took off his mask, revealing himself to be Thomas Sanders. Catherine was shocked and relieved nonetheless. She threw her arms around him and hugged him, "Tom, oh God, I'm glad it's you!" But a more urgent thought hit her. "You've got to get back to my father! He's inside-- he's been shot!" she told him frantically. "Please hurry and get father out of there and find Michael!"

"I will, don't worry," Thomas assured her. He seemed flushed with excitement to have participated in something as exciting as this. "I'll meet you and Michael as planned at the office at midnight."

Thomas leaned over to give her a goodbye kiss, when the window exploded with a crash behind him. He grunted in a silent cry and grabbed his throat. Blood gushed from a bullet wound. He slumped over, gasping for breath.

"My God! Tom!" Catherine screamed. She looked up to see the second agent pointing his gun through the broken window. It had a silencer on it and was aimed directly between her eyes. She saw the smirk on the agent's face and thought it would be the last thing she would see in this lifetime.

Suddenly the agent's mouth opened in a silent scream as he was attacked from behind. He gasped and dropped his gun as a knife stabbed him in the back not once, not twice but four times. He fell dead to the ground.

Catherine watched as an unfamiliar face stood in his place, wiping the knife clean on the Federal agents' clothing. Their eyes finally met. Catherine was so traumatized, she couldn't react. She couldn't even scream. Things were happening too fast.

The man saw her confused expression. "Go!" he shouted. "I'm not here to harm you. I'm here to help."

Catherine finally found her voice. "Who...are you?"

The man laughed, "Just think of me as your guardian angel."

Catherine's eyes flashed in confusion. He sensed she wanted more of an explanation.

"A friend from Miami sent me to you...that's all you need to know!" She started to speak, but the man quickly added, "No, not Corrigan! Your other friend in Miami."

"What other friend," she finally asked.

"I've got to go," he said evasively and disappeared into the shadows as quickly as he appeared.

Catherine had no time to think about what happened. She was in the middle of an emergency! She reached down to Thomas, bleeding and hovering at the edge of unconsciousness. She tore off part of her blouse as a bandage to stop the wound from bleeding, but realized it was too serious. Thomas needed medical attention-- and fast. She set him down and then started the car.

Catherine drove down the street and turned the corner. Up ahead was one of the ambulances parked nearby at the bus terminal. She headed for it.

Back inside the bus terminal, the remaining bomb squad member, still wearing his gas mask, examined Kencade's tattered suit. It was suitable for the part of the bum he had portrayed, but the bullet holes in his back didn't come with the costume. The man looked around; attempting to judge the direction the bullets must have come from to have hit Kencade from behind. He studied the tall windows on the side of the terminal, then saw the bullet holes spider-webbed in the glass.

He looked further across the street to the abandon office building, observing the second and third floors where the sniper must have aimed downward to shoot his rifle.

The bomb squad member turned his attention back to Kencade who lay dead on the ground. He noticed Kencade's revolver lying beside the man's body. He reached for it and slid it into his pocket, looking nervously at the window panes where the shots came from. Then it dawned on him what to do with the envelope he retrieved from the locker. If he had not been able to exit with the precious material without being caught, he originally intended to pass it over to Kencade, disguised as the bum. The man's only thought was stick with the plan, but for a different reason now. He gave a quick glance around the terminal to assure himself no one was watching him, then placed the packet inside Kencade's coat pocket for safekeeping. The man decided to take this precaution in case he, too, was shot as he left the terminal.

Once on his feet, the bomb squad member hurried for the front entrance and exited the terminal. Outside the entrance, he pulled off his mask and equipment revealing himself to be John Modini.

Modini's soldier instincts took over. He threw his gear to the ground and made a beeline to the structure across the street, Kencade's gun now in hand. He marched forward with stealth and determination, as if he were in enemy territory back in Vietnam. He headed around the side of the abandon building to the back entrance.

Modini looked upward and studied the premises. Then, with the revolver ready, he climbed the outside back staircase past the second floor level, heading upwards, where he surmised the shooting must have taken place. He glanced below as he reached the third floor. Behind the building was a railroad yard and on the other side of the tracks, was parked a white Jaguar. It was an unusual sight because the Jaguar stood out conspicuously in the surrounding area.

Modini turned back to a third floor open window and crawled through. He paused to listen. He heard footsteps above him, but they stopped just as quickly.

The room Modini stood in was empty. The building itself appeared to be an abandon business building. He opened the door to the hall and saw a staircase going up. He made his way down the debris strewn hall and steadied his nerves as he climbed the stairs and reached the upper floor.

It was very quiet. Modini strained his ears to pick up any sound, but heard nothing. He cursed himself for leaving the flashlight behind. He certainly could have used it now.

Modini made his way to the front of the building, with a half-formed plan to see whether he could find where the shots were fired. He moved to the open doorway of the room where he thought the sniper had waited. Cautiously he entered, his gun aiming straight into the room.

He saw an eight-inch opening in the front window. The illumination in the room came from the lights of the bus terminal across the street. Next to the window was a telescopic rifle standing on its end against the wall.

Modini continued to move forward, spot checking every inch of the room. He stayed close to the wall, so no one could make him out in the dark, staying out of sight from the window as best he could.

Modini finally reached the rifle, his eyes darting from side to side. He was ready for anything, now. His hand reached out to the rifle when he heard footsteps again, this time from the outer hallway, where he just came from. He quickly backed away into a darkened corner and checked the chamber in his gun. It contained only five bullets, one already spent. He clicked the chamber back into place and aimed his weapon at the open doorway.

The silence lasted several seconds. Then suddenly, a man's silhouette stood outside the entrance. More footsteps echoed through the empty hall as a man's voice called out, "Hey, who's there?"

The shadowy figure entered the room and swung a handgun at Modini. "Police! Hold it right there!" His shout summoned the second officer to the entrance way.

Modini could now tell that both men were police officers. They were both in uniform and were wearing badges.

Modini still aimed his gun at the first officer. The policeman shouted again. "Now drop the gun...drop it, *mister!*"

Modini froze to the spot, afraid to move. He shouted back out to the officer, "Show me you guys are *real* cops, first!"

The first officer was in the same standoff position as Modini was in, but decided he had the upper hand. "If you don't put the gun down in three seconds, we'll open fire...now *do* what I say, one...two...thr--"

Modini, his revolver still aimed, and still paralyzed with fear, didn't budge, but interrupted the countdown. "If you don't show me some identification real quick, motherfucker! I'll start pulling this trigger, and I won't stop! Is *that* understood!"

The second policeman in a low voice called to the first from the hallway. "I think you better show him some ID. Both of you could go down in this room if you don't! Since he hasn't opened fire yet he could be cool."

"Now, listen, whoever you are," the first officer said, "It's dark in here! How do you suppose we do this?"

Modini, a bit calmer now, thought quickly. "Let's all just back up slowly into the hallway, down the stairway and outside into the street," he suggested. "If you guys are for real, we can resolve this with no one getting hurt-- with *no* problem."

The first officer made the first move backwards, "Okay, we're backing into the hallway. Start coming forward!"

Modini slowly moved to the entrance way until he could see both officers backing toward the stairwell.

The two officers slowly started to descend backwards down the staircase. Modini followed, and paused at the top of the landing. "Okay, guys," he tried to sound casual, "Before we go any further, I have a question for you."

"What question did you have in mind?" the first officer asked as the two officers halted on

643

the stairs.

"I admit I'm no policeman.," Modini responded, "but I do know police procedures. Now, you, mister...You got a name?" he asked the second officer

"My name is officer Joseph Dalton," he said gruffly. "You want my badge number, too?"

"Sure, why not, "Modini said.

"My badge number is 102--" Dalton started to reply

Modini cut him off. "Good! Don't give me too much." He looked down at the first officer, still keeping his gun pointed at the second. "All right, Officer Dalton, number 102...tell me your partner's name, rank and number"

The second officer was silent for a moment and reluctantly answered. "Mister, I can't identify this officer because he's not from my precinct!"

"I thought you guys were working together."

"No," Officer Dalton told Modini, "I never saw him before until now."

Modini felt his suspicions growing. *It's better to be paranoid than dead*, he thought to himself. "Now, Officer Dalton, what I want you to do is ask this officer to identify himself to you. Have him show you his identification, is that clear?"

Officer Dalton, his gun still aimed at Modini challenged his fellow officer. "Well!"

The first officer, never taking his eyes off Modini, reached into his jacket for his ID. "This is ridiculous!"

Modini quickly urged, "Do not, I repeat, do *not* look at his ID until he identifies himself...is that clear!"

The first officer swore, handing over his wallet. "By the book, huh? All right, sweetheart, it's Frank Slaton, Precinct number--"

Before he completed his sentence, he swung his gun at Modini and fired. Modini was already prepared for something like this and twisted aside, when the officer moved. He dived onto the hallway floor, out of the sight of the two officers. But Modini didn't react as fast as he expected, and screamed out as he went down, his forehead bloodied.

"What the *fuck* are you doing, man?" Officer Dalton screamed at the first officer in anger.

"Shut up!" the first officer snarled, then turned his gun on Dalton, blowing him away. The bullet struck him in the head, and he tumbled down the stairs to the lower landing. This police officer followed Dalton's body to the bottom and headed down the first floor hallway.

Modini, still on the fourth floor, felt the side of his forehead. His fingers came away stained with blood. He was relieved he had only been grazed and listened to his heart thumping wildly in his chest. In the distance he heard the sound of a train whistle. He struggled to his feet, a bit dazed and stunned, and heard the footsteps of the assassin disappearing in the hallway below. Modini didn't know who the man was or if he intended to kill him specifically, but he would not let it rest. For all he knew, the man was the sniper himself. Either way, the killer was his only link to discovering who set them all up. He was determined to get some answers. It was now or never.

Modini proceeded down the staircase, gun in hand. As he reached the bottom of the stairwell, he saw the body of Officer Dalton lying at the foot of the stairs. The sudden sound of broken glass caught his attention. He stepped into the hallway and sprinted to the back of the building. He paused and looked through the doorway of the last room. The room was as empty as the others, but this one had a broken window. This is where the noise came from.

He hurried to the window and saw the killer leap the fence and running across the railroad yard behind the building, heading to the tracks. On the other side of the rails sat the white Jaguar. *That's why it was parked out there*, Modini thought to himself. *It was planted there as a getaway car!* He slipped the gun into his pants pocket and started his chase after the assassin.

But luck was against him. Modini heard the train whistle sound again, this time closer than he expected. He looked to his left. The engine of the Amtrak train was in sight, and it approached at a slow but steady speed. He ran to the back fence, climbed it and jumped into the railway yard, following the route of the killer.

It became a race between the train now and the assassin with Modini some distance behind.

He hoped beyond hope the train would force his prey to slow down, but had no such luck. The assassin ran faster to beat the train before it intersected his path.

The assassin reached the tracks as Modini made a frantic effort to dash across the yard. His prey made it over the tracks as the train screamed by, missing him by a few feet.

Modini didn't succeed and stopped in his path, gasping for breath, finding it difficult to draw in air. His lungs were on fire and cursed at himself through the deafening noise of the passing train. He started to pace back and forth like a madman, raging inside. This was obviously a mega-long train of passenger cars, and commercial boxcars. Desperate seconds ticked by as Modini tried to figure out how to get to the other side of the tracks.

Modini desperately wanted to collar this man before he got away. Growing more enraged and frustrated at each passing second, Modini attempted the impossible. He watched the cars pass one by one, timing them. In a judgment made by sheer instinct and adrenaline, he waited for the right moment and made a choice no sane man would make. As the first pair of wheels on a passenger car went by, he threw himself underneath the moving train.

Modini landed between the rails on the rough wood support beams and hugged the ground, hoping his momentum wouldn't carry him across the second rail. He succeeded and remained frozen on his stomach, hearing the train clatter over the top of him. He had less than three feet of space between him and the bottom of the boxcars.

He slowly raised his head and watched the wheels of the cars roll toward him and pass by either side of him. A split second glimpse to the side caught the blurred image of the Jaguar. Was the assassin inside it? He couldn't tell. Modini concentrated on the wheels of the train cars.

Modini waited for several cars to pass. He then braced himself and prepared to make his exit. For a moment he felt the fear go through him and wondered if he were only moments from death. He shoved the thought aside. *It's now or never* he told himself, and he waited for the next set of wheels to pass.

A split second after the wheels roared by, Modini rolled his body over the second rail and onto the other side of the track. He was so keyed up he didn't feel himself clear the rail. He continued his roll for three more yards. He was on his back now and gave God a silent thanks he was still alive. Thirty feet away the engine of the Jaguar roared to life. As Modini pushed himself up into a sitting position, the sports car drove away. It headed away along the side road in the same direction the train was traveling.

Modini hauled himself to his feet and took a couple steps in the car's direction before slowing down and stopping. His legs were trembling from the exertions of the last five minutes. The car was too far away to attempt to catch it. He reached for the gun in his pants pocket, but decided it wouldn't do him any good. He yelled out, cursing to himself, "Shit!"

Modini watched the never-ending train rumbled by. After catching his breath, Modini realized there was one chance left now, and he would not let it slip away. He turned toward the train and ran along side it.

Modini felt his lungs bursting as he reached out and grabbed onto a ladder on a boxcar's side. He held on for several long seconds, feeling his feet being dragged along the ground, then his adrenaline kicked in and he pulled himself upward. He was propelled on by sheer desperation now, climbing rung by rung until he reached the top of the car.

He pulled himself onto the train car's roof and shakily crawled to the center of the roof. Slowly he raised himself and traveled forward, fighting the wind, moving painstakingly along the length of the train, one boxcar at a time. The Jaguar was still up ahead. It was to his left as it raced along on a rocky and dirt road, paralleling the track. The Jaguar suddenly gained speed, moving closer alongside the train now. Modini wondered why. He peered at the horizon. About a mile ahead of them was a bridge and crossroad. Then Modini understood. The Jaguar was trying to beat the train to the crossroads before the train. Once across, the sports car could head off and lose itself in the countryside.

Modini moved as fast as he dared, to the front end of the train. The train seemed to pick up speed, now. The wind was tremendous, coming in strong periodic gusts. He almost lost his footing.

This is nuts he told himself. *I'd better not stumble or it will be the end of me.* He tried to keep a steady course on the rooftop as he inched ahead. He moved carefully to his goal, the front end of the train, doing his best to keep his balance. He glanced quickly to his left, keeping one eye on the Jag up ahead. After every two yards he traversed, he would check to see whether it was still there. Then something unexpected made him stop. He heard a peculiar noise above his head. A light streamed down from above and Modini discerned the reverberation of a helicopter's rotor blades above his head.

He watched the Jaguar until a helicopter with police markings swooped down at an angle to see what was happening on top of the train. Somehow the authorities were alerted and sent someone to check out the report of a man on top of the train cars. Could the call have been made from the Jaguar, or was it a coincidence he was spotted? Modini didn't care. He knew this meant more trouble.

The helicopter darted overhead and continued on the length of the train. The Jag raced onward, still on a parallel course to the left of the Amtrak. A flash of red and blue lights to the right caught Modini's attention. Half a dozen police cars, their light bars flashing, swerved onto the adjacent road next to the train. Modini heard their sirens screaming over the whipping of the wind. They were chasing down the train on a service road on the train's other side.

The chopper up ahead hovered over the bridge where the left hand road crossed the tracks. From their vantage point high in the sky, the police helicopter realized the Jag was trying to beat the train to this intersection.

The chopper made a move to prevent this. It descended over the road in front of the Jag, trying to make it slow down or stop. "Stop your vehicle," The loudspeaker voice from the helicopter ordered. "I repeat, stop your vehicle now."

The sports car slowed and swerved to one side, but continued roaring down the road, pinned by the light from the helicopter.

Modini knew the Jaguar would ignore the critical warning. It was desperate to get away.

This only gave Modini more motivation to realize his goal.

Sheriff Tom Winston thought he saw it all. He drove his new Sheriff's Department patrol car along side the train, watching as the figure of a man moved from one car to another. "What the fuck is that guy doing?" he said, bellowing at his deputy next to him, "Is he trying to kill himself?"

"Maybe he's high on drugs," the deputy offered.

"Why don't you make yourself useful. Get on the radio and see if you can contact that chopper up there!" Sheriff Winston ordered.

"Right," The deputy grabbed the microphone and contacted the chopper above. He asked what was happening.

The chopper's pilot reported in, "If you think that guy is nuts, there's a Jag right beside the train doing seventy or eighty! I'm sure it's trying to beat the Amtrak to the crossing at the bridge. What that idiot on the train is doing is-- well, your guess is as good as mine!"

Modini halted. The train was closer to the bridge now, arriving sooner than Modini expected. Time was running out. He knew the Jag would cross the tracks if nothing were done to slow it down or bring it to a stop. The sports car, meanwhile, punched the gas. It would try to beat the train after all.

With the Jaguar still in his sights, Modini moved over to the left edge of the boxcar and proceeded to climb down the side of a car. He lowered himself carefully and held onto a railing of the train with one arm wrapped around it. The chopper above him flew over him again. He ignored it. He knew what he had to do.

"Sheriff, are you there," the chopper pilot's voice radioed down to the Sheriff's car.

Sheriff Winston grabbed the microphone. "You see him? I can't see him now from this side? Did he fall off?" His questions came fast, like bullets fired from his revolver.

"No, he's still on the train...sort of?"

"What do you mean, sort of?" Sheriff Winston yelled.

"The idiot's hanging from the other side of the train. I think he's going to jump!"

"He'll kill himself for sure if he does! Watch him! Lemme know what happens."

Modini, of course, had no intention of jumping. Holding tight to the railing, he took Kencade's gun from his pants pocket. He tried to aim the gun at the accelerating Jaguar as best he could. The wind made his eyes tear, and he tried to steady his hand, fighting against the rocking and juggling motion of the train. He concentrated on his target as long as possible, then fired.

The first shot either hit or missed. Nothing happened. But the second shot alerted the assassin. It must have struck the car because the killer floored the accelerator and swung the car wildly to one side, almost losing it. Modini heard the driver pouring more power to the engine as it revved and leaped forward. Modini swore to himself. He had hoped for better results. He saw the lights of the bridge looming ahead. Maybe he'd get another chance to shoot. The Jaguar had to slow down to make the turn onto the bridge.

Modini prepared himself for one last shot as the train approached the bridge crossing. The sports car was about a hundred yards ahead of his position. He felt very tense, knowing he might have but two shots left. He wasn't sure. And there was a good chance the Jag would make it. Modini strained his eyes through the whipping air and peered at the intersection. The barriers on both sides of the track at the bridge were down, giving him that last chance. Yes! This meant the Jaguar would have to slow down at the turn, or it would break or crash through the barriers.

The loudspeaker from the helicopter boomed again trying to warn the rushing Jaguar. But the message came out garbled. Even Modini couldn't understand what the words meant. He still heard the police sirens on the other side of the train.

Modini took aim again as the Jag started to make its turn onto the bridge, barely slowing down. His finger was on the trigger ready to squeeze it, fighting to keep the revolver aimed at his target, the two barrier warning lights.

In the front engine of the train, two engineers spotted the Jaguar pulling ahead, ready to take them at the bridge. They couldn't believe the car attempted to outrun them.

"What does that fool think he's doing?" one of the engineers shouted to the other. The other engineer reacted swiftly, grabbing the emergency break, hoping any type of action on his part would make a difference. A train as long as the one he was operating would take several miles to make a complete stop.

The Jaguar pulled out all the stops. It was only seconds from the crossing now. On the side of the train, Modini was poised, steadying himself, aiming at the point of impact, waiting for the Jaguar to hit the crossing barrier. He was so intent upon his goal that time seemed to stand still.

The sports car raced up ahead and slowed at the last possible instant as it swung into a wide turn. Modini had a perfect split-second view of the assassin through the passenger side window. The gun exploded, BANG BANG BANG! Three shots in all, until the clip was empty. The gun's hammer clicked, all its rounds spent. Then the sports car plowed through the first barrier, splintering the arms.

One of the shots must have found it's mark. The Jag skidded and went out of control, twisting itself around in a 180-degree angle on the track, centering itself head on with the oncoming train.

"We're gonna hit it!" the Engineer screamed to his assistant.

As the officers in the helicopter watched, the Amtrak surged ahead and smashed into the front end of the Jaguar.

If the assassin had been conscious at all after the collision with the barriers, he would have been the first to witness the train through the front of the windshield. It hurtled toward the helpless car until it struck it head-on.

The impact crushed the front end like an egg shell, ripping the vehicle almost in half. It whirled off the tracks and into the air, exploding as it landed, half on and half off the tracks. The train hit the burning wreckage again, shoving it to the side of the rails as the train continued forward. It had already begun breaking, but it was too late.

Modini tossed the empty revolver away and hung on tight to the railing. He hardly felt the collision because of the train's enormous mass, but he did see the fire and explosion up ahead. As the Flaming debris slid past the side of the train, Modini held tightly to the railing, shielding himself from the flaming wreckage as it slid past.

Modini heard the emergency brakes on the train now, making the squealing noise below him. He waited until the train slowed down to a safe speed before climbing down from the side of the car. The helicopter chasing the train flew over. His first instinct was to get away. He was still on the left side of the track. There was no one in sight, so he ducked under the boxcar and emerged on the other side. There to greet him was twelve waiting police patrol cars. And there were twice as many deputy sheriffs and police officers aiming their guns and rifles at him.

Modini halted in his tracks, surprised by this overwhelming show of force. He forced a smile at them, feeling a bit elated after what just happened. "What took you so long?" he finally asked.

"Get your hands up...slowly," came the order.

Modini raised his arms to surrender to them without a fuss. He couldn't count how many officers stepped forward to hold him while they put cuffs on him.

"What a day this was for small town America...huh!" Modini couldn't resist saying aloud.

* * *

At Kirkland Air Force base in Albuquerque, New Mexico, the Dragon prepared for a briefing with the President of the United States. It was 8:45 p.m. and he waited outside a briefing room which included a large screen monitor where the President would appear live for the meeting.

As the Dragon prepared to be summoned inside for the President's telecast, his assistant asked him, "What are you going to tell him?"

The Dragon turned to the man and replied, "What can you tell any President when it comes time to inform him a group of his most trusted soldiers and friends in positions of high office have to go. I'll tell him what I've been telling all of them each term-- to clean house-- to clean up that son of a frickin' CIA! This agency has become a burden to every President. It has happened again this time as well. He'll have to force the resignations of those he bargained with and for those who, ironically, helped put him into office..."

"If he doesn't agree, then what?" the Dragon's aid asked curiously.

The door to the briefing room opened, and a four-star General nodded to the Dragon. "The President will see you now," the General informed him.

The Dragon answered his aid's question before entering the room, "Then he'll have to kiss a second term goodbye! I'm here to protect his ass, not wipe it! I'm not to cover it up!"

* * *

The following day in the Madison Police Department, located in the same building as the Madison City Hall, police lieutenant Fulton read the morning news headlines. "Judge Henry Kencade killed in explosive shootout at Greyhound Terminal! Five others are dead including local attorney Michael Bradley and a Madison police officer who had just graduated from the police academy four weeks ago, in what could be a possible drug sting gone awry! Two other bodies found are yet to be identified. The authorities are keeping a possible suspect under wraps now. He is currently in custody of the local sheriff's department!"

An FBI agent holding his badge interrupted the police lieutenant. "Excuse me, Lieutenant. I'm here to see the prisoner." William Rutland requested.

The Lieutenant examined the identification and nodded, "Follow me."

Lieutenant Fulton took Rutland to an observation room. The agent carried a large tan envelope, the kind used for important papers. As the men entered the room, the FBI agent heard John Modini being questioned, his voice coming though a speaker. On the other side of the interrogation window, he saw two plainclothes men standing next to a table. Behind it, seated in a chair, was Modini. He seemed not to be in a cooperative mood.

"Why? Why won't you let us help you if you won't even help yourself?" one of the men pleaded with him.

Modini looked at the plainclothes men. He was weary and bored with their questions. "Look, if you guys are truly on the level with me and want to help, you won't want to believe me when I tell you, these people will kill you, too...and I don't need any more bodies falling about because of me!"

The plainclothes man exchanged a strained expression with his partner. "Believe me, Mister Modini-- or whoever you say your name is. Nobody will kill anybody as long as you cooperate." They were being polite and courteous, treating him like the regular nut case.

Modini was all too aware of it. He looked up to the officer and answered skeptically. "Oh yeah? I wish you were right. They've been getting away with it for almost thirty years, now"

"Lieutenant Fulton, Sir?" A uniformed police officer entered the observation room. "You told me to let you know when Mrs. Rogers arrived. Oh, and here's the newspaper you asked for."

The Lieutenant took the dated newspaper and leafed through it until he found the article on John Modini's death. There was a much too youthful photo of him to go along with it. Lieutenant Fulton handed the article to the FBI agent, staring at Modini, wondering what type of man he was dealing with.

"Will that be all, sir," The officer asked the lieutenant.

"Thank you!" Fulton said. "You can show Mrs. Rogers into my office." When the officer left, he stared at Rutland, the FBI agent who read the article and studied Modini behind the interrogation window. "Mrs. Rogers was the one he made the phone call to. I think it's time we meet the lady."

Lieutenant Fulton and William Rutland introduced themselves to Catherine Rogers in the lieutenant's office. The agent handed her the newspaper article and asked, "Ma'am, do you know this man?"

Catherine looked at the article and picture. She nodded, handing it back to him. "He's all right, isn't he?"

"For the present. Do you have any idea what's happening here," Lieutenant Fulton asked.

"I might," Catherine responded. "Can I see him now?"

"Follow me please," Lieutenant Fulton directed. Catherine was escorted into the darkened observation room where she saw John Modini seated in the interrogation room. He looked tired and haggard.

"Is this John Modini?" the Lieutenant asked her.

Catherine walked to the window. "Yes!" There was no doubt in her mind. "Please, it's very important I talk to him immediately!"

Lieutenant Fulton looked at the FBI agent for his input on her request. Rutland shrugged his shoulders. It was as if to say it wouldn't hurt anything. But the Lieutenant was still concerned. "Mrs. Rogers, you're a prominent attorney. Why stick your neck out involving yourself with this nut case? Your father, God rest his soul, was one of the most outstanding judges in this country!"

Catherine spoke up sharply. "Yes, my father was, Lieutenant. But now he's dead. He was killed, sir, shot in the back by a bullet that was meant for me. And the man who killed him was the man Mr. Modini was chasing." She turned to both of them and spoke with urgency. "Now, if you can be patient with me and listen to what I have to say, we both could use your help!"

The FBI agent gave a surprised look at the Lieutenant.

John Modini sat alone in the interrogation room. The two plainclothes man left, but he knew they'd be back sooner than later. He had lost all track of time. He was frustrated because he didn't know what would happen to him next. He jumped as the latch on the door made a clanging sound as it opened. He realized his nerves were frazzled. Maybe it was because he was tired and wired all at the same time. Then Catherine entered the room.

Modini's eyes moistened as he saw her. He was exhausted. He hadn't had any sleep in the last thirty-six hours, but he got up from the chair anyway, wanting to go to her, to hold her. But he didn't. He took two steps forward, but kept his distance, fighting hard to restrain his tears. "Thank God, you're all right! I'm so sorry, Catherine." Modini still wanted to go to her but stayed where he was.

"I know..." Catherine replied, her voice catching in her throat. Her eyes were also moist.

Modini wiped his tears. "Your father...he was a good man. He actually sacrificed himself to save us. You know that, don't you?"

Catherine nodded, and the tension of the moment snapped within her like a taut thread. Her eyes were almost blind with tears now. She moved to Modini for comfort herself. They came together and embraced, hugging each other.

Modini needed that embrace. The feeling it gave him was worth all he had been through. He closed his eyes and held her tighter. They said nothing, lost in the moment.

Finally, Catherine whispered into his ear. "Oh, John...!" there was a quiver in her voice, "They killed Michael, too!"

Modini took her shoulders and looked into her eyes as if he were to blame. "Oh, God!"

"And...and Thomas was wounded. He's going to be all right, but..." Catherine's words trailed off. She couldn't continue. Modini saw the expression of tragedy and loss on her face. "What now?" Catherine finally said.

Modini lifted his hand and touched her cheeks. It was wet with tears. "You have to go to your father now to...to take care of things," he said softly.

Catherine looked at him hopelessly. "But John--"

Modini cut her off, "You *must!*" he said whispering into her ear. "The letter is with him. I planted it on him as he died in my arms."

The door opened. They were interrupted by the appearance of FBI agent Rutland. "Sorry to interfere with your reunion," Rutland said curtly to Modini, "but I thought you'd like to know the news." Modini stared at him blankly. Rutland continued, "I'm FBI agent Rutland. My office in Washington called to inform me that those responsible for last night's ordeal have been apprehended. The man killed in the Jaguar was a wanted felon. So barring the usual legal complications, you're free to post bail and leave."

Modini was surprised by the FBI agent's announcement, knowing his involvement in the train accident, plus his faked death, were no misdemeanors, but wasn't planning to make a protest.

Catherine faced the agent. "Do you mind if I ask you a question?"

Agent Rutland grinned. "If I can."

"What happened to those two men? Those two federal agents?"

Agent Rutland pursed his lips and shrugged innocently. "There are no reported federal agents here in Madison. Those men's identities are still being investigated."

"But they said they were Federal agents," Catherine said incredulously.

"We found no identification on them."

Catherine protested. "But Agent Rutland. I was there. They showed us their badges!"

"I know. That's what you reported, and I believe you," the agent agreed, "But what can I say? There were no such credentials on their person, no identification whatsoever-- that was the odd part. The FBI is studying it as we speak, but I know without any new evidence Washington will close the matter. It will probably be filed under the designation of drug trafficking."

Modini frowned. "Drug trafficking? What are you talking about?"

Agent Rutland slipped a case folder out of the large envelope he was carrying. Modini opened it to pictures taken at the lockers in the Greyhound bus terminal showing duffel bags of cocaine lined up side by side. "There's forty million dollars worth here, so you see, Mr. Modini, you actually helped in the discovery."

"What the hell!" Modini couldn't believe any of this. There was no sign of drugs anywhere in the terminal, let alone duffel bags full. "What about the rifle I found in the building across from the terminal where the police officer was found?"

Agent Rutland nodded. "Oh yeah, that! Well, to tell you the truth, Mr. Modini, we did find about five million dollars in one hundred dollar bills stashed in a closet...but no rifle..."

Modini's eyes closed, trying to suppress the fury. The cover up was starting again. Catherine squeezed Modini's hand, implying for him to let it go. But he turned to the agent one last time. "So that's it then...I can go?"

Rutland took back the case folder with the photos. "That's it for now. We'll probably get back to you for a few other things, but for now you're free as a bird. It's been a pleasure meeting the both of you. Again, Mrs. Rogers, I am truly sorry for your loss!" Rutland tucked the large envelope under his arm and left the room. Both Catherine and Modini just stared at each other.

Modini was well aware of what happened, but he was determined, with or without the government's help, to expose the cover up. Then suddenly there came the conflicting thoughts flooding his mind again. What if this was the Government's way to send him a message to keep quiet? What if they wanted all the details of this incident swept under the carpet? Whatever was happening, Modini knew, someone, somewhere was pulling the strings.

* * *

That afternoon, Catherine faced the unpleasant task of visiting the city morgue and identifying the body of her father. A sheet was wrapped over his body, an autopsy yet to be performed. The sheet was lowered, revealing his face.

"Yes, that's him. That's my father Henry Kencade," she said flatly, her eyes shiny with tears, her voice empty of emotion. The morgue supervisor nodded and covered the face again. "What became of the clothes he was wearing," Catherine asked the supervisor.

The man became uncomfortable. "His clothes, Ma'am?" He looked a little surprised and embarrassed then. "I don't believe I--" he paused in mid sentence. "Excuse me," he said suddenly and crossed the room to speak with two colleagues.

Catherine watched him exchange harsh words with the men. Then he joined her again. "I'm sorry, Miss Rogers, but there are no clothes."

"He was brought in wearing some old clothes, wasn't he?" Catherine demanded.

"Yes, of course, but...they were misplaced."

Catherine shook her head. "What do you mean?"

"They were put aside in the usual manner, but then they disappeared. No one knows what happened to them," the supervisor tried to explain. "They were either taken...or accidentally disposed after...after your father arrived."

"Disposed of...how?"

"We burn the unwanted items in the incinerator..."

"What about all of his belongings. His watch, his ring, any papers he was carrying? Weren't they put aside in a separate place."

The Supervisor shook his head with a regrettable expression. "I'm sorry, Ma'am... His jewelry has been put aside for you, but anything else was destroyed with his clothing."

Then the full effect of the loss dawned on Catherine. She could only close her eyes in horror. "Oh my God!" she said to herself.

Chapter Forty

"Resurrection"

Richard Franklin grabbed a *LA Times* newspaper at a stand in LAX and hurried to the boarding area for his flight to Indianapolis. As he waited in line he read the front page headlines:

"Commander of the Joint Chiefs of Staff Resigns!"

Franklin's eyebrows lifted. He continues to read on.

"The sudden departure for the commander was neither job nor health related, nor was the result of any mishandling of assignment within his assigned duties.

The resignation comes at a critical time for President Bush, prior to this fall's election. He has been hurting in the polls since the recent reemergence of H. Ross Perot, the Independent party candidate and Clinton's growing Democratic lead.

The Commander of the Joint Chiefs of Staff stated today he regretted leaving, but had planned to earlier within the next Presidential term. He said he needed to spend more time with his wife and children. The President has not announced yet who he will pick to replace him yet."

While waiting for his plane, Franklin observed the television monitors within the airport reporting the same story, as well as a related story concerning the CIA. The question again was raised concerning the revamping of the organization. Robert Gates, the CIA Director, announced there would be an investigation into any wrong doing within the agency, but felt everything was under control as the Iran Contra affair resurfaced to haunt them. Meanwhile, it was reported President Bush had all the confidence in the world in the agency and stated it is doing its job, continuing to keep the country free from evil dictators like Hussein and Noriega who want to corrupt the world.

On this last statement, Franklin picked up his carry-on bag and commented, "Yeah! I bet!" He then departed for his plane.

* * *

The black gloved hand of Catherine Rogers released its hold on a single rose, and it fell from her fingers into a newly dug grave to land on a mahogany coffin. Catherine stood above her father's open burial site and looked down into it. A million thoughts filled her mind during this time, but the only emotion she felt was one of overwhelming grief. But she wouldn't let the feeling overpower her...not now. She would deal with it later. Right now, she was going through the motions, as if obeying the common ritual and courtesy of a funeral.

She kneeled down and tossed in a fistful of dirt from her gloved hand, completing the ceremony, and turned to the others in the group.

The friends and relatives of Henry Kencade and Michael Bradley gathered together in what were designed to be a ceremony for two funerals. Judge Henry Kencade was buried next to Catherine's mother and Michael Bradley was interred a short distance away.

The day was still bright, but clouds were gathering above as the two grave sites accommodated the crowd of over three hundred people standing to give their condolences. Many close acquaintants attended Kencade's ceremony, including those from Michael Bradley's family.

When the priest finished with the service, he indicated everyone would move to Michael Bradley's grave site. Catherine left her father's grave accompanied by her colleagues, Jennifer and Thomas. Despite The bandage around his neck and throat, Thomas Sanders survived the attack that night at the bus terminal, but suffered with a temporary loss of his voice. He insisted on attending the double funeral against doctor's orders and looked as pale as a ghost. On his writing pad he assured the others he felt better than he looked. Nothing would prevent him from paying his final respects to Bradley. It was important to him. Also joining the observance was John Modini and Richard Franklin.

They proceeded to Michael Bradley's grave where they paid their respects. After the ceremony was concluded, Catherine turned to Bradley's father and mother and kissed them, giving them her condolences. Afterward, they departed to their waiting cars.

As the rest of the gathering started to disperse, Jennifer and Thomas shook hands with the guests, allowing Catherine her private moment at Bradley's grave site. Modini stood next to Richard Franklin and bid farewell to those departing as well. After what he considered a respectful time, Modini went to Catherine and stood by her side. He was determined to stay with her until she was ready to go. He glanced back at the departing guests and saw the Lieutenant and his partner from the Madison Police Department, watching them. They were keeping a respectful distance should anything unusual happen today.

Catherine became aware of Modini standing quietly next to her and gave him a little smile. She took his arm into hers as they, too, walked back where the cars were waiting.

"Michael was my best friend and nobody will ever change that," she reminded Modini.

"I know how you feel," Modini responded. "I've lost many close friends too." He was silent a moment, then added, "I even considered your father a friend..."

At the mention of her father, Catherine reluctantly confided in Modini. She couldn't help expressing the anxious thoughts filling her mind. "Dad, I believe, knew I loved him..." Catherine confessed. "I...I, never got to tell him how much. There were times I'm sure he wanted me to know what he was feeling. Now I think my father and Michael both died for nothing. Father was right about the letter. Look what happened!"

John remained quiet and let Catherine talk. They reached the others, and they all headed for their cars. She shook her head in disgust and disbelief. "God! What happens to us now? Did my father die for nothing? How can we come out of this without the letter or any proof of conspiracy and still sound credible?"

Franklin tried to comfort Catherine. "If history has taught us anything," he told her, "it has taught us this country of ours, America, has often continued to lick its own wounds and has repeatedly healed itself. If people can't change the system, or open a can of worms to show everyone what's wrong with it, then everything remains the same. But the key here is you want to remind them what you're fighting for-- like the Jews who constantly remind us not to forget the Holocaust."

A lone taxicab headed in their direction, coming from around the bend as the funeral procession from the two grave sites started to exit the cemetery. Franklin watched the taxi park near the other cars. Modini and Catherine paid no attention to it.

Franklin continued, "Anyway you look at it, we do have an obligation and a duty to present it to the public. But it all depends if we can get the right people on our side. There's a powerful media out there... Why not let them help us, as well."

Catherine was still filled with anger and bitterness. "I want to get those...whoever is responsible for all this!"

The five of them moved down the path and headed for their cars and Catherine's black limousine. Thomas pointed to a woman. He couldn't speak yet, so he gestured to Jennifer. The woman emerged from the taxicab, carrying a portfolio in her hand.

Jennifer didn't recognize her. "It looks as though we have some company," she told the others. "Does anyone know her?"

The woman approached Jennifer and asked to speak with Catherine Rogers. Jennifer gestured in the direction of Modini and Catherine as she reached her limo. The woman walked over to her. "Excuse me, are you Catherine Rogers?" she asked.

"Yes. Have we met?"

"You've probably heard of me. My name is Hilary Swank"

The name sounded familiar to Catherine, but she couldn't place it. "What can I do for you, Miss..."

"Mrs. Swank," she corrected Catherine. "This will only take a few moments of your time. I was the notary public witness Michael hired four and a half years ago. I was at the same hotel with Michael Bradley when Karl Hunter turned himself over for arrest."

"Earlier that morning, the day Hunter turned himself in, I was a witness to certain documents Hunter prepared before his arrest. As I told you, I was hired by Michael Bradley for Hunter's confidentiality and ordered to keep a low profile. I was the one who sent out the Manila envelope addressed to Henry Kencade, prior to Hunter's arrest and arraignment before your father's court. I cannot explain, but neither your father nor Mr. Hunter had any prior knowledge that your father would be handling the case against him. The materials I sent to your father were supposed to be kept confidential, even from Mr. Bradley. That was what I was instructed to do. Once it was known your father was the one to try the case; Mr. Hunter requested all the materials sent to the U. S Postal office in Madison until further notice. I also was responsible for seeing to other matters based on Mr. Bradley's orders." Mrs. Swank indicated the portfolio she held. "This is now yours. My responsibility ends here."

Catherine was bewildered why this woman would appear now. She took the portfolio and unzipped it. Modini watched her reach inside and check the papers. There was what looked like a manifest declaring what the two items were and to whom they belonged. Jennifer and Franklin now joined them near Catherine's limo.

"There are two white envelopes or letters that Karl Hunter asked me to hold for him," Hilary explained. "One letter stated if anything should happen to your father...after Hunter's materials were sent to him, Michael was to receive this complete portfolio. It now goes to your possession since you are now in charge of Michael Bradley's law firm..."

"What are you talking about? I'm not in charge--"

Mrs. Swank cut in. "Michael Bradley has left you his law firm in his will...of which we can discuss at a more convenient time."

Catherine was speechless. Jennifer poked her in the arm, more to snap her out of it. "Do you think we can still keep our jobs, boss lady?" she whispered to Catherine, hoping she could get her talking.

Catherine managed a little smile. She was still astonished by the news.

Mrs. Swank reached into her purse and took out two legal envelopes. She handed them to Catherine. "The first envelope is addressed to Michael Bradley. The second envelope concerns company business. Because of Michael Bradley's death you are now legally obligated to see that this letter is delivered to the person whose name is on it."

Catherine looked at the envelope. "Mrs. Swank..."

"Call me Hilary," she said to Catherine.

"Hilary, would you like to join us here at the car. I'd like you to be present when I open the first letter"

"Of course, if you'd like."

The six of them gathered around the limo.

At the black limousine Catherine read Bradley's letter aloud. "To Mr. Bradley. Upon my death, and the subsequent death of Henry Kencade, this letter is to be submitted directly to your attention for you to do with as you see fit upon its conclusions. The second letter is placed in your trust to be delivered by hand to the woman it is addressed. It must not be opened, nor the contents divulged to anyone, except upon request. It should be delivered by a person or persons you trust as stated on the manifesto."

Catherine took the second envelope and looked to see the name on it. There was the name of a woman printed on it, someone vaguely familiar, but now she couldn't make the connection.

But John Modini recognized it. His eyes widened in total astonishment. The name written on the envelope was Marian O'Leary. Modini was in shock. "Marian O'Leary?" he blurted aloud.

665

"Do you know her?" Catherine asked.

"Know her? She's my mother!" Modini exclaimed.

"What?" Franklin was as surprised as everyone. "Well, I know that's the name she goes by today-- from her second marriage. Are you sure of the name?" he asked skeptically.

Catherine held up the letter for him to see. "Yes, that's her..." Franklin agreed.

Catherine handed the letter to Modini. "Then here, John... Can I have your word you'll deliver it to your mother?

Modini took the envelope. "Certainly..." For a moment, he debated whether to open it then and there. Then he decided to wait until later and tucked it into his suit pocket.

Catherine continued with the reading of Hunter's letter. "This second letter will answer your questions why I will refuse to give testimony to you or the grand jury for the forthcoming trial. You will understand my attitude towards you and why I have to secure my silence. I appreciate your help, Mr. Bradley, so forgive me for what I'm planning to tell you. We all have been duped as much as our country has, this last quarter of a century. I'm sorry I didn't come forward sooner. Maybe if I did it would have made a difference. I have a reason for not cooperating with you. I am protecting someone!"

Catherine looked up to the others who, like Modini, were patiently listening to her. He nodded and gave her a half-turned smile. Her eyes returned to the letter. "These people would have gotten to me one way or another. I have provided Judge Henry Kencade with information upon my death. It will answer some questions and should convince him the reasons I am innocent. I have chosen Judge Kencade because he is one of the most important judges in the state. When my case goes to trial, I want Judge Kencade to be aware of the games the prosecution will use to condemn me without the truth ever coming to light.

"If Judge Kencade is the honorable man I think he is, he will use his authority to expose those who are guilty of framing me. I am also aware of the possibility those powerful enough to control the politics behind my frame-up in the state of Indiana, will maneuver to appoint Judge

Kencade as the judge for my trial. I pray this doesn't happen because Judge Kencade will be at the disadvantage of knowing the truth while involved in political blackmail to get me a speedy conviction. Whatever his decision, it will certainly weigh heavily on his conscience.

"As I have stated earlier. If you are reading this letter, my worst fears have come true and Judge Kencade is dead. You must then receive the materials I had provided for him including a tape recording of myself and a very important letter. Please listen to the tape and then use your own judgment concerning the information in the letter. This second packet of evidence was prepared in the eventuality something happens to the evidence in Judge Kencade's possession or it never reaches his hands.

"At the present moment, I have become the most dangerous man in America. I have been declared a bomb, someone who could go off at anytime. Once set off, I could destroy the Central Intelligence Agency forever-- at least in this lifetime. It is no secret the CIA has been knocking off world leaders for years thanks to the disclosure of the Pentagon Papers and evidence from Richard Milhous Nixon, so what I'm ready to say shouldn't shock many people who spent their lives investigating such issues. You should know, they planted the bomb within me, a bomb that would eventually destroy my credibility and eventually my life. Sure, they'll deny it, but that's their credo-- deniability. But, the enclosed letter will explain everything.

"The letter was written by my older brother ten years my senior. He raised me and made me who I am. He was a CIA operative working within an elite group in the 1960's that handled assassinations under the code name, 'Executive Action,' information of which should now be available because of the Pentagon Papers and freedom of information act. What it won't tell you is that the code was also used in connection to Dallas, November 22, 1963. My brother was a chameleon who moved within the Intelligence agencies. He was the contact man that day in Dallas for the Mafia, including Charles Nicoletti who was Jack Ruby's contact man as well as contact man for both Roscoe White and J. D. Tippit of the Dallas Police force. White had infiltrated the Dallas Police Department as an operative of the CIA, My brother ordered White to assassinate officer

Tippit, the man who had been ordered to kill Oswald once he was arrested and under their custody. At the last minute Tippit refused and backed out. Ruby was then ordered to finish the job!

"Following this, My brother was put in charge of cleanup. So began the mysterious deaths of so many people who were connected one way or another to President Kennedy's demise. I'm not telling you he went around killing people himself. He was the one who arranged the killings. He ordered them concluded through various means, from the mob, including Nicoletti under the control of Sam Giancana, to police departments across the country and even our own military. One by one they died: Oswald, Ruby, Tippit, White and, William Pitzer, a commander at the Naval Hospital in Bethesda, Maryland. Like me, Pitzer was a bomb ready to go off. He had filmed the Kennedy autopsy-- or I should say his second autopsy. You'll never be able to see the actual photographs or film-- nor will the Kennedy family, who the public and government thinks have them. My brother used those within a group, code named 'Queen Mary,' to coordinate both in Washington and Dallas prior to Kennedy's assassination and especially its aftermath. If you find out who 'Queen Mary' is, you'll find out how it was so easy and convenient to cover up!

"If anything would ever happen to my brother, he left a trail to the CIA. The letter in Judge Kencade's possession details all this and more. There is one last thing I must tell you. After the Vietnam war ended, my brother either was ordered, or had taken it upon himself, to eliminate members of my platoon for the knowledge we possessed concerning the POW/MIA situation and the fact it got out of hand concerning the illegal importation and distribution of drugs to the United States. Those of us who were involved in my platoon were set up to be terminated. It was after I found out my friends were becoming targets I decided to do something about it. I set myself in motion to track down and assassinate my own brother.

"But I had a heavy price to pay. I knew if I succeeded, I was, myself, to become the hunted-- not just for this, but for the knowledge my brother allowed me to possess. Both the letter and I had to be destroyed. What they accomplished and how they would do this can now only be told through the second letter to Marian O'Leary."

Catherine looked up from the letter. "And it is signed, 'Karl Hunter.'" As she handed the letter to Modini, she saw the shocked expression on his face.

Franklin breathed in deeply and felt a small bit of relief as he slowly exhaled. "I knew it! I fucking damn well knew it! This is what all of us originally on the House Select Committee came to believe!"

Catherine addressed Mrs. Swank. "Hilary, I appreciate your staying until I finished reading the letter.

"I didn't mind at all. If I hadn't heard it with my own two ears, I wouldn't have believed it!" she shook hands all around. "I'm glad to be of service to you. I'm very sorry for your loss."

Modini shook Hilary's hand and said appreciatively, "Thank you, thank you very much! You don't know how much this means to us."

Hilary smiled at this small group realizing the rough road lying ahead of them. "I'll be in touch with you soon, Mrs. Rogers."

"It's Catherine," she smiled. "The next time you see me, call me Catherine."

"I promise. And I wish you all luck..."

Hilary Swank departed from the group, heading for her taxi.

Franklin shook his head, pondering over certain points in Hunter's letter. He spoke with the others present. "The Mafia angle was a red herring. Ruby had a story to tell but Earl Warren didn't want to hear it! Why? Maybe the suspicion was to fall on Marcello and Trafficante, but the government, even if they wanted to pretend, would never be able to tie it to them-- especially J. Edgar Hoover who knew all along about Sam Giancana's involvement. Trafficante made it to out Committee, but behind closed doors-- and that was after Giancana was offed. Once Ruby was pointed toward the Chicago mob, there was no way they ever could control the direction of those members on the Warren Commission! Hell, no!"

Thomas, unable to talk, took out his note pad and wrote down his comments, then showed it to Franklin. "There is still evidence and witnesses out there that can confirm much of this, including the gentleman in Chicago who had actually viewed the film and photographs of Pitzer's work the day after the assassination at Bethesda!"

Franklin agreed and added, "And all of us on the Senate and House Select Committees can now come forward to break the code of silence and tell the truth about our own separate investigation and that the Zapruder film did not lie. It shows what had been the truth all along. I believe Kennedy's body should be exhumed, so the truth can be told if such autopsy photos no longer exist! But that will never happen, will it? John Connally's shrapnel still left within him from that day in Dallas should be measured and compared with Arlen Spector's magic bullet. This would then assure us that Gerald Ford is through lying to America. Ford would have to explain his part in the cover up and not continue to blame Alan Dulles, his commission partner!"

Franklin stopped a moment and looked to Modini who was encouraged by everyone's change of mood within these last few minutes. But then Franklin realized this wouldn't bring back Michael Bradley or Henry Kencade. It did mean their deaths did bring honor for them along with vindication for Karl Hunter. This was the man who came into their lives and set this extraordinary experience into motion. He looked over and noticed Jennifer was crying, not with sadness but with happiness.

All well and good," Modini agreed, "but no matter how hard we try, we always hit a brick wall. Isn't that the way it always happens? Look at me. When I played devil's advocate on how our government could take out our own president, I tried to write a movie about it, to get the facts into the public eye, but I got nowhere...nowhere at all! And hell, it was only a fantasy, for God's sake! Now I understand. To those it would expose, it would be a reality."

Franklin nodded, "That's what I've been trying to tell you!"

Something Modini said reminded Franklin now of a question that had been bothering him all these years since he had first read Modini's screenplay, *The Connection.*

"John, can I ask you about that person you were involved with in the early '80's concerning the financing of your film? No one but you knew whom he was, but you said he worked for the Nixon administration. I was told he bailed out of the project because Reagan's attempted assassination? Why? No pun intended, but what's the connection here?"

John Modini was aware the others didn't know what Franklin was talking about, so he explained this incident in another way. "Do you remember our meeting with Manderson, the ex-CIA agent, in Scottsdale, Arizona?" he asked Franklin.

"Yes."

"One of the things we talked about was that Day in Dallas in the Parkland Hospital-- after Kennedy was pronounced dead in front of Jackie Kennedy, and then to the world. Now what Manderson said to me were the exact words this person from the Nixon administration had said concerning my screenplay. They both adamantly stated that this movie needed to be made, that the people out there had the right to know! I'm saying to myself, know what? I didn't know what the first person was talking about let alone this second ex-CIA man, until the pieces started coming together like a jigsaw puzzle! It was always there! My subconscious mind was providing it to me piece by piece."

"What do you mean," Franklin asked.

"The simplest way to explain is to remind you what happened in Dallas after Kennedy was pronounced dead. When a murder happens in a city or state, the state authorities have jurisdiction over the victim's body. So in Dallas, Texas, the doctors of Parkland Hospital took the responsibility of preparing the autopsy on the President of the United States. Remember, this wasn't only their exclusive right, but this was also the law. But something odd happened there. With the President dead, the Vice-President who was also at Parkland Hospital, had to be sworn in. Johnson had always stated Robert Kennedy, the Attorney General responsible for this task, gave the order for the judge in Dallas to swear him in immediately. Remember that famous picture of Johnson being sworn in on Air Force One with Mrs. Kennedy standing by his side? Well, what everyone didn't know was Robert Kennedy never gave such an order. It wasn't that he wouldn't have-- I'm sure he would if that was his duty, too, but it was Johnson who didn't want to give

671

Bobby Kennedy, his sworn enemy, the satisfaction of letting him do it. And so Air Force One was stalled for two hours at the Dallas Airport until they got this woman judge-- who they lied to, saying Bobby Kennedy requested her to come and swear him in. Meanwhile, if you ask what was happening with the President's ordered autopsy, well, there *wasn't* one! Even though it was ordered by law!"

"Well, why wasn't there one," Jennifer asked.

"Because the secret service wouldn't allow it!" Modini explained. "There was something in Karl's letter that jogged my memory. Remember in the Zapruder film there was no sign of any Secret Service men protecting the President until Clint Hill ran to the car and pushed Mrs. Kennedy back into the seat and fell onto her and her husband. She was out there climbing onto the back trunk to pick up a piece of her husband's brain off the rear of the limousine. Kennedy was already dead on arrival before the official announcement a half hour later. One thing I discovered about that day was some Houston oil man was getting the Secret Service drunk the night before. And some of the Secret Service men were even sighted at The Carousel, Jack Ruby's bar and strip joint, while Kennedy was still in Fort Worth the night before."

"Yes, I seem to have read that somewhere," Franklin agreed.

"The other noted incident was Secret Service agent Youngblood was given a medal for saving and protecting Vice-President Johnson's life that day. This ceremony happened later after Johnson became President. There would be no medals for anyone who protected Kennedy. Johnson, for the next few months, spread the rumor Oswald was shooting at him as well, even after J. Edgar Hoover informed him the day later he wasn't in the line of fire. I guess this was why Youngblood got his reward...and to take the sting of bad publicity away from the Secret Service. You see, it was originally the Secret Service that started the controversy of a cover up following Kennedy's death. The Secret Service's job is to protect the President, to keep him alive, to risk their own lives if necessary...but no agent gave their life for President Kennedy that day, did they? And the President died! Since there was nothing the Secret Service could do following the death of the

President, they switched to their next assignment, to protect and serve the man next in line, which of course was the Vice-President. He would be swept up by those in charge and taken in protected custody until either sworn in or returned to Washington. Except some of the Secret Service decided to take it upon themselves to break Texas law on orders by someone. And it certainly wasn't the Attorney General! They seemed to have done a better job protecting President Kennedy dead than when he was alive."

"I think I'm losing you," Jennifer said. "How could the Secret Service protect Kennedy after he died?"

"They actually kidnapped the President's body while the Parkland Doctors were preparing his autopsy," Modini explained. "Dr. Earl Rose, the Dallas County Medical Examiner, protested and was shoved by an agent to the wall, with a muzzle of a gun forced in his mouth. The poor determined doctor must have pissed in his trousers! What did the Secret Service think these doctors were going to do, desecrate the President of the United States? If that was the case, you won't want to know what did happened to our President in the next twelve hours, including the fact his brain is still missing to this day. I believe if Jackie had stayed in Dallas that day and had her husband's autopsy completed by the Parkland staff, she would have never left the country nor married Aristotle Onassis and Bobby Kennedy would still be alive today. And likely Ruby would not have shot Oswald! And Oswald would have never been linked, let alone brought to trial. Talk about changing the course of history! Another thing...Jackie, Mrs. Kennedy, was waiting aboard Air Force One, standing by her husband's coffin in the rear end of the plane with special assistant Kenneth O'Donnell and David Powers, the President's friends and aids, all waiting for take off. She didn't realize Johnson and his party had taken over the front end of the plane and were now stalling for time. Mrs. Kennedy thought in the previous two hours Lady Bird and Lyndon Johnson had already left in Air Force Two back to Washington. It wasn't until Johnson asked her to come forward as he was sworn in to take the oath of Office of the President of the United States did she even know he was there! Talk about humiliation. This is where another mystery begins, what

673

happened to Kennedy's body?"

Jennifer spoke up, "Yes, this is the time the controversy started about Kennedy's coffin."

Modini nodded. "Right! The Secret Service seemed to be in charge again, but Jackie was determined to stay with his body, or in this case, the coffin. Even today there is speculation Kennedy's body really wasn't in the coffin! This came from certain eyewitnesses who were already present with the President's body as Jackie entered Bethesda Naval Hospital, where his autopsy had been completed. If Jackie who stated she never left her husband's side, was just now arriving, how could the autopsy already be over with?"

"What about the time Johnson asked her to witness the swearing in," Jennifer spoke up. "They could have taken his body then!"

Modini agreed, "Yes, you're right, Jenny, even David Lifton mentions this in his book on this exact subject. But when I interviewed Kenneth O'Donnell before he died in '77, he said there was always someone with the coffin continually besides the Secret Service, either himself or Dave Powers. He did say though, Dave and he also had to go to the swearing in and Jackie was determined to have one of them stay behind. Johnson was adamant about all of them to be front and center for his respect and honor to the Presidency toward the media. A military commander came forward to replace them temporarily. I don't know whether he was from the Navy or Army, but it was someone that Jackie had trusted so they all went forward to the front end of the plane for Johnson's oath. Still, if Kennedy's body were removed, this was the time it happened. I'm sure it was put aboard Air Force Two to be taken for a pre-autopsy somewhere prior to, or even at Bethesda!"

Franklin spoke up with his own comment. "That military commander, I wonder if it's the same military official who I suspect would be the Naval Commander who, during the middle of the autopsy, stopped the pathologist from probing the wound of the President's back or from recovering any bullet fragments inside it? John! Are you saying the Secret Service had something to do with Kennedy's murder?"

674

Modini quietly nodded. "They had a lot to do with it...they were the only organization to have full custody of the President's body within the government, both alive and dead in those hours between 11:30 a.m. when he arrived in Dallas, when he greeted the Texans at the airport, until 12:30 p.m. when he was shot. They took possession again after 1:00 p.m. and between 1:30 p.m. to 5:30 p.m. Eastern Time, when they brought it to Bethesda Hospital in Maryland. I'm not saying all the Secret Service was involved, but you remember what Manderson said. He said the CIA can and will infiltrate any organization, including those of this government, to convince these people they shall do their duty, whatever it takes to protect this country! Besides, I'm convinced now, after hearing Karl Hunter's statement concerning 'Queen Mary'-- you see...the White House code name for 'Queen Mary' is the Secret Service!"

"You think people will buy this?" Catherine said. "That they are doing their duty by assassinating their own president?"

Modini smiled grimly. "I see your point. No, I don't believe the people will believe it. But I do believe if it were carried out this way, the way Central Intelligence works, that is, these people would never know they were ever involved in the murder of a President. Not until it was too late and their demise was eminent. That's how I believe Tippit and Oswald were killed, they had no idea what they were getting themselves into. And no, I don't believe all the CIA were involved, only a chosen few, a secret group. But it's pretty obvious history has told us whom they were. There was a secret group. The one Nixon formed in 1955 with Alan Dulles, the CIA director, the same man who Kennedy fired after the Bay of Pigs. The same man who kept secrets from the other members of the Warren Commission. Why do you think all the files were closed for National Security reasons for seventy-five years? Those involved would be dead anyway, and by that time who's going to care. All you need to do is look back to see who benefited these last thirty years to see how easy it was to keep the lid on. I'm sure it'll stay that way, especially if any of the people who were involved or participated have children who one day will grow up to run for the Presidency themselves. They'll protect their family's name."

"Kenneth O'Donnell did say something very interesting about Kennedy, though. He said Johnson wasn't going to be replaced as Vice-President during the '64 bid for reelection-- which Johnson himself thought-- but he did say John Kennedy was going to restructure the Central Intelligence Agency and retire J. Edgar Hoover following the January 20, 1965 inauguration. So after the assassination, on the advice of two of the greatest generals, both Eisenhower and MacArthur, those one-thousand Vietnam advisors whom Kennedy ordered out, would soon be returning on orders by a new President, Johnson, who no one ever expected to be President in the first place. The deceit and disinformation to the masses worked well into the approaching decade, but who would ever think Richard Nixon would return suddenly as the Trojan Horse? Nixon if you really think about it, would never have been President without the murders of both John and Bobby. And following Nixon's election, anyone connected to Nixon would also make it to positions that would be impossible to attain if Kennedy had not died that day in Dallas. And the CIA? It was never restructured, was it?"

"No, It never was," Franklin shook his head. "Too many things happened to derail the process. But where was J. Edgar Hoover all this time? He was the link between both Johnson and Nixon. Why didn't someone hear from him?"

"J. Edgar Hoover had more power at that time than he ever had. With Watergate around the corner, Hoover benefited by realizing his goal in bringing down Martin Luther King and Bobby Kennedy within months of each other. The growth of the Mafia and the return of Jimmy Hoffa all benefited from the death of Robert Kennedy. And then there was the Treasury Department whom the Secret Service represents. Others like the Pentagon, the military Industrial Complex and Rockefeller and the Texas oil men, profited because of the Vietnam War. So what did Johnson say in his last years in office to Walter Cronkite that he didn't want repeated on National television? It was, of course, with a wink in his eye that it was the Texas oil men and the CIA that did in Kennedy. Now, was this a Freudian slip of the tongue or was Johnson allowing his maker to know he was finally coming clean, knowing he just had a few years to live and was no longer a candidate

676

for reelection? It's funny, isn't it? The media never followed up on the greatest story ever to fall into a reporter's lap. Nothing really stops a team of reporters, especially a coup like this one, no matter if their lives or jobs are threatened. But here, they were stopped. Reporters have an obligation to inform the public, and if you can keep the media's mouths closed then you have the ultimate cover up, don't you? This was an early Watergate! The United States of America was on trial here, and will always be until the truth finally comes out!"

Modini looked at all of them leaning up against the limo and then addressed Franklin, "You have the most to benefit, Richard, in your dedication and work. I'll even tell you who that person was who wanted to finance my film, if you really want to know. I thought I was protecting him all these years by saying nothing, but now I realize it doesn't matter. What matters is he believes in what we're trying to do and he's one man who, if he came out to say what he knows, would not benefit until others within the government also come forward to say what they know. For some reason, the truth is always the hardest to tell."

Modini now smiled as he began his disclosure. "This gentleman who worked side by side with Nixon, informed me there were crucial assassination attempts on President Nixon's life when he went to China. One of them was contracted out of Texas and both Dr. Kissinger and Nixon were in constant danger. The word was stop Nixon from setting foot on China soil. The Texas group who once saw Nixon as the great Republican fighter of Communism, now saw him as a Communist traitor to his own country. Funny...that's what those leaflets were saying about Kennedy when he landed in Dallas, stating he was 'wanted for treason,' because he signed a peace treaty with Russia stopping the cold war and a possible nuclear World War III. Someone in Texas was repeating the accusation Kennedy had gone soft on Communism, which made him, like Nixon, now a traitor. The funny thing was that Nixon was just trying to save his ass because of Watergate!"

Richard Franklin laughed, "Who is this person? Was he in the Secret Service?"

Modini looked straight into Franklin's eyes and answered him honestly. "Yes, Richard, he was...and that's all I'm going to say except...I realize now I feel sorry for him. Here's a man who worked for our government, our country. The man had the position of protecting the President of the United States, but what does he do after Nixon's resignation? He leaves his country forever, never wanting to be a part of it again...why? I don't know. Maybe he thought anyone seeking the real answers to our President's murder had no chance of succeeding. He did what Jackie Kennedy eventually did in the final outcome, which was to get the hell out when she did-- and that's what's so sad about our America the Beautiful! Though Jackie returned after Nixon's resignation, many those who were a part of it didn't or were eliminated."

Modini held back his tears. He bowed his head and prayed aloud for the first time, asking them to join him in the Lord's Prayer. In the middle of it, the others started to join in. When Modini was finished, he addressed them again.

"This is not over by a long shot. There's a lot more to do...but I want you all to know I thank you for being there, for saving my life!" Modini smiled at Catherine and she returned the smile. He took her hand and gently kissed it.

* * *

As the group split up and headed back to their cars. Catherine asked Modini if he would ride back to the office with her. She told the others to continue to the reception at a country club outside Madison to honor both Bradley and Judge Kencade. The two of them would join them later. Franklin departed with Thomas and Jennifer in their car, and everyone drove from the cemetery.

As Catherine and Modini headed back to the office in the limo, it was quiet for the first half of the ride. Modini didn't want to intrude on Catherine's grief, so he remained silent. He looked out the side window at the passing scenery. A few drops of rain hit the windshield. *Good timing*, he thought. *At least the weather waited until the ceremony was over.*

It was Catherine who broke the silence. "There's something I'd like to say to you,"

678

Catherine told Modini.

"I'm listening."

"I wanted to be alone with you, John, for a couple of reasons. One is that I wanted you to know I'm not sure if I can take over Michael Bradley's practice. The news came out of nowhere, and I'm...I'm completely overwhelmed. I thought you might have some ideas. The other reason is I thought maybe you wanted to be alone with your Mother's letter, and I wanted to provide you space for that. The fact the letter bothers me and makes me more afraid of it now more than ever."

Modini sighed. "Catherine, if it bothers you so..." he took the letter out of his jacket pocket and held it out to her. "Then you should quickly read it!"

Catherine pushed the letter back to him. "No, it's nothing like that! It's just a feeling I have. Remember in Washington D.C. when I asked you if..." she paused a moment, thinking, then shook her head. "No, you read it, John, I might be totally off base here. I think you should read it at the office. If you think I should see it, then I'll look at it."

Modini stared at the letter addressed to his mother. "This isn't even my letter. I shouldn't be opening it! But you're making so much out of this it's driving me crazy now." He half attempted a joke. "I hope this hasn't anything to do with my demise."

He turned the letter over in his hand and considered opening it right then and there. As he carelessly tore the top of it open, a photograph within the envelope fell out onto the floor of the limo. He didn't notice it, but Catherine did.

She reached down to pick it up and suddenly froze as she saw the image. She put her hand over her mouth in shock! "Oh, my God!" Tears formed as Catherine stared at the photo.

"What's wrong?" Modini asked.

"I thought so...I've had this feeling...something wasn't right. All this time a key to the puzzle was missing. But it was here...right in front of me!"

Modini took the photograph from Catherine and studied it, then handed it back to her. "Yeah, I know who this is. She's the girl in that porno film, the one framing Hunter. How is she a key to your puzzle?"

Catherine felt the anger within her from his offhand reply. "Men!" she muttered to herself. "John, read the letter and you'll find out why she's the missing piece!"

Modini took the letter and read it aloud:

"Dear Mrs. O'Leary, I'm writing to you, knowing I will have passed on. In the circumstances, I had no choice but to proceed in this matter, but I want you and Jack to know I had complete control over my intentions. Please, both of you, forgive me, for I know it is a cardinal sin to commit suicide! I want you both to know I have a daughter. She was born in Cambodia and will be turning thirteen soon as I write this. Her mother died in 1979 trying to escape the killing fields of the Khmer Rouge prior to Phnom Penh's capture! *No* one is aware of any of this now except you and Jack, whenever you notify him. Michael Bradley will be involved since he is responsible in getting this letter to you at the proper time."

Modini stopped to clear his throat. Catherine put a hand on his arm. "When I spoke with Captain Corrigan in Miami, he said something that started me thinking. He thought Carrie's father might be an American soldier held over from the war. I knew you couldn't be the father because you left Vietnam in 1969. Then the name of Karl Hunter came to mind as the person who might be the father. I had no proof, but I believed I might be on the right track."

As Modini turned back to read the letter, he could clearly hear the voice of Karl Hunter speaking within his mind. "Bradley will be the one to act as your legal counsel for proof in legal custody of my daughter. Her name is Carrie. There is one problem now that needs to be resolved before I jeopardize her safety-- as if it weren't already in jeopardy. I don't want Jack to be involved because then his life will be in danger. I want you to know I assassinated my own brother. He was the one taking the lives of our platoon during and after the war. He was ordered to eliminate every survivor by the end of the war and those who eventually made it back to the states. I did not find this out until after I investigated the reasons Father Conrad took his life. I had to stop my brother before he got to Jack. Meanwhile, my operatives within our own Intelligence Agency kidnapped my daughter to keep my mouth shut if I ever talked about my brother's background and the fact I had refused to defect for them to the USSR.

As their retaliation, I have just been introduced to a pornography film of my daughter to be used against me if I decided to take that stand in the courtroom, or speak out to anyone concerning this issue. This film shows a man who looks like me, a double, having sexual intercourse with my daughter. This was to assure my silence and keep me quiet. You cannot imagine the overpowering anger I felt at what they did to my only flesh and blood. I rescued my daughter from them and had her committed to a sanitarium for, I thought, safekeeping-- this under the protection of the Catholic Church by using our friend, Father Daniel Conrad's name as legal guardian. I knew Jack would connect everything eventually and figure out the odd coincidence, especially when he finds out Carrie's name would be the same his own, Modini!"

"Jack will-- if anyone can-- be able to convince those necessary it isn't me, Karl Hunter, in that film. And Jack, if you're reading this, I'm telling you this now, myself!

"I have surrendered myself to Michael Bradley and will soon be turned over to the authorities after completing this letter. I will be tried for certain heinous crimes I'm supposed to be accused of. I thought I could use the system-- this trial-- as a pulpit-- to communicate what really is going on here within our government. But now, I'm worried about the threat against my daughter's life. The Bradley firm has no knowledge of this as I want it kept that way. By God, I'm hoping through time, Carrie will be able to survive this horrible trauma and have a normal life. I guess only God can heal wounds as deep and devastating as something like this."

John Modini now looked up to Catherine trying to keep his composure but was, little by little, losing it as he continued to read on:

"The other matter is of equal importance. If I should learn my enemies have discovered the location of my daughter, I will not hesitate to commit my final act to save her. I'm talking about suicide, of course. This will be decided when there is no other choice for me to make, to keep them from her, or to use her like they did. So, Jack, I want you to know if I'm labeled a serial rapist or

681

murderer by whatever tag the intelligence communities want to discredit me with, I'm hoping you will do your best to take care of Carrie for me. This will be a huge trauma for her to handle, but I know I'm putting her in good hands. I love her very much...and I hope you will too. The name and address of the sanitarium where you can find my daughter are at the conclusion of this letter.

"You can see Mrs. O'Leary, why I didn't want you or your son Jack to be involved with my trial or with my life. My only concern is for my daughter's personal safety. And as you can see, right now this is a very delicate matter. Please be careful how you handle this. I don't have to tell you there is a fine line here concerning Carrie's psychological scars from this incident. I trust no one! I repeat--I trust no one! Please handle this case with caution!

"I am hoping once I'm dead they'll have no further cause to harm or inflict any danger upon my daughter's safety. This letter will confirm now that they will no longer have use of my daughter as blackmail and I pray to God she is still alive as you read this.

"The Bradley law firm can be trusted and will help you. God bless you, and you my friend, Jack. You were a true brother to me in my lifetime. Marian, you are so lucky to have a son who exists on this earth like him. I know he will make a good father for my Carrie. Again, please explain to my daughter how much I truly loved her and tell her my last words to her were, 'I love you'... And all my love to you both-- Karl Hunter."

Modini dropped the letter in his lap, his eyes brimming with tears. He almost couldn't see the last paragraph of the letter. He covered his face with his hand and rested his head on the window of the limo. He didn't want Catherine to see him crying. There was a downpour of rain outside giving a hint of God's sadness as well.

Catherine, sensing Modini's own personal sorrow, moved closer to Modini and reached out to him, taking him into her arms, holding him as he weeped.

They held tightly to one another as the limo drove on through the downpour.

Chapter Forty-One

"The Aftermath: Grace Under Pressure"

As CNN Broadcasted the nightly newscast, the woman anchorperson on the screen reported the latest developments in the BCCI scandal involving Senator Orrin Hatch of Utah. "The Senator seems to continue to turn a blind eye after his famous self-righteous and moral issue, long before the Anita Hill hearings. Hatch is the first Republican linked to the BCCI scandal who defended BCCI on the Senate floor. And therefore, the senator now is in the unfortunate position of being targeted in an investigation by the Justice Department. Prior to this, the Justice Department was not aggressively investigating the BCCI scandal. This may be due to the possible link between the BCCI, the Iran Contra affair and President George Bush, which were suggested by written entries documented in the office diaries of Colonel Oliver North.

"Former hostage Terry Waite released a CIA document that shows the U.S. Government was 'far more manipulative' in efforts to trade arms for hostages than he realized. The Wall Street Journal said the document shows ex-White House aide Oliver North implied in a 1986 meeting with Iranian representatives that Waite was North's agent, now jeopardizing Waite's life."

The reporter moved onto the next story. "Jennifer Flowers continues her claim of an affair with Democratic Presidential candidate Bill Clinton, saying it lasted through his Governorship in

Arkansas and had a phone conversation on tape to prove it. Experts in sound analysis will be investigating to determine if this is truly Clinton's own voice or if editing was done to merge his voice with hers within the recording. Meanwhile, tabloids are offering big money to get their hands on this."

She continued, "In other news, President Bush signed documents Tuesday requiring government agencies including both the FBI and the CIA, to release secret material on the assassination of President Kennedy..."

George Bush's face filled the television screen. He was speaking with a news reporter. "I signed this bill with the hope it would assist in healing the wounds inflicted on our nation almost three decades ago--"

The anchor woman appeared again to conclude, "The law sets down the guidelines for Congress, executive branch agencies and government research centers such as the National Archives and Presidential libraries, to release a mountain of still classified material from the November 22, 1963, assassination. This material ranges from top secret intelligence reports to news clippings and tax returns. In the interim, Bush has formed a five member panel appointed as a Commission to have the power to review documents that agencies refuse to release and to make public the disputed materials. In the case of executive branch documents, the President could overrule the commission and withhold documents, but only by showing that 'grave harm' would result by their release. One exception written into law is the file of photos and x-rays taken during the autopsy of Kennedy. The material will remain confidential, and access would be controlled by the Kennedy family. National Security will eventually have power to revoke any such detrimental documents from being released!"

Richard Franklin stormed from the television. He was furious from hearing all the negative news. "Fat chance anyone knows there are no x-rays or photos to be scrutinized in the first place! I like how Bush put in that last touch-- how access would be controlled by the Kennedy family when they don't have a clue where this evidence, let alone his brain, is! And, of course, National Security has the last word! Bush...well, he set the stage for a possible court battle over presidential power. As he says, his authority comes from the constitution and it cannot be limited by statute!"

Franklin looked over to Modini, Catherine, Thomas, and Jennifer who were sitting at a bar over drinks. He had called them together for an informal gathering to review their options. The intended goal was to find some way to reveal the information that the government wanted to keep secret to the American people. And right now it seemed as if they didn't have a plan.

Franklin gestured to the tv news program above the bar. "How does it happen that a man from the start of the Reagan administration that this man--" he pointed to the bar TV set and took a sip from his vodka tonic, "...then, Vice-President Bush, one-time CIA director, becomes next in line to become President after Ronald Reagan."

"What do you mean," Modini asked. He thought Franklin might have had a little more to drink than necessary.

"As Vice-President in Reagan's administration, he waged a war on drugs. During this 'war' the cocaine coming into this country was doubled! Whatever his anti-drug stance and program were then, it wasn't very effective! Why, since he's become President, I've been waiting for him to do something-- not carry us from one scandal to another." Franklin hiccuped, "Excuse me! So what should we do? We can't go to Bush, the President of our country with the information we now hold, can we. And we can forget about Danny Quayle! What a dupe he is, the way he could be bought and paid for like that if it will get him the Presidency!" Franklin snapped his fingers and got up from his seat.

"What other choices do we have?" Modini took a sip from his drink and looked at Catherine.

Franklin sighed, "We can't go to Perot...he'll be laughed off his own ticket if we provide him with this information. The CIA already has him branded as loony tunes before the nation as it is. They dare not kill him, because there would be some verification after all in what he has been saying all along."

Thomas scribbled something quickly on his writing pad and showed it to Franklin. "Unfortunately, you're right," Franklin told Thomas. "We have to ride this one out and allow nature to take its course. In fact, Perot is doing all right against Bush in the debates so far. Then again there's Clinton."

"I wonder if he'll be of any help," Catherine speculated.

"Yes," added Jennifer. "He's an outsider...from Arkansas, isn't he."

"Well," Franklin shrugged, "We can always go to this friend of Michael's in Clinton's camp-- if, of course, Clinton wins the election. That means we wait to see what happens next week, come election time!"

Thomas tried to speak up, forgetting about his throat, then proceeded to write it down. "Meanwhile, we have to decide who to entrust our information with."

Jennifer then added, "Someone in the media-- who to go to, for instance. You always said Roger Mudd was the one to speak for the media on this."

Franklin agreed, "And maybe also Robert McNeil, Ted Koppel for *Nightline*, Bill Moyers and Bill Kurtis. There are good newsmen out there that deserved this chance. Moyers, did work for Johnson, but I believe he is somewhat skeptical about our government and knows something. We might be able to trust him. I say we start with Mudd. The national networks ban anything that's negative to the CIA since it looks as if they control what goes on the air. Yeah, Roger Mudd, he is the best! It's too bad Chet Huntley is not around anymore!"

He finished off his drink and sat back down in his seat while the others stewed in their own thoughts about what the future would hold for them and their cause.

Catherine felt tired. It had been a long day for her and it would be even a busier day tomorrow. She stood and told the group, "I hate to be a damper on all this fun, but I think Mr. Modini needs to get enough sleep to handle his big day tomorrow."

"Why, what's tomorrow?" Jennifer asked.

Catherine grinned at Modini. "Tomorrow's the day he'll know whether he'll become a father or not..." The four people at the bar raised their heads in unison, all with surprised looks on their faces.

Catherine covered her mouth in embarrassment, totally red-faced. "Let me rephrase that..." she said quickly. "Tomorrow I introduce Carrie to her new father!" She pointed to Modini as the others nodded in unison and raised their drinks in a toast.

"Thanks a lot," Modini said, chiding her. His secret was out.

"I've had Carrie's adoption in the works for several months now," Catherine told the others, "and finally its coming down to the wire."

Modini got up and stood next to Catherine.

Catherine Leaned over to Franklin and put her arm around him. "Mr. Richard Franklin? I was wondering if entertainment law were the only restriction on your agenda for the rest of your life?"

Franklin caught his eye, then said to Catherine, "Why, what do you have in mind?"

Catherine exchanged an apprehensive glance with Modini, then finally said, "I've been thinking...if this doesn't work out for Mr. Modini and Carrie, I want to take some time off and become a mother to Carrie. She's seventeen and needs somebody right now, more than ever, and I want to be there for her full time, until she can be off on her own. Mr. Modini and I have talked it over and felt you would be the best candidate to run things at the law firm...so what do you say?"

Franklin was surprised. The others were in complete agreement.

Catherine smiled. "What do you say? Do you agree to help us out?"

Franklin shook his head, "Now, now...I didn't say I would, but if you twist my arm a few times and allow me to do my seminars occasionally, I'll think about it!"

"That means it's a deal," Catherine told Modini, and kissed Franklin on the cheek.

Modini congratulated him, shaking his hand. Franklin got off his bar stool to hug Modini and whispered into his ear. "I love you, brother!"

Jennifer kissed Franklin on the cheek as well. Sanders caught his attention and nodded.

"Now, don't you start with me boy!" Franklin told him jokingly. They compromised by giving each other a high five slap.

* * *

The next day on an early November morning, the weather called for snow. Modini and Catherine drove in her Honda Prelude to the Glen Ridge Convalescent Hospital. After parking on the grounds of the sanitarium, they entered the institution and were greeted by two attendants who escorted them to the office of the Head Chief of Staff, Miss Maxine Hightower. She was the same woman who continued to act as Carrie's charge since she was first brought to the sanitarium in 1988. Catherine greeted her with a friendly handshake and introduced her to John Modini.

"Carrie has been doing fine, Mrs. Rogers," Miss Hightower said. "You'll be surprised when you see her. She's turning into quite a young lady!" she gave a brief look to Modini, as her fingers fiddled nervously with a small silver whistle she wore around her neck. "Although, I must say I was expecting to see you alone today!" she said to Catherine. "I didn't realize you were going to bring a...friend."

"Oh, that's no problem," Modini assured her, feeling the unexpected friction. "I'll wait elsewhere-- in one of the waiting rooms," he forced a smile.

"Miss Hightower-- Maxine...may I have a word with you alone?" Catherine asked. She waited until Modini entered a waiting room down the hall. But Miss Hightower spoke first.

"I thought you understood Carrie was to have no visitors unless you had my permission."

"Well, I'm asking your permission today," Catherine said. She was determined to stand her ground. "During the last few visits with Carrie I asked her whether she would mind if I brought along a friend...a male friend. She told me she wouldn't mind."

"I think she would say that just to please you. I advise against it." Miss Hightower was alarmed.

Catherine spoke out, "Miss Hightower--Maxine... Carrie is a very bright and remarkable

688

child. You've shown me some of her medical charts. I'm aware she's been weaned off much of her medication in the past year and has made very good progress."

"Under my supervision," Miss Hightower announced, "I know what's best for Carrie! You know I've taken a personal interest in her case since she arrived here. I feel as though Carrie were a part of me. I do realize in another year or two she'll have to make the decision to leave this hospital or not."

Catherine interrupted her, "Listen to me, Maxine. Isn't it time to give her some responsibility, to let her control her own destiny? She should be allowed to meet other people-- especially those who care about her." She confirmed Maxine knew she was now referring to John Modini.

But Miss Hightower's position hardened. "Suppose I allow it? And suppose the sight of Mr. Modini puts her into one of her convulsions. Then what?"

"That's not going to happen."

"But it will, Mrs. Rogers." Maxine's voice became cold and impersonal. "I know what her reaction will be."

"What if you...what if you stood by with medication--something to stabilize her. Would you permit Mr. Modini to meet her then?"

"I told you she's not ready to meet any strangers!"

"And I think she is! The main concern here is to see how she reacts after she's off her medication. She's never met Mr. Modini, I know-- he's a stranger to her, but we've got to take that chance...the first step to give her back her life."

"Carrie hasn't required medication because she has been isolated. You should not be questioning our medical decisions."

"Please, Maxine," Catherine was feeling emotional now. "I don't want Carrie to spend the rest of her life in this place! No offense, but yes, I am resentful of her being here, especially at this stage in her life. As an adult, I went through what she went through as a child. You know that.

Allow her to make that decision herself. At least let me try to help. I've seen for myself she's growing into a beautiful, intelligent young lady. Do you know what I mean?"

"I know what you mean. And I, like you, want the best for Carrie. I've always done my best to protect her. It's just that I'm reluctant to have him or anyone...confront her now. I don't feel that she's ready for it."

"Then when will she be ready? In a year or two? When she reaches her eighteenth birthday? Her twentieth? It might be too late then."

Miss Hightower was silent a few moments. Her fingers played restlessly with the silver whistle hanging around her neck. What Catherine had said was true-- and she knew it as well. She finally nodded, making up her mind. "Very well. We'll try it your way. But it will be a controlled situation."

Catherine finally felt a small measure of relief. "Thank you." Slowly she took a breath.

The two women went to get Modini. The group walked down the ward to the common room. Catherine noticed the hallway sported newly drawn Thanksgiving, as well as Christmas pictures, and other decorations handcrafted by the children. They approached their destination and could hear the sound of children's voices singing in the background.

"You'll be surprised when you see her," Miss Hightower commented to Catherine as she escorted her to a classroom.

"Please wait out here, Mr. Modini," Miss Hightower said. The women entered the classroom where a group of children were singing, 'America the Beautiful,' conducted by Carrie herself. Catherine's eyes sparkled as she stood in the back of the room and watched Carrie, now a young lady of seventeen, take charge of the hospital's younger children.

Miss Hightower lowered her voice. "I think it best to bring Carrie to him. I'll see to it Mr. Modini is brought to the empty classroom next door," she said to Catherine, indicating the door to the next room. "Give me a few minutes."

Miss Hightower left closing the door behind her. Catherine turned back and watched

Carrie. She wore a simple blue dress and still had the locket around her neck, the same locket she had when Catherine first met her.

When Carrie finished leading her class in song, she looked up and saw Catherine standing at the back of the room. She smiled and waved to Catherine, genuinely glad to see her.

Carrie quickly excused herself from the children and came down to greet Catherine with a hug. "Catherine... Catherine... I'm so glad you came."

Catherine didn't know how much she missed hearing Carrie's voice until she heard the girl speak. Catherine hugged her.

"You must stay and hear our next song, Carrie said. "It's a special Christmas song I've been rehearsing with the other kids all week long."

"Certainly, Carrie. I'll stay and hear it. But I also have a holiday surprise for you, too."

"You do?" the young girl responded enthusiastically, her eyes lighting up. Then she remembered her restless children who were waiting for her to start the next song. "I'll talk to you later."

Carrie moved back to the front of the room and raised her arm to conduct, "All right you guys, give me your best!" Then she leaned over and whispered to them, "And make it good. A special friend of mine is watching." Her arm came down for the cue and the kids began singing the Christmas song.

John Modini impatiently paced back and forth in the next room listening to the children's voices raised in song. He had been accompanied to the room a few minutes before by Miss Hightower, and left alone.

As Modini listened to the familiar lyrics, he unconsciously mouthed the words to the children's voices, thinking simultaneously of his friendship with the man who saved his life more than once-- Carrie's father.

He glanced outside the window and noticed it had begun to snow. The image of the white falling flakes drifting to the ground combined with the children's voices in the background suddenly calmed him. He crossed to the window, feeling the heat coming from the radiator as he put his face to the glass. He settled here to watch as each flake of snow hit the ground. His eyes traveled upward into the gray sky where the flakes filled the air by the thousands, too numerous to count. He smiled and allowed the relaxed sensation to come over him.

His reverie was broken by Catherine's voice behind calling out his name, "John!" It was her third try that awakened him from his deep thoughts.

Modini realized there was silence now. The children's song had stopped. He turned around from his surreal world of falling flakes, to the real world of this hospital, in this room.

Catherine stood in the doorway of the adjacent classroom, smiling at him, Miss Hightower by her side.

"John Modini," she addressed him with mock formality, "This is Miss Carrie Hunter."

John didn't see Carrie who was hidden behind the women. Catherine stepped aside and allowed Carrie to enter the room.

Modini shifted, opened his mouth, then closed it again as he saw his friend's daughter for the first time. He instantly became enamored at this lovely half-caste young lady. Yes, she was Cambodian, but he could see that her nose and jaw line definitely belonged to Karl.

Catherine put her arm around Carrie to introduce her to Modini. "Miss Carrie, this is--" but before she could continue, there was a startled reaction from the teenager. Catherine saw Carrie's lively face suddenly tighten, grow hard and rigid, and her eyes open wide with panic. Without any warning, Carrie went into one of her fits. She gasped for breath and couldn't speak, one hand going to her throat. She went down on her knees, trying to grab for Catherine with her other hand. Then she began to panic, her eyes widening as a rush of tears flowed.

"Oh, my God! No!" Catherine's worst fears were finally coming true.

Miss Hightower must have expected the girl's response. She immediately went to Carrie's aid, trying to calm her. She pulled her off Catherine and placed herself between the teenager and Modini.

Modini wanted to step forward, to help, but held his ground. Any attempt on his part would only make things worse. Miss Hightower glared at Modini over her shoulder, as if he were evil incarnate. "Leave the room now, Mr. Modini!"

Modini was frozen to the spot, unable to respond. Miss Hightower's head swung around to Catherine. "I told you this wouldn't work out...didn't I?" She held on to the hysterical teenager with one hand and dragged her into a corner, where she couldn't escape. Then the determined woman reached into her jacket pocket and took out a small case and removed a hypodermic syringe she had prepared. *"Outside,* Mr. Modini!"

Modini had no choice. He went to the door.

"No! Stop!" Catherine shouted before Modini could leave the room. She saw the syringe and knew Miss Hightower had prepared for such a situation. Carrie now tried to scream. Before Miss Hightower could remove the protective plastic cap from the needle, Catherine slapped the hypodermic syringe out of her hand. When Miss Hightower went after it, she tried to get the sobbing girl's attention.

"Carrie...Carrie... Listen to me!" Catherine grabbed the girl's shoulders and held her firmly. "Stop this *immediately!"*

Carrie stopped screaming and drew a sharp breath, stunned by Catherine's sudden outburst. Catherine glared at Miss Hightower. "I don't have to be a doctor, Miss Hightower to know that this girl is having an anxiety attack!"

Catherine pulled Carrie to her and put her arms around the sobbing girl. "Carrie...stop this! Please... Listen to me. You've got to calm down..."

Carrie didn't move or scream again while Catherine hugged her, although she still sobbed, and tried to catch her breath.

Miss Hightower now retrieved the syringe, her anger growing each passing second. She was enraged by Catherine usurping her authority and taking charge of the situation.

"Carrie... You're hyperventilating. Please listen to me, sweetheart! "Take some deep breaths...slowly, now." Catherine spoke with Carrie in a calm voice, trying to soothe her.

Carrie listened to Catherine and obeyed her. Catherine pulled her arms away and guided the young girl to a chair. "Here...sit. Put your head down between your knees. Please, Carrie...do what I say!" She looked up to see Modini still at the doorway. "John? Find a paper bag, any bag will do--"

Modini began searching the room and checking the shelves stacked with paper and craft materials. He spotted a roll of paper towels and picked it up.

Suddenly, the silence of the room was shattered by the blast from Miss Hightower's whistle. She had stepped to the door and had sounded an alarm. She waved specifically to two male interns in the corridor. They hurried past her into the room. "Get these two people out of here! Now!" she ordered.

One of the attendants approached Modini who showed no resistance. "There's no need for any of this, I'll leave on my own accord!" he told the man. "I know you two have a job to do. Just give me a second."

Modini took a paper towel and folded it into a loose shape of a bag, then handed it to Catherine. He looked again at Carrie. "Don't worry little one," he told the young girl. "I'm leaving." He then turned around and exited with the attendant.

Catherine held the makeshift bag to Carrie's mouth. "Breathe slowly in into it... That's right...short, deep breaths, sweetheart." The other intern in the room shifted nervously, unsure whether to interfere with Catherine or not.

Miss Hightower, meanwhile, removed the protective cap from the needle. She looked up to see the attendant standing there. "I told you to get her out of here!" she told him.

The burly attendant grabbed Catherine's arm and pulled her away from Carrie. But Catherine fought back by stomping on the intern's foot. "Let go of me, you bastard!"

The man released her, wincing in pain. Miss Hightower ignored this altercation. She squirted the syringe, testing it, preparing to administer the sedative to Carrie.

Catherine threw herself forward to stop the woman, but Miss Hightower was ready for her. She slammed her elbow into Catherine's stomach and shoved her aside, then proceeded to the chair where Carrie was still seated.

The pain made tears come to Catherine's eyes as she tried to take air into her lungs. It took her a few precious seconds to recover.

Carrie still had the towel bag to her mouth and was breathing into it. But the girl was frightened because she saw everything that happened.

Miss Hightower grabbed the bag from Carrie and flung it aside. "Hold still," she told the girl, "you'll feel much better once you've had your medicine." She reached out to grab Carrie's hand.

But Miss Hightower never got that far. Catherine's intervention prevented her. She grabbed Miss Hightower's arm, the one holding the syringe, and pulled her away. Miss Hightower shook Catherine loose, but then retreated when Catherine swung her fist at her open face.

Catherine again approached to take the syringe from the woman, but the male intern grabbed her and swung her around. Catherine lost her balance and fell to the floor.

By this time Carrie had stopped hyperventilating, but anyone watching her closely could see she was visibly fighting to remain calm. She was terrified and bewildered by the spectacle happening in front of her.

When Carrie saw Catherine thrown to the floor, the overwhelming panic spread within her again. "No!" Carrie cried aloud, stunning everyone in the room.

As all eyes turned to the girl, Carrie grabbed at the chain holding the locket and tore it off her neck. She held it out in one hand to Catherine as if displaying something precious.

For a split second there was silence. Then Catherine spoke up. "What's wrong, Carrie." She started to get to her feet.

Carrie didn't answer. She held the dangling locket out to Catherine, as if she wanted her to have it. Before Catherine could understand what Carrie attempted to do, she saw Miss Hightower start toward the teenager again.

The instant Carrie saw Miss Hightower move, she clutched the locket to her chest. To everyone's astonishment, she bolted from the chair and rushed out the doorway.

"What are you waiting for," Miss Hightower ordered the intern, "Go after her!"

Carrie made her escape down the corridor, running as fast as she could. She glanced back to see the attendant emerge from the room and chase after her. With her heart pounding in her ears, Carrie raced down the hallway as if running for her life. But in reality, she wasn't running because she felt her life was in danger-- she was running *after* someone.

Miss Hightower also appeared and headed down the corridor chasing Carrie, followed now by Catherine.

Carrie, her arms pumping air, headed for the main entrance of the hospital. When she reached the end of the corridor, she stopped, almost out of breath. Then she spotted Modini exiting through the front doors, escorted by the other attendant.

Carrie heard the echoing footsteps of the attendant chasing right behind her. Holding tight to her locket, she sprinted to the entrance way, past the first intern and dove through the main doors.

Carrie paused at the outside entrance to the hospital, gulping for breath. She finally summoned enough strength and shouted. "Please! Don't go! Please, Mr. Modini, don't leave me!"

John Modini, startled by the girl's cry, stopped in his tracks and turned around to see Carrie behind him, calling his name. At that moment both male attendants emerged from the hospital and grabbed the girl.

Carrie was again consumed by a furious panic as she felt the men's hands upon her. Terrified and insane with fear she screamed aloud. "No... No! Let me go!" She struggled, writhing and twisting against the men's grasp.

Modini charged up to the men. "Let her go! I *said* let her go!" He pulled one of the men from her and shoved him aside. The other intern wrestled Carrie to the ground. She screamed and yelled in terrified protest.

Miss Hightower emerged from the building, Catherine right behind her. Carrie tried to escape from the attendant's grip, but he was too strong. He pinned her down, preventing her from getting away.

Suddenly, Carrie cringed when she saw the looming figure of Miss Hightower approaching from above. For a moment she froze in fear, but desperation gave Carrie strength to cry out, "*He* told me you wouldn't leave me! *He* promised me you would come for me! Mr. Modini, don't go! Please!"

Modini was suddenly startled by Carrie's unexpected outburst. "What did you say?" He saw the pleading look in the teenager's tear-wet eyes.

"Hold her down," Miss Hightower ordered the attendant. "I'll make sure she doesn't make any more trouble."

"No!" Carrie screamed as she saw the syringe in Miss Hightower's hand.

"Wait a minute! Have all of you gone nuts!" Modini yelled. "This stops here and *now!*" He stood beside the attendant. "*Get off her*"

"Don't listen to him," Miss Hightower snapped. "She's out of control!"

"No she isn't," Modini said to the attendant. "Carrie! You won't give anyone any more trouble, will you?" He focused on her severely, hoping she would give the correct reply.

Carrie trembled. She forced herself to remain motionless, battling with all her strength against the inner voices ordering her to yell and scream and attack the man grasping her. Then she obeyed, giving Modini her full trust. "No... I won't..." she said, shivering with apprehension.

"I said hold her down," Miss Hightower demanded. "She's going to get her medication before this happens again."

Modini defied Miss Hightower. "She doesn't look like she's out of control," he told the attendant. "Everything will be okay...I'll see to it."

Miss Hightower moved to Carrie, her syringe ready. Modini blocked her path. "Put that away or I'll take it from you myself," he threatened.

Miss Hightower stepped back, intimidated by his threat. Catherine stepped next to Miss Hightower and put a firm grip on her arm. "It's over...Maxine," Catherine told the woman. "I'm here...John's here... And we're not going to let anything happen to Carrie."

The energy seemed to drain from Miss Hightower. With the others present, she knew she had lost the command of the situation. She looked into Carrie's eyes, and watched the girl straining to overcome the fear and pain of this appalling situation.

Reluctantly Miss Hightower nodded. "Let her go," she told the attendant.

Modini kneeled down to Carrie and took the girl's hand. Then with calm determination he slowly helped Carrie to her feet.

Carrie stood next to Modini and swallowed hard. All eyes were on her, and everyone saw she was filled with apprehension. For a few seconds, Catherine thought she would make a run for it. Instead, Carrie took a step toward Modini, threw her arms around him and burst into sobs. Childlike, she clung to him trembling.

Modini was baffled by Carrie's actions as Catherine was. He stood there, hands raised, reluctant to touch the teenager or put his hands around her. Then, very slowly, he lowered his arms and enveloped her with a protective tenderness.

Catherine reached down and picked up Carrie's locket with the broken chain from where it fell during the struggle. She looked at Modini. He hadn't taken his eyes off her since Carrie embraced him. His eyes reflected the anxiety he felt, and he looked for Catherine for guidance. On impulse, Catherine held the locket out to Modini and gestured for him to take it. It gave him an excuse to disengage himself from the sobbing girl.

Modini took the locket, not sure what to do with it next.

When Carrie pulled her tearstained face from Modini's chest, her eyes blinked and smiled in pleased surprise as she saw the locket.

"*He* promised me you'd come for me," Carrie repeated to Modini, the same words before the attendant grabbed her. "You took a long time...but you kept your promise." She looked at the dangling locket in his hand. Again, the tears were in her eyes and she tried to wipe them all away.

"What do you mean, Carrie," Modini asked gently. He did not want to frighten the girl.

Carrie took Modini's hand, the one with the locket and peered into his bewildered eyes. "This is what I mean," she told him.

As Modini held the locket, Carrie opened it revealing two pictures, side by side. One was a slightly blurred and faded color picture of a Cambodian woman. A faded ballpoint pen scrawl on the bottom read 'MOM.' The other picture was sharper, showing two people: Karl Hunter in his G.I. fatigues, smiling, with an arm around John Modini. Below the picture was the name 'DAD' and 'JOHN MODINI.'

Modini was astounded. "That's me..." His amazement made him state the obvious.

Carrie nodded. She had regained some of her composure. "My father told me if anything ever happened to him, you would come for me," she explained. "That's the last thing he said to me, and I never forgot it. I never stopped wishing or hoping..."

"I would have come sooner if I had known, Carrie..." Modini reassured her. Tears were now stinging his eyes, and he no longer had the strength to hold them back.

Carrie gave a quick glance to Catherine, thanking her silently with the smile on her face. Catherine felt the tears clouding her eyes as well.

Modini leaned down until his eyes were level with Carrie's. "I hope you'll forgive me for making you wait so long." His words were genuine and sincere.

Carrie looked right back at him, unflinchingly. "Silly!" she said, jokingly, scolding him. She threw her arms around his neck before anyone saw her tears again.

Modini took her actions as a sign of forgiveness. He whispered in her ear. "I'm glad I found you, Carrie. Believe me, I'm glad I'm here." They both cried now, hugging one another.

Catherine approached Carrie and Modini and put her arms around them.

Maxine Hightower stood there, watching them, silent and immobile. She gestured to the attendants to go back inside. The past four years she did what she thought was best for the young girl, trying to help her overcome her trauma. Gradually she watched Carrie improve and encouraged her to come out of her shell to interact with the other children. Once Maxine thought she was the only one who could show Carrie the attention and love she deserved. Now she knew she was wrong. Carrie had found two others whom she trusted as much as she.

Tears came into Maxine Hightower's eyes. But she made sure no one saw them. She turned and went back into the building, walking away from the child she once thought she'd never be able to let go.

* * *

At the University of San Diego, 1993, in a forum and seminar for a majority student audience, a female student asked Richard Franklin a question, "How can the ex-governor of Texas, John Connally, state he believes in the final report of the Warren Commission, but also continue to say he was shot by a separate bullet from President Kennedy, thereby disproving the 'magic bullet theory?'"

"You make a very good point," Franklin acknowledged. "If you look at the anomaly of Connally's thoughts when he explained his intentions to the American people, you understand how this country came to divide itself in the Kennedy assassination. On one hand, you have Satan fighting Jesus for the souls of our good people. There is good on one side, evil on the other. Then, however, you have the fight between truth and falsehood. Connally wanted to be on the side of God by protecting the souls of all the good people. But Mr. Connally also wanted to be liked on both sides. He wanted to be loved by everyone. Now doesn't this sound like a true politician? This is what Connally wanted most. But to have the love of the people, he had to go along with his political peers and agree with the final Warren Commission Report or he could not be elected dog catcher. Perhaps you noticed his political maneuver. On orders of, I should say advice, of President Nixon, Connally suddenly switched political parties. Why? This is the man who was fighting to get out of his body, asking God to fight Satan for his soul by telling us he, Connally, was allowed to be a witness in JFK's assassination by actually being shot himself and to live to tell about it. Then he agreed with the Warren Report, knowing what many expert doctors and pathologists already knew, the bullet that went through two entrances of Kennedy and five entrances of his own body, was anything but a magic bullet. There are pieces of shrapnel from this bullet still within him to this day. It was a separate shot that wounded him, he's telling us, which means there had to be four or more shots that day in Dallas. The Warren commission established the time frame of Kennedy's assassination to be 5.6 seconds, set by the Zapruder film. Any more shots than the three fired in this window of opportunity would mean there was more than one gunman. Think about it. Oswald may or may not have shot off one round of anything. Since the magic bullet was the only bullet that could be connected to the Mannlicher-Carcano Italian bolt action rifle-- the one the Warren Commission alleged Oswald owned-- that's all they needed to make a case. What about the other bullets fired at the President. What happened to them? Oh, oh, oh, yes! I forgot. That would be the same one-- the one and only magic bullet! Wow, how stupid of me. That explains everything."

The audience in the auditorium roared with laughter at Franklin's sarcastic remark. He added at the close of the laughter, "You now see the anomaly in all this and why John Connally will always be a perfect example of how this country will always be divided trying to decide what the real truth is, or what really happened on that black day in Dallas, Texas, thirty years ago in November, 1963! The only thing that matters is, as Jesus told Satan, 'You shall not win! You shall be defeated!' In other words, no matter how long it takes, the truth will win out in the end!" Franklin looked up. "One more question in the back row."

A male student, one of Irish descent, stood up. Sitting next to him was a familiar face, ex-Green Beret and Lieutenant Colonel Donald Casson. He was dressed in normal civilian clothes as a spectator in this audience. He listened as the Irish student asked Franklin what he thought of the new book, *Case Closed* by Gerald Posner. "What will it do to the country when it presents proof Oswald was the sole assassin and dispels many conspiracy 'myths' surrounding JFK's

701

assassination?"

Casson waited to hear Franklin's reply. Franklin thought it over a few moments before answering. "Well, it'll be a sorry day if his book catches on. For one, my feelings tell me our government is surely behind it. The media will surely sell and promote it. It's their version all over again-- perhaps someone in our government, maybe the CIA, is financing Posner or recruited him with your taxpaying dollars. They're definitely behind this so to destroy Oliver Stone and his movie. More of their technique in providing disinformation! This means the country will shut down for a while until someone else like you or me can take this author's book and throw it right into the trash can where it belongs. Like I said, the truth, sir, will win out in the end. It depends which side of the truth you want to be on. This Posner was never within the House Select Committee to know what happened all those years behind closed doors. And until those doors are reopened, this case will never be closed. I already went through this before with a very good friend of mine. He's a Pulitzer-Prize winning photojournalist, and he, formerly, was in this Posner character's same shoes. So I know how the government can work its spell on all of us good people out there..."

Later, backstage, after Richard Franklin's lecture was over, some of those good people asked for Franklin's autograph. He jokingly said, "I feel as popular as Denzel Washington. I wish I had the money he makes!"

Lieutenant Colonel Casson waited in line with the autograph seekers who moved one by one to Franklin. But Casson wasn't here to get his autograph.

"Hello, Mr. Franklin. I didn't stand in line to get your autograph, I just wanted to meet you," Casson said, shaking his hand. "You mentioned at the end of your seminar until someone can prove Posner's book false, the cover up will continue or remain just as it is. I might be able to help you. My name is Donald Casson. I was a Lieutenant Colonel and ex-Green Beret of the Special Forces. If you have time, Sir, for a cup of coffee...I have a story you might be interested in hearing."

"What is this regarding?" Franklin asked.

702

Casson asked simply. "Do you know of a man named William B. Pitzer?"

Franklin recognized the name immediately. "You mean Naval Commander Pitzer of Bethesda Naval Hospital?"

Casson nodded. "The same. Then I think you'd be interested in what I have to say!"

A short time later in a little coffee shop a few blocks from campus, Casson and Franklin sat in a booth and ordered some freshly brewed coffee. Casson picked up the conversation where he left off. "When the General at Fort Bragg finally reported to me no one by the name of Randell Clarke existed in the Green Berets, I was appalled, especially when the Pentagon informed me he didn't exist. Hell, I had my own proof and paperwork on me and showed him Randell Clarke's name. I was at Fort Bragg in 1963, and 1965 I went to Vietnam, but after I saw Clarke in 1966 I never saw him again! I forgot about him until last year when those stories concerning Kennedy's assassination and those who died surrounding it came out. There was a program about the deaths of many of those who either witnessed or connected in some way to the Kennedy assassination. One name threw me for a loop-- William Pitzer. The hairs on the back of my neck rose, and I lost it. I've been trying to find Clarke ever since, but to no avail."

"Why?" Franklin asked Casson. "What can he do? What is it you think might have happened to him?"

"It's not about if he is alive or dead." Casson confessed. "Only he could answer a question. I have to settle in my own mind what transpired. After our top secret CIA training following the assassination, I returned from Vietnam in 1965. Then as Captain Casson of the Green Berets, I was approached by a representative of Central Intelligence who requested I volunteer for an important assignment-- in his words-- for the good of our country. It would take place the following year because of its immediacy and importance."

"And what did you do?" Franklin asked.

"I agreed to handle the assignment. I was asked to assassinate a person unknown to me at the time, but they needed confirmation when the time and location were worked out. I'm thinking they'll be sending me overseas again-- Europe, maybe, wherever, knowing the CIA's clandestine jobs happen strictly outside the country. So six months later I learn the man's name and the assignment to be completed before the end of the year-- before this man retired. And that it had to look as if it were a suicide!"

Franklin knew whom he meant. "Pitzer?"

"Yes," Casson acknowledged. "When I found out he was a Naval Commander, I was skeptical, but that didn't hinder my assignment. It was when this Central Intelligence Agent informed me it would happen at Bethesda Hospital that I decided to back out. I knew now something wasn't right. Overseas-- fine! But to assassinate someone here in the United States on a government base-- this is when I knew the CIA had stepped out of bounds. I simply refused any further participation, and contact was terminated. Next thing I knew, they approached my friend and fellow Green Beret, Randell Clarke, for the assignment. I decided to ask him whether he was taking it. He said he didn't want to talk about it. That was the last time I would ever see him again. In fact, I actually forgot about him until this past year. Like I said, when I saw Pitzer's name connecting him to Kennedy, that's when I started recalling things. I've surmised from the government's point of view Randell Clarke does not exist. This man has disappeared off the face of the earth. If he's dead he has no gravestone. If he's alive, he no longer has any military records. He no longer is among the Green Berets that have protected and served this country. But here is his name recorded with mine, and a picture of him taken in '63 with our unit!"

Casson handed Franklin a worn photo and continued. "He is real, Mr. Franklin, and I believe he took the assignment I had declined. Do you think for a moment I would be here today, if I had not backed out at that last moment? That is one of the unsettling questions that bothers me even now, Mr. Franklin! Think for a moment, sir, a Green Beret like myself was let loose like that, for a covert domestic assignment. A Green Beret that now doesn't exist. A Green Beret like me, sir, that would never have existed if it were not for President Kennedy himself. It was during his first term he created us to protect and serve our country!"

Catherine was driven in an unmarked Miami Police Department car to the Iron Gate home of ex-mob chief Costalanno. Captain Corrigan went with her but stayed behind as she entered Costalanno's seaside home for the second time.

She was escorted to a bedroom having all the conveniences of a hospital, except an operating room. Nurses tended to Mr. Costalanno, now a bedridden old man who was on a death watch. He had I.V. tubes going into his arms and an oxygen tube for his nose. His body was connected to a support system handling every need and care, intravenously feeding him food and supplying him with pain killers.

With all this care keeping him lucid, Costalanno smiled when he saw Catherine approach his bedside. Catherine moved forward as he weakly gestured to her. She took his hand as he spoke. "I want to thank you for coming!"

Catherine nodded and smiled at him. "I had to, sir. Don Costalanno... You saved my life...and you saved a very good associate of mine. Nothing could have kept me away."

Costalanno patted her hand, grateful to hear this, then told her, "I am going to die as you probably have guessed by now, with all this attention. I just wanted to know whether you found the answer you were looking for?"

Catherine squeezed his hand, letting him know there was a serenity within her now and proceeded to tell him about Karl Hunter's letter. It relieved her to talk about it. She felt less tension now than she did based upon their first meeting.

Costalanno blinked his eyes and tried to focus on her. "I want you to know it doesn't matter who killed Sam Giancana because what it comes down to is that the Federal Government was responsible for him," he told her, "They were in charge. Remember, he was to appear at the House Select Committee either the next day or sometime that week. It was the Federal Government that brought him across the state line from Mexico. It was they who assured the Committee he would appear before them. So whoever walked into Sam's place and whacked him had to be permitted by the Federal Government! You see, someone other than Sam allowed that person to enter and end Giancana's life right then and there."

"Like I said, we did not order it. Sam took the contract. The Federal Government ended it. Then it was Johnny Roselli's turn. If Hoffa hadn't opened his big mouth none of these committees would have existed! He couldn't leave well enough alone. But it doesn't matter. I can tell you this much, it's people like your journalist friend who keeps that torch in Arlington Memorial alive! I wanted you to know that."

* * *

Mickey Mouse and Minnie were dancing down Main Street USA in a Parade of Disney characters at Disney World in Orlando, Florida. Among the patrons participating in all the fun and gaiety and excitement of the amusement park, was John Modini and Carrie Hunter. They both shared a double vanilla and strawberry ice cream cone that belonged to Carrie. As they walked past the colorful characters on this late afternoon, Carrie stared at her half-eaten cone.

"You, know, Uncle John," she hinted, "I can afford to buy you one of these if you'd like one for yourself. It's not as though it cost a million dollars!"

Modini smiled at her as they passed the Mark Twain Mississippi River boat ride, strolling through Frontier Land. "Well, you must know I can't really eat ice cream, so--"

"Yeah, right!" Carrie said, cutting him off, laughing. "Tell me another story!" Modini laughed with her as she took his arm and wrapped herself around it.

Modini, meanwhile, lost all track of time. "What time is it?" he asked her.

Carrie looked at her watch and informed him. "4:45." And this reminded her as well. "Oh, John, what time were we to meet Catherine?"

Modini lessened her concern. "At five p.m. sharp. And we're right here! We have plenty of time!"

Carrie looked around. "This doesn't look like the Haunted House?"

Modini shook his head, "You weren't paying attention. We're going to the Haunted Mansion next after this. That's just up the street there, see!" He pointed to a gloomy looking mansion up ahead and turned Carrie around to another attraction, "This is where we're supposed to meet, inside the Hall of Presidents. Let's hustle on in so we won't be late."

The two of them followed a line of people into the Hall of Presidents attraction, entering the mezzanine where they were to wait prior to making their entrance into the auditorium. The room was fascinating. It was like walking into an art gallery, except the portraits here were of all the past Presidents of the United States.

Carrie's eyes widened in awe. "Wow!" she exclaimed and broke free from Modini to look around.

Modini looked around and was as impressed as Carrie was. He turned in a semicircle studying the portraits of Bush, Carter, Johnson and Lincoln, then stopped. Most presidents here were portrayed in a sitting position, but the one he viewed was standing, his head bowed, nothing surrounding him, no flag, no presidential seal-- just the man himself.

Carrie approached Modini from behind and slid her hands around Modini's waist. She leaned her head onto his side as she commented, "That's him, isn't it?"

There was a twinkle in his eyes as he smiled. "Yes, that's him." He noticed benches in front of each portrait. He had an idea. "Carrie, let's wait here at this bench. This would be the most obvious place to be noticed, right?"

Carrie agreed, and the two of them sat down beneath the portrait of the thirty-fifth President to wait. Meanwhile, people strolled by to gaze. Carrie noticed Modini searching for something and read his mind. "Are you looking for any other specific President?" she asked, her curiosity getting the better of her. He nodded his head slowly as he checked out the other presidential portraits. Carrie tugged on his arm. "If you're looking for Mr. Nixon, he isn't among them. Only half of the presidents are even here!"

Just then an eight-year old boy ran up in front of them to stare up at President Kennedy's portrait. His father soon joined him. "Look Dad," the boy looked up to his father, "This president held the office only for a short time!"

His father put his arm around his son and looked up at the portrait, remembering. "Yes, son, he held the office for over a thousand days but he was one of the great ones. He gave us more to dream and believe in than any other President who had served a full term."

Modini watched the father and son pair move off. He agreed with the man. He remembered the way he felt when he lived through that time.

A lady's voice came over the loudspeaker for all the guests to step forward. The doors for the auditorium prepared to open. The presentation was ready to begin. Modini and Carrie joined the others and mingled with the rest of the group. But the auditorium filled before they could get inside and were politely told they would have to wait for the next show.

Carrie shrugged her shoulders, "Oh, well...so we'll wait."

Modini looked at her, admiring her patience, "You don't mind?"

She showed a bit of disappointment, but brightened. "No, I don't mind." They walked back to the bench again. "I thought you said we would be noticed if we sat here. Those two people who were just here, the father with his son-- I think we were invisible to them. They didn't notice us at all."

Modini wanted to cry and laugh, but settled with hugging her. "I want you to know something. By finding you, Carrie, my life has been changed. Your father, with God's help and direction, allowed me to find myself."

Carrie hugged him again, then lifted his head with her two hands. She stared at him a moment and then asked a question he never would have imagined coming from anyone, let alone her. "Uncle John, do you mind if I called you...father or dad, once in a while?"

Modini placed his two hands on her round face, the twinkle still in his eyes. "Carrie...you can call me that anytime-- all the time, whenever you want. And when you do, I'll know you're saying to me, I love you-- and that, my lady, will be enough of a gift to cherish for the rest of my life." He kissed her on the forehead. Then he noticed someone else standing near by. "Guess who's here...and it's about time, too!" he said to Carrie.

Carrie turned around and was overjoyed as she saw Catherine. She responded to the both of them with a big smile. "I thought I'd find you two here. The minute I walked in this place and saw all these Presidents. Where else would I find my favorite two people?"

Carrie gave Modini that, 'Okay, you were right' look, then announced to Catherine, "We have to wait for the next show!"

"Sorry I'm late," Catherine apologized. "I'm sure you had a great time so far without me! Can I at least get a hug from you guys?"

Modini and Carrie exchanged hugs and kisses with Catherine. Carrie came right out and told her, "You missed the best time, Catherine!"

Catherine laughed, "Well, I don't know about that. You haven't seen the best yet. I heard this attraction is something else! And I better not hear you've already visited the Haunted Mansion without me!"

Carrie played up to her serious side, "Oh, Catherine, no! Are you kidding? Father would never go inside that house without you! You should have been there when we just walked right past it to get here. He was sooo scared!"

Catherine raised her eyebrow and gave Modini an odd look, "Father?" she asked inquisitively.

Modini smiled, "A new nickname," he explained quickly. "Carrie was right. I was very scared of the mansion! She had the impossible job of trying to protect me until you arrived!"

Carrie winked at Catherine and flexed her arm muscle, "What can I tell you? These ghosts here in Disney World are real mean machines!"

The three of them waited in the mezzanine for the next call to enter the auditorium. Carrie acted as guide while they walked through and around the gallery of portraits. She introduced them to each President giving them the background of each one, showing off the extraordinary knowledge she had learned.

Catherine whispered into Modini's ear. "Have we created a monster or what?"

Modini just smiled. "What she possesses up here--" he tapped his head, "--means she'll be able to knock anyone dead as she goes through life. She, my girl....is the future!"

Catherine stopped Modini and kissed him, whispering to him, "I think I love you!"

Modini reacted coyly, "You only 'think?'"

Catherine looked at him and blushed. "You mean you *want* me to love you?"

Now it was Modini who was dumbfounded by her audaciousness. He hesitated, the reply failing to form in his mind. He wanted then and there to tell Catherine his true feelings, but Carrie grabbed for Catherine's hand and prevented him.

Carrie answered her question for him, "Yes, Catherine, he does." She gave Catherine a knowing look. "You always wanted to be my mother didn't you? Well, bright eyes, here is your chance!"

Catherine was amazed by Carrie's candid remarks. She gave a bewildered glance at the both of them. "Are you guys trying to propose to me?"

Carrie responded with a condescending, "Duh!" To her it was obvious.

Modini put an arm around the teenager. "Carrie, I think, is doing a good job in saying it all!"

Carrie, gave them the 'Oh brother!' look, then pushed them on, guiding them through the Gallery of Presidential Portraits.

"This is Ulysses S. Grant, our eighteenth President of the United States. Like previous Presidents, Washington and Jackson and our thirty-forth President, Dwight Eisenhower, they each held a position as military General in four crucial wars in the history of our country. Grant was Abraham Lincoln's top general in the Civil War between 1861 and 1865 and he was--"

While Carrie continued to speak, Modini took Catherine's hand and whispered into her ear,

"See what I mean!"

When they announced the next show, Carrie, Modini and Catherine finally entered the auditorium and sat down in their seats waiting for the presidential attraction to begin. Modini asked Catherine, "So how was your friend in Miami?"

She turned to him and whispered, "He died twenty minutes after I left him. Captain Corrigan was with me, and I thanked him for saving my life and Tom's. And then I told him what we had discovered about the letter. He was surprised and told me the family would always be blamed in public forums. But now we discover the CIA and the mob had a pact with each other, and that we should understand how someone like Lucky Luciano could have worked for the U.S. Government-- and how Carlos Marcello and all the Trafficantes and Giancanas of the world could be called in to work for the government. The CIA used them in their expertise as they, the Mafia, used the CIA. The CIA would always be immune, while someone, one of their own in the family would have to take the fall. Our power, he said was in tradeoffs and the world changed because of it in just three days. Those three days he said were Dallas, Memphis and Los Angeles! Then he laughed."

Modini repeated Catherine's last statement, "He laughed?"

"Yes," Catherine explained, "He thought it ironic that the Texas oilmen were afraid the Kennedys would monopolize the Presidency for the next thirty years once JFK was elected. He said George Bush, no matter what he actually says he is, is a Texan and when he leaves office, his son, now the Governor of the State, will be the Republican party's candidate in the new millennium...and the whole cycle will begin again. Texas will be running this country once and for all again!"

Modini turned to Catherine as the lights in the auditorium dim, "Except one thing, there is still one son who has more power than anyone to take the Presidency, if he decides to follow in his father's footsteps that is--"

The curtains opened, and the program started. A narrated film began, a presentation of the

American Revolution. It explained the heritage of America before the birth of George Washington, and continued to the death of Abraham Lincoln. They listened to the patriotic music, too, from 'The Star-Spangled Banner' to 'America the Beautiful.'

The song concluded, and the screen rose above and the curtains widened to show several live animated figures of the Presidents of the United States. They were introduced to the audience, and everyone was amazed by their lifelike motions. The spectators applauded them, from the first to the last. The latest Presidents were included: Nixon, Johnson, Ford, Reagan, Bush, and the now newly elected Bill Clinton.

While the presentation continued, a series of historical images and voices raced through Modini's mind. It was not like the sanitized version of history, but just the opposite. It was filled with the obscure facts, the little details he had grown up with and lived with all his life. And it centered around the president whom he had the greatest reverence and respect for, John F. Kennedy. Many different impressions flickered through his brain, and something triggered his memory of a conversation between reporters to Lee Harvey Oswald and Jack Ruby.

Oswald: "I really don't know what this is about...nobody has told me anything, except I'm accused of murdering a policeman... I know nothing more... I do request someone to come forward to give me legal assistance..."

Reporter: "Did you kill the President?"

Oswald: "I didn't shoot anybody, no sir!"

Then there was the image of Marina Oswald sitting with her two babies at Lee Harvey Oswald's funeral. Then the voice and presence of Jack Ruby took over in his mind:

Ruby: "These people who have so much to gain and have such an ulterior motive to put me in the position I'm in...will never let the true facts come aboveboard to the world..."

Reporter: "How high up are these people, Jack?"

Ruby: "As high as you can go!"

Second Reporter: "Are you saying this is a 'complete conspiracy' Mr. Ruby?"

Ruby: "I have been used for a purpose. I was framed into killing Oswald. If you knew the truth, you would be amazed!"

Modini tried to concentrate on the presentation. He and Catherine watched the spotlight in the auditorium focus on John F. Kennedy. The figure rose and spoke the words he was most associated with: *"And so my fellow Americans, ask not what your country can do for you...ask what you can do for your country!"*

Modini glanced over to Carrie, then envision her father, Karl Hunter, leaving the Catholic funeral of Father Conrad in 1982. Modini remembered Karl taking him aside and into his confidence, "I want you to know this, Jack...the public must never doubt the competence of the intelligence machinery it can never see. Anything that threatens this trust also threatens National Security!"

Modini focused his attention on Carrie, seated in the auditorium. She appeared mesmerized by the show. He put his hand on hers, turning now to glance at Catherine, then back to Kennedy's figure on stage. He envisioned John-John the day of his third birthday as his father's coffin passed by in procession, the same day of his father's funeral. John-John turned from his mother to salute his father again. Kennedy's words continued in Modini's mind:

> *"For in the final analysis...our most basic common link is that we all inhabit this planet. We all breathe the same air. We all cherish our children's future...and we are all mortal..."*

EPILOGUE

"That Magic Bullet"

By the thirtieth anniversary of John Kennedy's death in 1993, William Jefferson Clinton, was the first Democratic President in history to take sides concerning Kennedy's assassination. In fact, he was the first Democrat in history who took sides supporting the Kennedys. Clinton announced to the world he agreed with the Warren Commission findings and conclusions that Lee Harvey Oswald was the lone assassin. This announcement followed the release of Gerald Posner's book, <u>Case Closed</u>. Presently, the fate of Kennedy's death is sealed and any possibility of finding the complete the truth seems further out of reach.

Mr. Clinton's decision became a mystery for some people since many Warren Report Commissioners didn't believe their own findings. President Johnson, before his death, revealed his feelings of his own appointed Presidential investigation, going so far to hint that it wasn't true. He then said candidly what he thought of the investigation!

The media, as well, could be blamed for not investigating every lead to this crime, especially ones that appeared more than a coincidence. These included reporters who had no excuse to lie, like Mr. Dan Rather who presented a false account of the actual Zapruder film in 1963. Look where Mr. Rather is today. He is the number one anchor at CBS News, the job Roger Mudd should have been rewarded following Walter Cronkite's retirement. No matter what Grandpa Cronkite said about what he thought the truth was about President Kennedy's assassination, remember, Cronkite was a newsman who his colleagues compared to Edward R. Murrow--one who lunched and dined with the same politicians who have never told the truth since the day they decided to run for political office.

Walter Cronkite received the announcement of Kennedy's demise at the exact moment as we all did on live national tv in 1963. His investigation into the Kennedy Assassination in 1988 yielded no further information than what Mr. Posner revealed in his book, in which he establishing his computer analysis and gave the 'Magic Bullet' theory life again. The national coverage Mr. Posner's book received made many people in government want to agree with him and his conclusions, including even the President. And following the thirtieth anniversary of Kennedy's death, both Richard Nixon and John Connally's death made the national news, as well as the death of H.R. Haldeman.

Nixon, today more than ever, has been revealed as the real, but secretive person he really was, based on his own incriminating tapes, subpoenaed during the Watergate hearings that caused much controversy and his downfall. Presently, we have heard a part of all the tapes to date.

Meanwhile the death of Mr. John Connally became ironic because he died from a poisonous chemical reaction from the shrapnel still left inside his body from the bullet that hit him that day in Dallas in 1963. Arlan Spector, the originator of the 'magic bullet' theory, said these bullet fragments were from the same bullet, fueling Gerald Posner's claims in the media today.

Two people who are still live today know the truth about this bullet, as well as the real feelings and thoughts of Mr. Connally, the one-time Governor of Texas and President Kennedy's Secretary of Navy. These two people would also know Connally's real secrets and thoughts about what really happened on November 22, 1963. They were aware of what Johnson, the future President, had told Connally that day also the truth about Alexander Haig and E. Howard Hunt, the fact Gerald Ford knew five days following the Watergate break-in of what went down and who did what. Congressman Ford would take the office of the Vice-Presidency and then the Presidency of the United States under a shroud of deceit. This is why Mr. John Connally found it difficult to run for public office. Years after the Kennedy Assassination, Connally would soon become an ally to both Nixon and BeBe Rebozo. And so, following Watergate and Nixon's resignation, he switched political parties and ran as a Republican.

This first person I talk about will remain nameless. He knew of Connally's decision to switch parties. He was his best friend and campaign manager who helped him run on the Republican ticket for President in the 1980's. The second person to know his secrets was his wife, Nellie. She could have settled the issue of this 'Magic Bullet' once and for all by allowing the authorities to perform an autopsy on her husband to extract all shrapnel evidence from his body. But she didn't! Why?

If you really want the truth, it is still out there, alive and kicking. You'll have to get off your duff and search for it yourself or find a way to make changes within this country by eliminating in the next elections all those political candidates who have been there for the last twenty to forty years and who have refused to examine this matter. You must give serious thought to and research the candidates when you decide to vote for a representative and servant for your state in our country's capital. Remember, this is the same government that originally destroyed one of the true heritages of this country, the American Indian. Lincoln and Kennedy's assassination too, were conspired by factions from the South with coordinated help. Here, we have an assortment of conspiracy theories beginning with the first President ever assassinated-- Abraham Lincoln, the first Republican President of the United States. Politics has never been the same since the two party split.

Thinking back on all this, it is easy to see the two most interesting Presidents in this century were John Kennedy and Richard Nixon-- one for what he tried to accomplish, but wasn't allowed to, and the other for what he did accomplish. One would rise like a shooting star especially after his death, the other would fall from grace to the lowest point of hell you can imagine. One, who the Mafia thought they had in their pocket, the other one whose hand was constantly in their pocket.

Both men were at the peak of their popularity in this country in June, 1959, one year before they would announce their candidacy for the President of the United States.

Nixon and Kennedy, in a chance meeting, arrived at the Chicago Midway Airport simultaneously. A press conference, set up and ready for Nixon, had reporters in awe standing by as Nixon and Kennedy disembarked from their plane. J.F.K., appearing as a shy Senator, arrived with Jackie, his wife, while Nixon, the Vice-President, took the initiative before the cameras and expressed his feelings concerning what could be a sneak preview for the following year. Little did anyone know neither had announced their candidacy. The reason Kennedy was shy was that the press conference was for the Vice-President's arrival and Kennedy didn't want to rain on his parade. But Nixon asked the young Senator from Massachusetts to join him with the press. These two men who started as congressmen together in 1946, took opposite sides, one as Republican, the other as Democrat. They continued their growth in politics by opposing the other as Senators, and now it appeared as if they were both contenders for the heavyweight championship of the world, standing together on national television. Nixon took Kennedy's arm and allowed him to share in the Vice-President's limelight. Kennedy, the Pulitzer Prize-winning novelist of Profiles in Courage and Nixon, as the second term Vice-President, appeared gracious. Nixon went as far as suggesting to Kennedy and to the press he should be the Democratic front-runner for President in next years' elections.

This was an eerie but remarkable moment in history, a triumph for Nixon, because you saw a side of him never to be attributed as being false. You saw Nixon in the raw for the first and perhaps last time as the man he could have been. Here he was, before the people, generous, personable, aggressive, and charming, showing himself up against a man he hoped one day he could be friends with. Next time these two men met together in public were on national television a year and half later in the fall of 1960 on the first national televised Presidential debate.

Most people thought the sweating Vice-President Nixon opposite the handsome and tanned John Kennedy was judged unfairly by his appearance. When it appeared Nixon lost the debate, and

717

followed through by losing the presidential election, everyone speculated he was through with politics. But he, too, one day would be President, no matter what friction happened between Kennedy and Nixon. These two men, like it or not, made a difference, showing different sides of the same coin. You could say their story was a bit like <u>The Prince and the Pauper</u>, except here, the Pauper wanted to be the Prince so bad he forgot to save the Monarchy, the nation, and its people. Instead, Nixon screwed up. Eventually, he was caught and ostracized, again becoming the ogre the media had made him out to be. The word shame branded him for the rest of his life like the scarlet letter worn by Hester Prynne. And so for the rest of his life, until his death, Nixon was branded with the nickname known as 'Tricky Dick!' It was unfortunate because this was a President who never allowed the public to get to know him.

The one thing Nixon never did was discuss Kennedy's assassination in public, nor any of the incidents on the day of November 22, 1963. Why? Because it was too much of a tragedy for him to think about or bring up, or was it because it was so painful to think about? He knew the reasons he was in both Houston and Dallas on that day, and the fact his personal colleagues and friends were there too, like J. Edgar Hoover. FBI Director Hoover was the first to break the news to the President's brother, Bobby. General Charles Cabell the ex-CIA Deputy Director was also there whose secret relationship with Nixon began in the mid-fifties with their covert assassination plots-- the participation of the failed coup, of the Bay of Pigs in Cuba whose brother, Earle Cabell, was the Mayor of Dallas and in charge of fixing the route of the Presidential motorcade.

Then there were Nixon's Watergate boys, the 'plumbers' from the CIA, E. Howard Hunt and Frank Sturgis, the latter connected to Charles Nicoletti who also was in Dallas that day. Nicoletti was the closest aide to Sam Giancana out of Chicago. And don't forget Giancana's man in Dallas was Jack Ruby or Rubinstein, known, like J. Edgar Hoover, to both Presidents Nixon and Johnson. And last, there were those Texan oil men, and one specifically who gained the most from these people publicly-- Nixon's own protege, George Herbert Walker Bush. Like the character of Norman Bates in the movie *Psycho*, this sweet old wimp of a man today gives us the impression he

718

wouldn't or couldn't even hurt a fly!

This group of human beings was connected that day either by being in Dallas or Houston within the first twenty-four-hour period leading up to the Kennedy assassination. The public were unaware of the people I speak of here until after the Watergate break-in almost ten years later, except for Hoover and Nixon, but by then Hoover was dead and Nixon was in his second term as President. If Hoover were still alive and still heading the FBI, I believe there never would have been a Watergate, nor the trail of evidence leading from it to Dealey Plaza. The character of John Modini did not believe in coincidences. To you who may or may not be skeptical, this must seem like quite a coincidence.

Let's explore another trail, this time looking closer at the 'Magic Bullet' theory. This shall not be Arlen Spector's trail, nor his theories. Remember, this was a theory manufactured to excuse the Warren Report's hidden mistakes. To those of you who have heard it over and over all these years, it seems to have become fact in your minds to believe this actually did happen that way. Your excuse was you believed in your own government like any American should, right? But before you can understand this odd theory, you have to know the story where this bullet actually came from.

The trail started with the Mannlicher Carcano rifle-- the Italian bolt-action rifle Oswald was alleged to have or owned. Remember, it's under the name Hidell, a name Oswald might or might not have used to order it, depending whose truth you believe. If it were Oswald's rifle, the "Magic bullet" did come from it, but was not necessarily fired from it. There could have been a connection here. The reason I say 'not necessarily' fired is that the bullet is in such a pristine condition it was most likely not fired, not into a pillow, let alone a rack of jello, and it is the only bullet used to connect Kennedy's assassination to Hidell--the name Oswald was supposed to be using.

Anyone would be suspicious on this fact alone, especially if I were a Gerald Ford or an Allen Dulles on the Warren Commission. But then again today, most of the population in America believed O.J. Simpson guilty of murdering his wife, Nicolle, and her friend, Ron Goldman, except twelve members of a jury. Another example has many people believing a six-year old girl was murdered by a perverted assailant who may be a possible member of the family in a small town in Colorado. This doesn't mean she was, but the big mystery that angered the people was why, at the beginning of the investigation, didn't the police department in the small town alert the public there was a killer loose. And why, as the years pass after finding her tiny body in the basement that Christmas morning, is the killer is still walking free?

For the most of us we see what the investigators don't see, that these killers are right in front of their faces-- so conveniently in front of them. Like the people the Warren Commission ignored and refused to interview. Can we as human beings believe a sports figure and hero would ever murder anyone, let alone his wife, or someone within a billionaire's family could molest and strangle their six-year old little girl, or, even a part of our government needed to be covered up! Why do we believe this, or why can't we?

Why do those who accept the death penalty of a Timothy McVeigh for taking part in the Oklahoma bombing, which killed 168 people and injuring countless others, when he was supposedly questioning the actions of Janet Reno? It was her order as the Attorney General to go in and murder religious fanatics in Waco, Texas, which resulted in the deaths again of many children as the Oklahoma incident. You can't say either was an accident since both went through with their intentions without thinking of the consequences. In Waco, there might have been a large arsenal inside that compound to threaten the people outside, but there still was not enough humans to start a war with the U.S. government no matter how you look at it. The public again was witness to this daily on national television as they were with the Ruby Ridge incident in Idaho. This doesn't mean we should take up arms and shoot our public officials. A gun is never an answer to the problem-- but that goes for our law enforcement authorities as well.

Our main problem is that people watch, but what they watch may not be the same as what they are told by the media or the government. Again, people are not stupid individually. They are beginning to see the lies told them between the words. I cite an example of the TWA 800 flight. There were countless witnesses on the ground and in the air including three airline pilots that saw a streak of light in that area, resembling the passage of a missile shot into the air. A respected member of the media, Pierre Salinger who had been John Kennedy's Press Secretary, shared proof it was a missile that was launched from a Naval submarine. Still the government told a different story through the media and all those witnesses were discounted. Yes, you can take Salinger with a grain of salt, but like in the JonBenet Ramsey case, years have slid by with no answered questions.

The government now blames the TWA flight explosion on TWA themselves. They announced the unfueled plane, before the flight, had a heat problem within the empty fuel tank that forced a fuel combustion to explode within minutes in midair after takeoff.

If the government said there was no terrorism connected to flight 800, there probably wasn't. But they omit mentioning the explosion might have been the result of friendly fire from the land or sea. It is easier to blame its destruction on a malfunction within the airliner than say it was a military error. I'm sure no intelligent airline pilot would ever fly a plane to endanger his passengers, let alone his own life.

What it comes down to is believing the theory of what happened, and that's why the witnesses, including Salinger, are sticking to their own beliefs. This brings us back to the theory of the 'Magic Bullet' based on one man's word that began as theory and now grew to be accepted fact.

Many people have already forgotten about all the stories I mentioned so far. You remember them because I reminded you of past events. Like the 'Magic Bullet,' they just won't go away. Still, there is a good chance people will forget about it once they finish my story. God gave us the gift to forget bad things, but the memory of certain events will continue to haunt us because many people are not satisfied with the final verdict of what others told us was their version of the truth.

So where did the theory of the Magic Bullet first get started. It began with the Mannlicher Carcano rifle. At the start of the investigation of Kennedy's murder on November 22, 1963, after the authorities had arrested Oswald and a German Mauser was found in the Texas School Book Depository, the weapon suddenly became an Italian Mannlicher Carcano rifle.

The rifle's history changed constantly throughout the following twenty-four hours and then again months later during the inquiries of the Warren Commission. This meant those involved lied from the very beginning to build the case linking Oswald to the trail of this bullet. And in the end, they made it fit their scenario like a glove.

It was at Parkland Hospital that either a Secret Service or FBI agent, reported to have found a bullet on President Kennedy's gurney. It was sent to Washington to Bethesda Hospital to match the hole in Kennedy's back during the autopsy-- which conveniently stopped any further investigation of that wound. There in the autopsy room it was determined that this was the bullet that caused the President's back wound.

After Kennedy was buried in Arlington cemetery, the Commission, in its investigation, found a discrepancy in this bullet. The government witness who discovered the bullet came to the hearings and stated he found the bullet on Governor Connally's stretcher after all.

Since the Warren Commission decided from the start that only three bullets were fired from the rifle at the School Book Depository and that Lee Harvey Oswald was the lone gunman, they now had some explaining to do. You can imagine the controversy when the Zapruder film depicting the actual killing of the President was revealed to the public by Jim Garrison during the trial of Clay Shaw. Careful analysis of the Zapruder film established the assassination of Kennedy occurred in a 5.6 second time frame. If only three bullets were fired, the Warren Commission had a problem. They claimed one of the bullets was the fatal head wound. They also had evidence one bullet missed the presidential motorcade, struck the curb, and nicked a bystander, Jim Tague, standing by the Triple Underpass. This left only one bullet to account for all seven wounds in Kennedy and Connally. This bullet, after smashing through flesh and shattering bone, supposedly emerged in pristine condition, later to be discovered on a stretcher in Parkland Memorial Hospital.

Since the single bullet (the magic bullet) explanation is the pivotal point of the Warren Report describing how Oswald acted as the lone assassin, if the Commission admitted there was a fourth bullet, it would be acknowledging there was *another* gunman in Dallas. And admitting there was another gunman meant admitting there was a conspiracy! Instead of admitting a conspiracy or investigating further, the Commissioners stuck to the theory that this one bullet did severe damage and remained in immaculate condition.

This explanation now gave credence to why Arlen Spector's theory became a reality. It all makes sense now-- as long as you believe the nonsense of Spector's 'Magic Bullet' causing seven wounds and still remaining in perfect shape.

Are you now semi-satisfied at least why this theory is so controversial? For thirty years everyone was satisfied with it, otherwise, why would these honest men investigating the crime of the century lie to us? Except it doesn't stop here. Months after the Warren Commission published their report, upset witnesses started to come forward saying their testimonies were changed or misinterpreted. One of these people who came forward was a Parkland Hospital attendant who said this 'Magic Bullet' found there was not on either Kennedy's or Connally's gurneys, that he had given it to a doctor who then gave it to a Secret Service agent who then pocketed it. He never heard about this bullet again until after the report was released to the public in the fall of 1964.

The bullet was found on an unattended gurney some might have thought was President Kennedy's. The attendant said it was discovered on a gurney used earlier by a man brought in thirty minutes before those shots were fired in Dealey Plaza. There was an ambulance near Dealey Plaza when a call came in minutes before the arrival of the motorcade. People said the man had an epilepsy fit in the middle of Dealey Plaza. The ambulance, which now would not be there for either Kennedy or Connally, took this unidentified man to Parkland Hospital. Once there, he was placed on a gurney and attended to but disappeared during the disorder and commotion from the arrival of the entire motorcade carrying both Kennedy and Connally. He was never seen again. It was on this man's gurney this pristine bullet, soon became known as the 'Magic Bullet,' had its original resting place.

It is the same infamous bullet Connally denied to his dying day that could not have made that trip through him nor the President as the Warren Commission states. If that is true, it meant

Connally never did believe in the Warren Commission report, as stated by the Mark Lanes and Jim Garrisons of the world all along. And that is why Nellie, his wife, refused to allow an autopsy on her husband, because she also was present as a witness in the presidencial car and knows the truth.

Since 1995, President Clinton had sought more power for the CIA. When a former CIA director was missing then found mysteriously drowned in a fishing expedition on the Colorado River, an expedition he attended alone. Pun intended here-- this sounds like a fishy story to me, especially if this was supposedly a suicide since the man in question was William Colby, an especially good swimmer. This is the same Colby who was the CIA director during the Nixon administration. And Nixon had many CIA directors during his administration, more than any President in history, beginning with Richard Helms. Colby was the director who opened his big mouth a bit too much at the Rockefeller Hearings in 1975 and was then fired by Gerald Ford and replaced by George Bush.

Also odd, is the fact another CIA official had also drowned here, before Colby, on the same Colorado River. Was this a dumping ground for suicidal, accidental prone CIA officials? Life does go on as they say, but again, we still wonder. As I stated earlier, you will forget what I have written in another week or two. Government officials including National Security, count on this, for the average person, to forget. So, as I said, life goes on!

Another Gerald Posner book recently published, stated why James Earl Ray killed Martin Luther King Jr. Within the past few years, Ray's rifle had finally been tested. The tests revealed the bullets do not match the rifle that allegedly shot Mr. King. King's own wife and family do not believe Ray was the assassin. They were working to get his release before his recent death.

Surprisingly, an investigation is now in the works concerning Lt. Commander William Pitzer's suicide at Bethesda Naval Hospital in Maryland on October twenty-ninth, 1966. The Freedom of Information Act showed there were contradictions in the autopsy report concerning how many bullets actually entered Mr. Pitzer's head, making it a homicide. Like the Kennedy assassination, it is more than likely another gunman was involved. If you have any information concerning Mr. Pitzer's death, you could be helping to solve not only one but possibly two assassinations, the other being the President of the United States. There is a connection! It was a connection that James Garrison the District Attorney could have exposed at the time of the Clay Shaw trial, since Mr. Pitzer was discovered on Garrisons witness list, which soon became his death list.

After I wrote this novel and it was in the editing stage, several prominent people have died or passed away, including John F. Kennedy Jr, whom I have dedicated this book to along with his sister Caroline. May God bless him and may Caroline continue as the beacon of the Kennedy name for both her father and mother, and now her brother?

David Powers, one of JFK's closest friends and aids in the white house, also passed away. His recently discovered motion picture camera and reel of film show Powers had photographed Kennedy's assassination on that day in Dallas. Powers was in the secret service car that followed behind the President's car. Powers stated in his will that no one was ever to view this shocking film.

Judith Campbell Exner, also passed away because of cancer. Newly discovered papers from Warren Commissioners have been released with half the Commission dismissing the findings. The inquiry of JonBenet Ramsey's death is in its fourth year and still is unresolved. And the incident at Waco is still undergoing a new investigation. A video tape shows inflammable tear gas canisters were launched the day of the fire after repeated denials by the FBI. What type of conspiracy will they find out about this apocalypse? Again the government is hiding something.

And the last item to report, the Chairman of the Board, Frank Sinatra died on the fourteenth of May, 1998. He was the greatest entertainer of the century-- period!

Before closing and leaving the reader to his own opinions, let me say it is natural for everyone to be concerned with their own problems. But it is important not to forget the children of this world. They must be taught the truth of what happened and guided from the lies and cover ups. It should be the goal of every one of us to concentrate on how to raise our own kids to be bright, respectful and honorable human beings, able to judge what is right and what is wrong. Then when this new generation of children becomes adults, they will be instilled within them a sense of responsibility and the knowledge to fight the hypocrisy of those attempting to deceive them. And those in our own government should be the first to right the wrong and be symbols and examples to our young. Truth will always rule in the end! Remember this!

God bless you all.

THE END

AFTERMATH : 10 Years Later

If you are a fan of the Colbert Report then you are familiar with his motto, "Truthiness." This is not a word, but this is the identification of Mark Fuhrman's book, *A Simple Act of Murder*. In other words, Stephen Colbert's definition of "Truthiness" is what you want the facts to be opposed to what the facts really are—what feels like the right answer as opposed to what reality supports. Along with Gerald Posner and his book, *Case Closed*, and the man responsible for painting the man the lone assassin, Warren commissioner, future Vice-President and President of the United States, Gerald Ford who just so happened to have lied in his own above confirmations, all agree it was Lee Harvey Oswald who assassinated the 35th President of the United States. All three, Colbert, Posner, and Ford (who died as this book went to press) agree that Oswald is a chronic liar, which makes me think of Jon Lovit's character from his "*Saturday Nite Live*" days. Everything that Oswald spoke of or said was contradicted or a lie. This means everyone else was telling the truth, which has to make Oswald no doubt, guilty! This was always the plan to paint Oswald who died 48 hours later by an assassin's bullet himself to the hour of John F. Kennedy's assassination in Dallas on that fateful day in November 22, 1963, forty-three years ago.

The big question should be why did Lee Harvey Oswald constantly lie about everything, knowing he would be contradicted by many witnesses? He did not know that he would be dead in 48 hours. This is just one of the reasons I dove into the mind of Oswald and wrote my novel entitled: *America the Beautiful* (now titled *America's Deceit*). This is a book Mark Fuhrman should have read, especially after five interviews with me on Fuhrman's radio show. If he had, I think he would have taken a different course or direction in the clues I incorporated, hidden within almost every chapter pointing to who really killed JFK. There are 42 chapters in my book. Instead,

Fuhrman in his book chose to ignore any evidence that has come forth in the last 40 years. He plays it safe really, with no controversy whatsoever, in his nonfiction book, but feels like fiction after reading two hundred or so pages, complete with colored pictures that I believe he drew himself. He details the forensic case and autopsy evidence based on the same conclusions of "Truthiness" as the four commissions who from, 1963-64 to 1976-79, had semi-completed already. Although, unlike, Posner, Ford, and Arlen Specter, Fuhrman does not believe in the "Magic Bullet Theory." Duh! This is the only thing that Fuhrman makes sense on? But why believe still that Oswald was the sole assassin, when this is really all the Warren Commission had, going in to convict him?

Three of four of the commissions and their members are mentioned in Fuhrman's book, but quite ironically he doesn't discuss or mention the third commission, the Church Senate hearings named after Idaho's state Senator, Frank Church. This important commission was the turning point in all the investigations, concerning the murder of our 35th President. There were more unanswered questions then were answered and hidden agendas, lies and more deaths of potential witnesses that were suddenly revealed to the public. Some of the biggest lies came from a future President, George W. Bush's father, H.W.! How does he fit in the picture? Well, how does one all of a sudden become the Director of the CIA in Ford's administration. And what were his credentials, other than being the Chairman of the Republican Convention, during the Watergate scandal of 1972 and President Nixon's former Ambassador of China? Why did he muster all this attention? Soon, you will see why, as the dots become connected.

The four commissions in order, beginning with the Warren Commission, 1963-64, headed by Chief Justice, Earl Warren, all had close ties to Richard Nixon. In fact, most the committee members had ties with this retired former Vice-President. With the exception of two members, Congressman Hale Boggs and Senator Richard Russell, both were threatened by the now, newly sworn in President, Lyndon Baines Johnson who played the fear card by announcing that the Russians were behind Kennedy's assassination, giving us the people the face of the enemy, Lee Harvey Oswald. Johnson promoted the idea right out of a spy thriller that the Russians and the KGB sent Oswald back to the United States, once a defector, now programmed as a Manchurian Candidate to assassinate the President, hence, the banning of the movie of the same name for the next 25 years. Does this sound familiar? Does 9/11 ring any bells? Incidentally, the bells are still ringing if you haven't noticed. This fear tactic to scare us silly, would soon die down and a new scenario would then happen. "**Operation Northwoods**" is a good example. Unclassified documents show that those in our government were considering using fake terror attacks on U.S. citizens. Kennedy debunked it, Johnson and Nixon considered it and Ford hired those back who thought of it, although Kennedy had demoted them on his watch. Let's try this scenario, as Johnson keeps us above board: Castro and his regime did it. No! Well, then how about this, the Cubans did it in retaliation for the Bay of Pigs. It goes on and on, especially after the commissioners get wind of Oswald being an F.B.I. informant within the first two weeks in January of 1964. Johnson, meanwhile, was approached by someone within his secret fraternity who is concerned with our new President. Lyndon seems nervous about the fact there are many people out here who believe that this former Vice-President somehow helped himself in getting this new position he suddenly inherited, following the demise of his predecessor. I mean, a lot of people feel this, even today, including after the fall of the U.S.S.R. in 1989 records show from the KGB that their leaders felt Johnson was involved, too.

This someone who apparently had great influence over Lyndon Johnson, told him to stop all investigations within the House and the Senate into JFK's murder. The Dallas Police Department suddenly is told to close their internal investigation. Now Richard Nixon enters secretly, no longer in government but still is the head of the Republican Party. Johnson is told, by again, this PERSON to ask the Republican leader to help him form the Warren Commission. Then Nixon's people enter, including House Speaker, Gerald Ford who represents J. Edgar Hoover, the head of the F.B.I. and Allen Dulles, the former head of the CIA. who was fired by Kennedy following the Bay of Pigs fiasco. How does Dulles rate to investigate the man who, we find out 12 years later during the Rockefeller commission, was taken out of Central Intelligence along with two others in 1961, of which we were falsely told that they resigned.

J. Lee Rankin became Head Counsel, but it is Nixon's personal attorney, David Belin who holds court by playing head games and shell games with authorities and eyewitnesses. In the end, both Democrats, Russell and Boggs, refuse to sign off on the Warren Commission. With another member of the commission, John Sherman Cooper, the three disagreed with Arlen Specter's "Magic Bullet Theory." Russell and Boggs do not believe Oswald did it alone, but Johnson wants the Warren Commission to come out with their reports months before the 1964 election—hence Mark Lane's book, *Rush to Judgment*. This was a book, Mark Fuhrman also should have read before embarking on his own. A deal was made with Johnson, under the influence of Gerald Ford and Specter as they convinced the two opponents that they would assure them the Warren Report would read in all aspects to Oswald's guilt: alleged, and a possibility of his involvement. In the end, Johnson had lied to his fellow Democrats as did Ford and Specter. The changes were never made, and Boggs and Russell never forgave the now newly elected President. Boggs would die in a mysterious plane crash and Russell gave life to the word "conspiracy" to Jim Garrison, the District Attorney of New Orleans who would take this conspiracy of Kennedy's assassination to trial in the late 1960's.

Let me tell you a story, one that most of you have never heard, and I promise you it is one that the Bush administration does not want you to know. Once upon a time, on a Halloween eve, 40 years ago in October of 1966, a strange suicide happened in the Bethesda Naval Hospital. Now, Fuhrman actually lists the people who were present in the Autopsy room in his book, where Kennedy was taken after flying his body back from Dallas. It was this hospital where Jackie Kennedy wanted her husband taken since her husband was a naval officer during WWII. In 1963 there were a few dozen people that would enter this room, including Generals, Marine guards and casket carriers, doctors, nurses, lab techs, as well as photo techs, those representing the Kennedy family, and Bobby Kennedy, the Attorney General, and more. Fuhrman lists every man but one, I'm not blaming Mark, but if he had read my book, I'd be very curious why this person's name was missing from participating in the room during the autopsy. Though, again, Fuhrman's concern was forensic evidence, but this alone does not make a case.

In my book, I take you to the Suicide on that Halloween eve in 1966; this gentleman who died in Bethesda was Lt. Commander William B. Pitzer, Head of the Photography Unit. I wrote that his death was not a suicide, but a murder, and I believe there were others, including his colleagues, family, friends and those in government who felt the same. It was this premise that prompt, this author to begin what has now become, my novel, *America the Beautiful*, which came out the day before 9/11, of 2001. I actually wrote the ending of my book two weeks prior to President Clinton's reelection, in 1996. I had no intention to make it into a book, what was then just a disk on the worldwide internet, in book form, but something strange happened. People were actually reading the first seven chapters I allowed on the internet that premiered in early March of the winter of 1997. Still by 1998, no one ever thought that the newly elected Governor of Texas,

George W. Bush, would ever be considered a candidate for President of the U.S. except me. By the November elections, Jeb Bush the younger brother of W. and the son of H.W. finally took the Florida governorship on his second try. It was now time to experiment with the two Bush brothers that papa Bush's cronies, such as James Baker, Dick Cheney, Dr. Henry Kissinger, and George Schultz, came together to see what choice between the two of them would make as a presidential candidate in 2000. I didn't know this at the time, but I tell you in my novel that I wrote back in October of 1996 which one of the two makes it. Jeb was never on my mind. How did I know? You are probably wondering how this relates to the above suicide/murder event. Well, it's like this, like the above, I know, Vincent Foster's death was not a suicide either; there is always a connection, and once the dots start connecting to show a much grander picture you will never know the truth. This is both Posner and Fuhrman's problem in thinking Kennedy's death was a simple act. Case closed! It wasn't. If it were true, there would never have been four commissions formed and countless conspiracy theorists out here trying to convince you differently. Thank God, that some of these people are still alive.

The death of William Pitzer took on a life of it's own, in what would be one of the biggest coverups by our own government since that day in Dallas. And both, like those dots, they are connected. The Kennedy assassination was simple in the way it was covered-up. How? Because you and I, we the people allowed it to happen! My book was suddenly removed from the internet within six months by my friend, the frightened owner of the web site, once he became a subject of investigation. Meanwhile, another incident happened early in 1998. Two gentlemen from Rochester, New York, were trying to contact me, but lost me once my book was taken off the internet. It was almost a year before I got word they had been trying to find me. I then finally contacted them, and now the truth can be told.

These two gentlemen began an investigation on the death of Lt. Commander. William B. Pitzer based upon the release of his files that were listed as top secret within the government archives now released through the Freedom of Information Act. Allan R. J. Eaglesham and R. Robin Palmer published their findings and evidence in January of 1998. They supplied their materials of what they wanted me to see, as well as, the 140-plus pages of FBI documents and the informal Board of Investigation Report to: Ms. Janet Reno, U.S. Attorney General; Mr. J.J. Curran, Jr., Attorney General of the State of Maryland; Captain J.F. Caffrey, Commanding Officer, Naval School of Health Sciences, Bethesda; The New York Times; The Washington Post, The Ithaca

Journal. That was back then, and still today I haven't seen any of the above report on the subject. It was Allan who contacted me and told me it was not their intent to connect any of their investigation to JFK, but it did, it led them to me and my book. They never got to read the rest of my book nor anyone else for that matter then. They would have found out; their conclusions were also mine.

Pitzer's death is linked to Kennedy's Autopsy and why you will never see the photos, film and the original reports connected to it. This is why Posner, Fuhrman and the expert doctors who testified at those four commissions, will never see the light of day concerning what is real, doctored, forged, drawn and stolen, beginning in Dallas at Parkland Hospital, with six doctors who had witnessed our President first hand, minutes after his assassination. It was by gunpoint to the head their jurisdiction was taken away from them by the United States Secret Service, the President's body taken sometime around 2:00 pm and brought to Washington after 7:30 pm Eastern time, and brought to Washington where the transfer of the body of evidence would end in Bethesda, for what Commander J.J. Humes thought was a second Autopsy. So why did he think this and what is the chain of evidence and responsibility of JFK's body between the time it left Parkland and the Dallas airport until it reached its destination at Bethesda, Maryland? Humes, found out the next morning when he called Parkland, in Dallas, that no doctor had done an autopsy. He then burned the original Autopsy report in his fireplace thinking someone had done something to the President's body prior to Bethesda. He had to draw a new one from memory that day, knowing it to be needed for any upcoming inquest.

Earl Warren would request it, to connect Oswald and his no longer alleged rifle, the Italian Mannlicher-Carcano, not a German Mauser that suddenly disappeared. Mark Fuhrman remarks in his book that even police officers can mistake a Mannlicher for a 7.65 Mauser, although three men from the Sheriff's Department and two from the Dallas Police Department witnessed it as a German Mauser, not the Italian Carcano. Seymour Weitzman and Eugene Boone did an affidavit and a Notary public on the gun to legally authenticate it. Will Fritz, Luke Mooney and Dallas Police Officer, Roger Craig who ran to the Grassy Knoll, after the shooting, would witness 15 minutes later, as an expert witness, a 7.65 German Mauser found on the sixth floor of the School Book Depository. Some of these Officers would retract their statements and identification of the rifle under pressure from the Warren Commission and their own department Heads, but Craig would refuse to change his mind since he had handled the gun himself and was an expert on both types of rifles. The Warren Commission decided not to take Craig's statement, which would mean a conspiracy, since at least two men would have been involved. Craig was later fired from the Dallas Police force. He would also be shot at while going to testify for Jim Garrison at the trial of Clay Shaw, alias 'Clay Bertram.' Someone then drove him off a mountain road in his car. He survived, but then was shot again in Waxahachie, Texas, the following year. If only Mark Fuhrman can relate to this. In 1975, as the Rockefeller Commission was beginning to take the public stage, Roger Craig would survive another attempt on his life as his car exploded after starting it in his garage. In May of 1975, Craig was found dead. It was later decided he had died because of self-inflicted gunshot wounds to the head, suicide— you know, like William Pitzer!

In Pitzer's case, both Eaglesham and Palmer found there were three investigations that had taken place following Pitzer's death:

(1) by the FBI; (2) the Naval Investigative Service, now known as NCIS; and (3) by an NNMC Informal Board of Investigation. They would all reach the same conclusions: the wound to Lt. Commander. Pitzer's head was self-inflicted. Pitzer's wife and family to this day, still exhibit doubt that suicide was the true cause of death. His wife and children never got to see his body, nor able to have any ceremonial burial.

Apparently, the three entities above never read each others report, other than agreeing on suicide, neither report was consistent with the other. The body of Pitzer was on the floor in one report, and it was questionable he was sitting behind his desk in another. Bullets, and this is plural, indicated two different guns were used, though a .38 caliber Smith and Wesson revolver was found near the body, there is nothing in any of the above reports that states that Pitzer's fingerprints were on the revolver, the spent cartridge, the live round, or on the blank cartridge. There were fourteen latent prints lifted from two chairs and three beer cans at the scene, none of those fingerprints matched those of Lt. Commander. Pitzer. In one report he was listed as "Victim," instead of "Deceased" in the other reports. A mysterious boot print, not linked to Pitzer, was photographed by the FBI for further study, but forgotten. This print found on one of the note pages from his desk, now on the floor, described as a style used by the Goodyear Rubber Company. Since the Military commission their uniforms and footgear from such companies, my guess is, at the time, this print could have come from someone in the Green Berets. Though Kennedy started the Green Berets during his administration, he sent the first group to Vietnam as advisers. Among them was my cousin who spent five terms there, 1961-62 through 1971-72 training the Vietnamese forces. His father, my uncle, was at the Pentagon during the Kennedy administration. The Green Berets were trained to become lethal weapons, but by 1966, like the CIA using the Mafia, they were commissioning particular Green Berets to be assassins. There is so much more to discuss here concerning the Pitzer case, it would boggle your mind, if it hasn't already. My book takes you into more areas of Pitzer's case. Both Eaglesham and Palmer have a case for those in charge in our government to reopen Pitzer's death that the physical evidence is inconsistent with suicide and indicates homicide. A homicide that has been covered-up big time to hide the fact that he would retire in two months, and had in his possession photographs and slides of John F. Kennedy on arrival at Bethesda Naval Hospital morgue. Most importantly he had in his possession a 16 millimeter film of the autopsy procedures, all of which disappeared following Pitzer's mysterious death. If there is no connection, then why did the U.S. Navy and the FBI cover up such an incident? Why?

Pitzer's obituary was hidden in the newspaper and did not appear for several days. By the end of the following week, on the 2nd day of November, something strange happened. This happened before any mention of Pitzer's death, let alone who he was, or what he possessed. But this day, the front pages of the newspapers across the country began the next phase of the coverup of JFK's assassination. This was to seal it completely as the headline's read: "Kennedy Autopsy Photos to be Preserved, in Secret" Basically, the Kennedy family was laying down the rules of certain photographs and X-rays of the late President that would be given to the National Archives under conditions which prevent the public from seeing them for over a generation. The pictures were not even seen by members of the Warren Commission which investigated the assassination, and both pathologists who conducted the autopsy, James J. Humes and J. Thornton Boswell, authenticated the pictures. Consent from the Kennedy family would be available to those officials in government who might reopen another investigation.

Then on the 5th day of November, 1966, President Johnson had other ideas and announced in the newspapers that any assassination probe on Kennedy will not be reopened! No one will ever see any photos or X-rays of Kennedy ever, and that Kennedy's brain was given to members of the Kennedy family. Johnson then commented that he was satisfied with the Warren Commission and this was the final word. Bobby Kennedy never did receive his brother's brain to the day he died in 1968, two years later. The brain of Kennedy somehow disappeared following the death of William B. Pitzer, as well as all his material. It just vanished!

On the same front page of Johnson's above announcement, November 5th, Richard

Nixon's name appeared for the first time in years. A coincidence? Nixon lashed out on Johnson as Johnson wanted to end the war in Vietnam and Nixon doesn't. By the 7th of November, Nixon is now in the Limelight and takes up the front page of the newspaper and begins anew. He is now on his way to establish himself for the election of '68. This is the same man who announced his retirement from the government, after losing both the Governorship and Senatorial races in the state of California, to the world and press in 1962, stating, "You don't have Richard Nixon to kick around anymore!" Richard Nixon, or should I say, "Tricky Dick," became his nickname, throughout the 50's and 60's. Nixon was out on the campaign trail helping the Republican Party, particularly what I call the "Four Musketeers," four members of the Republican party who were very close together that would go on to further Nixon's career by putting him in the White House in 1969. These four were Gerald Ford, House Speaker, Robert Dole; and Donald Rumsfeld, a first timer, in the race for Congress. All three would win, but the fourth musketeer was running in his second outing for a Senate seat from Texas. George H.W. Bush would lose in his first try in 1964 and again here in 1966. For some reason, Nixon was pushing this man. Why?

Nixon, while running for the presidency in 1968, switched this musketeer to run instead for Congress. Bush won, and this was at the same time that his oldest son, George W. Bush, was dodging the Vietnam draft, later getting on top of the list for the National Guard when his father took over a seat in the House of Representatives from the state of Texas. The "Four Musketeers" would join Nixon in his first term in the White House. Bush Sr. would become Nixon's Ambassador to China, but soon Dole bales out and leaves the Nixon camp in 1970. Dole forms his own camp within the Republican Party, as does former Democrat, Ronald Reagan. Both Reagan and Dole separate themselves from the Nixon Party. Dole doesn't give any reasons for his departure from Nixon except for the controversy concerning the direction of the Vietnam War and Nixon's persistence in his paranoia with Ted Kennedy. This was also the time of the Ellsberg office break in and the discovery of the Pentagon papers. Never the less, Dole was replaced, by a suggestion from Donald Rumsfeld that his old buddy, would be perfect as the fourth and final replacement musketeer, this man would be none other than, Dick Cheney.

Watergate began with a simple call from Howard Hughes to Richard Nixon about some information he knew that "Tricky Dick," would just love to get his hands on. This information went back to when Nixon was running against JFK back in 1960, information, that John Kennedy stopped his father, Joseph from using to destroy Nixon's career at the time. How did Mr. Hughes know this and why did Dick believe him? Very simple, just like the cover up of Pitzer's death and both Bobby and John F. Kennedy's assassinations, the coverup of Watergate that toppled a Presidency was always maneuvered by those in high places. But this time they were caught and some were brought to justice and some scattered, running for their lives, like the four musketeers, only to return when the coast was clear. The path was cleared all right, by secretly setting up Vice-President Spiro Agnew in a scandal that brought in Gerald Ford to replace him. Soon, the other three would join him once Nixon was taken out of office, a first in the history of the Presidency without actually assassinating a man— as long as the former President kept his mouth shut!

In June of 1968 Howard Hughes had contributed monies to almost every candidate running for the Presidency. He would eventually give Richard Nixon, in secret, $100,000 dollars prior to the election. Although Howard Hughes was not a fan of the former Vice-President, it looked like Nixon would take office as election time approached and Mr. Hughes wanted, like certain Mafia heads, to have the leader of the free world in their pockets. Hughes always wanted to be three steps ahead of his enemies. In 1956, he loaned quite a few thousand of dollars to Nixon's brother and it became quite a scandal, come the 1960 bid for the presidency. By 1968, Nixon had even bigger forces to contend with, mainly Robert Kennedy who now was a higher threat to the Presidency than his brother ever was because of the recent assassination of his friend, Martin Luther King, Jr., and the turmoil of the Vietnam War, which Bobby wanted to stop. But Nixon secretly had to attend to those who were trying to put him in the White House.

Nixon, meanwhile, hid behind a cloak of darkness, even this author did not see, when I voted for him in my first election in 1972, not until the truth was revealed by two persistent reporters named Woodward and Bernstein. The night that Robert Kennedy gave that famous speech at the Ambassador Hotel in Los Angeles, June of 1968, the Senator had taken the state of California in the primaries and would have taken the Democratic Nomination for President if it hadn't been for the tragedy that happened minutes later as he was embarking to leave the Hotel.

At this same time, in a secret rendezvous in Los Angeles, two Limousines met. One man, Lawrence O'Brien, would leave his car and enter the other. This man, Lawrence O'Brien, was Bobby Kennedy's chairman for the Presidential Election Committee and was for John F. Kennedy as well in 1960. The man he was meeting was Howard Hughes who believed that Bobby would surely become the next President of the U. S. He gave a cash amount of $10,000 dollars, the limit at this time for campaign contributions, to O'Brien. Sometime later, after Robert Kennedy's funeral, O'Brien tried to return the monies to Hughes, but instead, Hughes offered O'Brien a job to come to work for him. Robert Maheu, one of Hughes attorney's was the go-between the two, though Maheu himself had never met his employer. Maheu was the one who paid off Nixon by giving half of $100,000 up front to Nixon's secretive friend at the time, Bebe Rebozo who lived in Florida. During the late 50's, Maheu was instrumental in bringing together those in the CIA with members of the Mafia, to bring to power Fidel Castro, then to topple him. Soon after O'Brien was hired, Hughes fired Maheu. O'Brien would stay on with Hughes for the next four years until he was offered the job as National Chairman of the Democratic Convention in 1972.

The Headquarters would be at the Watergate Hotel, the location of the break in of the Democratic Headquarters, by what were known only as the five plumbers, really members of the C.I.A. Three Cubans, along with E Howard Hunt and Frank Sturgis, were all connected to Nixon since the 50's— Castro, the Bay of Pigs and assassination attempts on Castro, Hunt and Sturgis were both arrested in the train yard that is behind Dealey Plaza, on November 22, 1963 but then released, why? Whose office did they break into? What was Nixon so Paranoid about? What could they be looking for and who was Lawrence O'Brien? That information, back in 1960, of which Joseph Kennedy Sr. who wanted to destroy poor old Richard Nixon, had journeyed beyond both assassinated Kennedy brothers, but one man always had a connection to it. So Howard Hughes made the call to Richard Nixon, not knowing he would light the fire to what is now known today as Watergate.

Gerald Ford slipped in as the new replacement for Nixon, sneaking in the other three musketeers, with Dick Cheney becoming Chief of Staff; Rumsfeld, the Secretary of Defense; and George H.W. Bush, soon to be Director of the Central Intelligence Agency. They were no longer the four musketeers, but now became the 'Four Horseman of the Apocalypse!' Nelson Rockefeller, Governor of New York, was appointed to be Vice-President, a one time rival, sometime enemy of Nixon, but one who always wanted to be President. This was the closest he got. The Vietnam War finally settled to an end in April of 1975, but the turning point in the history of Kennedy's assassination happened in Ford's Administration, wracked with not one, not two, but three commissions, starting with the Rockefeller Commission named after the Vice-President who became Chairman. The usual suspects arrived again, though some had died since the Warren Commission Report. In fact, a death list had been growing rapidly. This time, David Belin was Head Counsel with Arlen Specter, right there beside him. Ronald Reagan, governor of California,

737

was listed as one of the commissioners. I would become friends with both Nancy and the future President after they left the Governorship and before his Presidency, through Frank Sinatra in the spring of 1978. A year later, Nancy asked me to campaign for Mr. Reagan, the only other time I voted Republican, but only for the first term. I did get invited to Reagan's reelection party in November of 1984. The last time I saw the Reagan's, Ronald was in poor health then and his mind going as early as before his second Inauguration, but it was not yet diagnosed. Whenever I saw Reagan on Television in his second term, sometimes he was the old Reagan I knew, but most of the time he was never the same. I would see the same thing happen to my friend, Arne, in Los Angeles who now has the disease.

I asked Mr. Reagan in 1978, what he thought about the Kennedy assassination, not knowing at the time that he was once a member of the Rockefeller Commission. He believed now, as well as then that JFK was assassinated within a conspiracy of our government and that President Jimmy Carter felt the same way, a man he'd be running against in two years. In hindsight, I feel, and only Nancy can confirm this, is that one of the main reasons Reagan, a staunch Democrat, switched to the Republican Party was that he thought Johnson was part of the conspiracy. Again, President Johnson had good reason to believe everyone might just think that.

Nixon, and now Ford's CIA director, William Colby came forward to admit that the CIA had a secret Executive Action order within their agency that meant assassination, connecting them to many throughout the third world countries among many other taboos that Colby confessed to. The information came from the break-in of Ellsberg's office in 1970, by those same plumbers who would get caught two years later at Watergate. This was really the beginning of the downfall of Richard Nixon, all because of the Pentagon Papers that brought out the sham of the Vietnam War. I wonder when the Iraqi papers will show up. Because of Colby's confession and honesty and wanting the agency to get a clean bill of health after hanging out its dirty laundry, Ford fired him and replaced him with George H.W. Bush. I didn't know who Bush was yet, and I didn't care. Apparently, neither did anyone else for that matter. The Republican party was in a desultory state and just wanted to get back on track without any more scandal. No one had to give any account to these people that were now running our country. The Democrats were about as lame then as they seem to be today.

Little did we know, that the Ford administration, which was never elected to run our country, was heading all of us Americans in the wrong direction, right to 9/11. Here is where it all got started, the 'Four Horseman of the Apocalypse,' their secret ties, with the Middle East and their plans to monopolize the oil market. Here, Hussein was born as was Manuel Noriega and Bin Laden, all under the tutelage of the four horseman; then there were the coverups: the atrocities of Vietnam, the dozens of incidents of mass murders of women and children there, and the Prisoner of War and the MIA's situation.

Count them, three commissions on the JFK assassination popped up, from Rockefeller to the Church Senate Hearings, where Senator Frank Church from Idaho wanted to know, based on what Colby spilled, if it were at all possible that the Executive Action program that began its inception in the mid-50's under the auspices of then Vice-President Nixon and Allen Dulles, had been red-lighted to turn on our own President, which might explain what could have taken place in Dallas on that day of November 22.

Not to worry though, that newly appointed director of the CIA confirmed that it wasn't possible! I am speaking of George H.W. Bush. Again, how does, a nobody who comes from the oil fields of Houston, Texas, rates a job as the director of the CIA, runs for President, then becomes the head of the Republican Party so quickly. Is it just money? I don't get it? Oh, maybe it has to do with his father, Prescott Bush, former Senator of Connecticut, banker for Adolph Hitler and the Third Reich before and during WWII. Prescott was one of the architects, along with Allen Dulles of the CIA, formed within the walls of that occult fraternity known as 'Skull and Bones' at Yale University, where both son and grandson attended. How special! Do you think it could help if H.W. were, let's say, the President of the Trilateral Commission for instance and would it help, if I mention that both former Presidents' Nixon and H.W.? When asked, where they were when President Kennedy got shot, they individually could not remember. How sad, neither of them should be recommended to any office, knowing this startling information. Nixon was caught in a lie years later when pictures started popping up and then just evaded the question ever since, as does H. W. who still can't remember.

Along with Johnson who became President while in Dallas and JFK who died there, both future Presidents Nixon and Bush were there, too! Gerald Ford would also be there within six months, to interview Jack Ruby, the assassin of Lee Harvey Oswald. Now I can see why it is possible that H.W. could certainly have been indoctrinated into the CIA. He was the Professor in teaching the art of lying to those who surrounded him to get to the top, from the CIA to the office of Ronald Reagan and Iran Contra, to his own years in office. And now, this former President's son is trying very hard to pretend that he is a born again Christian, isn't he? By his comments and his actions, George W. Bush has shown he has no clue what the word truth means.

Finally, in the final months of Ford's watch, a third committee was formed, the fourth and final commission, called the House Select Committee on Assassinations, 1976-79. How does Gerald Ford rate all this attention in just one term, a term he did not even get elected to. The House Select Committee introduced two more probes; besides JFK, the new evidence concerning both Robert Kennedy and Dr. Martin Luther King, Jr., were added to separate investigations and committees.

Representative Henry B. Gonzalez of San Antonio, Texas who was with Kennedy and Governor Connelly in the beginning stages of the motorcade trip through selected cities of Texas, and Richard Sprague of Philadelphia, was the committee chairman. They offered the committee to be open to the public and allowed all conspiracy theorists, if there were any credence to their claims, to offer up evidence to be questioned. This means Jim Garrison, the Mark Lanes and those with years of investigation could come forward. Robert Groden was the expert on the Zapruder film and had the top priority with the committee members. It was Groden who received under mysterious circumstances, a print of the Zapruder film in his mail box one day in 1966, yes, that same year that Pitzer was killed and Mark Lane's *Rush to Judgment* came out, as well as James Garrison's crusade on the trail of the assassins to bring Kennedy's killers to justice. Groden's version of the film is quite different from the one *Life Magazine* was trying to peddle on us. Though we could never see this film, like the autopsy reports, we got the same courteous of lies from the most prestigious of all magazines in this country. What we got to see or not to see, were frames reversed, missing frames, probably thinking because we were not allowed to see this famous film, it was far too gruesome for us folks to see at the time. The funny thing here is that CBS news reporter from Houston, Dan Rather was the only person attached to the media and us, to see this film, and he has lied to us ever since, even taking Roger Mudd's job from him, to replace Grandpa Walter Cronkite as head anchor for CBS News. Our government from the beginning was lying to us, why?

You have now, Posner, Fuhrman and people like Dale Myers out here giving you bull crap and the people are swallowing it because the government is giving these people a platform to sell you the big lie. If you continue to buy it, truth becomes the lie, it positively has these past 43 years. The government expects you to forget all this in a couple of weeks, and they are right, the negatives in your soul, the troubles you're having, the demons, you are struggling with, soon will replace the information you hear, and hopefully, you do go on with your life. This is what the Intelligence agencies, like the CIA, count on. Unless it is like a canker-sore that won't go away, like the Vietnam War or Iraq, even for some, it is Watergate and the Iran Contra scandals or Enron; someone losing their life savings and job. Sexual assault or rape, these are examples that may never go away. What the government does to relieve you of their mistakes or misgivings is to scare you to death by posting news item or news broadcast to make you forget that they are doing just that. A terrorist attack is a good example because they know this is foreign to us and can't relate to it. For me this Author, my canker-sore that just won't go away has been the JFK assassination, it just persists and I can't shake it off, especially when I have tried a thousand times. So people like Posner and Fuhrman, the Ford's and the Bush's do not faze me because I've grown accustomed to all their truthiness and when they try to prove with digital film like Dale Myers' reconstruction, with his computer-generated analysis of how the Zapruder film will make you believe that Oswald was the shooter, when no one really has any real proof Oswald was even in that window that the Mannlicher was even the gun, that Posner and Myers can prove that the "Magic Bullet" actually works. All I will say to this is that manipulation is the key to tricking the mind, but God gave us eyes to see for ourselves and common sense to distinguish truth from falsehood. If Steven Spielberg, who I worked within Hollywood, made you believe that dinosaurs could still walk the earth, then we have to surpass the facts presented to us and ask more questions.

Forty-three years ago *Life Magazine* lied to the world about the Zapruder film that they bought for $100,000 dollars. The frames were all we could witness on that day Kennedy was assassinated, until twelve years later in April of 1975, when Robert Groden would share his film to a television audience on what was called, *Geraldo Rivera's Midnight Show*. By this time, a few weeks prior to the program, it just so happens, *Life* sold the film they had bought in 1963 back to the family of Abraham Zapruder, deceased now, for one dollar. This prompted me to believe, *Life Magazine* was now excused from any impending lawsuits that might happen following this broadcast, once the lies of the past 12 years, had finally been revealed that *Life* and our government perpetrated this as did, Dan Rather. Ironically, Dan Rather would lose his CBS news anchor position by going into Bush territory too often. Besides Groden's version of the Zapruder film, there was new evidence provided by the Dallas Police Department, a dictabelt was found with recorded gun shots from a policeman's radio mounted on a motorcycle in John Kennedy's motorcade. It had been kept in storage all this time, but could have been discovered as far back as

741

the Warren Commission if President Johnson had not forced the Dallas Police to close down their internal investigation on Kennedy's assassination. This dictabelt has become a controversy over the last decade and is still being investigated today. The problem is the motorcycle officer they say it belonged to has denied that it was his. In 1978, at the House Select Committee, he said it was his but states today he was never in position near Dealey Plaza when the shots were fired. This particular dictabelt recorded the gun shots in Dealey Plaza coming from both the front, mainly the Grassy Knoll and from behind, the School Book Depository when the microphone button got stuck on the parade route. The problem is now that if you discard the evidence from the House Select Committee, the dictabelt, there is no Grassy Knoll shooter, which means they can rule out conspiracy, and that means, going back to square one and allowing the Warren Commission to live on, with Oswald again the lone assassin.

After reading Fuhrman's book, I could see he was accrediting for Posner's and Myers digital accounts to disprove any theory that there was a conspiracy or that Oswald was a part of one, though Fuhrman may agree there might have been a connection between Oswald and other conspirators. I don't deny this, I always felt that he was and this is what I display in my book, that he was working with those that were. But I also present to you the other side of the coin. I still believe with all my heart that neither Officer Tippit, nor Kennedy was shot by Lee Harvey Oswald. I can tell you that both Fuhrman and Posner never heard the sounds of the dictabelt. No matter, whose it was, this dictabelt belonged to someone and it was in Dealey Plaza. I heard the sounds from the dictabelt myself and can state definitely it was gunfire. In the end, Robert Blakely took over the House Select Committee after the infighting between the two commissioners, Sprague and Gonzalez and then the firing of the both of them. They were mainly arguing over the direction the committee was heading. It seemed that Gonzalez was hitting his stride by pursuing the CIA connection and Sprague was to keep it from going in that direction.

The consensus was Gonzalez was closing in on a breakthrough, and although more monies were appropriated for the Committees, both of the commissioners were fired and Robert Blakely who had worked with Robert Kennedy in the Attorney General's office, became their replacement. But also added was our friend, Arlen Specter! Hell, what would these commissions be without him. I believe he took over Head Counsel. Blakely ruined everything for everyone. He shut out the open house and everyone's invitation except those he so chose. He turned the committee into a closed session with Blakely as sole spokesperson for the commission, all other members had to keep their mouths shut for good, before, during, and after the Committees closed. He made every member to sign an affidavit to keep their word or be dismissed. If any leaks got out or anyone spoke out, even today, their jobs would be in jeopardy. This means that a Senator or Congressman would lose their seat in public office, a police officer or detective would have to resign or be fired, Judges and lawyers disbarred. The HSCA under Blakely dropped the other two committees on Robert Kennedy and Martin Luther King, Jr. This was when President Jimmy Carter was getting in positions of embarrassment that included the Middle East Peace Treaty with Anwar Sadat getting assassinated, Billy Carter, his brother and the American Hostages in Iran. Blakely drops another bomb this time, cutting the CIA out of the picture. He wants now to go in only one direction. This would be the Mafia.

In 1979 the HSCA came to the conclusion, or I should say Blakely did that there had been a conspiracy. With Groden's version of the Zapruder film matching to the sounds of gunfire heard from the dictabelt gave pause for the first time that there had been four shots to be accounted for, showing that two guns were fired that day in Dallas. I myself heard the shots fired in this dictabelt. What I heard was Seven shots and possibly more. Blakely and the HSCA also heard what I heard, but kept their findings as close to the Warren Commission and Arlen Specter's account of the "Magic Bullet Theory." The Conspiracy Theorists can have their Grassy Knoll shooter, though he missed, so says Blakely who accounts one shot from the Grassy Knoll and three from the School Book Depository. In the end, the HSCA contends that a conspiracy does now exist, though the Mafia did it and Oswald was the only successful shooter that day.

These are the words of Mark Fuhrman as he ends his book agreeing with the WC and Gerald Posner: "All the evidence shows that Lee Harvey Oswald fired three shots with his Mannlicher-Carcano from the southwest-corner, sixth-floor window of the Texas School book Depository, killing President John F. Kennedy and wounding Governor John B. Connelly. All evidence shows that Oswald acted alone. There is no proof of a second gunman, or any conspiracy, involving Oswald or anyone else." Fuhrman states: "These are the facts." He learned that I'm sure from Jack Webb, Fuhrman once being LAPD cop and all. He goes on to conclude: "Ever since John F. Kennedy was assassinated, his death has remained unresolved. We have grieved, yet we cannot move on. A cloud hangs over his murder and our nation because we refuse to accept what is so clearly the truth— that his assassination was a simple act of murder (hence the title of his book— how profound!) committed by a man who left evidence proving his guilt. (Or, just maybe, somebody else did!) It is time we lay JFK and his assassination, to rest. The case is solved." I hate to say this Mark, "But not by the hair, of my chinny-chin-chin!" And not by this book either.

After Jack Ruby shot Oswald, newscaster Howard K Smith said: We don't know whether Oswald really committed the crime and maybe we will never know." It is still the same today, the year 2006, forty-three years later. Fuhrman mentions 450 books have been written on the subject, 452 if you want to include his and my book, oh yes, I guess maybe mine doesn't count since it is a novel. It is interesting here to note that Mr. Fuhrman has interviewed me five times on his talk radio show four times at KXLY and one time at KGA between February of 2002 and November of 2004.

The last time I scared the hell out of him and we went off the air fast. Mark and I got along fine, and I believe both of us liked and respected each other very much, but he did not know much about our subject matter in the first few interviews as I overwhelmed him with, other than books he had read through the years. Our interviews were tape recorded so I pretty much can say from his book; he did not believe in any of the things that he expounded upon in his book or on his radio program. What has changed his mind? In fact, his radio listeners are probably thinking the same thing. He contradicts a lot from our conversation, one point specifically. I found his surprise fascinating when he found out after a recent tour and visited at the Texas School Book Depository, that I had never been there myself, especially those who have read my book and say, I describe Dealey Plaza perfectly as if I were really there. In my mind, I was and this surprised Mark. He continued in detail explaining how Oswald could not have been the shooter from that sixth-floor window unless he was a great shot (which Mark said, he wasn't with that type of rifle), either he had to lay on his stomach or possibly on his knees, because it was a floor window, it was inches off the floor which he thought incredible. In fact, Mark thought, like Oliver Stone explained in his film, *JFK* that the shooter's best shot was straight on as the motorcade turned off Houston Street and came toward the shooter down Main and to Dealey Plaza. This was just one contradiction. He told me and his radio audience, stating infallibly, that no one could have taken a shot standing up in that window as he described above.

Here is what he explains in his book: Fuhrman actually provides us a scenario, how Oswald felt as he loaded and reloaded his rifle and took aim at Kennedy, with a rifle, many say, did not work, including Fuhrman himself. Oswald remembers his training from the corps. "Breath, relax, aim, slack, squeeze three times until it's over in those few seconds in Dallas." Though Fuhrman portrays Oswald as an expert Marine (this is the first time I've ever heard this from anyone, including the Warren Commission) who he says, Fuhrman then provides us with an eye witness, really, one of two, the WC used in their conclusions to make Oswald the assassin. "Howard Brennan who sees a man standing up and resting against the left windowsill, with gun shouldered to his right shoulder and taking aim, then firing his last shot. Another witness, Amos Euins, looks back up at the window and sees the man shoot again. The bullet strikes Kennedy behind the head. At least three large bullet fragments exit the right parietal region of the skull. One fragment strikes the windshield, landing in the front seat of the limo. Another fragment also comes to rest in the front seat with the Secret Service, and a third fragment ricochets off the street, continuing to strike a section of curbing that wounds a pedestrian, James Tague, in the face." Amazing, now that's what you call a magic bullet, Mr. Fuhrman. And this is a person who doesn't believe in the "Magic Bullet Theory!"

Here is some new proof if you haven't heard by now, the "Magic bullet Theory" would not hold water in a court of law in 1964, if Oswald went to trial, nor today, especially when discovered that item #399 the pristine bullet known as "magic" had been handled by 4 to 5 individuals of which one of them was not even known until the 1990's. Like Mark Fuhrman's situation concerning O. J. Simpson's glove, was item #399, planted evidence? How did Item #399 become so magic? I won't go there to explain Arlen Specter's theory because you have heard it a thousand times and you have Oliver Stone's *JFK* to look at to see how it could not make the seven wounds, entering and exiting both Kennedy and Connelly, exit remarkably pristine. The commission exhibit #399 from Fuhrman's book which he probably followed the footsteps of the WC, weighed in at estimated 160.85 to 161.5 grains before firing it from the Mannlicher-Carcano. After exiting Kennedy and Connelly and scraping lead from the bottom of #399, for evidence that it was shot from the rifle, it weighed for exhibit: 158.6 grains— and mind you, this is accounting for the lead left in Connelly's body as well. Fuhrman can do the math, but he says it's possible, although he may not know that Governor Connelly died in the early 1990's still believing he was shot from a separate bullet—and that bullet's lead is what in the end that killed him. He died of lead poisoning. Why was there no autopsy performed on Connelly following his death to take the lead out to match the bullet or even the weight for that matter.

The widow, Nellie Connelly apparently refused. Why? So many questions could have been put to rest. Now "The Magic Bullet" lives on for another era. This bullet was said to be found on not one of two stretchers but three, the two being Kennedy and Connelly. It began with Kennedy, then the story switched to Connelly because it would make #399 work for the WC. But there was a third gurney, which an ambulance attendant brought in a man who had an epileptic fit in the middle of Dealey Plaza just minutes prior to the arrival of the motorcade. When Kennedy and Connelly arrived at Parkland Hospital, this man suddenly disappeared during all the chaos, never to be seen or heard of again. Both this man and Jack Ruby were there at Parkland during these early crucial minutes. Why?

If the Mannlicher-Carcano 6.5 millimeter rifle actually fired #399 and the gun found on the sixth floor of the Texas School Book Depository was really a German Mauser, this scenario would not make sense. The Mauser disappeared after Oswald was put in custody, an FBI, or someone from the Secret Service brought in the bullet that would fit the now replaced rifle tied to Oswald in the middle of Kennedy's autopsy at Bethesda in Maryland. This would become that famous bullet that spelled magic. Yes, #399 may have come from the Mannlicher-Carcano and might have been fired from the gun, as well as the other spent shells, but even if it had, there is no proof it was fired that day. Oswald used an alias name, Alex James Hidell.

Anyone that he worked for in the intelligence community could have ordered the Oswald rifle under his alias, and there's no magic to that. Oswald was put in that Depository for a reason one month prior to the assassination, and those who recommended him for the job, to the one source, and then that source, would make the call to the next source that put him in place for work. In the end, these same sources became witnesses to the WC, against Oswald, all tying in together, including the gentleman and his wife who witnessed Oswald taking to work, curtain rods. These two people are the one and the same as source #1 above. It is a merry-go-round, but it all comes together full circle. Incidentally, with today's DNA testing, is there any way that #399 would have any DNA on it that had allegedly passed through, from either, Connelly or the President in this late date?

Another thing, Posner's book is just full of holes and lies too many to mention, so I'll just give you a couple examples, which I believe I've done anyway, if only to help out Fuhrman's mess. Posner's book came out prior to the 30th anniversary of the JFK assassination in 1993, just in time to spoil Oliver Stone's film *JFK* that convinced 90% of the people to believe there was a conspiracy on that day in Dallas. The film went on to be nominated as the Best Picture of 1991, and I feel that at least it is half right in its depiction, and still say, it is the *Citizen Kane* of the 90's. Posner's book, let alone his theory, does not hold up, concerning the exact frame of the Zapruder film he describes in his book that he contends was the first shot that was fired in Dealey Plaza. First, where does this idiot come off stating there is no connection to Oswald and David Ferrie let alone them to Clay Shaw, alias "Clay Bertram," who District Attorney, Jim Garrison, brought to trial in the late 60's.

Ferrie, a commercial pilot and CIA operative was one of Garrison's witnesses who died of mysterious circumstances prior to Garrison's trial. Posner continues to roam the talk show circuit, as if he were the Messiah on the subject of closure in the JFK assassination. Far from it, more than likely, was hired by the CIA to stop Oliver Stone's crusade on Capital Hill to open the Kennedy files that have been top secret since day one. If Oswald did it, what is there to hide? Why spend hundreds of millions of dollars, yours incidentally, in keeping it a secret for over 75 years? Posner's book was a major best seller, a book of manipulation. Fuhrman, however, was only going back into the Stone Age, agreeing partly with both the WC and the HSCA. With all the circuits, Posner made headway with both Rather and Peter Jennings, but he made a mistake by appearing on PBS Frontline a show that does its homework. They treated him well until they caught him in a lie. Again, he says, there is no connection between Ferrie. History has it that Oswald had known David Ferrie before he was in the Marines, from 15 years old as a cadet in a civil air patrol unit, whose instructor was Ferrie, to Oswald's death at City Hall in Dallas, Texas.

Posner tells *Frontline* that there is no proof or any connection that Oswald was ever in a civil air patrol unit or that Ferrie was conducting one during this period of Oswald's life. Frontline then in a surprise coup, even to this author, provided to Posner a photograph of a 15 year-old Oswald at a youth training camp, as a cadet in the civil air patrol unit in New Orleans. There standing also with the group was their instructor, dressed as if he were George Patton himself, helmet and all, David Ferrie.

Jim Garrison had the same problem himself, taking Clay Shaw to trial for conspiracy in the murder of JFK. Two points he needed to prove in court, that Clay Shaw, alias Clay Bertram, was one and the same and worked for the CIA. The other point was that Shaw or Bertram knew and was seen with, both, Oswald and Ferrie. The first one was simple as long as Shaw could be proven that he was also Bertram, Garrison had a case and it so happened that when Shaw was booked after his arrest, he signed both his name and his alias onto the police report. Any court of law would call this a slam dunk, but not this court, someone high up in government got to this Judge. The proceedings stopped cold, and the next thing the Judge decided not to allow the police report with Shaw's alias on it to be used as evidence. This did not stop Garrison. He would just put the police officer who booked Shaw on the stand to testify. Again, the Judge would not allow it. His many years of hard work, was being abused in a court of law, by the Judge himself. His witnesses, including David Ferrie, were mysteriously dying off one by one.

One witness who knew all three happened to be a homosexual, taboo in those days, He last saw Shaw, Ferrie and Oswald at a 1963 Halloween party in Shaw's New Orleans mansion. The Judge dismissed this witness as unreliable, and so went Garrison's case. Soon after, Garrison would also disappear as well. He would be set up and defending himself in a court of law for tax fraud and tax invasion and, the real stumper, for taking bribes from the Mafia. It took many years, but he won and survived on all counts. Sometime later following the mysterious death of Clay Shaw in 1974, a new photograph appears. This Author has seen it, with my own eyes, a Halloween Picture to be exact, of the four of them, I believe dancing, dressed in costumes, but very much identified as Shaw, Ferrie, Oswald, and the witness from Garrison's trial, I believe his name to be Perry.

A year later, at the Rockefeller Commission, William Colby was not the only CIA Director that testified, his predecessor also testified, Richard Helms, whom I believe is still alive as I print this, A man who knows more secrets about what happened in Dealey Plaza and the deaths of Martin Luther King, Jr., Bobby Kennedy, and the dark side of both Presidents, Johnson and Nixon who he both served under. He knew their secrets and where the bodies were buried. He also was fourth man on the totem pole below the three men fired by Kennedy following the Bay of Pigs: besides, Dulles, there was the Deputy Director of the CIA, General Charles Cabell who also might have been in Dallas on November 22nd, 1963, His brother coincidentally was the Mayor of Dallas at the time. Charles Cabell was in Houston, Texas the day before with Richard Nixon and an oil Texan by the name of George H.W. Bush. Coincidence? Lee Harvey Oswald, coincidence? The third CIA operative was Richard Bissell, the architect of the Bay of Pigs who, then Vice-President Richard Nixon, gave the green-light to go ahead in late November, 1959. Now you know about what some of those missing minutes were about on Nixon's erased tapes. In 1975, like Colby, Helms spoke up at the Rockefeller Commission and confessed that Clay Shaw was an operative of the CIA after all. Still through the years Garrison was ruled a nut case usually by those in our government, the same that say Oswald is also a nut case. These remarks were started by WC and former President Gerald Ford. He is still alive as I write this (unfortunately he died as this book went to press). One last note, I got to put in a call to Jim Garrison in New Orleans in February of

1992. I was told he was on his death bed, and I was allowed to talk to his personal assistant at the federal court house since apparently this so-called nut case was still a Federal Judge the day he died, the day after my birthday that year, on October 21. She praised me for keeping Kennedy's eternal flame lit and would provide him and his family the new information I discovered concerning the Warren Commission's coverup of JFK's murder. How Oswald's "Historical Diary" is fake, forged by someone within the intelligence community. The evidence is in the WC report itself. You can't see it unless you have the original letters that Oswald wrote, particularly two of them that the WC deliberately misguided the reader. Those responsible for this hidden agenda were two people whose names keep creeping up in my story, Arlen Specter and the architect of the "Magic Bullet Theory," Gerald Ford.

Speaking of these two, I want you to know again the Magic Bullet could never have stood up against a candle in a court of law. Here, is the shocker, it wasn't Arlen Specter who made up this, "Magic Bullet Theory." I remember it was in the summer of 1997, July, to be exact, since my friend, James Stewart in Beverly Hills, had died the same day of this announcement. My book was still a disk on the worldwide web site. I received a call by someone to ask me how my book contains something that hasn't come out publicly yet. The answer is the same as what I tired to explain before, only God can explain my gift, I don't understand it myself. Maybe that's why I am finally writing this piece so the truth can, as I wrote in my book, set us free.

After I finished writing my book in late 1996, and following the deaths of both William Colby in a mysterious boating accident, and J. Lee Rankin, the Head Counsel of the WC, it was discovered by his son in his notes in July, 1997, that it wasn't Specter who invented the 'magic bullet theory' but Gerald Ford! They never could explain this bullet that came into the middle of the autopsy by someone within the Secret Service. Because Humes did burn the original report, no one would see any photographs or anything else for that matter, except their drawings altered by Mr. Ford. So the pictures depicted in both Posner and Fuhrman's books are forged and altered documents. What the future President did was make a bullet hole that was originally in Kennedy's back, below his shoulder blade, into a neck wound. This was because at the autopsy, Humes and the other pathologists at Bethesda, Colonel Pierre A. Finck and Commander J. Thornton Boswell, thought that the neck wound was an exit wound. They found out the next morning that the Parkland doctors confirmed it was an entrance wound from a shot from the front of President Kennedy — hence, the grassy knoll shooter. That these doctors had done a tracheotomy on the entrance wound confused the Bethesda doctors and that is why, Humes burned the original autopsy report the next day. What they also didn't know was there was another bullet hole even further down the President's back about another five inches, causing more confusion and changes in changing and falsifying drawn pictures and photos to fit their analysis of what would become the "Magic Bullet Theory." This second bullet hole wound was much smaller down his back, apparently by a different make of gun, possibly even the Mannlicher Carcano itself. This bullet wound would slowly disappear like everything else. This is the photo shown in Fuhrman's book without the second back wound. The photo now tells you what they did, Ford changed the bullet hole in the President's back five inches below the shoulder blade and settled it into his neck area so it would look as if the bullet was shot from behind, from the School Book Depository, having the bullet enter the back of Kennedy's neck, exiting the throat, and causing all those wounds in Governor Connelly. Fuhrman is basing his evidence and findings on forged and doctored photographs. He is also basing on eyewitness testimony that has been completely fabricated, planted or tainted, as complete lies in the WC. Seventy-five percent of the people have all committed themselves as proof positive that shots were fired from the Grassy Knoll, even over sixty cameras, moving and still shots, confiscated by the FBI, show crowds running to the picket fence including Dallas Police officers, but the WC ignored them and only concentrated on the fifteen percent that heard shots from the Texas School Book Depository, why? How was there so many FBI agents in Dealey Plaza to get all these film cameras confiscated so quickly and why are there so many of these pictures and film missing today?

In 1988, prior to the 25th anniversary of the JFK assassination, I remember in anticipation, getting ready to watch an ABC broadcast segment of *20/20*. It was to be a controversial program, investigated by Sylvia Chase who had explosive information commemorating that fateful day in Dallas. This was during the last months of the Reagan/Bush administration and H.W. just got elected President of the U.S. My fears came true then when I originally wrote *America the Beautiful* as a Hollywood screenplay back in 1983 as was in 1996 when I turned it into a novel. As I sat down in front of my television set in Glendale, California, to watch a possible breakthrough in the Kennedy assassination. Suddenly, as it was beginning, a disclaimer came on stating this segment of *20/20* will not be presented this evening. Apparently, someone high up in Washington or from the White House— and I can tell you it wasn't Reagan— ordered this part of the segment cut from the program. I remember how disappointed I was, because this segment was concerning a

750

dispute in the findings of Robert Blakely's HSCA and WC in their conclusions of Kennedy's autopsy reports. Chase had interviewed all six Parkland Hospital Doctors who had witnessed Kennedy's wounds, especially the described explosive head shot in the front, as well as the wound behind the head that had a large gaping hole protruding outward, like a volcano. Then there was the bullet entrance to the throat, all this within the first 30 minutes of the assassination. But what Chase showed the doctors from the commission's final reports, was not what they saw that day, on Nov. 22, 1963. Also, Chase interviewed Commander James J. Humes the pathologist from Bethesda on his testimony, against both the HSCA and WC conclusions.

Well, my disappointment was nothing compared to what Sylvia Chase must have felt. She quit *20/20* and ABC news as did Geraldo Rivera who walked out with her that very week. Fuhrman doesn't mention these doctors, nurses or staff who were the first witnesses of Kennedy's body brought into Parkland. Why? Because the WC apparently didn't either? The reason I can tell you about this now is that it was released eventually to the public finally in 1993, but without any fanfare. Chase's reporting of this subject still stands today as a landmark in getting to the truth. In the end, the doctors from all the committees and commissions and the three from Bethesda eventually allowed the big lie to catch up to them as they all agreed with the newly released autopsy reports and photographs that were presented to them because of Stone's fight to open the assassination files on JFK and the Freedom of Information Act. They were agreeing with the planted, forged and altered documents.

A shocking surprise happened when Sylvia Chase arrived after the same government official came knocking on the doors of the Parkland Hospital Doctors in Dallas for their assessment of Kennedy's autopsy reports and photographs in 1988. Only one of the six agreed, Dr. Marion Jenkins, or I should say changed his mind by intimidation of the altered photos of Kennedy's head. Dr. Robert McClelland was not fooled and would never change his mind. Both McClelland and Dr. Malcolm O. Perry who started a tracheotomy on Kennedy's entrance wound through the throat, along with three of the other doctors all disagreed with the government's conclusions, They remarked that when Kennedy entered the hospital, there was a tiny wound in the President's throat.

It was an entrance wound with no exit, nor visible bullet. What they were seeing now, was a wound that became a large gaping wound three times its size when Kennedy's body reached the doctors at Bethesda for the autopsy at around 7:30-8:00 p.m. in the evening.

Now, Reagan told me that if he became President in 1981 that he would continue to support the HSCA and refinance it, which Arlen Specter who, secretly behind the scenes was pulling the strings, prematurely closed its findings, This was after Blakely took over and changed the course in 1979. I decided then and there that Reagan was sincere, I knew he loved JFK. I told Nancy, what I had told myself over and over, that I would not vote for a Republican again, but I would campaign for her husband, knowing Carter did not have a chance. That is why the HSCA closed because those in the Republican Party were not supporting it. I didn't believe in Carter then as I do now, but the top candidate in the Republican Party to win the nomination was H.W. of all people. No way! For God's sake, who would in their right mind vote for someone who had been the head of the CIA, as President of the United States? This was not going to happen not in this country, not after Watergate! Although Reagan was about 12th in the running for the fortieth President and a movie star at that, the industry I was now working in, I voted for him. But still those who control the strings in high places, got Bush and his cronies into that White House anyway, didn't they? Within sixty days of his Inauguration President Reagan was shot by John Hinckley, and any chance for the HSCA to be re-appropriated as well as those POW and MIA's in Vietnam coming home, would be rescinded. Clinton who believed prior to his presidency, that there was a conspiracy that day in Dallas, changed his mind between the time of Vincent Foster's death in July and the release of Posner's book before the 30th anniversary of the JFK assassination. On the eve of November, 22nd, Bill Clinton announced that he now believes Oswald was the lone gunman. The only Democrat in history that I know believes that, and now after W. Bush becomes President in 2000, not even elected mind you, like Gerald Ford, with the same suspects in the White house, Bill Clinton becomes buddy-buddy with the President's father, his ex-opponent, George H.W. Bush. Clinton must now be a member of the Trilateral Commission. I just wonder when he first got in? Ten years after John Hinckley supposed to have shot Reagan and others, including Reagan's press secretary, James Brady and one of the Secret Service Agents who tried to cover him, the Doctor who attended Reagan and recovered the bullet was kept silent, until he spoke out during his successor's administration, now George H.W. Bush. He told the world for the first time it was a miracle that the President had lived through this because the bullet that had lodged just a half inch from his heart was no ordinary bullet; it was a dissolvable missile or what is known in the intelligence circles as an ice bullet. This bullet did not dissolve or explode within him for some strange reason, which definitely would have killed him. Now the big question becomes what was

752

Hinckley doing with such a bullet? Did he shoot such a bullet and why the false cover story of the Jodie Foster scenario, of which I know personally isn't true.

There are also multiple connections to the Hinckley family and the Bush family. John Hinckley is locked up in a mental hospital never able to speak with anyone in the media let alone, a court of law, about the real truth of what really happened that day in March of 1981. Another thing, the bullet described above was also mentioned or suggested in the 1960's, since this was at the first time I had ever heard of such a bullet that was used to kill President Kennedy. The Doctors witnessed at Parkland found nothing of bullet fragments that blasted out the back of his head causing a big gaping hole. Again these Doctors, unlike Jenkins' change of mind, all disagreed with the government's intimidation concerning this gaping hole. This is when experts began discussing for the first time such a bullet of this caliber.

Besides Clinton, you say, what about President Johnson— he also was a Democrat? Even Lyndon himself finally came clean but did anyone believe him at first? He rescinded after leaving office in 1969, tired of being used and abused by the same people who allowed him to be President. Now they did the same by positioning their new man into the White House, Richard Milhous Nixon.

Johnson decided not to run for a second term because he didn't want to stay the course in Vietnam, let alone Cambodia. He wanted to appease the masses of protesters who want to hang him up to the nearest tree. Johnson also felt that he may have only four more years to live because of a possible bad heart, and why not live it out on his beloved ranch.

Johnson would be right, a family history of heart failure seemed to be his concern. He allowed Walter Cronkite and CBS news to come on his ranch to do a 90 minute Television interview on his Houston Ranch. Though he formed the Warren Commission to destroy and make Lee Harvey Oswald the lone assassin and scapegoat, he confessed he didn't believe Oswald did it and if he were involved he surely was not alone. Then surprisingly Johnson proceeded to answer Cronkite who he thought did have his predecessor killed, shocking those from CBS news, but did grandpa, Walter, believe him? No matter if believed or not, CBS wanted to air it like is, but like Sylvia Chase's *20/20* piece, almost 10 years later, This section of the interview was cut from airing on National Television. Remember, no one at this point in time would know who these black hats were who control what we can see or even know. We just depend on them, because they must know what is best for our country. If this is what you believe, than you and everyone else that believes the same, all belong in Iraq, with George W., Dick Cheney, Donald Rumsfeld and Condoleezza Rice. Johnson's shocking answer to Grandpa Cronkite was this: the Houston Oil men and the CIA had John F. Kennedy assassinated! I suppose Cronkite's face would be white about now, white as a ghost. It didn't matter. Johnson, our 36th President would be dead soon and he probably felt he needed to get this off his conscience. Do you think so? So my guess, Walter, like Dan Rather, would continue to lie to us, which they did throughout their careers on our national newscast everyday. What you don't know can't hurt you, right? Tell that to Richard Nixon! To your husbands, fathers, mothers, sisters, sons and lovers who have died and still are dying in Iraq, a war that was a big lie, like yes, the Vietnam War, those who have died and are still suffering for it. Then there is 9/11, we still are not getting the whole truth which I blame on those Houston Oil men and who once again are in our, and I mean OUR, White House! It doesn't matter to them, when they leave in 2009, they will be awfully richer and financially secure for the rest of their, and their generations, lives.

What I have said above, makes Fuhrman and Posner's and those other books supporting our government's side kind of small doesn't it? This came out in 1993 when Posner's book was making quite a splash, and the O.J. Simpson trial was the biggest and most watched soap opera of all time, and poor Mark Fuhrman the police officer who was accused of planting evidence, Simpson's glove on his premises, following the murder of his wife, Nicole and her friend. Fuhrman then would leave the LAPD and Los Angeles in disgrace. Then he would come to the Northwest write books, get a prime time talk radio show and get rich and live happily ever after like G. Gordon Liddy and Oliver North. Except, after meeting Mark, I could relate to him because I've been accused falsely in Los Angeles as well, as a racist. I fought two and a half years to clear my name and won the battle in Los Angeles, but not the War, which brought me here to Spokane, my home town, by this Corporation's retaliation, of which I fought another 10 years, with corrupt attorneys and Judges, even those who wanted to coverup another's mistake. I would then lose this battle and the war as well, not because of the fight I continue to struggle with, but because no one wanted to be involved or lend any help. I was heart broken, I still am, but I continue to fight the good fight and I try, by God, I try to stay the course.

I don't believe Mark planted that glove at O.J. Simpson's house. Hell, he would have had to be very close to O.J. to know his whereabouts and that he was leaving town, or even to be having an affair with Nicole himself, and there is no evidence to prove any of this to be true, unless people lie and plant evidence, like in my case and in my position. Only God knows what prejudices are hidden in the mind of Mark Fuhrman. I don't believe Mark is a racist, and I definitely know I'm not. But Mark did make one mistake, mainly because, I imagine his anger at the time, I know how angry I was and how disgraced I was in my position, since my evidence was sold back with a high fee from my own law firm and part of the deal was, somehow, they were to get rid of me, the client. But in Mark's case, he held back evidence that could have helped the prosecution at the time to send O.J. Simpson to death or away for a very long time. Instead, he used it in his own best-selling book. So now we come back a full circle to the Zapruder film and evidence that everyone missed only because of the negative attacks on Oliver Stone who wasn't getting any attention anymore, the government calling him the same names that they used for Jim Garrison, the subject of his film, *JFK*. Another problem would arise concerning the timing of this new evidence, and it had to do once again with the O.J. Simpson case and Posner's book.

The impact of the original film shot by Abraham Zapruder is the best evidence for any of us to see with our own eyes and what God allows you and me to witness, this is a gift of intuition and those eyes give the brain the answer you can trust to be the right decision. Most people when they are allowed to see the original Zapruder film tend to be in full agreement. A good example was Oliver Stone's film *JFK*, on a much bigger and wider screen. Now if the film is altered, your eyes and the brain begin to play tricks on you, of which our government depends on and has done to you over the past 40 years concerning this subject. I would say this is the greatest crime committed in the 20th century against the American people. I told you earlier in this story what *Life Magazine* did to misguide you, under the direction of our government within the Zapruder film. Let me tell you something new about this film. Robert Groden, the expert on this original film, whom Sylvia Chase used on her piece from, *20/20* had made a similar mistake, as Mark Fuhrman did, concerning the O.J. Simpson trial.

Except this time it was for the defense side of the coin. After Fuhrman's exit and the racist card now being the subject of attention, if the glove doesn't fit you must acquit! First the glove, then comes the shoe, those Italian shoes my friend. Again Mark knew about them, but this pair of shoes would get Simpson off. The defense used an expert on altered and forged photos. This person was the very highly respected, Groden. But not for long because later during the Civil trial the Prosecution would find dozens of pictures of those darn Italian shoes, as well as footage showing O.J. walking up and down the field in those shoes from Monday Night Football on ABC sports.

Whoops!

Here, Posner's *Case Closed* would be for many, the beginning of the end of a long trail in the JFK assassination. Luckily, I wasn't paying any attention, I was mainly upset with our President, Bill Clinton, whom I met here in Spokane and decided he would be the first Democrat I would vote for. He seemed to be making an ass of himself in everything he didn't touch in his first six months of office. Also, I was in the second year of my lawsuit in the State of California, but what I missed, what we all missed, disappeared in the back pages of newspapers and was hidden because of mistakes made by those wrapped in deceit and greed. What we never noticed before in the Zapruder film is what happened in the beginning of the film. Most of us were only concerned with those gruesome scenes toward the end and then the concentration on the middle, starting with Kennedy and the motorcade disappearing behind the Stemmons sign. But what you and I and all those commissions didn't know was that a splice of two frames was missing in the film at the beginning when the motorcade takes that turn in front of the Texas School Book Depository. So tell me, why were two splices made at the beginning of the Zapruder film that wasn't discovered until recently and why isn't there another commission formed?

You don't need this. You can see for yourself in that your first instinct was right all along, so trust me, let me take you down that same path again and see what your eyes can do to relate this to your brain. In fact, why don't you close your eyes, while a friend reads these few seconds to you while you allow your brain to do all the work for you.

Homicides, such as the controversy over this President, are never a closed case. They stay cold, like the television series, *"Cold Case."* Fuhrman uses the archive frames from the Zapruder film; starting at frame #210 to allow the first of what he contends was only three shots fired from Oswald's rifle. I believe Posner starts the first shot at frame #199 because he uses for his proof, a little girl in a red coat running down the sidewalk across the street from the Texas School Book Depository. This was his marker, for she suddenly stops and reacts, as he puts it, to what is gunfire. This is what Posner says is the first shot, a shot he continues to say came from behind, from the Depository. I looked at a lot of film footage and found on her side of the street dodging in and out of people, this little girl running after the motorcade to get a glimpse of her President. When she stops, it looks to me that she had enough and just was tuckered out. No one else around her was reacting to anything here. The little girl just stands there and looks on, as the motorcade continues to pass the Depository. Her hope or wish of the car stopping, maybe, is dashed. If she were reacting to gunfire, I'm sure at least a few adults in the same area would have, too.

A few people did when they heard in succession, pop-pop-pop, some thinking it to be firecrackers. And there were those that thought that someone threw firecrackers into the car as they saw what were sparks hitting within the car itself. If that were true that would be three rifles going off at almost the exact moment. Maybe this allowed people to think back that they had heard echoes, following the shots, especially when word got out on the news broadcast that only three shots were fired. This is where the brainwashing began, and once Oswald was in custody, his face was broadcast all over the television networks before he even knew himself that he was a suspect. This was before anyone could truly identify him as the assassin. In the Zapruder film prior to this, as the Kennedy car turns towards the Depository, watching the little girl in the red coat running, something does happen. There is a glitch in the film that you wouldn't notice at Frame #154. Kennedy had been waving his hand to Jackie Kennedy's side of the car toward where the little girl was still running, two frames, #155 and #156 were spliced out of the sequence.

I was shocked once I saw this for the first time as Robert Groden discovered this and added the frames that were missing back into the sequence, and adding the dictabelt. It seems that those pulling the strings in our government today want to discard as evidence something new at frame #155. JFK hears what is now the first shot. The oak tree in front of the TSBD, as Kennedy's car passes now, would not allow any shooter, no matter if it were Oswald or not, to fire at this time from the sixth floor window. The branches are in the way obscuring the street below. The little girl wearing the red coat, Posner says, was still running, but Posner maybe right, when she does stop, about frame #199, but here at frames #155 and #156, she is still on the run as Kennedy hears the first shot, startled, he turns from Jackie and stops waving his hand for a moment and then turns toward where the shot came from, to the right of him and to the front, his eyes focus on the Grassy Knoll area as does Governor Connelly, like his testimony states, also turns to the right. The little girl continues to run until after the second shot. Kennedy relaxes and begins to wave again, proving here that the first shot missed.

A second shot is fired as Kennedy disappears in the motorcade as it passes behind the Stemmons sign. Kennedy is hit in the throat, his hands rising upward, as he reappears from the sign, reaching for his throat as if he were choking on a chicken bone. If the magic bullet is what it is, magic, then this bullet is both the third shot and the fourth shot combined. The third shot hit JFK in the back starting at frame #210 and the fourth shot hit Connelly in the back below the armpit at frame #224. The Zapruder frame #210 is the first shot from behind because of the live foliage of the oak tree that blocked any view of the shooter from the TSBD. This tree would be cut down and destroyed as was the Stemmons sign, which both had a bullet hole in it. Two to three more shots were fired. I believe one that missed and the last two at the end hit Kennedy's head simultaneously from both the front and the rear making it at least six to seven shots altogether. And this is the conspiracy our government will continue to hide as long as we allow them to.

What about that curb section in Dealey Plaza where James Tague was hit by a piece of it and removed by an FBI agent who stated that it was a bullet mark and not a bullet fragment as Mark Fuhrman states. Then there is the car itself that was hit, including that dent in the windshield trim made out of chrome or maybe steel that really didn't get investigated thoroughly for many different reasons, it sat at Parkland Hospital for 14 hours and I'm sure the Secret Service in the beginning stages of their investigation were not guarding it for evidence, having to handle both the President and Vice-President Johnson. Did some of the agents go back to Dealey Plaza and do some background investigation or did it all come down to just chaos? There was the premature reconstruction of the car after taking it to Detroit prior to the forming of the Warren Commission. Pictures again but were they reliable?

Then there was Officer Tippit's death and the reason Oswald was arrested in the first place. Four spent shells were found by the homicide detective at the scene of the crime and just like out of a "Perry Mason" episode. The detective finds himself on the stand being questioned by the WC, counsel member, David Belin who plays a shell game with the homicide detective. In the interview, the Oswald gun was to be matched by the four spent shells described above, all marked for evidence. But what the detective answered gave Belin a good scare and his face turned from white to red. The Detective told the Commission that they were not the same shells that he had found at the scene and, like Lt. Tragg of the "Perry Mason" series, he told Counsel member, Belin that he had marked each bullet with his initials. A strange thing happened. They stopped the proceedings here and told the detective he was dismissed for the present and would be called back to testify. When the detective did return, Belin gave him another set of exhibits numbered like the shells before, this time with the homicide detective's initials on them. That was that, Oswald was the assassin of Officer Tippit, this is how the WC worked and would come to their conclusions.

No matter, in the end God brings everything back full circle. Even when groups get together to document reenactments of Dealey Plaza or what they call the dog man behind the wall near the picket fence and the magic bullet theory as they have recently done on the *Discovery Channel*. This later program was like watching some pool hustler preparing himself for a match by proving he can make three, hole pockets, hitting three separate balls with one, the number seven solid. I'm sorry, but you still haven't any proof Oswald was even on the sixth floor of the Depository, since the WC can't let alone prove it either. Remember, Oswald didn't have three months to prepare like the pool hustler with the rifle, plus he only worked in the Texas School Book Depository about one month, and I'm sure a few of the employees would have noticed him taking practice shots. Or maybe you see it in Fuhrman's scenario, the ultra-cool marine. Either way, I got to hand it to the person from the Discovery Channel, not bad of a shot by actually inventing a possible magic bullet. There is also Dale Myers' computer analysis concerning the Motorcade and where and how everyone was sitting in the Lincoln Continental and the same perspective shots tied to no one but Oswald on that sixth floor.

In his letter to the First-Century church, the half brother of Jesus Christ, James who had never believed in his brother throughout his ministry here on earth, not until he witnessed the resurrection, wrote, "To him who knows to do good and does not do it, to him it is sin" (James 4:17). In a world filled with evil and darkness, followers of Christ have the opportunity to shine after light. That often means we must resist the urge to do nothing. Now when faced with the choice between doing good and failing to do anything at all, I must, like what I have tried to do here with you readers, and you must in the end, always choose to do what's right.

John A. Gaetano

2006

About the Author

John Anthony Gaetano, was an active member of the Screen Actors Guild of America from 1977 through 1988, whose writing talents and ambitions touch upon many areas of the motion picture industry. A serious student of Alfred Hitchcock, Frank Capra and Howard Hawks, John came to Hollywood, and in 1976 Mel Brooks chose him to appear as an extra in his film *Silent Movie*. Following that, John has appeared as an extra, bit-player, and supporting player in such motion pictures as *Coming Home*, *The Good-by Girl*, *Grease*, *Meteor*, *The Swarm*, *The Muppet Movie*, *All Night Long*, *The Competition*, *Annie*, *Flashdance*, and *Beverly Hills Cop II*.

John has appeared in Sidney Poitier's *Stir Crazy*, and Richard Brooks' *Wrong is Right*. He was not only an actor, but also a stuntman in Steven Spielberg's *1941*. His contributions in television include *M*A*S*H*, *The Rockford Files*, *Police Story*, *Columbo*, *Kojak*, *Battlestar Galactica*, *Beyond West World*, *Lou Grant*, *Hunter*, *Hill Street Blues*, *St. Elsewhere*, *Nightcourt*, *Friendly Fire*, and *Masada*.

Early in his career, John was a young live sports announcer, and at age 18, was the youngest disc jockey on FM radio station KPBX in Spokane, Washington producing, directing, and writing his own programs. Moving to Honolulu, Hawaii, he worked for CBS radio as a copywriter. He was also entertainment writer for *The Honolulu Gazette* and the *Glendale News Press*, a southern California newspaper, writing articles about film and the great motion picture directors: Alfred Hitchcock, Frank Capra, John Ford, Howard Hawks, George Stevens, and William Wellman.

John initially came to Hollywood to work on Hitchcock's last work in progress, *A Short*

Night, under the auspices of Dr. Jules Stein, Chairman of the board of MCA Universal Pictures. In the following dozen years he met some of the great film makers of all time, including Hitchcock, Capra, King Vidor, Orson Welles, William Wyler, Stanley Kubrick, George Cukor, Mervyn LeRoy, Henry Hathaway, Vincent Minnelli, Fred Zinneman, Woody Allen, Francis Ford Coppola, Michael Cimino, Sidney Pollack, Francois Truffaut, Milos Forman— and in 1986 interviewed Akira Kurosawa. John has worked with Steven Spielberg, John Huston, Richard Brooks, John Cassavetes, Sidney Poitier, Blake Edwards, and Hal Ashby.

In 1976, on the set of *Silent Movie*, Marty Feldman met John, and became a lifelong friend and it was Marty who inspired John to write his first script, which evolved into *Pawns*.

In 1977 while working on *Coming Home*, another friendship grew, this time between John and Hal Ashby, the director that lasted until his death in early 1989.

It was Hal Ashby who convinced John to produce and direct a 16mm demo film in Seattle, Washington. This thirty-minute film, based on John's script *Delusions*, was made in 1982 at a cost of only $3,800 under the company formed by John, named CAP-HITCHHAWK PRODUCTIONS. The story concerned a serial killer and the city he terrorized. Coincidentally, this was two months prior to the Green River strangler case in Seattle, and remains unsolved to this day.

After his movie *Delusions,* John wrote, produced, and directed another promotional film, *Pawns*. This eight-minute production featured sophisticated video effects and a teaser story line. John would like to turn *Pawns* and *Delusions* into feature length films, and is looking for investors for these production. He also put together a miniseries called *One Deadly Winter*, in the tradition of Hitchcock and Agatha Christie. The all star cast of this project can be be filmed in the Great Northwest. or the New England states.

www.ingramcontent.com/pod-product-compliance
Lightning Source LLC
Chambersburg PA
CBHW030326130626
46554CB00011B/3